The Six-Day War and World Jewry

Dedication

This publication is based upon papers presented at the international academic conference, "The Six-Day War and Its Impact on World Jewish Communities," which took place at the Hebrew University of Jerusalem, December 19–21, 1994. The conference was made possible by a generous grant from the research fund established by

ISAAC DONNER OF ENGLAND
AND HIS LATE WIFE HERMA, OF BLESSED MEMORY.

The Donners lived in Vienna, and after the Nazi regime was established in Austria, they fled to England, where they found shelter. Here, their children were born and their industries were developed in Wakefield, near Leeds.

The Donners have always encouraged family ties, the well-being of the community, and have maintained active links with Israel. Mr. Donner's valuable assistance in bringing about the conference is warmly appreciated, and in his honor we dedicate this volume.

THE SIX-DAY WAR AND WORLD JEWRY

Edited by
Eli Lederhendler

Editorial Board
Haim Avni,
Sergio DellaPergola,
and
Gideon Shimoni

THE AVRAHAM HARMAN INSTITUTE
OF CONTEMPORARY JEWRY
THE HEBREW UNIVERSITY OF JERUSALEM

UNIVERSITY PRESS OF MARYLAND

LIBRARY OF CONGRESS CATALOGING-IN-PUBLICATION DATA

The Six-Day War and world Jewry / edited by Eli Lederhendler.
  p. cm. — (Studies and texts in Jewish history and culture ; 8)
Includes bibliographical references.
ISBN 1-883053-59-5
1. Israel-Arab War, 1967—Congresses. 2. Israel and the diaspora—Congresses. 3. Jews—Politics and government—1948—Congresses. I. Lederhendler, Eli. II. Series.

DS127.S59 2000
956.04'6—dc21   00-036675

> We thank the Steven Spielberg Jewish Film Archive of
> the Avraham Harman Institute of Contemporary Jewry,
> The Hebrew University of Jerusalem,
> and the Central Zionist Archives
> for permission to use the photographs on the cover.

Copyright 2000. All rights reserved. This book may not be reproduced, in whole or in part, in any form (beyond that copying permitted in Sections 107 and 108 of the U.S. Copyright Law and except by reviewers for the public press), without written permission from the publisher, University Press of Maryland, P.O. Box 34454, Bethesda, Md. 20827.

STUDIES AND TEXTS IN JEWISH HISTORY AND CULTURE

The Joseph and Rebecca Meyerhoff Center
for Jewish Studies
University of Maryland

VIII

General Editor: Bernard D. Cooperman

UNIVERSITY PRESS OF MARYLAND

STUDIES AND TEXTS IN JEWISH HISTORY AND CULTURE
Bernard D. Cooperman, General Editor

I
Religion and Politics in the Ancient Near East
A. Berlin, Editor

II
Freedom and Moral Responsibility: General and Jewish Perspectives
C. H. Manekin, Editor

III
Land and Community: Geography in Jewish Studies
H. Brodsky, Editor

IV
A Life in Jewish Education: Essays in Honor of Louis L. Kaplan
J. Fruchtman, Jr., Editor

V
Religious and Ethnic Communities in Later Roman Palestine
H. Lapin, Editor

VI
Hitting Back: An Austrian Jew in the French Résistance
Dolly Steindling (H. Avni and S. Steindling, Editors)

VII
The Jews of Italy: Memory and Identity
B. D. Cooperman and B. Garvin, Editors

VIII
The Six-Day War and World Jewry
E. Lederhendler, Editor

IX
Rememberings:
The World of a Russian-Jewish Woman in the Nineteenth Century
Pauline Wengeroff
(H. Wenkart, Translator; B. D. Cooperman, Editor)

Contents

Preface .... *ix*

Introduction:
  The Six-Day War and the Jewish People in the Diaspora
  Eli Lederhendler 1

The Six-Day War and Israel-Diaspora Relations:
An Analysis of Quantitative Indicators
  Sergio DellaPergola, Uzi Rebhun, and Rosa Perla Raicher 11

The Diaspora's Contribution to Israel's Economic Development
  Haim Barkai 51

From David to Goliath:
  American Representations of Jews around the Six-Day War
  Deborah Dash Moore 69

The Impact of the Six-Day War
on the Organizational Life of Canadian Jewry
  Harold M. Waller 81

The Limited Impact of the Six-Day War on America's Jews
  Chaim I. Waxman 99

Jewish Cultural Confidence in American Letters:
  A Writer's Thoughts
  Nessa Rapoport 117

The Six-Day War and the "Jewish Question" in France
  Judith Friedlander 125

The Impact of the Six-Day War on a Zionist Community:
  The Case of Argentina
  Haim Avni 137

Repercussions of the Six-Day War in the Leftist Jewish
Argentine Camp: The Rise of *Fraie Schtime*, 1967–1969
  Leonardo Senkman 167

The Impact of the Six-Day War on the Mexican Jewish Community
  Judit Bokser-Liwerant 187

Consolidating the Consolidated:
  The Impact of the Six-Day War on South African Jewry
  Milton Shain 205

Jews in the Muslim Countries during the Six-Day War
  Haim Saadoun 217

The Psychological and Political Consequences
  of the Six-Day War in the U.S.S.R.
  Zvi Gitelman 249

New Documentation on Public Opinion and the Jewish Reaction
  in the U.S.S.R. to the Six-Day War
  Mordechai Altshuler 269

Polish Jewry, the Six-Day War, and the Crisis of 1968
  Daniel Blatman 291

The Six-Day War and Communal Dynamics in the Diaspora:
  An Annotated Bibliography
  Haim Avni and Jeffrey Mandl 311

Index 333

PREFACE
THE SIX-DAY WAR AND WORLD JEWRY

SOME EVENTS, when they occur, seem to divide history into a "before" and "after" all their own. Such an event was the 1967 Middle East War, the "Six-Day War" in common parlance. Unquestionably, the war altered the political map of the region, determined the manner in which Israel and the Palestinians confronted the issues of coexistence, and heightened Israel's role in the final chapters of U.S.–Soviet geostrategic competition.

In addition, however, the war found an immediate echo in the response of many Jews throughout the world. It resonated with their most intense, but mostly latent feelings. Few events since the Holocaust have conveyed as compelling a sense of the collective Jewish fate as did the war of 1967. It colored the postures of governments with regard to their Jewish citizens and in relation to Israel, and it affected the dynamics of Jews' interaction with others in their own societies. But was this a momentary crisis to be overcome or a watershed experience?

Today's attempts to craft a political solution to the issues that led to the war or that were its consequences represent a long-delayed sequel to the event itself. They demonstrate vividly its continuing significance. What is less clear is the nature of the war's sequel outside the region, in those same Diaspora communities that were caught unawares on a precipice of disaster in May 1967 along the road that led from the June war, what changed for these communities? What, if anything, remained fixed? Can we discern any Diaspora-wide commonalities: trends that would indicate Israel's magnetic effect on Jewish communities living in disparate cultures and under markedly different political regimes? Will Jewish life in the Diaspora be realigned yet again in the wake of a political resolution of the Israeli-Arab conflict?

The essays contained in this book address themselves to these issues from the vantage point of nearly thirty years after the event, but also with an immediacy that derives from its continuing "presence." The major Jewish communities are covered: North and South America and Soviet Russia, as well as Europe and South Africa. Themes range from new images of Jews projected in the mass media to intellectuals' and writers' responses to Israel and Jewishness in the post–1967 period; consensus and dissent within the Jewish community; the realignment of leadership groups and organizations; the economic and social implications of Diaspora support for Israel; and the psychological dilemmas caused by the war.

By comparing Diaspora communities with each other, certain similarities emerge. One consistent finding is that, as a result of the war, Jews of various kinds crystallized their ideas about "the right to be different." Always an important motif of Diaspora Jewish survival, the articulation of this demand was apparently reinforced in communities as diverse as Soviet Jewry, French Jewry, and Canadian Jewry in direct response to the 1967 war. In the United States and in Latin America, too, the war fed the cultural construction of a new Jewish self-image in light of Israel's ordeal. In the Soviet Jewish case, "being different" was a posture that brought some Jews into conscious opposition to the regime and its policies—a position that was not chosen by the Jews themselves but was nevertheless brought out into the open for the first time. In a very different way, we read about a newfound "cultural confidence" in American Jewish literary culture, in French Jewish intellectual discourse, and among Latin American Jewish writers.

The authors of the essays are recognized experts in their respective fields: Deborah Dash Moore in American studies, Zvi Gitelman in Soviet studies, Chaim Waxman in Jewish sociology, Sergio DellaPergola in Jewish population studies, and Haim Avni in Latin American studies, to name but a few of the twenty leading authorities contributing to this volume. Here they explore together how history intrudes upon the local rhythms and patterns of life. They ask, what is more compelling in the long run: do preexisting local forces reassert themselves, or are new patterns traced along an altered trajectory? What, in a word, is the true legacy of dramatic historical episodes and how are they incorporated in the lives of people and communities? That, indeed, is the underlying issue that this book takes up for consideration.

The Editors
Jerusalem 5760/2000

Introduction

THE SIX-DAY WAR
AND THE JEWISH PEOPLE IN THE DIASPORA

Eli Lederhendler

Avraham Harman Institute of Contemporary Jewry
The Hebrew University of Jerusalem

SOME HISTORICAL EVENTS acquire and retain iconic meaning. That is to say, the particular incident is significant more for the complex set of memories and circumstances associated with it than for its individual importance. This is undoubtedly true of many battles, wars and revolutions, natural or man-made disasters, great migrations—and the persons (celebrated or notorious) associated with them. To cite but a few American examples, we have only to recall the resonance possessed by the names, "Plymouth Rock," "Valley Forge," "Gettysburg," or "Lincoln," which are recognized shorthand for entire chapters of history and their manifold cultural associations. "Gettysburg" and "Lincoln," for example, refer to much else besides the particular moment, the battle, the speech and the president. They signify an American crusade; a nation deeply divided over the immense challenges of continental dominance; contradictions and wounds in the collective American psyche that have yet to heal to this day; and a man whose personal martyrdom echoed the varied martyrdoms of many others among the people.

Something similar appears to be true of the Arab-Israeli war of June 1967, popularly known as the "Six-Day War" and rightfully recognized as a defining moment in Israeli and modern Middle Eastern history. Here, again, much more adheres to the memory of the event than the war per se. At minimum the "Six-Day War" also includes the so-called "waiting period" from the middle of May 1967 till the morning of 5 June. Clearly, too, the name is intended to identify and set apart this particular war from among Israel's other wars, and hence a much longer chain of events is implied, both forward and backward from that brief but startling campaign.

To resort once again to American analogies, the Six-Day War was for Israel what the War of 1812 was to the United States: a continuation of the nation's war for independence. And, while one certainly cannot compare the two in terms of their origins and motivations, the Six-Day War's *outcome* for Israel bears comparison to the impact of the Spanish-American War on the United States: the emergence of the nation as a regional power. The quest for strategic security unavoidably involved a direct confrontation with those other nations whose lives and fortunes became subject to the victor's interests—initiating a process of protracted political conflict the end of which is, even now, barely in sight. Thus, our historical awareness of the event has a depth and complexity that could only have been guessed at during the actual event.

The present volume takes this level of abstraction as its point of departure. Moreover, not only are we interested in taking a broad view of the event, but we are also taking up a question that stands at one remove, at least, from the field of battle: Did the Six-Day War, a significant event in Israeli history, also significantly affect Jewish communities around the world at the time in question or subsequently? To what extent has the Six-Day War become an icon—a determining event of historic and symbolic depth—for Jews living outside Israel? What, in fact, has changed in the Jewish Diaspora as a result of that war?

We all "know" in an informal sense (for it has been asserted over and over again) that the 1967 war generated a groundswell of pro-Israel concern, enthusiasm and public activity in most if not all Jewish communities, even among people who were previously not engaged by Israel-related matters. Indeed, our impression that the response by Jews in the Diaspora in May–June 1967 constituted a significant change in patterns of behavior implies that many Jews could have been described, before the war took place, as somewhat apathetic regarding the State of Israel—an implication that does have some basis in fact, at least in some Diaspora communities. Hence, when change occurred, it appeared all the more dramatic. Thus, one of our authors affirms that "the perception of the Six-Day War as a historical watershed was due not only to Israel's victory but also to the expression of solidarity and the cohesion it brought about in Jewish communities abroad."[1]

We are hard-pressed to say conclusively, however, whether and to what extent people living far from the belligerents' borders were drawn into an engagement with the event in any concrete manner. Can they, indeed, be said to have been actual participants in the events and their aftermath?

---

[1] Judit Bokser Liwerant, "The Impact of the Six-Day War on the Mexican Jewish Community," *infra*.

What can we learn about this from a closer analysis of Jewish immigration (*aliyah*) to Israel after 1967 or of the Diaspora's share in fueling Israel's post-1967 economic boom?

Conversely, can it be contended that many Diaspora Jews were observers rather than participants, that they were affected more metaphorically than concretely—that is, affected, yes, but involved mainly in the verbal and symbolic echoes produced by the war, as is implied in at least three essays in this volume (dealing with Jewish intellectuals and writers in France, the United States, and Argentina)? To quote a rhetorical gesture from one of these: "We carry our heads high in America not only because the country has been home to us in an unprecedented way but because there is a country across the sea that is not home but homeland."[2]

Other questions arise as well. We are puzzled as to why the Six-Day War should loom so large in the public Jewish mind when, in terms of duration, human cost, political and symbolic significance, it was more than matched by Israel's War of Independence in 1948–1949. Why, for example, should anyone have been surprised in 1967 to discover that "Jews are fighters"—as if 1948 had never happened? Yet, this is a point that is made over and over by Jews from various Diaspora communities, as many of the essays in this volume attest.

Here we can only surmise that the establishment of the State of Israel and the War of Independence were subsumed in many Jewish minds under the overwhelming impact of World War II and the Holocaust, perhaps as a "resolution" of that tragedy ("rescue through statehood," as one writer has recently put it[3]), rather than as something new; whereas by 1967 Israel itself, a new but relatively little-known entity on the Jewish historical map, was being tested and acknowledged. Many of the essays agree that images of the Holocaust were invoked by Jews in May 1967, stemming from early fears of an Israeli defeat in battle. The surprised relief that attended the Israeli victory implies that the oppressive stigma of the Holocaust was not fully exorcised from Jewish thinking, even in 1967 (see, for example, the essays here by Mordechai Altshuler and Zvi Gitelman). But the results of the Six-

---

[2] Nessa Rapoport, "Jewish Cultural Confidence in American Letters: A Writer's Thoughts," *infra*.

[3] Aaron Berman, "Rescue Through Statehood," in *The Final Solution: Origins and Implementation*, ed. David Caesarani (London and New York: Routledge, 1994), 228–45.

Day War countered that stigma more convincingly than would have been possible in 1948, with the terror of the Holocaust then still so fresh.

Finally, we do not fully understand the degree to which the responses of Diaspora communities were determined by local conditions and events in each individual country. Perhaps some of this can be elucidated by carrying out a comparative study, as we have done here, thereby highlighting different patterns. In addition, if despite local variations, there were common features in the Diaspora Jewish response to the war and its aftermath, a comparison ought to bring that to light.

One underlying question that is implied in all of the above is this: Has the fact of Jewish statehood in Israel politicized the conditions of life in the Jewish Diaspora in any compelling way? That is, has Israeli statehood fostered a new form of Jewish political interdependence? Has it blurred or has it rather underlined the essential distinction between sovereign nationhood and Diasporic ethnicity?

As we shall see in the essays that follow, the answer to this fundamental question is mixed and sometimes paradoxical. In countries such as Poland, the Soviet Union, South Africa, Morocco, and Tunisia—that at the time contained Jewish communities that ranged from the miniscule to hundreds of thousands (in the U.S.S.R. some three million)—Jewish citizens were routinely seen as proxies for Israel and held accountable for Israel's deeds, as if Israeli nationality extended to Diaspora Jews as a matter of course. This political interdependence certainly did not improve the terms of Jewish existence in those countries—in most cases, quite the reverse. In effect, once Jews were seen as a politicized national group, their status and legitimacy in those countries could be questioned with impunity, whereas as a depoliticized ethnic minority, their status (if not always their welfare) had been legitimately assured in the past.

It was for this very reason, as our essay on Mexican Jewry argues, that the Jewish leadership there tended to avoid embracing a thoroughly political role, even while, within their own sphere, Mexican Jews were actively pro-Israel.

The war of 1967 proved to be a turning point for some Jewish communities (chiefly in Arab and Soviet-bloc countries) because it was the key event that triggered the changeover in their status in the eyes of the regime, from that of tolerated or legitimate ethnic minority to that of a group in political limbo. In those cases, emigration remained the only viable option.

Overall, the contrast between Israel's performance on the battlefield and the inability of Jews in these countries to determine their own political fate throws into stark relief the distinction that persists between minority ethnicity and sovereign statehood. Thus, while it is true that some Jewish communities were drawn into Israel's political orbit (sometimes in spite of their own interests or inclinations), it is not true that this resulted in their assumption of a new and viable political status, except for those who eventually immigrated to Israel, thus completing the process of re-nationalization. Interestingly, however, significant proportions of Jewish emigrants from those countries sought destinations other than Israel: Many Polish Jews headed for Sweden and Denmark, many North African Jews headed for France, and many immigrants from the Soviet Union, especially in the latter part of the 1970s, tended to prefer the United States or Germany.

In the United States, Canada, France, and Argentina, on the other hand, Jews succeeded in using their Israel-connectedness more for leverage in projecting a reinforced Jewish ethnic identity *within their own societies,* rather than as a mode of proxy Israeliness. Their status as ethnic minorities was not altered: that is, they did not become, nor were they seen by others as extensions or representatives of the Israeli polity, except perhaps by symbolic association.

Still, in some cases (the United States, Canada, and Argentina in particular) an enhanced ethnic identity and an improved system of mobilizing the communities' financial resources could also be parleyed into political dividends. Thus, in Canada, as Harold M. Waller argues here, a community that had been perceived as politically "passive" was encouraged to adopt a higher profile in Canadian public affairs. Likewise, there is little doubt that the political campaign waged in the United States to support the demands by Soviet Jews to emigrate was rapidly energized in the wake of the Six-Day War, evidence of a heightened sense of historical urgency and political efficacy among many American Jews. In Argentina, with its anti-Communist regime, the local Jewish leadership reaped some benefit from the fact that Israel had vanquished Soviet client-states in the Middle East, as Haim Avni's essay points out. Meanwhile, right-wing Argentinean nationalists in and around the military regime, usually known to sympathize with anti-Semitic groups, were in this case more apt to regard anti-Semitic extremists with less sympathy, or even with suspicion (although this change did not last very long).

In any case, we may say that the impact of the Six-Day War on these last-named Jewish communities tended to be positive in nature. This suggests that we can divide the subjects of our investigation into two broad categories: Jews living in ethnically monist and/or politically authoritarian societies versus those living in societies that were ethnically and politically pluralistic. Let us elaborate:

In countries dominated by strong nationalist currents and/or that were part of the Soviet bloc, the Six-Day War affected local Jewries strongly and negatively. In some cases, such as that of Poland, this effect was almost immediate, while in other cases, such as South Africa, this would become evident only later (and to a less drastic degree). Indeed, the essay on South Africa that we have included here tends to accentuate the more positive ramifications that attended the 1967 war. Nonetheless, two things are clear: South African society was extremely polarized (rather than pluralistic) on national-racial grounds, and the Jewish community there could not enjoy absolute security in its own right, since that security was to a greater extent than before dependent upon Israeli policies toward South Africa. This was true both before and after the fall of the apartheid regime.

Regarding the Arab states, as Haim Saadoun points out, not only were there the nationalist and pro-Soviet factors to take into consideration, but the nature of the confrontation between Arab and Jewish nationalism in the Middle East created a very specific dilemma for Jewish communities in the Moslem world.

In contrast, in those countries which were ethnically pluralistic, constitutionally republican, or both, the impact of the Six-Day War on Jewish communities tended to be positive, though perhaps less direct or intense. This is clearly true of the United States and Canada, but it applies, at least to some extent, to France and Argentina, as well.

France, with its strongly centralist nationalist culture, was nevertheless also a strong republican democracy; moreover, it was at that time entering into a new phase of radical self-questioning on the nature of French society and French national identity—a discussion in which French Jews, to the extent that they wished to do so, took an active part, sometimes carving out new ethno-cultural niches for themselves as Frenchmen and as Jews (see the essay by Judith Friedlander).

Argentina is *de facto* ethnically diverse because of the significant size of its immigrant population, though its national ethos eschews any recognition of such pluralism. The government had been deposed in June 1966 by a military junta determined to abolish Argentina's republican constitution, but at the time of the Six-Day War the country was enjoying some economic stability, the regime was attempting to curry favor with the United States, and the free elections held in 1973 returned a civilian government to power for a time. Thus, the country was in a long and uneven transition to the dictatorship that took power in the latter part of the 1970s (see Haim Avni's essay).

The basic distinction being made here—monist, centralist, and authoritarian societies as against heterogeneous, pluralist, and liberal societies (albeit with some borderline or "gray" cases)—ought to alert us to the fact that conditions for Jewish life in Diaspora communities in and around 1967 adhered to the same criteria that had held true throughout the modern era: Jewish life could be enhanced only under certain kinds of social and political regimes. In that sense, the basic rules had not changed. That Jewish life was affected positively in some countries and negatively in others *by the same event* is the tip-off that conditions other than the event itself were determinative.

Moreover, as we shall see, it was precisely in the relatively pluralist-democratic countries that Jewish life *changed least* as a result of the Six-Day War, probably because those Jewries were already enjoying a fairly comfortable way of life under secure conditions. As one of our essays puts it, "Several patterns involving the relationship of Diaspora Jewries with the general society in the respective countries had such deep historical, social, economic, political, and psychological roots that they did not appear to be substantially affected by one single event, even of the magnitude of the one examined here."[4] The terms worked out historically in those societies for Jewish integration and legitimacy were flexible enough to be able to afford Jews the chance to enhance their self-image, their communal apparatus, their cultural distinctiveness, and their ability to send resources overseas to a foreign country—and all without calling into question any basic change in their status as citizens and co-nationals. The Six-Day War offered those Jewries the opportunity to make use of the event (or not) as they saw fit. It will not come as too much of a surprise, therefore, to see it argued in some of the essays that only modest change took place in the internal workings of the Jewish community as a result of the Six-Day War (for example, in the United States, Canada, and Argentina).

A sea-change took place precisely and only in those countries where the basis for Jewish life was, to begin with, based on the assumption that Jews would not be permitted to accomplish any of the above-mentioned improvements (in self-respect, cultural distinctiveness, communal efficacy, and mobilization of resources for overseas) because they ran counter to the regnant ethos of the society or the regime.

Accordingly, the studies are presented here in the following order: First, we present two essays that seek to establish to what extent Diaspora

---

[4] Sergio DellaPergola, Uzi Rebhun, and Rosa Perla Raicher, "The Six-Day War and Israel-Diaspora Relations: An Analysis of Quantitative Indicators," *infra*.

Jews in general were either participants or, alternatively, less directly engaged, in the events and processes that surrounded the Six-Day War.

Second, we present a group of papers that deal with those countries that conform to the pluralist-democratic model—i.e., the United States and Canada, followed by France, and followed in turn by three borderline cases (by our criteria): Argentina, Mexico, and South Africa.

Third, we present papers on Jews in Moslem states, the Soviet Union, and Poland. This group of communities exhibits what may be the most significant and the most permanent change in the Jewish Diaspora to have resulted from the Six-Day War: Most of them have virtually ceased to exist due to large-scale Jewish emigration in the months and years after June 1967. While one may quibble with the inclusion of the Soviet Jewish case under this blanket statement—since Jewish communities still exist in the C.I.S., the successor to the U.S.S.R.—it is clear that at least two-thirds of the Soviet Jewish community of the late 1960s has left, leaving behind a Jewry that is not only much smaller but is also rapidly shrinking due to a lack of natural increase.

We may establish, therefore, that the Six-Day War served as the occasion or pretext for eliminating what in Israeli parlance have been called "Jewish communities in distress." The Diaspora as it exists today conforms much more completely to the pluralist-democratic paradigm, leaving the Jewish world in a bi-polar situation: a Diaspora with, for the most part, strong roots in relatively liberal, heterogeneous communities, and a sovereign Jewish state which (due largely to the consequences of the Six-Day War) is now engaged in a great internal debate to determine whether it, too, will decisively embrace the pluralist-democratic model or else draw closer to a monist-nationalist-religious type of society.

As for the Diaspora, the fact that Jews' lives continue, as before, to be rooted in the minority-ethnic situation within pluralist-democratic societies implies an answer to our underlying question: No, Israel, even during its moments of extreme crisis, has not brought about a definitive politicization or nationalization of Diaspora Jewry. In that sense, the Six-Day War has indeed underlined the essential distinction between sovereign nationhood and Diasporic ethnicity, rather than dissolved Diasporic ethnicity within the category of nationality.

Finally, we also offer the reader a bibliography of readings and studies that pertain to the subject of this volume—to our knowledge, the first such bibliography ever assembled—in order to facilitate further study.

Introduction

A few words need to be said about the genesis of this book. It represents a selection from papers that were delivered at The Hebrew University of Jerusalem, on 19–21 December 1994, at a conference on "The Six-Day War and its Impact on World Jewish Communities." The conference had been made possible by a generous grant from the research fund established by Isaac Donner of England and his wife, Herma (of blessed memory).

The papers we have selected for publication do not, obviously, cover every Jewish community (readers will certainly note the absence of large and significant Jewries, such as Anglo-Jewry, and smaller ones throughout the world). Nevertheless, as I have pointed out in this introduction, the essays represent different categories or types of Diaspora communities and fit within a scheme that, it is argued here, is generally applicable.

Overall editorial guidance, including the selection of papers, was provided by a distinguished committee of my colleagues at the Avraham Harman Institute of Contemporary Jewry: Haim Avni, Sergio DellaPergola, and Gideon Shimoni, whom it is my privilege to thank on this occasion. Further, it should be noted that Professor Avni was throughout, from the earliest conceptualization of the conference to the final adjustments to the book, the inspirer and guiding spirit of the project. Without his determination and prodding, this book would not have been possible.

I should like to thank, as well, three others at the Institute: Moshe Goodman, who, with his many years of experience in manuscript preparation as well as his willingness to assume the burdens of correspondence with both authors and publisher was invaluable to the project. Laurie Fialkoff, with whom it has been my pleasure to be associated on the editorial staff of *Studies in Contemporary Jewry*, devoted long hours to stylistic and copy editing on much of the original draft of the essays. The help of Alifa Saadya, whose skill at word-processing will be noted throughout the book, has also been indispensable.

A word of thanks is due as well to Leah Cohen of the World Zionist Organization and her staff who, in cooperation with the staff at the Institute of Contemporary Jewry, did yeoman labor on the preparations for the 1994 conference.

And finally, on a personal note, may I insert a note of appreciation to my wife Lisa, who gave me something to think about other than the pressures of deadlines!

The Six-Day War and Israel-Diaspora Relations: An Analysis of Quantitative Indicators

Sergio DellaPergola, Uzi Rebhun, Rosa Perla Raicher

Avraham Harman Institute of Contemporary Jewry
The Hebrew University of Jerusalem

AMONG THE FIRST TO OBSERVE that the Six-Day War provided an occasion to study the relationship existing between a particular event and an underlying longer-term trend was Prof. Jacob Katz. That was at an international meeting of scholars and public figures held soon after June 1967 at the residence of the President of Israel, Zalman Shazar, on the theme *Yahadut hagolah be-yemei "milhemet Eretz Yisrael"* (Diaspora Jewry during the days of the "war of Eretz Israel"; at the time, the term "Six-Day War" had not yet gained popular acceptance).[1] Katz noted the general difficulty in evaluating the exact impact of a certain historical event:

> Processes are continuous and slow developments that affect society on an ongoing basis. Events happen all of a sudden. Events constitute the truly important turning points in history. Through unexpected events, latent forces emerge that were previously unnoticed. However, the event and especially its character, can only be evaluated after it has occurred.... The potential of a certain latent force was discovered [in this case] thanks to unanticipated circumstances. The question is, what is the significance of this for the future? Obviously a solitary event cannot simply displace those ongoing trends that had concerned us all along about the state of Diaspora Jewry.... Great events and even catastrophes do not create anything new. They always strengthen preexisting trends.[2]

Thirty years later, having the benefit of some historical perspective, we can try to assess the impact of the Six-Day War on the relationship between Israel and Diaspora Jewry. One question of some interest is whether the

---

[1] Moshe Davis, ed., *Diaspora Jewry and Eretz Yisrael, Iyar–Sivan 5727—June 1967* (in Hebrew) (Jerusalem: Study Circle on World Jewry in the Home of the President of Israel, Institute of Contemporary Jewry, Hebrew University of Jerusalem, 1968).

[2] Ibid., 66–68.

Six-Day War was basically a factor of continuity or discontinuity regarding various preexisting aspects of the relationship, or—to broaden the question—concerning various central processes in Jewish history and society.

Questions of such broad import are usually dealt with by means of thorough historical analysis of the facts and their implications, and by attentive consideration of the role possibly played by memory in reshaping the nature and meaning of the past events themselves.[3] This chapter follows a much simpler course, by describing and briefly discussing a variety of trends concerning Israel-Diaspora relationships, all of which lend themselves to quantitative measurement. It is through the compilation and presentation of selected statistical materials, rather than through a well-defined theoretical construct, that we hope to shed some light on the question whether and to what extent the Six-Day War was a turning point in the mutual relationship between Jews in Israel and in the rest of the world.

To begin with, we consider what the theoretical expectations might be concerning the measurable relationship between an event occurring within a limited frame of time and the unfolding of a related trend. Figure 1 illustrates the gamut of existing possibilities. Two aspects in particular should be considered: (a) the *intensity* of effects generated by the event with respect to the general level and character of a given process, and (b) the *reversibility* of the effects generated. As graphically shown, a sudden event may leave its mark on a previous trend in a way ranging from *highly visible* to *not visible at all;* and the main thrust of the existing trend may range from *irreversible change* to *reversible change*, to *no change at all*. One should further consider whether the impact of specific events (if any) on existing trends operates through a direct relationship between determinants and consequences, or whether the observed effects rather are the product of intervening mechanisms, stimulated indeed by the given event but also having their own peculiar momentum.

Given these assumptions, we proceed to analyze various series of data mostly referring to movements of people and resources to Israel from the Diaspora, and vice versa. The series of data presented in the following pages relate to numbers of new immigrants to Israel and emigrants from Israel; tourists to Israel; Jewish volunteers who came to Israel to help

---

[3] See, for example, L. Fein, "Failing God: American Jews and the Six-Day War," in *The Impact of the Six-Day War: A Twenty-Year Assessment,* ed. S. J. Roth (Hampshire and London: Macmillan Press in association with the Institute of Jewish Affairs, 1988), 269–80.

FIGURE 1
SCHEMATIC REPRESENTATION OF POSSIBLE EFFECTS OF OCCASIONAL EVENT ON EXISTING PROCESS/TREND

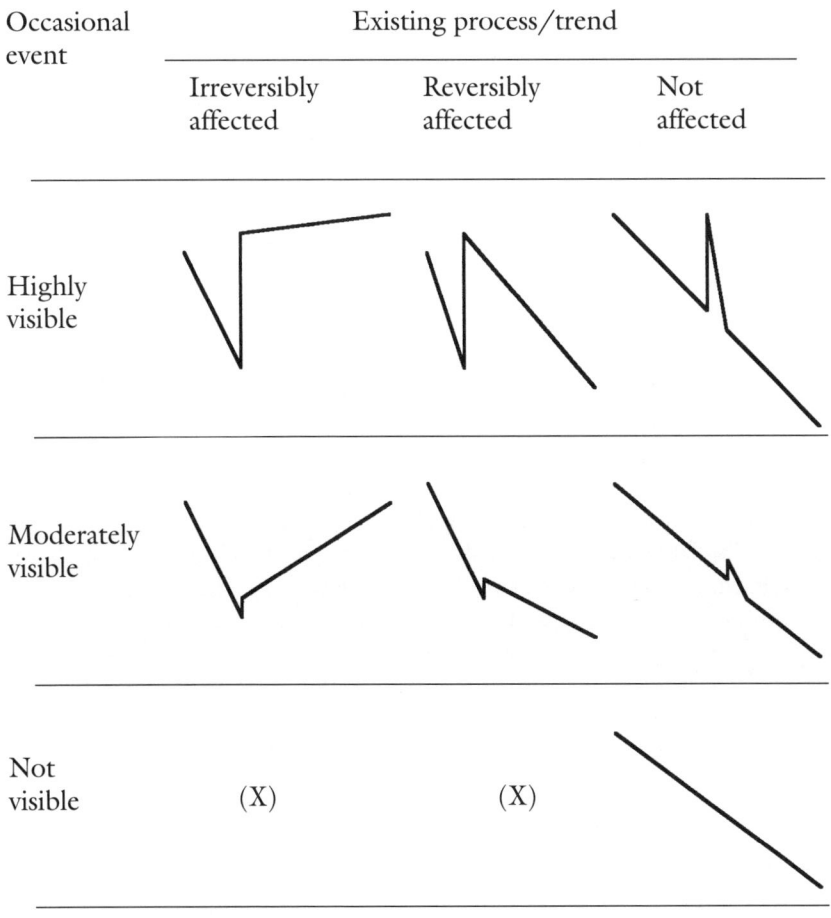

during wartime; participants in Jewish leadership training courses in Israel; Israeli emissaries, mostly educators, sent overseas by various departments of the Jewish Agency/World Zionist Organization; and money annually raised by the United Jewish Appeal and other Jewish organizations in regular and special fund-raising drives aimed at meeting Israeli needs. All of these are direct indicators of different dimensions of the broad expression of mutual solidarity and support supposed to exist between Israel and world Jewry, by way of population transfers, cultural-educational involvement, and philanthropic support.

The data presented typically cover the span of years between 1948 and 1996,[4] and refer to two different types of indicators:

1. cumulative counts of acts which reflect people's own individual decision-making;
2. aggregate results of acts which reflect the decisions and the implementation of those decisions by persons or organizations operating on behalf of others, and thus supposedly interpreting their collective will.

Such acts occur all the time, thus creating an underlying trend, or deviations from it. Observed changes in the frequency or intensity of such acts immediately and in the longer run after a particular event of interest—in this case the June 1967 war—and presumably in response to it, allow for understanding the historical impact of event on trend. As noted, the following analysis does not intend to verify a clearly pre-established set of assumptions, besides the central hypothesis that the Six-Day War should be expected to have affected in some measurable way each of the indicators examined. Some preliminary conclusions will be drawn only after a sufficiently diverse amount of data are described and compared.

IMMIGRATION TO ISRAEL

General Pattern

The question of the possible impact on immigration to Israel *(aliyah)* was raised immediately after the Six-Day War. Dr. Haim Yachil asked:

---

[4] A preliminary compilation of the data discussed in this paper appeared in Sergio DellaPergola, Uzi Rebhun, and Rosa P. Raicher, *Israel-Diaspora Relationships: A First Quantitative Analysis of Social Indicators* (Jerusalem: Avraham Harman Institute of Contemporary Jewry, Hebrew University of Jerusalem, Division of Jewish Demography and Statistics, Occasional Paper 1994–13, 1994).

> Will there be large-scale *aliyah* to Israel or not?... The question, in the first place, is whether one can find among the [Jewish] people those—even if relatively few—who might follow the gravitational pull of Jewish creativity; and whether the challenge of Israeli independence can bring them to identify with such a life and to devote themselves to that idea. If there be such, then many more will follow in their footsteps—whether the factors that operate upon them are pressures pushing them out of Diaspora countries or pull factors attracting them to Eretz Israel that brings them here.[5]

While asking a question of paramount Jewish interest, Yachil was also implicitly making reference to a basic explanatory model of the determinants of international migration. Conditions experienced by potential migrants in the places of origin, conditions perceived in the possible places of destination, and intervening mechanisms constitute indeed the basic infrastructure around which theories of migration are developed.[6] Evaluation of the impact of the Six-Day War on migration to Israel requires that the same general elements be examined in the framework of the longer time-span since Israel's independence to the present.

Viewed first in its totality and through absolute numbers, immigration to Israel unfolded through successive waves of variable magnitude (Figure 2A).[7] The first major wave associated with independence brought into the new country the remnants of Central and Eastern European Jewry after the Shoah (with the exception of Jews in the Soviet Union), and a large share of the Jewish communities in the Middle East and North Africa. Subsequently, immigration continued from a variety of countries of origin, the volume of each successive wave happening to be smaller than the previous one, until by the late 1980s, the impact of immigration on Israeli population could be judged to be approaching exhaustion. At this stage, beginning at the end of 1989, the major new wave mostly originating from the Soviet Union started, comparable in its size to the initial formative one.

---

[5] Davis, *Diaspora Jewry and Eretz Yisrael*, 64.
[6] See, for example, E. Lee, "A Theory of Migration," *Demography* 3, no. 1 (1966): 47–57.
[7] The Israeli concept of immigration includes people entering the country for the first time with a status of "new immigrant" or "potential immigrant," as well as tourists changing their status to that of "new" or "potential" immigrant. The data reported included Jewish immigrants and those non-Jewish immigrants accounted for in the framework of Israel's Law of Return. For a more detailed overview, see Sergio DellaPergola, "The Global Context of Migration to Israel," in *Studies of Israeli Society*, eds. E. Leshem and J. Shuval, vol. 8 (New Brunswick, N.J.: Transaction, in press).

The year 1967 came at the low point of a wave of *aliyah*—the third since Israel's independence—that started in 1961 and peaked in 1963 with about 65,000 new immigrants. Mostly connected with the end of the process of French de-colonization in North Africa, that wave had virtually emptied one of the last major reservoirs of potential Jewish migration. With few exceptions, Jews were now overwhelmingly concentrated in western countries, which had traditionally sent to Israel rather modest numbers of migrants; and in the Soviet Union, whose doors were locked. In 1966 the annual volume of *aliyah*—about 16,000—was the second lowest since 1948—a fact that could also be related to emerging economic recession in Israel.

In 1967, immigration to Israel further decreased to less than 15,000 but the following year the number increased to 21,000, and in 1969 it jumped to 38,000. In retrospect, the Six-Day War coincided with the beginning of a new wave of immigration, first including a strong representation of newcomers from western countries, which in previous years had constituted a barely marginal component in overall *aliyah*, and later dominated by the entirely new inflow from the Soviet Union. The new wave peaked in 1972, with 56,000 immigrants, followed by a strong 55,000 in 1973, and then sliding down again to lower levels.

Viewed through rates of change in the annual number of immigrants versus the preceding year (Figure 2B), 1967 represented the actual turning point in the ongoing trend of the mid-1960s, though this was manifested through a *less negative* rate of change rather than through an *actual increase* versus the preceding year. The two-stage character of the post–Six-Day War cycle of *aliyah*—from the West, first, and then from the U.S.S.R.—is clearly detected here.

Although the previous immigration waves had reached higher peaks in absolute terms, the intensity of change over the previous year, approaching a 100% increase (i.e., doubling) in 1969, was comparable to incidences already observed in 1949, 1955, and 1961. It was a far cry from the performance of 1948, the year of independence, versus 1947 (+450%).

In the years following the mid-1970s, the overall volume of *aliyah* tended to weaken, while keeping its basic wave-like profile, and so did yearly rates of change. The Six-Day War was the last truly stirring event in the history of *aliyah* until in 1989 the doors of the U.S.S.R. again opened wide to Jewish emigration. The subsequent new wave not only reached absolute values comparable to those of the initial mass immigration, but also established the all-time highest rate of change with an increase of over 700% in 1990 versus 1989. Taking into account this expanded time-frame-

FIGURE 2
IMMIGRATION TO ISRAEL, TOTAL, 1947–1996

A. Absolute figures

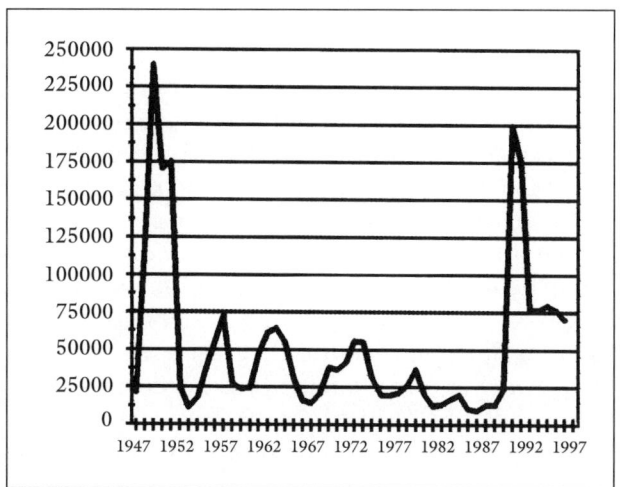

B. Percent change versus previous year

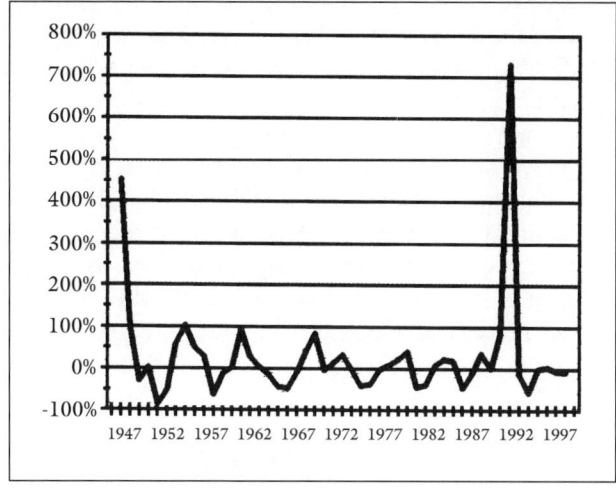

work, the post-Six-Day War spell of *aliyah* looked quite average, when viewed in the framework of Israel's unique history of migration.

Country Profiles

The time-series of immigration as illustrated above lends itself to interpretations focusing mainly on determinants that operate, respectively, in the countries of origin, or in the country of destination (Israel). In the former case, the main explanation should be found in negative factors stimulating the propensity of Jews to emigrate; in the latter, it would be factors related to the international position of Israel and to the quality of life in the country that would provide the main explanation. Most likely a combination of the two approaches is required for a satisfactory explanation.[8] To explore such an interpretation it is necessary to disaggregate *aliyah* features by examining the profiles of immigrants from each individual country separately. Indeed it is through the contemporaneous observation of movements from different countries that the case of Israel pull versus Diaspora push can be argued. Simultaneous waves originating in different places would provide initial evidence to the predominance of Israeli effects; significant country differences in the dynamics of *aliyah* would support the push hypothesis.

We turn to a comparison of the yearly profiles of migration to Israel from six countries: three—the United States, the United Kingdom, and France—are Western developed democracies; two—South Africa and Argentina—are less developed and more unstable western societies; the sixth is the U.S.S.R., eventually becoming the Former Soviet Union (FSU). All Western countries have in common a regime of free mobility; hence, fluctuations in the yearly number of immigrants can be interpreted as the product of free decisions taken in the context of changing circumstances in the respective countries of origin and in Israel. On the other hand, the possibility to emigrate from the U.S.S.R., until the recent changes that led to its dismemberment, was highly regulated over time and most the product of political decisions centrally made by the government in the framework of its broader strategic considerations. Figure 3A compares the

---

[8] These issues are discussed in a slightly more technical form in various papers by Sergio DellaPergola, "On the Differential Frequency of Western Migration to Israel," in *Studies in Contemporary Jewry*, ed. Jonathan Frankel, vol. 1 (Bloomington, Ind.: Indiana University Press, 1984), 292–315; idem, "Mass *Aliyah*—A Thing of the Past?" in *Jerusalem Quarterly* 51 (Summer 1989): 96–114; and idem, "Global Context of Migration to Israel."

absolute numbers of immigrants, and Figure 3B displays the yearly percentages of change in comparison with the previous year.

At first sight there is much similarity in the yearly profiles of *aliyah* from the United States, the United Kingdom, and France: quite low in numbers until the Six-Day War, a very significant increase soon after, returning during the early 1970s to moderately low levels—yet somewhat higher than during the pre-Six-Day War period. Examined more closely, the data reveal interesting differences:

1. *Intensity:* the historical peak for French Jewry (5,292 immigrants and potential immigrants in 1969) corresponds to about ten per thousand of a total Jewish population estimated at 500–550,000; the peak for the United Kingdom (1,763 *olim* in 1969) corresponds to about five per thousand of a Jewish population then estimated at over 350,000; the peak for the United States (7,364 *olim* in 1971) equals about one and a half per thousand of a Jewish population estimated at five and half million.

2. *Timing and duration: aliyah* from the United Kingdom began to surge in 1968 and peaked in 1969, followed by four years of decline before a new trend became apparent, possibly related to the Yom Kippur War. In France the initial surge occurred in 1967, peaking in 1969, and again followed by four years of steady decline before stabilization. In the United States, *aliyah* started to increase in 1968; it took three more years to reach the maximum level in 1971, followed by the customary decline.

These differences cannot be logically explained by the different time it takes in different communities to "prepare your luggage and go." Specific circumstances in each country seemingly added significantly to the common awakening of Jewish identity and sentiment which obviously was associated with the days before, during, and after June 1967. In France, two factors come to mind. One is the then-recent immigrant status and the existence of strong family relations in Israel among many of the newcomers from North Africa, which meant less-established roots in France and greater sensitivity to events in Israel, hence greater quickness and propensity to leave. The second factor that quite certainly operated as a booster of French *aliyah* was the famous speech of President De Gaulle, who, in response to the Israeli preemptive attack in June, defined the Israelis and by extension the Jews as "a domineering people, elitist, self-assured...." The French president was quite popular with the Jewish community, but his

FIGURE 3
IMMIGRATION TO ISRAEL FROM SELECTED COUNTRIES, 1948–1996

A. Absolute figures

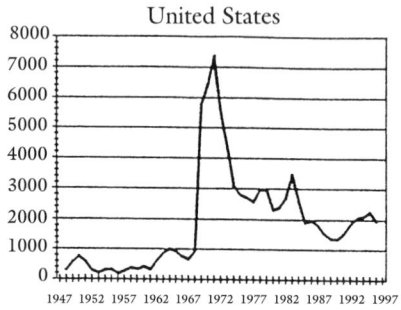

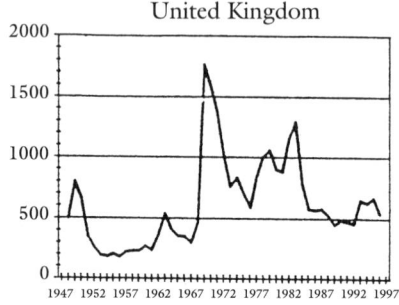

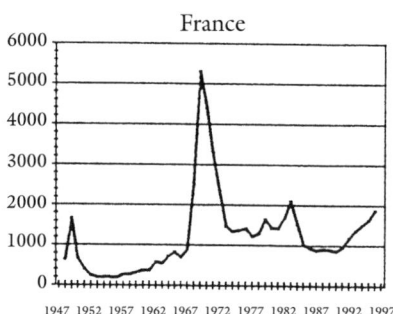

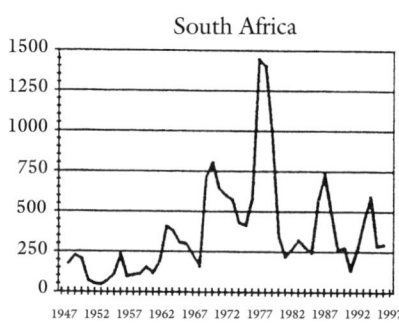

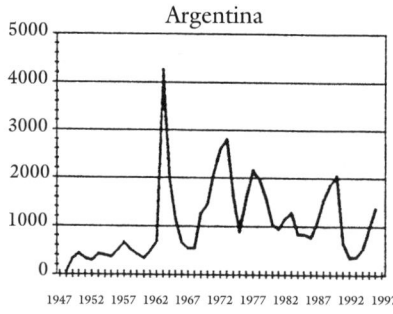

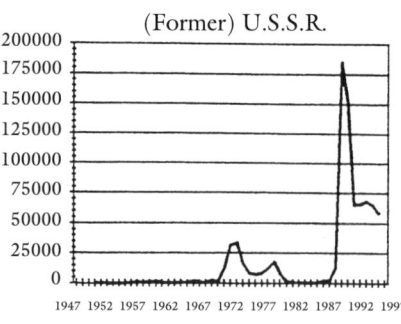

FIGURE 3 (*continued*)
IMMIGRATION TO ISRAEL FROM SELECTED COUNTRIES, 1948–1996

B. Percent change versus previous year

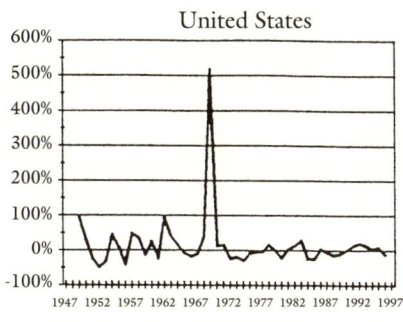
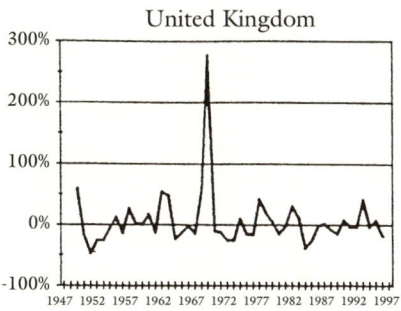
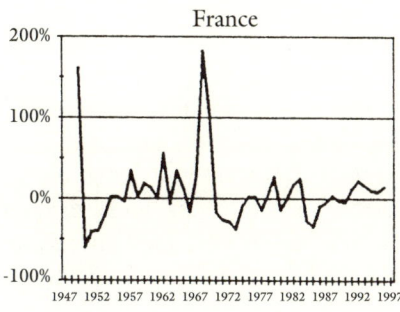
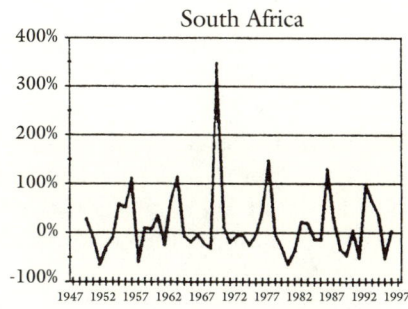
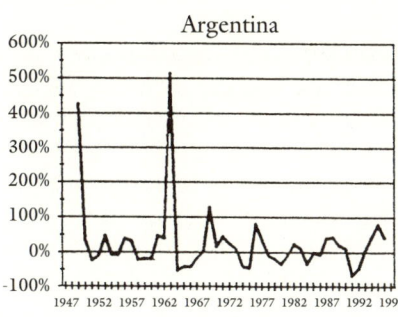
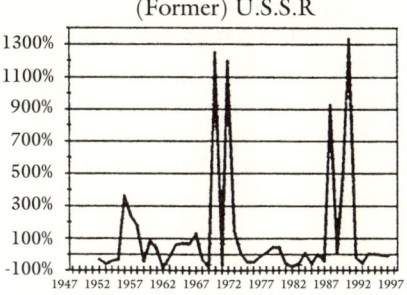

words suddenly undercut their sense of belonging and raised the specter of antisemitism. It was thus factors stimulated by the Six-Day War, rather than the Six-Day War itself, that apparently explain the intensified propensity of French Jewry to emigrate to Israel.

The temporary surge in *aliyah* from the United States is better interpreted in the context of general American emigration to other Western countries during the 1960s and 1970s. Such data have been analyzed, in particular American emigration to Canada and Australia.[9] While emigration to Israel during those years consisted mostly of Jews, migration to the other two countries presumably included a majority of non-Jews. The unfolding over time of the three migration flows displays some similarity (Figure 4A). In particular, the pace of American *aliyah* and of general American emigration to Australia significantly overlap. Since there can be no obvious connection between the Six-Day War and emigration to Australia, it appears more logical to explain the similarity of trends through the changing intensity of factors that were simultaneously operating in the United States. These are promptly located in the concerns related to the Vietnam War, intellectual unrest in American universities, racial tensions, particularly regarding the relationship of Black Americans to such heavily Jewish professions such as teachers and social workers, and the state of the American economy. The pace of response of 1968 and especially 1969 was, indeed, exceptional in its consequences for Jewish migration to Israel as shown in Figure 4B. Otherwise, it can be maintained that the Six-Day War was a catalyst for migration propensities in the Jewish community, directing them towards Israel, whereas contemporary non-Jews, and possibly some Jews less impressed by Israel's image and message, were looking for other outlets—primarily neighboring Canada, but also more distant countries such as Australia.

Turning now to the response in South Africa and Argentina, as relevant proxies for several other countries, the picture is quite different. In South Africa the role of the Six-Day War in stimulating *aliyah* is surely visible, but it is definitely much smaller than other effects related to unstable political and economic conditions in the country. Indeed, the strongest yearly percentage change in the number of immigrants occurred in 1969 versus 1968, and the following wave peaked in 1970, but the all-time highest number of immigrants was to occur in 1978, approaching 1,500 (over 12 per thousand of a Jewish population then estimated at 120,000). That clearly was connected

---

[9] A. Dashefsky, J. DeAmicis, B. Lazerwitz, and E. Tabori, *Americans Abroad: A Comparative Study of Emigrants from the United States* (New York: Plenum Press, 1992).

FIGURE 4
EMIGRATION FROM THE UNITED STATES TO ISRAEL, CANADA, AND AUSTRALIA, 1961–1985

A. Index numbers (1961–1985 average = 100)

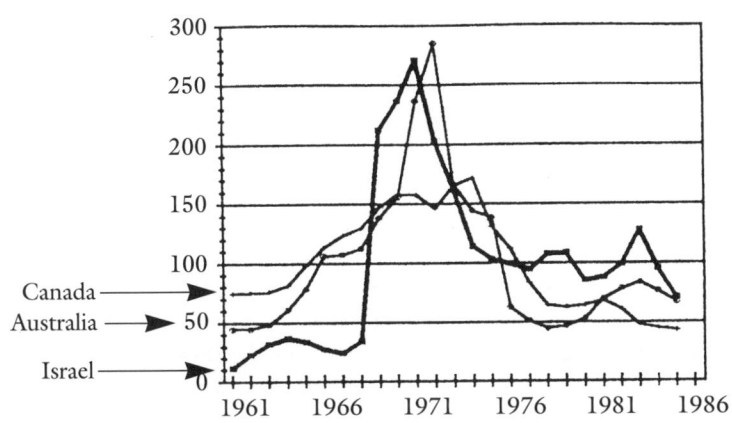

B. Percent change versus previous year

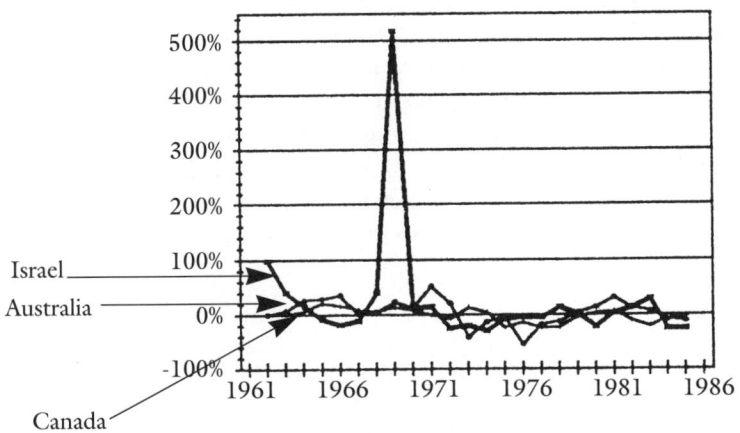

with the wave of public disorders originated by the uprising in Soweto that menaced stability in the country. Other major changes in the pace of *aliyah* (increases equal or above 100% versus the previous year) appeared in 1957, 1963, 1977, 1986, and finally in 1992, on the eve of the historic transfer of power from white rulers to the African majority, years in which the Jewish community felt less secure about its future.

A similar conclusion applies to Argentina, where factors related to the general situation in the country of origin, namely the repeated cycles of economic crisis/seizure of power by the military/return to civilian political rule, constituted a much more powerful determinant of *aliyah* than the idealistic call related to Israel, including the post-Six-Day War period. Both the all-time maximum volume of *aliyah* and the highest percentage change are recorded in 1963—over 4,200 immigrants or nearly 15 per thousand of a Jewish population then estimated at just over 300,000. That year severe economic crisis combined with terrorist actions by the Tacuara movement and unprecedented manifestations of anti-Jewish hostility— possibly fueled by the recent abduction from Argentina and trial in Israel of the war criminal Eichmann. That occurred at the moment of transition of power from a relatively liberal civilian (President Frondizi) to the military (Generals Guido and Ongania).[10] Further waves of Argentinean *aliyah* peaked in 1973 (Peron's return to power), 1977 (the Peron regime's final dismissal), 1983 (at the time of the "dirty war" staged by the military, during which the cases of Jewish *desaparecidos* largely surpassed the Jews' share in the total population), 1990 (the economic crisis terminating the Alfonsin presidency and the return of Peronists with President Menem). A new wave of *aliyah* was developing in 1996, conceivably stimulated by the dramatic terrorist attacks in Buenos Aires in 1992 against the Israeli embassy, and in 1994 against the central premises of AMIA—the politically crucial center of Jewish community life in Argentina.

With regard to the Soviet Union, as noted, *aliyah* belongs to a different context of extremely restrictive and changing emigration policies on the part of the sending country.[11] It is worth noting that already by the mid-

---

[10] On this period, see Haim Avni, "Jewish Leadership in Times of Crisis: Argentina during the Eichmann Affair (1960–1962)," in *Values, Interests and Identity: Jews and Politics in a Changing World, Studies in Contemporary Jewry*, ed. Peter Y. Medding, vol. 11 (New York and Oxford: Oxford University Press, 1995), 117–35.

[11] Zvi Gitelman, "The Soviet Jewish Revolution," in *Impact of the Six-Day War*, 281–98.

1960s, preceding the Six-Day War, small numbers of immigrants were allowed to come to Israel, determining strong fluctuations in the percentage of change versus the previous year, e.g., in 1966. In 1968, *aliyah* was again nearly nil, so that a modest increase in 1969 was sufficient to produce a sharp jump in the percentage of change. The long period in which doors were virtually shut ended abruptly in 1971. The Six-Day War had unquestionably produced an irreversible change in the national identity of Jews in the Soviet Union, but it was not until international pressure and especially U.S. legislation had become effective that the U.S.S.R. authorities released the built-up pressure for Jewish emigration. The *aliyah* peak, at this stage, occurred in 1973. The following fifteen years were a tale of contradictory Soviet policies, a new minor peak in 1979 being followed by several years of nearly total refusal to allow emigration. It will be recalled that during the 1980s most of the Jewish emigration allowed from the Soviet Union was going to countries other than Israel. The situation changed toward the end of 1989 when the whole superstructure of the Communist system in Eastern Europe began to collapse. The year 1990 marked the all-time maximum in both absolute numbers of *olim* and the percentage of change versus the preceding year, with 185,000 immigrants (including non-Jewish members of households)—over 120 per thousand of a Jewish population of about one and a half million at the beginning of 1989.

Overall, these data clearly indicate that the role of the Six-Day War in stimulating *aliyah* cannot be ignored. Once these effects are analyzed in a longer-term context of changing societal circumstances in a variety of countries, however, it is apparent that the general factors related to local political events and decisions and to changes in the economic environment in each country had the power to motivate much larger numbers of Jewish migrants to move to Israel.

Emigration from Israel

To complete a balanced review of trends in Jewish international migration, as related to the Six-Day War, one should also look at emigration from Israel. A general caveat, in this respect, concerns the availability and quality of data. For lack of better information, use is made here of a proxy customarily provided by Israel's Central Bureau of Statistics: the number of Israeli residents who left the country and did not return after a continuous stay of at least four years abroad.[12] Such data do not represent actual emigration

---

[12] Israel Central Bureau of Statistics (CBS), *Statistical Abstracts of Israel*, yearly publication.

figures, which are not readily available, but they do convey a good sense of the major trends and variations over time.

Before we look at the possible effects of the Six-Day War on emigration from Israel (Figure 5A), it is necessary to note three fundamental differences in the general profiles of immigration to and emigration from the country. First, the size of immigration generally greatly outnumbered the size of emigration, thus producing a steady positive balance of migration movements. Exceptions occurred once in the early 1950s, after the end of the initial major immigration inflow, and for a few years during the mid-1980s. Most of the time the annual number of Israeli emigrants ranged between 5,000 and 20,000; and between 1968 and 1972 it stood at relatively low levels between 5,000 and 10,000. Second, while the overall size of emigration increased over time, its rate per thousand inhabitants in a rapidly growing Israeli population was relatively moderate and stable (Figure 5B). One of the lowest emigration rates ever was reached in 1969. Third, unlike the major periodic waves that historically characterized immigration, emigration from Israel featured a continuous sequence of relatively short-lived cycles whose height and duration did not vary dramatically over time (Figure 5C).

The causal explanation of emigration from Israel tends to be related mostly to short-term economic trends (such as unemployment and inflation, not unlike other developed countries), to some extent the burden of military service, and more significantly to the echo-effects of immigration (as typical of all major immigration countries).[13]

Having noted the temporary increase in immigration to Israel from several countries soon after the Six-Day War, and having explained that increase at least partially with a revival of interest toward Israel and other cultural-ideological factors, one might also expect a temporary decrease in emigration from Israel during the same years. Indeed, in terms of both absolute numbers and rates per thousand population, emigration decreased for a while after 1967. This decline is seemingly related to the years of rapid Israeli economic expansion that followed the Six-Day War, with the significant introduction of new investments, the growing diversity of the economy, the new employment opportunities that, at least to some extent, were the product of enhanced immigration from the Western countries, and a marked improvement in the economic and logistical conditions of immi-

---

[13] R. Lamdany, *Emigration from Israel* Discussion Paper No. 82.08 (Jerusalem: Maurice Falk Institute for Economic Research in Israel, 1982).

FIGURE 5
EMIGRATION FROM ISRAEL, 1949–1995

A. Absolute figures

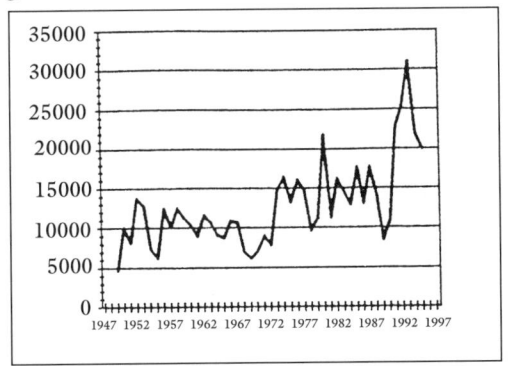

B. Rates per 1000 Israeli population

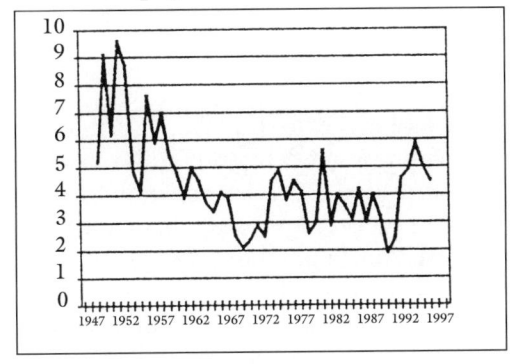

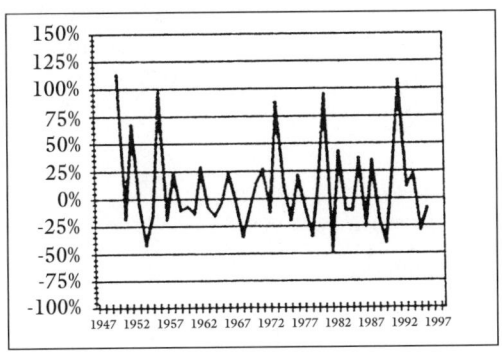

C. Percent change versus previous year

grant absorption. The rather optimistic mood, settlement expansion, and housing promotion in the period that ended with the 1973 Yom Kippur War can also be taken into account to explain the temporary diminution in emigration.

Among American immigrants who arrived in Israel between 1961 and 1972, 58% returned to their country of origin, and for the period 1961–1983, this rate was 52%.[14] The main explanations given for return were economic and family concerns, including lack of employment opportunities and the cost of living, cultural barriers, and estrangement to various aspects of Israeli society. Considering the "push" and "pull" factors involved, return migration was more a result of negative forced perceived in Israel than of attraction stimuli operating in America, although one may assume a latent presence of the latter all the time.[15]

Overall, however, the impact of these factors on the longer-term trend of emigration is of quite secondary import, once compared with the volume and strong fluctuations of immigration in the late 1960s and early 1970s, and throughout the history of the State of Israel.

TOURISM TO ISRAEL

General

Further insight on the role of the Six-Day War and other factors operating in Israel and in other countries in determining the volume of movements of people to Israel is provided by an examination of data on tourism.[16] Tourism lacks by definition the supposedly permanent intention to stay that characterizes international migration, though in the Israeli reality the boundary between the two types of movement is not extremely tight. A certain amount of new immigrants each year can be expected to leave the new country very shortly after arrival, to return to the country of origin or to re-emigrate to a third country. On the other hand, a certain fraction of tourists regularly ends by remaining in Israel, eventually changing their status to that of new immigrants. We examine first the overall volume of tourism, including Jews and non-Jews, followed by a more detailed examination of Jewish tourists.[17]

---

[14] Dashefsky et al., *Americans Abroad*, 120.
[15] G. Engel, "North American Settlers in Israel," *American Jewish Year Book* 71 (1970): 161–87; C. Waxman and M. Appel, *To Israel and Back* (New York: American Jewish Committee, 1986).
[16] CBS, *Statistical Abstract* (annual publication).
[17] The following analysis does not consider passengers arriving on cruise ships.

FIGURE 6

TOURISTS TO ISRAEL, TOTAL, 1951–1996

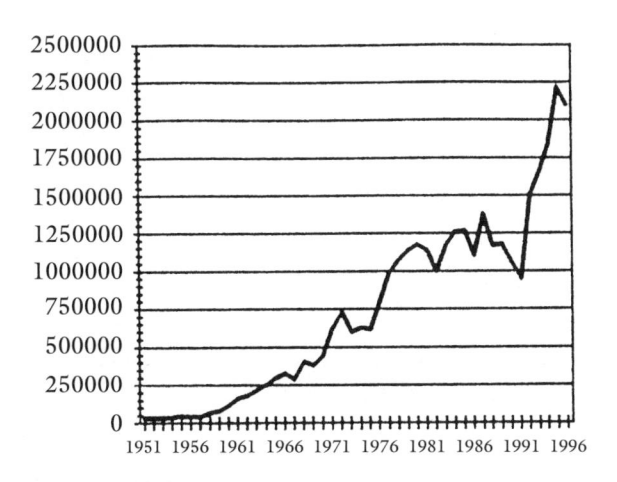

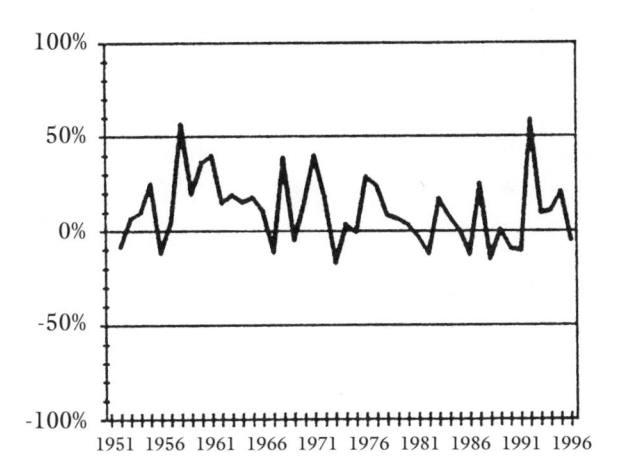

A. Absolute figures

B. Percent change versus previous year

The trend that emerges is one of consistent increase over time in the number of tourists to Israel, interrupted now and then by periodic crises (Figure 6A). In the long run, the figures point to the consistent strengthening of the State of Israel as an attractive site for tourism, thus providing a totally different picture from the long term profile of *aliyah* which—as we noted—was essentially dominated by the conditions prevailing in the countries of origin. Calculated in relative terms as the rate of tourists per thousand Israeli population, the pattern is very similar: in 1951 the number of incoming tourists corresponded to 20–30 per thousand Israeli inhabitants, whereas in the mid-1990s it was more than 400 per thousand of a largely increased Israeli population.

The effect of wars and other major moments of security stress was clearly negative, causing temporary falls in the number of tourists (Figure 6B). The year 1967, in this respect, was no different from the years 1956, 1973, 1982, and 1991, in each of which major military events affected Israel. The negative effects of terrorism on tourism are visible in the 1996 data. On the other hand, immediately after the Six-Day War as well as after each other war, tourism quickly recovered. In 1968, a 40% increase in the number of tourists occurred over the previous year. While significant, such relative increase was surpassed by the rates of change recorded in 1958 (based on much smaller absolute numbers) and in 1992, after several years of *intifada* and the Gulf War (based, this time, on much larger absolute numbers).

It can be assumed, however, that the Six-Day War played a particularly significant role with regard to tourism, by making Israel definitively better known and visible on the international scene. The augmented resort opportunities stemming from the territorial expansion and the incorporation of relevant sites following the 1967 war also probably played a role favorable to tourism, for Jewish and non-Jewish travelers alike.

Jewish Tourists

A more specific examination of the response of Jewish tourists to the Six-Day War is possible thanks to the availability of data from a special survey promoted by Israel's Ministry of Tourism during the years 1966–1970 (Figure 7A).[18] By comparing the available estimates of the number of Jewish tourists with the general data on tourists, it appears that Jews

---

[18] Israel Ministry of Tourism, *Tourist Survey*. Otot Surveys, Ltd., 1966, 1967, 1968, 1969, 1970.

FIGURE 7
JEWISH TOURISTS TO ISRAEL, 1967–1970

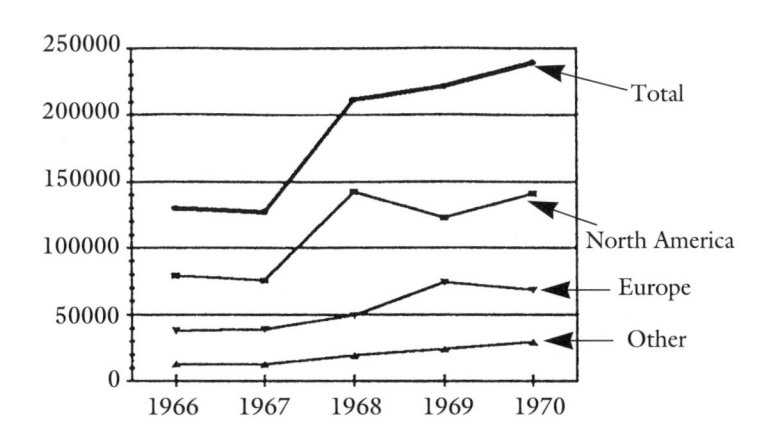

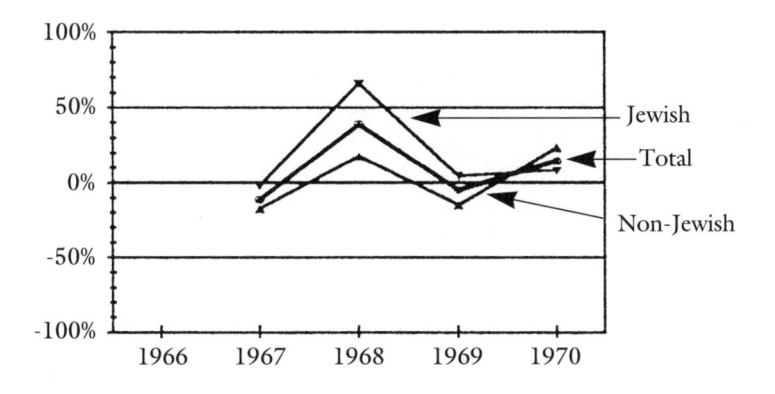

A. Absolute figures

B. Percent change versus previous year

responded much more quickly to the new situation following the war (Figure 7B). Whereas the total increase in tourists in 1968 over 1967 was about 40%, the increase in Jewish tourists was about 65%. Moreover, these different responses created for a few years a Jewish majority among all tourists to Israel, which had not been the case previously, nor presumably was in subsequent years. Jews constituted an estimated 40% of all tourists to Israel in 1966. That percentage rose to 44% in 1967, 52% in 1968, 57% in 1969, and was 54% in 1970.

With regard to the major geographical areas of origin of tourists to Israel, in 1966 Jews represented 76% of all tourists from North America, 25% of those from Europe, and 19% of those from other countries. In 1968 the respective shares of Jewish out of all tourists had become 85%, 24%, and 35%; and in 1970 they were 76%, 37%, and 42%, respectively. Visitors from North America continued to dominate Jewish tourism numerically, given their weight among Diaspora Jewry (Figure 7A). Jews also dominated numerically the overall North American tourism to Israel. North American Jewish tourists appeared to be the quicker to respond to the Six-Day War, followed in that order by European Jews and by Jews from other countries.

Jewish Activists Going to Israel

Volunteers

The Six-Day War also attracted several thousand volunteers, mostly young Jewish adult members of Jewish youth movements who wished to join Israel at a moment of greatest danger. Some of these young activists were ready to join the Israeli army to fight the war. The actual role fulfilled by most volunteers was to substitute for the Israeli civilian personnel that had been enlisted in the army, replacing them mostly in agriculture, industry, and essential services. After the cease-fire, most volunteers returned home, although quite a few remained for good, and many more returned to Israel and permanently settled over the following years.

An interesting comparison is made possible thanks to data collected by E. H. Cohen on the number and countries of origin of volunteers who came to Israeli on the occasions of the 1967 war and the 1973 Yom Kippur War (Figure 8A).[19] in 1967, a total of 8,232 volunteers was recorded. Of these, 1,749 came from the United Kingdom, 1,355 from the United

---

[19] E. H. Cohen, *Les volontaires juifs de France vers Israel durant la guerre de Kippour; Contribution à l'étude des relations Israel-Diaspora*, vol. 3 (Ph.D. diss., Université de Paris-Nanterre, 1986).

FIGURE 8
VOLUNTEERS TO ISRAEL, 1967 AND 1973–1974

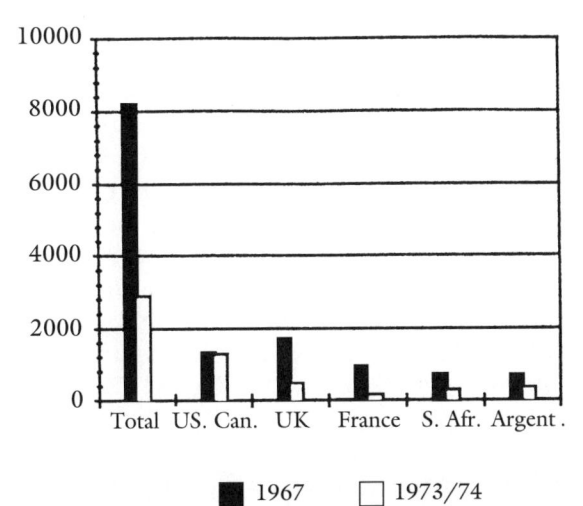

A. Absolute figures

B. Percent change

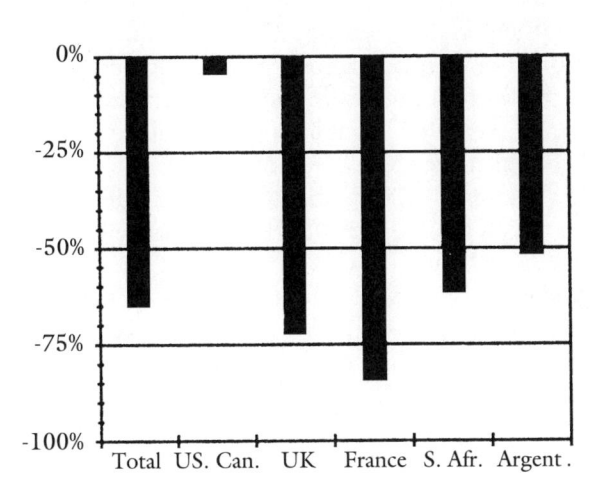

States and Canada, 951 from France, 733 from South Africa, and 714 from Argentina. In 1973–1974 the total of volunteers was 2,889, of which 1,300 came from the United States and Canada, 490 from the United Kingdom, 350 from Argentina, 285 from South Africa, and 155 from France. It thus appears that the frequency of response of volunteers to two of Israel's wars was quite unequal, especially when compared to the relative size of the Jewish populations in the respective countries of origin.

In 1967, relative to the total size of major Jewish communities, the highest amount of support came from medium-size communities in Western Europe (Belgium/the Netherlands/Italy), with a combined rate of 8.4 volunteers per thousand Jewish population, followed by Uruguay (6.9 per thousand), South Africa (6.4), the United Kingdom (5.1), Australia/New Zealand (3.3), Brazil, Mexico, Chile, and Venezuela (2.6), Argentina (1.9), France (1.8), with the United States and Canada at the bottom of the list (0.2 volunteers per thousand Jewish population).

The intensity of response was 65% weaker in 1973–1974 as against 1967 (Figure 8B), although in retrospect it would appear that the danger to Israel's security was actually greater during the Yom Kippur War. This was perhaps due to the fact that during the Six-Day War Israel had already proven its ability to defend itself militarily, which in a sense determined a lesser need for help from the outside. It was perhaps also a sense of *déjà vu,* or perhaps the more divided Jewish Diaspora facing Israeli policies after the Six-Day War, unlike the situation that had prevailed before it, which helped explain the blander reaction. The diminished response of volunteers did not distribute equally across the geographical board. The strongest decline came from some of the countries that had been more prominent in sending help in 1967: Uruguay (-94%), Belgium/the Netherlands/Italy (-93%), but also France (-84%), Mexico/Chile/Venezuela (-79%), Australia/New Zealand (-78%), and the United Kingdom (-72%). The only countries which basically kept to their contingent of volunteers were the United States and Canada, with a diminution of only 4%. This still left North America at the bottom of voluntarism in 1973–1974, in relation to its total Jewish population, whereas the country with the highest contingent of volunteers per thousand of Jews turned out to be South Africa (2.5 per thousand), followed by Brazil (1.7), and the United Kingdom (1.4).

Young Leaders

The Jewish Agency administers in Jerusalem an Institute for Leadership Training *(Hamachon lemadrichei hutz-le'aretz),* where activists in Jewish youth movements abroad come to spend a term (usually a year) of training.

The Institute has had quite an impact in creating a cadre of Jewish community activists. Quite a few of the former trainees eventually migrated to Israel.

The Institute grew especially during the early 1950s, when its student population passed from less than fifty to over two hundred (Figure 9A). In subsequent years the figures were quite stable, besides minor yearly fluctuations. Students totaled 225 in 1956 and 229 in 1981. Looking at the development over the 1960s and 1970s, one is perhaps surprised not to note any significant change of trends (Figure 9B). It would appear that the capacity of the Institute was not affected by the 1967 war, probably more because of budgetary constraints than because of a real shortage of possible candidates abroad. In this case, the Six-Day War does not appear to be associated with a substantial expansion of the activity undertaken by Jewish youth movements in the Diaspora, at least as reflected by the numbers of trainees at the Institute.

EMISSARIES SENT FROM ISRAEL TO THE DIASPORA

The World Zionist Organization develops its educational effort among Jewish communities in the Diaspora through the activities of two departments, one aimed at Jewish education and culture in general, and the other aimed at religious Jewish education and culture. This division of labor reflects the existence of different ideological orientations among Jewish schools in the Diaspora. Furthermore, in the framework of political arrangements within the Zionist executive, certain geographical divisions, such as specific countries or continents, have been dealt with by one of the two departments, regardless of the specific Jewish cultural orientation of individual schools. A conspicuous part of the departments' activity consists of sending to Diaspora communities a certain number of emissaries *(shlichim)*, mostly employed as teachers of Jewish subjects and to some extent as administrators in Jewish schools. In this section we analyze the changes in numbers of emissaries sent abroad by the two educational departments.[20]

Religious Jewish Education

The number of emissaries sent by the Department of Torah Education and Culture in the Diaspora steadily increased throughout the 1950s and the

---

[20] World Zionist Organization, *Report to the Zionist Congress*, Jerusalem, 1951, 1956, 1960, 1964, 1968, 1972, 1978, 1982, 1987, 1992, and unpublished data. Figures for the late 1980s and 1990s were derived from the known numbers of emissaries leaving Israel each year. Otherwise, the figures reflect the number of emissaries staying abroad at each date.

FIGURE 9
STUDENTS AT INSTITUTE FOR LEADERSHIP TRAINING, 1947–1981

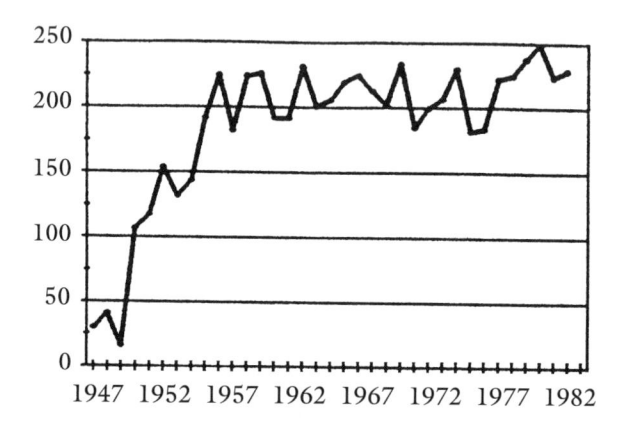

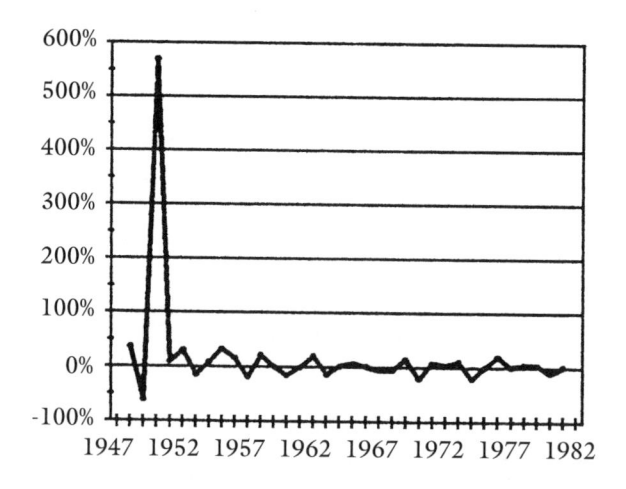

A. Absolute figures

Percent change versus previous year

1960s (Figures 10A and 10B). Immediately following the Six-Day War, the number of emissaries sent abroad in 1968 jumped from less than 150 to over 250. This increase clearly reflected the department's policy of greater involvement with Jewish education in the Diaspora, and possibly also greater demand for Jewish educators on the part of Jewish schools there. However, the data for the 1970s and 1980s point to a sudden slowdown followed by a progressive return to the levels that could be projected according to the rhythm of growth observed in years preceding the Six-Day War. The high figure of emissaries for 1968 thus anticipated the developments that would have naturally occurred in the course of time, more than it created an entirely new trend. During the 1990s the number of *shlichim* declined again and stood at 180 in 1996.

General Jewish Education

The picture concerning emissaries sent abroad by the Department of [general] Jewish Education and Culture in the Diaspora is quite different (Figures 11A and 11B). Indeed a moderate expansion in the number of *shlichim* is visible immediately after the Six-Day War, though its major effect is somewhat postponed to the school year 1968–1969. However, soon after, not only did the number of emissaries stop growing, but it actually diminished to a level well below that observed in the years preceding the Six-Day War. Renewed expansion during the 1980s was followed by retrenchment in the 1990s.

FUND-RAISING

Philanthropic fund-raising has long been one of the fundamental mechanisms in the life of Jewish organizations locally and internationally. It has voluntarily provided the financial basis for undertaking innumerable programs of rescue, relief, and renewal, thus helping to achieve fundamental Jewish social, educational, and cultural goals. More specifically, fund-raising in the framework of the United Jewish Appeal (UJA) in the United States, and in the framework of Keren Hayesod (KH) in other countries has provided a substantial share of the budgetary needs of Jewries worldwide, in Israel and in other countries.

For historical and political reasons, Jewish fund-raising in the United States was largely implemented through joint collection of funds for all purposes, including Israeli and other international needs, as well as communal activities aimed at American Jewry. The subdivision according to main budgetary destinations, between local and international needs, and then between Israel and other countries, was much more the product

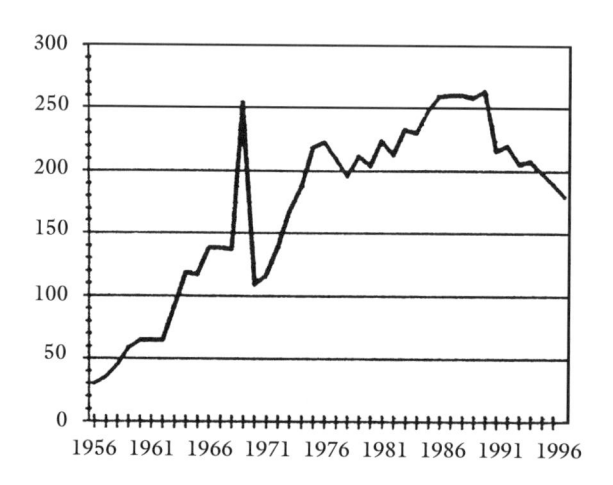

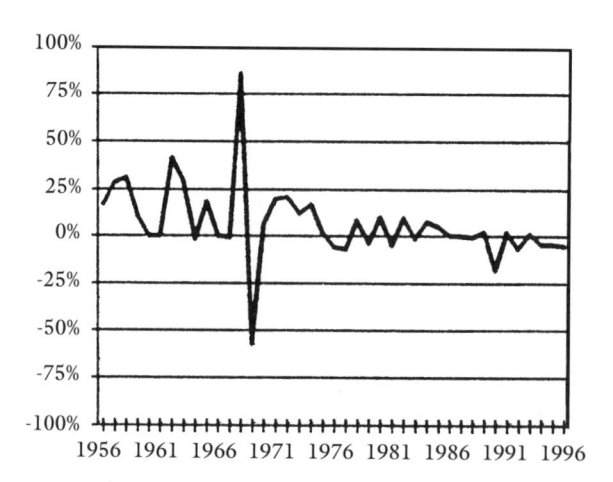

FIGURE 10
EMISSARIES, DEPARTMENT OF TORAH EDUCATION AND
CULTURE IN THE DIASPORA, 1955–1996

A. Absolute figures

B. Percent change versus previous year

Six-Day War and Israel-Diaspora Relations

FIGURE 11
EMISSARIES, DEPARTMENT OF EDUCATION AND CULTURE IN THE DIASPORA, 1966/67–1993

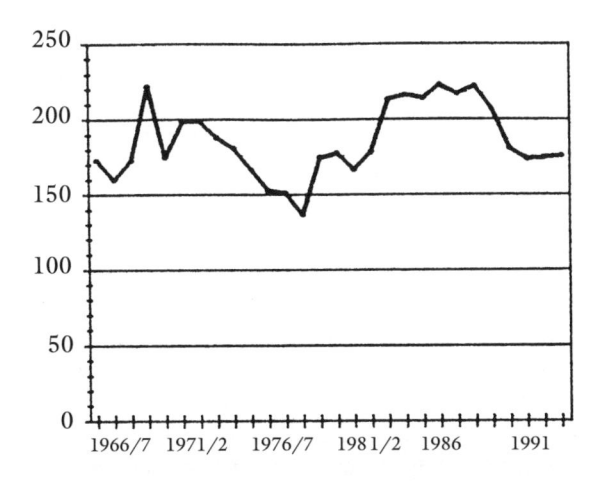

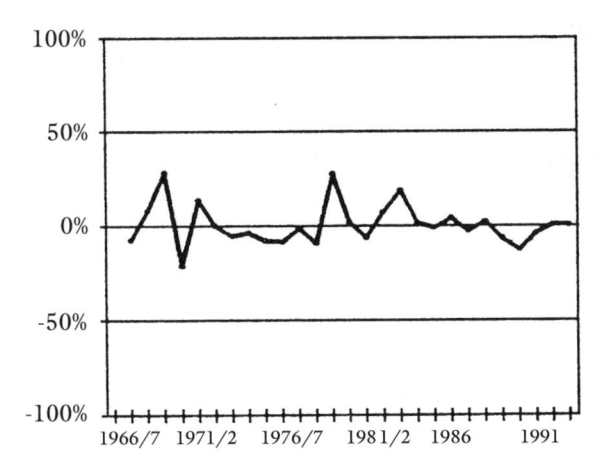

A. Absolute figures

B. Percent change versus previous year

of decisions made by the UJA leadership as the result of public considerations and of its negotiations with the Israeli and world Zionist leadership, rather than based on the actual preferences of individual donors.[21]

One of the central tenets of this mode of operating was that coupling local and international Jewish needs, especially those related to Israel, would produce a much more powerful and effective message and fund-raising mechanism. In the course of time, a demand emerged in the United States and in other countries for greater attention, hence greater allocation of funds, to the needs of local Jewish communities, in response to the emerging debate on Jewish assimilation and continuity. Part of this debate dealt with the rationale for the integrated concept of UJA and with the internal structure, efficiency, and controls concerning the major recipient organization at the Israeli end, the Jewish Agency for Israel (JAFI).

These major problems cannot be dealt with in this chapter. We rather focus here on general trends in fund-raising in the UJA framework, and examine trends in the allocation of UJA funds to JAFI through the United Israel Appeal (UIA). We then expand the focus on the global scope of Jewish fund-raising, incorporating both the funds channeled through the central fund-raising agencies in the United States and in the rest of the Diaspora (the *magbioth*) and the direct transfers to non-profit organizations in Israel, and briefly examine the impact of such fund transfers on the Israeli economy.

United Jewish Appeal Total Revenues

The development over time of regular annual and special UJA campaigns (here combined and expressed in U.S. dollars at current values) can be briefly described as follows.[22] In 1948 and 1949, respectively, $200 million and $160 million were collected in the United States (Figure 12A). The volume of fund-raising declined to a quite stable level ranging around $100–$140 million between 1950 and 1966. The Six-Day War marked a definite, and it would later appear, irreversible change versus the previous pattern. Funds collected more than doubled in 1967 to over $300 million, and after some decline in 1968, subsequently increased at quite a regular

---

[21] See E. Stock, *Recent Developments in Fund Raising for Israel* (in Hebrew) (Jerusalem: Institute of Contemporary Jewry, Hebrew University of Jerusalem, 1991).

[22] United Jewish Appeal, *Data and Reports on Campaign and Cash, 1948–1996* (Jerusalem and New York, various years). See also in this volume, Haim Barkai, "The Diaspora's Contribution to Israel's Economic Development."

FIGURE 12
UNITED JEWISH APPEAL REVENUES ($ MILLIONS), 1948–1996

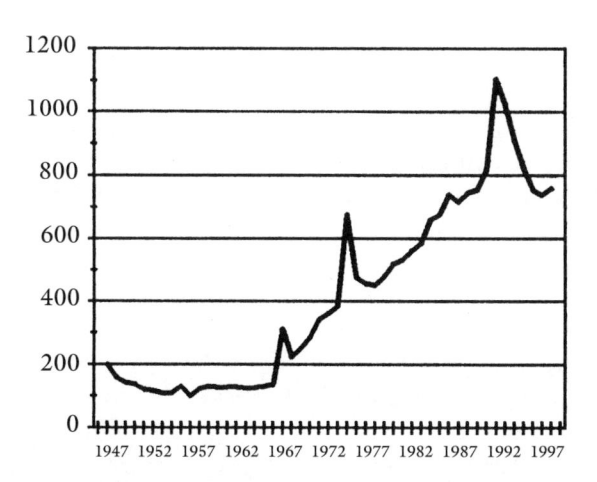

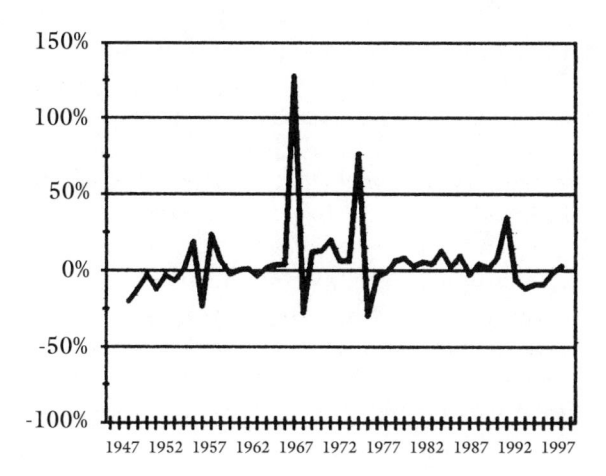

A. Absolute figures

B. Percent change versus previous year

pace throughout the 1970s and 1980s. Two further moments of significant increase in fund-raising occurred in 1974 following the Yom Kippur War, with a total revenue of about $700 million, and in 1990, following the start of "Operation Exodus"—support for the mass migration and resettlement of Jews from the (former) Soviet Union—when UJA revenues reached an all-time peak of $1100 million. The latest years covered here point to steady decline in UJA revenues, and perhaps to the beginning of a new era in the philanthropic relationship between U.S. Jewry and world Jewry.

Examined in terms of yearly percentages of change versus the previous year, possibly the leading year of change as against the previous year's revenues would be 1948 versus 1947 (not shown here). The exceptionality of the year 1967 stands out in comparison to the two other years of major increase in UJA returns, 1974 and 1990 (Figure 12B).

Allocation to Jewish Agency Needs

A different trend appears if we examine the percentage of UJA funds allocated through the United Israel Appeal (UIA) to JAFI to provide for Israeli needs (Figure 13A). As noted, the balance of funds were allocated to other Jewish needs outside the United States and to local American Jewish needs. JAFI allocation data provide an indication of the centrality of Israel in the framework of the overall concerns of the main American Jewish fund-raising agency at each point in time. Throughout the late 1950s and up to 1967, there appeared a tendency to gradually reduce JAFI's share, from around 40% to about 20% of the total amount collected by the UJA. The main exception was the year 1957, following Israel's Sinai campaign. The Six-Day War's impact is clearly felt in the 1968 allocation, which jumped to nearly 90% of total UJA revenues. This was followed by a period of twenty years during which the percent allocated to JAFI generally did not fall below 40%. Since 1988, with the exception of 1991, JAFI's percent has again tended to settle around 30% of the total revenues.

Percentages of change in JAFI's share convincingly illustrate the impact of the Six-Day War in the history of UJA campaigns (Figure 13B). The year 1968 stands out dramatically, with an increase of nearly 600% in the percent allocated to JAFI. Such short-term change in allocation favoring Israeli needs is unmatched over the whole period examined here, the two other major years of change being 1949 over 1948 and 1991 over 1990, each with an increase of about 100%.

FIGURE 13
PERCENT OF UJA REVENUES SENT TO JEWISH AGENCY FOR ISRAEL, 1948–1996

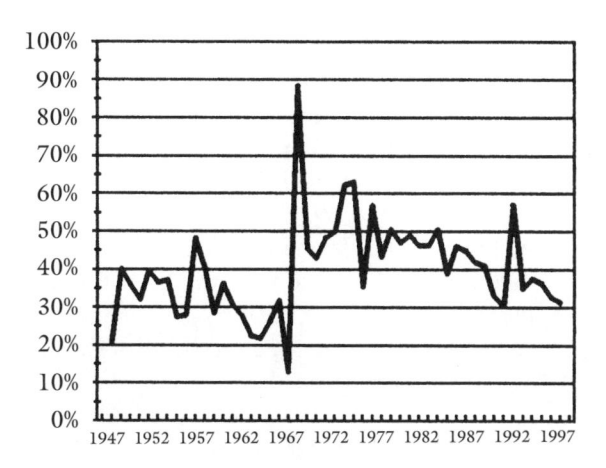

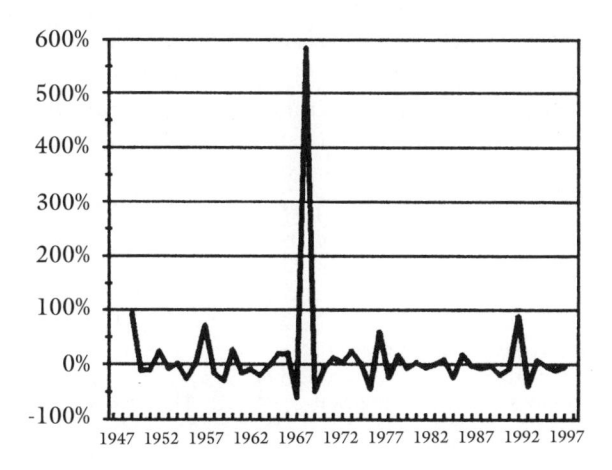

A. Absolute figures

B. Percent change versus previous year

Total Transfers from Diaspora Jewry to Israel

A better sense of the changing impact of Jewish fund-raising is obtained by adjusting the nominal values of the amounts collected to the real value of the U.S. dollar over the years. Unilateral transfers of funds from Diaspora Jewry to Israel in millions of dollars at constant (1955) values are reported in Figure 14A. The figures include funds transferred through the *magbioth* (UJA and KH) as well as direct transfers to non-profit organizations such as hospitals, universities, and other social, educational, and cultural organizations in Israel.[23] The steadily increasing trend that was apparent in Figure 12A is substantially reduced in Figure 14A (which relates to a much expanded scope of fund-raising), showing the distorting effect of inflation on nominal revenue values. A significant change of fund-raising levels indeed appears following the Six-Day War. However, following the brusque increase in 1967, the highest-ever Israeli revenue from unilateral transfers (in constant dollars) is clearly associated with the Yom Kippur War.

It is in terms of percent changes from year to year (Figure 14B) that the effects of the Six-Day War demonstrate again to be most the powerful ever over the whole period covered by these data.

Impact on Israel's Total Dollar Revenues

A final aspect of the fund-raising partnership between world Jewry and Israel relates to the economic impact of these transfers on the Israeli economy.[24] Figure 15A illustrates the percent of Diaspora Jewry unilateral transfers, inclusive of *magbioth* and direct transfers to non-profit organizations, out of Israel's total dollar revenues, inclusive of exports and other sources of income. The long-term diminishing impact of Jewish fund-raising over an economy of growing size and increasing complexity is evident. Whereas in 1955 transfers represented 15% of total dollar revenues, their share had declined to less than 10% by the mid-1960s, and to less than 4% by the mid-1990s. Nonetheless, the impact of special events is visible, starting with 1956, and jumping to a historical peak in 1967. The years

---

[23] Bank of Israel, *Report*, yearly publication.

[24] For an extended analysis of these trends, their background and implications, see Y. Don, "Diaspora Jewry and the State of Israel: The Dynamics of Economic Relationships and Thoughts Toward the Year 2000," in *"Israel 2020": Master Plan for Israel in the 21st Century. The Macro Scenarios: Israel and the Jewish People* (in Hebrew), eds. A. Gonen and S. Fogel (Haifa: The Technion-Israel Institute of Technology, and Association of Engineers, Architects, and Planners in Israel, 1996), 225–56.

Six-Day War and Israel-Diaspora Relations 45

FIGURE 14

UNILATERAL TRANSFERS FROM DIASPORA JEWRY TO ISRAEL
($ MILLIONS, 1955 VALUES), 1955–1993

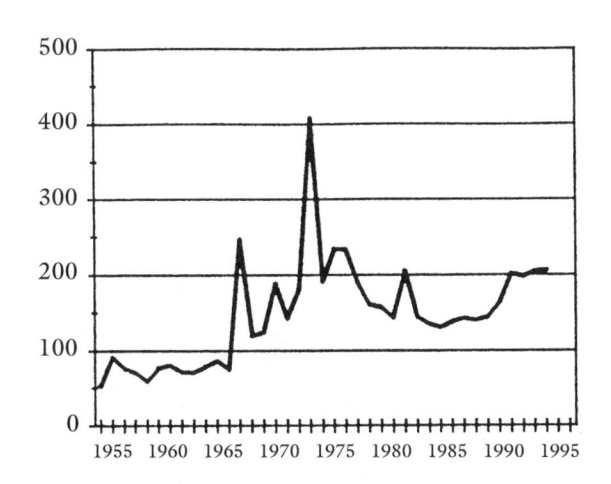

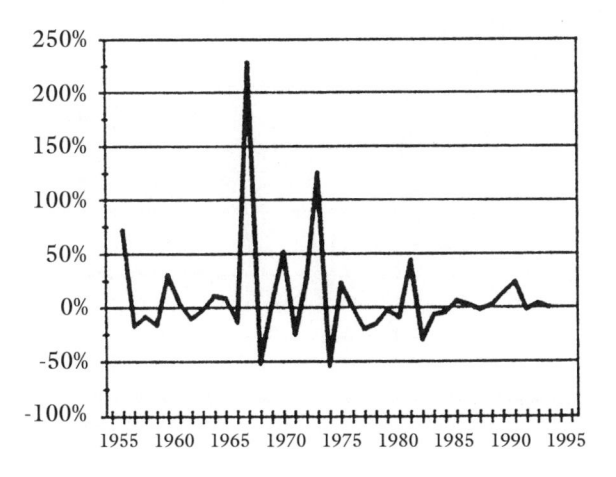

A. Absolute figures

B. Percent change versus previous year

FIGURE 15

DIASPORA JEWRY TRANSFERS
AS PERCENT OF TOTAL ISRAEL DOLLAR REVENUES, 1955–1994

A. Absolute figures

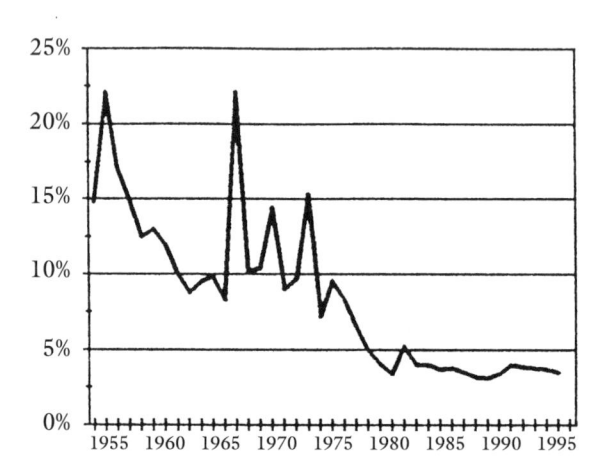

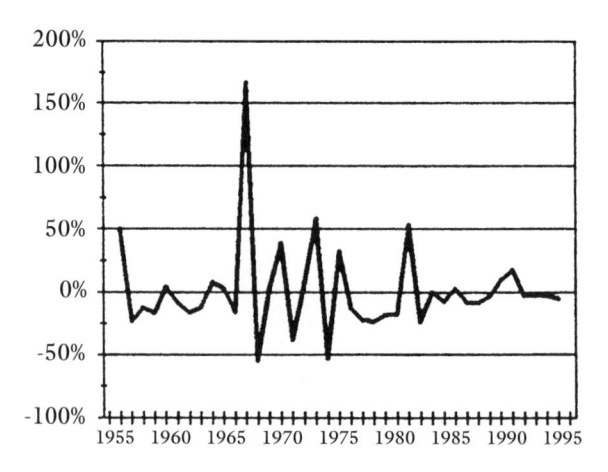

B. Percent change versus previous year

between 1967 and 1973 are not only characterized by strong fluctuations in the percent of Jewish fund-raising out of Israel's total dollar revenues, but also constitute an interruption in the general trend toward lesser dependency of the Israeli economy on Diaspora Jewry's financial help.

The Six-Day War again marks the moment of strongest change relative to the preceding year (Figure 15B). Since the second half of the 1970s, the overall impact of unilateral transfers from world Jewry on the Israeli economy tended to be rather modest, although it continued to be highly significant for the individual recipient organizations. The real significance of fund-raising tended to shift from its original financial role to the role of a meaningful indicator and a powerful booster of Jewish identification for the Jews throughout the world and in Israel.

SOME CONCLUSIONS

The data presented throughout this study constitute only an initial effort to explore the nature of the unfolding relationship between Israel and world Jewry. A broader range of indicators should be added to the analysis before one can reach firm conclusions on the general nature of the relationship, and on the role played by the Six-Day War in modifying it in the short and long run. It appears, nevertheless, that some preliminary conclusions can be presented on the face of the evidence examined so far.

Looking together at all indicators collected here, it is evident that the emerging patterns are quite different. They are even more diverse when separate countries are examined individually, as was done here selectively. We thus begin to realize that the Six-Day War was a factor stimulating change in the Israel-Diaspora relationship on some accounts, and it was not on other accounts. Significant and long-term effects appeared in the overall volume of fund-raising, both in relation to UJA in the United States and to a broader range of countries and of agencies operating on the Israeli scene. Significant short-term effects concerned the impact of Diaspora Jewry fund-raising on the Israeli economy, the percentage of all UJA revenues allocated to JAFI, the numbers of Jewish volunteers joining Israel in the moment of greatest danger, the outreach programs of the Department of Torah Education and Culture in the Diaspora, and the levels of emigration from Israel. The evidence for immigration to Israel is more complex and contradictory, but concerning *aliyah* from the more developed and politically stable countries, the Six-Day War certainly contributed to a significant short-term, followed by a moderate longer-term increase. In other, less stable Western countries, the effect was visible but of much lesser import in comparison with other effects related to the political and economic environment in the respective countries. More indirect effects on trends that were already at work can be discerned regarding tourism to Israel, and in more complex ways, *aliyah* from the Soviet Union. Little effects appear regarding such instruments of the World Zionist Organization as the educational programs of the Department of Jewish Education and Culture in the Diaspora and of the Institute for Leadership Training.

Translating these data into more general terms, the Six-Day War certainly raised the visibility and relevance of the State of Israel as one of the most meaningful foci for Jewish identification, both in the personal consciousness of many Jews and on the Jewish public agenda. Clearly the Israeli option for Jewish identification already existed before, but for many Jews living outside of Israel it was not clearly formulated or at best latent. The great fears and emotions that preceded and accompanied the military events of June 1967 gave the Israeli component greater relevance, attractiveness, and permanency within the overall complex of Jewish perceptions and identity worldwide. Unquestionably, the Six-Day War had a strengthening effect on Jewish identification patterns and such effect was irreversible, though the intensity and staying power of such effect is subject to questioning.

Furthermore, looking at the position of the State of Israel within the world system of nations, the 1967 war produced a significant strengthening of Israel's international status. One of the reasons was directly tied to the element of military victory. The fact, and perhaps even more the image of Israel's power, generated significant implications for broader international and internal processes that eventually were leading to industrialization and modernization of Israeli society. A victorious Israel would in turn become a stronger and more attractive destination for potential immigrants but also for international investment and other socioeconomic and political processes. Such a strengthened Israel would several years later have the resources to successfully absorb large numbers of new immigrants that in fact continue to arrive in the country at the time of this writing. Thus, various processes which either directly stem from, or are indirectly related to the Six-Day War irreversibly strengthened Israel's relation to the outer world and its centrality in respect to world Jewry.

On the other hand, some changes that might have been expected did not in fact materialize. This relates in the first place to the response of a certain segment of the Jewish organizational system whose decision-making behaviors, at least as reconstructed through our data, point to a pattern of "business as usual." This might have reflected objective budgetary constraints, but perhaps also a lack of inspiration and a failure to seize a historical opportunity when one appears—as was the case in 1967. Furthermore, several patterns involving the relationship of Diaspora Jewries with the general society in the respective countries had such deeper historical, social, economic, political, and psychological roots that they did not appear to be substantially affected by one single event, even of the magnitude of the one examined here. However, on some accounts the Six-Day War served as a catalyst helping to bring to the fore important processes that were already at work in a latent way.

For sure we cannot assume what might have happened to world Jewry if the Six-Day War had not taken place, and how the default processes would have looked like. Most likely, the weakening of Jewish communities in the Diaspora, and the incipient erosion in the mutual relationship between them and Israel which were already under way during the early 1960s might have continued their course. The Six-Day War slowed down and to some extent reversed such erosive trends. In some other respects, most prominently in the case of the Jews of the U.S.S.R., 1967 helped to generate a new consciousness which would eventually produce consequences of invaluable momentum for the Jewish population locally, for Israel, and for world Jewry.

Going back to the initial question about the relationship between unique events and long-term trends, one possible conclusion is that the Six-Day War, as assessed through measurable indicators, was a significant factor in enhancing continuity of world Jewry, in the light of preceding trends and in the face of their possible or likely weakening, more than in breaking revolutionary new paths in Jewish history and society. It should also be noted that viewed in historical perspective and in the context of the simultaneous reading of several indicators as attempted in this chapter, the Six-Day War stands out as the single most powerful source of direct and indirect consequences in the relationship between Israel and world Jewry since Israel's independence in 1948.

Concluding with a metaphor, and looking back at the graphical display of yearly change in the percent of funds allocated to Israel as part of Jewish fund-raising in the United States (Figure 13B), more than anything else, the Six-Day War amounted to one extra, powerful heart-beat on the long, resilient and convolute cardiogram of Jewish history.

ACKNOWLEDGMENTS

Research for this article was conducted at the Division of Jewish Demography and Statistics of the Avraham Harman Institute of Contemporary Jewry, the Hebrew University of Jerusalem. The authors gratefully acknowledge the collaboration of all those at the Central Bureau of Statistics, the Israel Ministry of Tourism, the Jewish Agency for Israel/World Zionist Organization, the Central Zionist Archives, and the United Jewish Appeal/United Israel Appeal, who facilitated research by providing access to published and unpublished data and other useful information. We thank in particular Dr. Erik H. Cohen, Todd Warnick, and Barbara Schipper-Bergstein. The research and preparation of this paper were assisted by the Isaac and Herma Donner (England) Fund for Research on Diaspora-Israel Relations.

The Diaspora's Contribution to Israel's Economic Development

Haim Barkai

Department of Economics
The Hebrew University of Jerusalem

THE SUBJECT OF THIS ESSAY is "The Diaspora and Israel's economy after the Six-Day War." This period refers actually to three decades which cover the interval between that war and the era of the second mass *aliyah*, which made its mark on Israel's society and economy during the first half of the 1990s, and which seemingly would be the hallmark of the whole closing decade of the twentieth century.

Development Patterns of the Israeli Economy

A short survey, mainly quantitative, of the trends and patterns of the economic system since the middle 1960s offers the relevant background to the study and analysis of the contribution of the diaspora to the development of the economy.

The data presented in Table 1, showing the growth of the economy in terms of an index of Gross Domestic Product (GDP), the best aggregate measure of production potential and of living standards, offers the proper short- and long-term perspective. Inspection of the series (Table 1, column 1) suggests that the economy grew by almost two times in the interval between the Six-Day and Yom Kippur Wars. Note that in the succeeding period, two decades (the interval 1973–1993) were required for the Israeli economy to grow by two times, a feat performed in the decade between 1966 and 1975. During these years, the economy had been subjected to a major leap, the expression of which in terms of aggregates was the rapid rise of national product, of national product per capita, and correspondingly, of living standards.

Although population growth accelerated too, the series of column 2 (Table 1) indicates that per capita product grew by 50 percent during the seven years between the two wars. This implies an annual average growth rate of living standards of about 6 percent—a high rate indeed by universal standards. This rate was cut by 2 to 3 percent only in the succeeding fifteen years (1975–1990). The decline in economic performance, and thus in the per capita growth rate, occurred even though this fifteen-year period was characterized by a dearth in *aliyah*, and correspondingly in the growth rate of the population. Yet in spite of that deceleration of growth, during the years in which Israel had been subjected to a high and accelerating rate of inflation through 1985, and in its wake, to a significant "slowdown" during the stabilization period interval (1985–1989), per capita product still during the three decades 1966–1995 more than doubled (Table 1). Thus, Israel's per capita product is about 62 percent of that of the United States and about 75 percent of the average of West European countries. It is by now higher than the per capita product of several members of the European Community, located at the tail end of the array of per capita product of this group of countries.

It is therefore reasonable to identify the post-Six-Day War decade as the decade in which Israel surfaced on the map of the international economy in terms of the size of its product and the volume of its exports and imports of goods and services (Israel's entrance into the world capital market occurred however, much later—towards the middle of the 1990s). The major leap in the production potential and in national product which was implemented during the post-Six-Day War decade was, however, not the only dimension subjected to major change. The quantitative change involved also a far-reaching change in the structure of the economy.

Farming, involving of course the setting up of agricultural settlements all over the country, but particularly along the borders (the 1949 armistice lines) was given the highest priority during the 1950s. This evidently was fully in line with the traditional economic orientation of the Zionist movement from the advent of Jewish settlement in Palestine in the third and particularly the closing quarter of the nineteenth century, and through the period of the British Mandate. During the 1950s, in the first half of which food was still rationed, the priority of agricultural settlement and production was reasonable from the short-term point of view. Pinchas Sapir, appointed to the portfolio of Trade and Industry in the fourth Ben-Gurion-led government, in 1955, already realized that future economic growth and rapid absorption of newcomers into productive activity, would depend on rapid development of manufacturing industries. He thus pushed openly for a change of the traditional Zionist agenda—a development policy giving top priority to manufacturing. It was not, however, immediately accepted.

Nevertheless, during his tenure as Minister of Trade and Industry (1955–1963) he began implementing that policy by initiating an industrialization drive. He continued his all-out support of the industrialization effort in the coming decade (1963–1974) in which he occupied the leading economic post in the government—as Minister of Finance. The focus of the first stage of the "Sapir industrialization drive" was inevitably the traditional manufacturing branches: food, textiles, and diamond polishing. Firms operating in the textile and food lines were already set up in the Mandatory period. They expanded rapidly during World War II when "shipping space" constraints effectively excluded competition from abroad and offered them rapidly expanding markets in the Middle East. The third line, diamond polishing, dominated by Jews in Belgium in particular, "emigrated" to Palestine as the war clouds were gathering over Europe in the late 1930s, as a result of which Israel acquired a leading position in the world diamond industries and trade in the postwar decades.

But the really significant conceptual reorientation leading to the identification of manufacturing industry as the engine of economic growth, and its implementation in practice, occurred only after the Six-Day War: effectively, in the seven-year period between 1967 and 1973. What happened during that short interval was not just a major effort directed towards the expansion of the manufacturing industry but also an overall restructuring—a move away from the traditional branches providing essentially consumption goods and basic inputs (steel, cement, etc.), towards high-tech industries in lines such as electronics, optics, and also organic chemistry.

The driving force of the process was the tremendous growth of the defense budget. Israel was forced to implement that policy by the transformation of the political and military environment in the Middle East in the wake of the Six-Day War. This change in the military balance reflected the "forward policy" adopted by the Soviet Union, the target of which was a rapid rebuilding of the Arab armies defeated in 1967. This led to the Soviet decision to arm the Egyptian and Syrian armies with the most advanced weapons systems—the first line of armaments of the Red Army: tanks, artillery, planes, and surface-to-air and missiles produced by Soviet industries. It also meant that the Soviet Union was ready to bear the cost of these supplies. This rapid rearmament of the Arab armies and the French embargo imposed on weapon deliveries (fighters and missile boats) to Israel (in flagrant breach of a commercial contract) by De Gaulle *before* the outbreak of the war, led to the Israeli government's decision to reduce the crucial dependence of the Israel Defense Forces (IDF) on the supply of major weapons systems from abroad. The policy adopted was designed to reduce the dependence of Israel's defense system on the political considerations of the major Western powers. Yet the quality of such major arms systems is crucially dependent on the most advanced technologies at the disposal of the weapons industries of the great powers. Israel's defense industry was thus challenged to produce and provide the "world"-quality weapons required by the Israeli Defense Forces. Later, this would also allow Israel to compete in the world market. This meant an allocation of resources to research and development in electronics, optics, and cutting-edge computing technologies, in order to adhere to the high and advanced standards characteristic of industries operating at the frontier of technology.

The major allocation of resources to this target can be approximated by the rising costs of Israel's defense system between the wars. The IDF's striking force in terms of manpower and equipment in the immediate pre–Six-Day War years had been dependent on the use of resources of about 8–9 percent of GDP. In those days this involved the total defense expenditure, the domestic cost, and the cost of weapon imports. But during the seven years leading up to the Yom Kippur War, domestic defense consumption rose to 11, 12, and finally to 14 percent of GDP. Rapidly growing defense imports were increasingly, and after 1970, almost fully, financed by U.S. aid, which in those days meant long-term credits. The cost of these imports added 3–4 percent of the GDP to the total cost. Defense consumption at its peak was thus more than 18 percent of GDP.

These ratios referred of course to a GDP which was almost twice as high at the end of that seven-year period. The defense budget, which thus grew by three times in real terms within these seven years, offered accordingly the main presumably dominant incentive to the development of Israel's manufacturing industries, and thus to the major restructuring of the economy. One decade after the Six-Day War, Israel's economy had a production potential more than twice as high as in 1966. The system underwent a correspondingly major change—it was transformed into an industrial complex per se, driven by a high-tech industry still focusing at that time on the production of weapons systems and the technology serving these systems, capable of competing in world markets and armaments purchased by defense establishments in the most advanced industrialized countries.

THE DIASPORA AND THE ISRAELI ECONOMY

Aliyah

The contribution of the Diaspora to the Jewish resettlement of Palestine and later of Israel involved first and foremost its impact on the population, expressed in terms of immigration—*aliyah*. Professor DellaPergola has discussed the demographic and sociological aspects of that ongoing process. My contribution to that subject refers essentially to the economic dimension of this cyclical process which had been going on over a period of more than a century. These waves of immigration did have an immediate and long-term ultimate impact on the economy.

The years preceding the Six-Day War were years of "recession"—a downturn in *aliyah* in the wake of the wave of the early 1960s (peaking in 1963). The number of *olim* in 1966 was only about a quarter of those arriving in the peak year of that wave. The group of *olim* from North Africa was the dominant group in that wave: they were 51 percent of the total of 315,000 immigrants who reached Israel between 1960 and 1967. Immigrants from Europe were only 31 percent of the total. The next wave, almost similar in size, turned up in the immediate aftermath of the war. Between 1968 and 1974 this involved about 280,000 *olim*. But the geographical dimension—the countries of origin of these immigrants—was quite different: European countries of origin contributed 57 percent of that flow, and America and Oceania contributed an additional 22 percent.

These figures are an indicator of a renewal of *aliyah* from the West; the number of immigrants from these countries of origin was three times higher than the number of arrivals from these countries in the 1960–1967 interval. But the dominant feature of that postwar *aliyah* was the small breach of the Iron Curtain after almost fifty years during which immigration from the U.S.S.R. was prohibited. Jewish emigration from the Soviet Union reached almost 100,000 between 1968 and 1974. Most of this could be attributed to the change in the East-West political dialogue in those days: in the context of the East-West "détante" of the late 1960s and early 1970s. Almost all those Jews who were allowed to leave the Soviet Union made *aliyah* to Israel.

It is well known that the dynamics of *aliyah* were from the very beginning generated and affected by "push" and "pull" factors. The direct impact of the Six-Day War increased significantly the identification of Jews all over the world with Israel and was accordingly a highly important "pulling in" device. This is undoubtedly indicated by the postwar *aliyah* wave from the West, relatively small indeed in absolute terms and even more so in relation to the size of the Jewish population in North and South America, in Western Europe, in South Africa, and in Australia. "Pushing out" factors in these countries were evidently minor or nonexistent in those years. Nevertheless, the younger generation was clearly affected by the "pulling in" factor. Many in this age bracket "discovered" Israel in the wake of the Six-Day War. Novel absorption devices were set up in Israel to promote their absorption into the Jewish social setting. The establishment of a School for Overseas Students by the Hebrew University immediately after the war is an innovation imitated later by other Israeli universities, an obvious case in point.

Yet the major relevance of the "pulling in" factor for the wave of *aliyah* from the Soviet Union was even greater than for Western *aliyah*. The political environment is highly relevant in this case. The very decision to apply for an emigration visa from the Soviet Union involved personal risk even in ordinary times. The immediate post-Six-Day War period—between 1967 and 1970, at the height of the Brezhnev reaction, before and in the wake of the Soviet invasion of Czechoslovakia—was evidently far from "ordinary." Nevertheless, many Jews took the risk and used the opportunity to slip through the small breach in the Iron Curtain which diplomatic pressure by the West, egged on by the appeal of the Jewish communities in the West to public opinion, had opened. A flow of tens of thousands annually from the Soviet Union reached Israel from 1968 onwards, peaking at 35,000 *olim* in 1973.

The contribution of this wave of *aliyah* to the economy was substantial, due to the quality of manpower in terms of education and training. The economic potential—the human capital—of this group was clearly higher than the average of the Israeli manpower at that time. The incentive for integration into the new social and economic environment and the urge to implement it rapidly was clearly strong in that group of *olim*, whose ideological motivation to immigrate to Israel was very strong. This also applies to the much smaller group of young *olim* from the West, mostly from the United States, which arrived in those days.

This high-quality manpower was relatively easily and rapidly integrated in an economy subject to strong aggregate demand pressures, and thus running at the limit of its capacity. The demands created by private and public sector consumption expenditures, boosted by that of the immigrants from the very day of their very arrival; the prosperity in the building industry generated by public sector projects designed to house the new *olim;* and correspondingly, the leap in private consumption expenditures by veteran Israelis created by rapid growth; and finally, the major demand pressure generated by the defense establishment which through 1970 had to fight the "War of Attrition," generated the very rapid growth process. Growth rates topping 10 percent annually (at an annual average of 10.6 percent for the 1968–1973 interval), were the order of the day.

The financing of immigrant absorption and the requirements of the defense system, imposed strong pressures on the public sector budget, which, year-in, year-out had a substantial deficit. The over-full employment situation from 1970 onwards, while the public sector deficit was large and growing, inevitably initiated an inflationary process. The take-off of Israel's "great inflation" thus occurred between 1970 and the Yom Kippur War. It accelerated in its aftermath, in the wake of the so-called "energy crisis" and peaked at three-digit rates in 1979–1985, after which the 1985 stabilization policies pulled it down rapidly. (It is, however, still running at an annual average of close to 10 percent in the 1990s.)

Contributions and the Independence Loan

The financial contribution of Jewish communities abroad to promote Jewish resettlement of Palestine and Israel was, from the very beginning, the focus of Zionist activity in the Diaspora. The personal contribution to the Appeal, was an indicator of both identification with the message of Zionism and an expression of personal financial capacity. The receipts of these appeals were transmitted to the coffers of the Zionist organizations in charge of the resettlement effort of Palestine. Later, after its establishment in 1929, the "Jewish Agency" (as a joint venture of the Zionist organization and "non-Zionist" Jewish organizations) was the recipient of the funds collected by the appeals and entrusted with their allocation. Besides the Jewish Agency, recognized by the Mandatory government as the political representative of the Jews in Palestine, other non-profit institutions such as universities and *yeshivot* operated as mechanisms supporting the establishment and maintenance of the Jewish presence in Palestine. Finally, the Independence Loan (Israel Bonds) organization, set up in 1950 after the establishment of the state, was to function as another device for the absorption of *aliyah* and the rebuilding of the country.

A flow of private Jewish capital was another factor contributing to that target before World War I, and particularly between the two World Wars. But in the post-World War II period, this was a small source and in the 1950s and 1960s, the two first decades of independence, private capital from abroad was indeed a miniscule source of finance for investment—compared with the flow of resources channeled into the economy by the appeals and by the Independence Loan organization. Things had changed significantly toward the middle 1990s. A major flow of private capital, much larger than anything comparable from 1939 onward, has been flowing into Israel's economy as direct funding of investment in Israeli firms—usually going concerns with "household" names—and also as financial capital moving into the Israeli capital market. A significant fraction of that flow consists, however, of funds which by no means might be identified as "Jewish private capital." These funds are essentially an investment of the world business and financial community implemented on the basis of clear-cut profit considerations.

The trend of the Diaspora's funding of the Israeli economy since the Six-Day War is described in Table 1 (columns 6 and 7). An inspection of these series, based on the series in constant dollar terms (in 1995 prices) shown in Table 2 (columns 5 and 6) reveals clearly the immediate financial response of the Jewish communities all over the world to the Six-Day War, the Yom Kippur War, and finally the major effort to fund the second mass immigration of the 1990s, in the wake of the collapse of the Soviet Union. The contribution index underlines the spontaneous response of the Diaspora to these major events. The flow of contributions grew 3.3 times within one year—between 1966 and 1967—and the total "aid" (which includes the flow of funds from the Independence Loan organizations) grew by a factor of 4.7. This means that the purchase of bonds grew at an even higher rate than the flow of contributions during the same period. The volume of contributions was indeed significantly smaller in the years succeeding the war, but it did not decline to the prewar level; it stayed at approximately twice the level of 1966, effectively, or approximately twice the level of the inflow during the whole prewar decade (1957–1966).

The figures in Tables 1 and 2, and data for the years between 1966 and 1995 not represented in these tables, indicate that in the three decades since the Six-Day War, the flow of contributions was between two to three times higher in real dollar terms than in the two decades before the war. This excludes of course the year of the Yom Kippur War, in which a leap in contributions allowed the appeals to transfer almost $2.5 billion (1995) to Israel (Table 2, column 5). This applies to the funds transferred by the Independence Loan organization too, as indicated by column 6 in that table. The flow of funds from that source in 1973 reached an all-time peak of about $1.2 billion (1995). Thus, total Jewish aid in 1973 was more than $3.5 billion (1995). A third peak in the flow of contributions, but not in the flow of total Jewish aid, can be identified from 1990, at the advent of the second mass immigration era. The flow of contributions during these years grew from about two to about three times the pre-Six-Day War flow. Note that in the Jewish aid series (Table 2, column 7, and Table 1, column 7), the flow of Independence Loan funds grew during that period at a lower rate than the contributions series. This reflects the weak performance of the Independence Loan organizations. This feature will be discussed below.

The survey presented above of financial aid of the Diaspora to Israel was based on the data of Tables 1 and 2, the base year of which is 1966. Though not presented in the tables, the available data on the flow of Jewish aid goes all the way back to 1952 and offers insight on this subject for almost the whole history of the State. Except for a single year—1954—in which contributions peaked at $654 million (in constant 1995 GDP prices), the flow of these contributions never reached 500 million dollars between 1952 and 1966. In 1956, the year of the Sinai campaign, in which contributions rose again, they were about half a billion; otherwise the annual flow was within the $300–$400 million range. This of course means that even though the analysis of the trend from the middle 1960s to the middle 1990s was based on the 1966 benchmark, it is *mutatis mutandis* applicable to the period beginning with the establishment of the State.

The data presented in Table 2, and the background time series for each year since 1952 indicate that the total "Jewish aid" flow had undergone a structural change somewhat after the Yom Kippur War. In the 1950s, the 1960s, and the early 1970s, the flow of funds from the Bonds (Independence Loan) project was with some deviations, about 40–50 percent of the funds transmitted by the appeals organizations. In the second half of the 1970s and in the 1980s, this ratio declined below the benchmark of 30 percent of the inflow of contributions. The Independence Loan funds are, however, not unilateral transfers. These funds represent medium- and long-term credit which must be repaid. The government of Israel had been redeeming these bonds punctually during the forty-five years since the project was initiated in 1951. In the 1950s, and through the 1970s, the interest rates carried by the Independence Loan bonds were indeed somewhat lower than the interest rates at which the government of Israel could borrow in the capital markets of the West. The difference between the promised yields on these bonds and relevant market rates involved of course a (small) subsidy—a kind of indirect contribution to Israel which purchasers of the bonds handed over to the State. But the gap between the yield on these bonds and market rates of interest were eroded in the late 1970s and 1980s, as inflation had been generating much higher real interest rates in Western markets, and as Israel's rating as a debtor had been improving. This meant of course that the risk premium on credit to Israel had been decreasing towards the "standard" rates of good debtors in world capital markets. The latter trend was reinforced in the 1990s in particular, as Israel's credit rating was moving closely to the median range (and beyond) of world capital market ratings, and simultaneously, real interest rates in the West had been declining. The Independence Loan funds offer effectively no net interest rate subsidies, from the early 1990s at the latest. Their decrease as a source of foreign currency liquidity for the State, which was a highly important feature indeed for the Israel of the 1950s, reflects the improvement of Israel's credit rating allowing the Israeli public sector, its banking system and business firms to borrow abroad at much better terms. Though still highly significant politically, the Independence Loan system is therefore hardly of any financial relevance toward the end of the century.

The new economic environment in which Israel operates in foreign capital markets, suggests that the maintenance of the Independence Loan organization as a going concern in the coming decade is hardly warranted by economic factors per se. It was warranted indeed by such considerations in the first two to three decades of its existence. The continuation of the Independence Loan operation in the future could be justified mainly in terms of public relations considerations—the significance of the links with the Jewish communities in the United States in particular. In any case, the Jewish economic aid to Israel which since the early 1950s was based on two legs—the appeals and the Bonds project—is from the late 1980s onwards dependent in practice on a single organization—the United Jewish Appeals run by Jewish communities all over the world.

JEWISH ECONOMIC AID: LEVELS AND COMPARATIVE TERMS

Contributions shown in Table 2 series (columns 1 and 5) had undoubtedly been the dominant component of Diaspora aid to Israel. The time series presented in that table indicate that during the thirty-year period between the Six-Day War and the mid-1990s, Diaspora contributions to Israel stood at an annual average level of $1 billion in constant (1995) dollar terms. The funds were transmitted in practice to the public sector, financing the budgets of the Jewish Agency and Keren Kayemet (Jewish National Fund), and also, by means of their separate collecting entities—Friends organizations of the universities, of *yeshivot*, and other non-profit public organizations such as museums, Magen David Adom, the Jerusalem Fund, etc. The latter organizations received a substantial fraction, and over the years an increasing share of total donations.

An important though not exclusive measure of the significance of these annual flows to the comings and goings of the economy, is the ratio of these annual flows to GDP. By the middle 1990s—1994 and 1995—the ratio of contributions to Gross Domestic Product was in the range of 1–1.5 percent of that aggregate. Yet though the flow of contributions between

1967 and 1970 in constant dollars was similar to that of the middle 1990s, its relative size was significantly greater. The real national product of the economy in the early 1970s was between 30 to 40 percent that of the GNP of the middle 1990s. This means that the resources provided by Jewish communities abroad amounted in those days to 3–4 percent of the GNP. Though in absolute terms the inflow of funds from contributions in the 1950s and 1960s was about 40–50 percent that of the post-Six-Day War period, the ratio of that annual inflow to GDP was even higher: it was about 6–7 in the early 1950s and 4–5 percent in the post-Sinai campaign decade. This of course expresses the much greater significance of the contribution flow to investment, living standards, and the growth of the Israeli economy in the first two decades of the State.

The declining trend of the ratio of Jewish aid funds and GDP certainly has influenced political thought in Israel. Some members of the political community suggest that Israel could afford to give up the funds transferred by the central appeal organizations which finance the budget of the Jewish Agency. These are now about 50 percent of the flow of contribution funds, involving about 0.5–0.7 percent of GDP. It is suggested that these funds should be used, say, for other Jewish communal purposes related to Israel: the funding of study groups of Jewish youth in Israel, or scholarships to students from the Diaspora coming for an extended studies program in one of Israel's universities.

If adopted, this proposal would eliminate two important functions of Jewish Diaspora communities. The first is the effective participation of Jewish communities all over the world in decisions on the allocation of a meaningful fraction of real resources at the disposal of Israel's public sector. Since the public sector allocates about 40 percent of the GDP, the effective influence of the Jewish communities on public sector allocations to public sector consumption and investment refers to 3–3.5 percent of government expenditure. Furthermore, the funds from the appeals abroad finance an even more significant chunk of long term investment—the investment in the formation of human capital—education and training, and the health system. The direct involvement of Jewish communities in the allocation and use of their contributions has grown significantly in the last decade. This involvement, which means participation in the planning of projects and frequent visits to oversee their running—namely, the imposition of controls on these funds by representatives of the contributors—contributes to the efficiency of their application. Inevitably, it leads to the strengthening of the links of the contributors with Israel.

The second function of the "appeals system," perhaps an even more important one, is the fact that this flow of an annual average of $1 billion during the last decades suggests to all and sundry the existence of an implicit hidden reserve at the disposal of Israel in times of danger. In "regular" times, Israel's relatively high ranking in the "league table" of financial risks means that its government, the banking system, and business can borrow substantial sums in the world capital markets. This reserve might, however, disappear overnight in the case of political complications or war. In this event, which could easily occur in the Middle East, the potential availability of Jewish aid is of a very high significance even for the operation of the capital markets and of course to the decision-making process of a political community under stress.

The significant rise in contributions during the Sinai campaign, their major leap in 1967 and an even larger jump in 1973, and again, their substantial rise twenty years later after the collapse of the Soviet Union and the advent of the second mass immigration in the 1990s (Table 2), suggest that the appeal organizations provide an implicit "insurance policy" underwritten by the behavior of Jewish communities. The provision of liquid working capital to an economic system operating in conditions of high levels of uncertainty requires the maintenance of the contribution organizations.

Therefore, I do not consider the trend toward the reduction of Israel's share of contributions collected by the appeals organizations as a problem. The effort to maintain Jewish cultural activities, in particular the running of Jewish schools—is clearly a highly important activity for the future of Jewish communities. Furthermore, from the Israeli point of view, it offers a kind of supplementary insurance, since a part of these additional financial resources could be diverted rapidly to Israel if and when unexpected serious developments on the political front recur. This does not mean at all that reduction in *absolute* terms in the flow of funds allocated for Israeli activities would be a reasonable policy. But in the present-day context, I do not see a big problem in a policy which would allocate a greater share of the forthcoming *rise* in appeals revenues beyond, say, the revenues in the early 1990s, to local needs of the communities in the Diaspora. This would of course mean that in the longer run, the relative share of funds transmitted to Israel would decline, though the absolute level of transfers would remain stable put and could even rise. Note that the adoption of such a policy would not do any harm to what I identified as the second function of the Jewish appeal system—that of providing an implicit "insurance" policy to the Israeli economy. In that case, the (implicit) reserve for an immediate transfer of funds in the case of an urgent need would clearly grow.

In the short and medium run, $400–$500 million for functions performed by the Jewish Agency are evidently still $400–$500 million. It would be a foolish move to forego the receipt of funds of this order, both from the point of view of the balance of payments and from the point of view of the involvement of representatives of Jewish communities in the allocation of public sector resources in Israel. The maintenance of the current flow of funds (in real dollar terms) at the annual average for the last three decades is therefore the most reasonable policy stance, even though their share in the revenues of the appeal system and as a fraction of Israel's GDP would decline.

Jewish Private Investment

The time series of "Jewish aid" presented in Tables 1 and 2 did not refer to figures of private investment by Jews and/or "Jewish" firms from the Diaspora. This, even though in the period of the Mandate, and particularly between the World Wars, private capital was the dominant component of capital imports to Palestine and the dominant source of funds for investment in the Jewish economic sector. Yet, since the establishment of the State and through the early 1990s, things were altogether different. The absolute size of the private capital flow, and its relative size compared to the inflow of Jewish aid, of foreign aid, plus German reparations to the State and individuals was small indeed. This is underlined by the heading of one of the sections of Professor E. Kleiman's recently published study, surveying "Philanthropy and Investment in Israel." This heading reads: "Why did the Jewish Diaspora donate but not invest?" (Kleiman 1996, p. 13). He summarizes his detailed estimates of the funding of investment for the three decades 1952–1982, saying: "With the exception of five years...the diaspora's private investment...never exceeded 10 percent...of domestic gross capital formation. For the whole period it averaged less than 6 percent."[1]

A significant change in that field occurred only recently, towards the middle of the 1990s. Investment funds of "foreign residents" had been financing 10 percent of gross investment. Furthermore, during the same period, flotations of Israeli business sector shares and bonds in the major international capital markets (mostly on New York's stock exchanges),

---

[1] E. Kleiman, "Jewish and Palestinian Diaspora Attitudes to Philanthropy and Investment: Learning from Israel's Experience" (Peace Papers, Truman Research Institute, The Hebrew University of Jerusalem, November 1996), 11.

were more than double the direct and financial investment of foreigners referred to above. This means that by the middle of the 1990s private capital imports to Israel had been financing about 25 percent of gross capital formation. Yet it would be wrong to identify these private capital inflows, and even the (net) direct investments of foreign residents, which are a component of the total inflow of these funds, with private investments of Jews residing abroad. Even the net direct investment and the purchase of stocks and bonds by direct placement or by firms quoted on the Tel-Aviv stock exchange are not necessarily made by Jews or "Jewish" firms. Amongst investors in Israel in recent years were firms such as Intel, IBM, Volkswagen, Siemans, Unilever, Nestle's, Motorola, and many other "household names." On the other side of the coin, Israeli firms, like Teva, Koor, ICI, Klal, and a great number of smaller firms operating mainly in the hi-tech branches have been floating their stocks and bonds in the major stock exchanges abroad.

The Israeli firms could not, of course, go it alone. They were advised and supported by the most important investment banks operating in the international financial markets. Furthermore, these investment banks had been recently opening offices in Israel and had been advising mutual funds and pension funds managed by them to buy Israeli securities. Yet this major inflow of funds in the 1990s and particularly between 1994 and 1997, cannot be identified as capital imports by Jews into Israel.

Financial and Marketing Advice

Nevertheless, a Jewish point does clearly surface in this context. Many top-line investment banks such as Merril Lynch, Goldman Sachs, Stanley-Morgan, Lehman Brothers, Rothschild, and others, all of which are involved in foreign investment activities related to Israel, have a great number of Jews operating in top management positions. This reflects a post-World War II trend which featured the entry of a significant number of Jews into the investment bank industry and their rapid climb to the top echelons. Several, and probably many of these financial experts and managers are involved in voluntary activities run by the Jewish establishment: the United Jewish Appeal, Israel Bonds, university appeals, the Jerusalem Fund, etc. This means, of course, the forging and maintenance of direct links with Israel, which endows them with inside information of the comings and goings in the economy and society. Thus, though they clearly maintain the profit considerations of their organizations as the prime criterion for financial involvement, their direct linkage and standing in the major financial markets in the world is helpful in gaining access for the business sector and the Israeli government to the pool of finance located in these markets.

Investment banks in the United States have served as underwriters and distributors of the $10 billion Israeli bond issue of Israel (guaranteed by the U.S. government), the sale of which will be completed in 1998. These banks serve similarly as financial advisors and underwriters to the Israeli business sector securities issues. It goes without saying that without these developments the entrance of Israel into the major capital markets of the world would not have been implemented, i.e., if its credit rating had not been significantly improved due to and in the wake of the 1985 stabilization policy, which put the system back into a reasonable economic environment featuring a single-digit inflation rate (albeit at the top end of that range) and the return to a pattern of rapid economic growth in the 1990s.

Comparative price stability, rapid growth in the wake of and related to the second mass immigration, and seemingly also the peace process evidently constituted the relevant menu which facilitated the rise of Israel's credit rating into the effective range of that applicable to the leading industrial economies. The size of product, the level of per capita income, the state of the balance of payments, the level of foreign currency balances, and last but not least a legal system similar to that of Western countries allowing the enforcement of contracts, were clearly preconditions for Israel's crossing the threshold of the worldwide capital market. But given these preconditions, one can hardly doubt that the great number of Jews operating in that field has helped in the past and will continue to help Israel's dealings in this highly-sensitive and sophisticated environment.

A somewhat similar contribution to the Israeli economy is the presence and activity of Jewish businesses in the marketing of consumer goods—a traditional function of Jewish entrepreneurs in the Diaspora. Marks and Spencer is evidently not the only example in this field. Scores of firms owned and run by Jews are operating in these branches in North and South America, and also in some West European countries. One can therefore not exaggerate their potential help in the marketing of Israeli products in view of the relative size of Israel's export sector. The current $30 billion annual export flow means that that sector creates demand to the tune of about 30 percent of GDP. Thus the advice of Jewish entrepreneurs operating in the retail business, and the openings into retail markets their firms could offer, have potentially great significance for the operation of Israel's production sector.

The contribution of Jewish entrepreneurs, of bankers, and financial analysts, of marketing experts and of leading agents in insurance, is evidently not quantifiable. But as Israel's economy grows and becomes more sophisticated, its dependence on foreign real and financial markets grows rapidly. The significant potential of that intangible but still highly effective contribution of the Jews living in the Diaspora grows correspondingly. The *conditio sine qua non* for this to happen requires at least the maintenance of the links between Jews in the Diaspora and Israel. But this is a subject for sociologists and political scientists, and last but not least the Israeli political leadership.

BIBLIOGRAPHY

Haim Barkai, "Economics," *The Hebrew Encyclopedia* vol. 6 (2) *The State of Israel* (Jerusalem: Sifriat Poalim, 1994), 551–88.

E. Kleiman, "Jewish and Palestinian Diaspora Attitudes to Philanthropy and Investment: Learning from Israel's Experience" (Peace Papers, Truman Research Institute, The Hebrew University of Jerusalem, November 1996), 3–17; A-1-A8.

Table 1

MEASURES OF NATIONAL PRODUCT, *ALIYAH*, POPULATION, AND "JEWISH AID" (1966 = 100)

Year	GDP (1)	GDP per capita (2)	Aliyah[1] (3)	Population: total (4)	Population: Jews (5)	Contributions[2] (6)	Total Aid[3] (7)
1966	100	100	100	100	100	100	100
1967	102	98	91	104	102	329	467
1970	143	125	230	114	110	267	365
1973	188	149	344	126	121	585	808
1975	206	157	126	131	126	335	397
1980	239	161	128	148	139	203	253
1985	276	171	67	161	150	193	247
1990	328	181	1250	181	168	277	299
1994	445	216	500	206	189[1]	297	344
1995	476	226	474	211	194[1]	298	372

NOTES:

[1] About 6000 *olim* who arrived between 1990 and 1995 on the basis of the Law of Return, but are not considered as Jews according to the *halacha*, are not included in this estimate. Their inclusion in the figures for the Jewish population would be expressed in indices of 195 and 200 for 1994 and 1995, respectively.

[2] The series represents annual (unilateral) transfers of the United Jewish Appeal, and the appeals of the academic institutions, *yeshivot*, museums, etc., in terms of constant 1995 dollars represented in Table 2, column 5.

[3] Represents the figures presented in Table 2, column 7, which are the sum of net transfers of appeals, contributions, and "independent loan organizations."

SOURCES:

Columns (1) and (2) according to Barkai (1994), Table 3, p. 555, and Bank of Israel, Table App. B-1, p. 193; column (3) Barkai (1994), Table 2, p. 554, and CBS, *Statistical Abstract of Israel 1997*, Table 5.1, p. 156; Columns (4) and (5), Barkai (1994), Table 1, p. 552, and *Abstract*, 1997, Table 2.1, p. 49; Columns (6) and (7) derived from entries in Columns (5) and (7) of Table 2 below.

Table 2

DIASPORA AID IN CURRENT AND CONSTANT DOLLAR TERMS
1966–1995

Year	Contributions[1] (1)	Independence Loan[2] (2)	Total Aid (1)+(2)= (3)	U.S. Prices[3] (4)	Contributions[3] (5)	Independence Loan[3] (6)	Total Aid (5)+(6)= (7)[3]
1966	97	7	104	100	408	30	438
1967	325	171	496	102	1341	706	2047
1970	290	135	425	112	1090	508	1598
1973	742	359	1101	131	2385	1153	3538
1975	510	138	648	157	1368	370	1738
1980	450	154	604	229	827	283	1110
1985	568	212	780	303	789	294	1083
1990	981	154	1135	365	1131	178	1309
1994	1050	417	1467	410	1211	295	1506
1995	1215	413	1628	421	1215	413	1628

NOTES:

[1] The Contribution series includes annual transfers in nominal dollars to the Jewish Agency and related institutions and transfers to non-profit organizations such as universities, *yeshivot*, etc.

[2] Net transfer of the Independence Loan Organization.

[3] Entries are in constant 1995 U.S. dollars in terms of the GNP implicit price index of the U.S.

SOURCES:
Columns (1) and (2) according to Kleiman 1996, app. Table 1a. Kleiman's table has been derived from CBS (special publication 767), *Israel's Balance of Payments 1952–1984*. The data from 1985 onwards is according to Bank of Israel *Report 1995*, Table VI-10, p. 226, and Table VI-12, p. 234, and similar tables in *Reports 1985* and *1993*;. Column (4) *Economic Report of the President 1996*, Table B-3, p. 273; Column (5) and (6), derived from entries in Column (1) and (2) respectively and the corresponding price entries of column (4).

From David to Goliath:
American Representations of Jews around the Six-Day War

Deborah Dash Moore
Vassar College

"One of the results of the Middle Eastern war," opined Vermont Royster in his column in the June 9th edition of the *Wall Street Journal*, "is that Israel has won a far more rewarding military victory without U.S. intervention than it could possibly have won with it,..." Though the war had not yet ended, Royster recognized "that the Israelis have thrown back the efforts of Mr. Nasser's creaky coalition to thrust them into the sea. And all this by a little country of sparse resources and only a fraction of the population of its surrounding enemies." Headline writers at the *Journal* appropriately entitled Royster's article "David and Goliath" for there was no doubt about his references. "So there is, first of all, the rewarding pride of a tiny David slaying a huge, if rather awkward, Goliath.... But the rewards of winning this way are much more than just to the spirit." Those rewards were tangible in Israel's newfound "firm status as a viable, independent nation," and not a "puppet nation" propped up and manipulated by U.S. power. Royster interpreted American caution in its diplomacy not as neutrality of mind, for "Arab aggression was too blatant to be disguised, and the American sympathies with Israel are too strong to be submerged." Americans were rooting for little David, cheering from the sidelines for the modern day Israelites to give the Philistines their "comeuppance."[1]

Representations of Israeli Jews as David and their Arab enemies as Goliath form a leitmotif in news reporting surrounding the Six-Day War. Popular press accounts, in such national papers as the *New York Times* and newsmagazines like *Time* and *Newsweek* present compelling imagery drawn not only from biblical depictions of Israelite struggles but also from more contemporary Zionist visions of Jews in the Jewish state. These represen-

---

[1] Vermont Royster, "David and Goliath," *Wall Street Journal*, 9 June 1967, 10.

tations express American understandings of the Six-Day War and influence American interpretations of Jews. Such a transformation of Jewish images was unexpected. "Neither the early Zionists nor their early American supporters anticipated that it would be as soldiers, and not as dreamers, that Jews would capture the imagination of the Gentile world," Peter Grose subsequently observed.[2] Despite the Six-Day War's overlap with American fighting in Vietnam, reporters evoke flattering sources of military might in their dispatches. Even without such specific references as Royster's, language used to depict Israelis suggest imagery congruent with the heroic struggle of David versus the giant Philistine.

Americans chose selectively from the biblical account. David's appearance, "ruddy-cheeked, bright-eyed, and handsome" in a recent translation, figure in the portrayal of Israelis, as did his youth and association with farming, albeit not sheep-herding.[3] By contrast, the biblical David's musical skill and his childhood home of Bethlehem with its link to the Christian savior, do not appear in American press accounts. Similarly, the unevenness of the battle between Israelis and Arabs, with the greater numbers, armament, and military might favoring the Arabs, contributes to an association with David's situation facing Goliath and the Philistine armies. However David's reliance upon the Lord and his depiction of the fight as one whose outcome depends upon the Lord does not seem to influence secular news writers and columnists. There are very few references even to miracles. Press accounts recognize Israeli military might although they ascribe it to the virtues of Israel's citizen soldiers. Thus American metaphors draw upon the biblical David selectively, merging his features with those of other American heroes. Most importantly, his solitary isolation—like that of his country Israel—resonates among a population accustomed to watching decades of westerns in movie theaters and on television with their lone heroes who fight successfully against incredible odds.

This Western movie tradition also has a specific Jewish incarnation that harks back to an earlier war, the Sinai campaign of 1956. A young American Jewish novelist and scriptwriter, Leon Uris, covered the fighting as a foreign correspondent. Uris was in Israel researching material for his third novel about the establishment of the state of Israel. When he arrived in

---

[2] Peter Grose, *Israel in the Mind of America* (New York: Schocken Books, 1984), 309.

[3] *Tanakh* (Philadelphia: Jewish Publication Society, 1985), I Samuel 16:12.

Israel in March 1956, he had a contract with MGM to write a novel that would become the basis of a movie. Uris logged thousands of miles conducting interviews, taping notes, and shooting photographs. Covering the Sinai campaign proved to be a revelation. "And the revelation was this: that we Jews are not what we have been portrayed to be. In truth, we have been fighters."[4] Uris incorporated his revelation into an epic novel, *Exodus*, which depicts Jews as heroes. As one critic observed, the Jews in the novel are ones "who have stopped running, hiding, scheming or pretending. They are Jews who fight, who die, who love and who *triumph*." An Israeli correspondent thought that the hero, "Ari Ben Canaan is not a Jew...[but] the very ideal of true blue American manhood...." When Otto Preminger cast blue-eyed, ruddy-cheeked, handsome Paul Newman for the title role in the film version, he represented Ari Ben Canaan's "ideal of true blue American manhood" as the prototypical Israeli, the new Jew for the generation of Americans who would watch the Six-Day War unfold.[5] The novel and movie provided Americans with a popular representation of Israelis as well as with a potential script with which to read events in the Middle East.

Life magazine made the connection between the fictional and real explicit. Next to a photograph of Yitzhak Rabin, "commander of Israel's land, sea and air forces," ran the caption: "General Rabin, a master of sabotage technique and a military planner respected for his cunning, was the man on whom Leon Uris based his fictional character Ari Ben Canaan in Exodus." The portrait shows Rabin in military dress, his shirt unbuttoned at the neck, his head raised as he looks up at Jerusalem's Western Wall pictured behind him. *Life*'s references to cunning and sabotage technique notwithstanding, the image presents a genuine hero, whose armies overran large swatches of blue territory shown in the black and white map above Rabin's head. The "extraordinary elan of Rabin's army" praised by the magazine also appears in the casualty rate, which includes a high percentage of officers and is portrayed graphically in a photo of rows of fresh graves in a cemetery outside Tel Aviv.[6]

---

[4] Uris quoted in Philip Roth, *Reading Myself and Others* (New York: Farrar, Straus, Giroux, 1975), 138.
[5] Frank Cantor, "A Second Look at Exodus," *Jewish Currents* (November 1959): 20–21 (emphasis in the original); Yehuda Lev, "Letter from Israel," *Sentinel*, 3 April 1959, quoted in Cantor, 40.
[6] *Life* (23 June 1967): 24B.

Life was not alone in drawing a connection between the movie version of Israel and its heroic Jews and the real-life version seen through other cameras. *Newsweek* also pictured Rabin. Its photo shows a smiling Rabin in military dress with his sleeves rolled up and hat pushed back, leaning forward, a cigarette between his fingers. Underneath the caption runs: "Rabin: Master of the juggernaut." If one reads the text below, the "bluff Chief of Staff" is quoted as saying "proudly," of the Israeli victory: "All this has been done by the Israel defense forces alone, with what we have, without anything or anybody else." The theme of single-handed victory, applauded as David's triumph in the *Wall Street Journal* article, is reiterated here by the hero who formed the prototype for Ari Ben Canaan.[7]

Rabin, of course, was not the only hero of the war. Moshe Dayan received plenty of news coverage as a military hero, including a *Time* magazine cover photo and a full-page color portrait in *Life*. The *New York Times* billed him as the "Hero of Sinai." Its profile emphasized Dayan's sabra roots; he was not an intruder as Arabs claimed Israelis were. Born in Degania, Dayan's Russian-born parents "moved the family to an even more primitive swampy outpost named Nahalal and young Moshe learned to plow and shoot." The emphasis is clearly on fighting, not farming. The article pictures him as a military man, standing sentry duty at age 12 years old against "marauding Bedouins" and joining the Haganah, described as "the Jewish militia," at age 14 for training. Dayan's heroism as a commando and his bravery as a scout during World War II when he lost his eye dominate the profile. The accompanying photo, however, shows a bareheaded Dayan in civilian dress, wearing a jacket, sweater vest, white shirt, and, yes, a tie. The caption reads: "He began standing guard when he was 12 years old."[8]

By contrast, the close-up photo of Rabin in the *Times* profile, titled "Hero of the Israelis," shows a youthful Rabin, in a three-quarter shot. The caption reads: "Prototype of fictional hero." The text itself begins with Rabin's words that conjures up single-handed courage and triumph: "The bulk of the Egyptian forces are fleeing in disorder and we have occupied most of Sinai. We have fought with our own forces, and nobody has aided us." After establishing Rabin's bravery in the 1948 fighting, the *Times* describes him at 45 as "still boyish looking." This "blue-eyed, sandy-haired, and rugged" hero "inspired many of the episodes in which Leon

---

[7] *Newsweek* (19 June 1967): 29.
[8] "The Hero of Sinai: Moshe Dayan," *New York Times*, 2 June 1967, 14.

Uris cast the fictional Ari Ben Canaan in *Exodus*." Like Dayan, the *Times* notes that Rabin was a sabra, born in Jerusalem, whose father spent fifteen years in the United States before coming to Palestine as a soldier in the Jewish Legion during World War I. The American connection, albeit a bit distant, nonetheless suggests a measure of rapport, especially in contrast to the Russian ties of Dayan's parents. Rabin's heroic American attributes with their biblical resonance are emphasized in the paragraph immediately following. Rabin, the *Times* reports, "hoped to become a farmer, restoring life to the eroded soil of Palestine." But, "he was recruited for the Haganah, the striking force that the British trained for sabotage and partisan activities to be carried out if the Germans, then at El Alamein, captured Palestine." Here the *Times* deftly links Rabin to the Allies in World War II. Compare the description of Dayan's wartime service: he is described as fighting Vichy France in Syria, not nearly the same dangerous enemy as Rommel's army at El Alamein. Yet, like Ari Ben Canaan, once the Nazis are defeated, Rabin is ready to fight for the Jews. As the *Times* reports, "when the Nazi threat passed, the young fighter used his training to combat the British blockade of Jewish immigration.... The raid against a British detention camp in Athlith, south of Haifa, to liberate more than 200 'illegal' Jewish immigrants, described in *Exodus,* was actually led by young Rabin." History and fiction merge seamlessly into a compelling narrative: Rabin actually led the raid that Ari Ben Canaan led in the novel. Here is a figure of the silver screen leading Israeli armies across the Sinai desert.[9]

In my history of Jews in Miami and Los Angeles, I argued that through *Exodus* Israel entered the popular American imagination as a romantic screen legend. Both the cinematic and novelistic portraits of Israel gave Americans, Jewish and Gentile, a hero to root for and to identify with: the plucky little Jewish state fighting for its freedom against overwhelming odds and personified in that singular, laconic, handsome, audacious leader, Ari Ben Canaan.[10] Ari Ben Canaan goes to war reluctantly, preferring the simple life of a farmer. In the Six-Day War, his image fuses with that of its prototype, Yitzhak Rabin, as Israelis in the Jewish state become modern biblical heroes. In an uncanny fashion newspaper headlines appear to follow a Hollywood script. First comes three weeks of increasingly unendurable tension: removal of U.N. peacekeeping troops, sealing the

---

[9] "Hero of the Israelis: Itzhak Rabin," *New York Times*, 8 June 1967, 16.

[10] Paul Breines, *Tough Jews: Political Fantasies and the Moral Dilemma of American Jewry* (New York: Basic Books, 1990), 56, goes further: "Suddenly, one might add, Jews were Paul Newman...."

Straits of Tiran, mobilizing of Egyptian and Syrian forces on the border, massing of tanks and guns and planes poised for invasion, inflammatory threats of destruction by Arab leaders, cautious diplomacy by Western nations. By the beginning of June, Israel stands completely alone—as a Hollywood hero should stand—against the massed military might of the entire Arab world. Then, in six brilliant, tension-filled days, the Israeli military not only single-handedly fights off the Arab armies of Egypt, Syria, and Jordan, but reunites Jerusalem, recaptures the Sinai, and triples the territory of the state. In the Six-Day War Israel lives up to its screen legend. Image and reality fuses: heroic visions become living history. This representation of Jewish David as a hero of westerns helps to account for American sympathy for Israel during the war.[11]

The power of the movie *Exodus* to influence visual imagery around the Six-Day War also appears in *Life* magazine's second feature devoted to the battles. Its first coverage offers the types of photos one might expect coming from battle: scenes of the wounded, of Israeli tanks riding through Jerusalem, of fighting in the desert, of handsome young soldiers standing in awe looking up at the western wall, and of surrender. The cover features a photo of Israeli soldiers, fully clad in battle gear, standing at a distance and looking at the raised hands of captured Egyptians who are lying face down in the lower left corner. The Egyptians are in civilian dress and the faces of the Israelis are not prominent. Contrast this with the exultant, smiling photo of an Israeli soldier, gun in hand, emerging from the Suez canal on the following week's cover. Ralph Cameron's photo suggests a generic blue-eyed hero, his muscular body visible beneath a wet uniform, surrounded by the brilliant blue of water that obliterates any horizon line or other point of reference. Without the caption that reads, "Israeli soldier cools in the Suez Canal," there would be no way of knowing that this man was an Israeli soldier. Even the weapon he is holding is not an Uzi but a Russian Kalishnikov, a captured trophy of the Six-Day War (close inspection reveals some Arabic on the gun).[12] *Life*'s cover presents Americans with a compelling portrait of a man with gun, a handsome grinning hero who, *Life* tells us, is Israeli.[13]

---

[11] Deborah Dash Moore, *To the Golden Cities: Pursuing the American Jewish Dream in Miami and L.A.* (New York: The Free Press, 1994), 248–60.

[12] *Life* (23 June 1967): cover; photo of Paul Newman in Moore, *To the Golden Cities*, facing page 215.

[13] Israelis, on the other hand, immediately identified the man: Yossi Ben Hanan, who built a career in the army and subsequently became a general.

Here is the new Jew reborn after his baptism of fire, emerging out of the waters of Suez. Why choose such an image for the cover? Where might Americans have seen such an image before? Those who remembered the movie *Exodus* would recall that the first time they saw Paul Newman, he was coming up out of the sea onto the shores of Cyprus. Newman is bare chested in the scene, wearing only a prominent star of David around his neck to identify him. It is night, not day, and Newman carries no weapon. But the palpable physicality of the hero's emerging from the water suggests why *Life*'s editors might have chosen the photo for the cover, instead of a Jerusalem photo or a shot of soldiers at the Western Wall. *Time* magazine described in words the new image of the Jew: "a bronzed and bare-chested figure somewhat larger than life...a handsome romantic idealist who furrowed his fields rather than his brow and was equally adept at digging wells for his country and graves for its enemies."[14]

These individualistic themes are not the only representations of Jews appearing in the media around the Six-Day War. Israel's citizen soldiers also received coverage linking them to their biblical ancestor who left his sheep to rescue his countrymen from the threats of Philistine destruction and humiliation. "Israeli forces are made up mostly of farmers, home builders and merchants who have had a long and gaunt struggle for survival," Bill Mauldin observed in a *New Republic* article on "those Israeli troops" titled "Not a Litterbug Among Them."[15] Mauldin's account appeared after the war but even in the week preceding the war, articles described reservists stationed in the Negev with humor and sympathy. An early piece in the *Times* was headlined "Israeli Soldiers in Negev Camp Shower While Awaiting Enemy; Backgammon Is Also Part of the Daily Routine of Young Reservists Called to Active Duty in Border Crisis."[16] Several days later, under a photo of a young boy cleaning refuse boxes from a bomb shelter in Tel Aviv, an article described the trials of Ron Ali, who left his wife and two-year-old daughter behind in Tel Aviv, along with his toothbrush and fresh clothes. In the male world of the military, Ron listens to the radio with the other men and yearns for home, but he is prepared to fight. "'It's our country,' he said, 'and we have to defend it.'"[17]

---

14 *Time* (9 June 1967): 40.
15 Bill Mauldin, "Not a Litterbug Among Them," *New Republic* (24 June 1967): 5.
16 *New York Times*, 25 May 1967, 17.
17 "Israeli Guards at the Border Shift Positions Daily," *New York Times*, 28 May 1967, 3.

Such steadfast courage infuses a portrait painted by *New York Times* columnist James Reston. "These people have gone to war with remarkable calm and kindliness to one another," he wrote on the first day of the war. "There is a curious combination of sadness and determination in their manner." Describing the "ancient Biblical roads" as transformed by war, Reston portrays the Israeli army as "a singing army, not polished but rumpled as if it had been in battle for months, not all young but all mixed up with young and middle-aged waving to the youngsters at the side of the road and smoking and singing like Hemingway's heroes at the start of the Spanish Civil War."[18] Theodore White, writing in *Life*, took a more sober view. Perhaps as a Jew he identified with the Israeli soldiers he describes because he explicitly links them to their past history of persecution and destruction as well as to an almost miraculous will to live. He defined "Israelis as Jews who have declared that they will not ever again be victims—and their army is an expression of this will." According to White, "the army expresses the fundamental politics of survival. As such, it unifies a people who will not die."[19]

Where, amid all of these images of secular Jewish heroes, are the religious men? Although few and far between, representations of religious Jews appear most often in conjunction with the reuniting of Jerusalem. *Newsweek*'s photos of the war by Charles Harbutt include steel-helmeted Israeli soldiers as well as one soldier in *tallit* and *tefillin*, praying. Terence Smith's front page *New York Times* account focuses on Israeli troops weeping and praying at the Western Wall. "The Israelis, trembling with emotion, bowed vigorously from the waist as they chanted psalms in a lusty chorus. Most had submachine guns slung over their shoulders and several held bazookas as they prayed," he wrote.[20] Photographers captured Rabbi Shlomo Goren carried on the shoulders of Israeli paratroopers as he blows the shofar beside the Western Wall. The caption beneath reads: "Victory trumpet: Israeli troops at the Wailing Wall."[21] Describing the same scene, UPI reported that "a bearded rabbi in a paratrooper's uniform blasted a call of triumph on the shofar. An officer wearing a skullcap hoisted a blue and white Israeli flag on a pole atop the Wailing Wall." Rejoicing in their

---

[18] James Reston, "A War's First Hours," *New York Times*, 6 June 1967, 16.
[19] Theodore White, "Mideast War," *Life* (23 June 1967): 25.
[20] Terence Smith, "Israelis Weep and Pray Beside the Wailing Wall," *New York Times*, 8 June 1967, 1.
[21] *Newsweek* (19 June 1967): 24.

victory, the Israelis shouted "Jerusalem is ours!" and then hugged and kissed each other. "Then they prayed. It took three days to regain what the Jews lost more than 2,000 years ago," the UPI report observed.[22] *Life*'s photo series includes a close-up of Goren at the wall, one hand holding a small prayer book and the other captured in rapid motion. These images all submerge the religious in the military.[23] In one of the few accounts of religious civilians, *Newsweek*'s reporter, himself Jewish, describes the "scene of wild joy" when he returned with Israeli soldiers through the Mandelbaum Gate to Jewish Jerusalem. "Hundreds of orthodox Jews, wearing the traditional caftans (long black coats), their long sideburns flying, waving Torahs, clamored to get to the Wailing Wall. One of them stopped me and asked me in Yiddish if I had touched the wall. When I said yes, he grabbed my hands and kissed them and the longing overpowered him and he wept. 'I am out of my mind,' he cried." This is one of the longest descriptions of religious Jews that I uncovered in the general press.[24]

The shift from representations of David to those of Goliath begins in some of the retrospective accounts of the war. *Newsweek* titled its long overview on June 19th, "Terrible Swift Sword," calling to mind the "Battle Hymn of the Republic" and its association with fraternal strife as well as God's vengeance upon a wicked enemy. (The verse reads: "Mine eyes have seen the glory of the coming of the Lord / He is trampling out the vintage where the grapes of wrath are stored / He hath loosed the fateful lightning of His terrible swift sword: / His truth is marching on.")[25] The article itself draws attention to Israeli power, observing that "though the Egyptian, Syrian and Jordanian troops had fought and died bravely in a score of nameless desert battles, neither they nor their leaders had proved anywhere a match for the brilliant planning and execution of the Israeli attack—nor for the studiedly implacable ferocity with which it was carried out." The Six-Day War made Israel "the dominant power on the map of the Middle East that its armies had just redrawn." Yet the same account credited one part "of this incredible Israeli blitzkrieg" to "a

---

[22] *New York Times*, 8 June 1967, 17.
[23] *Life* (16 June 1967): 36.
[24] *Newsweek* (19 June 1967): 24, 26, 29.
[25] Edmund Wilson, *Patriotic Gore: Studies in the Literature of the American Civil War* (New York: Oxford University Press, 1966), 92–96, suggests that Julia Ward Howe, who wrote the hymn, probably was influenced by Isaiah 63: 1–6 and Macaulay's "Battle of Naseby," part of his *Songs of the Civil War*. He also notes that the song was sung by soldiers like psalms.

rugged forty-year-old who was a chicken farmer until recalled to service." Thus imagery suggesting David—the farmer who leaves his farm to defend his homeland—coexists with representations of Israel as Goliath, a ruthless power. *Newsweek* even characterized Dayan as "turning mice into lions." Then the lions became dragons.[26]

The movement from David to Goliath becomes manifest most clearly in the realm of pop art heroes where both representations are contained within one Jewish image. The process of imagining Jews, albeit disguised, as Goliath, actually begins before the war, as Leslie Fiedler noted in a 1966 essay. "This shift of the Jew from archetypal 'Baddie' to mythological 'Goodie,' and its connection with the shift from folk culture to mass culture is immensely important," he observed because it provided a vulgar alternative to anti-Semitic stereotypes. Fiedler is writing about comic book heroes created by American Jews, especially the Superman comic strip. The Six-Day War brought the Jewishness of such heroes out of the closet. A popular poster united David and Goliath into one image of Super-Jew. The color poster features a skinny, bearded hasidic Jew with *peyes* and glasses, wearing a large black hat, long black coat, black socks and shoes, standing in a red telephone booth. He is grinning and looking up at the viewer, so that the glasses appear to be sliding off of his nose. He has pulled his coat open to reveal his true self: underneath the external garb of a religious Jew he wears red underwear and a white shirt with the Superman logo on it. But in place of the "S" on his shirt is a bold Hebrew letter "shin" signifying Superman's essential Jewish identity. *Time* reproduced the poster in its June 16th issue under the heading "Blintzkrieg" that featured a host of jokes circulating in response to the war. "'It was our finest hour,' boasted an Israeli spokesman. 'Or did it take longer than that?'"[27] The placement of the poster in such a context reinforces its humorous attributes, even as it speaks to a new openness about American Jewish fantasies of power that Fiedler found hidden in pop culture heroes.

How did American Jewish intellectuals respond to these representations? Milton Himmelfarb, writing in *Commentary,* expressed surprise "that some Jews still had to find a reassurance about themselves in the military valor of the Israelis. One would have thought that that had been taken care of in 1948," he mused. However, American Jews still seemed to need Israel to give them "a kind of contemporary pioneer or cowboy ances-

---

[26] *Newsweek* (19 June 1967): 23–36.
[27] *Time* (16 June 1967): 17.

try, reassuring us by showing us what we wanted and needed to have shown—that while Jews can be pretty good with a fountain pen and briefcase, they can also if necessary be pretty good with a rifle or tank." Himmelfarb's parallelism of fountain pen and rifle, briefcase and tank, suggests the importance of masculinity in this representation of Jews. Surprisingly, such imagery did not change fundamental American Jewish attitudes he concluded. "[I]f by Zionism is meant agreement with Zionist ideology, we are no more Zionist than we used to be."[28] Veteran Zionist Marie Syrkin saw matters differently. "Israel does not want to play the perennial role of David. To play the part three times in 19 years is excessive," she complained. "The image of the Israeli warrior now cheerfully being acclaimed is not of her seeking. The wastes of the Negev to be irrigated, the stony hills of Jerusalem to be re-forested afford enough challenge to Israeli energy and will," she affirmed, articulating the classic Zionist vision of the *halutz* (pioneering) ideal and rejecting representation of Israeli Jews as singular romantic western heroes. "Israel refuses to be permanently cast in the role of fighter extraordinary against monstrous odds," she insisted. Yet even Syrkin could not resist describing the "miracle" of military victory in terms of "such imponderables as the free spirit of the kibbutzniks, artisans, white-collar workers and intellectuals who constitute the Israeli army."[29]

Why such ambivalence characterized Jewish intellectuals' responses to American representations of Jews during the Six-Day War can be found, perhaps, in their unease with American popular culture, especially its vulgar simplicity. Unwilling to embrace Ari Ben Canaan and skeptical of any form of hero-worship, they were unsure of how to celebrate real-life Israeli prototypes. Neither David nor Goliath proved satisfactory.

Most Americans didn't have such difficulties. Like a Nebraska farmer who called Senator Jacob Javits's Capitol Hill office, they took sides and chose the Jews. "I'm not Jewish," the farmer announced, "but I want you to know that all us farm people out here are with you and hope you beat the hell out of them Arabs."[30] If the national press offers any guide to American attitudes, then Jews emerged as popular heroes in the Six-Day War. Americans elided Israelis and American Jews, rooted for David to tri-

---

[28] Milton Himmelfarb, "In the Light of Israel's Victory," *Commentary* (October 1967): 53–54.
[29] Marie Syrkin, "The Right to be Ordinary," *Midstream* (June/July 1967): 6.
[30] *Newsweek* (19 June 1967): 35.

umph over the contemporary Philistines, and cheered when David became the new Goliath of the Middle East because they knew that he stood like Superman for truth, justice and the American way.

THE IMPACT OF THE SIX-DAY WAR ON THE ORGANIZATIONAL LIFE OF CANADIAN JEWRY

Harold M. Waller

McGill University

CANADIAN JEWS, along with their brethren in many countries throughout the world, could not view the Six-Day War with detachment. Psychologically and emotionally they were very much involved in the events that were to shape Israel's future for many years to come. In retrospect, the war had a very great impact on Canadian Jewry; its effects, both direct and indirect, can still be observed. The purpose of this paper is to analyze the impact of the war on Canadian Jewry, particularly in its organizational manifestations. Indeed, the evidence shows that the war had a profound and lasting effect on the organizational life of the community. Even to the present day, disputes within the community regarding the disposition of territories which came under Israeli control in 1967 remain visible, highly charged, and a source of dissension. Thus the effects of the war are still being felt in communal life.

Of course the war affected Canadian Jews in their individual capacities as well, in many cases intensifying Jewish and/or Zionist commitments and involvement. However, there is insufficient data available on individuals to generalize. Hence the focus of this paper is on the formal and collective expressions of the Canadian Jewish community.

Prior to the war, a tradition of political passivity, which resulted mainly from deep-seated fears of anti-Semitism, made political involvement and organized community action vis-à-vis the government difficult for Canadian Jews. The nature of Canadian life was such that Jews, like other minorities and ethnic groups, felt themselves to be fairly weak when trying to penetrate into the political life of a society that focused primarily on the French and English Canadians. All Canadians were considered to be hyphenated, at least informally, a practice that accentuated the differences between the newcomers—the twentieth-century immigrants—and the two dominant groups that had formed the Confederation in 1867. Jewish political ineffectiveness, related in part at least to feelings of insecurity and vulnerability, was particularly evident during the Nazi period, when Jews were unable to modify an unfeeling Canadian immigration policy. This experience became a permanent reminder of the costs of political impotence.

After World War II, Canada gradually was transformed into a *de facto* multicultural society, a development that was increasingly recognized during the 1960s and 1970s. This complicated the task of conceptualizing the nature of Canadian society, which could no longer be explained in terms of a straightforward English-French dichotomy. It led to tension between the French and English, as the French, with their falling birthrate, began to worry about the stability of their own position in the Canadian constellation. The trend toward multiculturalism also contributed to increasing resistance to immigrant groups. Thus two major developments of the past thirty years—the rise of Quebec separatism and the emergence of the Western-based Reform party—are both related to the country's ethno-cultural development.

During the postwar period, the Jews, exhibiting a greater sense of security and belonging, began to respond to historic events, especially those concerning Israel, as "passivity gave way to action."[1] Israel became a paramount focus of concern and provided a common bond that helped to unite the community. What emerged was a conviction that what happened to Israel affected Canadian Jews and was important to their lives.[2] By 1967, Canadian Jews felt comfortable with this situation and were hardly expecting the emergence of the existential threat that Israel faced that year.

As in other Diaspora communities, the Six-Day War was a watershed that mobilized the Jewish community and fostered strong identification with Israel and its cause. For Canadian Jews it marked a transformation from a relatively passive posture to an activist stance, reflecting the view that the destiny of Canada's Jews was inextricably linked to the fate of Israel. It certainly intensified the feeling of Canadian Jews for Israel, making many feel a shared sense of identity with the citizens of the Jewish State. The war drove home to Canadian Jews the vulnerability of Israel and the importance of the state to Jews everywhere.

---

[1] David Taras, "From Passivity to Politics: Canada's Jewish Community and Political Support for Israel," in *The Domestic Battleground: Canada and the Arab-Israeli Conflict*, eds. David Taras and David H. Goldberg (Montreal: McGill-Queen's University Press, 1989), 37.

[2] Ibid., 45–46.

The community had long had close ties with Zionism, the Zionist movement, and then the State of Israel itself. As a result, Canadian Jews identified closely with Israel and its destiny and responded to its crisis. There is little doubt that the war had an extensive effect on the conduct of Jewish community life in Canada. In organizational and political terms these effects can be analyzed with reference to three periods. The first was the *crisis* period, the weeks and months in 1967 surrounding the war itself. After that came a period of *consensus,* which lasted from 1967 to about 1982. The third period, *division,* lasted from then until the 1992 Israeli elections.

Crisis

The weeks leading up to the war, the week of the war itself, and the months following it represented a crisis for the Canadian Jewish community, which united in support of Israel, raised unprecedented sums of money, and enthusiastically supported the positions of the Israeli government. Israel became a dominant concern for the community and remained so afterwards.

Canadian Jews perceived the crisis in stark terms: Israel's future was at stake. Some even feared a second Holocaust. As a result, the idea of doing their part to help to save Israel became an imperative for action among Canadian Jews. Whatever the actual military and security situation, they felt an obligation to do what was in their power to assist the Jewish State in its hour of need. Toward that end, the Coordinating Committee for Emergency Aid to Israel was set up.[3] Its establishment reflected the view that fund-raising was the one area where Canadian Jews could do something concrete on behalf of Israel. Several hundred members of the community, among them about twenty-five physicians, actually went to Israel as volunteers, but the bulk of the community's energy went into fund-raising. As the waiting period ended and hostilities began on 5 June, the heroic achievements of the IDF and the people of Israel proved inspirational and uplifting, thereby stimulating donations to the committee. Moreover, the crisis brought marginal Jews closer to the community as the reality of the crisis was driven home to people who had not been strongly affiliated.

---

[3] David H. Goldberg, "Ethnic Interest Groups as Domestic Sources of Foreign Policy: A Theoretical and Empirical Inquiry" (Ph.D. diss., McGill University, 1986), 130.

The highlight of the fund-raising effort was a meeting held on 4 June, the day before the fighting started. It was convened in Montreal by Samuel Bronfman, who was clearly the *de facto* leader of Canadian Jewry and the only person with enough clout to make a success of such a venture. He summoned over 100 community leaders from across the country to join him at the Montefiore Club.[4] He had two major objectives for the meeting: to set a target for fund-raising between then and the fall and to raise the down payment on that sum immediately. He accomplished both objectives, gaining a commitment from those assembled to raise $25 million for Israel over the summer and soliciting pledges for immediate gifts.[5] He announced that he was personally tripling his pledge to the annual UJA campaign and asking the rest to follow suit. He expected pledges of about $2.5 million on the spot, but in fact raised over $13 million at that one meeting.[6]

As a result of the Montreal meeting, emergency committees were formed in each community across Canada. The money that they raised was separate from the regular annual UJA campaigns—and considerably larger. Local and countrywide organizations, such as the welfare funds, the Federated Zionist Organization of Canada (FZOC), Canadian Jewish Congress (CJC), and B'nai B'rith Canada (BBC) were all involved in various aspects of the ambitious pro-Israel effort.

The key personal role played by "Mr. Sam," as he was known, cannot be overemphasized. As the wealthiest Jew in the country and as a person who had labored long and hard on behalf of community causes over the years, including long service as CJC president, which was then the most prestigious post in Canadian Jewry, Bronfman had unparalleled influence throughout the community. He used his stature to great advantage during the 1967 crisis, focusing his efforts both within and beyond the community. Among his activities during the crucial period were a trip to Ottawa on 26 May to meet with government officials in order to bolster political support for Israel, the meeting of 4 June to set fund-raising goals, a later trip to Ottawa to meet with Prime Minister Lester Pearson, and several speeches at rallies held in behalf of Israel. This display of leadership set the community in the desired direction as it attempted to cope with the

---

[4] Michael R. Marrus, *Mr. Sam: The Life and Times of Samuel Bronfman* (Toronto: Viking Press, 1991), 447.
[5] Ben Kayfetz, "Canada," *American Jewish Year Book* (1968), 384–85.
[6] Marrus, *Mr. Sam*, 447–48.

pressures of the moment. Furthermore it set an example for future political work, demonstrating how the community could unite behind the Israeli cause despite the real differences between the various organizations.

The overall effect of the crisis of May and June 1967 was to drive home to Canada's Jews the dangers that Israel faced and the fragility of its security situation. It united the community politically and organizationally and made evident the extent of previously unimagined resources. Finally, the crisis drove home the importance and value of unified political work on behalf of Israel. Even though Canada was surely not one of the great powers, it was a country with some influence on the international scene. And regardless of its international standing, the Jews accepted an obligation to see to it that Canada's diplomatic posture was as sympathetic to Israel as possible.

Consensus

During this period, Canadian Jewry built on the foundation established during the crisis period in 1967 to create the instrumentalities of pro-Israel action on a permanent basis. Activity on behalf of the state moved from the status of emergency to that of routine. It was widely accepted among community leadership that the kinds of activities initiated in 1967, especially in the political sphere, would have to become part of the Canadian Jewish agenda. This represented a break with the past and a new emphasis in community life.

For more than a decade after the war, Canadian Jewry remained united behind the Israeli cause as defined by the government of Israel. The community reorganized itself so as to be a more effective advocate of Israel's position. David Taras has argued that the war was "a vital catalyst in the political transformation of the Canadian Jewish community."[7] One of the key manifestations of this transformation was the establishment of the Canada-Israel Committee (CIC), a joint venture of the CJC, Canadian Zionist Federation (CZF—the successor to the FZOC), and B'nai B'rith Canada. But in addition, the aftermath of the war enabled the local community federations to assert themselves as the address in Canada for Israel. They made Israel the focal point of their fund-raising efforts and the engine that produced their revenue stream. In doing so, they supplanted the CZF. This was also a factor in their increased importance in community life relative to the CJC. The federations, which controlled the major share

---

[7] Taras, "From Passivity to Politics," 48.

of the community's fund-raising, became the most dynamic element in the community during this period. They, especially the Montreal and Toronto federations, were the focal point for the connection between members of the community and Israel. The CZF, in contrast, suffered from severe financial limitations, lacked an energetic lay leadership, and appeared to be mired in an organizational politics that reflected outdated ideological struggles.[8]

The consensus eventually began to break down with the Israeli election of 1977. The division in the community over issues that largely related to the outcome of the Six-Day War became most apparent during the Lebanon War of 1982, although a number of events occurred during the period of Likud government that imposed strains on community cohesion. The community's consensus regarding Israel did persist throughout the 1970s. It enabled the community to channel resources into activities that served to increase support for Israel, not just among Jews, but in government, the media, and the general public. Thus the function of Israel advocacy became a permanent feature of Jewish life in an increasingly professional manner.

In the months following the Six-Day War, the Joint Public Relations Committee, which had been set up on an *ad hoc* basis during the conflict, was slow to develop into something with a broader focus. The need for a foreign policy interest group, which could lobby the government and bring Israel's case to the public, had become apparent to many in community leadership positions. But the Joint Public Relations Committee failed to transform itself and adapt to the new requirements. Its organizational character remained ad hoc and it lacked the professional sophistication and internal cohesion that were necessary in the postwar environment. However, by the end of 1967, it had become the Canada-Israel Committee (CIC), and was assigned the role of being the formal link between the Jewish community and the government.[9] Its formation was deemed necessary because the community had been unprepared for the 1967 crisis. Afterwards there was a general agreement that the community should have

---

[8] A fuller discussion of the challenges faced by the CZF during the 1970s is found in Harold M. Waller, "Canada," in *Zionism in Transition*, ed. Moshe Davis (New York: Herzl Press, 1980), 111–20. See also Daniel J. Elazar and Harold M. Waller, *Maintaining Consensus: The Canadian Jewish Polity in the Postwar World* (Lanham, Md.: University Press of America and the Jerusalem Center for Public Affairs, 1990), 39–53, 441–44.

[9] Goldberg, "Ethnic Interest Groups," 130–31.

a permanent political presence focused on Israel. CIC was the chosen vehicle.

The CIC depended on the support of three constituent groups, which did not always see eye to eye, even then. The three were CJC, CZF, and BBC. At that time the involvement of the federations was not seen as necessary, despite their role in fund-raising. A problem involving B'nai B'rith led to a split in 1971, but it was patched up. The problem resulted from the fact that BBC was not involved in CIC at the beginning. Between 1968 and 1970, serious efforts, especially by Sol Kanee of CJC, were made to bring it into the fold. There were lengthy discussions, especially over the issue of funding. Essentially BBC wanted an equal voice on policy, along with CJC and CZF, but was not willing to pay an equal share of the cost. Eventually a compromise was reached. By late 1971, the CIC had been reconstituted with Myer Bick, a young Montreal lawyer, as its first director. It was Bick who saw the CIC through its important formative years, establishing the patterns of operation that have been followed subsequently.

Bick advocated a more politically aggressive role than that to which the community had been accustomed. He believed that Jews should use whatever political resources they had, including electoral strength when appropriate, influence, and a willingness to speak out on the issues.[10] This approach contrasted sharply with the more cautious style of the older leadership, many of whom feared that a more aggressive posture might foster an anti-Jewish backlash. Thus the basis for tension and conflict was endemic to the organization from the start. As newcomers with a sense of confidence and mission, the CIC ran the risk of stepping on toes, a risk that was inherent in a structure that provided for an autonomous body that supposedly was under the direction of three other distinct organizations.

It was not surprising that one of the key problems faced by CIC over the years was preserving internal cohesion, or maintaining the consensus of the sponsoring organizations over both substance and tactics. Actually, there were more disputes over the latter than over the former. Over the years there was considerable conflict between the three organizations that had little to do with Israel *per se* but more likely reflected domestic organizational considerations. Nevertheless, the CIC helped to maintain a public consensus on the major issues, thereby reflecting well the prevailing view among the rank and file of the Canadian Jewish community. Generally that meant backing the position of Israel's government.

---

[10] Myer Bick, interview by author, 15 November 1994.

Bick himself saw the creation and the operation of the CIC as a direct response to the Six-Day War, which had had the effect of intensifying Canadian Jewry's identification with Israel.[11] With Israel as the focal point of Jewish identity for many, CIC was able to provide an important way to manifest that identity. In addition, community leadership saw that there was potential danger in the emerging criticism of Israel in the media and intellectual circles, criticism that focused on Israel as occupying power, as an alleged violator of human rights, and as the denier of the political aspirations of the Palestinians. Counteracting such criticism became one of the tasks of the CIC.

Another task involved interaction with the Jewish community itself. CIC saw the need for political education within its constituency, though the perceived encroachment on the turf of existing bodies led to some disputes. Furthermore, the focusing of Israel, the number one community issue, in the hands of the CIC contributed to a diminution in the importance of the three sponsoring organizations. Each of the three had to make major adjustments in terms of their mission and role in the community during the quarter-century after 1967. This was not due solely to the changing role of the CIC, but Israel-related matters certainly played an important part in these changes. In addition, the direct connection between Israel and the local federations was developed during this period, a development that weakened both CJC and CZF, the latter being especially hurt. The federations, which channeled more than half of their fundraising to Israel, used Israel and Israeli personalities to induce people to make their annual pledges to the Jewish community appeals. The Israeli government cooperated, sending its political and military leaders to appear at federation functions and events. Furthermore the federations began to carry out such projects as sponsoring Project Renewal in specific Israeli towns; brought leadership missions to Israel in which the participants could hobnob with top government officials and visit key defense installations; and gradually expanded the scope of missions to include more of the rank-and-file in the community. Thus Canadian Jews interacted with Israel to a much greater extent through the federations than they had ever done through CZF. Throughout this period of major shifts in emphasis in community life, the CIC remained in a strong position and in fact emerged as one of the priorities of the community.

The emergence of the CIC also marked the maturation of Canadian

---

[11] Ibid.

Jewry as a political community. It became more self-confident in dealing with the media and government. This was largely a new activity for community organizations, which had been much more insular in the past. Bick identifies this change as the "Canadianization of the Jewish community," when the Jews recognized the need to be active on the Canadian political scene in order to pursue their objectives. They finally felt strong enough to stand up and speak out. It also provided Jews with a way to be partners with Israel that was separate and independent from contributing money. Thus, whereas formerly a Canadian Jew could be involved with Israel only by contributing funds, now he could participate by helping to generate political support. This certainly made the work novel and exciting. It helped Israel and it surely provided a benefit to Canadian Jews themselves.

Another benefit to the community was the fact that the CIC brought into organized Jewish life prominent and well-connected people who had been uninvolved before, except perhaps to donate funds to the community campaigns. These were people with access to the highest reaches of the political system, who had influence with policy makers. The CIC helped to mobilize them to serve the community politically and to maintain such activity for a sustained period. Furthermore, the general political awakening that accompanied the CIC's rise to prominence helped to make Jews, and not just the prominent ones, conscious of their political potential in general. In more technical terms, the activities of the CIC contributed to a heightened sense of political efficacy among Canadian Jews. This new sense of what was politically possible had an important impact on the community's political posture in the subsequent years. Thus the expectations of Canadian Jews with respect to politicians and government officials were raised.

The early years of the CIC during the 1970s coincided with a crisis for organized Zionism, which sought a renewed sense of purpose during a time when conventional manifestations of Zionist ideology were of declining importance and salience for Diaspora Jews, including those in Canada. The Zionist movement, by then represented by the CZF and its constituent organizations, found that it had been eclipsed by bodies with greater vitality, sense of purpose, and, most importantly, resources. In the years following the Six-Day War, the Zionists lost their privileged position regarding fund-raising for Israel to the federations, which learned that by combining funds for Israel with funds for local needs in one annual campaign it was possible to increase the yield dramatically. In fact, Israel had become the big drawing card in Jewish life, which meant that the programs for local purposes rode on Israel's coattails. Beyond that, the federations became the local "address" for Israel-related activity. Thus when important Israeli public figures such as Moshe Dayan, Shimon Peres, Yigal Allon, or Yosef Burg would come to Canada to speak, for example, it was the federations who generally sponsored the events. CZF might have been a co-sponsor, but the federations were in the driver's seat, using the visiting dignitary's presence to drum up financial support, part of which was used to support local community needs. The CZF—which did not face the same legal restrictions as the federations, which were registered charities—concentrated on public relations and political action. These might well have been important activities, but they lacked the glamour and panache of the fund-raising. Thus, even though CZF was a constituent partner in CIC, it never was able to capitalize on the Israel connection. It declined in importance through the 1980s. Not surprisingly, by the end of that decade, the federations had also become constituent partners in CIC. So even though CZF remained part of the formal structure, it was relegated to a fairly minor role.

The question of the CZF is connected to another important point. One of the underlying issues in Canadian Jewish life after 1967 concerned the significance of Israel in world Jewish life and sometimes led to internal conflicts within the community and specifically the CIC. The CZF, as a Zionist organization, accepted the Israel-centered view that is inherent in its ideology. This point was self-evident to Zionists, but that was not necessarily the case with other sectors of the community. In general, insofar as the community was not about to pick up and make *aliyah* on a wholesale basis, it was committed to perpetuating itself and its institutions in Canada. Most Canadian Jews, no matter how intensely they supported Israel, did not accept the view that Israel was necessarily the center of Jewish life, but rather saw the Diaspora as having a legitimacy of its own. One's position on this key point often influenced positions on the issues that the community had to face. In particular, it had an impact on how one reacted to attempts from Israel to exercise leadership on policy matters. Ultimately it became clear that community leadership remained in the hands of people who did not necessarily hold an Israel-centered view. Ironically, this occurred at the same time that Israel had become such a vital interest to Canadian Jewry.

From the Yom Kippur War to the Lebanon War

This was a period during which the community had digested the changes that followed in wake of 1967 and had begun to adjust to a new reality in which political responsibility had become a feature of organized Jewish life. By the time the Yom Kippur War had ended, the question of tactics, which had emerged in 1967 when the value of traditional quiet diplomacy was questioned, had been resolved in favor of a significant activist component. Quiet diplomacy had not been abandoned, but more visible tactics had become an important supplement at the very least. The CIC was very active and increasingly self-confident from 1973 for several years afterwards. It focused on such diverse issues as U.N. votes, the Arab boycott, and the relocation of the Canadian embassy from Tel Aviv to Jerusalem, as well as more time-bound matters. It also became involved in working with the media, making that a major emphasis in its agenda.

By the middle of the decade, the CIC operation was working fairly smoothly and enjoyed support from the key community organizations. However, the election of Likud in the 1977 election began to undermine the apparent consensus. Until that time, Diaspora Jews had only had to deal with Labour governments in Israel. The style and content of Menachem Begin's new government were unsettling to some Canadian Jews and began to lay the groundwork for what eventually became substantial expressions of dissent from Israeli government policies by 1982. "Beginning with the Israeli military action in Lebanon in the early 1980s, expressions of skepticism began increasingly to be heard within the community, though they were still generally voiced internally. In a sense the precondition for growing dissent had been set with the election victory of the Likud party of Menchem Begin in 1977. A large majority of Canadian Jewish activists...had been nourished on a Labour party model of Israeli Zionism and were uncomfortable with the apparent militancy, right-wing nationalism, and rhetorical style of Likud."[12]

Under Begin both the issues and the arguments changed. Likud supporters in Canada, who had played a very low-key role for decades, suddenly emerged on the scene in community politics, expecting to take a leading role comparable to what their colleagues had obtained in Israel. They became more activist and pressed the CIC to embrace the government's new line. Issues such as the Jerusalem embassy, which became entangled in Canada's 1979 election campaign, constituted a source of division—"how hard does one press the Canadian government on this

---

[12] David Taras and Morton Weinfeld, "Continuity and Criticism: North American Jews and Israel," in *The Jews in Canada* by Robert J. Brym, William Shaffir, and Morton Weinfeld (Toronto: Oxford University Press, 1993), 303.

one?"—but for the most part consensus was maintained in favor of devoting the energies of the community to supporting the positions of the Israeli government. Solidarity with the government of the day in Israel prevailed over specific policy differences. One participant described this as a period of confusion, not consensus. Nevertheless there was indeed a pretty broad consensus that any outside observer would have noted. Begin's efforts to maintain that consensus, by working with the community's leadership, were quite important. Certainly the solidarity of Canadian Jewry with Israel was a key feature of that period. The CIC role in all of this was critical, precisely because it provided a unified structure through which Israel and Canadian Jewry could interact. Moreover it was comprehensive in the scope of its representation, especially once the federations became formal constituents. As a result, it became a combination of AIPAC and the Presidents' Conference in one small operation, to use an American analogy.

In looking at the entire fifteen-year period from 1967 to 1982, as a result of the international pressures that Israel faced, Canadian Jews became more aware of their political responsibility vis-à-vis Israel. At first the pressure was the intense opposition of the Arabs that characterized the threat of the 1967 crisis period. But later on the pressure took the form of international isolation of Israel. In either case the necessity for Canadian Jewry to play a supportive role was accepted and recognized by members of the community, who acknowledged that political action on behalf of Israel had become a permanent feature of Jewish life. These developments enhanced the importance of the CIC in the life of the community, giving emphasis to the community's stand on issues such as the embassy and the boycott. Independent events, such as Begin's election and the achievement of the Camp David Accords, helped to solidify the centrality of Israel in the communal affairs of Canadian Jewry.

Division

The emergence of a coherent opposition to the Likud government's view solidified the divisions that characterized the decade from 1982 to 1992. These divisions emerged first in Israel but were quickly mirrored in Canada (and elsewhere as well) and largely concerned the disposition of the territories that came under Israeli control during the 1967 war. Whereas in the early years after the war there was a broad consensus within the community regarding the wisdom of the government's policies, the emergence of a significant segment of the Israeli population that opposed the continued and indefinite occupation of the territories spawned a comparable movement in Canada, which eventually took the form of Canadian Friends of Peace Now, an organization that had a membership of several hundred. In a number of community contexts beginning in the early 1980s, the Peace Now people began to challenge the community's conventional wisdom and argued for the policies that were eventually adopted by the Rabin government in 1993: recognition of the PLO and a willingness to withdraw from nearly all the territory that came under Israeli control in 1967. The political environment within the Canadian Jewish community was generally inhospitable to these ideas until the Israeli government itself changed course. Consequently there were a number of conflicts that erupted within community organizations that often became quite intense and which undermined the consensus for which community leaders had traditionally fought so hard. The community as a whole remained committed to Israel, but the details of that commitment varied much more widely than previously. An underlying theme of the period was the desire to support the position of Israel's government, that public dissent was appropriately confined to Israel. Thus the form of the disputes that occurred was frequently over the propriety of dissent, rather than its content.

The Lebanon War of 1982 proved to be a turning point, probably from the perspective of domestic Israeli politics but certainly in terms of Israel-Diaspora relations and the internal politics of the Canadian Jewish community. Although Canadian Jews certainly supported Israel's goal of assuring peace on its northern border, many believed that the transformation of the war goals represented excess, and that Israel had gone too far.[13] The objective of protecting the security of the north had given way to more ambitious political objectives that included a new regime in Lebanon and the ouster of the PLO from that country and its elimination as a force which Israel would have to deal with politically. In this situation, the CIC was under strain, facing internal problems, a strengthened and articulate opposition, and disaffection of many of its friends. For the first time, divisions within Israel were reflected in the public positions of constituent groups of the Canadian Jewish community. It was a novel challenge for the community to face the dilemma of how to reconcile a devotion to the State of Israel and its cause with legitimate criticism of the government, its leaders, and its policies. However, the official position remained one of support for Israel and its government's policies, one that only intensified the commitment of the dissenters to their own positions.

---

[13] Taras, "From Passivity to Politics," 58.

The underlying commitment of the Canadian Jewish leadership was to follow the lead of Israel's duly elected government and not to embark in an independent policy direction. This made it progressively difficult to hold the community together, as the dissenters became increasingly vocal and articulate. Those in positions of power were reluctant to co-opt the dissenters into leadership posts, a stance that reflected an underlying if unstated belief that public expression of dissent from Israel's policies by Diaspora Jews was unpatriotic and would undermine Israel's international position. They assumed that it was essential to have a united front in Canada in order to maximize the likelihood that the Canadian government would provide political support to the government of Israel. In fact, the Canadian government was rarely as supportive of Israel as the American government was, but it was markedly more supportive than most other Western governments. The Canadian Jewish leadership took pride in the degree of support that was achieved, viewing this as a concrete way in which they could help Israel politically. It was frequently argued that evidence of dissent among the Jews would allow the government greater license to adopt positions that were critical of Israeli policies and actions. When the dissenters, largely Peace Now people, found their objective of shifting Canadian Jewish public policy thwarted, they only became more determined to succeed and more willing to escalate the pressure.

The *intifada* and Israel's response to it increased the pressure on the community after 1987 because it provided Canadian government and opposition politicians greater license to distance themselves from Israel and emboldened them to express criticism of Israel. By 1988, the Secretary of State for External Affairs, Joe Clark, was hinting that Israel should negotiate with the PLO. There was a major confrontation at and after that year's CIC parliamentary dinner, which brought together MPs and members of the Jewish community for an evening of speeches by foreign affairs spokesmen of the political parties. After making a speech that did not sit well with the Jewish part of the audience, Clark faced a barrage of criticism that led him to back off within a short time.[14] But the parliamentary dinner, which once had been an opportunity for Canadian political leaders to celebrate their devotion to Israel and its achievements had now become a platform for stern rebukes to Israel for its treatment of the Palestinians.

During the late 1980s, the gap between the community's leadership

---

[14] David H. Goldberg and David Taras, "Collision Course: Joe Clark, Canadian Jews, and the Palestinian Uprising," in *The Domestic Battleground*, 215.

and at least part of the grass roots widened, with official bodies urging members of the community not to criticize the Israeli government publicly. The official line was that any dissent aided Israel's enemies. According to Robert Brym, this phenomenon was more pronounced in Canada than in the United States. In any event, Canadian Friends of Peace Now, through public pronouncements and advertisements, appeared to be challenging the official positions of the CIC and its constituent bodies. By 1990, the gap between official communal positions and those of the dissenters became increasingly pronounced. The Montebello Affair in 1988 had driven home that point. External Affairs people had encouraged a small group of Jews (largely Peace Now supporters) to meet secretly with a group of Arab Canadians at the Chateau Montebello resort in order to try to reach an agreement on a common position for the resolution of the Arab-Israeli conflict, particularly the Palestinian problem. Eventually word of the meeting leaked out, provoking outrage in the Jewish community that such an unrepresentative group of Jews had been selected and that the whole thing had been carried out surreptitiously. As a result the follow-up meeting was cancelled and the initiative shelved.

By the end of the 1980s, it was evident that the question of communal discipline had become a central one. Dissent from the Israeli government line (and that of the official Canadian Jewish community as well) was open and widespread, particularly among intellectuals, but also among some community leaders such as Milton Harris, a former CJC president. In a 1989 article, he came out in favor of a Palestinian state and against enforced communal solidarity.[15] The notion of a Palestinian state was anathema to the community leadership, and most Canadian Jews as well, at the time. Harris complained that "this solidarity precludes any discussion of territorial compromise." Also in 1989, Mel Shipman, Michael Marrus, and Harold Troper, all associated with CFPN, challenged CJC president Les Scheininger to ascertain the true state of public opinion among Canadian Jews.[16] Such debates, though initially carried out within the confines of communal organs, eventually got out into the general media. The Peace Now group appeared to challenge the CIC's right to speak on behalf of all Canadian Jews.[17]

Although Canadian Friends of Peace Now never became one of the constituents of the CIC, it was accepted as an affiliated organization of the

---

[15] Milton Harris, "Why Dissent," *Viewpoints* (31 August 1989): 1.
[16] *Canadian Jewish News* (7 September 1989), 11.

CJC. Through Harris it did have some access to CIC. CFPN had little influence on CZF, largely because it did not try to influence an organization that was rather ineffective anyway. Its impact was to publicize and legitimate a dissenting position, one that eventually was reflected in many ways in the policies of the Labour-led government in Israel between 1992 and 1996. Because of the quality of its spokespeople, the way in which the message was transmitted through the media, and the congruence between its views and those widely articulated by non-Jewish opinion leaders and commentators, CFPN had influence far beyond what one might have expected given the number of members.

Over the ten-year period from the beginning of the Lebanon War of 1982 until the election of a Labour government in Israel in 1992, the situation in Canadian Jewry evolved substantially. Debate over policies with regard to the territories, the idea of a Palestinian state, and how to deal with the *intifada* came into the open and became major issues of contention. Dissent moved from the fringes of the community to eventual legitimation once Labour came into power. The task of the CIC, representing Canadian Jewry's position on Middle East issues to government and non-Jewish Canadians, became more complex and difficult to carry out. By 1993, the initiatives of the Israeli government reduced the significance of pro-Israel Diaspora activity. Nevertheless the twenty-five years after the Six-Day War were eventful for Canadian Jewry and had what one can expect to be a lasting impact on the community.

Conclusion

The Six-Day War challenged Canadian Jewry's historic passivity and stimulated the creation of a politicized community that had no choice but to respond to the Middle East events that have occurred since 1967. Canadian Jews have experienced these events as though they were personally and directly involved. This greater sense of personal identity with Israel is surely one of the legacies of the war.

The Six-Day War also has had a long-term impact on Canadian Jewry because it stimulated a basic change in the way that the community handled Israel-related issues and the priority that it accorded to such action. The Canada-Israel Committee was a direct outgrowth of this change in

---

[17] Harold M. Waller, "The Canadian Jewish Polity: Power and Leadership in the Jewish Community," in *The Jews in Canada*, 265–66.

behavior and organizational approach. "CIC was definitely a response to the Six-Day War.... It was also a response to what the Six-Day War unleashed, both positive and negative. For example, it was a response to a much wider identification with Israel on behalf of Jewish constituencies that heretofore were not necessarily attached or committed to Israel."[18] The role that the CIC has played ever since and the manner in which the Jewish community related to it are reflections of the impact of the Six-Day War. From a period of great communal solidarity with Israel and its policies, a situation that prevailed for years after 1967, to the serious communal divisions of the 1990s, the CIC has been at the center of Israel affairs within the Jewish community of Canada.

There is also another manifestation of the long-term impact of the war. The territories that came under Israeli control in 1967 and the attendant issue of the Palestinians have been the focus for political debate within Israel for years. Eventually that debate surfaced among Canadian Jews as well and became a source of division within the community.

In retrospect it is now clear that the Six-Day War spurred the Canadian Jewish community to adopt policies and take actions that reflected strong and usually uncritical support for Israel while at the same time sowing the seeds of internal division and conflict fifteen to twenty years later. The legacy of the war remains a key factor in understanding the political evolution of the community since 1967.

THE LIMITED IMPACT OF THE SIX-DAY WAR ON AMERICA'S JEWS

Chaim I. Waxman
Rutgers University

THE SIX-DAY WAR is widely seen as having had a major impact on American Jewry, including its relationship with Israel.[1] Whether the changes brought about in that relationship were "revolutionary," as suggested by some, is another question.[2] In any case, there is considerable evidence that Israel moved from the periphery to the center in the structure and culture of the American Jewish community.

Viewed from the perspective of the institutional structure of American Jewry, Israel undoubtedly plays a central role in American Jewish life and much of that role developed as a result of the Six-Day War. In the *American Jewish Year Book*'s annual listing of "National Jewish Organizations," for example, more than eighty organizations specifically devoted to Zionist and pro-Israel activities are listed. For many others, objectives and activities such as "promotes Israel welfare," "support for the State of Israel," and "promotes understanding of Israel," appear with impressive frequency. In addition, more than fifty of the largest and most active of these national Jewish organizations are affiliated with the Conference of Presidents of Major American Jewish Organizations, for which Zionist and pro-Israel activity is the major emphasis. The Conference of Presidents shares an address with the U.S. headquarters of the Jewish Agency and World Zionist Organization, and virtually all of its chairmen have had long records of extensive previous activity on behalf of Israel.

Israel became central to the American Jewish philanthropic structure as a result of the Six-Day War, as Menahem Kaufman has indicated, to the

---

[1] Arthur Hertzberg, "Israel and American Jewry," *Commentary* 44, no. 2 (August 1967): 69–73.
[2] Cited in Menahem Kaufman, "From Philanthropy to Commitment: The Six Day War and the United Jewish Appeal," *Journal of Israeli History* 15, no. 2 (Summer 1994): 161.

point where leaders of the United Jewish Appeal are supportive of almost every decision of almost every Israeli government, at times becoming actual lobbyists for Israeli government policy.[3] The leadership acts in this manner out of its own convictions and also with the tacit support of a broad cross-section of the American Jewish population. For example, in 1990, more than 70 percent of American Jewish baby boomers agreed with the statement that, "The need for funds for services and programs in Israel is greater now than five years ago."[4] Although that figure has probably decreased somewhat as the result of widely publicized assertions by some prominent Israelis that Israel is a modern, growing, society and no longer needs American Jewish charity, Israel still plays a major role within the American Jewish philanthropic structure.[5]

In terms of the overall pro-Israelism of the American Jewish community, the empirical evidence indicates very strong support for Israel among the community's leadership. For example, a 1989 survey conducted by Steven M. Cohen that included "key professionals and top lay leaders from some of the most influential organizations in American Jewish life" (as well as a small number of academics who are involved with Israel) found that 99 percent of the respondents had been to Israel at least once and 84 percent had been there three times or more. Moreover, 78 percent identified themselves as "Zionists" and 54 percent had "seriously considered living in Israel." When asked, "How close do you feel to Israel?," 78 percent responded "very close" and 19 percent "fairly close." Only 2 percent stated that they feel "fairly distant" and none stated "very distant."[6] Jewish communal leaders not only feel close to Israel and identify with Zionism in the American sense of that term—i.e., pro-Israelism[7]—they also appear to subscribe to the Zionist tenet of the centrality of Israel. Thus, in response to the statement, "Jewish life in America is more authentically and positively Jewish than Jewish life in Israel," 81 percent of Cohen's sample disagreed and only 10 percent agreed.[8] The ways in which Jewish organi-

---

[3] Ibid., 161–91.
[4] The data are from the National Jewish Population Survey. Specifics on the population involved will be discussed later on in this article.
[5] *Long Island Jewish World*, 11–17 February 1994, 2.
[6] Steven M. Cohen, *Israel-Diaspora Relations: A Survey of American Jewish Leaders* (Ramat Aviv: Israel Diaspora Institute, Report No. 8, January 1990), 26–28.
[7] Chaim I. Waxman, *American Aliya: Portrait of an Innovative Migration Movement* (Detroit: Wayne State University Press, 1989), 105–18.
[8] Cohen, *Israel-Diaspora Relations*. If it were based solely on this statement,

zations have been strongly involved in defense activity for Israel have been amply documented.[9]

Israel has also become increasingly central in the realm of American Jewish education. If, in 1968, Alvin Schiff found that Israel was taught as a separate subject in 48 percent of all Jewish schools, including all-day, weekday afternoon, and one-day-a-week schools under Orthodox, Conservative, Reform, communal, and secular auspices,[10] by 1974, as Barry Chazan found, 63 percent of the school curricula listed Israel as a separate subject, and "a general increase of attention paid to Israel in all subject-areas as compared with 1968."[11] Although there are no more contemporary empirical data, anecdotal "evidence" and personal observation conveys the strong impression that this pattern has only intensified over the years. As for the role of Israel in American Jewish education, its increased importance is evidenced in a wide variety of ways, not the least of them being that Israel is a today a major source for curriculum materials in the field of Jewish education. In certain respects, the biblical vision, *ki mitzion tetzei tora* (from Zion shall Torah flow) has been realized; i.e., in the publication of Judaica and a wide variety of Jewish curriculum materials.

Israel also has become an integral part of the synagogue service of American Jewish denominations. As David Ellenson and I have indicated, almost all of the standard American Jewish prayer books now incorporate some prayers for the State of Israel as a part of the weekly service. Thus, the

---

Cohen's interpretation of the responses to this question as a measure of Zionism would be somewhat questionable. Those who responded negatively may not have been affirming the centrality of Israel. Perhaps they merely do not subscribe to the "centrality" of America; that is, they may hold Israel and America as of equal importance. That would be in line with the findings of a study of Reform Jewry's national leadership in which an almost identical percentage disagreed with the statement "It is easier to lead a fuller Jewish life in Israel than in the U.S." (Mark L. Winer, Sanford Seltzer, and Steven J. Schwager, *Leaders of Reform Judaism: A Study of Jewish Identity, Religious Practices and Beliefs, and Marriage Patterns* [New York: Research Task Force on the Future of Reform Judaism, Union of American Hebrew Congregations, 1987, 63–64]). However, in light of the responses of Cohen's sample to other Israel-related questions, his interpretation does seem appropriate for the majority.

[9] See, e.g., Daniel J. Elazar, *Community and Polity: The Organizational Dynamics of American Jewry* (Philadelphia: Jewish Publication Society, 1976), 288; Jonathan S. Woocher, *Sacred Survival: The Civil Religion of American Jews* (Bloomington, Ind.: Indiana University Press, 1986), 76–80.

[10] Alvin I. Schiff, "Israel in American Jewish Schools: A Study of Curriculum Realities," *Jewish Education* 38, no. 4 (October 1968): 6–24.

[11] Barry Chazan, "Israel in American Jewish Schools Revisited," *Jewish Education* 47, no. 2 (Summer 1979): 10.

official prayer book of the American Reform Movement, *Sha'arei Tefillah* (*Gates of Prayer*), published in 1975, is radically different from its predecessor, the Union Prayer Book, in many ways, not the least being its inclusion of a prayer for the State of Israel as part of the weekly and Holiday service. The movement's holiday liturgy, as set down in *Gates of the Seasons* (1983), incorporates Israel's Independence Day *(Yom Ha'atzmaut)*, into the religious calendar and the ritual service. Although the most popular edition of the Orthodox Art Scroll *Siddur* does not contain any reference to the State of Israel, there is an abundance of data which substantiate that the Orthodox have the most extensive and deepest attachments to Israel.[12]

Perhaps even more dramatic is the impact of the Six-Day War on the culture of the American Jewish community. In their assessment of the extent to which Israel has become central within the American Jewish community since the Six-Day War, published in the *Encyclopaedia Judaica* in 1971, Eventov and Rotem indicated that Israel now occupies "an important place in synagogue activities, sermons, and various religious celebrations," including Israel Independence Day. They continued:

> The Israel flag is frequently displayed in synagogues and community centers. In many synagogues, prayers for the welfare of the State of Israel and world Jewry are recited on Sabbaths and holidays following that for the welfare of the United States.... Hebrew songs and Israel folk dances have become American Jewish popular culture: at weddings, bar mitzvot, and on many college campuses....[13]

Although Israel has become part of the religious behavior of American Jews, as Charles Liebman observed,[14] or even *the* religion of American Jews, as Nathan Glazer observed,[15] it is nevertheless the case that America's Jews are a "non-religious" group, even as they might define themselves as a religious group. Understanding this requires recognition of the differ-

---

[12] David Ellenson, "Envisioning Israel in the Liturgies of North American Liberal Judaism," and Chaim I. Waxman, "The Changing Religious Relationship: American Jewish Baby Boomers and Israel," Papers presented at the conference, "Envisioning Israel: The Changing Ideals of North American Jews," Ben-Gurion University of the Negev, June 13–15, 1993; also see Chaim I. Waxman, ed., *Israel as a Religious Reality* (Northvale: Jason Aronson, 1994).

[13] *Encyclopaedia Judaica*, 16: 1147.

[14] Charles S. Liebman, *The Ambivalent American Jew* (Philadelphia: Jewish Publication Society, 1973), 88–108.

[15] Nathan Glazer, "American Jews: Three Conflicts of Loyalties," in *The Third Century: America as a Post-Industrial Society*, ed. Seymour Martin Lipset (Stanford: Hoover Institute Press, 1979), 233.

ence between the American Jewish community and the American Jewish population. They are certainly not one and the same. In fact, a majority of American Jewish baby boomers are not affiliated with the American Jewish community. They are not members in any Jewish organization; they do not subscribe to any Jewish publication; and, they are not members in any synagogue or temple—even the ones they don't attend.

A careful examination of the evidence on the behavior and attitudes of American Jewish baby boomers strongly suggests that the impact of the Six-Day War is actually significantly less than a look at American Jewish communal life might indicate. The data that will be presented below underscore a basic fact of American Jewish life, namely, that there is a vast difference between the American Jewish community and the American Jewish population.

The population with which we are concerned—American Jewish baby boomers—are those who were born between the years 1946–1964 and who, when asked in the 1990 National Jewish Population Survey (NJPS), "What is your current religion?," identified themselves as Jewish. This age group was selected for analysis because it represents those currently ascending to leadership and dominance in a variety of institutional spheres in American society. Thus, for example, the election of Bill Clinton as U.S. president was widely seen as symbolic of the ascendancy of the "baby boom" generation to political dominance.

Without getting too technical about it, it is important to know that the NJPS sample consists of 2,441 respondents. Each of the respondents provided the information for himself or herself and also for each member of their household. Thus, the survey obtained information on almost three times as many people as the actual number of respondents, or 6,514 individuals. The resulting data were subsequently statistically weighted, so that the sample of Jewish households would then represent more than three million American households nationally.

The question, "Who is a Jew" is an important one not only on the Israeli political scene but also for social scientists studying Jews and Jewish communities. The problem may be even more difficult for social scientists in that they cannot resort to ideological definitions; they can only follow the empirical evidence. Moreover, people may define themselves as Jewish by different criteria. That is, some may define themselves as Jewish by religion, some as Jewish by ethnicity, some as Jewish by birth, and others as Jewish by emotion, i.e., they "feel Jewish."

Since the vast majority of those who identify as Jewish say that they are Jewish by religion, and since the vast majority of those who identify as

Jewish but say that they are not Jewish by religion manifest very low levels of Jewish identity and identification, I selected for analysis only those who when asked, "What is your current religion?" responded "Jewish." Thus, the NJPS sample selected for analysis consists of 801 Jewish baby boomer respondents. There are several reasons that only actual respondents were selected for analysis. In general, I have problems with relying on data obtained from anyone but the respondent himself. Even more importantly in terms of this article is the fact that many of the questions probing Jewish identity were asked only of respondents.

Since there has been somewhat of a debate among the social scientists most directly involved with NJPS as to exactly which, if any, weighting procedure should be used in many instances,[16] and especially when dealing with Jewish cultural issues, all of the tables presented below are of three sets: one consisting of unweighted percentages, one using an alternative weighting procedure suggested by Steven M. Cohen, and one using the NJPS weights. Although the figures differ, depending on which set is used, the most important findings are not the very specific percentages but the patterns, and in the patterns there are no basic differences between the different sets.

TABLE 1

NUMBER OF TIMES JEWISH BABY BOOMERS HAVE BEEN TO ISRAEL

	Unweighted	SMC Weight	POPWGT
Once	15.0	15.7	12.8
Twice	5.0	5.5	4.8
Three times	1.5	2.2	1.9
4–9 times	3.5	4.3	3.3
10+ times	0.5	0.4	0.4
Born in Israel	1.1	1.5	1.4
Never	73.4	70.4	75.3

[16] For example, see Steven M. Cohen, "Why Intermarriage May Not Threaten Jewish Continuity," *Moment*, 19, no. 6 (December 1994): 89ff.

The Limited Impact on America's Jews

It should be emphasized that these figures are for the national American Jewish population, and there are regional differences. A major study of the New York Jewish population found that New York Jews rank higher in their ties with Israel, as well on most indices of Jewish identification and identity, than do Jews nationwide. Thus, among New York Jews ages 18–34, 40 percent stated that they had been to Israel, and among those ages 25–49, 37 percent did.[17]

How one interprets these figures is obviously a matter of perspective. To those who accepted the figures frequently bandied about by representatives of the Jewish Agency and/or World Zionist Organization, to wit, that only about 10 percent of America's Jews have ever visited Israel, the data may be good news. However, if one considers the facts that Israel is, supposedly, a key component of American Jewish identity, and that America's Jews are relatively well-off socio-economically and, presumably, travel considerably, the figures would appear to suggest something quite different.

TABLE 2

NUMBER OF TIMES BEEN TO ISRAEL,
BABY BOOMERS AND MIDDLE-AGERS

	Ages 26–44	Ages 46–64
Once	12.8	19.8
Twice	4.8	5.0
Three times	1.9	1.5
4–9 times	3.3	3.2
10+ times	2.0	2.0
Born in Israel	1.4	.3
Never	75.3	68.3

---

[17] Bethamie Horowitz, *The 1991 New York Jewish Population Study* (New York: UJA-Federation, 1993), Table 2.2, p. 52.

The meaning of the baby boomer figures takes on additional significance when we compare their rates of visits to Israel with those of what may be called "middle-agers," those aged 45–65 in 1990.

It might be suggested that the reason most American Jewish baby boomers have not visited Israel is due to the fact they are busy with their families, especially their children and, at this stage in their lives, or have too many financial obligations to visit Israel (even though they do find the time and money to visit elsewhere). Instead, it may be more revealing to look at feelings about Israel rather than actual visits. However, when we look at the data on the emotional attachments of American Jewish baby boomers to Israel, the picture is not all that different. Some 70 percent say that they are either "Not attached" or "Somewhat attached," and only about 30 percent say that they are either "Very attached" or "Extremely attached."

TABLE 3

EMOTIONAL ATTACHMENTS OF JEWISH BABY BOOMERS TO ISRAEL

	Unweighted	SMC Weight	POPM1WGT
Not attached	19.6	17.7	24.2
Somewhat attached	49.8	48.6	47.0
Very attached	20.1	22.0	18.2
Extremely attached	10.5	11.7	10.6

Here, again, we find that the baby boomers' levels of emotional attachment to Israel are lower than those of the middle-agers. Since emotional attachments do not, in and of themselves, cost money, the lower levels are, indeed, significant.

America's Jews are highly pro-Israel. Indeed, 85 percent of those sampled in a 1988 *Los Angeles Times* survey, favor strong U.S. support for Israel.[18] Such a high percentage of pro-Israelism is obviously a manifestation of Israel as an important factor in American Jewish identity.[19] However

---

[18] Robert Scheer, "The Times Poll: U.S. Jews for Peace Talks on Mideast," *Los Angeles Times*, 12 April 1988.

[19] Chaim I. Waxman, "All In the Family: American Jewish Attachments to Israel," in

TABLE 4

EMOTIONAL ATTACHMENTS TO ISRAEL OF BABY BOOMERS
AND MIDDLE-AGERS

	Ages 26–44	Ages 46–64
Not attached	24.2	15.0
Somewhat attached	47.0	38.0
Very attached	18.2	33.2
Extremely attached	10.6	13.7

to place this in proper perspective, it must be recalled that Americans as a whole are quite favorably disposed toward Israel.[20] One should also be cautious in interpreting the significance of the sharp rise in pro-Israelism among American Jews in 1967. It was probably not as clear a reflection of the centrality of Israel in American Jewish identity as some have suggested. It was also a reflection of the "Americanization" of America's Jews in that many of them felt by then comfortable enough as Americans to express their support for Israel, especially since the United States supported Israel, whereas in earlier times, e.g., 1956 and 1948, they were less comfortable doing so lest they be viewed as less than complete Americans. That support for Israel is today completely compatible with being American is evident from a remark made recently by a 55-year-old—slightly older than baby boomer—New York Jewish "radio personality," who said about Israel: "I'm glad it's there. I viscerally support them in their wars with the various Arab states, but I'm an American and I'm going to live and die in America most likely."[21]

A number of observers have suggested that the Six-Day War conjured up fears of another Holocaust.[22] Accordingly, ties to Israel are, in part,

---

A New Jewry? America Since the Second World War (*Studies in Contemporary Jewry*, Vol. 8), ed. Peter Y. Medding (New York: Oxford University Press), 134–49.

[20] A good analysis is Peter Grose, *Israel in the Mind of America* (New York: Knopf, 1984).

[21] Quoted in Jon Kalish, "The Roots of Radio," *The Jewish Week* (Queens Edition), 14–20 October 1994, 25.

[22] Chaim I. Waxman, *America's Jews in Transition* (Philadelphia: Temple University Press, 1983), 114.

related to feelings of security in the United States. In fact, that the condition of American Jewry is positive is unprecedented. Perhaps Charles Silberman captured it best when, about eight years ago, he called them "a *certain* people."[23] American Jews have made in into American society in ways that could not have been predicted even as recently as mid-century. Socially, Jews seem to have made it into American society. Although much publicity was given to a recent ADL report showing that one in five, or 20 percent, of Americans hold anti-Semitic beliefs and attitudes, what was not given notice was that this reflects a decrease in anti-Semitism. Indeed, all studies since World War II indicate a rather steady and consistent decrease in anti-Semitic beliefs and attitudes by white Americans.[24] Does this mean that there is no anti-Semitism in the United States or that we shouldn't be concerned about it? Certainly not! It does exist, as the ADL report indicates, and it is greater in some parts than in others. For example, it seems fair to assume that in cities such New York, where the economy has suffered periodically and where there is the greatest competition between Jews and blacks, hostilities will be greater. Moreover, Jews are disproportionately urban, so there is an even greater probability of such competition. And, if there is one lesson that history has taught us it is that we must constantly be vigilant to anti-Semitism, no matter how unrepresentative of the society it appears to be.[25]

Also, although surveys of non-Jewish Americans consistently indicate a decrease in anti-Semitic attitudes, most Jews continue to believe that anti-Semitism is a serious problem in the United States. For example, approximately 82 percent of American Jewish baby boomers stated that they believed anti-Semitism to be a serious problem in the United States. Anti-Semitism has long been a force in maintaining Jewish group identity and in maintaining ties to Israel, and one might assume that, with such a high level of perception of anti-Semitism, the bonds will continue to remain firm.

---

[23] Charles E. Silberman, *A Certain People: American Jews and Their Lives Today* (New York: Summit Books, 1985).

[24] Leonard Dinnerstein, *Anti-Semitism in America* (New York: Oxford University Press, 1994).

[25] For a thoughtful challenge to the thesis of "American exceptionalism" as it pertains to anti-Semitism, see Benjamin Ginsberg, *The Fatal Embrace: Jews and the State* (Chicago: University of Chicago Press, 1993).

The Limited Impact on America's Jews

TABLE 5

RESPONDENT: ANTI-SEMITISM IS A SERIOUS PROBLEM IN THE UNITED STATES

	Unweighted	SMC Weight	POPM1WGT
Strongly disagree	2.5	2.2	3.4
Somewhat disagree	14.9	15.1	14.3
Somewhat agree	33.5	30.7	34.9
Strongly agree	49.2	52.1	47.4

However, when we look at the percentage who say that they personally experienced discrimination because of their Jewishness, the percentages drop radically, with more than 90 percent of Jewish baby boomers stating that they have never experienced discrimination.

TABLE 6

RESPONDENT PERSONALLY EXPERIENCED DISCRIMINATION

	Unweighted	SMC Weight	POPM1WGT
Yes, getting job	1.2	1.8	1.3
Yes, promotion	2.8	2.9	2.6
Yes, both	2.0	2.1	1.6
Yes, other	2.4	2.4	2.3
No discrimination	91.2	90.3	91.5
Did not try for job	0.4	0.5	0.6

And, although the percentages were somewhat lower, when asked for their agreement or disagreement with the statement, "In a crisis, Jews can only depend on each other," approximately 60 percent disagreed "somewhat" or "strongly."

TABLE 7

IN CRISIS JEWS CAN ONLY DEPEND ON EACH OTHER

	Unweighted	SMC Weight	POPM1WGT
Strongly disagree	30.5	28.6	31.6
Somewhat disagree	30.5	28.6	30.0
Somewhat agree	14.5	16.1	14.6
Strongly agree	24.5	26.7	23.8

There is ample evidence that Jews are making it into spheres of American society which were traditionally closed to them. Evidence from studies of occupational patterns indicates that Jews can now be found in virtually every occupational sphere and at the highest levels. Even more, they are able to reach these spheres and levels without denying their Jewishness. They don't have to change their names and make a secret of their Jewishness.[26]

TABLE 8

ASSESSMENT OF THE IMPORTANCE OF NEIGHBORHOOD JEWISHNESS

	Unweighted	SMC Weight	POPWGT
Not important	19.9	17.7	21.7
Not very important	25.8	24.4	25.0
Somewhat important	38.2	39.2	38.2
Very important	16.0	18.7	15.1

---

[26] For example, see Samuel Z. Klausner, *Succeeding in Corporate America: The Experience of Jewish M.B.A.'s* (New York: American Jewish Committee, Institute of Human Relations, 1988).

The Limited Impact on America's Jews

However, the "symbolic" rather than ideological and/or structural nature of their Jewishness is evident in a variety of manifestations. To cite but one example, when we look at the character of the neighborhoods in which American Jewish baby boomers live, we find an interesting paradox. On the one hand, a majority says that the Jewishness of their area is either somewhat or very important.

On the other hand, when we look at the actual Jewish character of their neighborhoods as they describe them, we find that more than 60 percent state that there is little or no Jewish character to their neighborhood.

TABLE 9

JEWISH CHARACTER OF NEIGHBORHOOD

	Unweighted	SMC Weight	POPWGT
Not Jewish	31.2	28.5	33.0
Little Jewish	31.8	31.2	32.1
Somewhat Jewish	28.3	30.7	27.0
Very Jewish	8.7	9.6	7.9

The era of the "melting pot," in which being ethnic was a stigma, is over. The change from an ideology of the melting pot to that of "cultural pluralism" took place during the 1960s. One of its first manifestations was the election of a Catholic, John F. Kennedy, to the presidency. Not only was JFK a Catholic, he was of Irish descent, and when he visited Ireland, he spoke proudly of his Irish homeland. In earlier times, that would have been heresy! To be president, one has to be actually born in the United States. As Theodore Roosevelt once said, hyphenated Americans are unacceptable.

The change to cultural pluralism was quickly picked up by Madison Avenue. The late Pan Am Airlines had an ad campaign which proclaimed that all Americans have two homelands—the United States and that from which they or their parents emigrated; that you should visit your other homeland; and when you do, of course, you should fly Pan Am. In another example, during the mid-1960s, Rheingold Beer had a television ad campaign in which they showed a series of ethnic festivities, one for each ad spot, such as an Italian wedding. They showed the ethnic songs and dances and at one point, everyone would lift their glasses of beer—Rheingold, of course—in blessing, salute, or what have you. Such ad campaigns were a clear celebration of ethnicity, something which earlier would have been "un-American."

When I moved to New Haven, in 1965, it was extremely rare to see a *kippa* at Yale. Today, that is not so rare, and one sees *kippot* on the heads of prominent doctors in major hospitals, in Wall Street offices, law offices, and even, several years ago, worn by the chief of the public defender's office in Los Angeles in the television series, *The Trials of Rosie O'Neal*. And, frequently, no mention is made and attention is paid to the *kippa*. It's very natural.

That Jews have "made it" into American society is also evident in the increasing numbers of Jews running for public office at the national level, and they serve while retaining their Jewish affiliation. Senator Joseph Lieberman of Connecticut is one outstanding example, and there are more.

One final manifestation of Jews having made it into American society is, much as it causes us pain, the significant rise in intermarriage. As the NJPS clearly shows, intermarriage today is basically different than it was in the past in that the Jewish spouse is no longer expected to renounce his or her Jewishness. On the contrary, the non-Jewish spouse frequently finds the spouse's Jewishness attractive. This, again, is reflected in the media. Remember Michael and Hope on *Thirty-Something*? In a sense, it's "in" to be Jewish today. Several years ago, Joel, the doctor from New York, on *Northern Exposure,* a very popular, prime-time weekly television show, proclaimed, "I am not white. I'm Jewish." And you can be sure he was not looking for a Jewish wife in Alaska! In fact, the next season he proposed to his colleague, Maggie O'Donnell.

Nor is it only with respect to mate selection that Jews are increasingly bonding with non-Jews. Approximately two-thirds of the Jewish baby boomer respondents said that none or few of their closest friends are Jewish.

Again, New York Jews are significantly different. Among those between the ages 18–34, 57 percent stated that most of their close friends are Jewish, and among those between the ages 35–49, 61 percent did.[27]

---

[27] Horowitz, Table 2.2, p. 52.

TABLE 10

JEWISH BABY BOOMERS' CLOSEST FRIENDS WHO ARE JEWISH

	Unweighted	SMC Weight	POPWGT
None Jewish	5.9	4.7	6.3
Few or some Jewish	58.4	53.1	60.4
Most Jewish	26.7	31.4	24.3
All Jewish	9.0	10.8	9.0

What we are dealing with is what Herbert Gans calls "symbolic ethnicity."[28] Traditional ethnicity meant submerging the individual self to the demands of the group. The group has strong social control. Today, the group has no control and the individual does not submit. Symbolic ethnicity is modern; it is an attempt to synthesize individualism with what Robert Nisbet referred to as the "quest for community."[29] But not community in the traditional sense that has power over the individual. Rather, it is a "community" with which one chooses to "identify" emotionally. It is, perhaps, a psychological community but not a sociological one. Even in choosing to identify with an ethnicity, the individual picks and chooses that which he can accept and that which he rejects, much as modern religion has become pick and choose religion. Charles Liebman also suggests that much of American Judaism is of a symbolic nature.[30]

James Davison Hunter has analyzed the "culture wars" raging in the United States today.[31] The more traditional element in U.S. Jewry is much

---

[28] Herbert J. Gans, "Symbolic Ethnicity: The Future of Ethnic Groups and Culture in America," in *On the Making of Americans: Essays in Honor of David Riesman*, eds. Herbert J. Gans, Nathan Glazer, Joseph R. Gusfield, Christopher Jencks (Philadelphia: University of Pennsylvania Press, 1979), 193–220.

[29] Robert A. Nisbet, *The Quest for Community* (New York: Oxford University Press, 1970).

[30] Charles S. Liebman, "Ritual, Ceremony, and the Reconstruction of Judaism in the United States," in *Art and its Uses: The Visual Image and Modern Jewish Society*, (*Studies in Contemporary Jewry* 6), ed. Ezra Mendelsohn (New York: Oxford University Press, 1990), 272–83.

[31] James Davison Hunter, *Culture Wars: The Struggle to Define America* (New York: Basic Books, 1991).

more involved with Israel. How that will play itself out if the less traditional element in Israel moves farther away from the "civil religion" of Israel remains to be seen. Likewise, the greater the strength of the *haredi* element in Israel becomes, the more it is likely to alienate the American Jewish non-traditionalists as well as a smaller but significant percentage of those in the traditional fold. Again, what will emerge from such developments is difficult to predict.

What seems clear is the nature of the American Jewish-Israeli relationship has undergone substantial change since the Six-Day War. There is no solid evidence, despite suggestions to the contrary by both American Jewish communal leaders and others[32] that visits to Israel are the *causal* factor in intensifying Jewish identity and identification. There is evidence that Israel plays an important part in American Jewish identification, and the American Jewish community needs Israel much as Israel needs the American Jewish community. However, as the evidence presented indicates, fewer Jews now identify with the organized American Jewish community and with Israel.

Yet, it might be argued that perhaps there actually has not been any diminution in American Jewish attachments to Israel, despite the evidence they have. Perhaps those have declined simply as a result of the broader decline in American Jewish attachments to what might be called the "public Judaism" of the organized American Jewish community. Some have argued that despite the decline in these type of attachments, there has been no decline—indeed, some suggest an increase—in "private Judaism," that is, informal as well as formal Judaism within the private sphere, especially family, without the formalized institutional connections.

Reassuring as that hypothesis sounds, the evidence does not appear to support it. With respect to attachments to Israel, in particular, the data presented relate to "private" as well as "public" spheres. Emotional attachments are most certainly within the private sphere and, as Table 4 indicates, they have declined among baby boomers. Furthermore, if it were only the attachments to Israel in the public, formal institutional sphere that have declined, we might have expected that, for example, the rate of *aliyah* among baby boomers to have, at least, remained constant. *Aliyah*, after all, is "doing" rather than "joining." Hard data on recent American *aliyah* is

---

[32] For example, see David Mittleberg, *The Israel Visit and Jewish Identification* (New York: American Jewish Committee, American Jewish-Israel Relations Institute, 1994).

meager. What is evident is that, although the median age of American immigrants to Israel (*olim*) remains in the 25–29-year-old cohort, as it has been for at least several decades, there was a steady decline in the number of American *olim* during the 1980s, and the 1990 figures were the lowest since the 1960s.[33] So there does not appear to be anything in the Israel-related evidence, of a private-sphere or public-sphere nature, to suggest that the diminishing of Jewish identification and identity is only of a limited nature. Although there may be sporadic and short-lived surges of manifestations of "symbolic Judaism," especially with respect to episodic American Jewish attention to Israel, there has been a decline in attachments that are socially meaningful and significant, that is, that involve the individual for any length of time in ways that can be empirically demonstrated. An important question then becomes whether those weakening ties will strengthen those in Israel who already wish to distance themselves from the American Jewish community, and what the impact of such a trend may have on both the American Jewish community and Israel.

---

[33] Chaim I. Waxman, "In the End Is it Ideology?: Religio-Cultural and Structural Factors in American Aliya," *Contemporary Jewry* 16 (1995): 50–67.

Jewish Cultural Confidence in American Letters
A Writer's Thoughts*

Nessa Rapoport

In 1990, the critic Ted Solotaroff invited me to join him in co-editing a new anthology of contemporary American Jewish short stories. In embarking on the project, we had to initiate—and then endure—the inevitable discussion about what Jewish writing really is and who can be deemed a Jewish writer. Thankfully, the conversation did not last long, because it was clear to both of us that we shared a very capacious view of the matter, one that is reflected in the pages of the ensuing collection, *Writing Our Way Home*.

The more interesting question from a Jewish vantage point was not what did we mean by Jewish writing, but what did we mean by contemporary? Ted proposed that we use the Six-Day War as the cutoff date for our oldest stories, on grounds he presents eloquently in the book's introduction—that 1967 was a watershed in American Jewish intellectual and literary self-awareness. The decision pleased me not only on American but on Jewish grounds. In a country where an anthology called *Best American Short Stories* is released each year, who but the Jews would define "contemporary" as any story published within the last thirty years?

In the many stimulating conversations Ted and I held as we planned the book, one thesis was central. Rather than documenting the slow attrition of a literary tradition from the glory days of Bellow, Roth, and Malamud, we claimed that American Jewish writing was entering a stage in which the representation of Jewish life and manners—whether immigrant or suburban—was only one of many possibilities for a rich literary culture.

---

* This essay develops ideas I explored initially in "Text, Language, and the Hope of Redemption," in *The Writer in the Jewish Community: An Israeli-North American Dialogue*, ed. Richard Siegel and Tamar Sofer (Fairleigh Dickinson University Press, 1993); and in an address given at the Jewish Museum, New York, in 1993, published in *The Jews in America: A Treasury of Art and Literature*, ed. Abraham J. Karp (Hugh, Lauter, Levin Associates, 1994).

In my own share of the book's introduction, I wrote about what I called "Jewish cultural confidence," a confidence I believe is owed in no small measure to the existence of the state of Israel. Of course, the changing idea of Israel in the minds of American Jews—from the existential anxiety of the weeks preceding the Six-Day War of 1967 to the miraculous triumph that ensued, from the shock of the Yom Kippur War and its demoralized aftermath to the heady days of the Soviet Jewish exodus and the salvation of Ethiopian Jewry—is a drama of interpretation in the Jewish mind: Are we all-vulnerable as we always have been, or invincible as we dreamed we could be? Are we a high moral light to the nations or too much like every other nation? But Israel's presence has been a fact, not an interpretation. And that fact has coincided with a period of unprecedented flourishing and influence for Diaspora Jews in the United States.

Jews are disproportionately educated and disproportionately represented, not in all aspects of American life, but in many that ally with cultural influence. Much of the writing that Jews produce in numbers far exceeding their share of the American population is not about Jewishness in any overt or conscious way. Much of it is written by Jews who have no intimacy with the Jewish literary tradition, with our sacred texts and their interpreters, with even one Jewish language—whether Ladino, Yiddish, or Hebrew; writers who have little familiarity with Jewish history, ideology, philosophy, or community.

But no matter how "un-Jewish" those Jews' work may seem, it reflects two extremely Jewish forces—a ferocious drive for education, inherited from immigrant forebears, and a passion for words, writing, and language that is at the core of the living Jewish enterprise. That passion has been, I would argue, what has sustained the Jews throughout many centuries, countries, and travails. It has even, through the rebirth of Hebrew, been indispensable in the enterprise of Zionism, for long before 1948, Zionism took root as a written idea.

So whenever I am compelled to counter the marginalization of culture and literature in the identity crisis taking place within American-Jewish life, I like to remember a journalist and playwright, writing in his diary less than a hundred years ago. It was a time when repression and pogroms had resumed in Russia; when xenophobia was rising in Western Europe. Even in an era of nineteenth-century nationalism, Theodore Herzl's vision of a homeland for the Jews was seen as impractical, preposterous and—that terrible indictment of writers—dreamy. And yet, in the fall of 1897, he wrote: "At Basel I founded the Jewish state.... Perhaps in five years, and certainly in fifty, everyone will recognize it."

Fifty-one years later turned out to be 1948. So before we decide that a vision for Jewish writing in America can only be incidental to the intermarriage statistics and the eclipse of Jewish culture in the multicultural hegemony of the marketplace of ideas, let us remember that writers and writing have saved the Jews.

In proposing that a new generation of Jewishly educated and culturally confident writers is emerging in the United States, I want to evoke the inescapable conclusion of our history: Jews have never had the most power, money, or number of citizens—and we never will. Our strength and gift lie in the great book we have given the world, in our traditional insistence on the indispensability of language to the highest human callings—whether law or prophecy, and in our unique interpretive legacy that demands a linguistic precision sanctioned as theological.

Looking at our history, we are entitled to feel a confidence in our literary culture, which has prevailed for thousands of years against extraordinary obstacles and odds. Nevertheless, there are many people, including Jews, who do not even recognize that Judaism is a distinct literary culture of its own. They continue to mistake our sociological success in America for our cultural success.

In today's multicultural wars, played out not only on campus but on the street, Judaism is seen as a subset of a frequently despised Western culture instead of the informing culture of both the West and the East, through Islam. Rather than the beleaguered minority culture we truly represent—for our literature is mostly unknown, even by Jews, and our culture was devastated by the murder of one-third of our people—Jews are disenfranchised in the multicultural debate, dissolved into the great white majority that is seen as afflicting victimized minorities with unwanted dominance.

Which only proves that these debates are really about race and class rather than culture. For if there's one thing that can be said about American Jews today, it is that for many their authentic Jewish commitment has not had the advantage of being illuminated by an equally authentic Jewish education, an immersion in the writing, dreaming, and modes of perception that have allowed advocates of Jewish culture, like me, to feel so rich.

At the same time, there is an outpouring of books, both academic and popular, on a breathtaking range of Jewish subjects that testifies to a growing Jewish literacy and interest taking place right alongside our deepening assimilation. Unlike Israeli writers, who must overcome, if they wish to use the Jewish written tradition, the unhappy marriage of contemporary religion and politics, American Jewish writers can be nourished, in

Ted Solotaroff's words, "by a nascent contemporary Jewish culture that lives on easier and perhaps more fertile terms with religious Judaism...and seeks to draw upon its vast literary tradition."

I am not making the case here for an explosion of religious writing in America. My point is that Jewish writing in American life can be a reflection of Jewish letters; it can draw not only on the lives of Jews but on the Jewish tradition—the myths, structures, and allusions of our own distinctive literature. In a conference sponsored by the National Foundation for Jewish Culture in Berkeley, California, to examine the place of the writer in the Jewish community, the late esteemed critic Irving Howe postulated that with the end of immigrant Jewish marginality in America—that almost shocking acceptance of Jews in public life and, even more surprisingly, in private life as suitable spouses for non-Jewish sons and daughters—Jewish writers would face what Howe called "a crisis of subject matter," "a spiritual vacuum... a glaring emptiness at the center of American-Jewish life." This is a view that is useful to many people, some of them classic Zionists, for whom it is important to believe that a nuanced, sophisticated Jewish culture cannot possibly flourish in the Diaspora. It is useful to polemicists in Israel and America, to politicians, and to exhorting Jewish leaders of various ideological persuasions. But I do not believe it to be true.

As I said in my introduction to *Writing Our Way Home,* even if one wanted to look at American Jewish literature from a sociological perspective alone, one could still point to entire communities of immigrant Jews from whom a fascinating literature may emerge. I am thinking of the waves of immigration that succeeded the Eastern European one—that is, Syrian, Israeli, Iranian, South American, Soviet and, once again, Eastern European.

These Jews have brought with them their own languages and modes of perception. Their writers will, like the immigrants who preceded them, have something to say about their communities within America, about the tensions between their cultural inheritance and America's in a time when the melting pot has been banished as an organizing metaphor and ethnic/racial identity is everything.

But national origins are not the only starting point for writers. I had a great mentor, Wolfe Kelman, who claimed that the most important contributions to American Jewish life would come from women, converts, and children of Holocaust survivors. Certainly in literature, Jewish women are transforming the subject matter and viewpoint of American Jewish fiction. Previous anthologies of American Jewish stories included a token woman or two. In ours, slightly more than half the writers were women, not because of any political correctness or quota but simply because the stories were new, depicting Jews we had not yet met on the page, in predicaments and attitudes that were fresh and distinctive. So, too, I expect to hear from others who have been conventionally outsiders: Sephardim, descendants of *conversos* in the American Southwest, lesbians, and gay men. Each of these groups has an idiosyncratic experience and perspective out of which imaginative writing may prosper.

But ultimately, sociology is only one ground—and the least interesting one—to dispute a verdict of cultural extinction. There is a larger, grander reason, a literary one, which supports my belief in the ongoing flowering of Jewish letters in America. Jews, as a covenantal community, are necessarily a literary one. An engagement with words has been both our history and our destiny. Bound by a passion for one book, we have produced thousands of books, commentaries, arguments, parables, laws, legends, meditations, poems, and songs. These writings constitute an astonishing literary civilization, which, like the best imaginative writing, exemplifies an intoxication with language, stunning formal inventiveness, imagery resonant with millennia of living use, a dazzling range of style from the sacred to the satiric, and a relentless resistance to nostalgia, cliché, and verbal decadence.

American Jewish writing before the Six-Day War transformed American letters by drawing on and legitimizing recent Jewish experience. But our fiction can equally be a dialogue with earlier Jewish books; it can retrieve the materials and resources of an august and infinitely rich imaginative tradition for art.

Such a strategy requires a Jewishly educated and culturally confident community of writers. My prediction is that we shall witness such a community. Unlike many literary phenomena that artists create and critics then dissect, in America there is a critical infrastructure waiting for its fiction. For more than a decade, critics have explicated the Bible as literature. Robert Alter, Harold Bloom, Geoffrey Hartman, and younger men and women have examined the Bible not as a religious artifact but as the literary influence it continues to be.

Recently, several collections of essays by Jewish writers have looked at Biblical texts imaginatively—to both critical and popular reception. In the fall of 1994, two collections by women writers appeared: *Out of the Garden: Women Writers on the Bible,* an anthology of essays by Jewish and Christian women; and *Reading Ruth: Contemporary Women Reclaim a Sacred Story,* a collection of essays by Jewish women writers solely addressing the book of Ruth. The books have been immediately successful, selling many thousands of copies within weeks of their release. They are testimony both to the recognition of Jewish writers that our sacred texts and reading tradition are worthy of literary attention and to the hunger of Jews, especially women, to have more direct access to the enduring cultural wealth of the Jewish people. For the first time, there are young Jews with a strong Jewish education who are becoming critically acclaimed American artists. Whereas once, with rare exceptions, the quality of art by Jews seemed to be in inverse proportion to the depth of the artists' Jewish education, today that need no longer be the case. What kind of art will be born when such singers and dancers—and writers—begin to explore the integration of their gifts and their profound Jewish imaginations?

I ask this question not out of the atavistic pride that enables some of us to name every movie star who was born a Jew, but out of genuine cultural curiosity. Jews are both enough at home in America to see such a generation of artists emerge, and distinct enough as a culture to shape American culture in our image.

I believe the Six-Day War and the fact of Israel play an essential role in the "at-homeness" of American Jews. By this I mean that any thinking Jew, even a man or woman who knows very little of Jewish texts or life, cannot fail to recognize that he or she was born in a century in which millions of people tried to eradicate the Jews, and millions of Jews were unprotected from that fate. I have seen in even my most assimilated friends, who are marrying non-Jews without much of a qualm, an awareness of Jewish vulnerability that is, I think, unconsciously offset by the existence of the Jewish state. I would go further and say that we carry our heads high in America not only because the country has been home to us in an unprecedented way but because there is a country across the sea that is not home but homeland. For writers like me, for whom Jewish texts and a Jewish way of reading are defining, Israel is a living engagement, a country whose people, national life, literature, language—and myth—are at the vital core of my idea of myself, writer and Jew. I do think I have a freedom in relation to the Jewish literary tradition, the one between "two thousand years ago" and "then in 1948," that many Israeli writers cannot allow themselves. But I know what I don't have: a language in which Jewish literature is inherent, not self-conscious; and the ability to extend Jewish imagination to the realm of sovereignty.

My Israeli writer friends remind me of the place of writers in the life of Israel; they continue to be far more central to national discourse than American Jewish writers can ever be. We can, as I have said elsewhere, create a Jewish culture but not a Jewish government; we will never have public transportation whose front seats bear the sign, *mipnei seivah takum*, quoting from Leviticus to remind us to stand so that we honor the elderly. We can play with English, shape and influence the language to a remarkable degree, but we will never hear on national television that the outcome of a football game or an election is *teiku*, the Talmudic term that means an unresolved debate whose outcome must await the Messiah. But the end of days is my cue to end this exploration. Even a dreamer like me cannot allow myself, especially in Jerusalem, to get started on the Messiah.

The Six-Day War and the "Jewish Question" in France

Judith Friedlander
Graduate Faculty of Political and Social Science
New School for Social Research

MY OBSERVATION OF THE INFLUENCE of the Six-Day War on France will focus specifically on French intellectuals of the generation of 1968, who assumed a political or cultural identity as Jews in the years immediately following the war. I refer to individuals representing three broadly defined groups. The people described here all see themselves as Jews firmly rooted in the Diaspora. While deeply committed to the existence of Israel, they refuse to make Zionism the defining feature of their new identity. Still, I argue, the Six-Day War and the violence that followed, in both the Middle East and France, played a major role in challenging Jewish intellectuals of the generation of 1968 to think seriously about their identity as Jews. The three groups I discuss are: (1) minority nationalists—secular Jews committed to cultural diversity and the possibility of developing their ethnic, not religious identity, in a multicultural, multi-ethnic society; (2) secular Jews who, after experimenting for a while with minority nationalism identify once again with the assimilationist ideals of the French Enlightenment; and (3) ultra-Orthodox Jews.[1]

Although the three groups differ from one another in significant ways, they all take as their point of departure eighteenth-century debates about the "Jewish Question" in France, invoking, frequently challenging, the terms spelled out for emancipating the Jews at the time of the French Revolution. In 1789 Stanislas de Clermont-Tonnerre defined these terms with his famous proclamation: "We must refuse the Jews everything as a nation and give them everything as individuals; they must constitute neither a political group nor an order within the State; they must become

---

[1] This paper is based on previously published material. See Judith Friedlander, *Vilna on the Seine: Jewish Intellectuals in France Since 1968* (New Haven: Yale University Press, 1990).

citizens as individuals."[2] Like other eighteenth-century champions of democracy and the French nation-state, Clermont-Tonnerre believed that an individual's religious affiliation was a private matter that should be neither regulated *nor* recognized by the state. Using the language of the times, Clermont-Tonnerre argued that there should be only one nation (or national culture) within the state. To become citizens of France, the Jews had to be French. But as Frenchmen they did have the right to practice the religion of their forefathers, if they did so discreetly, behind closed doors. The price of emancipation was assimilation. Jews had to become Frenchmen of the faith of Moses.

In the years following the French Revolution, the acceptability of this eighteenth-century formulation was not always taken for granted. Time and again, political groups appeared to challenge the idea that Jews could, or should, be French. Usually, however, those opposing the terms of Jewish emancipation were non-Jews representing the extreme Right. Now Jewish intellectuals identified with the Left were raising objections, denouncing those who embraced the Enlightenment and who recommended that Jews assimilate. While some Jewish intellectuals of the generation of 1968 eventually returned to the universalistic ideals of the Enlightenment, many others continued to reject assumptions long held sacred in France. Challenging the old adage about being Frenchmen on the street and Jews at home, they called for the right to be Jewish everywhere.

The Jews described here come, for the most part, from middle-class assimilated families, Ashkenazim and Sephardim. Students and young teachers in the late 1960s, many of them played significant roles in the movement that led to the student uprising in 1968. In the early days of this period of political unrest, they joined extreme leftist groups, associating in many cases with the Trotskyists or the Maoists. Soon, however, they abandoned these groups, as the "gauchistes" took virulent stands against Israel, which verged, at times, on anti-Semitism. By the mid-1970s, activists who were Jewish had become Jewish-identified activists, seeking ways to live like Jews in contemporary France. Today, a number of these Jewish-identified activists hold professorial chairs in the French university system and research posts at the Centre national de la Recherche Scientifique (CNRS). Others have achieved distinction in the media and the press. Still marginal

---

[2] Cited in Léon Poliakov, *Histoire de l'antisémitisme* (Paris: Calmann-Lévy, 1968), vol. 3, *De Voltaire à Wagner*, 234, note 2; Eng. trans. *The History of Antisemitism*, (New York: Vanguard, 1975), vol. 3, *From Voltaire to Wagner*.

in 1980, when Dominique Schnapper published *Jewish Identities in France*,[3] many of these "militants," have since gone on to influence the larger Jewish community in France.

As we look more closely at these Jewish-identified intellectuals of the generation of 1968, we see that they divide themselves according to their age at the time of the student upheaval. While there are exceptions, for the most part those who were already professors in 1968 founded secular Jewish movements. Those who were in the *lycée*, or beginning students in the university, followed their professors in the early years of the upheaval, but then turned away from national/secular solutions and sought inspiration from their religious heritage. Some became Orthodox Jews, others merely students of sacred texts.

A number of demographic and historical factors bear heavily on any discussion of the Jewish community in contemporary France: the deportation of Jews during the Second World War, the establishment of the State of Israel, the emigration of North African Jews to France in the 1950s and early 1960s, the Six-Day War in Israel, and the escalation of armed conflict in the Middle East that occurred in subsequent years.

Of the Jews described here, many of them came of age in the shadow of the Shoah, their childhood years filled with a longing for relatives who would never return. Others suffered less as they grew up on the southern shores of the Mediterranean Sea. Their families, too, lived through difficult times, but the traumas they faced rarely compared to the misfortunes of Jews caught in Europe during the Second World War. However, soon after the war ended, the French colonial period did, too. And as the French armies retreated in the late 1950s and early 1960s, many Jews living in North Africa left as well, moving either to Israel or France.

With the outbreak of the Six-Day War in 1967, the French Jewish community saw a significant rise in the number of young people emigrating to Israel.[4] Even for many who remained in France, the eruption of violence in

---

[3] Dominique Schnapper, *Juifs et Israélites*, (Paris: Gallimard, 1980); Eng. trans. by A. Goldhammer, *Jewish Identities in France: An Analysis of Contemporary French Jewry* (Chicago: University of Chicago Press, 1980).

[4] Between 1944 and 1959, 5,000 Jews emigrated to Palestine/Israel. Between 1960–1979, the number rose to 33,000. See: Doris Bensimon and Sergio Della-Pergola, *La Population juive de France: Socio-démographie et identité* (Paris: CNRS, 1986), 36. The highest single year was 1969, two years after the Six-Day War, when 5,292 Jews made aliyah from France. See Sergio DellaPergola and Uzi Rebhun, *Israel-Diaspora Relationships: A First Quantitative Analysis of Social Indicators* (Jerusalem: Occasional paper, no. 13, Division of Jewish Demography

the Middle East awakened a fierce sense of loyalty to the Jewish state. To work for Israel became a way of affirming their ethnic and national identity.

But as the crisis deepened in the 1970s many Jewish intellectuals with ties to the Left had difficulty defending Israel's claim to the West Bank and the Gaza Strip. They refused to join mainstream Zionist organizations and embrace policies they considered to be acts of aggression, but they vigorously opposed the Palestinian Liberation Organization too, defying Arab threats to destroy Israel. Caught in the middle, some wanted to serve as intermediaries. A handful of artists and intellectuals began trying to help as early as 1967 and their numbers increased in the 1970s as socialist Zionists started sending representatives to the Middle East on a regular basis to meet with like-minded Israelis and Palestinians.

As the Israeli-Palestinian conflict escalated in the late 1970s, Jews in France became targets of terrorist aggression. Between 1979 and 1982, bombs killed and wounded innocent people with alarming frequency. In some cases, Palestinian groups took responsibility for the attacks; in others, French neo-Fascists. During the same period, Robert Faurisson, a literature professor from the University of Lyons, claimed that gas chambers in the German death camps had never existed, and his work received the enthusiastic support of a group of extreme leftists.

For many in the generation of 1968, it was this wave of violence, both physical and ideological, that pushed them to consider the problems of Jews in the Diaspora. As they focused their attention on the situation back home, they began to look at themselves, wondering why they claimed they were Jewish when they identified so little with Jewish tradition. To correct this embarrassment, some joined groups seeking ways to establish national and secular Jewish culture in France, while others turned to religion.

Minority Nationalists

Jews interested in questions of minority nationalism had begun forming circles in the late 1960s to study the experiences of ethnic groups in France and compare them to those of communities living in states where cultural diversity existed. Determined to replace the historical French model of "one nation (one culture) within one state," they made alliances with political movements organizing among the Bretons, Occitans, and other ethnic

---

and Statistics, Avraham Harman Institute of Contemporary Jewry, Hebrew University, 1994), 3; and their article in this volume.

groups in the country and eventually found ways to influence government policy. In the 1980s the French Socialists actually adopted aspects of their program for the new party platform on the rights of minority cultures.[5]

In 1967 Richard Marienstras founded Le Cercle Gaston Crémieux.[6] Shakespearean scholar and professor of English at the University of Paris VII, he was one of the first to analyze closely the contradictions imposed on assimilated Jews in France.[7] With a group of one hundred and fifty professors and students, Marienstras studied Jewish history from the perspective of Simon Dubnow, the great Russian apologist for Diaspora Jewry, and looked for ways to develop a secular Jewish culture in France. Influenced as well by the Yiddish-speaking Bund, Marienstras envisioned creating in France a national Jewish tradition tied neither to the synagogue nor the State of Israel. Committed to the development of Jewish cultures in the Diaspora, Le Cercle Gaston Crémieux encouraged Jews to seek ethnic autonomy in a joint political effort with other minorities.

While the Cercle recognized the importance of the State of Israel in the life of contemporary Jews, it challenged those who would make Zionism the central ideology of Jews living in the Diaspora. Deeply opposed to cultural uniformity and to the expansionist policies of all nation-states, the Cercle often criticized Israel and opposed the willingness of the French Jewish establishment to support virtually every decision made by the Jewish state. The Cercle similarly opposed the synagogue and religious Judaism, insisting instead on the importance of the cultural and political traditions of Jews outside the religion. To promote a secular Jewish culture in France, the Cercle organized study groups in Jewish history, classes in Yiddish and in Jewish cooking, as well as workshops to discuss what it meant to be a Jew in the Diaspora today. Most importantly the Cercle sponsored major events to introduce France to the accomplishments of secular Jewish cultures outside Israel. Although its programs reflected only the contributions of Yiddish-speaking Jews from Eastern Europe, the

---

[5] Henri Giordan, *Démocratie culturelle et droit à la différence* (Paris: Collection des rapports officiels, La Documentation Française, 1982); Giles Verbund, ed., *Par les langues de France*, 2 vols. (Paris: Edition du Centre Georges Pompidou, 1985).

[6] Lawyer, journalist, poet, and socialist, Gaston Crémieux was killed by the French Government in 1871 for having supported the Paris Commune. At the time, he was president of the departmental commission representing the Commune of Marseilles. A member of a distinguished family, Gaston Crémieux was the cousin of Adolphe Crémieux, founder of the Alliance Israélite Universelle and architect of the 1870 decree that recognized Algerian Jews as citizens of France.

[7] See: Richard Marienstras, *Être un peuple en diaspora* (Paris: Maspéro, 1975).

group endorsed efforts that promoted Ladino, Judeo-Arabic, and even Hebrew cultures in the Diaspora. Identifying neither with the State of Israel nor with institutionalized forms of Judaism, the Cercle wanted to create living Jewish cultures in France that went beyond the consensus politics of such influential organizations as the CRIF (Conseil Représentatif des Institutions Juives de France) and the "official" Judaism promoted by the French Jewish *consistoire*.

Given their outspoken positions on Israel and the synagogue, the Cercle never received much support from mainstream organizations in the French Jewish community. Still, members of the group have played an important role in setting the terms of the debate about minority cultures in the country today. Thanks to the Cercle, everybody knows the contemporary French rendition of the Bundist ideal of minority nationalism—"le droit à la différence." Furthermore, even though the group waxes and wanes, having lost most of its influence by the late 1980s, former members of the Cercle continue to generate a great deal of interest in the history and literature of Eastern European Jewry before the Second World War. The number of books, films, cultural events, and university courses on the subject produced by people who participated in the Cercle is impressive, the reception by Jews and Gentiles enthusiastic.[8]

SECULAR JEWS WHO, AFTER EXPERIMENTING FOR A WHILE WITH MINORITY NATIONALISM, IDENTIFY ONCE AGAIN WITH THE ASSIMILATIONIST IDEALS OF THE FRENCH ENLIGHTENMENT

For the most part, older members of the Cercle Gaston Crémieux were of East European origin. Richard Marienstras himself was born in Warsaw and came to France with his mother as a very young boy, before the Second World War. His father died in the Warsaw Ghetto. The younger members of the group were more mixed ethnically and included a significant number of Sephardic Jews of North African origin.

---

[8] See, for example, the work of Rachel Ertel, who has edited several series of French translations of Yiddish poetry and novels (most recently for Editions Julliard). She has also written *Le Shtetl: la bourgade juive en Pologne* (Paris: Payot, 1982) and played a major consultative role in Nat Lilenstein's television documentary *Les Révolutionnaires du Yiddishland* (1984). Another founding member of Le Cercle Gaston Crémieux is Pierre Vidal-Naquet, classicist and author of the internationally acclaimed *Les Assassins de la mémoire* (Paris: Editions La Découverte, 1987), English tr., *The Assassins of Memory* (New York: Columbia University Press, 1992).

By the mid-1970s, younger members of the generation of 1968 had begun questioning whether national definitions of being a Jew in the Diaspora had meaning for their lives today. Many of those who had been students at the time of the university revolt shared a similar political history. First they joined the extreme Left, dividing themselves essentially between the Trotskyists and the Maoists. As the Left became increasingly critical of Israel and, so it seemed, of Jews more generally, many quit their parties and continued to struggle as minority nationalists, becoming members of groups like Le Cercle Gaston Crémieux. But unlike Marienstras and his contemporaries, these students, for the most part, could not respond to the ideals of the Yiddishists. While they wanted to know more about the history of Eastern European Jews, they could not see reviving or creating a secular Jewish culture in France. The lost world of Polish and Russian Jews was a haunting nightmare, not a dream for the future. In his book *The Imaginary Jew*, Alain Finkielkraut, the son of Polish Jewish immigrants and a provocative spokesman for the younger members of the generation of 1968, wrote the following:

> The need for roots is the *mal* of the last quarter of this century. But how can I possibly plant myself in pre-war Galicia or Warsaw? All I know in Polish and Yiddish are a few swear words, a few affectionate expressions, two or three little sayings. This world, assassinated, concerns and haunts me.... [Yet] I do not look for myself there, but for who I am not and can no longer be.[9]

Finkielkraut's target was not Le Cercle Gaston Crémieux—in fact he praised Richard Marienstras in a footnote—but the emptiness today of his own secular Polish Jewish heritage. He could not identify with a way of life that had been monstrously destroyed before he was born. Finkielkraut had not suffered personally during the war and he had little experience with Jewish secular or religious traditions from Poland or anywhere else. When he used to evoke his Jewishness during the turbulent student years, his declarations were nothing more than a political travesty, he claimed—an image he drew on when it was convenient, his most interesting way of attracting attention. There was no substance to his "Juif," it was little more than a narcissistic label:

---

[9] Alain Finkielkraut, *Le Juif imaginaire* (Paris: Editions du Seuil, 1980), p. 51 (my translation); English trans., *The Imaginary Jew* (Lincoln, Neb.: University of Nebraska Press, 1994).

'I am Jewish,' said I, and this phrase condensed all that I knew about Judaism, my profound truth, my dignity refound. The only language I spoke was the one that made demands. Settling down to a life of *defiance,* I spent many happy days on the edges of the social order, enchanted with the part I was playing. It was this posing of mine that kept me away from Jewish culture more than social pressure or any obligation to assimilate.[10]

Finkielkraut claimed that history did more than spare his peers the sufferings of those who had lived through major tragedies. History had literally passed them by. Reduced to spectators, but eager to find a role for themselves, they tried to play a number of parts from the sidelines, before assuming the empty shell of their own. Over the years, they had dressed up as colonized natives with Frantz Fanon, as American Blacks with Malcolm X, as guerilla fighters with Che, Giap, and Ho Chi Minh. Now they were playing Jews and in doing so, reversing the famous formula associated with their people's emancipation in the eighteenth century: they had become universal men at home and Jews on the street. Asserting their right to be different in public, they returned to their assimilated selves back home.

When Finkielkraut decided to look seriously at his Jewish heritage, he first went to meetings of Le Cercle Gaston Crémieux, but he found the group's Yiddishist program inadequate for his needs. He then turned to the study of philosophical texts, becoming a student of Emmanuel Lévinas and following his mentor in an exploration of the ways Jewish thought enriches the humanistic ideals of Western European culture. Inspired by the work of a philosopher of Lithuanian Jewish origin, Finkielkraut now vigorously rejects the call to elaborate cultural or ethnic differences and embraces instead the universalistic ideals of the Enlightenment. Today he defends the values of the French nation-state, defiantly supporting secularism and "one nation within one state," against those who insist that the French government endorse the open expression of religious beliefs and diverse national traditions in public institutions and contexts.[11]

---

[10] Ibid., 215.

[11] See, for example Alain Finkielkraut, *La Sagesse de l'amour* (Paris: Gallimard, 1984), idem, *La Défaite de la pensée* (Paris: Gallimard, 1987), English ed., *The Defeat of the Mind,* trans. J. Friedlander (New York: Columbia University Press, 1995).

THE ULTRA-ORTHODOX

Still other members of the generation of 1968 continue to criticize the universalistic ideals of the Enlightenment in terms similar to those of Le Cercle Gaston Crémieux. But they too have moved away from minority nationalism. Embracing particularism with a vengeance, they eventually abandoned the secular Yiddishists and turned to religion in order to live, in their eyes, more fully as Jews.

In 1976 a few of the younger members of Le Cercle Gaston Crémieux invited Eliahou Abitbol, a rabbi of Moroccan origin, to give a lecture on Jewish life in the Diaspora. Their initiative challenged the group's policy of not sponsoring talks by religious leaders. Rabbis, the Cercle maintained, had other places in which to speak. Abitbol's talk caused such an uproar that those responsible for arranging the event left the group and decided to pursue their inquiry elsewhere. A few of them subsequently joined the yeshiva community that Abitbol had established in the Alsatian city of Strasbourg, modeling his institution on the great yeshivas of early nineteenth-century Lithuania. Founded in 1967, La Yéchiva des Étudiants is a place where young people with little prior background in Judaism have come to study and live as strictly observant Jews.

By the mid-1980s Abitbol had attracted over 100 Jewish families to his yeshiva, many of them veterans of the student movement. He attributes his appeal to the decline of political ideologies. According to Abitol, although many Jews of the generation of 1968 remain critical of Western values, they have also lost faith in the alternatives offered to replace them. Responding to their profound sense of intellectual and political loss, Abitbol has provided these former activists with a new way to reject the nation-state and the ideals of the Enlightenment.

Comparing the situation today to that of the nineteenth century, Abitbol said he could understand why Jews in the past embraced the Enlightenment and welcomed the promises held out to them by those committed to their emancipation. But now things were different. Dismissing secular ideologies in general, Abitbol singled out Zionism for special criticism.

As far as the rabbi was concerned, many Jews wasted their lives with the "Zionist adventure," an effort, he said, that legitimized some of man's basest instincts—nationalism and the nation-state. It upset him, he explained, to think that people continued to renounce the sacred texts to pursue lowly matters of no enduring significance.

Among Abitbol's disciples in the mid-1970s was Benny Lévy. Born in Egypt, his family moved to Belgium in the late 1950s, following the Suez crisis. Lévy then came to Paris in the early 1960s where he was accepted as a student at the École Normale Supérieure. He quickly got involved in the

French student movement, becoming a major leader on the extreme Left. Known by his alias "Pierre Victor," Lévy founded La Gauche Prolétarienne, a Maoist faction. Abandoning political activism in 1973, he became the secretary and intellectual companion of Jean-Paul Sartre, remaining with him for the last seven years of the philosopher's life. With Sartre, Lévy began studying philosophy again, an interest he had dropped during his activist days, and through philosophy he discovered—or rather rediscovered—Emmanuel Lévinas, whose work led him to embrace Judaism:

> The name of one person is important, a person to whom I must confess my indebtedness, Emmanuel Lévinas. Here was someone who had the very same philosophical training as Sartre, the same roots in phenomenology and humanism. Here was someone who was very close to Sartre in his philosophical language, and yet profoundly different, because he had roots in the Talmud. This was extraordinary to me. I had two great philosophical moments in my life: in my youth it was Sartre, and then it was Lévinas, when I came away from the Left in 1973–75.[12]

As Lévy read Lévinas and then the sacred texts, he discussed Jewish history and thought with Sartre. In 1980 before the philosopher died, Lévy published three interviews the two had recorded jointly. Sartre's "last words" caused quite a furor, for it seemed the young man had convinced the philosopher to change his mind on a number of issues, including the "Jewish question," a subject he had first treated in 1946 in his highly controversial book *Anti-Semite and Jew*.[13]

In the interview, Sartre explained that he had changed his mind thanks to three Jewish friends he had made after the Second World War: Claude Lanzmann, Arlette Elkaïm(-Sartre) whom he eventually adopted, and Benny Lévy. Through these friends, Sartre grew to accept that the Jewish people had a history, something he had categorically rejected in his book. This was no minor concession, for to revise his position, he had to reject Hegel's definition of history, the terms of which had dominated European thought for more than a century and had helped justify the position that Jews should assimilate and become Frenchmen of the faith of Moses. According to Hegel, a people had a history only if they lived together on their own land, as a sovereign political entity, clearly recognized as such by

---

[12] Stuart L. Charmé, "From Maoism to the Talmud (With Sartre Along the Way): An Interview with Benny Levy," *Commentary* 78, no. 6 (December 1984): 50.

[13] Jean-Paul Sartre, *Réflexions sur la question juive* (Paris: Gallimard, 1954 [1946]), Endligh ed., *Anti-Semite and Jew*, trans. G. Becker (New York: Schocken, 1965).

similarly organized states. When Hegel proclaimed that the Jews had no history, he was speaking about a people who had not lived together in a single territory for nearly two thousand years.

Sartre finally freed himself from Hegel and began reading about the history of Jews in the Diaspora. In the process he learned to recognize a certain "unity of dispersed Jews," a people scattered all over the world who had nevertheless remained culturally and spiritually connected.[14] Jews managed this extraordinary feat, Sartre concluded, not by living together, but by continuing to read the same body of texts and by maintaining the same relationship to their God.

Had Lévy used Sartre in these interviews to mouth his own words? Many felt he had, in effect, done exactly that and they questioned the authenticity of the philosopher's voice as recorded in the pages of *Le Nouvel Observateur* where the interviews first appeared. Manipulated or not, Sartre, a confirmed atheist, grew to appreciate in abstract terms the vitality of the culture of religious Jews in the Diaspora, a way of life that had survived for two thousand years in small communities scattered all over the world. With his newly acquired insight, Sartre joined members of the generation of 1968 in challenging his earlier dismissal of the traditions and history of a people who did not live together under a single flag. And with Lévy as his guide, Sartre accepted a position that went beyond the one held by other critics of the French nation-state—one that justified, ironically, the former Maoist's decision to become an ultra-Orthodox Jew.

Conclusion

Before Lévy challenged the hegemony of French culture with his version of "the right to be different," Jews of the generation of 1968 had two main strategies for opposing assimilation: minority nationalism and Zionism. For Jews committed to living in the Diaspora, Zionism, in the end, was an empty solution. It only allowed them to identify as Jews long-distance. What is more, for Jews who saw their struggle in France as a struggle against all nation-states, they opposed the Israeli nation-state as well. In particular, they objected to Israel's treatment of Palestinians, drawing unflattering parallels of Israel with France. Still, even if many Jewish intellectuals of the generation of 1968 rejected Zionism as a way to express their Jewish

---

[14] Jean-Paul Sartre, "L'Espoir Maintenant.... (III)," *Le Nouvel Observateur*, 24–30 March 1980, 58; "The Last Words of Sartre," trans. A. Foulke, *Dissent*, (Fall 1980).

identity, socialist Zionists played an important role in the early days following the Six-Day War in trying to serve as intermediaries between progressive Israelis and Palestinians, reaching out to kindred souls in the Middle East who seemed to share their ideological opposition to nation-states.

Zionists of other persuasions have also contributed to debates taking place in France about the Jewish question. Important among them is Shmuel Trigano. Born in Algeria, he came to France with his family in 1962, when he was fourteen years old. Calling himself a spiritual Zionist, he was influenced by Ahad Ha'am, the great Russian Jewish thinker of the turn of the century who vigorously opposed the Enlightenment ideal of the French nation-state. Disillusioned by France's strategy for assimilating the Jews, Trigano endorsed Ahad Ha'am's proposal to save Jews from disappearing in the West by creating a spiritual center for them in Israel. Eager to make aliyah, Trigano went to Jerusalem after the Six-Day War and studied there for several years, but he quickly rejected Israel as being a poor imitation of a Western European nation-state, hardly the realization of Ahad Ha'am's dream.

Now Lévy has offered a third possibility. Insisting on the right of his people to cultural autonomy in the Diaspora, he, like Marienstras, rejected territorially based cultures in any form, including Trigano's more benign model of the spiritual Zionist State. But he also challenged the secularization of the French Enlightenment and chose to live as an ultra-Orthodox Jew.

When Lévy joined Rabbi Abitbol's Yéchiva des Étudiants in Strasbourg, he became a member of an autonomous Jewish community that has, in effect, recreated some of the very conditions Clermont-Tonnerre opposed in the late eighteenth century, when the count and others made their celebrated case for emancipating the Jews and integrating them into the French nation-state. The yeshiva, of course, does not threaten the political structure of the state, for it exists legally as part of the private sector, like any other personal interest group. Still, the followers of Eliahou Abitbol have dropped out of French culture and recreated firm ethnic boundaries in ways reminiscent of the days when Jews still lived as "a nation within a nation."

The Six-Day War may seem far removed from the debates I describe in these pages, but the heroic war and tragic conflicts that followed contributed in significant ways to the renewal of Jewish life and thought in France among intellectuals of the generation of 1968. Inspiring several thousand French Jews to make *aliyah*, the Six-Day War led many more to seek ways to build a new life for themselves in the Diaspora, one that directly challenged the French Enlightenment and the ideal of assimilation.

The Impact of the Six-Day War on a Zionist Community: The Case of Argentina

Haim Avni
Avraham Harman Institute of Contemporary Jewry
The Hebrew University of Jerusalem

THE ORGANIZED JEWISH COMMUNITY in Argentina has been the subject of several scholarly analyses and descriptions.[1] The image that emerges from them is of a highly centralized community—despite its internal diversity and divisions—a community that wholeheartedly espoused Zionism, and one whose dominant culture is reminiscent of pre-Holocaust Eastern European Jewry—a comparison that pleased Argentina's Ashkenazi establishment. The regnant image of this community is also one of permanence and remarkable stability. It is this static image that begs closer examination in the context of a discussion of the Six-Day War and its impact on Diaspora Jewries.

It is universally accepted that the war was a traumatic event that rocked Jews everywhere, and most perceive it as well as a turning point in Jewish life in the Diaspora. In this article, I shall try to test the proposition that the war was also a turning point for the Jewish community in Argentina, and to delineate those areas of communal life in which its effect was felt. The result of this inquiry, it is hoped, will be a better understanding both of the dynamic quality of Jewish life in the Diaspora and of modifications in communal Zionist frameworks in the wake of the Six-Day War. By comparing such modifications in Argentine Jewry—which has for so long been self-defined as "Zionist"—with other Jewish communities that may not always have defined themselves in this way, we ought to reach an enhanced understanding of processes that did—or did not—occur in all sectors of the Jewish people.

---

[1] Irving Louis Horowitz, "The Jewish Community in Buenos Aires," *Jewish Social Studies* 24, no. 4 (October 1962); reprinted in idem, *Israeli Ecstasies—Jewish Agonies* (New York: Oxford University Press, 1974), 133–67; Haim Avni, "Argentine Jewry: Its Socio-Political Status and Organizational Patterns," *Dispersion and Unity* 12 (1971): 128–62; 13–14 (1972): 161–208; 15 (1972): 158–215.

We shall begin by reviewing the general political situation that prevailed in Argentina, in particular as it affected the personal security of Argentinean Jews at the outbreak of the Middle East crisis. The Argentine government's policy vis-à-vis the Middle East will then be examined, followed by an overview of the organized Jewish community and its reactions to the events that unfolded after 15 May 1967.

Having done that, we shall proceed to the *practical* results that emerged in the form of aid to Israel, always bearing in mind that even so organized and Zionist-oriented community as that of Argentina is established—like all communities in the Diaspora—on a voluntary basis. The long-range effects of the Six-Day War will also be considered, in two major spheres—first, *aliyah* (did the war affect its place on the agenda of the organized Jewish community in Argentina, and what was the actual extent of *aliyah* in the postwar period?); and second, its effect upon the Zionist movement in Argentina and the composition of its leadership. We shall conclude with an analysis of this volume's central issue, seeking to determine to what extent the Six-Day War influenced the wider historical processes that shaped Argentine Jewry both before and after June 1967.

Two important events in Argentine political history provide local points of chronological reference: the military revolution of 28 June 1966, led by General Juan Carlos Onganía, and the free general elections of 11 March 1973, which returned the Peronists to power.

Argentine Jewry and the Military Government

War erupted in the Middle East a bit less than a year after the military junta led by Gen. Onganía had taken power in Argentina. That event brought great anxiety to Argentine Jewry, since one of the first acts of the junta had been to issue a manifesto that proclaimed the creation of a "new Argentina": nationalist and Catholic. The manifesto was intended as a first step, to be followed by the drafting of a constitutional document nullifying those sections of the republican constitution that conflicted with the spirit of the manifesto. Jews feared that the constitutionally guaranteed equality of non-Catholics might be endangered. Moreover, national-Catholic anti-Semitic organizations had enthusiastically endorsed the new regime, and several persons known for their anti-Semitic views had been appointed to senior positions in the new government. The fear was that violent, organized anti-Semitism—which had been the lot of Argentine Jewry for years preceding the military revolution—might now be transformed into state-sanctioned anti-Semitism. "We must now sit down and learn a new chapter: *underground* Zionist organization, initiative and activity," wrote Elimelech Gutkin, chairman of the Organización Sionista Argentina (OSA), two weeks after the coup. These words, like the report in whose margins he had written them, expressed the sentiment that Zionist activity, like that of the organized Jewish community as a whole, was in danger of being delegitimized by the new government.[2]

On 12 July 1966, Onganía received a delegation of leading members of the Jewish community, led by Dr. Isaac Goldenberg, chairman of the Delegación de Asociaciones Israelitas Argentinas (DAIA), the political umbrella organization of Argentine Jewry. According to a memorandum that was prepared in advance in consultation with Onganía's press bureau, the delegation wished the new government every success, expressing as well the hope that it would continue to foster a climate in Argentina that guaranteed full liberty, "whose achievement necessitates acceptance and encouragement of the various religious and cultural expressions of all of its inhabitants." Underscoring its point, the delegation noted the Jewish community's "anxiety as an ethnic entity fully integrated into the country, at the persistence of extremist groups who do not conceal their threats against it." Onganía thanked the delegation for its good wishes, stressing that the manifesto, which had called on citizens to take a share in the "new Argentina," had been addressed to all Argentineans, irrespective of religion and race, and that it had "implied the continuation of the traditional ethical and religious values of Argentina, which have always stood for toleration and the respect of the human being." He then declared, as a true Catholic and as the president of the republic, his firm resolve "to proceed with full strength against all extremism, whether of the Left or of the Right, which threatens the peaceful and productive unity of all the citizens." The memo, distributed to the press soon after the meeting, was widely quoted in the print and electronic media. This was reassuring to the DAIA, as it appeared to ensure—at least for the time being—that the status of Argentine Jewry was not in jeopardy. It also served Onganía's purpose in helping to allay apprehensions that the military had aroused in world public opinion.[3]

---

[2] E. Gutkin to Zvi Lurie, Head of the Organization Department, CZA S5/12611; Haim Avni, "Antisemitism in Argentina," in *Approaches to Antisemitism: Context and Curriculum*, ed. Michael Brown (New York: American Jewish Committee; Jerusalem: International Center for the University Teaching of Jewish Civilization, 1994), 65–67.

[3] "Información de la Presidencia de la Nación," 12 July 1966, DAIA Archives

Five days after this meeting, the new constitutional document, styled the "Charter of the Argentinean Revolution," was published. Although the document did include a number of "Christian-Western" clauses that contradicted—and thereby annulled—the liberal spirit of the constitution of 1853, widespread violence against Jews and systematic government obstruction of their rights did not materialize. Onganía's cabinet included several nationalist Catholics, but during the first months of his regime their influence was countered by right-wing liberals to the extent that nationalist anti-Semites labeled the new regime a "revolution without revolutionaries."[4]

On balance, then, the status quo vis-à-vis the Jews was not noticeably changed: anti-Semitic incidents that went unpunished by the authorities continued to be quite common, as in the past, and called for ongoing alertness on the part of the Jewish political leadership. Meanwhile, Onganía's regime achieved a certain level of stability—to some extent attributable to the successful economic policy of Minister of the Economy Adalberto Krieger Vasena (himself of half-Jewish parentage). By June 1967, the regime enjoyed wide acceptance and was being credited with the considerable economic progress then being felt in the country. The Jewish community had to deal with no more than the "normal" extent of security problems.

Governmental stability continued until May 1969, when student protest rallies in several cities in the interior of the country eventually resulted in a series of violent clashes with the military and the police. They reached a peak late that month in Cordoba where fourteen students were killed. From that point on, there was an increase in acts of terror carried out by two armed underground groups: the "Montoneros," formed by left-wing members of the outlawed Peronist party; and the "People's Revolutionary Army," composed of Marxist and Trotskyite elements. The terrorist attacks, together with a deterioration in the country's economy, led to the overthrow of Gen. Onganía by his military colleagues and his replacement by Gen. (Res.) Roberto M. Levingston on 8 June 1970. Levingston held

---

(henceforth DAIA Ar.), Box 11; testimony of I. Goldenberg in letters to the author, 29 June 1996, and 16 September 1996; and his draft notes, dated 21 July 1966: "Sintesis de la situación politica-social en sus implicancias con el problema judío"; and 27 July 1966: "Algunas aspectos internos del proceso." I am grateful to Mr. Goldenberg for placing this important material at my disposal.

[4] The phrase "Revolución sin Revolucionarios" appeared in *Azul y Blanco,* the anti-Semitic organ of Marcelo Sanchez Sorondo, quoted in *Oficina de Prensa DAIA* 41 (1 December–20 January 1967): 3. For a listing of the incidents, and the DAIA's protests, see *Hasta Cuendo?* (Buenos Aires: Ediciones DAIA, 1967).

power for a mere nine months. On 23 March 1971, he was deposed by yet another junta, which appointed in his stead Gen. Alejandro Agustin Lanusse, the army chief of staff. Lanusse's government sought ways to reinstate a constitutional government, and some two years later, following protracted negotiations, Argentina went to the polls in fully free and democratic elections for the first time since 1946. The election was won by a united front of parties led by Hector J. Cámpora, who was nominated by exiled Gen. Juan Domingo Perón. When Cámpora was sworn into office on 25 May 1973, seven years of military rule came to an end.[5]

Back in June 1967, however, the military government was firmly in place and the Jewish community relatively secure. At this time, too, Argentina had a significant role to play in international politics: it was serving as a non-permanent member of the U.N. Security Council. Two factors stood in Israel's favor at this juncture. First, Argentine leaders were still anxious to legitimize their regime in the eyes of the West, which militated against their adopting an anti-Israel stance. In addition, Argentina had no vital interests in the Arab states. On the contrary—as fervent anti-Communists, Argentine leaders could be expected to oppose Soviet influence in the region by refraining from supporting the Arab belligerents.

Argentina's first declaration of policy on the Six-Day War was issued the night after hostilities began, when the government called for an immediate cease-fire, to enable all sides to work toward a just and lasting peace. At the same time, the Argentine delegation to the United Nations was instructed to uphold the principle of free passage through international waterways. This stance clearly supported Israel's own demand for free passage through the Straits of Tiran, although it was prompted more by Argentina's dispute with Chile over navigation rights in the Straits of Magellan. More significant was Argentina's abstention in the Security Council vote on a resolution sponsored by the Soviet Union that branded Israel an aggressor and demanded the immediate withdrawal of its forces. In a special session of the General Assembly, Argentina's foreign minister, Nicanor Costa Mendez, justified his country's abstention by noting that Israel's guilt had not been proven, nor had convincing reasons been given to support the Security Council's demand; furthermore, he claimed, Israeli withdrawal would not in itself ensure peace for the Middle East. In all these

---

5   Paul Lewis, "The Right and Military Rule, 1955–1983," in *The Argentine Right: Its History and Intellectual Origins, 1910 to the Present*, eds. Sandra McGee Deutsch and Ronald H. Dolkart (Wilmington, Del.: Scholarly Resources, 1993), 161–70.

statements, the Argentine government emphasized its commitment to neutrality and impartiality, affirming its sympathy for both the Arab and the Jewish communities in Argentina. In effect, however, such statements were essentially supportive of Israel.

Throughout the entire period of hostilities and in their immediate aftermath, the Argentine government maintained an unswerving policy consistent with Israeli interests.[6] This policy remained intact despite the efforts of five Arab ambassadors—from Egypt, Syria, Lebanon, Algeria, and Morocco—who came as a joint delegation to the Foreign Ministry on 5 June, followed by Husein Zulfikar Sabry, special envoy of Egyptian president Gamal Abdel Nasser, who arrived in Buenos Aires on the second day of the war to meet with the foreign minister and the president.[7]

The major Argentine dailies openly supported Israel. The two conservative papers—*La Nación* and *La Prensa;* the widely circulated afternoon daily *Clarín;* the socialist *La Vanguardia,* as well as the vast majority of papers appearing in the interior of the country, all deemed Israel's action a justified defensive war and expressed the hope that it would lead to regional peace. Other powerful bodies in Argentina supported Israel, or at least refrained from coming out against it. Church leaders, who happened to be meeting in a national convention when the hostilities broke out, called upon the Catholic faithful to pray for peace and to try to prevent violence between Jews and Arabs in Argentina. Some time later, they joined the Vatican in calling for international efforts to ensure that Jerusalem be declared an "open city." The Confederación General del Trabajo (C.G.T., trade union confederation) called for peace, "which all eagerly await." Argentine military circles tended to admire Israel's decisive victory. This was to have significant consequences: their positive attitude acted as a counterweight to propaganda by nationalist anti-Semitic groups that could normally count on solid support from the army.[8] In fact, only papers published by such groups—publications with limited circulation—came out in support of the Arab states, despite their otherwise anti-Soviet position.

---

[6] Paul Warszawski, "La Actitud de Argentina," Mundo Israelita, 17 June 1967; see also *La Prensa,* 6 and 7 June 1967; and *Clarín, La Nación, La Prensa, Crónica,* and *El Cronista Comercial,* all from 28 July 1967.

[7] *La Prensa,* 6 June 1967, 6; 7 June 1967, 12.

[8] *Oficina de Prensa, DAIA,* no. 44 (June–July 1967); no. 45 (1 August 1967–15 September 1967); no. 46 (16 September 1967–15 November 1967); see also Paul Warszawski, "La repercusión del Conflicto Arabe Israelí en la Argentina," CZA C1\10.

Members of anti-Semitic groups, first and foremost the violent Tacuara organization, organized a rally near the Syrian embassy, and such pro-Arab activities caused a certain amount of anxiety among the Jewish leadership.[9] With hindsight, however, it is obvious that during the war and its immediate aftermath the State of Israel—and with it, Argentine Jewry—enjoyed the sympathy of the vast majority of Argentineans.

Argentine Jewry: An Organizational Overview

As of June 1967, Argentine Jewry was represented by three leading federations that had come into being during the previous two decades.

The first and largest organization was DAIA, which, as previously noted, was the political umbrella organization comprising virtually all of Argentina's Jewish communal, ethnic, social welfare, and political groups. The only groups not represented in the DAIA were the Communists (who had been expelled in the 1950s) and the Instituto Judeo-Argentino (IJA), an affiliate of the American Jewish Committee, composed of a small group of wealthy Argentine Jews. Like the AJC, they did not accept DAIA's claim to be the only and exclusive representative of the Jewish community.

The second organization, known as the Va'ad HaKehillot (the Federation of Jewish Communities of Argentina), focused on the provision of communal services (as opposed to promoting political activity). The most influential constituent member of the Va'ad HaKehillot was the Asociación Mutual Israelita Argentina (AMIA), the communal organization of the Buenos Aires Ashkenazic community. Sephardic organizations in the capital and communal associations outside of Buenos Aires played a minor role in the Va'ad.

The third major federation was the OSA, the Zionist Organization of Argentina, which included all of the Zionist political parties. These drew their membership almost exclusively from the ranks of the Ashkenazic Jewish community, as did also the non-Zionist Bund and Communist organizations.

Alongside these three federations was an outside entity that wielded significant influence: the Israeli embassy. During the period under survey, the presidents of DAIA and the OSA, together with a representative of B'nai B'rith (who was also active in the IJA) formed in effect a steering committee that frequently met in the embassy under the auspices of the

---

[9] *Así*, 3ra. Año II, 92 (17 June 1967).

legation's first secretary.[10] The importance of the Israeli embassy is more readily understood in light of the key role played by the various Zionist parties. In 1966, for example, AMIA held elections for its governing council. Of a total of ninety seats, forty-four were won by a Labor alignment consisting of representatives from Mapai, Ahdut Ha'avoda, and Poalei Zion. Other Zionist parties accounted for another forty-two seats, leaving just four seats in the hands of the non-Zionist Bund. Tuvia Kamenszain, elected as the new president of AMIA, was a leading figure in the Labor alignment—as were Isaac Goldenberg of the DAIA and Elimelech Gutkin of the OSA. Thus the Labor alignment essentially controlled the central organs of organized Argentine Jewry.

Virtually all of Argentine Jewry, including the non-Ashkenazim, affiliated themselves, either ideologically or organizationally, as Zionists. The only significant exceptions were the Bundists and the Communists. Intramural politics permeated the life of most of Argentinean Jewry's larger cultural and sport associations (like Hebraica, Maccabi, and HaKoah), as well as the major Jewish financial institutions—mainly cooperative credit societies—that contributed large sums to educational, cultural, and political activities.[11]

Ironically, however, the OSA, which represented all the Zionist parties, had little real authority. Matters concerning *aliyah* and Zionist education were in the hands of the *shlichim*—emissaries from Israel—and the OSA organization suffered from a chronic lack of funding.

Shortly before the outbreak of the Six-Day War, both the OSA and the DAIA held conventions. The DAIA's original agenda was indicative of the low profile the organization was maintaining during this period: matters to be dealt with included "the structure of the community and the organization of the DAIA; communal and religious relations; Jewish identity and the organization of the Jewish people," with no mention made of the problematics of how to function under an authoritarian military regime. By the time the convention got under way, however, war was imminent, and events in Israel had eclipsed local issues. On Friday, 26 May 1967, after a closed session, attended by fifty-seven delegates from twenty-two provincial cities and fifty representatives from the capital, the convention made public the decisions it had adopted: a supreme emergency council would

---

[10] Dr. Abba Geffen to the author, 16 June 1996. The representative of B'nai Brith (and a prominent member of the IJA) was Captain Korenblum. I am grateful to Dr. Geffen for this information.

[11] Avni, "Argentine Jewry," parts 2 and 3.

be established in Buenos Aires, comprising representatives of the DAIA, Va'ad HaKehillot, and the OSA. Similar councils would be organized in every important city in the interior. All Jewish organizations would be placed on alert for thirty days, holding domestic consultations and mobilizing volunteers to canvass the communities on behalf of Israel. The declared objective was to reach every Jew in Argentina. The convention also issued an official manifesto—a call to Argentine public opinion—warning that Israel was under threat of war because its neighbors had refused to recognize its existence, had transgressed the principle (to which Argentina adhered) of free passage of the seas, had supported armed infiltration across Israel's borders, and had plotted to destroy a site created by the enlightened nations "as the expression of a reality rooted in the ancient land of the Prophets and which was intended to be a historical reparation for a thousand-year-old injustice infinitely aggravated by the crimes of the Nazis."[12]

That same day, the Jewish press reported that a festive gathering initiated by Keren Hayesod in honor of the Argentine Day of the Revolution (celebrated on 25 May) had turned into an *ad hoc* meeting of hundreds of public leaders who had decided to immediately launch a special fund-raising campaign on behalf of Israel. On 28 May, a public announcement by Keren Hayesod listed the addresses of all the Jewish economic associations and neighborhood offices to which donations for Israel could be brought. Three days later, the local Yiddish press published an official call issued by the Zionist Executive in Jerusalem to all Jews in the Diaspora. World Jewry was asked to act immediately in four specific ways: "to enlist the sympathy and support of the countries of the world and their leaders for Israel's just struggle"; "to increase *aliyah* to Israel"; "to encourage the best of our youth to come to Israel and work, in order to replace those who are called up to defend the county," and "to make a heartfelt and maximum effort to contribute financially so that the state of Israel will be able to bear up under the heavy burden placed upon it." The call from Jerusalem was discussed at an assembly of about five hundred leaders of the various organizations and associations convened on 1 June by the supreme emergency council.[13]

---

[12] *Di Presse*, 27 May 1967, published the Spanish text of the manifesto also printed in *La Prensa, El Mundo,* and *La Capital* of the same date.

[13] *Di Presse*, 26, 28, 31 May, and 2 June 1967; *Di Yiddishe Zeitung,* 26 and 31 May, and 2 June 1967; *El Mundo Israelita,* 27 May 1967.

Spontaneous vs. Organized Support for Israel

Alongside the rapidly organized nationwide fund-raising campaign, Argentine Jewish leaders began to plan a mass rally of support for Israel, which was scheduled to take place in Buenos Aires on 6 June. On 5 June, fighting broke out in the Middle East and the Buenos Aires police immediately cancelled the rally, on the grounds that it could lead to riots and cause offense in Arab countries. Hearing the news of the war, Argentine Jews reacted with an outpouring of spontaneous activity. A group of Holocaust survivors, dressed in their striped concentration camp uniforms, gathered in front of the Soviet embassy. Many young Jews arrived at the offices of the OSA to volunteer for service in Israel. Some 1,700 people showed up on the very first day at the Ezra Jewish Hospital to donate blood; many others, impelled by the desire to do something—without knowing what was most needed or where to contribute—went to various Jewish institutions with donations of food and clothing. At the designated fund-raising locations, meanwhile, unprecedented financial contributions were the order of the day.

Seeking to create order in this somewhat chaotic situation, the supreme emergency council quickly responded with a series of open directives. First it called upon the public to channel all financial contributions through Keren Hayesod. Food and clothing, it declared, were not needed, although blood would continue to be collected at the Ezra Jewish Hospital (on 8 June the blood collection was also halted). In lieu of the mass rally that had been cancelled, Jews throughout the country were urged to gather in synagogues, community centers, and schools on 7 June for prayer meetings and local rallies. According to a later estimate by Nachman Radzichowski, president of the OSA, some 70,000 Jews took part in such meetings on the night following the third day of the fighting.[14]

The general Argentine press gave wide coverage to these events, reporting as well on the arrival of the SS *Theodor Herzl* in the port of Buenos Aires on 9 June. This was a ship bound for Israel with some fifty Uruguayan Jewish volunteers for Israel among its passengers. A first group of Argen-

---

[14] "Communicado del Comité Central Especial," nos. 1–5, 5–9 June 1967, DAIA Archives, Box 10; "Mobilization of Jewish Youth" (in Yiddish), *Di Presse,* 7 June 1967; *Di Yiddishe Zeitung,* 7 and 22 June 1967; *El Mundo,* 9 June 1967. For the statement by Nachman Radzichowski, see *Di Yiddishe Zeitung,* 7 July 1967.

tine volunteers for Israel set out the following night, and was accorded even wider press coverage. Papers such as *El Mundo, Clarín,* and *La Prensa* featured photographs and interviews—though in some cases, a measure of doubt seemed to be cast on the "Argentineism" of these enthusiastic young volunteers.[15]

As previously noted, pro-Arab sentiment was marginal among the general Argentine population. Apart from the notorious Tàcuara group, there were only small factions within the Peronist movement, trade unions, and radical youth movements that issued statements in support of Egypt or Syria.[16] Nonetheless, the supreme emergency council issued a request that any anti-Semitic attacks be reported to the authorities. Not content to rely upon police protection, the Argentine Jewish community also mounted guards at various Jewish institutions. In one instance, these guards thwarted an attack; in another, police blocked a group of youth that were advancing toward the Israeli embassy. Bombs were hurled at two Jewish institutions in Cordoba, and there was a false alarm about a bomb placed aboard a flight from Buenos Aires to Brazil, among whose passengers were a number of volunteers for Israel. Although widespread anti-Semitic violence did not materialize, there was a good deal of apprehension in the Jewish community at this time.[17]

Even before the war, a number of prominent non-Jewish Argentines had come out in support of Israel. On 27 May a public statement signed by sixty authors, historians, sociologists, and psychologists—most of them non-Jews connected with the moderate socialist Left—warned that war was imminent and called for an effort to preserve the peace for the benefit of Jews and Arabs alike.[18] Admiral Isaac Rojas, a vice-president in a prior military government, had been invited to participate in the mass rally; when it was cancelled, he issued a strong statement in support of Israel's military action. On 10 June, as the Israeli victory was complete, Americo Ghioldi, a professor and leader of the outlawed Social-Democratic party, joined two dozen other members of the Universidad Nacional de La Plata

---

[15] *El Mundo,* 9 and 10 June 1967; *La Razón,* 9 and 10 June 1967; *Clarín* and *La Prensa,* 10 June 1967.
[16] *Crónica,* 13 and 16 June 1967. The groups mentioned were Movimiento de la Juventud Radical, Movimiento Nueva Argentina, Juventud Revolucionaria Argentina, and Sindicato de Obreros Navales.
[17] *La Prensa,* 9 June 1967; *Crónica,* 13 June 1967.
[18] "Manifesto de los Intelectuales," *Nueva Sion,* 17 May 1967. Fourteen persons added their signatures to those of the original forty-six signers.

in a statement celebrating the end of fighting and condemning the Arab nations' twenty-year attempt to destroy Israel.[19]

Even more impressive was the press conference of 8 June that was convened by an imposing group of intellectuals, including the writer Jorge Luis Borges, the historian Arturo Capdevila, and Carlos Sánchez Viamonte, a noted jurist and statesman who had represented Argentina on the U.N. Human Rights Commission until the Onganía coup. The group announced the establishment of the Argentine Commission for the Defense of Embattled Israel and issued a manifesto that opened with a quote from the statement made on 26 May by Egyptian President Nasser: "the battle with Israel will be a total one. Its fundamental objective is the destruction of Israel. I would not have been able to say these things three years ago, but today I have confidence in the forces at our disposal." As Argentineans who aspired to justice and peace, the signers appealed "to all lovers of peace to express their solidarity with the democratic State of Israel in its struggle for existence in the Holy Land, from which came forth the ethical principles that provide the basis for mutual co-existence of all civilized men." The manifesto was signed by 102 eminent authors, historians, social scientists, and statesmen, later joined by others. The text of the manifesto was first delivered to Israeli ambassador Moshe Alon, and later, similar initiatives were taken in cities of the interior. In Rosario, Argentina's second-largest city, an exact copy of this manifesto was signed by seventy-six local dignitaries.[20]

Simultaneously, another act of solidarity with Israel was taking shape among Argentina's cultural elite. It culminated on 27 June when a large delegation of stage and television artists, painters, and sculptors, musicians, and authors came to the Israeli embassy and presented Alon with a declaration signed by no fewer than 450 artists, which read, in part,

> we are free men, and as such we come to the defense of all nations unjustly attacked, as is the case in this dramatic moment for the world, with the State of Israel.... [T]he fact that Israel, despite innumerable vicissitudes, has regained its legitimate and unrenunciable right to possess its own land is not only the fulfillment of the aspirations of a nation, but at the same time contributes to the progress of humanity.[21]

---

[19] *El Mundo,* 9 June 1967; *El Dia* (La Plata), 11 June 1967.

[20] *Di Yiddishe Zeitung,* 9 June 1967; *La Nación, La Prensa, Crónica,* and *El Mundo,* 16 June 1967; *La Capital,* 28 June 1967.

[21] *La Prensa, La Nación, Clarín, La Razón,* 27 June 1967; *Crónica,* 27 and 28 June 1967. At a meeting of the Executive Board of the DAIA on 19 June, the

By the time these declarations and manifestos were made public, the sense of anxiety that had caused them had been replaced by profound relief and enthusiastic admiration of Israel's astounding victory. In this supportive atmosphere, the Argentine army also displayed a willingness to help out, allowing its labs to process large quantities of fresh blood into plasma. This plasma, along with drugs and medical supplies that had been collected, was rushed to Israel—the normal bureaucratic procedures having been waived.[22]

VOLUNTEERS AND FINANCIAL AID TO ISRAEL

In early July 1967, Eliahu Dobkin, the head of the Jewish Agency's youth and Hehalutz department, reported to the Agency that 4,917 volunteers had arrived in Israel since the outbreak of the war. Of these, 260 were from Argentina. By September, the figures were 7,025 and 603 respectively. (Only about half of the volunteers were past or present members of Zionist youth movements.) Even if we take into account the fact that the Six-Day War had broken out during the southern hemisphere's winter semester—as opposed to the northern hemisphere's summer break—this is not a large figure, given that the Argentine Jewish population totaled just over 286,000 at this time. The South African Jewish community, which had less than half that number, had sent 801 volunteers to Israel by the end of September—a figure, be it noted, that also exceeded the total of volunteers from the United States (707).[23] In the absence of more thorough research

---

organization of these two impressive groups in support of Israel was described as spontaneous initiatives on the part of the intellectuals and the artists themselves; see DAIA Actas, Reunion no. 368, 19 June 1967, 96. Even today, the former president of DAIA and the first secretary in the Israel embassy in 1967 cannot decisively point to any Jewish body which organized or was responsible for this striking exhibition of solidarity with Israel. In letters to the author, dated 16 September 1996, Isaac Goldenberg and Abba Geffen both attributed responsibility for the mobilization of this impressive support to the institution that the other represented.

[22] Report by Gregorio Faigón, through Rachel Edelstein, 15 July 1967, CZA S5/12612.

[23] For the figures for early July, see *Letzte Neies*, 6 July 1967; for those for the end of September, see Moshe Kitron, "Survey of Volunteers from South America" (six-page mimeographed report in Hebrew), delivered before the Organization of Latin American Immigrants, which handled the volunteers in full coordination with and under the direction of the Volunteers Bureau of the Jewish Agency, that supplied the figures. See also Tamar Horowitz and M. Cialic, in association with J. Hodara, *Volunteers for Israel (In the Wake of the Six Day War): Their Motives and Work Careers* (in Hebrew), (Jerusalem: Henrietta Szold Institute Research Report no. 127, Publication no. 473, 1969).

on the costs and logistical difficulties connected with the volunteering effort (e.g., travel costs, the availability of flights or ship crossings, lost hours of work and study) and the manner and extent to which each community aided this effort, it is difficult to use such figures as a yardstick for measuring the war's immediate impact on Jewish communities.

More data is available concerning Argentine Jewry's fund-raising campaign. According to a report based on remarks made by the vice-president of the DAIA during a trip to Israel in July 1967, "the sum raised (non-Jews also contributed) came to 20 million dollars. We hope to reach 24 million dollars." In a more authoritative report that summarized contributions made to Keren Hayesod from Latin America as a whole, cash sums received in Jerusalem from donations raised in 1967 totaled $30,185,900—compared to a mere $2,387,300 in 1966. Interestingly, and assuming that this information is indeed correct, this enormous increase in contributions was accompanied by a much smaller increase in the *number* of individual contributions: from 69,655 in 1966 to 98,050 in 1967.[24]

The Argentine Jewish press devoted a good deal of coverage to individual acts of philanthropy: that of children at the Jewish orphanage, who were willing to forego their bi-weekly visit to the movies; residents of the Jewish old age home who brought small sums they had managed to raise; teachers in the Sholom Aleichem school system, who donated a month's wages; doctors on the staff of the Jewish hospital, who put aside part of their salary. One of Argentine Jewry's most famous artists, Leon Poch, donated all of the income from the sale of his paintings at a special gallery exhibition; and all the proceeds from a public annual auction of works of art at the Hebraica Society were funneled to the Israeli Magen David Adom.[25]

On 18 June, hundreds of public leaders from Buenos Aires and other cities convened in the conference hall of the AMIA to discuss how best to continue the fund-raising efforts. The decision was made to designate

---

[24] "First and Second Emergency Campaigns, 1967 and 1968," Jerusalem, 19 January 1969, CZA, KH, S5/12612, file 103/2; number of contributors taken from report dated 30 November 1967, file 103/2. The actual sums collected in the various countries were probably higher than those that appear in the table in the report, for in each country, including Argentina, certain agreed-upon sums were deducted before their remission to Israel. We have no information as to the amounts involved.

[25] *Di Presse*, 21 and 28 July 1967; *Di Yiddishe Zeitung*, 9 and 26 June 1967, 5 July 1967; see Z. Wasserzug, "Uplifting Moments" (in Yiddish), *Di Yiddishe Zeitung*, 18 July 1967; *La Razón*, 29 June 1967.

1967 as an "emergency campaign for Israel" year, so that "all the committees of the various organizations and associations, the cooperatives, sport clubs, social clubs, schools, congregations, *Landsmanschaften,* women's associations, etc., will continue their efforts to have each and every member contribute to Keren Hayesod." To this end, it was also decided that "no Jew will be allowed to arrange his religious, social or economic affairs until he presents the organization to which he applies with an affidavit from Keren Hayesod–United Jewish Appeal affirming that he has fulfilled his obligation toward the State of Israel." Such organizational enforcement, of course, was contingent upon the willingness of the various autonomous organizations and associations to comply. For its part, the United Jewish Appeal (UJA) adopted its own compliance procedure: all committees were requested to supply names of individuals who had not contributed—as well as those who had made outstanding donations—along with lists of new volunteers who were especially zealous in their efforts. Moreover, the "ethics committee" at the central office, which for years had been dealing with those who refused to contribute, was expanded into a national unit. A council of representatives of all the major Jewish organizations was also established, which began to operate out of the Hebraica Society building. It was hoped that these means would help the Argentinean Jews to defray the voluntary "tax" which was mandated by their identification with the State of Israel.[26]

As a community whose entire organizational structure was grounded upon an organic relationship with political parties in Israel and with the World Zionist Organization, Argentine Jewry was probably more inclined than other communities to take up the challenge of the four objectives set by the Zionist Executive in Jerusalem. Its task was made easier by the fact that Argentine government policy at this time was consonant with Israeli interests (as was not the case, for example, in France). Mobilization of public opinion was extremely successful, apparently requiring little extra organizational effort on the part of the community leadership.[27] It remains to be ascertained exactly what proportion of Argentine Jewry participated in the overall effort to support the Jewish state—whether the donation was

---

[26] *Di Presse,* 21 June 1967; for the full list of committee members, see *Mundo Israelita,* 8 July 1967; DAIA, Actas, Reunion no. 368, 19 June 1967, 96, for the appointment of the DAIA member on the ethics committee.

[27] Naum Radzichowski, Simja Sneh, and Shalom Heiman to Zvi Lurie, in their official report summing up the activities of the emergency committee of Argentine Jewry, CZA S5/12612.

in the form of money, goods, blood, time, or physical labor. Statistics concerning such matters as the amount of money raised, the number of volunteers sent to Israel or the quantity of blood donated tell only part of the story: there were also many individuals who tried to donate blood but were turned down; many who signed up for volunteer work in Israel but were not sent; multitudes who participated in rallies or who simply followed media reports about developments in Israel. All of these people had a share in the emotionally charged atmosphere that followed upon Israel's victory.

It remains to be seen what were the longer-term effects of the war—especially in the areas of *aliyah,* and structural change within the Argentine Jewish leadership, organizational framework, and public affairs agenda.

CHANGES IN THE PATTERN OF *ALIYAH*

Following the cease-fire of 10 June, leaders of Argentine Jewish organizations began to visit Israel in droves. On their return to Argentina, they brought with them a message: Israel was expecting a new and large wave of immigration.[28] On 14 July, the Argentine Jewish press published a joint communiqué of the Israeli government and the Zionist Executive, which included the following plea:

> Every Jewish family must participate in this wave of aliyah.... [W]e need men and women who will take upon themselves pioneering tasks. Israel needs financial investments to create new industrial plants, scientists, professional intelligentsia and skilled craftsmen in all fields who can give of their experience and knowledge in the service of the nation.[29]

Early in July, the Organization of Latin American Immigrants in Israel convened to discuss how immigration to Israel could be encouraged and how the absorption process could be improved. Both topics were the subject of widespread discussion in Israel; one proposal, dubbed "One

---

[28] Hardy Swarsenski, president of the emergency campaign, reported that "Israel has been fundamentally transformed and they expect there great help and masses of immigrants from the Jewish people throughout the world," *Di Yiddishe Zeitung,* 14 July 1967. Among those who visited Israel at this time were Haim Finkelstein, secretary-general of the Left Poalei Zion party in Argentina, Tuvia Kamenszain, president of AMIA, and Isaac Bokser, president of Herut in Argentina.

[29] *Di Presse,* 14 July 1967.

Hundred Thousand Immigrants," was to send delegations that would include high-ranking military figures, intellectuals, and representatives of kibbutzim and moshavim to a dozen Diaspora communities.[30] The proposal was modified somewhat in the case of Argentina: in November—designated "*aliyah* month"—a delegation of representatives of the Organization of Latin American Immigrants in Israel made the rounds of Argentina's interior cities. This was followed by an "*aliyah* conclave" in Buenos Aires that was chaired by Israeli ambassador Moshe Alon, Arie Pincus (chairman of the World Zionist Organization and the Jewish Agency), and Leon Dulzin (head of the Agency's finance department). According to one source, the conclave was attended by 525 delegates representing 172 organizations (not all of them Zionist) and communities from Argentina and neighboring countries. The message transmitted was that *aliyah* was just as urgent and important as security for the continued existence of Israel. Every Jew in Argentina who was in some way connected to the organized Jewish community or read the local Jewish press was that month exposed to the call for *aliyah*, and to the ideological and pragmatic messages connected to that call.[31]

The atmosphere was quite different from that of a year before, which had been marked by a well-attended public discussion of *aliyah* and *yerida* (emigration from Israel). To one of the questions posed then—"Why do community leaders not immigrate to Israel?"—Tuvia Kamenszain, president of the AMIA, had responded, probably in the spirit of statements made at the 1965 conference of the Poale Zion party, "Israel looks to the Diaspora"—meaning that Israel wished to see the Diaspora communities strengthened.[32] Now, however, Jewish leaders were being asked to set an example by *leaving* the Diaspora.

Aliyah was a major story in the Argentine Jewish press during the last months of 1967 and throughout 1968. The topic was also raised from time to time during the hectic preparations for the Twenty-Seventh Zionist

---

[30] For the increase in *aliyah*, see *Di Yiddishe Zeitung*, 17 July 1967, and an article by Miriam Wohlman of Tel Aviv, *Di Yiddishe Zeitung*, 24 July 1967; the call for 100,000 immigrants in an article quoting Itzhak Korn, secretary-general of the Mapai World Union, *Di Neie Zeit*, 28 July 1967.

[31] DAIA, *Boletin Informativo*, Año 3, no 10 (November–December 1967): 23; *Di Yiddishe Zeitung* and *Di Presse*, 19 November 1967; and further articles in both papers on 31 October 1967 and 16 November 1967. The number of delegates, according to Y. Zudiker, *Letzte Neies* 7 (December 1967). See also *La Luz, Nueva Sion*, and *Mundo Israelita*, November 1967, passim.

[32] "Report of the Executive 1961–1967" (in Yiddish), 9, CZA S5/12612.

Congress, which convened in Jerusalem in June 1968. Early in 1968, Mapai, Ahdut Ha'avoda, and Rafi joined forces in Israel to form the Labor Alignment. This presented an opportunity for the party to call upon its Diaspora affiliates—leaders and rank-and-file alike—to come on *aliyah*. Simultaneously, a movement known simply as Tnuat Aliyah (*Aliyah* Movement) was created in Argentina as a framework for those who committed themselves to immigrate to Israel within a limited period of time.[33]

Although the Six-Day War placed *aliyah* higher on the agenda of Argentine Jewry, the actual results in the field were not very impressive. Figures published by the OSA show that only 820 people emigrated to Israel during 1967, admittedly an improvement over the number of immigrants in the previous year (a time of deep economic recession in Israel). The difference, however, does not point to a revolutionary change in the extent of *aliyah*. Figures published by the Israeli Central Bureau of Statistics (CBS) were slightly lower for these years (see Table 1), but do not change the overall picture. A former Argentinean who was in Buenos Aires during the summer of 1969 on an official mission of the World Zionist Organization declared:

> What is most evident is that there is a speedy process of settling down here, as a result of the relative economic stability.... True, sympathy for Israel and its struggle has not decreased, even though it has somewhat diminished in certain circles and classes—but there is no sign, in the foreseeable future, of any real change over and above the traditional sense of identification [with Israel] in the direction of increased *aliyah* or preparation for a serious wave of immigration.

That this was the true state of affairs emerges from the internal report prepared by the OSA covering April 1968–March 1969, the period during which the Zionist Congress was convened and declarations and discussions concerning aliyah were at their peak. The report shows that in these twelve months no more than 839 Argentinean Jews emigrated to Israel.[34]

---

[33] *Di Presse*, 2 June 1967; *Di Yiddishe Zeitung*, 4 and 5 June 1967, 1 March 1968; see also David Schers and Hadassah Singer, "The Aliya Movement," *The Structure of Latin American Jewry* (in Hebrew) (Tel Aviv: Report of the David Horowitz Institute for the Research of Developing Countries, 1975), 7–16.

[34] Asher Brushtein to Avraham Schenker and Yehoshua Haran, 12 August 1969, "Informe sobre actividades de las Organización Sionista Argentina, Abril 1968–Marzo 1969," CZA S5/12613.

TABLE 1

NUMBER OF IMMIGRANTS TO ISRAEL FROM ARGENTINA,
1966–1969 ACCORDING TO ZIONIST ARGENTINE AND ISRAELI SOURCES[35]

Year	OSA	CBS (Israel)
1966	499	664
1967	820	547
1968	920	559
1969	1,350	1,274
1967–1969	3,090	2,380

Economic stability in Argentina reached its peak in 1969; during the following years, there was an increase in the number of immigrants to Israel (see Table 2).

TABLE 2

NUMBER OF IMMIGRANTS TO ISRAEL FROM ARGENTINA,
1970–1973 COMPARED WITH 1967–1969

1970	1,457
1971	2,107
1972	2,598
1973	2,809
Total 1967–1969	2,380
Total 1967–1973	11,351

Source: Central Bureau of Statistics (Israel)

It would appear that the Six-Day War had only an indirect influence on *aliyah* from Argentina: it led to economic expansion in Israel at a time when Argentina was approaching a period of political and economic instability. Moreover, Israel's victory thrust the issue of *aliyah* into public

---

[35] Sergio DellaPergola and Uzi Rebhun, *Israel Diaspora Relationships: A First Quantitative Analysis of Social Indicators* (Jerusalem: The Hebrew University of Jerusalem, Avraham Harman Institute of Contemporary Jewry, Division of Jewish Demography and Statistics, Occasional Paper 1994–13), table 1; AMIA, *Archivo de Recortes de Prensa* [=AMIA, *Recortes*], 1966, 217; 1967, 206; 1968, 221; 1969, 227.

consciousness. The efforts of such elements as Tnuat Aliyah, youth movements, and the various departments of the World Zionist Organization that conducted seminars for adults both in Argentina and Israel, certainly had some weight with prospective immigrants to Israel, although they, too, were more decisively influenced by news of economic stability and development in Israel and the facts of the crisis at home in Argentina. Notwithstanding, the actual extent of *aliyah* was far from living up to expectations. A comparison of the figures following the war with those of the peak years of Argentinean *aliyah*, 1962–1963 (this was a time of economic crisis and heightened anti-Semitism in Argentina) lends credence to our supposition. In 1963 alone, 4,255 Argentines immigrated to Israel and the total for the three-year period 1963–1965 was 7,407. This total is nearly two-thirds of the total number of Argentine immigrants to Israel in the seven-year period following the Six-Day War.[36] Thus, despite the fact that Argentinean Jewry was strongly identified with Zionism, the Six-Day War itself did not generate any basic transformation in its rate of *aliyah*.

THE ARGENTINE ZIONIST MOVEMENT IN THE WAKE OF THE SIX-DAY WAR

In the euphoria that followed upon Israel's victory, expectations were high that the Zionist movement would undergo an organizational shake-up. In Argentina, such hopes were quickly dashed when preparations for the Twenty-Seventh Zionist Congress got underway. Although a WZO official had expressed the hope that "there will be room in the delegations for a meaningful changing of the guard...*and members of the younger generation*," the Argentine delegates were not elected at the polls but appointed by the various parties according to an agreement among them and in the exact proportion to the previous congress. Moreover, explicit resolutions passed at the 1968 congress calling for organizational changes and opening up the ranks to include new forces and young people had very limited impact. An OSA report of April 1969 noted that "excluding the participation of Tnuat Aliyah," no real organizational changes had taken place.[37]

---

[36] DellaPergola and Rebhun, Occasional Paper 1994–13, Table 1.

[37] Quoted from a letter of Michael Levin, director of the Latin American section of the Organization Department, 22 November 1967, CZA S5/12612 and from the report of the OSA, 14 April 1969, which includes the Organization Department's guidelines for preparing the report, stressing that it must include the steps taken to implement the Zionist Congress's resolutions concerning organizational changes.

Tnuat Aliyah, however, was swiftly taken under the wing of the WZO. The movement, whose members obligated themselves to make *aliyah* within a three-year period, was allocated both funds and—somewhat later—*shlichim*; a study conducted by David Schers and Hadassah Singer in 1973 noted that "at any rate, its leadership admitted that they were not lacking in resources."[38]

Between its inception in 1968 and 1973, Tnuat Aliyah's objectives became more diversified. While continuing to be a "pragmatic" movement that was mainly concerned with easing the process of *aliyah*, it gradually became more institutionalized (with salaried, as opposed to an all-volunteer staff) and more committed to local objectives such as transforming the nature of the Zionist leadership in Argentina into one that personally fulfilled the new "Jerusalem Program" of the WZO, which called for "ingathering of the Jewish people...through Aliya from all countries." According to figures provided in 1973 by Tnuat Aliyah activists, there were 2,000 names on the movement's mailing list, though only 200–250 people participated in the weekly activities that were held in various branches throughout Argentina.[39]

A second innovation in Argentine Zionism was the establishment of the Movimiento Sefardi Sionista (MSS), or Sephardic Zionist Movement, immediately after the Six-Day War. The moving spirit behind the MSS was Nissim Elnecave, a long-time Zionist and veteran journalist, editor and owner of the biweekly *La Luz*. He intended the new movement to be a framework for Zionist activity for non-Ashkenazim in Argentina, and later, in other Latin American states. Although it immediately joined the OSA, the MSS utilized existing social and communal frameworks and avoided any identification with the established Zionist parties. It sent four delegates to the Twenty-Seventh Zionist Congress and petitioned the organization department of the WZO for financial aid, but insisted upon preserving full independence.[40] Not surprisingly, the Ashkenazic community expressed reservations about the movement's "isolationist tendencies." Elnecave, moreover, was no favorite of the Ashkenazic and Zionist establishments. He had particularly irritated them by publishing a number of

---

[38] Schers and Singer, "Aliya Movement," 13.
[39] Ibid. 13–14.
[40] See the report of the movement's activities since its founding convention to the end of 1968, its program and proposed budget for 1 April 1969–31 March 1970, CZA S5/12613.

articles that alleged mismanagement and even fiscal irregularities in Jewish organizations.[41]

In preparation for its activities during 1969–1970, the MSS submitted a comprehensive program to the WZO Organization Department in Jerusalem, which included proposals for seminars, young leadership courses, publications, contacts with cities of the interior and an extension course in Israel. The budgeted cost was $10,420; but only $2,000 was actually allocated in 1968 and 1969 (much of this amount was deducted by the Jewish Agency's finance department to cover upkeep of the Agency's central office in Argentina). An article that appeared in *La Luz,* in which it was claimed that the Israeli embassy was trying to gain control of the Argentine Jewish press, led to further tension between the movement and the WZO. Deprived of organizational backing, the MSS was unable to transform itself into a movement with real standing.[42]

OSA activity in one field created, for a while, a quite successful campaign to gain the attention of the second and third generations of Spanish-speaking Argentine Jews for Zionism. During his visit to Argentina in connection with the "Aliyah Conclave," Arie Pincus became convinced that the OSA should be helped to publish a high-level Zionist monthly for all of Latin America. He promised to allocate the sum of $54,000 to cover the cost of establishing an editorial board and publishing the first few issues. During the following year, the monthly *Raices* (Roots) began to appear, edited by the veteran journalist Simha Sneh, who also doubled as secretary of the OSA. However, the journal's income was far from covering its expenses, and the calculations in 1970 were that each issue would cost $5,686 beyond the income from advertising. This was without doubt an enormous amount, when considering the total sums needed for Zionist

---

[41] M. Gilad to Rachel Edelstein, 10 June 1966, concerning withholding the budgetary allocation from Elnecave in 1963 because of criticism of the manner in which the wave of immigration from Argentina to Israel in 1962–1963 was handled; report of the OSA executive for July 1961–1967, p. 9, where Elnecave and *La Luz* are censured by OSA President Elimelech Gutkin for publicly disclosing a fraud in WIZO (Women's International Zionist Organization) funds with which the OSA had to contend; both in CZA S5/12611.

[42] See Rachel Edelstein to A. Schenker, 16 October 1968, which included a proposed budgetary allocation; the proposed plan of activities of the MSS, dated 11 December 1969, and Schenker's reaction, 27 March 1969; letter of Enrique Zvik of the Financial Department in Buenos Aires to his counterpart in Montevideo, Isser Ben-Zvi, 28 May 1969, concerning the implementation of the allocation; and A. Schenker to Z. Divon of the Foreign Ministry, 31 October 1969, about the Embassy-Elnecave affair, all in CZA S5/12612.

activities in Argentina, and even more so when compared to the allocation made for purposes like the Movimiento Sefaradi Sionista. Yet the WZO did continue to fund the journal for a few more years until it finally gave up.[43]

Perhaps the most ambitious effort to bring about organizational change was *mif'al ha'haverut*, a direct membership campaign for the WZO that was designed to replace the traditional party-affiliated membership. Judging by the numbers, the campaign in Argentina cannot be judged a success: by the opening of the Twenty-Eighth Zionist Congress in January 1972, Argentina had only 19,600 registered Zionists—a very small percentage of the Argentine Jewish community, particularly when compared to those of other Latin American Jewish communities. In neighboring Brazil, for instance, there were 11,500 Zionists out of an estimated Jewish population of 100,000; for Mexico, the respective figures were 3,350 and 35,000. Moreover, the Canadian Jewish population—approximately the same size as that of Argentina and, like Argentina, considered strongly Zionist in orientation—boasted 32,000 registered Zionists.[44] Yet another symptom of weakness was the low turnout in the October 1971 elections for the Argentine delegation to the Zionist congress: of approximately 14,000 eligible voters, only about half actually showed up at the polls.[45]

For the Ashkenazi community of Buenos Aires—represented most prominently by AMIA—the period following the Six-Day War was seemingly one of growth and development. AMIA's membership grew annually, standing at 46,300 in 1969 (an increase of more than 10,000 since 1966). Its budget in 1969, more than $4,500,000, covered an ever-expanding range of activities, with special resources allocated to *aliyah* and Israel-related activities. Special emphasis was placed on the Jewish educational system. The introduction of longer school days in the Argentine educational system had cut the ground from under the Jewish schools, which until then had mainly provided after-school education. A decision was reached to transform these after-school programs into comprehensive

---

[43] R. Edelstein to A. Schenker, 2 February 1969; A. Schenker to I. M. Giladi, Head of the Finance Department of the Jewish Agency, 10 February 1969, both in CZA S5/12613.

[44] Executive of the World Zionist Organization, "Report of Activities from Tishri 5732 to Teveth 5738, 20 September 1971 to 31 December 1977, Presented to the 29th Zionist Congress, Jerusalem, Adar I 5732" (in Hebrew), 19; Sergio DellaPergola, "Demographic Trends of Latin American Jewry," in *The Jewish Presence in Latin America*, eds. Judith Laikin Elkin and Gilbert W. Merkx (Boston: 1987), 101, 104–5.

[45] *Nueva Sion*, 23 May 1972, 3.

day schools, despite the heavy financial burden this entailed. In September 1968, AMIA dedicated a magnificent new building, popularly known as the "Palace of Education," which housed all of the Jewish higher educational institutions of Buenos Aires: the elementary teachers' seminary, the college for high school educators (Ha-Midrasha Ha-Ivrit), and the pedagogic center. However, the economic crisis that hit Argentina during the latter half of 1969 severely affected the Jewish credit cooperatives that were a major source of support for the schools. As the schools' economic distress increased, so too did AMIA's financial burden. Eventually, it turned to donors in Israel and in the United States to help fund its educational system.[46]

AMIA's increased numbers and influence encouraged its leadership to believe that members were actively interested in the association—yet many of the younger members were actually couples who had been enrolled automatically when they registered for a religious wedding. In the expectation of a record turnout for the May 1969 elections for the AMIA council and executive, eight tickets openly canvassed for support in a lively campaign that was conducted on the pages of the Argentinean general press, in posters exhibited in Jewish neighborhoods, and in public rallies and meetings (all of this took place despite the military government's dislike of democratic public activities of this nature). The outcome, however, was disappointing: a total of 13,169 voters came to the polls, instead of the anticipated 15,000–17,000. Although this number was a slight increase over the previous elections of 1966, it represented only 31.7 percent of the eligible voters.[47] In view of AMIA's greatly expanded membership, the turnout was seen as a setback.

The situation became even more severe in the next elections, when only 7,360 AMIA members troubled themselves to vote.[48] These elections, it is true, were marked by controversy—the left-wing Mapam-Hashomer Hatzair party boycotted them—yet the inescapable conclusion was that

---

[46] Avni, "Argentine Jewry," Part 2, 181–86, 206–8; see also *Mundo Israelita*, 7 March 1970, 13, and 3 April 1971, 10.

[47] Report of Marc Turkow to the president, chairman, general secretary, and council members of the World Jewish Congress, May 1969 (no exact date), which included a description of the campaign, the expectations and an analysis of the results. The number of AMIA members is on the basis of information supplied by its Membership Department, CZA C1/13. The number of eligible voters was 41,513 according to Teresa Kaplanski de Caryevschi, *Características de los Socios de la AMIA* (Buenos Aires: 1970), 4.

[48] *Nueva Sion*, 23 May 1972, 3.

AMIA, the major organization of Argentine Jewry and the primary support for the Va'ad HaKehillot, was essentially losing membership. Because AMIA had a monopoly on the burial of Ashkenazic Jews, a service that provided 90 percent of its income, it was not forced to cut its budget or the various services it provided. For the period under review, then, AMIA was in the paradoxical position of suffering a continuous decline in public support while maintaining its central role in the Argentine Jewish community. The Six-Day War, despite the prestige it lent to the Israeli "mother parties," apparently did not greatly influence the development of their Argentinean affiliates that controlled the AMIA.

Major changes in organizations are usually the outcome of changes in leadership. With this in mind, it is useful to determine just who constituted Argentine Jewry's leadership cadre during the years under review, and to what extent this group appeared to be permeable. Partial answers to these questions can be obtained from a systematic survey of the Argentine Jewish press, which was carried out using the Spanish language Jewish press: the weekly *El Mundo Israelita,* the bi-weekly *La Luz,* and the monthly *Nueva Sion.* All of these papers, it should be noted, had a clear organizational affiliation: the first with the Zionist Labor alignment, the second with the Movimiento Sefaradi Sionista, and the third was the organ of Mapam-Hashomer Hatzair. Thus, the picture of the Argentine Jewish community that each presented was somewhat incomplete. Nonetheless, these journals constituted the major sources of information for Spanish-reading Jews in Argentina. Every news item, feature story, and advertisement having some relevance to Jewish public life in Argentina between 1966 and 1973 was noted, and the names of leaders and activists mentioned in them were registered. Attention was given to the central political and economic bodies of the Ashkenazic and Sephardic communities, while institutions such as *Landsmanschaften* were omitted from the analysis. The following pattern emerges from the survey:

A total of 396 individuals were mentioned in the newspaper items during the seven years under review, of whom 220 were mentioned only once or a very few times; these can be considered as belonging to the second echelon of Jewish communal activists. Another 115 people were mentioned often enough to be classified as major leaders. The remaining 61 individuals can be considered the top-ranking leadership, although this last group included five "past leaders" who by the time of the survey were filling honorary positions, plus seven rabbis of particular standing (representing Ashkenazic, Sephardic, Syrian, Moroccan, Conservative, and Reform congregations). The top leadership, then, consisted of 37 individuals, who were joined in the course of the period under survey by 12 others who advanced from more junior positions. Of this limited group of 49, only eight emigrated to Israel during the years under study.[49]

Thus, the dominant circle was quite limited, and very few succeeded in rising in the ranks to the top. Moreover, there was a good deal of overlap within the dominant circle; leading positions, such as the presidency of AMIA, the OSA, and the major credit cooperatives rotated among very few leaders, and there were even several cases of one person holding more than one position simultaneously. The call to open up the leadership ranks, particularly to those who were not members of the World Zionist Organization, had no appreciable impact on the Argentine Jewish establishment.

We cannot venture an opinion at this stage as to what extent this "closing of the ranks" on the part of the local Zionist leadership gave rise to a sense that the movement was in crisis, rather than undergoing a surge of momentum in the wake of the Six-Day War. As early as 1968, and even more so in the following years, there were repeated complaints concerning both the absence of "new generations" from public activity in the Jewish community, and of the apathy that was spreading through its ranks. Simultaneously, there was a growing involvement of young Jews—including members of pioneering Zionist youth movements—in Argentine politics, particularly the revolutionary left-wing underground organizations, but also within nationalist Peronist circles. Efforts of the Zionist establishment and *shlichim* to win the youth back via special projects such as organized visits to Israel failed to reverse these worrying trends.

Conclusion: The Six-Day War and Historical Processes

There is no doubt that the Six-Day War produced shock waves in most segments of the Argentine Jewish community. For many Argentine Jews, deep concern for Israel was combined with personal anxiety for the welfare of family members who had gone there to live. Since the ratio of *aliyah* from Argentina in relation to the size of the community was probably one of the highest in the West—at least in the early 1960s—we must not overlook this dimension when we compare the reaction of various Diaspora communities to the Six-Day War. The frenzied responses to what seemed to be

---

[49] The lists of names of community leaders and notations of the contents of the journals are deposited in the Division for Jews in Latin America, Spain, and Portugal of the Avraham Harman Institute of Contemporary Jewry, The Hebrew University of Jerusalem.

Israel's immediate needs—clothing, food, and above all, blood donations—were an expression of this anxiety, which was shared also by the non-Jewish public. The outstanding response of the Argentinean intellectual and artistic elite to the call to support Israel was striking evidence to this effect. Though the number of volunteers who actually reached Israel was not very great, the willingness to volunteer was evidently much greater. Yet, the main response, which was absolutely necessary and effective was the sustained and highly successful emergency fund-raising campaign.

The sharp increase in the income of Keren Hayesod and the United Jewish Appeal breathed a new spirit into the Zionist establishment in Jerusalem. The sense of crisis, on both the ideological and organizational levels, that preceded the Six-Day War was replaced by a feeling of renewed momentum. In the wake of the war, new programs were planned for the Diaspora communities and expectations were high that those communities would be the scene of revitalization and renewed Zionism. However, whereas the new developments in Jerusalem were organizational in nature, revitalization in the Diaspora was contingent upon a voluntary search for renewed ideals and values—the extent of which was disappointing.

Paradoxically, what may be regarded as a disappointingly limited effect on the organizational structure and leadership of Argentine Zionism may instead reflect the fact that Argentine Jewry had essentially been "conquered" by the Zionist parties some two decades prior to the Six-Day War. A close relationship between the local communal establishment and the political parties of Israel had already existed from the time of the establishment of Israel.[50] Israeli political parties were well involved in elections campaigns for the AMIA from the 1950s—a condition that held true even in the 1980s. And while the "mother parties" in Israel called upon the leaders of Argentine Jewry to emigrate to Israel, non-compliance did not lead to sanctions. On the contrary: competition between the parties within the WZO caused them to have a certain degree of dependence upon their subsidiaries in Argentina, both before the Six-Day War and afterwards. The war did not obligate Argentine Zionists to make any ideological reassessment, but rather it reinforced their conviction that they had chosen the right path. As a result, those disintegrating processes that the OSA and its controlling parties had been undergoing prior to the events of June 1967 continued in the wake of Israel's victory.

---

[50] Yosef Goldstein, "The Influence of the State of Israel and the Jewish Agency upon Jewish Life in Argentina and Uruguay, 1948–1958" (in Hebrew) (Ph.D. diss., The Hebrew University of Jerusalem, 1993), especially 261–330.

Developments in world Jewry after 1967, above all the struggle on behalf of Soviet Jewry, left their mark on the political agenda of the organized Argentine Jewish community. Protests and demonstrations against the Soviet Union now accounted for a greater part of the DAIA's activities, in addition to its regular and almost routine efforts to combat anti-Semitism in Argentina. Political and economic developments in the country were the dominant factors influencing the activities of DAIA, as they did other sectors of the Argentine community. Thus, for example, the foundations of communal organization were rocked during the economic recession of 1969–1970, when several Jewish credit cooperatives failed. Financial scandal—notably the embezzlement of enormous funds by the officers of some of these cooperatives—further undermined the faith of the Jewish community in its organizations.[51]

Still another change in Argentine Jewry—the dramatic decrease of Yiddish culture—occurred without any relation to the Six-Day War. In 1967, Argentina's Jewish community still boasted two Yiddish dailies and another fourteen regularly published journals of various types, and at least nineteen Yiddish books were published that year, including works of poetry, belles-lettres, and research. By 1973, both dailies had shut down and the number of journals and books had greatly dwindled.[52]

Yiddish culture was inevitably replaced by a Jewish counterpart in Spanish, which was quantitatively far behind the diverse and ramified culture whose decline was so evident. Hebrew, despite its becoming almost universally taught in the Argentine Jewish educational system, did not in any way replace Yiddish; though many more people learned to converse in it, there was no appreciable rise in the number of Hebrew readers.[53] In this

---

[51] See the decision of AMIA to remove fifteen directors of the Cooperativa de Credito Viamonte, *Mundo Israelita*, 27 June 1970, 10.

[52] AMIA, *Recortes* 1967, 159–71, 192–93. When a group of young people in one of the cities of the interior protested in 1971 that the chief rabbi of Argentina, David Cahana, had addressed the congregation in Yiddish, they were roundly criticized at a session of the Va'ad HaKehillot. However, the protest only brought home what many Argentine Jews already knew or felt only too well: the cultural milieu of the founding generation was agonizingly fading away. *Mundo Israelita*, 12 June 1971, 13. The protest occurred during the visit of Rabbi David Cahana in Bahia Blanca.

[53] AMIA, *Recortes* 1967, 192–93. *Tzohar hadarom* and *Rimmon*, two very small Hebrew journals that appeared in 1967, ceased publication when those who took an active interest in them emigrated to Israel. See also Baruch Ben-Yehuda, "Educational Mission to South America" (in Hebrew), appended to a letter of Eliezer Argov of the Jewish National Fund, 1 January 1969, CZA S5/11613.

sense, too, the Six-Day War led to no changes, save for increased opportunities for visits to Israel and contacts with native Hebrew speakers.

In sum, the Six-Day War, with all the anxiety and euphoria associated with it, was a milestone in the collective memory of those Argentine Jews who lived through it. From a vantage point some thirty years later, however, it seems to have had little effect on the major historical processes that shaped the Argentine Jewish community.

Repercussions of the Six-Day War in the Leftist Jewish Argentine Camp: The Rise of *Fraie Schtime*, 1967–1969

Leonardo Senkman

The Hebrew University of Jerusalem

In memory of Simon Lewinthal

THE SIX-DAY WAR ideologically influenced Argentine Jewish intellectuals affiliated with the Communist party (PC), progressive Jewish centers tied to the Idisher Cultur Farband (ICUF), as well as non-organized independent Jewish intellectuals on the Left. The ICUF was created in Argentina in 1937 and united with cultural centers and Jewish schools that maintained a Communist orientation under the Federation of Jewish Cultural Organizations of Argentina (Federacion de Entidades Culturales Judías de la Argentina).

This article's objective is to analyze the ideological and institutional consequences that the commotion of the Six-Day War provoked in certain dissident groups of the ICUF and the several Jewish affiliates of the Argentine PC. The circumstances that produced the rise of a new postwar ideological trend of Judeo-Argentine solidarity with Israel (*Fraie Schtime –Voz Libre–Free Voice*), as well as its incorporation into the institutions of the Argentine-Jewish community, will be analyzed. Furthermore, as we review a number of important essays written by certain Leftist intellectuals we will observe there again the influence of the Six-Day War on patterns of Jewish identity in Argentina.

THE LEFTIST JUDEO-ARGENTINE CAMP

The repercussions of the Six-Day War constitute an interesting opportunity to study new forms of Jewish national identification during the 1960s in Jewish communities such as Argentina's. The Argentine Jewish community included both a strong presence of immigrant leftist ("progressive") Jews bound to the PC, as well as native-born intellectuals who were thoroughly politicized by their involvement in left-wing movements.

The commotion among the rank and file of the ICUF on the eve of, during, and after the Six-Day War, has until now been covered only by journalists who wrote with the ideological positions of their leaders in mind. These reports are not sufficient to understand the changes that the war engendered within certain institutions linked to the ICUF, as well as among native Jewish intellectuals affiliated with, and/or sympathizers of, the PC.

The two groups that we will analyze are distinct both in terms of generation and occupation. The majority of those affiliated with the ICUF and its cultural and social institutions in the capital city and the cities in the interior (La Pampa, Rosario, and Cordoba) were Yiddish-speaking immigrants from Eastern Europe (predominantly Poland). They immigrated to Argentina in the early 1920s and shortly thereafter began a rapid process of de-proletarization. These artisans, laborers, and traveling salesmen *(cuentenikes)* soon became prosperous businessmen and textile factory owners. As with the Italian and Spanish immigrants, a number were active in the Communist party, specifically the Yiddish-speaking section. Furthermore, they participated in cultural and cooperative activities of the immigrant aid associations of former Polish residents *(Landsfarein)*. A smaller number participated in the Popular Jewish Theater (IFT), arguably the most important cultural institution of the ICUF, as well as in its network of schools.[1]

In contrast to the immigrants, the Jewish intellectuals affiliated with the Communist party were native Argentineans who, prior to joining the PC, were active in the Communist Youth Federation and in university organizations controlled by the Communists during the Peronist regime. In the 1960s they were well integrated into the political and national life of Argentina. Often they worked as liberal professionals, academics, and intellectuals. These native Jewish Argentines were quite uninvolved with the cultural activity of the ICUF and of the *Landsfarein*, as well as with the institutional representative structures of the Jewish community.

To date no thorough research has been conducted on either of the two groups. There is still no systematic study of the ideological schisms within the Argentine Jewish community, nor the dilemmas of Jewish national identification in the organizations around the ICUF, since the Molotov-

---

[1] See Edgardo Bilsky, "Etnicidad y Clase Obrera: La presencia Judía en el movimiento obrero argentino" *Bibliografía Temática sobre Judaísmo Argentino*, No. 40: *El Movimiento Obrero Judío en la Argentina* (Buenos Aires: AMIA, 1987), t.1, 24ff; AANN, *Libro de Homenaje a los 50 Años del Teatro IFT* (Buenos Aires: 1990), chapter 1; Efraim Zadoff, *Historia de la educación judío en Buenos Aires (1935–1957)* (Buenos Aires 1994), 405–16.

Ribbentrop pact of August 1939. The first investigation related to the Jewish Communists was undertaken as part of a study on the anti-Zionist camp and its attempts to politically control the Buenos Aires community board *(kehilla)*, the AMIA, in which they won a third of the votes in the 1948 elections.

The impact of the creation of the State of Israel on the national identification of the Jewish Communists, as well as the repercussions of the ICUF decision to mobilize their affiliates to collaborate with the special campaign in favor of the creation of the state of Israel is also unknown.

Equally un-investigated are the repercussions on the national identification of the Communist Jews immediately after the Communist Jewish institutions were expelled from the Jewish communal representative institutions (AMIA, DAIA, Va'ad Hachinuch) as a consequence of the 1952 Prague trials.[2]

However, an examination of the impact of the Six-Day War on the non-Zionist leftist camp cannot be carried out without taking into account the catalytic role that the leftist Zionist movement played, particularly those groups connected to the Israeli-based Kibbutz Artzi and Mapam, in the second half of the 1960s. The leftist Zionist camp prompted anti-Zionist and anti-Israeli intellectuals, as well as with those groups connected with the ICUF and the PC, to vent certain ideological issues.[3]

Obviously, the growth of leftist Zionism in Argentina as a consequence of the Six-Day War must also be looked at in the light of the anti-Communist reaction that set in during the military dictatorship of General Juan C. Onganía (1966–1970). Whereas the subsequent military regime, under

---

[2] See the pioneering doctoral work of Dr. Silvia Schenkolewski-Kroll, where she analyzes the ideological and organizational confrontation between the Argentine Zionist movement and the Communist Jews who were mobilized in the 1930s into the Organización Popular contra el Antisemitismo (People's organization against anti-Semitism): "Zionism and the Zionist Parties in Argentina; 1935–1945" (Ph.d. diss., Hebrew University of Jerusalem, 1984), 224–51. See also, idem, "La Conquista de las comunidades: el movimiento sionista y la comunidad Ashkenazi de Buenos Aires (1939–1949)," *Judaica Latinoamericana* II, ed. by AMILAT (Jerusalem: Magnes Press, 1993), 198–200. The political antecedents that caused the separation of the Jewish Communists from the DAIA as a result of Stalin's anti-Semitic crimes and the Prague trials were analyzed by Schenkolewski-Kroll in "Zionism against the Left," in *Zionism and Opposition in the Jewish World,* eds. Haim Avni and Gideon Shimoni (Jerusalem 1990). See also *Yahadut Argentina-maamda ha-hevratit udemuta ha-irgunit* (Jerusalem: 1972).

[3] See the newspaper *Nueva Sión* 1962–1970 and *Voz Libre* (which began publication in December 1967).

General Jorge Videla (established in 1976) repressed leftist Zionist activities, under Onganía, the anti-Left campaign stopped short of outright repression. Leftist Zionists, their publications, and Jewish intellectuals succeeded in enduring his regime, despite the political harassment of the national universities, the exodus of important Argentinean-Jewish scientists, and the restoration of a Catholic nationalist cultural program.[4]

DISSIDENT VOICES AMONG THE JEWISH COMMUNISTS PRIOR TO THE SIX-DAY WAR.

Certain Argentine-Jewish intellectuals associated with the PC began to denounce the anti-Semitism present in Socialist countries such as Poland, Hungary, and even the U.S.S.R. after returning from private trips dating back to 1956. The most notorious case was the denunciation of anti-Semitism in the U.S.S.R. by the renowned psychoanalyst José Blejer in 1964. Blejer's condemnation of Soviet anti-Semitism culminated in a joint declaration with six other Jewish intellectuals in December 1965 that hastened their estrangement from the Party.[5]

These Jewish intellectuals disagreed with the Party line on global political ideologies, particularly with respect to the "Jewish Question" in the U.S.S.R. The Soviet position vis-à-vis Israel, before and after the 1967 War, presented them with a propitious opportunity to critically distance themselves from the PC. Due to their prestige, their condemnation of

---

[4] The intensity and violence of anti-Semitism noticeably decreased between 1966–1970 until the outburst of violence after the fall of General Onganía in 1970. See Guillermo O'Donnel, *El Estado Burocratico Autoritario* (Buenos Aires: 1982), chapters 3 and 4; Haim Avni, "Anti-Semitism in Argentina. The Dimensions of Danger," in *Approaches to Anti-Semitism. Context and Curriculum*, ed. Michael Brown. (New York: American Jewish Committee and Jerusalem: International Center for University Teaching of Jewish Civilization, 1994), 61, 66. See DAIA's declaration of 29 September 1968 on anti-Semitic attacks: DAIA *Boletin Informativo*, December 1968. In the crisis that led to the resignation of President Onganía anti-Semitic acts stood out, for example, the attack on the La Plata AMIA headquarters, 16 May 1970, perpetrated by ultra-Right officers of the 7th infantry regiment. See the denunciation in *La Razon*, 8 August 1970 and *Nueva Sión*, 28 May 1970.

[5] Dr. José Blejer and six other Argentine Jewish intellectuals signed a public declaration in December 1965 condemning the Soviet delegates' comparison of Zionism with Nazism, anti-Semitism, and Neo-Nazism as forms of racial discrimination before the Social and Cultural Council of the General Assembly of the United Nations. See the "Manifiesto de Siete Intelectuales Argentinos," *Nueva Sión*, 23 December 1965.

Soviet anti-Semitism had an impact on other Jewish activists linked with the ICUF.[6]

Furthermore, a small group of Communist-Jewish activists in the institutions of the ICUF, such as the Jewish neighborhood centers and the *Landsfareinen*, did not accept the ICUF's 1952 decision to sever relations with the special economic campaign for Israel. These small groups, together with fellow activists from cultural centers connected to the ICUF in the interior cities of Rosario and La Plata, had been disenchanted with manifestations of Soviet anti-Semitism for a long time. Over several years, and with much hesitation, they searched for a sufficient motive to disassociate themselves from the ICUF. Previous attempts to create a dissident group on their own initiative were not successful. Such was the experience of the group Claridad, which included Nuchem Burshtein and Simon Lewinthal, two former activists of Jewish institutions affiliated with the ICUF and members of the Yiddish-speaking division of the Communist party, who were penalized for "Zionist deviation."[7]

On the eve of the Six-Day War these small dissident groups were requested by Mapam activists in Buenos Aires not to accept the PC and/or the ICUF position on Israel. Mapam invited them to join the Emergency Campaign Committee for Israel (Comite de la Campaña de Emergenica en pro de Israel) and to publicly condemn Arab aggression. The timing was propitious in that some constituencies of the ICUF's institutions (such as schools, social and cultural centers, *Landsfareinen*, and the IFT theater) began to express Jewish national sentiments. Thus, they aligned themselves with Israel, contrary to the PC line, which condemned the "imperialist aggression" of the Zionist state. The catalysts of this national identification were certain rank-and-file activists of the Mapam-Hashomer Hatzair party in Buenos Aires.[8] However, certain preexisting bases of Jewish national and social attachments were evident among many ICUF sympathizers living in the industrial neighborhoods of San Martin and Villa Lynch (suburbs of greater Buenos Aires). For their own reasons they needed to hear a Jewish national position different from that of the PC. Therefore, on the eve of the Six-Day War, they were willing to consider an Israeli leftist position regarding the Middle East conflict. The national

---

[6] See José Blejer, Moises Polak, José Itzigsohn, Arnoldo Liberman, and Bernardo Verbitzky in the documentary reader *Israel, un tema para la Izquierda* (Buenos Aires: 1968), 14–100.

[7] Simon Lewinthal, interview by author, Buenos Aires, 20 September 1994.

[8] Enrique Cwik, interview by author, Buenos Aires, 13 September 1992.

Jewish sentiment that animated these groups in 1948, when they took an active role in the emergency and solidarity campaign after the creation of the state of Israel, apparently persisted, despite the fact that ideologically they continued to define themselves as non-Zionists.[9] As we shall see, shortly after the Six-Day War broke out, this sentiment was reinforced by the fear that the state of Israel would be destroyed.

In ICUF-affiliated centers in Rosario—the Argentine-Jewish cultural club "19th of April" (Ateneo Judeo Argentino "19 de Abril"[10])—and in La Plata—the Jewish Literary Center and Max Nordau Library (Centro Literario Israelita y Biblioteca Max Nordau)—certain Argentine-born professionals who were involved in specific political PC youth groups began to participate, thus replacing the older immigrant generation of founders and leaders. While they did not commit themselves ideologically to Zionism, they were opposed to a political fight against Israel. Their behavior in this respect is contrary to that of first-generation ICUF and PC leaders. These younger native activists, as a result of their non-Zionist ideological position, refrained from joining Mapam's militant leftist Zionist circles. Indeed, in the months prior to the war's outbreak, some even identified with the ideological line of the dissident Israeli Communist party, Maki.[11]

Nevertheless, at the end of the war, the ICUF official position strictly followed the Argentine Communist party line of condemning the "Israeli aggression," indiscriminately aligning itself with the "attacked" Arab countries. The two official ICUF publications, *Renovación* and *Unzer Lebn*, editorialized against the "Zionist-imperialist aggression," conforming to the official PC line and adopting the official position of Rakach, the Israeli-Arab-Jewish Communist party (led by Meir Vilner and Tewfik Toubi), which followed the Moscow line, calling for complete identification with the Arab countries. Ruben Sinay, the leader of ICUF, stated that all solidarity with Israel signified support of "American imperialism."[12]

---

[9] Enrique Cwik, interview by author. Cwik refers to Nuchem Burstyn, who was one of the few former ICUF members from the 1950s who was active in the *Landsfarein* and identified with Mapam-Hashomer Hatzair leftist Zionism. Burstyn was also active in the RAT (General Assembly of Representatives) of the Buenos Aires *kehilla* in the 1960s as a Mapam party representative.

[10] The date is that of the outbreak of the Warsaw Ghetto revolt in 1943.

[11] Mauricio Tenenbaum, interview by author, Buenos Aires, 10 November 1994.

[12] *Renovación*, 8 and 12 August 1967.

As a result of the commotion provoked by the war, the ICUF leadership began to fear the presence of dissidents among its ranks. Instead of admitting the different trends among the ICUF-affiliated institutions arising out of legitimate ideological questions, the two periodicals decided simply to negate them. In August 1967, the ICUF violently attacked Mapam and its local newspaper, *Nueva Sión,* accusing it of "Zionist provocation." According to the ICUF, Mapam allegedly attempted to sow division in the ranks of its associates regarding the question of Israel and the Arabs.[13]

Politically, the ICUF followed the official position of the Argentine Communist party, without reservation. The PC put forth a call shortly after the war's outbreak "for the immediate end of the imperialist aggression against the Arab people, for the respect of self-determination of the Arab people," and attributed the war "to imperialism, to the reactionary government of Israel and the feudal forces of the Arab world."[14]

In comparison, the position of the Chilean PC was quite different. Its political committee issued a public statement on 6 June, strongly affirming the "legitimate right of the existence of the State of Israel," and proclaiming "that the chauvinist positions that arise on both sides of the belligerents are completely foreign to the Chilean PC." At the same time they attributed the outbreak of the war to "Yankee Imperialism," which allegedly had opened another international conflict in order to divert world attention from Vietnam. In addition, the Chilean PC accepted for publication in its official paper, *El Siglo*—albeit with reservations—a public declaration in favor of Israel's right to exist, signed by one hundred intellectuals who condemned the call for Islamic holy war against the Jewish state and called for a peace agreement in the Middle East.[15]

In spite of the political confrontations between the PC and Argentine national leftist currents, the PC's anti-Israeli position was shared with other sectors of the anti-Communist Left.[16] The public expression of this combined anti-Israel sentiment of the leftist camp, as well as Argentine

---

[13] See the dispute between *Renovación* and *Unzer Lebn* with *Nueva Sión: Nueva Sión,* 8 September 1967.

[14] See *Nuestra Palabra,* 8 June 1967.

[15] See *El Siglo,* 5 July 1967. Among the signers of "For a Fair and Permanent Peace in the Middle East," figured certain friends of the Communist daily where noteworthy leftist Jewish intellectuals appeared, including, Professor Alejandro Lipschutz, Alejandro Brodsky, Linda Volosky, Isidro Guelfenbein, Claudio Kogan, Sara Weitzman, and Rodolfo Bolzman.

[16] On the anti-Communist Left, see Oscar Arevalo, *El Partido Comunista* (Buenos Aires: 1983), 63–65; Norberto Galasso, *La Izquierda Nacional y el FIP* (Buenos Aires: 1984), 46–47.

Communism, was the widespread distribution of an anti-Israel poster on the streets of Buenos Aires in August 1967, entitled "Together with the Arab people," that condemned Israeli racism. It was signed by intellectuals and members of a varied spectrum of the Argentine Left, including known Communists and leftist Peronists. The names of John William Cooke (Leftist Peronist), together with Juan Carlos Coral (Socialist), Alcira de la Peña and Hector Agosti (PC) stood out, as did those of student leaders of the Argentine University Federation (Federacion Universitaria Argentina), and various unionists, together with the directors of the ICUF, Ruben Sinay and José Goldberg, and the Argentine-Jewish Peronist writer German Rozenmacher. This anti-Israel manifestation provoked indignation in the ranks of other progressive Jews associated with the ICUF. Various Communist Jewish intellectuals who refused to sign this manifesto suffered sanctions as a result.[17]

Jewish activists claimed that certain arguments of the Argentine Left's anti-Israel campaign coincided with arguments of the Argentine anti-Semitic Right. Such was the case of the periodicals *Azul y Blanco* and *Ulises*. These important Argentine nationalist publications printed articles whose anti-Zionist and anti-Israel arguments mirrored those of such leftist magazines as *Propósitos* and *Política Internacional*.[18]

This violent anti-Israel campaign of the PC and the National Left inspired a political split in the orthodox Communist camp between Jewish dissidents, long alienated from both the ICUF and the PC. It also prompted leading leftist Jewish intellectuals to take a pro-Israel position and identify with Jewish nationalism.

IMPACT OF THE SIX-DAY WAR ON ICUF: THE RISE OF *FRAIE SCHTIME*.

In the institutions and periodicals sympathizing with the ICUF it is possible to detect immediately after the Six-Day War a serious uneasiness and a desire to revise the official anti-Israel position of the PC. Towards the end of November 1967, the directors of the ICUF were presented for the first

---

[17] *Nueva Sión*, 8 September 1967, 2; Dr. José Itzigsohn, interview by author, Jerusalem, November 1994.

[18] See *Azul y Blanco* 39 and 40 (1967); *Política Internacional* 89 (July–August 1967) and 90 (September–November 1967); *Propósitos*, 6 and 15 June 1967, 15 and 20 July 1967, 26 October 1967. See the response to Leónidas Barletta by the Progressive Jewish writer Bernardo Verbitzky, who wrote "Carta a Leonidas Barletta," before the war. See *Israel, un tema para la Izquierda* (Buenos Aires: 1968), 14–29; Dr. Pedro Szylman, interview by author, Jerusalem, 20 May 1994.

time with a formal proposal from members of affiliated institutions for revising the official position of the PC with respect to the State of Israel. The proposal was contained in a memorandum addressed to the presidium of the ICUF. It questioned in particular the position maintained by the Rakach Communist line in Israel and supported by the ICUF. The party line, reads the memorandum, "neither expresses the feelings or the desires of our popular masses, nor those of the progressive population of Israel." The memorandum requests the return to the line of the constituency of the ICUF that "pledged to defend Jewish culture against both its internal and external enemies and to develop and improve in the spirit of progress."[19] The initiators of this memorandum were then co-opted to the presidium of the ICUF pending the designation of a new leadership to be elected in 1968. However, the ICUF congress, held in October 1968, dashed the hopes of the rank and file who for a year had demanded a change of position regarding Israel and the Middle East conflict.

The resolutions adopted by the ICUF congress, which were strictly molded by the official political position of the U.S.S.R., disillusioned a number of Jewish Communists. This contributed to their decision to abandon not only the ICUF, but also the PC.

Nevertheless, important affiliated centers, such as the Max Nordau Library in La Plata, preferred to criticize the ICUF from within, rather than break with the organization, as did the Argentine Jewish cultural club "19th of April" in Rosario.[20]

The Soviet invasion of Czechoslovakia in 1968 helped secessionists arrive at their decision to leave. Based on interviews with a number of ICUF dissidents, the political impact of the Soviet invasion that put an end to the "Prague Spring" and the anti-Jewish campaign by Gomulka in Poland was evident. These incidents provoked an even larger, second group of dissidents. Both groups of intellectuals and dissident activists from the rank-and-file—not exceeding twenty people—finally formed the new progressive Jewish cultural organization *Fraie Schtime* (Agrupacion Cultural Judía Argentina Progresista Fraie Schtime) in 1968.[21] Before its establishment as an association, the first group of dissidents, shocked by

---

[19] See "Organo Judeo-Argentino de Información y Esclarecimiento," that united ICUF dissidents who conformed to the Israeli Maki party line. *Fraie Schtime* 2, no. 2 (December 1967).

[20] Abraham Escovich, interview by author, Rosario, 5 August 1993.

[21] Simon Lewinthal and Bernardo Treister, interviewed by author, Buenos Aires, 20 September 1994 and Tel Aviv, 26 November 1995.

the impact of the Six-Day War, edited the first issue of the bilingual newspaper *Fraie Schtime–Voz Libre*. The first issue in October 1967 explained that the new publication responded to the need to demonstrate solidarity with Israel and to react to the attacks by the anti-Israel Argentine Left, whom the editors accused of falsifying the true nature of the conflict. The reactive character of the paper arose in its editorial titled "¿Por Que?," in which the editor confided, "We will be surrounded by all those progressive Jewish people who react with astonishment and pain in the face of so many false accusations voiced against Israel in the name of the highest human ideals." This first edition of *Voz Libre* contained translated articles about the Arab-Israeli conflict from the Yiddish paper *Frai Isroel*, an organ of the Israeli Maki party, as well as *Freiheit*, a dissident American Yiddish Communist paper. One article directly criticized the position of the ICUF toward Israel, and another one refuted anti-Zionist and anti-Israel arguments, addressing in particular the Argentine Left's poster (cited earlier), "Together with the Arab people." Also included in the first edition was a declaration by the Movement for a Progressive Israel and Peace in the Middle East (El Movimiento Por Israel Progresista y la Paz en el Medio Oriente).[22] Toward the end of 1968, the newspaper succeeded in becoming the voice of a new cultural progressive Jewish institution, the Judeo-Argentine cultural association Voz Libre (Asociación Cultural Judeo-Argentina Voz Libre), with approximately fifty members. The group was composed of intellectual dissidents from the PC, former ICUF activists, and native Jewish Argentines from the National Left.

The first public declaration reads:

> a) The problem of the Near East is an issue that is a central concern of the Jewish communities the world over. We are convinced that the Six-Day War, independent of speculations harbored by the imperial powers, was a defensive war, dictated by open threats of a new genocide and the effective and juridical liquidation of the State of Israel.

The declaration goes on to identify the signers with the national line of the Israeli Left. Equally, it assumes the group's obligation as progressive Argentine citizens and calls for active political solidarity with the state of Israel and Jewish communities around the world. It asserts a vigorous synthesis of Jewish and Argentine identities. In addition, it alerted the Argentine Left:

---

[22] See H. Glauber, director, *Fraie Schtime*, 1, no. 1 (October 1967), 1, 7. See also the article of the Israeli Communist newspaper in the Yiddish section of *Frai Israel*, Latin American ICUF Congress, Montevideo, 6.

inviting it to recognize that its acceptance or silence in the face of an anti-Zionist fight, ultimately unleashed in certain socialist countries, calling for the juridical liquidation of the State of Israel and its extermination proclaimed by the Arab states, has nothing in common with socialism, and only endangers it.[23]

In conclusion, *Fraie Schtime* adopted the political position of the Israeli Communist Maki party, led by Moshe Sneh, regarding the Middle East conflict and the national Jewish line.

Through translated Yiddish articles of the Israeli writer Meir Lipsky and the American writer Itche Goldberg, *Fraie Schtime* in 1968 and 1969 presented to the Argentine public a non-Zionist line, but one that adhered to a national conception of the problems of the Jewish people and Israel. In this vein, Jewish intellectual dissidents of the PC, such as José Itzigsohn, Moisés Polak, Mimi Pinzon, Arnaldo Liberman, Héctor Yanover, and others, wrote noteworthy articles.

Fraie Schtime decided to participate in the May 1969 elections of the AMIA, the Ashkenazi Kehilla of Buenos Aires, but not with its own list. Their voters were basic members of the Kehilla. Coming from immigrant origins, they were dissident members of institutions and *Landsfareinen* tied to the ICUF. They preferred to give their vote to the Bund list, which obtained 697 votes (five seats, one more than in the previous elections of 1966), rather than to Mapam-Hashomer Hatzair, which obtained 1,112 votes (8 seats, two less than the 1966 elections). As early as the 1972 elections, *Fraie Schtime* participated with its own lists of candidates, receiving 596 votes—almost equal to the total number of Bund votes, thus entering five members into the Rat (Plenary Assembly of Members—Asamblea Plenaria de Socios): Simon Lewinthal, Lanwl Pzredborsky, Gil Rozen, Aizik Schliapochnik, and Nachman Drechler. Only one member of *Fraie Schtime* joined the AMIA Executive Committee.[24] Immediately after it was constituted as a cultural association, *Fraie Schtime* joined the DAIA, the major Jewish umbrella organization in Argentina.

This same process of integrating members of the Yiddish-speaking immigrant generation with Argentine Jewish intellectuals who were seek-

---

[23] *Fraie Schtime*, 7–8 (January 1969).
[24] Haim Avni, *Yahadut B'Argentina*, 60. The joint Communist list in the 1955 AMIA elections obtained 4,638 votes, and in 1957, 2,311 votes. They didn't participate in the 1960, 1966, and 1969 elections because the Jewish Communists were excluded from the communal institutions, *Nueva Sión*, 15 May 1969, 1. 1972 electoral data for *Fraie Schtime* provided by Simon Lewinthal.

ing to enter the mainstream of local communal Jewish life can be observed in the activities of the Argentine Jewish cultural club "19th of April" in Rosario, and in the Max Nordau Literary Center and Library in La Plata. While the center in La Plata, in spite of the pro-Israel dissidents, continued to be affiliated with the ICUF for a number of years, the center in Rosario adopted independent activities prior to 1967, later disassociated itself entirely from the ICUF. There were also some differences between them in the manner in which they demonstrated solidarity with Israel. In August 1967, the club in Rosario organized a demonstration together with the local community, issuing a declaration whose slogan was "For peace in the Middle East, solidarity with the State of Israel, for the consolidation of Jewish life throughout the world." The club, as a consequence of the Six-Day War, adopted the principle that affirmed "Israel is a reality that rejects any formula of negation, and we, Argentine Jews, have the obligation to stand for it." These same ideals were furthered by its director, Dr. Abraham Escovich, who spoke at a public event on 28 October in Buenos Aires. This ceremony was organized by Mapam and the Movement for Peace in the Middle East. The "19th of April" club played an important role in the organization of this event, and participated in the local *kehilla* in spite of divisive personal rivalries and ideological suspicions.[25]

The leaders of the Max Nordau Center in La Plata also expressed solidarity with Israel and participated in the United Emergency Campaign. In addition, they fostered among Jewish youth various volunteer programs in Israel. However, they were not involved in the rally on 28 October, nor did they issue their own declaration. But it is important to note that the process of dissidence in the Nordau Center had been initiated as early as 1963, when its leaders made known their criticism in plenary and congresses against certain ICUF political positions.[26] Starting in 1978, the Center of La Plata stopped paying membership fees to the ICUF, and since 1980 its youth has not participated in the ICUF's social and athletic events. Since 1985 they have worked with emissaries from Kibbutz Artzi.[27]

---

[25] Abraham Escovich, interview by author; see Escovich's pro-Israel speech, *Nueva Sión*, 3 December 1967, 2.

[26] For example, in the VIII and IX ICUF Congresses of 1965 and 1968 these leaders criticized ICUF's withdrawal from the moderate and popular Jewish plans for educational and cultural activities of its affiliated institutions, as well as denouncing the silence of the Communist Jewish Argentines in the face of Soviet anti-Semitism.

[27] See Simon Kossak and Mauricio Tenenbaum to ICUF, 25 June 1985; *75 Aniversario Centro Literario Israelita Biblioteca Max Nordau, 1982–1987*, pp. 29–31; 49–56.

Completely distinct from the path of the La Plata center was the reaction of the Jewish Cultural Association of Cordoba (Asociacion Cultural Israelita de Cordoba—ACIC). Also affiliated with the ICUF, the ACIC continued to toe the Communist line without reservation. The ACIC used the occasion of a rally for Israeli Independence Day in 1970 to attack Zionism as an imperialist enterprise and to defend the official position of the U.S.S.R. regarding the Arab-Israeli conflict. This provoked a violent reaction by local Zionist youth as well as a repudiation from Cordoba Jewish communal institutions and the central DAIA. The DAIA in Cordoba attacked not only the anti-Israel ideological propaganda of the ICUF in the interior of the country, but also its pro-Soviet ideology.

This episode suggests that, in spite of the anti-Communist military intervention in Cordoba a few weeks after the fall of General Onganía, the ICUF did not sufficiently fear the anti-Communist ideological repression of the new military regime that appointed General Roberto Levingston as President. ICUF publicly expressed its pro-Soviet position and attacked so-called Israeli militarism, despite the fact that the Israeli army was admired by the Argentine military, seen by them as an example of defense against Communism and the fight against terrorism in the West. At the same time, violent repudiation of the DAIA and the Argentine Jewish Youth Confederation (Confederacion Juvenil Judeo Argentina) suggests that the Jewish communal leadership had no objection to politically fighting ICUF's anti-Zionism by making use of anti-Communist discourse in similar language to that used by the Argentine military regime.[28]

The impact of the Six-Day War among ICUF's rank-and-file pressured the leadership to take new initiatives. For the first time since 1949, the ICUF organized a massive public demonstration in 1969 at the IFT theater in Buenos Aires to celebrate Israel's twentieth anniversary. In effect, the internal debate at the heart of the ICUF regarding the position of Israel focused on thirteen lay directors who questioned the official position upheld by the executive director, Ruben Sinay. The split among ICUF members that resulted from the breakaway of *Fraie Schtime* forced the ICUF directors to take note of the position of the group of thirteen,

---

[28] Gerardo Lopez Alonso, *Cincuenta años de Historia Argentina, 1930–1980, Una cronologia basica* (Buenos Aires: 1982), 250; Paul Lewis, "The Right and Military Rule, 1955–1983," in *The Argentine Right. Its History and Intellectual Origins, 1910 to the Present*, eds. Sandra McGee Detusch and Ronald H. Dolkhart (Wilmington: 1993), 169–70; *Nueva Sión*, 20 March 1970.

and thus agreed to organize an event commemorating Israel's independence. Thus, the ICUF participated in the massive independence celebration organized by the central institutions of the Jewish community and attended by Golda Meir.[29] For the first time since its expulsion from the DAIA in 1952, an institution tied to the Argentine Communist party issued a formal invitation to the Israeli ambassador in Buenos Aires to deliver a speech. (The ambassador could not attend, but he sent his regards.) The official orators saluted the Israeli labor movement, the kibbutzim, and the working Israeli masses, without attacking the Zionist movement. They did, however, criticize the pro-American politics of the Israeli government. On the other hand, no Arab country was criticized, and only Ahmed Shukeiri, the leader of the Palestinian Liberation Organization, was the object of invective. It should be pointed out that the anti-imperialist slogans and support for abstract internationalism voiced by spokesmen of the ICUF were not applauded by the public. Furthermore, the popular song "Jerusalem of Gold" won an emotional ovation from the audience.[30]

But the rank-and-file of the ICUF were not satisfied with official speeches to commemorate the twentieth anniversary of Israeli independence. Some members of the ICUF continued their ideological fight in the suburban centers of Greater Buenos Aires, demanding a change in the anti-Israel line of the leadership. The most significant case occurred in the I. L. Peretz Cultural Center of Lanus, where it was demanded that Moisés Polak be the keynote speaker. Polak, at the time was a dissident from the PC line, president of the Movement for Peace in the Middle East, and affiliated with the *Fraie Schtime*. Furthermore, the Lanus center's leadership committee solicited organizational help from Hashomer Hatzair for the artistic part of the planned event. "We do not want those who lied to us during the past twenty years to speak during the anniversary of Israel," said one director of Mapam. Despite attempts by the "orthodox" ICUF stalwarts to disrupt the event, Dr. Polak successfully continued his speech, comparing the "just fight for the existence of Israel during the Six-Day War" to the cause that he personally defended against military intervention in Argentine univer-

---

[29] Gregorio Lerner, interview by author, Buenos Aires, September 1994; Bezalel Blitz, interview by Efraim Zadoff, Buenos Aires, April 1985. See *Como lograr la paz arabe-israeli? Respuesta a un interrogatorio* (Buenos Aires: Federacion de Entidades Culturales Judías de la Argentina, 1969).

[30] See report of the event and reaction by Jewish centers affiliated with ICUF, *Nueva Sión*, 11 June 1968; and ICUF newsletter, *Renovación*, 24 May 1968, in which Bezalel Blitz's speech is reproduced.

sities, and against American armed intervention in Santo Domingo and Vietnam.[31]

REPERCUSSIONS IN THE NON-COMMUNIST LEFTIST CAMP

The creation of the Movement for Peace in the Middle East immediately after the Six-Day War was the fruit of a united effort among Mapam and Hashomer Hatzair radical intellectuals and their Mordejai Anielevich student division, non-Communist leftist Jewish intellectuals, and PC dissidents tied to the Judeo-Argentine newspaper *Voz Libre*.[32]

The first declaration of the Movement for Peace in the Middle East was read at a well-attended rally at the Astral Theater of Buenos Aires on 29 October 1967. The event was organized by the newspaper *Nueva Sión*, the Rosario "19th of April" Jewish cultural club, Mapam, the Anielevich student division, and the Martin Buber Jewish cultural club. Organizers felt that it was one of the best-attended public events in the Jewish community of that last year. Dr. Moisés Polak spoke, as did Dr. Natan Trainin of the Weizman Institute, who had emigrated from Argentina to Israel in 1949.[33]

The movement grew during the year that followed, thanks to the recruiting of adherents among leftist Jewish intellectuals, basically dissidents of the PC, such as Miguel Polak, José Blejer, and José Itzigsohn, as well as the participation of noteworthy independent progressive intellectuals such as Delia Etcheverry, Oberdan Calleti, Abelardo Castillo, Andres Lopoz Acotto, Segio Bagu, Norberto Rodriguez Bustamente, and Bernardo Kordon. Despite the declared intention of the movement to supply unbiased information to the public on the situation in the Middle East and to clarify the nature of the Arab-Israeli conflict, some of the leaders of the group openly took a partisan position favoring the recognition of Zionism as a national Jewish liberation movement and unconditional support for the left-wing sectors in Israel. In May 1968 the group organized a symposium of South American intellectuals for peace in the Middle East. This meeting was inspired by the similar gathering of five hundred European

---

[31] *Nueva Sión*, 11 June 1968, 2; Dr. Carlos Polak, interview by author, Buenos Aires, 19 September 1995.
[32] Among the first to stand out were Drs. Leon and Perla Perez, Dr. Bernardo Kliskberg, Dr. Najum Solominsky, Dr. Moshe Roit, Dr. Pedro Szylman. Following them were Dr. José Itzigsohn, Dr. José Blejer, and Dr. Moisés Polak.
[33] The movement's declaration was endorsed by leading Jewish and non-Jewish intellectuals; see *Nueva Sión*, 3 December 1967, 6–7.

intellectuals in Paris the previous April, organized by the Bernard Lazare Circle and the leftist Israeli magazine *New Outlook*. In Buenos Aires, with the cooperation of Mapam-affiliated intellectuals such as Drs. Leon and Perla Perez, and Uruguayan writers such as Professor Carlos Rama, the dramatist Mauricio Rozencoff, and the Chilean Miguel Saidel, Argentinean intellectuals and academics participated together with members of the Departments of International Studies, Middle Eastern Studies, and Economics of the Colegio de Mexico. The movement did not succeed in editing a magazine of it own, but rather published its communiqués in the national and the leftist Jewish press. It sponsored two books, with the intention of clarifying the Middle East conflict, which were published and financed by the local branch of Mapam.[34]

Cuba's position on Israel also influenced the Argentine leftist dissidents, many of whom greatly admired Fidel Castro. The Cuban government did not take responsibility for the anti-Israel resolution of the Tri-Continental Conference held in Havana in January 1966, which called on the anti-imperialist revolutionary movements of Latin America, Asia, and Africa to break off political relations with Israel and condemn Zionism as racism. Cuban-Israeli diplomatic relations were not affected at the time. The leftist Argentine and Uruguayan delegations abstained from the anti-Israel vote. Leftist political groups, university student associations, and distinguished pro-Cuban Argentine and Uruguayan intellectuals repudiated the resolution of the Tri-Continental Conference. Both the Argentines and the Uruguayans sent a communiqué to the press and a telegram of protest to the conference.[35] Not only did Castro refuse to break off diplomatic relations with Israel after the Six-Day War, but at various international forums held in Havana after June 1967, he even intervened per-

---

[34] *Nueva Sión*, 24 May 1968, 2–3. *Nueva Sión* and *Voz Libre* offered to publish public declarations of the Movement for Peace. The movement was supported by Mapam-HaShomer HaTzair, who wanted an organization similar to the Israeli Committee for Peace affiliated with the World Council of Peace and integrated representatives of the Israeli parties Ahdut Avodah, Mapam, Maki, and Rakaj. See the manifesto of the Israeli Committee for Peace of November 1967, in *Nueva Sión*, 15 December 1967, 11; see also *Nueva Sión*, 2 August 1968, 5; *Israel, un tema para la Izquierda* (Buenos Aire: 1967), and *Informe sobre Medio Oriente* (Buenos Aires: 1968), both edited by *Nueva Sión* and widely distributed by the Committee for Peace.

[35] See the reaction of the Israeli Committee for Peace and its communiqué to the Israeli press of 8 February 1966, *Al HaMishmar*, 9 March 1966; for the names of Argentine and Uruguayan intellectuals who repudiated the resolution, see *Israel, Un tema para la izquierda*, 225–27.

sonally to abort anti-Israeli resolutions. Castro's personal intervention at the International Congress of Intellectuals in April 1968 to prevent the presentation of a declaration of the intellectuals of the Arab bloc condemning Israel and comparing the situation in the Middle East with the Vietnam War had special repercussions among the non-Communist Jewish intellectuals of Argentina. In spite of the fact that Israeli leftist intellectuals were not invited, due to the threat by Arab intellectuals that they would not attend, Castro offered his political support to Chancellor Raul Roa at an important juncture. Roa authorized, in spite of the Arab delegates' veto, the uncensored circulation of the pro-Israeli speech by Arturo Schwartz, a Egyptian Jewish Trotskyist living in Milan. Schwartz publicly denounced the intended genocide on the part of the Arab countries, aimed at erasing Israel from the map.[36] The position adopted by Cuba regarding Israel influenced the leftist dissidents of the PC up until the Yom Kippur War. Among the resolutions adopted by the Colloquium for Peace in the Middle East in May 1968 was a resolution explicitly phrased in this regard.[37]

The Jewish Argentine leader, Ismael Viñas, a member of the National non-Communist Leftist party (Movimiento de Liberación Nacional—MLN), was a delegate at the Tri-Continental Conference in Havana. Viñas defended Israel, declaring that leftist and anti-imperialist Israeli forces should have been invited to the conference, and opposed the resolution condemning Zionism. On the eve of the Six-Day War, the MLN issued a declaration against the outbreak of the war, repudiating Arab aggression and recognizing the right of Israel to exist. After the war in June, the MLN issued a communiqué demanding a just peace between Arabs and Israelis.[38]

---

[36] See the antecedents that led to the intervention of Roa and Castro in *Nueva Sión*, 10 May 1968. Schwartz's speech was published under the title "Imperialismo y Racismo," *Nueva Sión*, 19 August 1968, 6–7. It was later circulated in various publications of the Argentine Left.

[37] The symposium was organized by the Argentine Movement for Peace in the Near East on 18–19 May 1968. See *Nueva Sión*, 1 August 1968, 3. Castro's declarations on the reasons for not breaking diplomatic relations with Israel were published in the Leftist Argentine press.

[38] Movement for National Liberation, 9 June 1967, *Nueva Sión*, 16 June 1967, 14. Ismael Viñas, interview by author, Jerusalem, October 1986.

Intellectual Implications of the Six-Day War: Written Reflections on Jewish-Argentine Identity

Starting in 1967 prestigious Argentine Jewish intellectuals of the Left wrote significant works about Jewish identity that were directly influenced by the circumstances preceding the Six-Day War, specifically in relation to the question of Israel's right to exist. Indeed, the support of the U.S.S.R. for the Arab cause, the radical questioning of the anti-imperialist Left and the Socialist camp regarding Israel's right to exist, provoked in the Jewish intellectual camp an ideological answer to anti-Zionism. This was not simply a matter of geopolitical polemics, but was also an expression of reflections on Argentine-Jewish identity. Without a doubt, one of the most fruitful consequences of the war's impact among certain talented intellectuals was their pondering, for the first time, their profound sense of being Argentine Jews and their need to affirm their identification with the Jewish people and with the local Jewish community. It is no coincidence that influential writings from the period 1967–1972 were written as a result of the existential threat to Israel. These include essays such as "Ser Judío" (To Be a Jew) by Leon Rozitchner, "La Identidad Reprimida" (The Repressed Identity) by Leon S. Perez, "Una Experiencia Judía Contemporánea" (A Contemporary Jewish Experience) by José Itzigsohn, and the essay-novel *Etiquetas para los Hombres* (Appellations for Men) by Bernardo Verbitzky. This heterogeneous and wide-ranging body of writings represents the first serious Latin American attempt to tackle the existential questions of Jewishness, and to substantiate from a secular and politically liberal perspective the right for Jewish cultural distinctiveness, both individual and collective, in Argentina. In spite of their dissimilar conceptual approaches and narrative genres, the authors shared a common critique of the anti-Zionist Left on the subject of Israel's right to exist, and at the same time intended to legitimize the possibility of being a pro-Israeli Argentine Jew without simultaneously alienating themselves entirely from the Leftist camp.[39]

---

[39] Leon Rozitchner, "Ser Judío" (Buenos Aires: 1967); Juan José Sebreli, "La cuestión Judía en Argentina" (Buenos Aires: 1968); José Itzigsohn, "Una Experiencia Judía Contemporánea" (Buenos Aires: 1969); Leon S. Perez, "La Identidad Reprimida" (Buenos Aires: 1969); Fernando Runa Camba, *Tránsito Hacia mi Mismo* (play) (Buenos Aires: 1971); Bernardo Verbitzky, *Etiquetas para los Hombres* (Buenos Aires: 1972). See Leonardo Senkman, *La Identidad Judía en la Literatura argentina* (Buenos Aires: 1983), 390–412. Itzigsohn's book, the only prestigious intellectual dissident who wrote a book denouncing Soviet anti-Semitism, for which he received strong criticism from the PC

These works could not have been created had the authors not been familiar with their Israeli counterparts. All of them had links to the Committee for Peace in the Middle East and were influenced by the moderate ideas of *Les Temps Moderne* and *Cahiers,* edited by Jean Paul Sartre, and views disseminated by the Bernard Lazare Circle in Paris. Also, they were acquainted with the ideas of left-wing Israeli magazines such as *New Outlook*. Finally, all of them wrote in Jewish leftist Buenos Aires-based periodicals such as *Nueva Sión* and *Voz Libre*.

The production of this body of writing amid the climate of internal self-inspection in the months previous to, during, and after the Six-Day War requires a specific study of each author and work separately, which lies outside the scope of this essay. Here it is simply worth pointing out that the whole of this corpus influenced the new formulations that were conceived by Jewish intellectuals intent upon constructing forms of identification that included solidarity with Israel, the Jewish people, and the Argentine Jewish community.

Conclusion

The Six-Day War had repercussions on the leftist Jewish camp from an ideological perspective and influenced a process of Jewish national identification that was previously much less in evidence. From the organizational point of view, the most important group that split from the ICUF as a consequence of the Six-Day War was that which was to become the nucleus of the *Fraie Schtime*. This organization began publishing the journal *Voz Libre*. Its influence was not quantitative, but rather, qualitative. *Fraie Schtime* received 600 votes in the Buenos Aires Kehilla elections. These voters were mainly Yiddish-speaking immigrant members of the AMIA. In contrast, the group's leaders were prestigious native Argentinean profes-

---

newsletter. See the anonymous article (attributed to the Communist leader Rodolfo Ghioldi, "Crónica de una degradación," *Nuestra Palabra,* 12 November 1969. After the war, Dr. José Itzigsohn renounced the PC and was invited to participate in forums on ideological analysis and in positions within the framework of the DAIA. In 1976, a few months after the rise of general Videla's military dictatorship, he immigrated to Israel together with his family. Leftist political leader, Ismael Viñas, another active intellectual in the framework of the Movement for Peace in the Middle East, also immigrated with his family to Israel in 1976. See his analysis written in Israel on the socio-economic causes of anti-Semitism: "Los Judíos y la Sociedad Argentina. Un análisis clasista retrospectivo," in *El Antisemitismo en la Argentina,* ed. Leonardo Senkman (Buenos Aires: 1989), 329–89.

sionals and intellectuals who helped instigate serious political-ideological debates between the rank-and-file in the ICUF-affiliated centers of Rosario and La Plata and independent progressive Jewish intellectuals. These intellectuals founded and promoted the Committee for Peace in the Middle East. They were heard with respect on the DAIA board and executive committee. Also, from 1972, distinguished intellectuals of *Fraie Schtime* were elected to the AMIA executive board and were in charge of AMIA's Office of Culture. However, ideologically and organizationally they remained an independent group, refusing to participate in the local Zionist movement (OSA). In spite of the concern for peace in the Middle East that they shared with the leftist-Zionists, they did not join Mapam in communal elections.

The Six-Day War also created an ideological controversy and a climate of crisis among the leftist politicians who joined the dozens of intellectuals as well as leftist non-Communist intellectual Jews in expanding such organizations as the Mapam-Mordejai Anielevich youth group and the Martin Buber cultural club.

Furthermore, these controversies spurred a flurry of writing by certain well-known leftist Jewish intellectuals regarding existential and communal aspects of the Jewish condition in Argentina and which reflected their gravitation toward Israel.

THE IMPACT OF THE SIX-DAY WAR ON THE MEXICAN JEWISH COMMUNITY*

Judit Bokser-Liwerant
Universidad Autónoma de México
Universidad Iberoamericana, México

ON 10 JUNE 1968, the 27th World Zionist Congress met in Jerusalem. Arie Pincus, then head of the World Zionist Organization, presented an analysis of conditions that prevailed in the Jewish world twenty years after the creation of the State of Israel, and a year after the events of June 1967. He stated: "The Six-Day War is not an integral cure for all diseases."[1]

It is evident that a statement of this nature sounds unusual. How can it have been meant, and when can warfare act as a remedy? What diseases was it expected to treat?

The war's immediate impact was a generalized Jewish awakening. It turned the routine into passion, fusing a new organic solidarity. Moreover, the Six-Day War seems to be the kind of event that is felt to be historic at the very time of its unfolding. Given the perception of a life-threatening situation, the rapidity of the developments, the magnitude of Israel's victory as well as the type and intensity of the responses it elicited, it was defined as a watershed while it was still happening. In this sense, the *response* evoked by the war was seen as a remedy, an everlasting renewal of Jewish life. Nevertheless, Pincus's statement may be seen as a harbinger of concerns shared by different sections of world Jewry wary of the difficulty involved in turning such a sudden arousal of enthusiasm into a permanent phenomenon. In other words, it reflects an effort to minimize the accidental nature of the situation, lest it should become impossible to discern in it any permanence.

In Mexico, the response of the Jewish community to the outbreak of hostilities was massive and enthusiastic both in human and material terms.[2]

---

* I would like to thank Haim Avni, Ignacio Klich, and Halina Rubinstein for their valuable comments as well as Katia Weissberg for her helpful collaboration.
[1] Arieh Pincus, *The 27th Zionist Congress*, June 9–19, 1968, Jerusalem, World Zionist Organization.
[2] On 29 May the Jewish Central Committee, the Zionist Federation, and the Ash-

This effort involved the whole community, straining existing institutional limits. It included fund raising as well as the collection of clothing and medicines. The pressing need for identification turned blood donation into a symbolic act. Young people were willing to participate directly in combat, even though the number of volunteers to Israel was comparatively small—sixteen. The prevailing atmosphere registered by memory was that of solidarity and willingness to sacrifice.[3] With the Jewish state's military victory, the feeling was one of sharing in Israel's euphoria. Various training frameworks for young people in Israel reached significant numbers.[4] The financial contributions to Keren Hayesod were outstanding.[5]

These responses indicate the way in which a moment in history can act as a "founding event" where different dimensions converge: reality, symbolism, and the imaginary. Discourse and social action met, and together stretched the boundaries that define the scope and meaning of *us*. In the words of the actors themselves, each Jew was defined as a potential citizen of Israel and the menace to the state was a threat to the entire Jewish people: "The people of Israel is one undivided unit."[6] Thus, the perception of the Six-Day War as a historical watershed was due not only to Israel's victory but also to the expression of solidarity and the cohesion it brought about in Jewish communities abroad.

Nevertheless, a year later, there were those who strove not to see the war as an instant cure-all. One has to ask about the "diseases" which gave rise to this sentiment. Were these afflictions related to the new conditions of Jewish life in general, or to the emerging situation that organized Zionism had to confront after the war? In the new situation of unity and increased mutual links between Israel and the Diaspora, the role each party

---

kenazi Kehila launched an Emergency Campaign and joined efforts in an Emergency Committee.

[3] Gregorio Shapiro, President, Central Committee, *Minutes of the Executive of the Central Committee (MACC)*, Archives of the Central Committee (ACC) 4 July, 1967; Simón Feldman, President, Ashkenazi Kehila, *Minutes of the Meeting of the Council of the Ashkenazi Kehila (MAKA)*, Ashkenazi Kehila Archives (AKA), 19 June, 1967.

[4] The same year, eleven doctors traveled to Israel as volunteers and more than twenty youngsters went to *hachshara* (training). An immediate increase in *aliyah* of 55 people was reported. Shraga Peri, *Report on Aliyah from Mexico and Latin-América during 1967*, AKA, México, 8 January, 1968.

[5] In the framework of the rise in the world campaign which increased from $14,476,515 in 1966–67 to $51,676,520 in 1967–68, Latin America's contribution increased from $2,382,622 to $29,012,284. *Keren Hayesod Report, 1966–1993* (Jerusalem: 1993).

[6] *MAKA*, 29 May 1967.

was called upon to play could be defined in different ways. Consequently, the perception and definition of the war as a "remedy" could mean different things under different circumstances, that is to say, as a remedy for different types of ills.

From the vantage point of the World Zionist Organization, Pincus's message was geared toward the leaders of the State of Israel as well as to Israeli public opinion. It came as a response to the doubts expressed regarding the relevance of organized Zionism, aroused precisely by the intensity of the awakening caused by the war, which apparently rendered Zionism no longer necessary. This became evident when it was reported that of the 8,000 volunteers who arrived in Israel during the first year after the war, fifty percent had not had any previous contact with Jewish or Zionist organizations.[7] In parallel, the absence of a massive *aliyah* from the non-Communist world after the war tended to reinforce the uncertainty surrounding the relevance of organized Zionism.

But precisely because of these arguments, for Pincus the Zionist movement had challenges to meet. Yet there were diseases for which the war was not a sufficient remedy. First, the immediate Jewish response to the war situation could be a temporary phenomenon and, therefore, the consolidation and expansion of Zionist activism had to continue. Second, the challenge of incorporating youth into Jewish life was still a task that Zionism had to confront; in this sense, Zionism defined itself once again as a means toward achieving continuity and as a tool against assimilation.

Organized Zionism in Mexico shared some of these concerns and had its own worries. Paradoxically, these challenges emerged simultaneously with the State of Israel's new centrality among Diaspora Jews, both as an organizational axis and as a source of legitimization. While the first dimension finds its frame of reference in significant transformations within the Jewish community, the latter points to its interaction with the society at large. The situation that emerged eventually showed that while the war's immediate impact was impressive, the concomitant changes it brought about were heterogeneous and even contradictory.

THE ORGANIZATIONAL AXIS: REDEFINITION OF SPACES

One of the main paradoxes brought about by the magnitude of the response to the war was that it inaugurated a process which diluted the

---

[7] Ricardo Levy, representative of the Volunteers Organization in Israel, *27th Zionist Congress*, 54–55.

boundaries between Zionism and non-Zionism to the extent that a pro-Israeli attitude came to be equated with Zionism. As a result of the massive and spontaneous expressions of Jewish support during the conflict, Zionism's organizational boundaries and identity became diffuse. The organized movement had to confront new ideological and organizational definitions regarding its validity as well as its specificity and self-definition.

Certainly, the war demonstrated the heightened mutuality in the ties that bound the Mexican Jewish community with Israel. Through solidarity with Israel, the community also expressed the legitimacy of its own existence. In the words of one communal leader, "The events of 1967 changed dramatically the relationship between the Diaspora and the State of Israel. They showed their unity, changing the vision of those in Israel who claimed that every Jew must live there. Jews in the Diaspora and Jews in Israel are all members of a single and mutually dependent people."[8]

Solidarity meant responsibility and, by implication, Israel was called upon to legitimate the Diaspora's separate existence. Israel legitimated the Diaspora by attaching great importance to its support for the Jewish state. In this sense, the Diaspora's solidarity with Israel legitimized its place and the channeling of energy into reinforcing its communities.

However, insofar as the State of Israel posed *aliyah* as a central criterion to evaluate the success and limitations of the Zionist movement after the war, it confronted Zionism with different and sometimes contradictory historical objectives: its final goal and *Gegenwartsarbeit* (work in the present). After 1967, a*liyah* offered both the possibility of converting the Jewish ferment into a permanent phenomenon and of giving back to the Zionist idea its own specific profile. Paradoxically, for the organized movement, the absence of a massive *aliyah* demanded the reinforcement of its activities, not necessarily along new lines, thereby justifying its own permanence.

In this new context, Mexican Zionism found itself caught between two different perspectives: on the one hand were Israel's expectations of a massive increase of immigration; on the other, while Zionist identity appeared as a synonym of Jewish continuity, involvement in Jewish life in the Diaspora as such was validated. Thus, the challenge was how to transform the awakening into a stable form of participation in organized Jewish life in Mexico.

---

[8] Horacio Jinich, *First Convention of Jewish Communities in Mexico,* Mexico, November 1973.

While approaching this dilemma, the first expressions of an inter-generational clash emerged. In the framework of the Aliyah Congress that took place in Mexico in November 1967,[9] youth movement spokespersons accused the Zionism of their parents of being "comfortable" and demanded a reinvigorated, *aliyah*-defined Zionism.[10] For its part, the older generation justified a wider conception of the objectives of the movement based on the assumption that *aliyah* is always a *result* of Zionist activism and education.[11] In this sense, Zionism in Mexico pursued continuity rather than change, reinforcing the prevailing pattern initiated during the twenties, when it aspired to "conquer the community," not only as a strategy to guarantee support for its cause but to ensure Jewish life in the new country.

From the point of view of Mexican Zionism's internal dynamics, the new developments added two more problems to this first and essential dilemma: one, regarding the campaign for inner democratization of the movement, that took the form of demands for individual membership rather than the traditional affiliation through political parties; the other, related to the loss of institutional relevance of the Zionist movement within the community vis-à-vis the emergence of other organizational spaces. These inherent dilemmas were intertwined in the more basic question of whether Zionism and the communal influence of the Jewish state were necessarily related.

In order to adapt itself to the new conditions, the World Zionist Organization called for the creation of new and more representative Zionist federations organized not only along party lines but also based on individual membership.[12] The Zionist Federation of Mexico, in its aim to protect the interest it had in the maintenance of the status quo, challenged

---

[9] As part of the call for a massive *aliyah* from the free world, the World Zionist Organization, the Government of Israel, and the Department of Aliyah and Absorption invited Latin American communities to hold congresses dedicated to the theme of *aliyah* in Mexico City, Buenos Aires, and Rio de Janeiro. *From the Department of Aliyah and Absorption to the Zionist Federation of Mexico*, AKA, 25 September 1967; Shraga Peri, *Report on Aliyah*.

[10] *Youth Declaration, MAKA*, November 1967.

[11] It was agreed to encourage study trips and a year of service, among other ideas. Shraga Peri, *Report on Aliyah*.

[12] The Action Committee agreed in July 1969 to carry out a vigorous campaign of individual membership. Zionist Federations were asked to declare 1970 as the year of Zionist Affiliation. *Minutes of the Meeting of the Zionist Federation*, Archives of the Zionist Federation (*MAZF*), 7 October, 1970.

this recommendation.[13] The generational clash showed itself again at the organizational level, with the breaking away of a group of young members who created the "Renewal Front" for the advancement of individual membership and who demanded that elections be held both for the federation as well as for the 28th Zionist Congress.[14]

Throughout the membership campaign, there were confrontations between the Zionist Federation and the Renewal Front.[15] The struggle between both groups was resolved through an agreement to respect the two membership recruiting structures and to hold elections.[16] However, even though both electoral processes took place, participation was low[17] and the recruiting of new members was limited,[18] pointing to the fact that it was difficult either to benefit from the Jewish awakening caused by the war or to regain a central role in community life. Hence, from the Zionist point of view, the effervescence related to the war failed to be translated into a permanent circumstance, either in terms of *aliyah* or in terms of communal participation. In this respect, one should remember that although 1967 brought about a growing demand for elections as a way toward democratization, they were never a customary pattern of political behavior in the history of organized Zionism in Mexico. Voting continued

---

[13] Mexico's Zionist Federation agreed to it on 5 February, 1969, even though it was initially opposed. By 1970 it was agreed to establish another committee in the Federation itself. *Minutes of the Meeting of the Zionist Federation*, 7 October 1970. On the struggle to establish a United Territorial Zionist Federation in Mexico following the resolutions of the 19th Zionist Congress, see Judit Bokser, *The Jewish National Movement. Zionism in México, 1922–1947* (in Spanish) (Ph.D. diss., UNAM, Mexico City, 1991), 193–201.

[14] The emissary Simcha Genossar was in charge of the individual membership campaign and criticized both the Zionist movement and the community as a whole for their ineffectiveness in introducing democracy in their internal life. *MAZF*, 3 February 1971.

[15] From the beginning of 1971 the Zionist Executive Committee in Jerusalem accepted the establishment of different organizational frames for this campaign. Two structures operated—the Zionist Federation (consisting of the General Zionists, the Labor Movement, *Mizrachi* and *Herut*) and the Renewal Front (consisting of Mapam, the Sepharadic Zionist Federation, the General Zionist Confederation, the women organizations and the youth movements).

[16] *MAZF*, 11 February, 3 and 17 March 1971.

[17] In August 1971 participation was low in elections held by the Zionist Federation. Of 3,200 members, only 13% voted. *AZF*, 18 August 1971. Elections for the 28th Zionist Congress were held in November 1971.

[18] The total number of those affiliated was 3 329, of which 2 469 were recruited by the Federación, and 860 by the Front. The final list, accepted by the Electoral Committee, numbered 3,113. *Report by the Department of Organization and Information, Archives of the Zionist Federation (AZF)*, 18 August 1972.

to be an irregular practice, for decisions taken at the top remained the common rule. In this sense, the impact of the war was historically structurally rather limited.

The radicalization of the youth movements exposed the Zionist Federation to severe criticism. As a result of the war, the youth organizations became stronger: the existing ones increased their membership and new ones appeared, especially within the Sephardic groups. This was the case of Lochamei Herut among the Syrian Jews' Maguen David community and of Hatikwa among other Sephardic groups. Due to this growth, youth movements claimed a more active role in organized Zionism as well as economic independence.[19] Their ideological commitment, however, did not prevent them from encountering difficulties in advancing their own program. For example, in 1972 their ranks consisted of 1,100 members and *aliyah* was almost nil. Nevertheless, they acquired a significant presence within the community, which would increase throughout the decade. The Yom Kippur War would act as a catalyst in this process: while in 1967 Mexico recruited only 16 volunteers for Israel, during 1974 Mexico sent 120 volunteers for a period of between six months and a year.[20] This should indicate to us the importance of the cumulative and dynamic effects of historical events.

Simultaneously, regarding its institutional role within the Jewish community, the Zionist Federation based its actions on the awareness of its displacement in communal life and its loss of prestige and authority. It tried by different means to reverse this trend, with its attempts varying in orientation and intensity during the early seventies.[21] The Zionist leadership explained the self-perceived loss of influence by way of contradictory arguments. They continued to refer, above all, to the lack of economic support for local Zionist activities and the excessive importance given to fund raising—an activity that did not translate into membership—as the main reasons behind their functional shrinkage.[22] They were increasingly critical of the apathetic attitude prevailing among the Zionist rank-and-file and could not come to terms with the fact that Israel's centrality would no longer be reflected only through traditional institutional frameworks.

---

[19] *Correspondence between the Latin American Section of the Organization and Information Department and the Mexican Zionist Federation, 1972–1973*, AZF.
[20] A. Hazan to Rafael Rafalín, 11 June 1975, *AZF*.
[21] AZF, 23 February 1972; *Annual Reports of the Zionist Federation, 1972–1973*.
[22] Letter to A. Schenker, 21 September 1972, *AZF*; MAZF 1 December 1971. Throughout the 1970s, the Zionist Federation continued operating with lack of funds; letter to A. Schenker, 29 March 1973.

The fact is that as a result both of the 1967 experience as well as the institutional differentiation and functional specialization prevailing, the community tended to a redefinition of the channels through which the links with Israel would take place. The once-predominant role of mediator that organized Zionism historically had played was questioned, and other existing institutions began to play an increasing role in the community's relationship with Israel.

One of those institutions was the Central Committee, the umbrella organization of Mexican Jewry. Although this body defined itself as an apolitical organization, after the Six-Day War it expressed an increasing solidarity and identification with the State of Israel and urged the diverse community sectors it represented to adopt a more active stance in Israel-related matters.[23] Simultaneously, it tried to maintain a balance between solidarity of this sort and its own organizational autonomy, thus reflecting the changes in the community's dynamics as well as those taking place within the World Jewish Congress, with which it was affiliated.

Another institution which gained a recognized space for direct links between the community and Israel was Mexico's Ashkenazi Kehila Nidje Israel, which already during the war became the center for the collection of material aid and the enlistment of human resources for Israel. Even though Zionists had "conquered" the Kehila at the outset, remnants of rival political parties and movements could still be found. These ideological vestiges were marginalized by the 1967 War.[24] At the same time, the Kehila had to confront the fact that the relationship with Israel and Zionism did not belong solely to the Ashkenazi community. While the Sephardic community had established close bonds with Zionism in the past, now other communities were attracted to the cause, like the Arabic-speaking communities of Alianza Monte Sinaí and Maguen David. While an analysis of the impact of the war on these two sectors would require a special study, it is important not to lose sight of the fact that their engagement with Israel and Zionism was complex. Their growing identification with Israel was interwoven with a process of secularization which also included a generational clash: Israel offered the new generation the opportunity to move away

---

[23] *MACC.* 5 March 1968 and 3 February 1970.

[24] For T. Maizel of the Bund, Jewish life continued to be focused on the Diaspora, especially in education. Nevertheless, after the Six-Day War, he understood that education had become an instrument of support for Israel. This belief was reinforced by the Kehila leadership, which considered that the youth response to the Six-Day War should be seen as part of the achievements of Jewish education. *MAKA*, 19 June and 10 July 1967.

from religion as the only focus of identity and to stress Israeli statehood as a complement of ethnicity.

Finally, the educational sphere would especially reflect Israel's rising profile as well as the redefinition of spaces for its expression. This sphere would be of increasing importance, notwithstanding the fact that the schools rejected the notion of inviting the youth movements into their framework immediately after the war.[25] Certainly, the impact of the 1967 hostilities brought to the fore a profound ambivalence regarding the place of the Diaspora in messages projected by the schools. As far as *aliyah* was concerned, they were focused around the old-new polemics regarding the affirmation or rejection of the *Golah* (Diaspora). Progressively, the State of Israel became active in different realms of educational life.[26] In order to coordinate educational efforts, the creation of a pedagogical center was recommended by the Zionist General Council in 1971, an idea which would not reach fruition before 1974.[27] From then on, Israel would strengthen its role as axis of joint educational efforts with regard to human resources as well as educational projects. This renewed function also responded to the continuing growth of the student body in Jewish schools after the war.[28]

Throughout this process of institutional change and redefinition, the Zionist Organization of Mexico was not able to achieve a proper equilibrium between autonomy and collaboration at the organizational level, precisely when it was most required. While ideologically Israel became a focus of identity for growing circles within the community, organized Zionism experienced profound misgivings regarding the challenge to join efforts with other organizations without giving up its own specificity. This may be seen in different attempts which, while offering organized Zionism the possibility of widening its range of action, brought to the fore its dilemma regarding the dilution of its function. Such was the case, among others, of the attempt to establish an Aliyah Committee formed by representatives of different institutions in the community, immediately after the

---

[25] *MAZF*, 8 September 1971. This was not the case of the Tarbut school, whose director N. Syrkin took on the role of supporting the activities of youth movements. The New Israelite School, under the direction of Mr. Blachinsky, also took a positive attitude. Ezra Shabot, interview by author, 16 November 1994.

[26] MAKA during this period; also: *First Convention of Jewish Communities in Mexico, 1973 (passim)*.

[27] *MAZF*, 5 July 1972.

[28] In 1970, 4,400 pupils attended the six schools, while in 1973 the number reached 5,370. *First Convention of Jewish Communities*.

war. This experiment in collaboration between Zionist and other community leaders preceded other attempts both at the local and worldwide levels.[29]

It is essential to point out that there was another still side to these phenomena. As a result of the war, Israel also went through transformations which, in turn, modified how it related to the Diaspora. Looking at it from a wide perspective, after the Six-Day War, its ideological and political spectrum was redefined. Left and Right were gradually emptied of their ideological contents and would concentrate almost exclusively on topics such as the occupied territories and the Palestinian question.[30] This political trend would remove the subject of its links with the Diaspora from the center of the Israeli agenda. Thus, it reduced and weakened the Zionist dimension of the political parties in Israel and made them less relevant in the Diaspora precisely when the Six-Day War brought Israel to the center of the community's agenda.

An Interactional Axis: Source of Legitimacy

Since social and political life cannot develop without a system of acknowledgments and rationalizations, it becomes an arena of legitimization efforts. Individuals and groups must exchange symbolic goods, not only inside but outside the group as well. In this process, in which discourse has a central role to play, mutual recognition and legitimacy are shaped and nourished.[31]

While Israel's transformation as an organizational axis shed light on the community's changing institutional patterns, its changed image influenced its role as a source of legitimization for Mexican Jewry vis-à-vis society at large.

The short- and long-term alteration of Israel's image would confront the community with new tasks. The way in which they were undertaken expressed and defined some of the profound dilemmas that accompany the reconstruction of Mexican Jewish identity.

---

[29] A paradigmatic example of the latter would be the reorganization of the Jewish Agency that maintained a trend inaugurated by the war by bringing together Zionist and community leaders. Daniel Elazar, *People and Polity. The Organizational Dynamics of World Jewry* (Detroit, Mich.: Wayne State University Press, 1989), chapter 6.

[30] S. N. Eisenstadt, "Changes in Israel's Society Since the Yom Kippur War," paper presented at the colloquium "From War to Peace: 1973–1993," Jerusalem, Hebrew University of Jerusalem, 24 October 1993.

[31] Pierre Ansart, *Ideología, Conflictos y Poder* (México: Premia, 1983), 12–14.

Identities may be seen as fluent junctures at which the past, the present and the future coalesce in such a complex way that they never become fixed images. Identities are also defined by boundaries and interaction: both are crucial to ascription and self-ascription.[32]

With the war, an image of a triumphant Israel emerged; its accomplishments reinforced Jewish pride. The Jewish state became a source of self-respect and a compensatory factor for the historical image (reinforced by the Zionist diagnosis of Diaspora life) of weakness. Israel's accomplishments and triumphs became those of the Mexican Jewish community.[33]

Insofar as self-perception is nourished by the "other's" discourse, the way in which, generally speaking, the press covered the conflict was consonant with the community's perception of Israel's achievements.[34] The Mexican press was favorably disposed toward Israel.[35] In the main, Israel was depicted as displaying defensive behavior both before and during the war,[36] and second—in addition to Israel's technical and military proficiency—Israeli society and its army were seen as morally superior.[37]

With the unfolding of the conflict, the Mexican government's positive stance toward Israel seemed to reinforce the open and public identification of the Jewish community with Israel.[38] The community's comfortable

---

[32] Fredrik Barth, *Ethnic Groups and Boundaries (The Social Organization of Culture Difference)*, (Oslo: Universitetsforlaget, 1970).

[33] O. Gorodzinsky, interview by author, 28 October 1994; Ezra Shabot, interview by author, November 1994.

[34] Editorial "Report on U. Thant"; Ramón de Ertze Garamendi, "Danger of War"; and Miguel Guardia, "Victimizers or Victims?," *Excélsior*, 29 May 1967; Editorial, "The Development of the Crisis," *Excélsior*, 31 May 1967; "Russia and Palestine," *Excélsior*, 31 May 1967; Sergio Veraza, "Danger in the Middle East," *El Día*, 30 May 1967; Editorial, *El Día*, 22 June 1967; Octavio González Cárdenas, "Mexico and the Middle East," *Ovaciones*, 24 June 1967; José Alvarado, "Intentions and Chronicles. The Middle East: crisis in the UN," *Excélsior*, 8 June 1967; Editorial, *El Universal*, 30 May 1967.

[35] *MACC*, 4 July 1967.

[36] While we consulted various Mexican newspapers, we concentrated on *Excélsior*, a progressive journal that is a forum for diverse political opinions. This allowed us to discern changing patterns of public opinion throughout the period. Ramón de Ertze Garamendi, "Ten Against One"; and Pedro Gringoire, "Israel Fights for its Existence Three Times in 19 Years," *Excélsior*, 6 June 1967; Raúl Carrancá y Trujillo, "Johnson's Five Points," *Excélsior*, 24 June 1967.

[37] Ricardo Garibay, "Israel: Fiction and Reality," *Excélsior*, 9 June 1967; Arturo García Formenti, "Arabs and Jews," *El Universal*, 24 June 1967.

[38] The government manifested its interest in finding solutions for a conflict that equally threatened two cultures and two peoples who had greatly contributed to human development. *Excélsior*, 6 June 1967.

feelings during 1967 were obvious as they requested President Gustavo Díaz Ordaz to mediate in the conflict. Thus, the war provided the Jewish community an unequaled opportunity for expressing its identification with Israel openly.

However, already during the war, some parts of the Mexican press expressed certain negative themes that would become reinforced in the coming years. Among these were prejudices related to Jewish economic power.[39] Besides, while throughout the conflict criticism against the Arab world was focused on its leadership—its self-interest, its ambitions, its errors[40]—as distinct from their people's behavior, Israel was perceived as a monolithic entity. This tended to promote the exoneration of the Arab people as the prisoner of the mistakes of its leaders, on the one hand, and the condemnation of Israel in undifferentiated terms, on the other. Similarly, Israel was perceived as a persevering, dynamic, modern, and Western country, while the Arab world was characterized by social gaps, traditionalism, and resistance to change. Eventually, due to Mexico's alignment with the Third World, this dichotomy would have a negative impact on Israel's image.[41] Whereas Mexico would not join the Non-Aligned Movement, its foreign policy, especially during the term of office of Luis Echeverría Alvarez (1970–1976), tended to support a degree of opposition to the Western world and support for what was considered then part of the socialist bloc.

The growing complexity of the Palestinian question would play a central role in this process. Black September (1970) was a turning point. Solidarity with the Palestinians became intertwined with anti-imperialist discourse that justified terrorism as a legitimate means of expression.[42] As highlighted in the writings of Jorge García Granados, in the past this had benefited the Zionists[43]; in the 1970s, however, it worked in favor of the

---

[39] Prejudice was evident in some of the commentary, along with pointing out the interest of the super-powers in the zone. Thus: "the Israelis do not need any help since they receive enormous amounts of money from Jews all over the world...," Editorial, "Crisis in the Middle East," *Excélsior*, 20 May 1967. Another argument stressed that U.S. support for Israel resulted from the strength of the "Jewish vote" in that country. Armando Camacho, "Mexicans Point of View," *Excélsior*, 24 May 1967.

[40] *Excélsior*, 1 and 2 June 1967.

[41] Editorial "Mao in Egypt," *Excélsior*, 24 May 1967; Cartoons by Abel Quezada, *Excélsior*, 27 and 31 May 1967.

[42] Froylan Lopez Narvaez, "Palestinians and Others. Battles of Today," *Excélsior*, 9 September 1970.

[43] Jorge García Granados, *The Birth of Israel* (New York: Alfred A. Knopf, 1949).

Palestinians. Progressively, the concept of guerrilla would substitute that of terrorism, as opposed to that of Zionism.[44] This new situation was congruent with a worldwide tendency developed during this period.[45]

The change in Israel's international position and its newly emerging negative image were built up in the Mexican press during the seventies. The questioning around Israel and Zionism gradually focused on the division between "good" and "bad" Jews, between the anti-Fascists of the pre-state period and the imperialists and militarists of the present.[46] Progressively, Israel's repositioning modified the meaning of the hero's role in history, which is always related to the binomial interaction strength/weakness, good/evil, etc. In other terms, within a short period of time, Israel went from hero to pariah.[47]

In fact, right after the Six-Day War there was a growing awareness of what was defined as the attempt to distort Israel's and Zionism's image. The 27th Zionist Congress of 1968 rejected the "antagonistic enemy's propaganda from the Arab camp, neo-Nazi groups and certain Communist movements."[48] At the same time, it denounced the differentiation between Zionism and Judaism as a criminal attempt aimed at promoting a negative public opinion of Israel while hiding anti-Jewish elements. Among other things, it was suggested that in its public-relations work, Israel try to restore its image as a seeker of peace, progress, and international cooperation, and of Zionism as a national liberation movement. For that purpose, Zionist institutions which were dealing with public opinion had to be strengthened, and training of activists in public relations had to be developed. The push to update Israel's public relations was aimed at reaching Jewish youth.[49]

The resolutions of the Zionist General Council of June–July 1971 continued this strategy and added new ones. It reiterated the need of Zionist Federations to strengthen the existing information committees or,

---

[44] Jacobo Mondlack and Hamdi Abouzeid, Ambassador of Egypt, Letters to the Editor, *Excélsior*, 21 September 1972.
[45] Robert Wistrich, ed., *Anti-Zionism and Antisemitism in the Contemporary World* (London: MacMillan, 1990).
[46] Fernando Carmona Nenclares, "Nasser. The Arab Heart Passed Away," *Excelsior*, 29 September 1970.
[47] See, for example, Irving Louis Horowitz, "From Pariah People to Pariah Nation: Jews, Israelis and the Third World," in *Israel in the Third World*, eds. Michael Curtis and Susan A. Gitelson (New Brunswick, N.J.: 1976), 361–91.
[48] *The 27th Zionist Congress*, 506–507.
[49] Ibid.

if needed, to create new ones, and stressed the need to cooperate with other communal institutions. This time, however, the focus of attention was also directed to the need to work with international non-official institutions and with students and intellectuals, Jews and non-Jews alike. Based on the awareness of the possibility that through the campaign against Israel the whole of the Jewish people was also under attack, other institutions within the Jewish world joined efforts to counteract the anti-Zionist propaganda.[50]

Within the Mexican Jewish community there was a growing concern that the change in Israel's image could affect its own and would have a negative impact on Jewish life in Mexico.[51] Therefore, the need to engage in the building up of Israel's image became not only a constant demand from Zionist central authorities but a common pressing concern.

However, confronted with this new task, the Mexican Jewish community was unable to fulfill its role either ideologically or organizationally. Paralysis as well as confusion characterized its lack of response. It failed to create the appropriate institutional tools and to develop a discourse oriented to satisfy the community's inner needs and to transcend its boundaries. This condition implied serious risks regarding the realm of legitimacy.

Even though communal institutions were conscious of the need to modify the existing dialogical structures,[52] the task was never successfully undertaken. With respect to Israel's persistent calls for a more active stand that was expected to act as a countervailing power, the recurrent answer coming from the local Zionist movement was that unless funds and guidelines were provided, there was no alternative but inaction.[53]

Unable to carry out this task alone, and following the suggestions from the central authorities, the Zionist Federation sought cooperation with other institutions. Together with the Central Committee it agreed on the need to act jointly to counteract the growing impact of damaging propaganda. Once again, the discourse emphasized Israel's need to provide the appropriate economic support for this purpose. After a long and difficult process of negotiation, both institutions decided on the publication of a bulletin, *Forum,* first printed in December 1974. In April 1975 sugges-

---

[50] *Resolutions of the World Jewish Congress,* January 1970, AKA.
[51] *MACC,* 19 September 1972.
[52] See, for example, *MACC,* 29 April 1969; 15 July 1969; 27 August 1970.
[53] See, for example, *MAZF,* August–September 1970; *MACC,* 8 and 15 June 1971.

tions were made for improving its quality as well as to involve the Israeli Embassy and the Institute of Mexican-Israeli Cultural Relations in order to widen its reach.[54] Only five issues were published. Surely, this brief effort was neither sufficient to counteract anti-Zionist propaganda, nor capable of transcending the boundaries of the Jewish community itself.

Time and again, the idea to create a public relations office remained only a blueprint.[55] The idea was broached again in May 1975, and it was agreed that the project would be financed by the Central Committee, the Zionist Federation, and the Israeli Embassy, but nothing came of it.[56]

The slow pace and unclear nature of the community's response led Israel to become the main force behind the public relations task. This was evident in the Diaspora Convention held in Jerusalem, on April 1974.[57] The World Zionist Organization was forced to play an increasingly active role in this function.[58] However, its recommendations regarding political strategy derived from its own perception and assessment of the conditions prevailing in Latin America, which did not necessarily correspond to reality.[59]

The overall lack of success in this sphere may be measured by the internal as well as external impact of propaganda work. The community was incapable of providing valid arguments and resources to be consumed by those sectors that were directly exposed to the questioning of Israeli legitimacy, as was the case with Jewish intellectuals and university students.[60]

---

[54] *MAZF*, 9 April 1975.
[55] *MAZF*, August–September 1970. *First Convention of Jewish Communities in Mexico, 1973.*
[56] *MAZF*, 21 and 28 May 1975.
[57] *Report of the Diaspora Convention*, Jerusalem, April 1974, *AZF*.
[58] Thus, for example, Israel asked for a list of non-Jewish intellectuals to whom informational material could be sent. *AZF*, 16 January 1974. The Latin American Section of the Organization and Information Department sent information about Arab activities on the Continent. 13 February 1974, 27 March 1974, *AZF*.
[59] See, for example, Isaac Goldenberg, Herzl Inbal, and Abraham Argov, *Report on Latin America*, *AZF*, Jerusalem 1975. This evaluation, by overemphasizing economic motivations for anti-Zionist attitudes and downplaying its political dimension, could not provide an adequate strategy to face the problem.
[60] Mexican universities were the main sphere of action for the Mexican Left, which was divided vis-à-vis the war. A minority, despite their identification with the Socialist world, expressed support for Israel. Many others perceived the conflict as an escape valve for super-power rivalries and tried to maintain balanced arguments. The majority saw Israel as an alien state in the region and defined the war as a conquest, with echoes of colonialism. See, among others, Francisco López Cámara, "The Middle East War and the Political Technocracy," *El Día*, 12 June 1967; idem, "The Middle East: neither conquests nor genocide," *El Día*, 27 June 1967; Leopoldo Zea, "The Middle East and the Cold War," *Novedades*, 27

Notwithstanding the fact that after 1967 the topic of youth was at the forefront of the community's agenda, the scope of efforts in this regard did not extend to non-Jewish society.

Public opinion was not influenced; links were not established with political and social organisms; proper channels of interaction and communication were never developed. This inability to create spaces of convergence with other social sectors that could act as allies to counteract the effects of the delegitimation of Zionism and its negative impact on Jewish identity had its utmost expression in 1975, when Mexico voted in favor of the U.N. resolution equating Zionism with racism.

Therefore, a complex set of interrelated questions emerge: was the loss of legitimacy of Israel and, consequently, of the Jewish linkage with it, related to the failure in information management? Was the Mexican Jewish community's negligence in developing appropriate institutional tools and in developing a discourse for inner and external purposes a consequence of its leadership's errors, or was it due to a more substantive lack of ideological resources? Finally, was this deficiency a product of the increasingly active role of the central authorities in Jerusalem that inhibited local action?

As the identification with Israel—the transition from the feeling of interdependence to that of unity—grew within the community, so did the inability to use both the private and the public spheres as realms for expressing a legitimate collective identity. The difficulty lay in the lack of public collective visibility for the Jewish community in Mexico.

The euphoria that accompanied identification with the State of Israel could not cross the threshold of Mexican society's expectation of national homogeneity as a *sine qua non* for national belonging. These external constraints regarding the public manifestation of national-cultural differences and the collective nature of Jewish life lie behind this situation. Confronted with the complexity of this situation, the case might be made that it was easier for the community's leadership to blame other causes for the paralysis rather than to recognize this fact.

In the final analysis, the community's legitimacy depended heavily on the conditions set by the society at large. The conception of Mexican national identity, defined as a terrain where diversity is seen as a challenge to national integration, made the acceptance of otherness difficult.[61] The

---

June 1967; Froylan Lopez Narvaez, "Palestinians and Others. Battles of Today," *Excélsior*, 9 September 1970.

[61] Judit Bokser-Liwerant, *Jewish National Movement*.

Jewish collective condition as an enclave within the national society was especially difficult. The public sphere never came to be an adequate space for the Jewish community to manifest its collective identity. The inability to modify the discourse of the public sphere reduced the community's ability to bring to the public realm subjects or values such as collective identity or autonomy, which could have acted as ulterior sources of legitimacy.

The events of 1967, then, modified the internal structure of Zionism and Jewish life in Mexico, and of its links with the State of Israel, but it did not modify the patterns of interaction between the Jewish community and Mexican society. One is tempted to ask if indeed those events could have had a more significant impact on the conflicting understanding of individuality, community, and public identity.

The answer has to do not only with volition and social action but also with historical structures. Surely, the war did not help to minimize the polar tensions that articulate the collective identity of the Mexican Jewish community. Therefore, this problem may also be approached in terms of the difficulties inherent in building the links between claims concerning individuality and arguments concerning the value of community.

It is evident that the formulation of this question requires a different spatial, temporal, and circumstantial perspective, largely unavailable to the participants themselves, for whom the possibility of a question such as this was limited by the contextual constraints. Nevertheless, its omission was of enormous consequence.

CONSOLIDATING THE CONSOLIDATED: THE IMPACT OF THE SIX-DAY WAR ON SOUTH AFRICAN JEWRY

Milton Shain
University of Capetown

GAUGING THE IMPACT of the Six-Day War on South African Jewry necessitates an appreciation of the importance of Zionism in South African Jewish life long before the stunning military victories of the Israeli Defense Forces in June 1967. It also demands a sensitivity both to the effect of the Holocaust on South African Jewish consciousness and the subsequent popular associations of the Holocaust with the rebirth of the State of Israel. That is to say, Zionism and the Holocaust have for some time comprised vital components of a national mode of identity, a civil religion informed at least in part by notions of destruction and rebirth. Such associations were enhanced at the time of the Six-Day War.

Zionism has deep roots in the community, going back to the establishment of the South African Zionist Federation (SAZF) in 1898—the first countrywide Jewish organization. Gideon Shimoni attributes the organization's importance to a number of factors: the community's "Litvak legacy,"[1] the peculiar nature of South African pluralism; support from the South African state; and the absence of opposition from acculturated Jews (the Reform movement was not officially established in South Africa until 1933).[2] Added to these factors was the vulnerability felt by Jews—and whites generally—at the tip of Africa with the onset of postwar decolonization across the continent. The potential for instability was ever present, and thus, Israel assumed the status of a lifeline, a place of refuge in the event of turmoil.

Zionist sentiment, however, was not simply a product of expediency. It was firmly based in the South African Jewish experience. Limited opposi-

---

[1] "Litvaks" are Jews who came from Lithuania and Belarus. A very large proportion of Jews who immigrated to South Africa were Litvaks.
[2] Gideon Shimoni, *Jews and Zionism. The South African Experience 1910–1967* (Oxford: Oxford University Press, 1980), 180.

tion from the oldest synagogue—the Anglo-dominated Cape Town Hebrew Congregation—evaporated with the Balfour Declaration in 1917, as did left-wing antagonism with the embourgeoisement of South African Jews in the course of the twentieth century.[3] By the 1930s, a deepened Zionist consciousness had evolved against a backdrop of growing anti-Semitism and hostility toward the influx of Jewish immigrants, including German-Jewish refugees.[4] Two visits by Ze'ev Jabotinsky, the first in 1935 and the second in 1937, ensured vibrant Zionist debate and lively involvement with the Yishuv (the Jewish community in Palestine). By the late 1930s, three Zionist youth movements—Betar, Bnei Akiva, and Habonim —had been established. According to Shimoni, these movements had "a profound effect on the Jewish community of South Africa," deepening both Jewish awareness and commitment to Zionist ideology, as well as educating toward *aliyah*.[5]

Jewish awareness became heightened during the war years, when South African radical rightists questioned the Jewish presence in South Africa and opposed the war with Hitler.[6] As news of the destruction of European Jewry spread, Jewish consciousness and support of Zionism grew even stronger.[7] South African Jewry offered unflagging support for the Yishuv in its struggle against the British, despite the fact that South Africa was part of the British Commonwealth. Not even the anti-British activities of the Irgun dampened the community's support, although the Jewish press did make it clear that it found some of the Irgun's actions unacceptable.[8] Apart from those on the extreme Left, virtually all South African Jews supported the Zionist enterprise. "In the two years preceding the creation of the State of Israel," writes Shimoni, "Zionism in South Africa reached the peak of its

---

[3] For the Jewish Left which challenged Zionism see Evangelos Mantzaris, *Labour Struggles in South Africa: The Forgotten Pages 1903–1921* (Durban: Collective Resources Publications, 1995).

[4] See Edna Bradlow, "Immigration into the Union, 1910–1948: Policies and Attitudes" (unpubl. Ph.D. diss., University of Cape Town); Shimoni, *Jews and Zionism*, ch. 6, passim.

[5] Shimoni, *Jews and Zionism*, 261–62.

[6] See Patrick J. Furlong, *Between Crown and Swastika: The Impact of the Radical Right on the Afrikaner Nationalist Movement in the Fascist Era* (Johannesburg: University of Witwatersrand Press, 1991)

[7] See Michael A. Green, "South African Jewish Responses to the Holocaust, 1941–1948" (unpubl. M.A. thesis, University of South Africa, 1987).

[8] See Lauren Singer, "The South African Jewish Press and the Problem of Palestine 1945–1948" (unpubl. paper, Department of History, University of Cape Town).

hegemony over the life of the Jewish community."[9] Prime Minister Jan Smuts's *de facto* recognition of the State of Israel two days before his election defeat in May 1948, followed by formal recognition a year later under the newly elected National Party, further ensured a comfortable environment within which Zionist activity could flourish. Almost 800 South African Jews joined the Mahal army volunteers during Israel's War of Independence, and of these, about 300 remained in Israel.[10] In addition, substantial numbers of South African Jews answered the Zionist imperative and made *aliyah*.[11] In July 1949, Israel opened a diplomatic mission in South Africa, although it was not until 1972 that South Africa reciprocated with full diplomatic relations.

By the time Israel was established, most South African Jews recognized its centrality for the Jewish people. Moreover, the European catastrophe was linked with the Jewish nation's rebirth. Thus in 1952, the South African Jewish Board of Deputies (hereafter referred to as the Board) established an official date for commemorating both the Holocaust and the casualties of Israel's War of Independence.[12] Survivors of the European tragedy wanted to ensure that future generations appreciated these connections and, most importantly, the enormity of the "war against the Jews." To this end, the task of education was taken up by She'erit Hapletah, a survivors' group. At its height, the organization numbered more than 200 members. Its efforts were complemented by those of the Jewish establishment, which was disturbed that the anguish of the older generation appeared not to be shared by South Africa's Jewish youth. It was deemed essential that young Jews "come to realize what these years meant to Jewish destiny and what the Jewish people owe to the Jewish resistance."[13]

Indifference on the part of youth was considered to be the fault of the older generation that was disinclined at first to dwell on the horrors of Nazism. To correct this situation, South Africa's network of Jewish day

---

[9] Shimoni, *Jews and Zionism*, 197.
[10] Lionel Hodes, "South African Volunteers in the War of Liberation," *Jewish Affairs*, May/June 1988.
[11] Carol Novits, "60 Years of Aliyah," *Jewish Affairs*, July/August 1990.
[12] South African Jewry was to hold official services on 22 April 1952 and Jewish organizations were requested not to arrange any functions on that date so that there would be mass participation in the official functions throughout the country. The later date was appointed by the first Israeli Knesset in preference to 19 April, the official date of the Warsaw Ghetto Uprising, so that the official commemoration would never fall in the Passover period.
[13] "Children's Lessons for a Day of Mourning," *Jewish Affairs*, March 1955, 55–57.

schools—established in the postwar period—incorporated the study of the Holocaust in its curricula. Using simple language and without putting too much emphasis on the horrible details of the Holocaust, teachers told children the truth about the Nazi plans for extermination, the execution of these plans, and Jewish resistance. The courage and heroism of the Jewish resistance were in turn linked to the establishment of the State of Israel.

Holocaust education in the schools was complemented by a "national traditional" curriculum. Ronnie Mink notes the rationale for this curriculum: "The Jewish child needed not only to be fortified by a religious tradition, but had also to be made fully conscious of the renaissance of Jewish national life, which had culminated in the State of Israel."[14] Part of the educational process included, albeit for relatively few, an intensive Hebrew *ulpan* or other Israeli experience. These educational initiatives appear to have been successful. By the mid-1950s, Jewish youth were conspicuous at commemorative services, and in 1960 a special memorial service was arranged jointly by the Board's youth department and the Zionist Youth Council of Johannesburg.

Throughout the 1950s, Zionist organizations played a central role in South African Jewish life—"considered the most Israel-centered in the English-speaking world."[15] This was evident in communal activities sponsored by general Jewish organizations, the Jewish youth movements, and most importantly, the Jewish day schools. South African Jews not only followed events in the fledgling state with great concern, interest, and pride, they also made their own substantial contribution in the form of funds that were from both wealthy and poor Jews. According to Shimoni, each fund-raising campaign in the 1950s attracted an average of 20,000 Jewish contributions—one-fifth of the Jewish population.[15] Zionist politics were also vibrant and often stormy.[17] At the height of the Suez crisis in 1956, the community's concerns resulted in the SAZF's launching its biennial Israel United Appeal (IUA) campaign four months ahead of schedule.[18]

---

[14] Ronnie Mink, "Education," in *South African Jewry. A Contemporary Survey*, ed. Marcus Arkin (Cape Town: Oxford University Press, 1984), 119.
[15] Moshe Davis, ed., *The Yom Kippur War. Israel and the Jewish People* (Jerusalem: Institute of Contemporary Jewry, The Hebrew University of Jerusalem, 1974), 155.
[16] Shimoni, *Jews and Zionism*, 239.
[17] See ibid., ch. 8, passim.
[18] *Jewish Affairs*, December 1956, 4.

During these years, the ruling National Party, although favoring an Arab-oriented policy, maintained cordial relations with Israel. Government leaders were therefore shocked when Israel joined an anti-apartheid vote at the United Nations in 1961. In retaliation, the government decided no longer to allow the continuous direct transfer of fund from the IUA to the Jewish Agency in Israel: applications now had to be made for each individual transfer and a cap was set on the amount that could be sent in any given year. This marked the first rupture in relations between South Africa and Israel and the first occasion on which questions of Jewish loyalty were raised. The somewhat strained relations between the two countries were evident in March 1963, when Israel did not participate in South Africa's premier trade fair. In September of that year, the Israeli minister plenipotentiary, Simcha Pratt, was recalled from South Africa, although the Israeli delegation remained.

Notwithstanding substantial discomfort, very few Jews distanced themselves from the Jewish state. IUA fund-raising continued energetically, with solid support from the majority of contributors. To the extent that there was a falloff in contributions (from 20,000 contributors in the 1950s to 17,000 in 1963 and 12,600 in 1966[19]) this was offset by increased support for the United Communal Fund, which was used for local needs.[20] The 1963 Zionist conference in Johannesburg reaffirmed "the bonds of history, religion and culture between all Jews and Israel, and the determination of South African Jewry to continue its participation in the unparalleled historic process that is taking place in the land of Israel."[21]

By the following year, campaigns were continuing as before, with increased totals in the IUA and the Women's Zionist campaign. Funds in excess of transfer permits were banked against future commitments.[22] Zionist activity was once again on an even keel, and at its twenty-ninth biennial conference, the SAZF agreed to reappraise efforts at mobilizing the full Zionist potential of South African Jewry.[23] This translated into an

---

[19] Shimoni, *Jews and Zionism*, 239.
[20] Edgar Bernstein, "South African Jewry," in *American Jewish Year Book 1964* (New York: American Jewish Committee; and Philadelphia: Jewish Publication Society, 1964), 342.
[21] Ibid., 345.
[22] Edgar Bernstein, "South African Jewry," in *American Jewish Year Book 1965*, 493.
[23] Edgar Bernstein, "South African Jewry," in *American Jewish Year Book 1966*, 455.

increased number of fund-raising campaigns in 1965, and in the annual rallies held in honor of Israel Independence Day (Yom Ha'atzmaut).[24]

The War

With tensions mounting in the Middle East in the spring of 1967, huge crowds attended celebrations of Israel's nineteenth birthday in Cape Town and Johannesburg. By May, offers of assistance—even from people not previously involved in communal work—began to arrive at the offices of the SAZF and the Board. The IUA launched an Israel Emergency Campaign at the end of the month, and it was agreed that for the entire month of June all other financial campaigns would be put on hold. Institutions were asked to contribute block amounts in addition to those contributions made by individuals. Besides raising funds, the SAZF put together a program for those wishing to volunteer six months of non-combatant service in Israel. The volunteers would replace mobilized soldiers in the towns and kibbutzim, helping to gather the harvest and maintain industries and vital civilian transport and medical services.

Some 1800 individuals applied for the program, with an initial contingent of 782 volunteers setting out two days before the outbreak of the war. At this point, the Jewish Agency informed the SAZF that there was no need for any more volunteers. In relative terms, the South African group was the largest of any Diaspora Jewish community. Among the volunteers were nearly 100 university students who were sacrificing an academic year for the Jewish cause.[25]

South African Jewry also led in the realm of fund-raising. Within weeks, 20,000,000 rand (at that time the equivalent of more than $27,000,000) had been collected from some 25,000 contributors.[26] Israel's Magen David Adom made an arrangement with the South African Blood Transfusion Services to have blood plasma sent to Israel on condition that the South African Jewish community would rapidly replace it. The response was enormous.

With the outbreak of war, "a wave of public sympathy for Israel swept over South Africa."[27] Jews were glued to their radios, awaiting news bulletins at every opportunity. All Hebrew congregations were requested to

---

[24] Edgar Bernstein, "South African Jewry," in *American Jewish Year Book 1967*, 458.
[25] See Shimoni, *Jews and Zionism*, 353.
[26] Ibid., 239.
[27] Ibid., 352; *SA Jewish Times*, 9 June 1967.

hold special prayer services—the first one taking place at Temple Israel in Johannesburg two days after the outbreak of the war. Huge crowds heard Rabbi A. S. Super announce that Israeli forces had taken Jerusalem's Old City and that the chief chaplain of the Israeli army, Rabbi General Shlomo Goren, had sounded the shofar at the Wailing Wall. "In kinship with our brethren in Israel," exhorted Rabbi Super, "it is proper that we start this service today with the blowing of the shofar." These were electrifying moments—and indeed days—for South African Jewry, who flocked to thanksgiving services throughout the country.[28] In Cape Town alone, twenty-six hugely attended services were held simultaneously.[29]

Although South African government policy was formally neutral, many non-Jews made contributions to the SAZF's fund-raising effort. More importantly, the government responded sympathetically to a joint Board and SAZF delegation which requested special permission to transfer appeal proceeds to Israel. This was agreed to, on condition that the funds would be "used by charitable non-governmental organizations in Israel solely for humanitarian purposes." The government, in short, gave no blank check; it was made clear that the amount sent out of the country would "from time to time be determined in the light of South Africa's economic position and interests.[30]

"Israel's Fight for Peace," as an editorial in the Board's journal, *Jewish Affairs*, put it, had rallied world Jewry as never before. Jews realized, the editorial continued, "that the Arab threat to Israel was in fact a challenge to the right of Jews everywhere to exist as free men." Notwithstanding its melodramatic tone, the editorial was correct in its assessment that the war had been perceived by Jews worldwide in apocalyptic terms. It had conjured images of destruction that, for South African Jews at least, had resonated powerfully; they shared with world Jewry a sense of cataclysm.[31]

Hardly a Jew remained uninvolved in the war. Fund-raising activities were extensively publicized and lavishly illustrated by photographs in the popular press. The war, moreover, forged new bonds of understanding

---

[28] Edgar Bernstein, "South African Jewry's Solidarity With Israel," *Jewish Affairs*, June 1967.
[29] *SA Jewish Times*, 9 June 1967.
[30] Edgar Bernstein, "South African Jewry," *American Jewish Year Book 1968*, 533–34. The official transfer conditions were that R1,000,000 was able to be transferred immediately; R1,000,000 in each of the following five years; and the balance in non-resident governmental bonds of R2,000,000 per year which could be sold overseas and the money transferred to Israel.
[31] "South Africa's Response," *Jewish Affairs*, June 1967, 6.

between Jews and non-Jews and eroded the tensions surrounding Israel's participation in anti-apartheid actions at the United Nations. The obvious sympathy of the white population in general also ended any lingering bitterness of the memories of the 1930s and early 1940s when, as noted, the Jews had faced substantial hostility from the radical Right. The South African government's gesture to facilitate the transfer of funds was viewed as a particularly hopeful sign that "a new chapter [would] be opened in relations between Israel and South Africa."[32]

In the Wake of War

As previously discussed, the massive involvement of South African Jews with Israel had its beginnings long before the Six-Day War. South African Jews had always supported the Zionist enterprise; they needed no prodding. The war, however, did consolidate and confirm the centrality of Israel for the community, as it did the memories and lessons of the Holocaust that had been carefully nurtured over the previous two decades. But community leaders took the matter even further, appropriating the war for their own purposes. The editor of *Jewish Affairs* was quite explicit:

> We believe that the concern over Israel's fate was more than a concern for the safety and well-being of the 2½ million Jews living within the borders of the State. In the last resort it was an affirmation of Jewish identity, of Jewish loyalty. The task facing us is therefore to make explicit the connection between these pro-Israel feelings and the, as yet, implicit concern for the maintenance and strengthening of Jewish life everywhere....[33]

In other words, echoes of the Holocaust and the existential fears aroused by the Arab threat to Israel were also to be used for boosting Jewish concerns within South Africa. Jewish educators were easily able to build on the sentiment generated by the victory—as indeed were other socializing agencies, including the Jewish youth movements.

Another outcome of the war was an enhanced sense of Jewish self-confidence. This became evident four months after the cessation of hostilities, when another crisis in South African-Israeli relations broke. The occasion was an anti-apartheid statement by Israeli delegate Joel Barromi at a United Nations debate in October 1967, at which he called for concerted action against South Africa. Coming so soon after the South African gov-

---

[32] Ibid.
[33] "Israel's Crisis—and Ourselves," *Jewish Affairs,* July 1967, 4.

ernment had rallied to Israel's cause, Barromi's comments were denounced by the media as a slap in the face.[34] Many South African Jews were also angered and they looked to a response from the chairman of the Board of Deputies, Maurice Porter.

Porter's statement expressed disappointment in Barromi's comments, especially in light of the South African government's conduct during the Six-Day War. The difference between the South African government and Israel, he suggested, would need to be settled by the respective administrations:

> As citizens of the Republic, we sincerely hope and trust that the relations between the two countries will improve. Even if differences of viewpoint may not entirely disappear, we believe that the traditional friendship between the two countries rests on solid foundations.[35]

Porter's response did not entirely satisfy those who had hoped for a more forthright rejection of Israel's behavior. The question remained, where did South African Jewish loyalty ultimately lie—Israel or the Republic? In response to charges of dual loyalty, the Jewish press reflected a new-found confidence. It rebutted the accusation, noting that Jews had repeatedly proved their loyalty in both war and peace; thus, hostile accusations could not untie the close connection between South African Jews and Israel.[36] Such confidence was again evident when Porter addressed the Board's biennial congress in November 1967:

> The religious, historical and cultural bonds which bind us to Israel do not in any way impair or weaken our unqualified loyalty to the Republic of South Africa. I am indeed sorry to see that the bogey of "Jewish loyalties" has again been discussed by some people. These bonds with Israel are independent of the policies of whatever particular group or party may be in power in Israel at a given time. In any event, the government and people of Israel alone determine the policies of their land, over which the Jews of the Diaspora cannot have any say.

The Board unanimously adopted a resolution echoing the hope that current difficulties between Israel and South Africa would disappear. The resolution recorded appreciation for the goodwill shown to Israel by the government of South Africa, but also reaffirmed the bonds linking south

---

[34] Edgar Bernstein, "South African Jewry," *American Jewish Year Book 1968*, 535.
[35] Ibid., 536.
[36] Shimoni, *Jews and Zionism*, 354.

African Jewry with the Holy Land, and pledged the community's continued endeavors to give maximum legitimate support to Israel.[37]

The Six-Day War, it appeared, had dealt a final blow to the age-old stereotype of the obsequious Jew.[38]

The heightened enthusiasm and communal unity that came in the wake of the war could not be maintained indefinitely. Nonetheless, record contributions accrued to the 1969 campaign when former Prime Minister David Ben-Gurion and Major General Chaim Herzog launched the IUA campaign.[39] There was also very large attendance at Holocaust commemoration services from the late 1960[40]—in part a product of the feelings aroused during the Six-Day War. In the early 1970s, contributions declined as a result of a stock market collapse. Jewish fund-raisers were also increasingly pressured to provide for local needs, especially for the burgeoning Jewish day schools. The growth of these institutions was itself partly a result of the war, although their academic excellence and the introduction of "Christian national education" in state schools added to their attraction.

By the late 1960s, some 8,000 children were receiving a full-time Jewish education, with approximately 5,000 additional children in a part-time Jewish educational framework.[41] Significantly, the *ulpan* scheme, which involved a three-month study visit to Israel, had increased in appeal. Starting with twenty-three pupils in 1963, it increased to thirty-six in 1965, fifty-two in 1966, eighty in 1967, 120 in 1968, and 152 in 1969.[42] Although the gradient was steady, the increase after the Six-Day War was nonetheless noteworthy. Summer vacation camps sponsored by the various Zionist youth movements also attracted large numbers—some 7,000 youths, mostly teenagers—by 1970.[43] Finally, the Six-Day War stimulated *aliyah*. Whereas between 1960 and 1964 an annual average of 226 South African-born Jews moved to Israel, the figure increased to an

---

[37] Edgar Bernstein, "South African Jewry," *American Jewish Year Book 1968*, 535.

[38] For the evolution of the anti-Jewish stereotype, see Milton Shain, *The Roots of Antisemitism in South Africa*, (Charlottesville, Va.: University Press of Virginia, 1994).

[39] Edgar Bernstein, "South African Jewry," *American Jewish Year Book 1970*, 532.

[40] Edgar Bernstein, "South African Jewry," *American Jewish Year Book 1969*, 452.

[41] Edgar Bernstein, "South African Jewry," *American Jewish Year Book 1970*, 532–33

[42] Edgar Bernstein, "South African Jewry," *American Jewish Year Book 1969*, 583.

[43] Edgar Bernstein, "South African Jewry," *American Jewish Year Book 1971*, 455.

annual average of 293 between 1965 and 1969, and shot up to an average of 549 per year from 1970 to 1974.[44]

ZIONIST POLITICS

The war, of course, could not heal ideological rifts in the community, and divisions soon reappeared in Zionist activities. A decision of the Jewish Agency to terminate its allocations to local Zionist parties was criticized by SAZF leaders, who feared the prospect of fund-raising campaigns being injected into local communal politics.[45] The Board subsequently resisted plans by the Zionist Revisionist Organization (ZRO) to run a party fund-raising campaign.[46] Despite the cutback in Israeli funding, Zionist politics remained lively. The Zionist Revisionist Organization, for instance, benefited from the visit of Israeli opposition leader Menachem Begin in October 1971.

In the elections held that year in preparation for the World Zionist Congress, the ZRO garnered 36 percent of the vote, followed by the United Zionist Association (25 percent), Habonim Zionist Youth (16 percent); Mizrachi-Bnei Akiva (12 percent), and Labour Zionist (Poalei Zion, 11 percent). This represented a substantial shift in party alignments from the previous elections held in 1952.[47] The actual voting turnout was also lower in 1971—45 percent. This was not because of a lack of Zionist commitment (one in five Jews registered in the 1971 elections) but because the Jewish State was a *fait accompli*, and little useful purpose seemed to be served by accentuating Jewish divisions in South Africa.

Israel had thus become a defining feature of South African Jewish identity in the wake of the Six-Day War. Over time, moreover, the further crisis brought the South African government and Israel into closer cooperation. While some individuals expressed consternation at these emerging ties, the rapprochement did give a new sense of confidence to South African Jews. Back in 1969, Ben-Gurion had held talks with the government during a visit to South Africa, and there were indications at that time that South Africa's foreign policy was moving away from its pro-Arab orientation.[48]

---

[44] Sergio DellaPergola and Allie A. Dubb, "South African Jewry: A Socio-demographic Profile," *American Jewish Year Book 1988*, 59–140.
[45] Edgar Bernstein, "South African Jewry," *American Jewish Year Book 1969*, 452.
[46] Ibid.
[47] Edgar Bernstein, "South African Jewry," *American Jewish Year Book 1953*, 402.
[48] See Naomi Chazan, "The Fallacies of Pragmatism: Israeli Foreign Policy Toward South Africa," *African Affairs*, April 1983.

The emergent harmony was damaged by Israel's decision to give financial aid to the United Nations for the Organization of African Unity freedom fighters. Amid substantial tension, not to mention embarrassment, the Board and SAZF jointly condemned support "for terrorism from whatever source." South African Secretary of Finance Gerald Browne announced the suspension of fund transfers from South Africa to Israel, though Minister of Finance Nico Diederichs softened its effect by explaining in a radio broadcast that the government had decided on the action as a temporary measure pending clarification.[49] Under pressure from the Knesset, the Israeli government decided to reroute its donation to the office of the U.N. High Commissioner for Refugees in Geneva to be used for educational purposes among African refugees, and the South African government in turn lifted its suspension.

This episode failed to divert Israel and South Africa from establishing closer relations. In 1972, South Africa opened full diplomatic relations with Israel. During the 1973 Yom Kippur War, government leaders expressed sympathy for the Israeli position. One year later, Prime Minister B. J. Vorster visited Israel to cement ties. Thus began a close partnership between the two "pariah" states. While the makings of that relationship were complex and manifold, a turning point was clearly the Six-Day War. And for South African Jewry, the Six-Day War in essence consolidated its relations with the Jewish State. Unlike many other Diaspora communities, South African Jews needed no goading to appreciate the importance of the Jewish State for the Jewish people in general and for South African Jews in particular. The notion of *klal Yisrael* (Jewish solidarity) has always been powerful; and the centrality of Israel in that formulation had hardly ever been in doubt.

---

[49] Edgar Bernstein, "South African Jewry," *American Jewish Year Book 1972*, 587.

JEWS IN THE MUSLIM COUNTRIES DURING THE SIX-DAY WAR

Haim Saadoun
Open University, Tel Aviv
Haifa University

IN 1968, A YEAR AFTER THE SIX-DAY WAR, a session of the Study Circle on Diaspora Jewry—which convened regularly in the official residence of the President of Israel—was devoted to "Diaspora Jewry and Eretz Yisrael, June 1967." Among those participating was Charles Jordan, a director of the American Jewish Joint Distribution Committee ("Joint"). This was to be his last visit to Jerusalem; a short while later he was murdered in Prague under mysterious circumstances. It is no surprise that such a senior official of such an important Jewish organization was charged with the task of surveying the condition of the Jews in the Arab countries. Jordan's report to the seminar began:

> I have been asked to speak briefly about fact and fiction, for a check of reports that reach us from various sources, both through the press and directly, has shown that quite often there is no correlation between the facts on the ground and the information contained in the reports, which turn out, in truth, to be no more than rumors. These rumors are quite ghastly, but the facts are even more horrendous.[1]

Jordan made that statement on the basis of myriad reports that flowed to him at the Joint, from Jewish communities throughout the world. Fielding that information was no easy task. Even from a vantage point of thirty years, the historian still faces difficulties when attempting to place the events of 1967 in their proper perspective.

In this article, I shall describe the condition of the Jews in the Arab countries during the Six-Day War[2] and try to analyze the role of the war in the totality of events that accelerated the process that virtually put an end

---

[1] "Diaspora Jewry and Eretz Yisrael, Iyar–Sivan 5727 • June 1967" (in Hebrew) (Jerusalem: Study Circle on Diaspora Jewry in the Home of the President of Israel, Series 2, 1–2; 1968), 51 (hereafter, "Diaspora Jewry").

[2] The location of source materials for such an analysis is most difficult, for most

to Jewish presence in these countries. This will be done on three different levels. The first will deal with the Six-Day War and its significance for Jews in all Arab countries. On the second level we shall concentrate on North Africa, which in 1967 contained the largest Jewish communities in Muslim lands. Furthermore, North African Jewry was, physically, furthest removed from the core of the Arab-Israeli conflict, and can therefore provide a criterion for a comparative analysis of the measure of anxiety experienced by the various communities on the one hand, and of the actual blows they suffered, on the other hand. The moot question is, to what extent was the condition of the Jewish communities in the Arab countries a direct continuation of processes which they were undergoing prior to the war, or of new processes that were the direct outcome of the Six-Day War itself?

The third level will focus on one country—Tunisia. An in-depth study of conditions in a specific country can provide terms of reference for a comparison with what happened in other Arab lands. For several reasons, Tunisia provides an interesting case study. First of all, it was a western, secular and democratic state in which Jews could fairly easily maintain their Jewish way of life, almost without sensing any discrimination. Second, in Tunisia there was no traditional severe hatred of Jews; moreover, very few exceptional events had marred Jewish-Muslim relations within its borders. Last, Tunisia was in the vanguard of those states that broke away from the monolithic Arab policy on the Arab-Israeli conflict. Its remoteness from Palestine, the core of the conflict, enabled Tunisia to make appreciably more moderate statements on that issue. For all these reasons, the case of Tunisia can provide a yardstick to measure whether it was possible for Jews to exist in an independent Muslim country.

---

of them are still classified. There is interesting information available in contemporary Israeli and foreign newspapers and periodicals, especially the *American Jewish Year Book* (hereafter, *AJYB* and the relevant year). Most relevant archival sources are deposited in the Central Zionist Archives (CZA) in Jerusalem, in the record groups containing the files of the World Jewish Congress, those of the Zionist Executive, and the files whose provenance was the office of Nahum Goldmann. Very little of the research literature has dealt with this period, except for N. A. Stillman, *The Jews of Arab Lands in Modern Times* (Philadelphia and New York: 1991), 173–74, 550–51. See also M. M. Laskier, *North African Jewry in the Twentieth Century* (New York and London: 1994), 287–309. This is a most important survey of the development of Tunisian Jewry from Tunisian independence until 1967. For the condition of the Jews during the war see also R. De Felice, *Jews in an Arab Land: Libyan Jews between Colonialism, Arab Nationalism and Zionism (1838–1970)* (in Hebrew) (Tel Aviv: 1980), 307–14; M. M. Laskier, *The Jews of Egypt 1920–1970* (New York and London: 1992), 290–94. See also Bat-Yeor, *The Jews of Egypt* (in Hebrew) (Ramat Gan: 1974), 125–37.

Fear and Anxiety on the Eve of the Six-Day War

For almost a month the armies of Israel and its Arab neighbors deployed, preparing for war. Security conditions deteriorated and the likelihood of open hostilities increased—the Six-Day War was not to take anyone by surprise. During that month, fear for the very existence of Israel was widespread, spurred on by the joint threat of the Arab countries against the Jewish State. This sense of anxiety took different forms in the various Jewish communities throughout the world. On the basis of their reaction to the threat of Israel's annihilation, we may divide them into three groups. The first, of course, were the Israelis themselves, whose apprehension took on a physical and very tangible form, resulting from the threat of an all-out war to be launched against Israel by all Arab countries, and from the fact that many of them had been mobilized into the reserve units of the Israel Defense Forces. Furthermore, many Israelis had family members still living in the Arab countries, and the danger they faced added to the anxiety of their relatives in Israel.

The second group included Jewish communities in the Diaspora that faced no physical danger but exhibited a great sense of solidarity with threatened Israel, more than ever in the past. Thus, for example, the French Jewish monthly *L'Arche* came out with a special issue in June 1967 whose front cover proclaimed "Israel Vivre!" while another French Jewish periodical, *L'Information Juive*, warned that "Israel is Endangered." Such headlines contributed to an atmosphere of anxiety and insecurity among Diaspora Jewish communities. André Neher, a leading French Jewish intellectual, described at the sessions of the Study Circle the fear that prevailed among the Jews of France. When the Middle East crisis erupted, he said, French Jewry underwent "a deep shock, dread that touched their very souls, a crisis which led to their identifying with Israel."[3] He then went on to describe the efforts of the French Jewish community, which reflected both fear and solidarity. Among these was the convening of an assembly, attended by representatives from all over France, "whose atmosphere was reminiscent of the great historic 'covenants' that the People of Israel made with itself as a nation...an outburst of popular mysticism...fund raising ...silent marches and parades through public streets and squares."[4] We

---

[3] "Diaspora Jewry," 31.
[4] Ibid. See also Sh. Di-Nur, "The 'Six Days' of French Jewry" (in Hebrew), *Bitefutzot Ha-Golah* 10, nos. 1–2 (Summer 1968): 116–24.

have dwelt at some length on the fear that gripped French Jews, for many of them still had relatives in North Africa, making their anxiety more tangible.

In the third group, the subject of this article, were the Jews living in Arab countries, over whom hung a threat of physical danger, since they were, in effect, hostages. The press of their home countries was full of news items and background stories on the tension between Israel and its Arab neighbors, on the forthcoming hostilities and on the Arab victory that was sure to come.[5] For two reasons, these Jews could not give expression to their anxiety on the eve of the Six-Day War. There were no Jewish periodicals in these countries, in whose pages they could give vent to their emotions; this state of affairs renders moot the question whether the authorities would have allowed such descriptions to have been published[6]; and Jews in the Muslim countries did not have direct mail or telephone contact with Israel. Whatever information was available was transferred through various channels in Europe and the United States.

One can attempt to ascertain the extent of the anxiety that gripped the Jews living in Arab countries by using two measures or sources of information: the testimony of Israeli emissaries in these countries and of representatives of international Jewish organizations; and the extent of *aliyah* (immigration to Israel) in the period immediately preceding the war or in its wake. This latter is a rather problematic yardstick, for the authorities did not always allow the Jews to emigrate freely. We should also bear in mind that the number of immigrants after the war reflects to no small degree the reaction of the Jews to the Six-Day War rather than the extent of their anxiety.

The condition of the Jews varied from state to state, depending upon factors such as the size of the Jewish community, how the authorities tended to relate to their Jewish citizens, and the extent to which each country was influenced by the Arab-Israeli conflict. On the eve of the war, the situa-

---

[5] See, e.g., items from the Arab press collected in *Daily Digest of Middle Eastern Press* (in Hebrew), prepared by the Intelligence Corps of the IDF (hereafter, *Daily Digest*).

[6] The last Jewish periodical to appear in Tunisia was *al-Nejama (L'Étoile)* which ceased publication in 1961. No Jewish paper was published in Algeria after 1962. *L'Information Juive*, the organ of Algerian Jews in France, was edited in Paris, not in Algeria. In Morocco, *La Voix des Communautés* continued to appear until 1963. The disappearance of a Jewish press in these countries dealt a significant blow to Jewish political life; in effect it put an end to independent "Jewish politics" in the new states of North Africa. It is therefore difficult to ascertain the extent of Jewish anxiety and apprehension at this time, and the reaction of the Jewish communities to the events of May–June 1967.

tion of Turkish Jews, for example, was quite comfortable. There had been a great wave of emigration to Israel in the years immediately after the establishment of the Jewish state, and Turkey's Jewish citizens were allowed to maintain contact with Israel. In Syria Jews lived under extremely harsh restrictions. They were not allowed to emigrate and any contact with Israel or other Jewish communities abroad was strictly forbidden. They lived in a Jewish ghetto under the strictest supervision of the authorities and had to bear identification cards in which their nationality *(Moussoi)* was clearly noted.[7] The condition of Egyptian Jews deteriorated after Nasser came to power in 1954. Special laws dealing with the status of the Jews and their property led to the flight of many Egyptian Jews from the country between November 1956 and March 1957.[8] In Iraq, Abd al-Salem 'Aref's rise to power worsened the situation of the relatively few Jews remaining in the country after the mass immigration to Israel, which came to an end in 1951. Various regulations placed obstacles before those who wished to leave Iraq and increased economic pressure upon the Jewish community.[9]

Two main factors influenced the extent of Jewish anxiety in Muslim countries. The first of these was their dwindling numbers. In 1948, when the State of Israel was established and fought its War of Independence, there were 890,000 Jews in Muslim states; on the eve of the Six-Day War there were only about 244,000. Quite simply, the vast majority of them had decided to emigrate, primarily to Israel. Yet they still accounted for sizable and not inconsequential communities, such as 70,000 in Morocco, 23,000 in Tunisia and 6,000 in Lebanon (see Table 1). To these one should add the 80,000 Jews living in Iran. Jewish communities of such dimensions indicate that prior to the Six-Day War these Jews believed in the possibility of a continued Jewish existence in Arab or Muslim countries.

The second factor influencing the extent of Jewish anxiety was the threat of war. Armed conflict between Arabs and Jews in Palestine and

---

[7] H. J. Cohen, *The Jews of the Middle East 1860–1982* (New York, Toronto, and Jerusalem: 1973), 46–47.

[8] Ibid., 52. Cohen claims that 21,000 were expelled between November 1956 and September 1957, and that by the beginning of the 1960s the number of Jews who had left Egypt reached 36,000, most of them forced to leave behind almost all of their property. This dealt a severe blow to Jewish autonomy, especially in personal matters. On this aspect see Laskier, *Jews of Egypt*, 252–90, and Bat-Yeor, *Jews of Egypt*, 125–37.

[9] N. Kazzaz, *The Jews in Iraq in the Twentieth Century* (in Hebrew) (Jerusalem: 1991), 305–7.

TABLE 1

NUMBER OF JEWS IN MUSLIM COUNTRIES[10]

Country	1948	1966
Morocco	286,000	70,000
Algeria	130,000	3,000
Tunisia	70,000	23,000
Libya	30,000	6,000
Egypt and Sudan	75,000	2,500
Iraq	90,000	6,000
Yemen	45,000	2,000
Syria	20,000	4,000
Iran	50,000	80,000
Lebanon		6,000
Aden	8,700	400
Pakistan		300
Afghanistan	5,000	800
Turkey	80,000	40,000
Total	889,700	244,000

[10] Data from *AJYB* 1948 and 1966. Though the *AJYB* is generally quite reliable, the figures provided here are not beyond challenge. See, for example, U. O. Schmelz, "Mass Aliya from Asia and North Africa: Demographic Aspects" (in Hebrew), *Pe'amim*, 39 (1989): 18–19. Schmelz arrived at a total of more than 1,100,000 since he included Jews in Ethiopia, Oriental Jews in the former Soviet Union, the Sudan, and elsewhere. Due to the difficulty involved in estimating the number of Jews in Arab lands, we prefer to base our data on another, quite reliable source and compare the figures for 1948 and 1966. The number of Jews in Lebanon in 1948 is not given, since in that year they were included in the figures for Syria. The number of Jews in Tunisia is actually greater (estimated at 105,000), since the figure given does not include Tunisian Jews holding French citizenship who were counted in censuses as French citizens. Iran is the only Muslim state to show an increase in its Jewish population, due to the policy of the Shah and Iran's relations with Israel. See A. Tartakower, "The Fate of Jews in the Arab Countries" (in Hebrew), *Ha-Poel Ha-Tzair* 38, no. 42 (11 July 1967): 4–6; also published in *Hadoar*, 14 July 1967, 591–93.

Israel had erupted from time to time over the past few decades.[11] Since the 1920s, the Arab-Jewish conflict has continued to play a role in the situation of Jews in Arab lands, though its impact varied from country to country. I shall not attempt to analyze how the Arab-Israeli conflict in its entirety influenced the condition of Jews in Arab countries, since research into that issue is still in its infancy. However, we should note several factors that account for the conflict's different measures of influence upon the various Jewish communities. Thus, the physical proximity of the various countries to Israel—the core of the conflict—was most important, for in the neighboring states anti-Israel and anti-Zionist propaganda was nastier and more prolonged than in countries that were not directly involved in armed conflict with the Jewish State. In addition, Arab leaders, fearing that local Jews would serve Israeli espionage agencies, doubted the loyalty of their Jewish citizens. An example par excellence is the ill-fated Israeli operation in Egypt, in the summer of 1954, in which a group of young Egyptian Jews were involved. Accusations of espionage were often leveled against Jews in Egypt, Syria, and Iraq. The relative remoteness of Yemen, Afghanistan, or even North Africa from the stage upon which the events were being played out tended to lessen the impact of this factor on their Jewish communities.

A third element that influenced the effect of the Arab-Israeli conflict on local Jewish communities was the character of the various regimes and their attitude towards Israel. In this respect, there is no comparing Iran and Turkey in the years preceding the Six-Day War to Libya, Egypt, or Syria. The condition of the Jewish communities in the first two countries was inestimably more comfortable due to the character of the regime and the subordinate role of Islam as a factor in the political fabric of the country. All this notwithstanding, certain political and social tendencies common to all Arab countries, such as pan-Islamism, could have a negative effect upon the Jews living there, especially during periods when Arab-Israeli tension peaked. The Six-Day War is an example, par excellence, of the manner in which the Arab-Israeli conflict shaped the condition of the Jews in these countries.

---

[11] H. Saadoun, "The 'Palestinian Element' in Violent Eruptions between Jews and Muslims in Muslim Countries" (in Hebrew), *Pe'amim* 63 (Spring 1995): 86–131, esp. 91–93 (hereafter, Saadoun, Palestinian Element). Norman Stillman was among the first scholars to emphasize the importance of this issue.

Fear and Anxiety in Tunisia on the Eve of the Six-Day War

Israelis sent to Tunisia in the mid-1960s to work with the Jews there reported a sense of relative calm, peace, and physical security for Jews. "It is probable," wrote one of them, who was well informed on conditions in Tunisia, "that those still in Tunisia... which either do not want to leave the country or cannot do so, and it seems that the number of Jews will remain more or less stable in the future, unless there is a drastic change in the political or economic situation."[12] Another claimed that there was a slowdown in the rate of immigration to Israel of Jews from northern Tunisia and the capital city, Tunis.

> For the first time in years, young couples show a clear tendency to continue living in Tunisia. In the past, this was very unusual, as couples that married and established a family unit left Tunisia, either for France or Israel. Those that remain prefer to stay either because they lack the courage to get up and leave, or because of the property which they cannot take with them, or because of rumors concerning the economic situation in Israel, or for some other reason. The Jewish population of the capital city, Tunis, has remained unchanged, or may even have increased somewhat, for the remnants of the communities of Sous, Sfax and Bizerte come to settle there.[13]

The two major factors which contributed to a lack of any real anxiety among Tunisia's Jews during the weeks immediately preceding the Six-Day War were the policy on treatment of the Jews adopted since that country achieved independence, and the posture assumed by President Habib Bourguiba regarding the Arab-Israeli conflict.

The Condition of the Jews in Independent Tunisia until the Six-Day War

The character of independent Tunisia was influenced by the nature of the party in power—Neo-Destour; the almost bloodless struggle for independence[14]; Tunisia's role in the Maghreb states and in the Arab world; its pro-Western inclinations; and the domestic problems it faced during the first

---

[12] Classified archive, letter (in Hebrew), 3 October 1966.
[13] Classified archive, letter (in Hebrew), 3 January 1967.
[14] For that period and its effect on the Jews of Tunisia, see H. Saadoun, "Aliya from Tunisia during the Struggle for Tunisian Independence" (in Hebrew), *Pe'amim* 39 (1989): 103–23.

years of independence. These factors were not inconsequential influences on the character of Tunisian Jewry and on the manner in which Israel handled the issue of immigration from Tunisia. The ideology of the Neo-Destour party was reflected in a personal, off-the-record conversation between one of its leaders, Mohammed Masmoudi, and Marc Jarblum, a French socialist and a leading member of its Jewish community, before Tunisia gained its independence:

> It is our objective to establish a Tunisian polity that will be grounded on democratic foundations, on Western civilization and on elements of secular life. Naturally, we are not going to renounce Islamic culture—we will adopt from it and from the Qur'an all their humane elements and these will go hand in hand with modern civilization. Combining the humane elements of the Qur'an with Western civilization will form the basis of our efforts in the field of culture. We reject any fanaticism or intolerance, and demand internal autonomy for Tunisia. We do not demand full independence, nor do we intend a complete break with France, which still has great influence in Tunisia. We are following the path set by Bourguiba, who represents the majority of Tunisians both actually and morally.[15]

Independent Tunisia's policy vis-à-vis its Jews favored their full integration into the new Tunisian society.[16] Thus, for example, all Tunisians were given the franchise in elections to the Constituent Assembly; ten Jewish judges were appointed to the country's courts to judge cases dealing with Jewish litigants; and although the rabbinical courts were abolished, special courts dealing with matters of personal status were established within the Tunisian legal system that were open to Jews just as they were to all other Tunisians. The Jewish community council was disbanded and replaced by an "Interim Committee for the Management of the Affairs of the Jewish Community" until "associations for religious matters" would be established. As to their role, the manner in which their officers would be elected and their conceptual foundation, the planned "associations for religious matters" were quite similar to the "consistoires" which the French had established in Algeria in 1845.[17]

---

[15] Marc Jarblum, "Tunisian Affairs—Talk with Minister Masmoudi," Mapai World Union Record Group, file 55/101, Mapai Archives, Beit Berl; the document probably dates from 1955.
[16] Research on the Jews in independent Tunisia is still far from satisfactory. The present discussion is based primarily on R. Attal, "Jews in Independent Tunisia" (in Hebrew), *Bitefutzot Ha-Golah* 8, nos. 2–3 (37–38) (1967): 87–96.
[17] Ibid., 90.

Two of the steps taken by the authorities for the development of the capital city of Tunis proved detrimental to the Jewish community: transfer of the old Jewish cemetery to another site and the razing of *Harat al-Yahud*—the Jewish quarter. These were carried out as part of an urban renewal plan in which the Muslim cemetery was also removed to a new location. Aware of the Jews' sensitivity, Bourguiba personally supervised all work related to the transfer of the Jewish cemetery, during which the Tunisians displayed a reasonable degree of consideration for Jewish feelings.[18]

The years from Tunisian independence (1956) until the events in Bizerte in 1961, were marked by a decrease in tension between those Jews who remained in the country and the authorities.[19] Jews were appointed to some of the positions vacated by the French, and Yom Kippur was proclaimed an official holiday, enabling Jews to absent themselves from work. The Jews' sense of security and the degree of their identification with Tunisia are exemplified in the role they played in the "Campaign for the Dinar" (in which all Tunisians were called upon to shore up the declining value of the Tunisian dinar). "The spontaneous donations made by the Jews were so many and so large, exceeding to such a great degree those of the Muslim citizens, that the daily papers ceased publishing lists of the contributors. The Association of Goldsmiths alone donated fifteen kilograms of gold, and it is well known that 90% of its members are Jewish."[20]

The reports of Israeli representatives in Tunisia at the time also reflected the congenial atmosphere in which its Jews lived. Zvi Heitner wrote: "Only rarely is anything negative said of the Jews…official documents generally include only praise for them; on every occasion praise is lavished upon the Jews and they are declared to be part of the Tunisian nation."[21] He noted the reasons why Jews were in no hurry to emigrate to Israel or to any other country: the security situation in Israel frightened them; rumors from Israel to the effect that it was difficult to find employment, and that North African immigrants suffered from discrimination; the extensive financial assistance of the Joint that encouraged Jews in southern Tunisia to stay put; the restrictions which the authorities placed on the sale of

---

[18] See A. Attal, "The Old Jewish Cemetery of Tunis" (in Hebrew), *Pe'amim* 67 (Spring 1996): 29. For a more detailed account see Ch. Haddad De Paz, *Juifs et Arabes au pays de Bourguiba* (Aix-en-Provence: 1977), 197–215.

[19] Attal, "Old Jewish Cemetery," 91.

[20] Ibid., 92.

[21] Zvi Heitner, letter, September 1960, Mapai World Union Record Group, file 60/101, Mapai Archives, Beit Berl. Heitner was in Tunisia as a representative of the Immigration Department of the Jewish Agency.

property and the transfer of capital out of the country; and the need to present the authorities with many affidavits before emigrating. Heitner believed that Tunisian Jews preferred to emigrate to France due to their status as French citizens, the French culture which they had absorbed in Tunisia, and the fact that in France Jewish children were eligible for financial assistance until they finished secondary school.[22] The extent of *aliyah* to Israel in those years also reflected the general climate of opinion in Tunisia. In 1955, over 6,000 Jews emigrated to Israel, while in 1956—the year of Tunisian independence—another 6,500 arrived. In following year, however, the figure dropped to about 2,600, and was even lower in the succeeding years until the events in Bizerte in 1961.[23]

The treaty granting Tunisia independence left the naval base in Bizerte (a strategic port in the north of the country) under French control. In 1961 Bourguiba demanded that the French withdraw from the base. Their refusal led to armed hostilities in which the French gained the upper hand, but military success does not always guarantee victory in the political sphere. The French were forced to evacuate the naval base after signing a new agreement with Tunisia. Fear for the fate of Bizerte's Jewish community, which numbered about 1,000 persons, led to a decision to evacuate them. This was done in a joint effort by representatives of the Jewish Agency in Tunisia, representatives of the Israel Ministry of Defense in France, and the French armed forces. Though the Jews were not directly threatened by either side in this conflict, as the fighting continued the possibility of Jewish casualties increased. One Jewish resident of the city related that "there was an Arab school opposite our house, in which Tunisian soldiers took up positions. French soldiers held our house. Only a street separated the two buildings. They fired at one another from the windows, and the house was destroyed."[24]

In a report by André Dreyfus, an official of the World Jewish Congress who visited Tunisia in September 1961,[25] he explained that the events in Bizerte had dealt a blow to the French presence in Tunisia and there was some ground for fear that Bourguiba might deviate from his democratic,

---

[22] Ibid.
[23] Saadoun, "Aliya from Tunisia," 111.
[24] A. Tirosh, "How the 'Mossad' Extricated the Jews of Bizerte" (in Hebrew) *Ma'ariv*, 19 February 1988, 3; A. Bensimon, "Le Pourim des Juifs de Bizerte," *Tribune Juive* 1010 (February–March 1968).
[25] A. Dreyfus, "Report on a Visit to Tunisia" (in French), 27 September 1961, CZA Z6/1558.

Western-oriented policy. Dreyfus claimed that there had been a few events that could be labeled anti-Semitic, but these were isolated cases and had not been instigated by the authorities. For example:

> Muslim students yelled "Death to the Jews" during a certain demonstration. Swastikas were painted on a synagogue near the Porte de France. The authorities had them erased. Jews were beaten. A street sign bearing the name of a Jewish hero of the period of Nazi oppression was torn down in Ariana...only after protests by a Jew who was "someone" in the Neo-Destour party was it replaced and apologies made.[26]

In Dreyfus's opinion, the Tunisian authorities were careful not to harm their Jewish citizens since that might have a detrimental effect upon Tunisia's international standing, especially after the "act of folly of Bizerte." Dreyfus went on to clarify that

> during what is called the "War of Bizerte" the authorities kept a close watch on the Jews. A few were detained on suspicion of anti-Tunisian acts such as conversing with foreigners and expressing opposition to the government or its policy. This was reminiscent of the Hitlerite period in Tunisia in early 1943.[27]

After intervention by leaders of the Jewish community, Dreyfus reported, the situation had become somewhat more stable, but the Jews were still taking various precautions and were more wary than in the past. On Yom Kippur, 1961, the governor of Tunis attended services in the synagogue as the representative of President Bourguiba. He declared that the president looked upon Tunisia's Jews as full-fledged citizens. In summing up the Bizerte affair, Dreyfus wrote that

> despite their love of Tunisia, the Jews believe that they are destined to emigrate. Even if the Tunisian flirt with France is renewed, the confidence of the Jews will never be restored. Thus, it is important that Tunisian Jews leave the country as fast as possible.

He believed that Bourguiba would not place any obstacles in the way of Jewish emigration because of his obligation to international organizations and the esteem in which he was held by their members, and also because of the election of Mongi Selim as president of the General Assembly of the U.N.

---

[26] Ibid. The description seems somewhat exaggerated, especially considering that the writer at times reported events to which he was not an eyewitness.
[27] Ibid.

The events in Bizerte increased the Jews' doubts as to their future in Tunisia. The French military presence, limited as it was, was a sort of lifebelt for them and made them feel more secure. The best proof of their new sense of insecurity after 1961 lies in the figures for Jewish emigration during these years. Of the 65,000 Jews in the country in 1960, 60,000 remained in 1962; while in 1965 the Jewish population of Tunisia amounted to no more than half of that in 1962. In less than five years, over 30,000 had left the country, most of them professionals, businessmen, or laborers. The extent and character of Jewish emigration during these years are quite similar to that of the period which immediately preceded Tunisian independence.[28] Those who remained were primarily the elderly.

In the interim period between the Bizerte affair and Bourguiba's proposals for a solution of the Arab-Israeli conflict, the condition of Tunisia's Jewish community deteriorated. After a plot to assassinate Bourguiba was uncovered in 1962, many Jewish families closed down their businesses and emigrated to France. Gradually, it became forbidden to send letters and parcels to Israel, and direct telephone communication between the two countries was cut off. Only Jews bearing French citizenship were allowed to leave with their belongings, and only if they were able to present proof of their citizenship and an affidavit certifying that their destination was France. Jews holding Tunisian citizenship could leave the country without their property, except for thirty dinars and some clothes. Thirty-five Jews from Djerba were arrested on suspicion of trying to smuggle gold from Tunisia to Libya. They were imprisoned, tortured, and tried in court, where they were very heavily fined. Only intervention by the community leadership managed somewhat to alleviate their condition.[29] Nevertheless, as we have seen, during the years immediately preceding the Six-Day War, Tunisian Jews appeared to have recovered a sense of security.

BOURGUIBA'S POLICY ON THE ARAB-ISRAELI CONFLICT AND THE CONDITION OF TUNISIA'S JEWS

Bourguiba surprised the Arab world when, in February–April 1965, he on several occasions declared that the Arab-Israeli conflict could be solved

---

[28] Population figures for Tunisian Jewry are from *AJYB* for the different years, and from data included in various reports at our disposal.

[29] E. Haddad, "Tunisia's Jews Call Out for Help" (in Hebrew), *Ha-Aretz*, 18 September 1964; see also idem, "The Economic Condition of Tunisia's Jews Deteriorates" (in Hebrew), *Ha-Aretz*, 29 April 1964.

through understanding and peaceful means rather than by war. He made public his thoughts on the matter during visits in the Middle East and in several European capitals. In a press conference conducted in the palace of King Hussein of Jordan in East Jerusalem, he laid down the guidelines of his policy. He claimed that the conflict was of an imperialistic nature and should therefore be solved in the manner in which such conflicts were brought to an end in the past. He presented the Tunisian model of non-violence as worthy of emulation.

> By the very act of putting an end to imperialism we actually extended our hands in cooperation, friendship and fraternity to the nation that had ruled us. We looked upon the blood that had been spilled during thirty years as the price of liberty and honor, and turned a new page that is founded on the respect of one man for another and on mutuality with France.[30]

In reply to questions from the press, Bourguiba postulated that the Palestinian problem was the result of "conditions, the international situation, world wars, the efforts of the Jews and the mistakes of the Arabs over the past twenty-five years and their strategy in this conflict." Returning to the Tunisian model, he leveled indirect criticism at Egyptian president Gamal Abdul Nasser:

> I never incited the Tunisian people to bloodshed, and often stood in the breach to prevent it. In the long run, events have proven my concepts and thoughts to have been correct. When I proclaim a cease-fire with imperialism, I have no fear. The same holds true for concessions.

Bourguiba emphasized that, in his opinion, "it is possible to cooperate with the Jews on the basis of mutual respect, with our hands joined, for they are the 'People of the Book,' and the two religions [Islam and Judaism] are closely related. There is also much room for cooperation on the basis of respect of our freedom and honor; all this is possible." When asked what role Tunisia would play in settling the dispute and whether he had a specific plan to that end, Bourguiba reiterated his traditional argument that Tunisia is far removed from the core of the conflict. He did not have a specific plan, but was prepared to sit down with the region's leaders and draw up such a scheme.

---

[30] See *Daily Digest*, appendix to digest no. 58, 7 March 1965. The press conference was reported in that day's issue of the Jordanian daily *Filastin*. All quotes below are from the *Daily Digest*.

No matter how one interprets Bourguiba's declarations, the fact that he made them publicly on several successive occasions is proof of his serious intentions. Reactions in the Arab world ranged from cool to furious, especially in Egypt and Iraq. Tension between members of the Arab League and Tunisia heightened, leading to anti-Tunisian demonstrations. Bourguiba repeatedly claimed that there was nothing new in these ideas and proved to one and all that he had held them for over twenty years.[31]

Alexander Easterman, a senior official of the World Jewish Congress who was a frequent visitor to Arab capitals, noted that Bourguiba's declarations were the event that aroused the greatest degree of public interest there since the establishment of Israel, the 1948 war and the Sinai Campaign.[32] He believed that diverse motives lay behind Bourguiba's statements. Among domestic reasons, Easterman pointed out that just three months before, Bourguiba was almost unanimously (96.34%) reelected to another five-year term. One of the first steps he took in his cabinet was to depose Mongi Selim, then serving as president of the U.N. General Assembly, known for his enmity toward Israel and the only person who could challenge Bourguiba's leadership. The president also appointed his own son as minister of foreign affairs.

Easterman also ventured the opinion that this might have been part of a struggle for hegemony in the Arab world, for Bourguiba's stance was directly opposed to that of Nasser. It was as if he were warning the Arab governments and nations that Nasser's policy would lead to war. When Bourguiba spoke of Arab unity, he was referring first and foremost to the unity of the Maghreb as opposed to that of the Mashrek, under the influence of Nasser. Moreover, there was also personal enmity between the two leaders, deriving primarily from Nasser's support of Salah Ben Youssef, Bourguiba's major rival in Tunisia. Since Tunisian independence, Bourguiba had adopted a most independent policy and would brook no intervention whatsoever by any foreign element in Tunisian affairs.

---

[31] See B. Etienne and N. Sraibe, "Bourguiba et Israel," *Annuaire de l'Afrique du Nord*, 1965, 151–62. (hereafter *AAN* with the appropriate year).

[32] Easterman to Goldmann, 15 April 1965, CZA, Z6/1164. As for Morocco, see Y. Tsur, "The Prince, the Diplomat and the Deal" (in Hebrew), *Ha-Aretz*, 18 November 1994. Tsur claims that King Hassan adopted a very moderate stand on the Arab-Israeli conflict. Hassan is quoted as saying: "The State of Israel is a fact, a reality. No one can deny the existence of Israel. Furthermore, that country is far removed from us and does not have direct contact with Morocco. But the Middle Eastern Arab states are our sisters and we cannot overlook that fact. My actions must take that into account. If matters would depend solely on the will of Morocco, I would suggest co-opting Israel into the Arab League."

Easterman believed that the timing of Bourguiba's pronouncements had been carefully planned and was most propitious. Nasser's reputation had been damaged by his ill-fated military adventure in the Yemen and he had been unsuccessful in attempting to have other Arab states follow his lead in cementing close relations with East Germany. Bourguiba, on the other hand, enjoyed the financial support of West Germany. Thus, his policy could also be construed as a step to counter Nasser's European strategy.[33]

Bourguiba's stand vis-à-vis the Arab-Israeli conflict did not seem to leave much of a mark upon the Tunisian Jewish community, even though his speech pointed to a moderate policy on that issue and an intention to continue his Western-oriented strategy.[34] The testimony of Israeli representatives on the eve of the Six-Day War, quoted at length above, indicate that conditions were rather agreeable for the Jews at the time. Further evidence of such an atmosphere is a book by Hashmi Baccouche, author, journalist, and member of a leading Tunisian family, published during the first half of 1965.[35] In his book, Baccouche warmly supports French-Tunisian cooperation and criticized Nasser's domestic and foreign policy. Moreover, he also considered the relations between Jews and Muslims in North Africa in general and Tunisia in particular to be a positive phenomenon. He expressed his understanding of what led some Jews to leave their country and emigrate to Israel despite their deep attachment to Tunisia, and his sorrow at the fact that some of these emigrants had turned their backs on their home country. As for the Arab-Israeli conflict, he wrote:

> Despite everything, I am sure that one day Israel and the Arab nations will find a way to reach an understanding. I should very much like Tunisia to be the first of all the Islamic countries to recognize Israel, if for no other reason than because of the many Jews whom I knew and loved and are now there. That is my national aspiration.[36]

As we have seen, the two events prior to the Six-Day War which had the most direct influence—though in opposite directions—on the condition of Tunisia's Jews were the Bizerte Affair in late 1961 and President Bour-

---

[33] Easterman to Goldmann, 15 April 1965, CZA, Z6/1164.
[34] It should be reiterated that we do not have many sources from within the community that describe what its members thought and felt at this time.
[35] M. Yishai, "Tunisian Author Calls for Peace between Israel and the Arabs," *Bama'aracha*, June 1965, 10. I have not been able to consult this volume and am therefore relying on the information supplied by Yishai. To the best of my knowledge, this was the only mention of Baccouche's book in the Israeli press.
[36] Ibid.

guiba's policy on the Arab-Israeli conflict, to which he first gave public expression in February 1965. While events in Bizerte increased the Jews' apprehensions as to their future in Tunisia, Bourguiba's pronouncements encouraged some of them to stay. The two years between Bourguiba's statement of policy on the conflict and the outbreak of the Six-Day War, therefore, was a period of comparative calm for Tunisia's Jews and of some amelioration in their condition.

THE SIX-DAY WAR

Events in Tunisia during the Six-Day War

Any analysis of violent incidents between Jews and their neighbors is problematic and should be done with great care.[37] This is even more so when we have only scant sources documenting the course of events.[38] The eyewitness account of incidents in Tunisia during the Six-Day War, published by Stillman, is the most detailed.[39] We shall begin with a description

---

[37] Saadoun, "The Palestinian Element," 87–90.
[38] Stillman *Jews of Arab Lands,* 550–51. See also: *AJYB* 1968, 527–28, where the report was written by Victor Malka. This is an important source, generally based on the reliable sources of the World Jewish Congress. For further information see Sh. Gaon, "The Jews in the Arab Diaspora" (in Hebrew), *Bama'aracha,* 94 (February 1969): 8–9; Jordan, "Diaspora Jewry and Eretz Yisrael," 51–54. The description of events in Tunisia, 51–52, is somewhat longer than that of any other country, which points to the importance Jordan placed on developments in Tunisia; "The Jews in Arab Lands during the Middle East Crisis" (in Hebrew), *Gesher* 2–3 (September 1967): 48–52; "The Jews in Arab Lands after the Six-Day War" (in Hebrew), *Bitefutzot Ha-Golah* 10, nos. 3–4 (Fall 1968): 90–93. See also: *The Plight of the Jews in Arab Lands* (in Hebrew) (Jerusalem: Information Services of the Prime Minister's Office, 1969). The variations between the several sources are small and inconsequential, more indicative of the authors and their tendencies rather than of their grasp of actual events. The similarity of these description may be evidence of the paucity of sources at the disposal of various Jewish bodies or, on the other hand, of an attempt by some body—perhaps Jewish—to play down descriptions of events precisely in a country such as Tunisia. The events in North Africa were also described in *AAN* 1969, 301–5, esp. 303–4 for Tunisia. There is no information here that adds to what was published in the Jewish reports, despite different sources of information. This French annual most naturally places more emphasis on domestic political developments in the countries surveyed than on Jewish issues.
[39] Stillman, *Jews of Arab Lands,* 550–51. Though written in August 1968, this memo is by an eyewitness, probably on the staff of the Joint (Stillman found it in the archives of the JDC in Jerusalem; I was unable to consult the file for further information when writing this article). This is the only first-hand report that we have used in our study.

of the violent incidents as reported by this witness and then compare it to other sources at our disposal.

> The outbreak of hostilities in the Middle East on 5 June saw a major outburst of anti-Jewish demonstrations in Tunis. Shortly before noon a crowd arrived at the British Embassy and in short order the entire building was sacked and the library on the ground floor completely burned out. As the afternoon wore on, the crowd grew larger and different bands attacked the American library, the offices of TWA, and the American Embassy.... But by far the heaviest damage was done to Jewish retail establishments throughout the city. The gangs came prepared with gasoline as well as heavy metal cutters with which to open iron shutters. Over 100 shops were affected, this representing the major part of the shops that were in existence.

The eyewitness goes on to relate that the reaction of the authorities was too little and too late. Meanwhile, the mob continued on a rampage, causing damage to Jewish cars and even penetrating into the main synagogue of the city, where they desecrated some forty Torah scrolls and urinated upon them, and ripped memorial plaques off the walls. A number of smaller synagogues throughout the city suffered the same treatment. One floor of the Tunis Jewish Community building was also damaged. During the afternoon, a group of thirty demonstrators arrived at JDC headquarters. They set fire to the front door but were unable to enter the building. After they left, the staff managed to put out the fire.

> By 1:30 P.M. Tunis looked like it had been bombed. Smoke was pouring out of scores of Jewish establishments, and the mobs continued to dominate the streets. Tunisian troops, who are quartered in barracks within ten minutes of the center of the city, did not arrive until four in the afternoon and then quickly drove the mobs off the streets. The mobs consisted mostly of youngsters between fourteen and twenty years of age, but I saw as well a considerable number of young men in their twenties who were haranguing and leading them on.

Henri Elfen, the author of this memo, was convinced that the demonstrations had been organized. Though the authorities referred to "Algerian troublemakers," Elfen believed that members of the Neo-Destour party were also involved. Furthermore, pillaging was systematically conducted and what was even more significant—no one was hurt during the rioting. "An eyewitness reported seeing a Jew who had lost his nerve as his establishment was being pillaged, begging the mob not to hurt him. He was told that no one had any intention of hurting him, he was simply to go home!

The police reacted feebly when they reacted at all, and it took five hours to get troops into the city."[40]

Only intervention by President Bourguiba, in the afternoon, brought the demonstrations to an end. In a speech broadcast over the radio and the television, he called on the mobs to stop the riots and denounced them severely. His action prevented even more severe attacks on the Jews, especially in the smaller towns. No Jews were attacked in the cities of southern Tunisia throughout the entire week of the war, with the exception of one case in which stones were thrown in one town. Bourguiba kept military units, including armored cars, posted for several weeks at strategic locations within Tunis. The radio station, for example, was under strict military guard. For a few weeks it was unclear just how much Bourguiba controlled affairs; the cry "Jew Bourguiba" was heard in the streets.

On Tuesday, 6 June 1967, four ministers of the Tunisian government came to the Jewish Community Council to express their regret at what had happened, promising that rioters would be punished and the damage repaired. And indeed, damaged store fronts were repaired, as was the synagogue, until no signs of what had happened were visible. Several of the rioters were imprisoned.

The immediate result of the incidents, according to Elfen, was a mass flight of Jews from Tunisia. During the first month, over 2,500 fled the country, mostly children and women who were sent in advance of their fathers and husbands. Some of them returned, to prepare their final departure from the country. Though there were difficulties in receiving passports in the southern cities, none was encountered in the capital. Due to the mass exodus, there was an immediate decline in the community's income from the sale of Boukha[41] and from the tax levied on kosher meat.

The report published in the *American Jewish Year Book* paints a more moderate picture of the events of 5 June, and will be briefly summarized

---

[40] Some of the details in this report seem to be exaggerated. The number of Jewish shops damaged and pillaged was much smaller, as was the number of Torah scrolls desecrated during the rioting. On the other hand, damage to the community offices fits in with the attack on the main synagogue, for they were situated immediately behind it. I am indebted to R. Attal for the information he provided on this matter, though all responsibility, of course, rests with the author. Attal also pointed out that the authorities forbade taking photos of these events and confiscated those that were made.

[41] Boukha is a Tunisian Jewish alcoholic beverage produced from figs and drunk with meals. The Bokobza Boukha distillery was the largest plant in Tunisia that produced this beverage.

here.[42] According to this source, rioting opened with calls of "Into the sea with the Jews" and "Let's burn the Jews." The Magen David (Star of David) on the front of the great synagogue of Tunis was set afire, as were about a dozen Jewish cars; damage was inflicted to Jewish establishments, including the Bokobza Boukha distillery. The report concerning damage to the Magen David seems to be erroneous, due to the great difficulty the rioters would have had to reach the spot where it was affixed to the wall. Interestingly, only Jewish-owned cars suffered damage during the rioting.[43] Does this indicate that the riots were organized and planned? In contrast to the eyewitness report published by Stillman, the *AJYB* does note that "many young Jews were attacked and beaten." Bourguiba's intervention, according to this source, came only in the evening, and his television and radio message—in which he termed the demonstrators "irresponsible fanatics"—was broadcast on the following day. Eighty of the rioters were arrested and would face heavy sentences. According to the *Year Book*, eyewitnesses claimed that the riots were organized and the police did nothing to prevent them. The authorities, naturally, denied that the demonstrations had been planned, though the chief of police in Tunis was sacked. The new situation in Tunisia and especially apprehension that Bourguiba's standing would be undermined by growing domestic opposition were among the major reasons that sparked a wave of Jewish emigration from Tunisia beginning in August 1967.

The differences between the two descriptions seem to lie in their different perspectives. Whereas the eyewitness report published by Stillman was a personal description, that of the *AJYB* seems to have been based upon testimony culled from several sources, including official Jewish bodies in France that received the Tunisian Jewish émigrés and helped them settle down. Furthermore, the eyewitness account was a confidential memorandum that its author could write without inhibitions, whereas the editors of the *AJYB* knew that their report was open to all. This, quite likely, accounts for the more moderate tone of the description in the *Year Book*.[44]

---

[42] *AJYB* 69 (1968): 527–28.

[43] I am once again indebted to Robert Attal for this information. I also learned from him that the matza bakery was destroyed and that since the 1967 riots, the Jewish community of Tunisia imports matzot for Passover from France.

[44] The following summary description of events in Tunisia (see Gaon, "Jews in the Arab Diaspora") was published in an Israeli journal—the leading organ at that time of the Sefardic and Oriental Jews in Israel: "The Six-Day War caused a cruel and sudden outburst in Tunis. Even the Bourguiba government was taken by

Information as to the course of the riots is repeated in almost all the sources at our disposal. Data concerning Jewish casualties appears in only one report,[45] but since this cannot be corroborated from other sources we prefer to consider such information unreliable. Descriptions of the damage done to the main synagogue in Tunis also seem to be exaggerated. The events of 5 June raise several questions to which we cannot provide clear-cut answers: Were the riots organized? Were they intended to strike only at the Jewish community, or did they also target foreign embassies in order to clearly show Bourguiba's weakness when facing the great powers? If the latter is the case, then the attacks on the British and American embassies fall into place. Or is this a case of the well-known pattern in which the Jews were scapegoats in domestic Tunisian conflicts?

A most interesting question is how the Tunisian authorities reacted to the rioting. It can be dealt with only by careful scrutiny of whatever information is available. Police reaction, which was most hesitant, enabled the rioting to go on unchecked. That probably explains why the local chief of police was sacked soon after the incidents in Tunis ended.

Of greater interest is Bourguiba's reaction. According to one source, he intervened during the afternoon of 5 June, while another delays his action to the evening. In any case, his intervention came too late, but we have no knowledge of when Bourguiba learned of the riots. What we do know, however, is that immediately after rioting ceased he adopted several measures with the object of calming things down, and their importance lies in the fact that this was done openly, with much publicity. First of all, he went on the electronic media, condemning the riots and promising that the perpetrators would be punished. Second, some of the rioters were

---

surprise. The Jews were not the only target of the street demonstrations that were also directed against the American and British embassies. The central synagogue was pillaged and many stores were set afire. President Bourguiba took sharp measures to counter the rioting. Due to his ill health, his physicians did not allow him to appear personally before the leaders of the Jewish community. He therefore sent two of his senior ministers, together with the mayor of Tunis, who apologized, and even promised proper restitution for all the damages and that the perpetrators would be quickly brought to trial. In a television broadcast, Bourguiba strongly denounced the rioters. Their leaders received heavy sentences. Since 8 June, many Jews began to emigrate from Tunis, taking refuge primarily in France. Though the government did not encourage this exodus, it raised no obstacles, and those wishing to leave Tunis could do so freely."

45 *Bitefutzot*, "The Jews," 93, refers to one Jew who was killed, one wounded and several women who were raped. This journal also informed its readers that 700 out of the 900 Jews of Sfax had left the country, and that two of the rioters had been sentenced to fifteen years in prison by a military court.

arrested (one source places their number at eighty), and the Tunis chief of police was fired. Third, Bourguiba dispatched senior government ministers to meet with the leaders of the Jewish community, express the president's deep regret and promise to repair the damage—an obligation that was speedily executed. Moreover, compensation for property damaged during the riots was promised—and paid. Fourth, in view of internal developments within Tunisia, Bourguiba did not prevent the Jews from leaving the country, though he would have preferred that they stay. All these are indicative of his sincere attitude towards his Jewish citizens, and of his sensitivity to the possible repercussion of the rioting on world public opinion.

How can one provide an explanation for the events of June 1967, in which the Jewish community was hard hit, when the two preceding years were marked by a diminishing impact of the Arab-Israeli conflict on Muslim-Jewish relations in Tunisia? It would seem that we must seek the roots of the matter in the domestic Tunisian political scene.

Two foreign-oriented elements strove to undermine Bourguiba's rule in Tunisia: the Algerians and the Nasserists. The cry "Long Live Nasser" was heard in demonstrations held during the war; there were also subversive acts by leftist circles or by supporters of Ben Yussuf, Bourguiba's chief opponent, who was supported by Nasser. The *Annuaire* reported: "Whatever the facts may be, these events prove that despite efforts by the Tunisians to keep things calm, the populace of Tunis exhibited great sensitivity in all that related to the Arab world and was easily swept to an outburst of emotion."[46] This state of affairs may explain Bourguiba's speedy and forceful intervention, which flowed from domestic considerations, but no less from his sincere appreciation for the Jewish community.

The Bizerte Affair and the events during the Six-Day War had something in common: the manner in which they affected the communal life of Tunisian Jewry. In 1961 the Jews sensed that they were no longer safe in Tunisia. The rioting that accompanied the Six-Day War reinforced this feeling, despite Bourguiba's efforts and conciliatory policy. Charles Jordan told the participants of the "Study Circle" in Jerusalem that the Tunisian ambassador in Paris had summoned several Tunisian émigrés and apologized in the name of President Bourguiba. However, he went on:"

> the ships and planes leaving Tunisia are packed with émigrés and refugees; I believe that since the cease-fire, between three and six thousand Jews have left Tunis, and they continue to stream out. France is

---

[46] *AAN* 1968, 314, and esp. the analysis, 338–41.

the destination of all planes and ships, and the Jewish communities there, under the leadership of the Rothschilds and in cooperation with our organization [the JDC], quickly organized reception committees at the Orleans airport and the seaport of Marseilles.[47]

Events in the Maghreb during the War

Of the four Maghreb countries—Morocco, Algeria, Tunisia, and Libya—the condition of the Jews in the latter was most severe.

> In 1967, when the Six-Day War broke out in Israel, anti-Jewish riots erupted in Tripoli. They were organized by the Palestinian Office in Libya and by the association of the schools run by teachers from Egypt. They began in the morning of Monday, 5 June 1967, but police intervention came only during the evening. A curfew was declared and the police transferred about 800 Jews to the Jurjy camp (about four km. from Tripoli) which was under police protection. Three women and one young man were murdered in the rioting... two Jewish families were taken from their homes by a police officer ...and their fate remains unclear to this very day. The other Jewish families remained inside their homes for almost three weeks; their major source of assistance came from Italian neighbors, who kept them supplied with food. In a few cases, Arab neighbors also helped them and brought them food. The government gave all Jews wishing and able to leave the country permission to do so. Policemen made the rounds [of the homes] and told them: "If you are considering leaving Libya, we will help you and supply you with the necessary documents and a permit to leave the country, but if you decide to stay, the government will not be able to assume responsibility for your safety." As a result, all of Tripoli's Jews (about 4,500) left the city and emigrated to Italy. There are only two families left, totaling about twenty souls.[48]

Just as in Tunisia, this violent outburst followed several years of comparative calm for the Jews who remained in Libya.[49] De Felice's study brings to light additional facts: Jews were transferred to the Jurjy camp only after serious rioting in Tripoli during which Jewish shops in the city's

---

[47] *Diaspora Jewry,* 52.
[48] F. Zouaretz et al., eds., *Libyan Jewry* (in Hebrew), 2nd ed. (Tel Aviv: 1982), 62. The first edition of this work, published by the Committee of Libyan Jews in Israel, appeared in 1959.
[49] De Felice, *Jews in an Arab Land,* 306. The work by this important Italian historian is based on press reports. De Felice's description of the events, to the best of our knowledge, is the only study of a Jewish community in an Arab country that deals so extensively with the effects of the Six-Day War (pp. 306–16).

main streets were looted and set afire. The incidents continued for several days, though not with the intensity of 5 June. Over and above damage to property, there were also cases of personal injury, though the sources are not in agreement as to their extent. According to de Felice, there were more than twenty casualties during the war and immediately following the hostilities, including two families, numbering thirteen souls in all, who "disappeared" and were probably murdered.[50] Tens of Jews were wounded, and very heavy damage inflicted upon property.

With reason, de Felice compared the violent outburst in June 1967 to two earlier such events in Libya, the first in November 1945 and the other in June 1948. In 1945, more than 130 Jews were murdered, while in 1948 those killed numbered "only" fourteen. As a result, almost all of Libya's Jews emigrated Israel and to Italy. A comparative analysis of the acts of violence points to a high degree of similarity from the standpoint of timing, the course of the riots, their causes, and the reaction of the participants. The difference between Tunisia and Libya was that Tunisia, as we have seen, did not have a record of violent incidents, especially during the final years in which there was still a Jewish community in the country.

The Jewish population of Algeria in 1967 was only about 3,000 out of more than 160,000 who had lived there in 1962, the year in which French colonial rule came to an end. We know of no Jews who suffered physical injury, but some anti-Jewish articles appeared in the press. Mass riots caused damage to the British consulate and the United States Cultural Center. What is interesting about the Algerian case is that the government created units of volunteers to join in the fighting in Israel, and placed a special budget at their disposal. The Algerian armed forces were put on alert as early as 26 May. After hostilities began on 5 June, Algeria's ports were closed to ships flying flags of countries considered to have friendly relations with Israel.[51]

Morocco's press also carried articles critical of Zionism and of Moroccan Jewry. A general strike was called in Casablanca and there were also anti-British and anti-American demonstrations. A boycott of Jewish stores was organized, anti-Jewish broadsheets were distributed, and two Jews murdered in Meknes.[52] Another source goes into more detail: a young girl

---

[50] Ibid., 309.
[51] *AAN* 1967, 302.
[52] Ibid. It is also reported that on 7 July 1967 *L'Avant-Garde* published lists of Jewish members of the Chamber of Commerce and other such organizations who were suspected of supporting Zionism. See *Plight*, 23–24.

and boy were the victims in Meknes, one Jew received knife wounds in Rabat, and a woman was beaten in Casablanca.[53] But for the timing, there does not seem to be any connection between the double murder and the Six-Day War. Moroccan Jews turned for help to the representatives of the World Jewish Congress. At the "Study Circle" deliberations, Charles Jordan said, in reference to events in Morocco:

> We were informed that synagogues had been burned in Casablanca, Rabat and Meknes. We checked out this information through our teams, and it turned out that all this had no basis. There were a few cases of killings—two Jews were killed in Meknes. From our check it transpires that this had nothing to do with the tension then prevailing. I believe that we must try to relate to these cases objectively and not create imaginary events that could lead to misunderstandings.[54]

It would seem that Jordan's comment was not directed only at reports emerging from Morocco but related to the ease with which this type of information is accepted during periods of such great tension.

Common to all the incidents in the Maghreb during the Six-Day War was that they occurred against a background of quite serious domestic political tension, of which anti-Jewish rioting was only one expression. The drama was played out in three concentric spheres. The first of these was the relationship between the government and Egyptian-influenced opposition circles in each country. In Morocco, for example, it was the Istiqlal party (Moroccan Party of Independence), together with certain elements in the trade unions, that were responsible for the economic boycott of Jews, the publication of anti-Jewish articles in the press, and even the riots against Western diplomatic missions. The situation in Tunisia and Libya was similar to that in Morocco. In Algeria, on the other hand, it was the government that encouraged the rioters, while the role of opposition elements in such activities was almost nil.

The second sphere related to the relations between each of the Maghreb countries and the Western powers, primarily Great Britain and the United States. In each country, there were demonstrations and riots against the diplomatic missions of these two states, during the course of which much damage was done. This is an interesting aspect of the effect of the Six-Day War upon the Maghreb which put the blame for events in the

---

53 *Bitefutzot*, "The Jews," 93. See also *Gesher*, "The Jews," 51. The latter source notes that the two Jews were murdered on 11 June, after it became obvious that the Arab states had suffered a defeat.

Middle East on the Western powers, despite the fact that both Tunisia's President Bourguiba and Morocco's King Hassan II had adopted a pro-Western foreign policy, primarily out of economic and political considerations, to the great displeasure of those Arab states that looked to or were already receiving aid from the U.S.S.R. The anti-Western rioting was conducted by opposition elements with the objective of undermining their governments' relations with the West, and this out of both ideological-religious as well as pan-Arab motivation. Such acts reached their peak in Libya, where a mob tried to attack an American Air Force base. Within a few days, more than 7,000 foreign residents had left Libya and a greater exodus was prevented only when the Libyan armed forces managed to gain control of the situation.[55]

The third concentric sphere was that of relations with the Jewish community. Undoubtedly, it was the masses, perhaps incited by the opposition, which inflicted injury upon their Jewish neighbors. By this means the opposition forces simultaneously achieved two objectives: first of all, to express solidarity with the Arab states who were fighting Israel and shedding their blood in battle; second, to undermine public order and thus weaken the government. With the exception of Algeria, the reaction of the ruling circles in every country was quite similar. We have already discussed at length the steps adopted by Bourguiba to placate the Jewish community of Tunisia and to demonstrate that neither he nor his senior officials had any part in inciting the rioting mobs. Charles Jordan devoted part of his report to the efforts adopted by the Moroccan monarch during the crisis:

> Grave anti-Jewish demonstrations broke out in Morocco, but King Hassan immediately adopted two measures. One was a request that the Jewish emigration offices be closed down.... The king's prime minister dropped them a broad hint that they should close their offices, which resulted in their staff leaving Morocco. His intention was to head off confrontation with pro-Nasserist Arabs.... Despite this, the king has control of the situation in the cities, primarily in Casablanca, he has brought in many policemen and is taking pains to prevent emotions from getting out of hand.[56]

---

54 *Diaspora Jewry*, 52–53. The *AJYB* 1968 accepts at face value reports of the burning of a Jewish community center at Fez, the dual murder in Meknes, and of the woman who was beaten in Casablanca.

55 De Felice, *Jews in an Arab Land*, 308–9.

56 *Diaspora Jewry*, 52. Another source informs us that Hassan II and his officials tried to placate the Jewish community: they promised to punish those responsible for the riots, did put on trial certain opposition leaders, and roundly condemned the instigators. See *Gesher*, "The Jews," 50–51.

Of special interest is the report that with the outbreak of hostilities in the Middle East King Hassan II called upon his people to refrain from violence. "The king himself declared that it was his government's policy to consider the Jews of Morocco as citizens having equal rights, irrespective of what was happening between Israel and its neighbors."[57]

In Libya a declaration of a state of emergency and a curfew prevented the spread of rioting, though it did not cease completely. The minister of the interior was deposed; the Jews were collected from their homes and placed under guard in a camp near the capital, and there was even an armed skirmish between government forces and a group from the village of Zawia which had volunteered to fight against Israel and intended to march on Tripoli.[58] What is obvious is that though the authorities were unable to prevent the outbreak of violent incidents, they definitely succeeded in preventing their spread throughout the country and did manage to limit the damage inflicted upon the Jews.

The overwhelming reaction of Jews in North Africa to these events was to speed up their emigration. The Jewish presence in two of the four countries dealt with in this article came to a complete end: it may be said that to all intents and purposes the Jewish community in Algeria ceased to exist as early as 1962. Those who left in the wake of the Six-Day War were primarily Jews employed by French companies still active in the country. This was not the case in Libya, where about 10% of its former Jewish population continued to live until 1967. Their exodus to Italy was quite similar to the waves of Jewish emigration from Libya after the violent incidents of 1945 and 1948 described above. The impact of the events of 1967 was so great that, in effect, it marked the end of Jewish presence in Libya.

As for Tunisia and Morocco, the war encouraged many to emigrate, but there still remained Jewish communities in these two countries. In both of them, the events of June 1967 were in sharp contrast to the relatively peaceful relations between Muslims and Jews that had been the rule prior to the war. Even after about 20,000 Jews left Morocco, its Jewish community remained the third largest in Muslim countries, after that of Iran and Turkey. We may, therefore, safely conclude that the Six-Day War

---

[57] Ibid., 52. This information is not corroborated by other source. However, this report of the king's action follows the pattern known to us from the War of Independence. See Saadoun, "Palestinian Element," and Appendix A to that article.

[58] De Felice, *Jews in an Arab Land,* 308–9.

accelerated a tendency to emigrate from the Maghreb countries that had been apparent since they received their independence. The destinations of these émigrés were first and foremost France and Italy, and only marginally Israel—if at all. It would not be erroneous to say that on the whole it was political reasons that gave the impetus to this latest wave of emigration, which lacked the "messianic" motivation of *aliyah* to Israel after the establishment of the Jewish state.

Conclusion

The Six-Day War marked the first time since their severe military and political defeat in the Israeli War of Independence that a majority of Arab armies launched a joint attack on Israel. The Arabs termed the Six-Day War *al-naksa* (failure), rather than *al-nakba* (catastrophe), as they called the War of Independence. Obviously, then, they considered their military defeat in 1967 to be less severe than that of 1948. The outcome of the War of Independence came as a great shock to the Arab states and the Arab League, and brought their action against the Zionist entity and the young Jewish State to a standstill. "The defeat in Palestine in 1948 was the first such shock suffered directly by the Eastern Arabs.... The shock of defeat in 1948, in place of the expected victory parade, was all the greater in that it was inflicted, not by the mighty imperial powers, but by the despised and familiar Jews."[59] The Six-Day War was a milestone in the development of the Arab-Israeli conflict, as Bernard Lewis has noted because "the Israeli victory of 1967...extended Israeli rule to the whole of Mandatory Palestine."[60] In addition to territorial gains, a new situation now prevailed in which Israel ruled over an Arab population of more than one million persons "with an active and vocal political and intellectual leadership."[61] The war transformed the Palestinians into an active element in the conflict and turned them into the leading agent in the formation of Arab policy in the struggle against Israel.

An analysis of the condition of the Jews in Muslim countries during the Six-Day War is important if for no other reason than that they faced imminent physical danger more than any other Jewish community in the

---

[59] B. Lewis, "The Arab-Israeli War: The Consequences of Defeat," *Foreign Affairs* 46 (1967–1968): 332.

[60] B. Lewis, *Semites and Antisemites: An Inquiry into Conflict and Prejudice* (New York and London: 1986), 164.

[61] Ibid., 186.

world. Their fate became ever more intricately linked to that of the State of Israel.

In July 1943, while World War II was still raging but after fighting had ceased in North Africa and the Middle East, Eliahu Dobkin, then head of the Immigration Department of the Jewish Agency, claimed:

> The very day which will be a day of redemption and deliverance for the Jews of Europe will be the most dangerous day for the diasporas in Arab lands. When Zionism enters upon the stage of implementation and we shall be engaged in the momentous struggle to achieve a Zionist solution here in Eretz Israel—it is then that a great danger will threaten those Jewish communities, the danger of a terrible massacre that will make the slaughter in Europe seem less horrendous than it seems today. Thus, the first objective we face is to rescue those Jews.[62]

In November 1948, only a few months after the establishment of Israel and the outbreak of the War of Independence, Y. Zerubavel, director of the Jewish Agency's Department for Jews in the Middle East, said: "Eastern Jews are concentrated in states which attacked us. Every step which hastens our victory may make their condition more serious."[63] Obviously, even before the establishment of Israel the leaders of the Yishuv were aware of the impact which the Arab-Jewish conflict would have upon Jews living in Arab countries. Dobkin erred, of course, in comparing the possible fate of Eastern Jews to the Holocaust in Europe, but their condition did grow more serious and over the years they lost their confidence in the possibility of being able to live in Muslim countries as citizens with equal rights.

The linkage between the condition of the Jews living in Muslim lands and political developments in the Middle East, especially the Arab-Israeli conflict, increased as time went on. The Six-Day War, of course, did not lessen the fears of these Jewish communities. In September 1967, a session of the Islamic Congress that was convened in Amman issued the following statement:

> The Jews of the Arab lands did not respect the protection granted them by Islam for many generations. The encouraged Zionism throughout the world and in Israel in its aggression against the Arabs. The congress declares that should it be corroborated that the Jews

---

[62] Minutes of the Mapai Central Committee, 12 July 1943, Mapai Archives, Beit Berl, File no. 23/43.

[63] *Minutes of a Conference of Representatives of Jews from Middle Eastern Countries, Jerusalem, 18 November 1948* (in Hebrew) (Jerusalem: 1948).

living in Muslim lands have any contact with Zionism or Israel, they should be considered enemies of Islam, and the protection which Muslims traditionally grant to the Jewish and Christian religions should be withdrawn from them. The congress further declares that all Muslim governments must view these Jews as constituting an enemy force; all Muslim nations, both as entities and as individuals, are duty bound to have nothing to do with the Jews and to treat them as sworn enemies.[64]

The following table summarizes emigration from Muslim lands after the Six-Day War, which was substantial both in numbers and significance.

TABLE 2

NUMBER OF JEWS IN MUSLIM COUNTRIES
FOLLOWING THE SIX-DAY WAR[65]

Country	1966	1969
Morocco	70,000	50,000
Algeria	3,000	1,500
Tunisia	23,000	10,000
Libya	6,000	100
Egypt and Sudan	2,500	(excluding Sudan) 1,000
Iraq	6,000	2,500
Yemen	2,000	—
Syria	4,000	4,000
Iran	80,000	80,000
Lebanon	6,000	3,000
Aden	400	—
Pakistan	300	250
Afghanistan	800	800
Turkey	40,000	39,000
Total	244,000	190,150

---

[64] *Bitefutzot* "The Jews," 90.

If we overlook the two large communities in which there was no real change in the number of Jews—those of Turkey and Iran—it transpires that more or less within one year of the Six-Day War some 73,000 Jews left the Muslim countries, about half of them emigrating from North Africa. The latter figure points to the gravity of the situation in the Maghreb as compared to other Muslim countries. Lebanon is an interesting case: most of its Jews emigrated even though the government adopted all possible measures to safeguard that community. The post-Six-Day War period was marked by a great increase in immigration to Israel from all over the world, but it seems that only the emigration from Muslim countries—including to Israel—was a result of political developments, and did not flow from other, more subjective, motives.

That being the case, we can now better understand what Arieh Tartakower—who in no small degree can be considered the historian of the World Jewish Congress—meant when he wrote:

> It is still too early for a final summation, but even now it is clear that Jewish misery in most Arab lands has increased.... [I]n only two of them Jews did not suffer, or almost did not suffer. They did not suffer in Lebanon which remained neutral—if not formally, at least in practice—during the Six-Day War, and it seems that no one attacked Jews there; they also did not suffer in Morocco (with the exception of the murder of two Jews in one of the provincial cities), where the government quickly intervened and silenced the inciting propaganda that could have led to mob violence (though according to the latest information the Jews are the target of an economic boycott which will be quite damaging to them). In contrast, in all other Arab countries the Jews were hard hit, whether by restrictions and persecution by the authorities, or by many acts of violence by rioters from among the general population.[66]

Tartakower was of the opinion that the Six-Day War caused a deterioration in the condition of the Jews in Arab lands. His reasoning ran as follows:

> The fate of the Jews in the USSR has long ceased to be a secret in the Arab countries, just as it is no longer a secret anywhere in the world. No matter what explanations or refutations are offered by the Soviet authorities, the Arabs readily interpret these as signs of an unmistakable anti-Jewish tendency, which suits their purposes. As far as the Arabs are concerned, the USSR's anti-Israel policy becomes

---

[65] The additional data for 1969 are taken from *AJYB* 1969.
[66] Tartakower, "The Fate of Jews," 591–93.

one with its anti-Jewish policy—and they just may be right. Thus, not only is there an increasingly hostile attitude which rejects any idea of peace with Israel, but—whether consciously or unconsciously – there is a growing sense among the Arabs that it is permissible to repress the Jews, for this is in the spirit of Soviet policy.[67]

This study of the situation of the Jewish communities in the Muslim countries began before the signing of the Oslo Accords but after the peace process between Israel and its neighbors had gotten underway, one in which Morocco played a central role. PLO presence on Tunisian soil, together with the Oslo process, placed Tunisia, too, in a position to mediate between Israel and the PLO. Reduced tension in the Arab-Israeli conflict together with pragmatic economic and political interests were among the primary causes that led Israelis who had formerly lived in Muslim states to strengthen their ties with the remnants of the Jewish communities in these countries, primarily Morocco, Tunisia, and Egypt.

In the wake of reactions to the Six-Day War in the Muslim countries, a closing of the gap between Israel and these states seemed implausible. An end to the Jewish presence in the Muslim world was deemed to be no more than a question of time or timing. The Oslo Accords, however, now place these communities at the beginning of a new process—one of expansion, economic prosperity and the ability to conduct a fairly normal communal life.

From the perspective of years, historical processes take on a somewhat different form than that discerned when one is close to the events. Is it possible that the remnants of Jewish communities in Moslem lands will be able to conduct flourishing communal life like their brethren in Europe and the United States? Had this study been completed a decade ago, it would not have such a possibility. Today there are signs, in a few of the Muslim countries, of processes indicative of different tendencies which themselves should be the object of careful study.

---

[67] Ibid. It is advisable to pay attention to any evaluation made by Tartakower because of his special status as representing the World Jewish Congress. His files are in CZA, Z6.

The Psychological and Political Consequences of the Six-Day War in the U.S.S.R.

Zvi Gitelman
The University of Michigan

PERHAPS NOWHERE ELSE in the Jewish Diaspora was the Six-Day War to have as revolutionary and long-lasting effect as it did in the Soviet Union. In the short term, the war galvanized a segment of Soviet Jewry to assert its identification with Israel and to reject the Soviet Union as hostile to Jews. Identification with Israel and rejection of the Soviet Union led logically to a demand for "repatriation" to Israel and to the emergence of a dissident movement for *aliyah* whose seeds had been scattered and planted long before. Concurrently, there was a change of priorities on the part of the world Jewish community vis-à-vis the Soviet government. Until the war, the main concern had been the general deprivation of civil rights suffered by Soviet Jews. Beginning in the late 1960s, the target was shifted to that of free emigration from the Soviet Union to Israel, which as a result of the war had been firmly established as a haven for Jews worldwide.

By the early 1980s, it seemed that the *aliyah* movement had run its course. After 1975, a majority of Jews leaving the Soviet Union went to the United States. The total number of émigrés declined precipitously with the deterioration in Soviet-American relations in the 1980s, and began to rise only in the Gorbachev era of *glasnost* and *perestroika*. Even then, emigration was not propelled by Zionist motivation.[1]

The later *aliyah* was not at all directly influenced by the events of 1967. In a survey I conducted among over 800 Soviet *olim* (immigrants to Israel) who came to Israel after 1989, only eight people (one percent) identified the Six-Day War as the "most important event in twentieth-century Jewish history." The establishment of the State of Israel was mentioned by 43

---

[1] For detailed histories and analyses of the development of Zionist sentiments and activities among Soviet Jews, see Yaacov Ro'i, *The Struggle for Soviet Jewish Emigration 1948–1967* (Cambridge: Cambridge University Press, 1991); and Benjamin Pinkus, *T'hiya ut'kuma leumit* (Sde Boker: Ben Gurion University Press, 1993).

percent, and the Holocaust by 34 percent. When asked which event during the course of the life of the interviewee had influenced him or her most of all, only ten percent mentioned the Six-Day War.

Nonetheless, it was the events of 1967 that made later emigration possible. Although the Six-Day War did not directly sustain *aliyah* or Jewish cultural-religious revival, it did set off processes of profound change in the outlook and activities of Soviet Jews, which ultimately resulted in the largest *aliyah* since the 1950s, a significant accretion to the American Jewish population, and a corresponding rapid depletion of Soviet Jewish population.

The Six-Day War was an unmistakable historical turning point for Israel and world Jewry. Surviving a threat to its very existence, Israel expanded greatly in terms of both territory and population under its control. For world Jewry, the Israeli victory was an affirmation of the viability of the Jewish state. Jews shared vicariously in the victory, feeling a sense of pride and vindication that affected their behavior not only toward Israel, but also vis-à-vis the populations among whom they lived as minorities. In the case of Soviet Jewry—the third largest Jewish population in the world—the war had an additional impact. They were citizens of a state that had most visibly supported the Arabs, being the largest supplier of the physical means by which Israeli Jewry might well have been destroyed. Yet the Jews were not only powerless to change their country's policy, they could not even protest it. Soviet Jews were acutely embarrassed by both these realities. Some were moved to reject the land of their birth and adopt Israel as their homeland whether in mind or—later—in deed. For those already convinced that Zionism was the solution to the "Jewish problem," the war served to reinforce their beliefs; for many others, it caused an awakening to the precariousness of their situation as Jews, activated their latent discontent and forced them to examine the viability of their status as Soviet Jews; even those who continued to view themselves as unquestionably loyal Soviet citizens were made uncomfortable by their country's policy during the war and in particular, the powerful anti-Zionist propaganda campaign that followed it. Thus, the war both reinforced and engendered feelings of alienation from the Soviet system.

The most prominent foe of Israel outside the Middle East, the country in which emigration was virtually unknown, the state in which no Zionist activity was permitted, became the single largest source of *aliyah* both following the war and, in a second wave, two decades later. Though its effects are longer direct, the processes set off by the Six-Day War continue to operate. To understand why this is so, it is necessary to examine the situation of Soviet Jews before 1967; the Soviet Union's role in the events leading up to the war and in the course of the fighting; and the consequences of the war both for Soviet policy and the Soviet Jewish population.

SOVIET JEWRY UNTIL 1967

In the decade following the Russian Revolution, Bolshevik authorities mounted a campaign against religion, Zionism, the Hebrew language, and Jewish political and cultural organizations. As a result, the traditional Jewish way of life was largely destroyed, with some remnants driven underground. While the long-range alternative was meant to be assimilation into other cultures, the Bolsheviks sponsored an intermediate substitute: a socialist, Yiddishist culture that was to serve as a bridge between "bourgeois-clerical" Jewish culture and the universal culture that was to emerge from the mutual "drawing together" and assimilation of nationalities. This, however, proved to be unpopular both among the older generation still loyal to traditional Jewishness and among the great majority of young Jews, who were drawn instead to the developing Soviet socialist and industrial urban culture. Overall, there was a strong tendency toward acculturation and assimilation. For about twenty years after the revolution, Jews enjoyed great social mobility and unparalleled opportunities in education, culture, politics, the professions, and the military. For the first time in Russian history, they suffered no restrictions or disabilities beyond those imposed upon the population as a whole. The state actively fought anti-Semitism—considered to be a "survival of the capitalist past"—and the "Jewish problem" seemed to be on the verge of solution. As Jews streamed from the *shtetlakh* to the cities, learned Russian and mingled with non-Jews, interest in their own culture faded, intermarriage rates rose steeply, and Jewish identity seemed increasingly irrelevant.

This vision of acceptance and integration proved to be illusory. By the end of the 1930s, the campaign against anti-Semitism was long dead. Soviet Yiddish culture was on the wane, and the heavy hand of terror had stifled even the most innocuous expression of national sentiment. At this point (between 1939 and 1941), the Soviet Union annexed eastern Poland, the Baltic states, and parts of Romania, and nearly two million largely unassimilated Jews became Soviet citizens. In this fashion, Soviet Jews became partly reconnected with their cultural heritage and with developments in world Jewry. Although many Zionists among the newcomers were imprisoned or exiled, they did manage to communicate their political ideas and convictions to at least some Soviet Jews.

The Holocaust, which took the lives of about 1.5 million Soviet Jews, dispelled many illusions concerning national equality and assimilation. Not only did the Nazis single out Jews for "special handling," irrespective of their Jewish commitment, but segments of the Soviet population collaborated in violent anti-Semitic activity. After the war, disillusionment was deepened by the loud silence that surrounded the Holocaust. Jewish suffering could hardly be mentioned: Jews were accused of having "fought the war in Tashkent," that is, far from the combat areas—despite the fact that half a million of them had been in the armed services. The double blow of losing so many Jews to the Nazis and then being slapped in the face by their fellow citizens awakened many Soviet Jews from their dream of "friendship among peoples."

Yet another blow was dealt shortly thereafter, this time from the very top of the system. Josef Stalin, "father of all the peoples," initiated a campaign against "rootless cosmopolitans"—a code word for Jews—who were presumed to have roots neither in the Soviet Union nor in any other country. Large numbers of Jews were expelled or demoted from their positions. The doors to higher education, once a main entrance to upward mobility, swung closed. Only Stalin's death in March 1953 prevented what appeared to be a major move against the Jews, perhaps including mass deportations to Siberia.

Following Stalin's death, overt governmental anti-Semitism abated, though nothing was done to counter anti-Semitism on the societal level. There was only a symbolic revival of Jewish cultural institutions. The first Yiddish book since the presses were closed down in 1948 came out in 1959, but only six books were published from that time until the end of Nikita Khrushchev's regime in 1964. Moreover, beginning in 1957, Khrushchev mounted a large-scale campaign against religion. Synagogues were singled out for special censure as nests of "speculation" and "economic crimes," and most of them were forcibly closed. This did not stop the government from accusing a disproportionate number of Jews of economic crimes; the proportion of Jews among those executed for such crimes was extraordinarily high.

Notwithstanding, Jews found it possible to enter higher educational institutions once again. Although they remained excluded from sensitive governmental and party posts, the fields of science and technology appeared to be open to them, and they went in those directions in large numbers. Nevertheless, it seemed quite clear to Jews (as well as others) that they were no longer equal members of society, but rather a tolerated marginal group that was excluded from the mainstream and relegated to particular sectors.

"Now we have our own cadres," Khrushchev's associates said, explaining to foreigners why Jews were no longer to be seen in governmental and party posts. Obviously, Jews were not considered "our own," and this perception was picked up quickly by the Jews—most of whom wanted nothing more than to belong. Faced, however, with unmistakable signals that their position would be marginal, some Jews reacted by dropping out of society, searching for alternatives in political reform, total dedication to one's work, religious experiences, or political cultural endeavors.

Khrushchev introduced a major shift in Soviet foreign policy that also indirectly affected Soviet Jews. Rejecting Stalin's view of the world as divided into two irreconcilable camps—the capitalist and socialist ones—Khrushchev identified a third camp of newly independent states, including the Arab world, whose allegiances would have to be won in competition with the capitalists. Beginning in 1955, the Soviet Union began to cultivate the Arab states. One consequence of this policy was a deterioration in Soviet-Israeli relations and an acceleration of anti-Israel and anti-Zionist messages in the Soviet media. Israel was identified with the "capitalist" and "imperialist" camp and its claims to being a socialist country were ridiculed. Few Jews were allowed to emigrate to Israel—between 1954 and 1964, only 1,452 Jews left directly for Israel—and occasionally there were articles in the Soviet press reporting their disappointment in the "promised land." Nevertheless, Jews were learning more about Israel as a result of contact with Jewish tourists from the West and Israeli diplomats and visitors. Concerts by Israeli performers drew overflow audiences; visiting Israeli athletes were cheered; and Israeli participants in the 1957 Moscow Youth Festival were besieged by local Jews, some of whom displayed remarkably detailed knowledge of that distant Jewish state.

The very creation of Israel had fired the imagination of many Jews of all generations. As physicist Mark Azbel recalls,

> Our sensation in 1948 was like that of an incurable paralytic who was suddenly told he would yet run. Life had 'anti-educated' Jews for too long, raising them as internal anti-Semites, almost ashamed of themselves.... And suddenly, the Jews fight, and like David, they are victorious. One could straighten up inside.[2]

In their enthusiasm, some young Soviet Jews even volunteered to fight for Israel. The authorities soon arrested them, but such repression did not put

---

[2] Mark Azbel, "Autobiography of a Jew," in *In Search of Self*, ed. David Prital (Jerusalem: Mount Scopus Publications, 1982), 61.

an end to interest in Israel—though as Soviet policy changed, people became more circumspect about demonstrating that interest. There were various perfectly legitimate ways of doing so. A former Leningrader, for example, described a series of public lectures on the Middle East given in the 1960s. Most of the audience was Jewish. The lecture on Israel drew the largest crowd of all, as people struggled to find a place even to stand. The lecturer, a specialist in Arab countries, turned with good humor to the audience and remarked: "I'm pleased to see that there's so much interest in lectures on Asia and Africa." The crowd laughed in appreciation.[3]

The return of Zionist prisoners from camps and exile in the mid- and late-1950s also contributed to interest in Israel and knowledge of Zionist ideology. Several years later, the Eichmann trial of 1961 reminded younger generations of the fate of the Jews during the Holocaust. But the single most effective force for the growth of national consciousness was social and governmental anti-Semitism. The Soviet authorities themselves did more to preserve Jewish identity—through the system of official nationality identification and policies that singled out the Jews—than did any efforts by "Zionist conspirators" and their allies.

Yosef Mendelevitch, later imprisoned for trying to leave the country illegally, described how he felt as the only Jew in an elementary school class. He waited "like a hunted animal" as the teacher went around the room asking students their nationality: "'Jew,' I breathed with effort. The whole class burst into laughter. From that point I no longer grew up like an ordinary Soviet citizen and I did not like the Soviet Union."[4] Similarly, Alla Rusinek described her dread each year when on the first day of school each child had to announce his or her name, nationality, and father's occupation:

> She asks my nationality and then it begins. The whole class suddenly becomes very quiet. Some look at me steadily. Others avoid my eyes. I have to say this word...which sounds so unpleasant. Why? There is really nothing wrong with its sound, *Yev-rei-ka* [Jew]. But I never hear the word except when people are cursing somebody.... Every time I try to overcome my feelings, but each year the word comes out in a whisper: *Yev-rei-ka*.[5]

---

[3] Ben Kohrin, *Mah koreh sham* (Tel Aviv: Am Oved, 1970), 182–83.
[4] Yosef Mendelevitch, *Mivtza khatuna* (Jerusalem: Keter, 1985), 14.
[5] Alla Rusinek, *Like a Song, Like a Dream* (New York: Charles Scribner's Sons, 1973), 20.

Some children learned early on that they were different from all the rest, and that difference was not in their favor. For others, the awakening came later—when denied entrance to a university for which they qualified, or for a job for which they had all the credentials, or a promotion, or a trip abroad. Twenty years earlier they would have accepted their fate with resignation, but by the 1960s many were determined not to be reconciled any longer. At a time when terror had receded, some reacted by taking a chance and asserting themselves rather than hiding.

About a decade before the Six-Day War, several of the leading Zionist activists in the Baltic republics had begun to express a new mood of national affirmation in amateur musical and dance groups. Jews of several generations began to sing in a choir or meet in small groups to learn Hebrew or discuss topics of Jewish interest. They also began to go to mass memorial meetings held at the graves of those murdered by the Nazis. At first these were attended by only a few dozen people, but from year to year the numbers grew: recalling the fate of their fellow Jews, they could not help but ponder their own.

A different kind of gathering also became popular at about the same time. In the major cities—where, at best, one synagogue remained open— young Jews began to congregate on the joyous holiday of *Simchat Torah*. They turned it into a social and national festival, meeting and socializing, exchanging views, information, or simply telephone numbers. They did not come to pray, largely because they did not know how. Soviet Jews were coming together as a community of fate, not of faith.

THE SOVIET ROLE IN THE SIX-DAY WAR

As tension between Israel and Syria mounted in the spring of 1967, Soviet officials told a visiting Egyptian parliamentary delegation (headed by Anwar Sadat) that Israel was concentrating troops on the Syrian border in preparation for an attack on Syria. Some have argued that the Soviets deliberately exaggerated the Israeli threat to Syria. Leonid Chuvakhin, the Soviet ambassador to Israel, refused an invitation to inspect the border area for himself. Meanwhile, Soviet newspapers reported that "tension is mounting" in the region and that various Arab states had pledged their support to Egypt.[6] Joseph Govrin's careful analysis of Soviet actions at this time concluded that "the Soviet Union wanted to secure the stationing of

---

[6] See, for example, *Pravda*, 25 May 1967.

Egyptian forces in Sinai as a force threatening Israel from the south, while Nasser's decisions taken as a result [demanding the evacuation of United Nations troops from Sinai and closing the Straits of Tiran to Israel] were his alone."[7] Soviet leaders did not believe that Israel would launch a preemptive strike against Egypt: "Soviet support for the Egyptian decisions was therefore intended to buttress the Syrian regime by warding off the Israeli threat and to award Egypt political-military gains as compensation for her readiness to come to the aid of Syria."[8]

A Soviet specialist on Israel, Galina Nikitina, later explained that Egypt's actions in the Sinai were "defensive measures" and that Israel had planned her "aggression" at least six months in advance. Defending Egyptian President Nasser's demand for the withdrawal of U.N. troops from the Sinai Peninsula, she argued that "one of the motives for this request was that the presence of U.N. troops...would give Israel military advantages in the event of an armed provocation against Syria."[9] Closing the Straits of Tiran to Israeli vessels merely reaffirmed Egypt's "undisputed sovereign rights to the Gulf of Aqaba"; essentially, all that Egypt wanted to do was to force a "broad examination of the problems of Arab-Israeli relations at an international forum, and this, to some extent, undoubtedly lay at the back [sic] of the restraint displayed by the U.A.R. leaders on the military-strategic level." In other words, it was Israel that insisted on a military confrontation.[10] The absurdity of Nikitina's arguments and her significant use of qualifiers ("to some extent") reflect the difficult position the Soviets were in when they attempted to explain the course of events as something other than an embarrassing fiasco.

Soviet authorities very quickly depicted Israel's "aggression" as part of a larger "imperialist" effort. The Central Committee of the Communist Party, in one of the first such statements soon after the war, proclaimed that "Israel's aggression is the result of a plot by the most reactionary forces of international imperialism, first and foremost the U.S.A., directed against one of the detachments of the national-liberation movement...."[11] Israel's militancy was said to be motivated by the desire for territorial expansion

---

[7] Joseph Govrin, "The Six-Day War in the Mirror of Soviet-Israeli Relations, April–June 1967," Jerusalem: Soviet and East European Research Centre, Hebrew University of Jerusalem, Research Paper No. 61, November 1985, 11.
[8] Ibid., 17
[9] Galina Nikitina, *The State of Israel* (Moscow: Progress, 1973), 317.
[10] Ibid., 318.
[11] *Pravda*, 22 June 1967.

and a concern to protect the interests of the oil companies (!). Other Soviet commentators cited Israel's desire to topple "progressive" regimes in Syria and Egypt and move other Arab states closer to the West.[12] The media relied mostly on the Arab press and radio—though they were always careful to point out the sources of their reports—and on Soviet correspondents in Cairo and Damascus. Some Western observers assert that the Soviet press did not fully report Israel's victories, but an examination of the various Soviet newspapers reveals that the attentive Soviet reader would have had no trouble discerning the extent of the Israeli advance and of the Arab defeat.[13] On June 7, for example, the Soviet press reported that Israel had captured Gaza and quoted General Yitzhak Rabin, the Israeli chief of staff, as he announced the capture of Jenin in the West Bank and several points in the Sinai.[14] The next day, *Pravda* reported that the Egyptian army had "retreated to the second line of defense," as Israeli tanks were on their way to the Suez Canal and Israeli troops had taken a series of "inhabited places" in Jordanian territory.[15] Evgeny Primakov, then chief correspondent for *Pravda* in Cairo, reported that same day that Israeli aircraft had bombarded Helwan and industrial suburbs of Cairo and that Israeli warships could be seen around Alexandria[16]; *Izvestiia* quoted Reuters on the extent of the Israeli advance in the Sinai and mentioned that Israeli troops had taken "Old Jerusalem, the Jordanian half of the divided city."[17] During this time, realistic reports about conditions in Cairo and Damascus were filed by Soviet correspondents. On June 11, *Pravda* reported the capture of El-Kuneitra on the Golan Heights, noting that the city was fifty-five miles from Damascus, and acknowledged as well that Israeli planes had bombed Damascus and Homs.[18] By June 13, an *Izvestiia* correspondent noted that "the Israeli army is in position in the Suez Canal region, on the West Bank of the Jordan River, and on Syrian territory."[19]

One somewhat difficult task for the media was to explain the loss of the "progressive" and numerous Arab forces to the outnumbered Israelis. A

---

[12] L. Sheidin, "The Arab Peoples' Just Cause," *International Affairs* 8 (1967): 40.
[13] See *Jews in Eastern Europe* 3, no. 7 (November 1967): 57.
[14] "Ozhestechennye boi," *Vechernaia Moskva*, 7 June 1967; "Voennye deistviia prodolzhaiutsiia," *Zaria Vostoka*, 7 June 1967.
[15] "Voennye deistviia na blizhnem vostoke," *Pravda*, 8 June 1967.
[16] "Boi prodolzhaetsiia," *Pravda*, 8 June 1967.
[17] Soobshcheniia o voennykh deistviiakh," *Isvestiia*, 8 June 1967.
[18] "Siriia vedet oboronitelnye boi," *Pravda*, 11 June 1967.
[19] L. Koriavin, "Na provode-Kair," *Izvestiia*, 13 June 1967.

major theme of the explanation was the element of surprise, labeled "blitzkrieg" in order to arouse invidious associations with the German attack on the Soviet Union in 1941. It was admitted by some that the Israelis were well-trained and well-educated, though it was asserted that they had "military men of Jewish nationality from Western armies" to assist them.[20] In contrast, most of the Arab soldiers were poorly-educated peasants:

> This was the big difference. On the one hand was a modern army of invaders under the black banner of colonialist enslavement, an army of fanatics just like Hitler's army was at the beginning...while on the other hand, we had an army of peasants and workers, upholding their just cause, peasants and workers who manned tanks and self-propelled guns, but who had not yet mastered them completely.[21]

It was not mentioned where those weapons had come from.

Of course, many Jews did not rely on Soviet sources alone for their information. Any Western or Israeli broadcast was listened to with great attentiveness. Alla Rusinek has described how a Jewish couple from Riga found two issues of *L'Express* in their Kiev hotel room, bribed a maid not to confiscate them, and brought them back to Riga where they were translated and circulated widely in *samizdat*.[22] The remarkably efficient system of informal transmission of information was working overtime among the Jews, who were mining every conceivable source of information about the war. But even those who confined themselves to the Soviet media managed to get a fair idea of the war's outcome, even if the account was scanty in details and biased in analysis.

THE IMPACT OF THE SIX-DAY WAR ON SOVIET JEWRY

Different groupings among the Soviet Jews perceived the impact of the Six-Day War in various ways. Ironically, it was the committed Zionists who were probably the least affected by it; the war's outcome merely reinforced their convictions about both Israel and the Soviet Union. For example, Hillel Butman, later a defendant in the Leningrad airplane hijacking trial of 1970, had begun his Zionist activities some years before the war; he does

---

[20] Radio Peace and Progress in English for Asia, quoted in Yaacov Ro'i, *From Encroachment to Involvement* (Jerusalem: Israel Universities Press, 1974), 448.

[21] Ibid., 449. Nikitina later added the arguments that the Israeli Communist Party had been suppressed, eliminating domestic opposition to the war, and that Israel had used especially brutal tactics, including napalm bombings.

[22] Rusinek, *Like a Song*, 259.

not even mention the war in his memoir.[23] Ilya Ehrenburg, in contrast, was a respected member of the Soviet establishment and the author of a famous article condemning Israel in 1948. In a private interview, he said that it was a good thing that the Israelis had not be "exterminated" by the Arabs:

> There is still this unpleasant feeling that it's "natural" for Jews to be massacred. If, following in Hitler's footsteps, the Arabs had started massacring all the Jews in Israel, the infection would have spread: We would have had here a wave of anti-Semitism. Now, for once, the Jews have shown that *they* can also kick you hard in the teeth; so now there is a certain respect for the Jews as soldiers....[24]

As Mark Azbel has noted:

> The war...was the most exciting experience of a lifetime to thousands and thousands of Soviet Jews. None of us thought of anything but the war during that agonizing week. We hovered over our radios, hardly daring to breathe.... Overnight we recognized how close was the fate of Israel to our hearts.[25]

Mark Dymshitz, born into an assimilated Jewish family, married to a Russian, with children registered as Russian by nationality, had encountered anti-Semitism in his work as a pilot. But what turned him into an active Jew was the fact that

> at the very time in which the Egyptian dictator was loudly declaring his aim of destroying Israel, here was my country, the Soviet Union, supporting and arming this would-be exterminator. This shook me. I was powerless to decry this one-sided Soviet stand from within. And then the thought came to me that if I cannot oppose Soviet policy ...from the inside, I had better leave and go to where I could say what was in my heart, to Israel.[26]

A young librarian in Odessa came to a similar conclusion. "I understood that I could have no future in the country in which I was born," she explained. "I began to interest myself in everything connected with

---

[23] Hillel Butman, *Leningrad-Yerushalayim, vekhanaya aruka beineihen* (Tel Aviv: Kibbutz Hameukhad, 1981).
[24] Alexander Werth, *Russia: Hopes and Fears,* 218–19, quoted in William Korey, *The Soviet Cage* (New York: Viking, 1973), 124–51.
[25] Mark Y. Azbel, *Refusenik* (Boston: Houghton Mifflin, 1981), 214.
[26] Mark Dymshitz, interview, *Jerusalem Post,* 4 May 1979.

Israel, and friends who felt as I did discussed the possibility of leaving for Israel."[27]

It is an exaggeration to claim that "most Jews were awakened as Jews by the Six-Day War."[28] As we have seen, Jewish consciousness had long been stimulated on the one hand by anti-Semitism and second-class status and, on the other, by positive feelings toward Israel and various aspects of Jewish culture. What did happen was that in the month before the war many Soviet Jews realized how endangered the Jewish state was and how much their own country had contributed to the danger. During and after the war their pride in being Jewish—and thus being associated with Israel—was increased tremendously. A sixteen-year-old girl at the time recalls that "we were changed completely.... I remember coming to class the morning after hearing on the BBC that the Israelis had reached Gaza. There were several Jewish students and we discussed it openly...as we had never before dared to do. We felt so exhilarated.... I felt that I was born just then." In a family that had "never...exhibited any signs of their Jewishness," a party was made to celebrate the victory, "as if we had taken part in the war ourselves."[29] Jewish dignity and self-confidence, eroded by years of impotence in the face of discrimination, were restored. Alla Rusinek notes that "it is difficult to describe how Jewish backs were straightened after the War.... And the more anti-Israeli articles appeared in the Soviet press, the surer we were that Israel and we were right."[30] As Mark Azbel comments, "What a different world it became when the most notable event in one's national consciousness was not the familiar tide of persecution and defeat, but a triumph that would live in history."[31] A man who later jumped ship in order to get to Israel remembers that the war

> made a tremendous impression on me.... I had been brought up to believe that Jews were weak and would always remain that way. Suddenly those weak individuals...had become strong and overcame mighty enemies. Israel became the symbol of bravery and courage for me.... Imperceptibly my links with Israel and the Jewish people were growing stronger.[32]

---

[27] Raiza Palatnik, quoted in Leonard Schroeter, *The Last Exodus* (New York: Universe, 1974), 242.
[28] Sylvia Rothchild, *A Special Legacy* (New York: Simon and Schuster, 1985), 105.
[29] Ibid., 52.
[30] Rusinek, *Like a Song*, 260.
[31] Azbel, *Refusenik*, 215.
[32] Aryeh Gur, *The Escape: From Kiev to Tel Aviv* (Ann Arbor: Translation Press, 1982), 30.

The war also affected non-Jewish perceptions of the Jews. On the one hand, Soviet Jews were associated with Israel in the minds of Soviet non-Jews, and respect for them grew with Israel's victory. Nearly 60 percent of several hundred Soviet Jewish emigrés who were interviewed reported that non-Jews drew a connection between Jews and Israel.[33] Azbel no doubt exaggerates when he claims that "no pro-Israeli or pro-Jewish propaganda...could have done half as much to defeat popular anti-Semitism as this war,"[34] but the Jews unquestionably gained respect in the eyes of their neighbors, at least temporarily.[35] A Latvian-born scientist recalls that "the Six-Day War moved not only Jews but also Russians, who suddenly discovered that Jews know how to fight. The always hostile Latvians respected the Jews as allies resisting the Soviet regime."[36] The situation was different in Central Asia, with its large Muslim population. There, hostility toward the Jews rose, as the local population believed that the Israelis had engaged in an anti-Islamic war and had seized and desecrated Muslim holy places. Nearly 70 percent of Central Asian Jewish émigrés questioned reported that non-Jews connected them with Israel.[37]

The events in the Middle East were given great prominence in the Soviet media; one could hardly avoid the barrage of excoriation that was aimed at Israel. Meetings were held throughout the country to protest Israeli occupation of Arab territory and alleged atrocities. A review of the Soviet press reveals that no fewer than 260 meetings protesting Israel's "occupation" were held in Soviet factories in the week of June 10 alone, and there were undoubtedly many more such meetings that were not reported in the press. Hundreds of letters were sent to newspapers by groups and individuals protesting Israel's actions. Support was pledged to "the Arab peoples," though its precise nature was not usually specified. One can easily imagine how Jews felt when participating in such meetings or even just reading and hearing about them.

---

[33] Survey conducted by Zvi Gitelman, Israel, 1985.
[34] Azbel, *Refusenik*, 216.
[35] The identification of Jews with Israel in the minds of other Soviets is illustrated in the following anecdote, widely circulated at the time. A Jew appears in court to complain against a Soviet officer who had attacked him. The accused explained his actions. "The radio said the aggressors had taken Gaza. Then I heard that they had reached the Suez Canal. Then I turned around, and I saw the aggressor had already reached Moscow. I had to defend our country against the aggressor, so I hit this Jew."
[36] Herman Branover, *The Return* (Jerusalem and New York: Feldheim, 1982), 97.
[37] Survey by Zvi Gitelman, 1985.

These meetings were only the beginning of a massive propaganda campaign condemning Israel and Zionism. A prominent theme in the campaign was that the Israelis were committing atrocities in the territories they had captured. Prime Minister Alexei Kosygin said at the United Nations that "atrocities and violence in the captured territories bring to mind the heinous crimes perpetrated by the Fascists during World War Two."[38] Israelis were accused of murdering prisoners of war, expelling people from their homes, and publicly hanging women and children.[39] The Soviet satirical magazine *Krokodil* portrayed Moshe Dayan as a Nazi and labeled him "Moshe Adolfovich Dayan."[40] At this point, Jews were not mobilized to express public condemnation of Israel, but this later became standard Soviet practice.

The first massive anti-Zionist campaign was launched in late July 1967. William Korey suggests that its purpose was to identify a scapegoat that would explain why the Soviet's clients had suffered such a major defeat, and why the Soviet Union itself had not succeeded, through diplomatic means, in forcing an Israeli withdrawal from captured territories. "Tiny Israel" could not be the explanation for these failures, and so "the enemy must rather be presented as a hidden, all-powerful, and perfidious international force, linked somehow with Israel."[41] This was Zionism. There is no doubt that the Soviet government was deeply embarrassed by the outcome of the war. In some respects, it reacted childishly: it struck out irrationally at forces that had little to do with the defeat; it shifted blame for its own miscalculations to others, and it conjured up some uncontrollable malevolent force as the cause of the catastrophe. Jonathan Frankel views the campaign somewhat differently, suggesting that it came in response to "an essentially internal issue, a crisis even,"—namely, mounting pressure by Soviet Jews for emigration to Israel.[42] However, Frankel focuses primarily on the later campaign of 1969–1971, whereas Korey describes the campaign launched immediately after the 1967 war. The two approaches are quite compatible: what may have begun as a campaign designed to explain away the Soviet political and Arab military defeat in 1967, changed

---

[38] Quoted in Ro'i, *Struggle for Soviet Jewish Emigration*, 452.
[39] *Izvestiia*, 15 June 1967, quoted in *Jews in Eastern Europe*, 8, no. 7 (November 1967): 77.
[40] *Krokodil* 19 (July 1967).
[41] Korey, *Soviet Cage*, 144.
[42] Jonathan Frankel, "The Anti-Zionist Press Campaigns in the USSR 1969–1971: An Internal Dialogue?" *Soviet Jewish Affairs* 3 (May 1972): 5.

into an "internal dialogue" of the Soviet government and the Jews. Zev Katz adds to these explanations the possibility that the Soviets wanted to dampen internal opposition to their Middle East policy, counter a certain amount of criticism on the part of East and West European Communists, and demonstrate their support for the Arabs.[43] Whatever its motivation, the escalation of the campaign was unmistakable. According to one count, seven books attacking Israel were published in 1967. Two years later, the number rose to ten, and between 1970 and 1974, 134 such books were published. In 1967, there were at least 110 articles in the press on Zionism and Soviet Jewry; in 1970, there were 332.[44]

One of the salient themes in the anti-Zionist propaganda was the equation of Israel with Nazi Germany. As early as July 5, 1967, when Party Secretary Leonid Brezhnev addressed the graduates of a military academy, he said "the Israeli aggressors are behaving like the worst of bandits. In their atrocities against the Arab population it seems they want to copy the crimes of the Hitlerite invaders."[45] A month later, a Ukrainian newspaper sounded what was to become a common theme: "In essence, Zionism is a species of racism, a variety of fascism."[46] Yeshayahu Nir's analysis of political caricatures in the Soviet press demonstrates that, in *Pravda*, Nazism was linked to Israel more often than to the colonels' regime in Greece, the Vietnam war, or NATO: "The parallel with the Nazis was focused almost exclusively on Israel, especially during the summer of 1967 and the winter of 1970. The names of Nazi concentration camps were mentioned solely in an Israeli context."[47] One of the more virulent "specialists" in Zionism, Evgeny Evseev, yoked Zionism to capitalism, fascism, and Israel. Israel's military appetite was said to be whetted by

> the support of an unseen, immense and powerful empire of Zionist financiers and industrialists, which is on no map of the world but which exists and operates everywhere in the capitalist camp.... In the practical application of Zionism to the affairs of the Near East, geno-

---

[43] Zev Katz, "The Aftermath of the June War—Soviet Propaganda Offensive Against Israel and World Jewry," *Bulletin on Soviet Jewish Affairs* 1 (January 1968): 21–23.
[44] Benjamin Pinkus, *Yehudei russiya ubrit hamoetsot* (Beersheva: Ben-Gurion University Press, 1986), 398–99.
[45] *Pravda*, 6 July 1967.
[46] *Pravda Ukrainy*, 5 August 1967.
[47] Yeshayahu Nir, *The Israeli-Arab Conflict in Soviet Caricatures 1967–1973* (Tel Aviv: Tsherikover, 1976), 81.

cide, racism, perfidy, aggressiveness, annexation—all characteristic attributes of Fascism—are present.[48]

Traditional anti-Semitic images of "unseen, immense, and powerful" empires were combined with the linkage between Zionism and Israel.

The identification of Israel and Zionism with Nazism may have been designed to "explain" Israel and its ideology in a manner that was concrete, terrifying, and repulsive. The great majority of the Soviet population, after all, had no real knowledge of the Jewish state. If they looked on a map they would have to ask themselves how such a small country could be so successful in defeating enemies who were considerably larger and more numerous. While few Soviet citizens could have any idea of Zionism, they knew only too well what Nazism and Fascism represented. By linking Zionism and Israel to the ideology and country that had caused the death of more than twenty million Soviet citizens and that had destroyed much of the country, Soviet propaganda was attempting to excite genuine passion among a population who might otherwise have remained quite indifferent to a regional war involving peoples with whom they had little contact and for whom they had little sympathy. Jews were disgusted and enraged by this identification of the Jewish state with those who had murdered six million Jews, but this, of course, did not restrain the Soviets. While the theme may have aroused more anti-Israel and anti-Zionist feeling among the population at large—there is no way to ascertain this empirically—it almost certainly reinforced a Jewish sense of alienation and embarrassment. Just as the events of 1967 increased the alienation of many Jews from the Soviet Union, so too did the subsequent anti-Zionist campaign.

Conclusion

The 1967 Middle East war opened a new era in the history of Soviet Jewry, though in some ways a short one. On the one hand, the war served as a catalyst activating interest in Israel and Jewishness that had been developing among some Soviet Jews. On the other hand, it jolted many out of indifference to their own Jewishness. It strengthened Zionists in their beliefs about the impossibility of Jewish life in the Diaspora and the desirability of living in a Jewish state. It convinced people that the State of Israel was viable. On these grounds, many began to apply for emigration to

---

[48] Evgeny Evseev, "Lackeys Running Errands," *Komsomolskaia Pravda*, 4 October 1967, translated in *Bulletin on Soviet Jewish Affairs*, 1 (January 1968): 29–30.

Israel, launching a mass movement that was to last for six years, until the emigration movement began to shift direction and Jews headed in greater numbers to the United States. The period 1967–1973 was marked by an unexpected mass *aliyah* from a country that had hitherto allowed only tiny numbers of Jews to go to Israel.

For one segment of the Soviet population, the effect of the war was compounded by the Soviet invasion of Czechoslovakia the following year. That forceful intervention with the attempt to fashion "socialism with a human face" convinced many in the Soviet Union—a large number of Jews among them—that the Soviet system would not tolerate reform, not even in allied states. Many who had pinned their hopes on internal reform changed gears and joined the growing numbers of Jews who were seeking to go to Israel.

As Jews began to emigrate, the number of Jews admitted into institutions of higher education began to decline. Jews also found it more difficult to gain employment or promotion. From the official Soviet point of view, this was only logical: if Jews were potential émigrés and hence "traitors" to their country, why should the Soviet Union educate them, promote them, or put any faith in them? Following the war, a qualitative change came about in the relationship between the regime and the Jews. It may not have been the result of a comprehensive policy, but it emerged from the actions and reactions of the two parties. It seemed as if the relationship was deteriorating to the point of a final divorce. Reconciliation between the regime and the Jews became impossible, as each side felt injured and betrayed by the other.

A second major consequence of the war, more easily reversed than the first, was the diplomatic rupture between the Soviet Union and Israel. On June 10, 1967, the Soviet Union broke diplomatic relations with Israel, a step followed by Yugoslavia and all members of the Soviet bloc save Romania. Joseph Govrin suggests several reasons for the break: it was an attempt to stop Israel's advance on Syria; a reaction to pressure from Marshall Tito of Yugoslavia, who was Nasser's ally; an alternative to military intervention; and a means of curbing the national awakening among Soviet Jews by eliminating Israeli activity in the country.[49] On the last point, the Soviet action did in fact reduce the immediate Israeli impact on Soviet Jewry, though in the following years Israeli influence might have even grown as radio and personal communication intensified. The break in

---

[49] Govrin, "Six-Day War," 24.

relations, followed by similar action on the part of the Soviet Union's allies, certainly helped to isolate Israel diplomatically. Israel struggled for twenty years to recover from the pariah status it began to acquire following the Six-Day War (which worsened in the aftermath of the Yom Kippur War). Ironically, the Soviet Union's ability to play a role in the international politics of the Middle East was thereby reduced. While it continued to be a major arms supplier to the region, the Soviet Union found that its ability to act as a negotiator, go-between, and peacemaker became limited over the years by Israel's logical insistence that such roles be filled only by those states with whom it had full diplomatic relations.

In addition to its effects on Soviet Jewry and the Soviet role in the Middle East, the war contributed to instability in Eastern Europe. Part of the Czechoslovak intelligentsia was dismayed by the alacrity with which their government followed the Soviet lead in breaking relations with Israel despite the fact that most Czechs were sympathetic to the Israeli side. At a Czechoslovak writers' congress in November 1967 a number of speakers pointed to the government's action as an example of its toadying to the Soviet Union rather than being responsive to its own public. This was one of the expressions of dissent that led to the political crisis which brought Alexander Dubcek's reformists into power. In Poland, the consequences were different. Painfully aware that substantial segments of Polish society sympathized with Israel during the war—if only because Israel was fighting against Soviet clients—Wladyslaw Gomulka warned that such sentiments would not be tolerated. If there were Jews whose loyalties were divided between Poland and Israel—as he asserted there were—they had best leave the country. Indeed, some Polish Jews reacted to the war as Soviet Jews had done. A former Polish army officer commented:

> For us, Jews...the last illusions about the Soviet Union were shattered.... Reality made us conscious of the fact that we shared a common fate with the Jews of Israel who were in danger.... A feeling of identification with Israel developed in a natural way, even among those who had regarded the Jewish state as alien until now.... At that time one could observe an interesting phenomenon, how people who had distanced themselves, or tried to, from Jewishness, felt suddenly that they were Jewish.[50]

---

[50] Kalman Nusboim, "Al hayehudim bepolin akharai milkhemet sheshet hayamim —keta zikhronot," *Shvut* 12 (1978): 131. As the author was in the minority of Polish Jews who immigrated to Israel after 1968, one cannot be sure whether this reaction was as widely shared as he claims.

The "Zionist" issue was then seized upon by Mieczyslaw Moczar and other political enemies of Gomulka, who accused him of heading a regime that was shot through with Zionists. Moczar and others demanded a purge of the Jews, which took place (their ultimate goal appears to have been to replace Gomulka with their own group, which they failed to do). Ironically, Gomulka's speech in March 1968—in which he said that Jews in Poland who felt tied to Israel were "going to leave our country sooner or later," was reprinted in *Pravda,* triggering hope among some Soviet Jews that socialist countries other than Poland would allow emigration to Israel.

The war moved the Soviet Union closer to the Arabs, and after they broke relations with Israel, the Soviets found that their room for maneuvering among the players in the Middle East was more restricted. They also found that the Arab-Israeli conflict became a major issue in their relations with the United States, so much so that in the next war, the October 1973 conflict, the two sides came close to an armed confrontation.

Thus, the 1967 Arab-Israeli war proved to be a true turning point in several places outside of Israel. In the Soviet Union, it crystallized and made visible certain tendencies toward national affirmation and assertion that had been building up in the previous decade. Among some Jews it brought a shock of recognition, that both their position in Soviet society was precarious and that, like it or not, they were affected by what went on in Israel. It changed the self-image, the behavior, and the tactics of many Jews in the Soviet Union. It accelerated the tendency toward *aliyah,* although by the late 1970s that tendency had been transformed into one of *yetziah* (emigration *from* the Soviet Union rather than *to* Israel). The war changed the Soviet position in the Middle East. More than a quarter century after the war, nearly a million Soviet Jews have emigrated; Jewish communal life is being reconstructed on the territories of the former Soviet Union; the Soviet regime no longer exists; and none of her successor states plays a major role in the Middle East.

This essay draws heavily on my article, "The Soviet Jewish Revolution," in *The Impact of the Six-Day War,* ed. Stephen Roth (London: Macmillan, 1988); selections quoted by permission of Macmillan Press, Ltd.

New Documentation on Public Opinion and the Jewish Reaction in the U.S.S.R. to the Six-Day War

Mordechai Altshuler

Avraham Harman Institute of Contemporary Jewry
The Hebrew University of Jerusalem

UNTIL RECENTLY, scholars could avail themselves of two major types of source materials concerning the reaction of non-Jews and Jews in the U.S.S.R. to the Six-Day War: (a) the Soviet media; (b) testimony presented by persons who had emigrated from the U.S.S.R.

The most important sources were the Soviet printed and electronic media—the press, radio, and television. These presented the official policy of the authorities, both in current news reports as well as in-depth articles and editorial commentary.

During the latter half of April 1967, the Soviet press published reports of military clashes along the Israel-Syrian frontier, emphasizing that Israel bore the major responsibility for the tense situation in the Middle East.[1] On 5 June the radio and the afternoon press notified the Soviet public of an Israeli attack against the Arab states.[2] According to the next day's editorials, this was an attack mounted against freedom- and peace-loving states, and was no less than an imperialist plot directly encouraged by the United States. Soviet correspondents in Damascus and Cairo reported during the next two days that the Israeli offensive had been unsuccessful and that Egyptian armor was speedily advancing on Tel Aviv.[3] However, on 8 June the press noted that the Egyptian forces were retreating to a second line of defense having inflicted heavy casualties on the Israelis.[4] To old-timers who remembered the Second World War, such reports were reminiscent of the staggering defeats of the Red Army, when the Soviet media used similar phraseology. By now, the U.S.S.R. leadership realized that the Arab states

---

[1] V. Popov, "Proiski reaktsii obrecheny," *Krasnaia Zvezda*, 30 April 1967.
[2] *Vechernaia Moskva*, 5 June 1967.
[3] *Pravda*, 7 June 1967; *Vechernaia Moskva*, 7 June 1967.
[4] *Pravda*, 8 June 1967; *Izvestiia*, 8 June 1967.

had suffered such a resounding defeat on the battleground as to necessitate a Soviet reaction. On 9 June it convened an urgent meeting of representatives of the Communist parties of the satellite states, including Yugoslavia, at which resolutions were adopted condemning Israeli aggression and expressing absolute support for the Arab states. Only Romania refused to sign.[5] From now on, any statement critical of the Arabs—even if referring to the distant past—would not be tolerated, and any hint of a positive evaluation of Israeli leaders would not be condoned. Two instances will suffice to illustrate this state of affairs.

On 14 June 1967, the Armenian newspaper *Aireniki Dzain* (Voice of the Homeland) published an article entitled "The Armenian Nation's Struggle against the Caliphate," tracing a history of Armenian defense against Arab invaders. Though written by the Armenian historian Aram Tergevozhdian long before the Six-Day War, and published in a paper meant primarily to foster relations between Soviet Armenia and Armenians living outside the U.S.S.R., the timing of its publication led the authorities to view it as being detrimental to Soviet relations with the Arab world. Upon the orders of Andropov, chief of the KGB, all copies of that issue were confiscated and the editor, Vaagan Dovtian, was removed from his post because he was found lacking in political awareness.[6]

On 12 July the *Literaturnaia Gazeta*, the organ of the Union of Writers, reproduced—under the heading "Another Feature"—a photo of a medallion bearing the likeness of Moshe Dayan that had been minted in Germany. Dayan's features were those of a normal human being, not the demonic visage by which he was depicted in cartoons in the Soviet press. The Propaganda Department of the Central Committee of the Communist Party considered this to be a grave mistake and so notified the journal's editorial board, which convened to discuss the matter. On 19 July, the editors wrote to the Propaganda Department explaining that their intention had been to point to "another feature" of Moshe Dayan—i.e., his connections with West Germany, generally represented in the Soviet media as a hotbed of Fascism. The Propaganda Department, however, did not accept the editorial board's explanation and next day sent a letter to the Central Committee, terming the publication of the photo of the medallion a grave error on the part of the editors of *Literaturnaia Gazeta* which

---

[5] "Zaiavlenie Tsentral'nykh Komitetov kommunisticheskikh i rabochikh partii i pravitel'stv...," *Pravda*, 10 June 1967.
[6] Secret letter from KGB Head Andropov, 16 June 1967, TsKhSD collection [fond] 5, inventory [opis] 59, file [delo] 27, p. 98.

"objectively contributed to the popularization" of Dayan. It even appended a proposed resolution condemning the editor and demanding that the editorial board take steps to ensure that such mistakes would not be repeated. The matter was raised before the Central Committee, which apparently realized the ridiculousness of the situation and decided to strike the matter from its agenda.[7] This case is indicative of just how sensitive were those whose job it was to control the media in the U.S.S.R. to any information which might—even indirectly—be construed as being in any way a positive evaluation of Israel.

Simultaneously with the application of stricter control over the press, from 9 June onward a well-coordinated team of propagandists began to operate throughout the length and breadth of the U.S.S.R. Their task was to explain away the stunning defeat suffered by the Arab states and Soviet weaponry. In certain regions Party functionaries who normally did not engage in influencing public opinion were mobilized to further this objective.[8] Organized protest meetings were conducted not only in cities but also in each and every village.[9] The extent of these propaganda efforts can be gauged from a report by the First Secretary of the Communist party of the Ukraine. During one week, from 9 to 16 June, 4,984 protest rallies were held in the Ukraine alone, in which 1,334,000 people participated and no less than 19,563 spoke.[10] This intensive propaganda campaign, most likely, was intended to counter the widespread distrust in the efficacy of Soviet arms and the Soviet high command, and to foster a quasi-"on the eve of war" atmosphere. From 13 June onward, the papers and the electronic media were increasingly filled with reports that thousands of Arab refugees had been forced to flee their homes; two days later the press began to describe "atrocities" perpetrated by Israel soldiers in the occupied territories. These descriptions were an almost exact repetition of the accounts

---

[7] Ibid., file 25, pp. 171–74.
[8] For information on 200 persons who were mobilized for this purpose in the Kirghiz SSR see ibid., file 1, p. 72.
[9] For information on protest rallies in the villages of the Lvov District, see reports dated 5 July 1967 in Arkhiv L'vovskogo obkoma Kompartii Ukrainy, collection 3, inventory 10, file 105, pp. 124–28.
[10] During the afternoon and evening of 10 June, 123 such meetings were held in the Ukraine alone, drawing audiences that totaled 36,500 persons. Tsentral'nii Derzhavnii Arkhiv 'Gromads'kikh Obednan [hereafter: TsDAGO], collection 1, inventory 24, file 6289, pp. 10, 36. Within three days, over 10% of the entire population of Altaiskii Krai, in the eastern part of Western Siberia, had attended protest rallies against Israel, and almost 15% of that of the Vladimir District. TsKhSD, collection 5, inventory 59, file 1, p. 70.

of Nazi behavior during World War II with which Soviet citizens had been indoctrinated and that lived on in the consciousness of most of them—perhaps to a greater extent than in any other European country. The newspapers reported that in a number of villages, far from the front lines, Israeli troops had executed villagers as a warning to others, and that in one village they gathered peaceful residents in a house and then set it afire, killing all within. There were also many reports, emanating from Damascus, that the Israelis were executing all Arab villagers who refused to abandon their homes.[11] On 16 June, *Pravda*, the central organ of the Communist party of the U.S.S.R., which set the tone for all the Soviet news media, published a leading editorial in which Israel was accused of genocide against the Arab population of the occupied territories.[12] Taking its cue from *Pravda*, the Soviet press revived accounts familiar from the days of the German invasion of the U.S.S.R., describing how Israeli soldiers first raped Arab women and then shot them.[13] And indeed, the next day *Nedelia* printed an article explicitly equating the behavior of Israel in the occupied territories with that of the Nazis in the occupied regions of the U.S.S.R.[14] In the Soviet media, the Six-Day War was presented not only as an imperialistic war, but in fact couched in language meant to remind the public of World War II.[15] That the comparison of Israeli to Nazi behavior did strike root in certain segments of the population is evident from the following statement by a member of a *kolkhoz:* "We still remember the abuse suffered at the hands of the German fascists during the Second World War, and from reports in the radio and press it is obvious that the Israeli marauders are now doing the same."[16]

The second category of sources at the disposal of scholars was mainly the memoirs and testimonies of various persons who had managed to leave the U.S.S.R. There is no doubt as to the importance of these sources, since

---

[11] "80 tysiach bezhentsev," *Sel'skaia Gazeta*, 13 June 1967; "Bolee sta tysiach chelovek," *Pravda*, 14 June 1967; L. Medvedko, "Net eshche mira pod olivami," *Izvestiia*, 15 June 1967; "Ostanovit' prestupleniia," *Pravda*, 16 June 1967.

[12] "Eto genotsid," *Pravda*, 16 June 1967.

[13] L. Kuznetsov, "Tragediia v pustine," *Komsomol'skaia Pravda*, 18 June 1967; "Prestupleniia izrael'skikh okupantov," *Trud*, 18 June 1967.

[14] L. Koriavin, "Prestuplenie v Sinaiskoi pustine," *Nedelia*, 17 June 1967.

[15] One example of a Soviet periodical's description of Israeli troops: "Their insolent faces precisely bring to mind Hitler's rogues who in 1939 set Poland aflame, in 1940 trampled France underfoot and in 1941 pillaged and murdered the residents of villages and cities in Russia, Ukraine and Byelorussia," Vl. Pavlov, "Tanki idut k granitsam," *Ogonek*, 25 June 1967.

[16] TsDAGO, collection 1, inventory 24, file 6289, pp. 1–2, 10–11.

for the first time these people could freely express their thoughts and emotions. However, since these testimonies were often set down in writing or presented orally years after 1967, they were at times influenced by hindsight and not always free of the attribution of later reactions to the events of June 1967.[17]

In the present article we shall, for the first time in research on this issue, add to these two categories a third to which access has been possible only since the dismantling of the U.S.S.R., which has—at least partially—opened up access to Soviet archives. This third category presents us with a more variegated reaction of the Soviet public in general, and of the Jews in the U.S.S.R. in particular, to the Six-Day War. Though this material does not as yet enable a quantitative evaluation of the various opinions held by the public or justify comprehensive conclusions, it does add another dimension to what we have known until now.

The archival material presently at our disposal relates primarily to the immediate reaction to the Six-Day War, until the end of July 1967. It consists mostly of reports by secretaries of the Communist party in various districts concerning public sentiment on issues of importance to the Soviet Union. The Six-Day War, though seemingly lacking direct relevance for the majority of Soviet citizens, was deemed an issue worthy of inclusion in these reports. The fact that the hostilities in the Middle East and their result were given so much attention is proof of the supreme importance that the Soviet authorities attached to these events.

The data upon which the district Party secretaries based their reports were culled from communications sent in from sub-districts, factories, and the like. As was the case on other important issues, the information relating to reactions to the Six-Day War was based on two major sources:

(A) What was said by those who addressed the protest rallies organized by the authorities to condemn "Israeli aggression"—lengthy quotes from these speeches were included in every report. As expected, they toe the Party line leaving little room for innovation,[18] though each speaker delivered the official message couched in his own language and in accordance with his own cultural background and personal feelings.

---

[17] See: B. Pinkus, *National Rebirth and Reestablishment: Zionists and the Zionist Movement in the Soviet Union, 1947–1987* (in Hebrew) (Sede Boqer: 1993), 255–324, 618–29.
[18] Report of P. Shelest, First Secretary of the Communist Party of the Ukraine, 9 June 1976, Ts DAGO, collection 1, inventory 24, file 6289, pp. 1–2, 10–11.

(B) Reports to the Party of what was said in private at places of work and elsewhere. From the 1930s onward, if not earlier, it was obligatory for a loyal Party member to report overheard conversations, rumors and so forth of consequence to the secretary of the Party branch to which he belonged. The secretaries in turn—in order to ensure that they would not be accused of withholding important information—would generally pass these reports one rung up the ladder of hierarchy. Thus, supplying information on private conversations became an almost normative act. The person who reported them was not considered to be an "informer" but rather a loyal member who "fulfilled his obligation to the Party," even though he generally noted the name of the person in question and gave a precise description of the circumstances in which the statement had been made.

A third type of documentation is letters sent to the editorial offices of newspapers and journals. Very few of these were ever published—primarily those consistent with Party policy, and not even all of these found their way into print. For the higher echelons of the Communist party, however, letters to the editor were one means of assaying public sentiment on key issues. The important papers and journals, therefore, were obligated to file detailed reports on letters received concerning such issues, and the Six-Day War was one of them.

In the reports received from Party functionaries as well as those sent in by the editorial boards of newspapers and journals, special attention was given to sentiment among Jews.

On the basis of the archival sources presently at our disposal we can come to three preliminary conclusions: (a) it was in the interest of the Soviet authorities to keep abreast of public sentiment, which may have been taken into account when making policy decisions to an extent greater than researchers outside the former U.S.S.R. have assumed; (b) the Six-Day War and its aftermath were considered an issue of such importance as to make the ascertainment of public opinion about it a matter worthy of special attention; and (c) Jews were expected to react differently than the Soviet populace at large and were therefore to be accorded special attention.[19] As noted by the Deputy Chairman of the Organization Department

---

[19] A. Grigorenko, Secretary of the Tchernovitz District, ended his report of 16 June on public opinion with the observation that "Party committees at the district, municipal, sub-district and factory levels...all understand the importance of ascertaining the sentiments and statements of citizens of Jewish nationality." Ibid., p. 7.

in the Central Committee of the Party: "The Party's committees are continuing to report about the mood of the Jewish population."[20] Our discussion will follow the same pattern: public opinion in the population at large, and the reaction of the Jews in the U.S.S.R.

GENERAL PUBLIC OPINION

The involvement of millions of people in tens of thousands of public protest rallies and meetings in factories, organizations, and institutions instilled in Soviet citizens a sense of being on the verge of a state of war, which they conceived in terms of the Soviet-German war in which millions had lost their lives. This atmosphere became more intense as the days passed and the propaganda campaign continued. One Polish priest by the name of Kikets, for example, told a congregation of worshipers in the district of Wohlyn: "The Americans want the Soviet Union to intervene in this conflict, for then the Chinese will attack Mongolia and invade Siberia and West Germany will invade Poland," placing the U.S.S.R. in a most difficult situation.[21] One unskilled woman worker in the Krym furniture factory seemingly expressed widespread sentiment when she said: "The memories of the horrors of the last war are still fresh and vivid in our minds, and we do not want them to repeat themselves. [We do not want] bombs to fall on the heads of our children."[22]

War seemed so imminent that the Party secretary in one district pointedly praised the residents of the region for not running panic-stricken to the stores to buy and hoard foodstuffs, as was usual on the eve of hostilities.[23] At one of the protest rallies in the Cheliabinsk district, held before 13 June, a participant asked whether severance of diplomatic relations with Israel meant that the U.S.S.R. would become actively involved in military action.[24] Obviously, to most of the Soviet public the Six-Day War was not just an issue in Soviet foreign policy, in which few took any serious interest, but an event that directly affected every person—for he or a member of his family might have to pay the price in human life. In letters sent to the edito-

---

[20] TsKhSD, collection 5, inventory 59, file 1, p. 71.
[21] TsDAGO, collection 1, inventory 24, file 6289, pp. 38–39.
[22] Report by the Deputy Chairman of the Organization Department in the Central Committee of the Communist Party, 14 June 1967, TsKhSD, collection 5, inventory 59, file 1, p. 70.
[23] Ibid., p. 71.
[24] Report by the Secretary of the Cheliabinsk District, 20 June 1967, ibid., file 5, pp. 63–64.

rial boards of papers and journals, as well as on more public occasions, not a few young Muslims expressed their willingness to volunteer for immediate military action in defense of their Arab brethren.[25] It is not surprising, therefore, that events in the Middle East were uppermost in the minds of even simple folk who generally took no interest in political issues.

Developments in the Middle East were particularly worrisome to those of military age who feared they might become possible battleground casualties. The sentiment expressed at an anti-Israel rally organized at the polytechnic institute in the city of Cheliabinsk is, therefore, not surprising: the students supported Soviet aid to the Arab states but vigorously opposed any direct military involvement in the Middle East.[26] It is reasonable to assume that this was repeated elsewhere.

In the intensive propaganda campaign that involved, in one way or another, millions of people, some less forthright statements were also made, whether in the form of a question[27] or as the outright expression of an opinion. Some 40% of the letters received in the editorial offices of *Izvestiia* by 15 June 1967 expressed some reservations as to Soviet policy in the Middle East.[28] Through the media, in their explanation of the severe defeat of the Arab armies, the Soviet authorities placed special emphasis on the surprise by which the Israeli attack took the Arab states, comparing it to the surprise Nazi invasion of the U.S.S.R. in 1941. However, not a few Soviet citizens did not buy that line of reasoning, noted the chief editor of *Izvestiia* in his report on letters to the editor received until 15 June:

> Most of those who support aiding the Arab states do not accept the explanation that their defeat was due to the surprise of the Israeli attack, because the possibility of a pre-emptive strike was clear even to people whose only source of information was the news media....

---

[25] See, e.g., letters of B. Magomedov from Rostov, O. Dzhavadov from Baku, G. Mamedov from the Armenian SSR and Faidulin from the District of Perm, TsKhSD, collection 5, inventory 59, file 26, pp. 79, 95–96.

[26] Report by the Secretary of the Cheliabinsk District, 20 June 1967, ibid., file 5, p. 65.

[27] In mid-June, the Central Committee of the CPSU composed a list of questions that its speakers were generally asked at meetings and rallies. It included queries such as "What is the explanation for such a speedy defeat of the United Arab Republic and other Arab States?"; "Is it true that most UAR planes were destroyed on the ground, in their bases, on the first day of hostilities?"; "Should Israeli aggression continue, will the Soviet government extend direct military aid to the Arab states?"; "Will we succeed in putting a brake to Israeli aggression or will a large-scale war break out?"; see ibid., file 1, pp. 73–74.

[28] Report by the Editor in Chief, L. Tolkunov, on letters to the editor concerning the Middle East, ibid., file 25, p. 136.

The Arab defeat is a moral blow to our military technical capacity [and undermines faith] in our instruction procedures and military training, for it is a well-known fact that the Arab states were supplied with large quantities of our military equipment and Arab officers were trained in our military establishments, in addition to Soviet military advisors who were stationed in the Arab states.[29]

Such "heretical" letters were not printed, of course, but the Soviet authorities were definitely aware of their existence, and it is plausible to assume that their contents caused them no little anxiety.

The feeling that the defeat meted out to the Arab states by the Israelis was a severe blow to Soviet national pride was apparently shared by many segments of Soviet society. That is probably why many plucked up the courage to ask incisive questions. A few of those who wrote letters to the editor doubted whether the U.S.S.R. would gain anything from the enormous amount of aid it had tendered the Arab states.[30]

Since faith in Soviet weapons and the U.S.S.R.'s armed forces had been shaken, and war seemed imminent, fear of danger from China increased, leading to several pointed questions being asked about the situation in the Middle East during the organized propaganda meetings. Moreover, many Soviet citizens were surprised at the independent stance adopted by Romania, which refused to join the other Communist parties of the satellite states in a joint condemnation of Israel and did not even sever diplomatic relations. These issues, too, were often the subject of questions asked at the rallies organized by the authorities in support of the Arab states.[31]

Obviously, then, developments in the Middle East in the wake of the Six-Day War were not confined to the realm of Soviet foreign policy. They were topic of great interest for wide segments of the population in which a sense of imminent war was prevalent. Furthermore, support for the Arab states was not unambivalent, as the Soviet media would lead us to believe.

---

[29] Ibid., pp. 136–37.
[30] Ibid., p. 178.
[31] The report on letters to the editor received by *Izvestiia* during June–July 1967 noted that "in the last few days many letters have been received requesting clarifications as to the foreign policy of Romania," ibid., p. 172. Concerning questions of this type raised by students at the polytechnic institute of Cheliabinsk see ibid., collection 1, inventory 24, file 6289, p. 65. The intelligence services at this time were actively collecting information on developments within Romania, with special emphasis on the Jewish community and its relations with Jewish organizations abroad in general and with various organizations in Israel in particular. See "Informative Memorandum from Travelers to Romania on Private Affairs," compiled by the head of the KGB in Odessa, 22 November 1967, ibid., file 6313, pp. 79–89.

Reaction of Soviet Jews

The Soviet media, like the great majority of citizens of the U.S.S.R., did not actually differentiate between the State of Israel and the Jews. All Soviet Jews—even those who had never evinced any special interest in Israel, now faced a new reality, a situation replete with dangers already hinted at in letters to the editors of journals and newspapers. Of those that were sent to *Izvestiia*, the editor labeled five of them as being "unmistakably anti-Semitic."[32] A Moscow veteran of the civil war and the Second World War wrote the editor of *Pravda*:

> We Russians...who at the cost of our lives saved the Jews from the brutal fascist troops; [we who promised] our Jewish brothers equality, happiness and wealth in the Soviet Union...[believe] that the only way to do away with the source of anything [i.e., the State of Israel] is by destroying it.[33]

The failure to differentiate between Jews in the U.S.S.R. and the State of Israel was characteristic of most Soviet citizens, who saw in every Jew a potential fifth column. One example of this attitude is a letter written by three women in Moscow:

> We demand that the synagogue in Moscow, that center of espionage and provocation, be closed down, and that the entire Jewish population of the capital be forced to undergo an investigation in order to purge it of clandestine Zionists and all types of scoundrels and rogues. They [i.e., the Jews] are a fifth column.[34]

A resident of Leningrad wrote *Pravda*:

> In our factory there are also Jewish employees who are embittered because they believe that our government seems to be exaggerating on purpose the danger [to the U.S.S.R.] and is encouraging anti-Semitism.... They openly discuss this among themselves, adopting a hostile and virulent tone.... I was never anti-Semitic, but the behavior of the Jews is causing antagonism toward them. They do not act like decent people, there is something in their manner which is anti-Soviet.... I believe that this behavior is a result of their sense of identification with the Jewish financiers in America.... Comrade editor...on the basis of this letter I could be accused of anti-Semitism, but I am not an anti-Semite. I am simply recording the whole truth.[35]

---

[32] TsKhSD, collection 5, inventory 59, file 25, p. 178.
[33] Ibid., file 26, p. 81.
[34] Ibid., p. 83.
[35] Ibid., p. 89.

It was but one short step from such an exposition to a description of the Jews, including those in the Soviet Union, as being even more despicable than the Germans, as one worker from Minsk (who signed only his last name—Ilin) wrote to the editor of *Pravda*:

> The Germans went to war twice in twenty-five years, whereas the Jews did that in ten years. This shows that the Jews are warmongers and aggressors even more than the Germans. These two nations think they are smarter than the whole world.... Many Germans and Jews consider themselves a master race.[36]

Another person from the city of Snizhansk in the Ukraine stressed in his letter that "the Jews want blood...but their desire will be thwarted."[37] This attitude toward the Jewish populace of the U.S.S.R. was not always confined to letters to the editor, most of which were never published, and at times took various forms of violent action. One example comes from the city of Saratov, which—according to the census of 1970—had a population of 1,000 Jews. Rioters burned alive a Jewish woman and her daughter, and the synagogue was stoned.[38]

Soviet Jews, therefore, were directly influenced by the outcome of the Six-Day War and its aftermath and they sensed that both the authorities and the Soviet public awaited their reaction. Indeed, in several letters to the editor written by non-Jews, the writers frankly expressed their anticipation that precisely at such a critical moment the Jewish population would proclaim its loyalty to the U.S.S.R.[39] Mindful of the deportation of German nationals in the U.S.S.R. during World War II, each and every Jew felt that the results of the Six-Day War had a direct bearing upon his fate. It is not surprising, therefore, that Soviet Jews reacted more intensely to the war than did the public at large. In his reports, the editor of *Izvestiia* noted that 80% of the letters received concerning the war in the Middle East until 15 June were written by Jew[40] as were about 50% (some 200 out of 400) of those received between 16–25 June.[41] The report filed by the

---

[36] Ibid., p. 85.
[37] Ibid., p. 82.
[38] Ibid., file 25, p. 178.
[39] The editor notes that "Writers of letters [to the editor] note that a public statement in the press by Soviet Jews concerning their stand on Israeli aggression and on the condition of members of the Jewish race in the Soviet Union would be most useful." Ibid.
[40] Ibid., p. 136.
[41] Ibid., p. 177.

editor of *Pravda* noted that about one-third of the letters dealing with this issue had been sent by Jews.[42] Despite this intensive involvement, we cannot speak of a uniform Jewish reaction.

There were some Jews who—either of their own free will or under coercion—spoke at mass meetings and wrote letters sharply denouncing Israel and its actions, expressing their wholehearted support of Soviet policy in the Middle East.[43] There were even those who on their own initiative proposed, in letters to the editors, to encourage Soviet Jews to sign a declaration denouncing Israel, or even to convene a world Jewish congress for that purpose.[44] The editors who filed their reports frequently noted such opinions as proof of the efficacy of Soviet education and indoctrination, since the Jews—so the editors believed—were expected to react in a manner different from the majority of Soviet citizens. Many Jews sensed that both the authorities and their fellow citizens held them responsible for the actions of the State of Israel and feared what might ensue from such a situation. Therefore, their reaction to the Six-Day War was to a great extent influenced by the implications it might have for Soviet Jewry as a whole, as was claimed by a Jewish doctor in Chernovitz who told his friends in private that little Israel should not have gone to war with the Arab states because "Israeli aggression will have a negative influence upon the condition of the Jewish population in the U.S.S.R."[45] That being the case, it is not surprising that a few Jews hinted in public, at mass meetings, that there is absolutely no legitimate ground to identify Soviet Jews with Israel. At a protest rally in Lvov, one Zeldin—a reserve officer—proclaimed that "the criminal policy of the Israeli government places all Jews in public contempt," while A. Gorodetskii of Moscow wrote the editor of *Pravda* that by its action, the Israeli government "desecrates the graves of millions of Jews who were murdered in concentration camps, at Auschwitz, at Babi-Yar and in the Warsaw Ghetto." Another Jew, from the city of Osh in the

---

[42] "I identified the Jews by their names or by statements to that effect made those who wrote the letters."
[43] Letters of this sort were sent to the editor of *Pravda* by four Jews from Moscow: A. Kestler, L.Kal'tsman, E. Likhter, and L. Linshtein but, as far as we could ascertain, they were not published. D. Davydov, from the Odessa district, wrote: "I myself am a mountain Jew...but am prepared to go and defend the United Arab Republic." P. Kaplan, from Sevastopol, wrote: "I, a reserve officer [aged 58]...am prepared to fulfil my duty...and to fight the hated enemy." Ibid., file 26, pp. 84, 95, 97, 102.
[44] Ibid., file 25, p. 178.
[45] TsDAGO, collection 1, inventory 24, file 6289, p. 6.

Kirghiz S.S.R., wrote in a letter to the editor that "we are used to having the role of oppressors and occupiers...filled by other nations, not by the Jews," and therefore the behavior of the Israeli leadership besmirches the entire Jewish People. Similar sentiments were expressed by one Nahum Kutik, an engineer employed in one of the factories in Lvov.[46]

On the basis of the experience gained during the Sinai Campaign of 1956, when prominent Soviet Jews were encouraged to publicly condemn Israel, officials in the Soviet propaganda apparatus decided to avail themselves of that means in the present crisis. At the instigation of the Propaganda Department of the CPSU and the editors of *Pravda*, a group of leading Soviet Jews was forced to draft a letter condemning Israel, which was brought before the Central Committee of the Party on 19 June 1967 for approval. Since this important document has never been published, the full text is recorded here in English translation.

Letter to the Editor

In these days, the hearts and thoughts of all men of good will are turned to the events in the Middle East where, due to imperialistic machinations, tranquil life has been interrupted, the blood of innocent people has been spilled, cities and villages are being wrecked and treasures of human civilization that were created over a lengthy period of time are being destroyed.

For the past twenty years, peace does not reign in the ancient lands of Egypt, Syria, Israel, and Jordan even though the fate of the Jews and of the Arabs are inextricably bound up together. Thus, peace and reconciliation are absolutely necessary. [There is need of] a constructive attitude toward the solution of vital issues.

We Soviet Jews, engaged in various professions, people of various ages and holding various opinions, artists and scientists, writers, persons active in the social and political spheres, are very much perturbed by

---

[46] Similar statements were made by Barnett, a factory machinist in Zhitomir; by Shneiderman, a foreman in Lugansk, and many others. An especially vicious letter was written by Iosif Khersonskii from Tashkent, in which he specifically equated Israeli leaders with Hitler and his associates, claiming that they will be tried before an international tribunal as war criminals and will end up on the gallows. He accused the Israeli leadership of "causing great injury to all Jews throughout the world, because it is making things easier for the antisemites who are prepared to accuse all Jews [of criminal acts]." In a similar vein wrote S. Girshfeld from Moscow, while P. Abramov, in his letter sent from Baku ostensibly in the name of all the "mountain Jews" of Azerbaijan, called for an immediate halt to the war because "the Jews are opposed to it." The same sentiments were expressed in letters sent to *Pravda* by Solomon Kantor of Roslavland and Kh. Finkel'stein of Riga. TsKhSD, collection 5, inventory 59, file 26, pp. 93, 98–102, 104–6, 107–113.

the situation that has developed, one that may have far-reaching consequences for both the Jewish and the Arab nations.

All the world knows what a momentous loss of life was suffered by the Jewish nation during the Second World War. In the course of their criminal invasion of the U.S.S.R., Poland, Czechoslovakia and other peace-loving countries, throughout the war the Nazi Hitlerites carried out a campaign, monstrously cruel in character, to exterminate the Jewish population. As a result of the crimes committed by the fascists, six million Jews were put to death in the gas chambers and the ghettos—the elderly, women, and children. That is why our hearts are sorrowed by the results of the aggression instigated by Israeli military circles against their Arab neighbors: tens of thousands of dead, wounded, refugees, and homeless.

By nature, the Jewish People is a peace-loving nation that has always been singled out for its humanity. This has even become a part of [Jewish] mythology. The Jews have always sought peaceful solutions, expressed for example in the ancient words of the Prophet: "And they beat their swords into plowshares" [Isaiah 2:4]. The progressive tendencies of the Jewish People, both in the past and in the present, are expressed in their aspiration to always live in peace with other nations with which they share a common fate. Together with those nations, the Jews participate in the struggle for social justice and a better future, contributing greatly to the advancement of contemporary civilization. The talented Jewish nation has given the world Marx and Sverdlov, Einstein and Mendelssohn, Levitan and Sholom Aleichem.

We find it difficult, therefore, to understand what moves the Israeli leaders to involve their nation in a hazardous and tasteless war that can only be detrimental to Israel itself. It is absolutely certain that Israel will not make any tangible gain from its aggression, but will for a long time be inscribed in the collective memory of millions of simple folk the world over as a state that adopted terms such as "conquest of *Lebensraum*," "blitzkrieg" and so forth, terms which carry a negative connotation from the recent past.

We cannot view these developments passively. As Soviet citizens of Jewish origin, we say to the Israeli extremists: take yourselves in hand, put a stop to madness, look at things realistically and learn the lessons of the past. Israel's short-term victory is a Pyrrhic victory.

We unconditionally condemn Israel's aggression against the Arab states and demand that peace and tranquility be restored to the suffering nations. We demand an immediate withdrawal of Israeli forces from the territories of the Arab states. We deeply thank our Soviet government which, with foresight and a sense of great responsibility for the future of humankind, has brought to bear all of its power and prestige for the attainment of peace in the Middle East. Like all men of good will, we place much hope in the General Assembly of the United Nations and expect its members to pass wise resolutions that will ensure peace and tranquility in the Middle East.[47]

Among the fourteen who appended their signatures to this letter was Professor Semen Vil'fkovich (1896–1980), a member of the Soviet Academy of Sciences, whose achievements and innovations in the field of chemistry afforded him high status among Soviet scientists. Another signer was Professor Iosif Kasirskii (1889–1971), a member of the Soviet Academy of Medicine, who headed the School of Hematology. The document also bore the signatures of Iurii Faier (1890–1971), conductor of the Bolshoi Ballet; Grigirii Roshal (1899–1983), a famous film director who, on the eve of the Second World War, made the anti-Nazi movie "The Oppenheim Family" based on the novel by Lion Feuchtwanger; Iosif Tolchanov (1891–1981), professor of theater and a famous actor; Iosif Chaikov (1888–1986), a painter and sculptor who until the mid-1920s was involved in Jewish culture and designed the scenery for the Jewish theater of Byelorussia, but later became primarily an important Soviet sculptor; and Aron Vergelis (b. 1918), editor of the Yiddish literary periodical *Sovietish Heimland*. The economic sphere was represented among the signers by Aleksander Birman (b. 1910), head of the Finance Department of the Moscow Institute of the National Economy and several Jewish directors of important concerns in Moscow. From the field of applied sciences came Petr Atlas (b. 1926), scientist and ship designer, and Mikhail Gurevich (1892–1976), one of the leading designers of the MiG fighter plane. Obviously, those who appended their signatures to the document were prominent Jews from many walks of life, and it is logical to assume that they carefully considered its text.

The tone of this letter departed from the Soviet propaganda line of the time, which did not differentiate between Jews per se and the State of Israel. It conveys two distinct messages: the first expresses reservations and condemnation of the Israeli leadership while voicing concern over the effect of the war upon the population of Israel; the second greatly emphasizes that the Jews have always been a peace-loving nation, pointing to their humane practices in whatever lands they reside and to the contribution of the Jewish People to human civilization. The letter, it would seem, reflected the sentiment of not insignificant segments of the Jewish community of the U.S.S.R.,[48] but it did not conform with Soviet propaganda, which depicted the Jews as being aggressive from the beginning of their

---

[47] Ibid., pp. 52–55.
[48] A letter sent to both *Pravda* and *Izvestiia* on 8 June by Isaak Tsudel'kovski from

national history, avaricious, and haughty with respect to other nations. It is more than likely that the CPSU authorities tried to pressure the signers into making substantial changes in both the content and the phrasing of their letter, so as to conform to the views expressed in the Soviet media. Each of the fourteen, however, was preeminent in his respective profession, and was—at least to some extent—no longer influenced by the climate of fear characteristic of the Stalinist period. More than likely, they refused to succumb to the pressure, so the Propaganda Department of the CPSU decided on 3 July to strike the letter from the agenda of the Central Committee.

That very month thirteen Yiddish writers, undoubtedly with the approval of the authorities, published a message of protest against Israel in the Yiddish literary journal *Sovietish Heimland*. Its full text is given here in English translation.

> In this difficult moment, when peace in the Middle East has been undermined by a futile war and has yet to be restored, we Soviet Yiddish authors cannot remain indifferent. Together with the entire Soviet nation we express our unqualified support of the policy of the Soviet government, adopted with the objective of bringing the conflict to an end and smothering the fires of war in the Middle East by peaceful means, to the benefit of the nations that inhabit the region.
>
> The Jewish People, which lost six million of its sons and daughters during World War II, is well aware of the dangers inherent in armed conflict in our days.
>
> It is precisely in such days that we must bear in mind the insightful warning voiced by the eminent scientist and thinker Albert Einstein, who at one time pointed out to the leaders of Israel that the existence of Israel as an independent state would be ensured only if peace reigned between that nation and its Arab neighbors.
>
> The people of Israel have no need of foreign territories, nor do they wish to undermine the peaceful existence of the neighboring Arab states. Conquest and annexation are the modus operandi of adventurers, themselves pawns in the game played by the imperialist countries. And indeed, that course of adventurism is fraught with danger to the very existence of Israel as a state.

Osh, in the Kirghiz SSR expressed those very same sentiments, albeit in much more caustic language and using crude terms to depict the Israeli leaders. A physician by the name of E. Lesnik, from the Tula district, declared in the opening phrases of his letter that "I am shocked and most upset by the fate of my nation, to which I belong and which I love greatly." Inasmuch as I have been able to ascertain, these letters and others written in the same vein were never published. Ibid., file 26, pp. 139, 141; file 26, p. 87.

Addressing the special session of the General Assembly of the United Nations on 19 June 1967, Soviet Prime Minister Alexei Kosigin made it very clear that the U.S.S.R. does not oppose Israel but rejects the aggressive policy adopted by the ruling circles of that country.

The U.S.S.R. has consistently supported the right of nations small and large to develop and preserve their independent statehood. It was this principle which led the U.S.S.R. to vote in the General Assembly of the United Nations in November 1947 for the resolution that called for the establishment of two states—one Arab and the other Jewish—in the [territory of] the British colony in Palestine.

We call upon all progressive Jewish writers and men of culture, upon Jews everywhere, to raise their voices for peace in the Middle East, for an Israeli withdrawal of forces across the cease-fire lines and for the creation of an atmosphere of respect for the just interests of all the states and the nations of the region.[49]

This protest was intended primarily to be read by Jews outside the U.S.S.R. and—to the best of our knowledge—was never published in Russian. The Soviet authorities probably believed that drawing attention to the Holocaust and to the U.S.S.R.'s support of the establishment of the State of Israel did not go hand in hand with the tone of the propaganda campaign then being conducted in the media. It should be noted that in both of the above documents as well as in many letters sent to the editors of newspapers and periodicals outrightly condemning Israel—including those written by Jews—the writers made reference to the Holocaust and its victims.

It is reasonable to assume that the letter rejected by the authorities more truly reflected the sentiments of many Soviet Jews than did the protest penned by the Yiddish authors, which was couched in accepted Soviet political phraseology. Many Jews in the U.S.S.R. sincerely feared the dangers that they believed the Six-Day War held in store for their brethren in Israel, especially in view of the possibility of direct Soviet intervention. This climate of opinion is reflected by one simple Jew from the city of Zaporozh'e who began his Yiddish letter with the salutation "Brieder und shvester fun Yisroel" (Brothers and sisters of Israel) and then continued:

> Think about where you are sending your husbands, brothers, sons and daughters...bear in mind the example of the war against Hitler in which the greatest suffering was the lot of the Jews, hundreds of thousands of whom were buried alive, and babes murdered before

---

[49] *Sovietish Heimland*, no. 7, 1967: 118.

the eyes of their parents. Citizens of Israel, I do not wish that your eyes should behold what happened here. Take yourselves in hand before it is too late.[50]

Over and above such sentiments, the fourteen signers of the letter were hurt to the very depths of their souls by the description of the Jewish people as an aggressive, cruel, Nazi-like nation. The voices of such Jews were never heard in the Soviet media, nor were their opinions ever made public even in the West until this very day. Only the opening of Soviet archives has enabled us to peek into their hearts and to learn of the dilemmas faced by Soviet Jews, even those estranged from their Jewish heritage.

A few Jews—some in private conversation and others in public[51]—whether in an effort to fathom Israel's unique predicament or out of their personal reading of the lessons of Jewish history, tried to understand and justify the Israeli action. They expressed their opposition to the one-sided Soviet attitude towards the Middle East war. Thus, for example, in a private conversation one Glasman, a department head in the Kharkov Technical Institute, claimed that "Israel had no alternative but to defend its rights by the force of arms, and the stand of the U.S.S.R., which places full responsibility [for the hostilities] on Israel alone is unjust."[52] A Lvov physician, Mark Reikhman, said that "Israel was justified to open war on the Arabs, because the Arabs have always oppressed the Jews."[53] In other letters sent by Jews to the editors of *Izvestiia*, generally typewritten and unsigned, the claim was made that

> the Jewish nation has the right to a political entity...; Israel is always in a hostile environment and has been the target of attacks by bands of terrorists.... The present policy of the U.S.S.R. is therefore [in effect]...the abandonment of Marxist theory, for in encouraging "genocide" [the U.S.S.R.] is negating the right of the [Jewish] nation to self-determination.[54]

Thus, the one-sided and anti-Israel propaganda, which took on a clearly anti-Jewish character, was a cause of worry to many Soviet Jews, as was

---

[50] TsDAG, collection 1, inventory 24, file 6289, p. 3.
[51] In one case, an unskilled worker in the local power station by the name of Yoffe came to the offices of the Party's secretariat in the city of Narva, Estonia, and declared "that he justified the steps adopted by Israel." TsKhSD, collection 5, inventory 59, file 1, p. 72.
[52] Report of P. Shelest (above, n. 18), p. 3.
[53] Arkhiv L'vovskogo obkoma Kompartii Ukrainy, collection 3, inventory 10, file 105.
[54] TsKhSD, collection 5, inventory 59, file 25, p. 137.

admitted by Israel Kil of Lvov in a private conversation with a group of friends: "The U.S.S.R. is conducting an exaggerated anti-Israel campaign in the press and is thus arousing anti-Semitic sentiments among Soviet citizens."55

No wonder then that at many protest rallies a not inconsiderable number of Jews felt as if they were in the role of the accused, having to bear the glaring looks of the other participants. Under these conditions they quite understandably tended to avoid being present at such anti-Israel meetings and rallies, and this, too, made them suspect to the authorities as being disloyal to their country—the U.S.S.R. The Party Secretary of the Chernowitz District, for example, reported that at such a meeting held in the Post Office on 8 June, "not one employee of the Jewish nationality showed up," and these included members of the CPSU such as the Chief Accountant A. Roitman and M. Kitelman, a department head.56

Alongside Jews who tried to understand and justify Israel's motives for going to war were others who absolutely identified with the State of Israel and considered the Six-Day War to be a campaign on behalf of the entire Jewish People which personally committed them as well. Thus, on 9 June, the First Secretary of the Communist Party of the Ukraine reported that one Beninson, the director of a musical instrument store in Chernowitz, openly declared before his entire staff that "the Jews must now take up arms and aid Israel in its war against the Arabs," while a Jewish mechanic by the name of Gobis, employed in a factory in that same city, "expressed his willingness to go to Israel as a volunteer."57 Shloima Melamud, the director of a cafeteria in that city, publicly declared that "he is willing to take to the streets as part of a Jewish protest against the Soviet radio broadcasts against Israel."58 The Party Secretary of this district did, indeed, include the following description in his report dated 26 July:

> Events in the Middle East... continue to attract the greatest attention of a certain segment of the Jewish population. A few citizens of Jewish nationality who have nationalist inclinations express their dissatisfac-

---

55 Arkhiv L'vovskogo obkoma Kompartii Ukrainy, collection 3, inventory 10, file 105, p. 5.
56 TsDAGO, collection 1, inventory 24, file 6290, p. 5.
57 Report of P. Shelest (above, n. 18), p. 3. A senior employee in one Chernowitz factory, G. Zakon, declared in the presence of all his fellow workers: "I am prepared to volunteer to fight alongside the Israelis against the Arabs, and I am overjoyed that they have captured much Arab territory." TsDAGO, collection 1, inventory 24, file 6289, p. 6.
58 Ibid.

> tion with the purportedly non-objective policy of the U.S.S.R. in relation to the Middle East and the "mistaken" commentary of events there in the Soviet press, radio and television....
>
> One resident of Chernowitz, Mendel Yankel, born in 1933, employed as an assistant craftsman in the Chernowitz Textile Works, zealously defended the aggressive policy of the ruling clique in Israel in a conversation with workers and clerks in his place of employment ...while at the same time making false statements about the Soviet state and its policy in relation to the Israeli aggression.[59]

This fellow's statements were reported to the KGB who summoned and warned him that further expression of such opinions would have far-reaching consequences.[60]

Joy at the Israeli victory and the Arab defeat served for some Jews as a form of catharsis from the tensions of anxiety, and was at times expressed openly by simple folk in diverse places. In his report of 16 June 1967, the Party Secretary of the Chernowitz District noted that the director of the supply department in one factory—Abraham ben Leib Pertsov—declared in the presence of the entire staff that he congratulates Israel for capturing so much war materiel, and that one Kirzhner, upon arriving at his place of employment, told his fellow workers that he had heard good news on the radio—that the Israel Defense Forces were nearing the Suez Canal. Jews sensed that the Israeli victory in the Six-Day War was a boon to the self-respect of Jews everywhere, and also enhanced their standing among their fellow residents. In the words of a certain Lifshitz from Lvov: "The Jews proved to the entire world what they are capable of doing and never more will anyone claim that Jews do not know how to fight."[61]

The Six-Day War had a tremendous impact upon wide segments of the Jewish community of the U.S.S.R. After the 15th of May 1967, many of them—even those who had previously taken little interest in the fate of the State of Israel—were in a state of anxiety, lest millions of their brethren be annihilated in Israel. This state of mind was obviously connected with the memory of the Holocaust, which lived on in the collective memory of Soviet Jews, many of whom had lost close relatives during those fateful years. Anxiety reached its peak when the Soviet media announced great

---

[59] Ibid., file 6313, p. 57.
[60] Ibid., p. 58.
[61] Ibid., p. 38.

victories of the Arab armies, soon to be replaced by apprehensions of another type.

The Soviet authorities launched an unprecedented propaganda campaign, creating a "brink of war" atmosphere. One result was that Jews, whom Soviet public opinion also identified with Israel, were held responsible for a war that could lead to many casualties and much suffering for many of the nations of the U.S.S.R. This led not only to increasing suspicion and hostility to Jews on the part of the authorities but in a very wide cross-section of Soviet society as well. A community numbering millions of Jews suddenly felt like an enemy minority, even though it had had nothing to do with the new situation that was developing in the Middle East.

From the archival material now at our disposal we may conclude that there were different and diverse reactions of Jews to the condition in which they suddenly found themselves, and that these reactions were perhaps expressed more frequently by rank-and-file Jews than by members of the Jewish intelligentsia, excluding of course the small circles of avowed Zionists then active within the U.S.S.R.

Some Soviet Jews wholeheartedly supported official Soviet policy and, out of a sense of unqualified loyalty to the U.S.S.R., demanded that the Israeli "war criminals" be severely punished. As far as we can ascertain from the material at our disposal, these were primarily elderly persons—such as pensioners—whose character had been shaped in the 1930s and 1940s, and for whom blind obedience to the authorities was second nature.

Other Soviet Jews opposed the Israeli action out of sincere and emotional anxiety for the fate of the Jewish community in Israel, should further developments lead to direct Soviet military intervention.

For many—probably very large sectors—of Soviet Jewry, their reactions to the hostilities were shaped by anxiety for the well-being of the Jews within the U.S.S.R. itself. They emphasized that it was necessary to differentiate between the Jewish People and the State of Israel, while dissociating themselves from Israel and primarily from its policy, and stressing the positive attributes of the Jews as a peace-loving nation whose sons were always loyal to the countries in which they resided.

There were also some Soviet Jews who fully identified with Israel's action and for whom Israel's war was fought on behalf of all Jews everywhere. Not only did such Jews not censure Israel—they took joy and pride in its victories.

The kaleidoscope of Soviet Jewish reactions to the Six-Day War point to the intricate situations and difficult dilemmas with which Soviet Jewry was confronted during those tense days, and which each individual had to face up to without the opportunity to clarify them in frank and open discussion with others.

POLISH JEWRY, THE SIX-DAY WAR, AND THE CRISIS OF 1968

Daniel Blatman
Avraham Harman Institute of Contemporary Jewry
The Hebrew University of Jerusalem

ABOUT A WEEK AFTER THE GUNS of the Six-Day War fell silent, Wladyslaw Gomulka, the head of the [Communist] Polish United Worker's party (PZPR), delivered a speech to participants at the Sixth Congress of the Polish trade unions. This speech of 19 June 1967, in which he termed the Jews a "fifth column," marked the beginning of an anti-Jewish campaign that led to the final chapter in the history of the organized Jewish community in postwar Communist Poland. In his speech, Gomulka asserted:

> We do not create difficulties for Polish citizens of Jewish nationality who wish to relocate to Israel. It is our attitude that every Polish citizen should have only one homeland...Poland.... However, in view of the challenges that are confronting world peace and, accordingly, Poland's own security...we cannot remain indifferent to people who side with aggressors, enemies of peace, and imperialism. Those of whatever nationality who feel that these remarks are aimed at them should draw the appropriate conclusions.[1]

The aggressive propaganda campaign against Zionism and the State of Israel that followed the Six-Day War was not peculiar to Poland. It was prosecuted with much vehemence in other East bloc countries, led by the Soviet Union. In Poland, however, it had unique significance and consequences. Those few Jews remaining in Poland were portrayed as tacit partners in an unrelenting imperialistic conspiracy aimed not only against Poland but, more generally, against "world peace." Their allegiance to the state in which they lived was openly questioned; at the same time, there arose an opportunity to leave. Thus, the political shock that swept Poland in 1967–1968 led, *inter alia*, to the last Jewish exodus from Poland.

---

[1] Wladyslaw Gomulka, "Przemowienie na VI Kongresie Zwiazkow Zawodowych," *Przemowienia 1967* (Warsaw: 1968), 201–2.

The Six-Day War was a signal event in post-Holocaust Jewish history. Naturally, its effects were most pronounced in Israel. Yet the war was also a catalyst for change and upheaval throughout the Western Diaspora and the Soviet bloc. With respect to the Jews in Poland, the Middle East crisis of June 1967 should be examined from a slightly different perspective. Although it ties in with the nearly final eclipse of Jewish life in Poland, a broader inquiry into the demographic, economic, and social processes within the Polish Jewish community of the 1960s makes it clear that other factors were more central in the community's demise.

POLISH JEWRY AFTER WORLD WAR II: A COMMUNITY ON THE WAY OUT

In April 1966, the American Jewish Joint Distribution Committee (JDC) executive in New York held a discussion on Polish Jewry. Among the participants was Akiva Kohane, director of the JDC European office in Geneva, who for nearly a decade had been active in coordinating various programs for Polish Jewry. Kohane's assessment was not optimistic: "If there had been no emigration after World War II," he noted, "we would have in Poland today a Jewish population of over 350,000. Of that number, 330,000 have left the country through the years—that is, almost 95 percent. Of the small remainder, the Jews are still emigrating and will continue to emigrate."[2]

Emigration had been a fixed reality of Polish Jewish life since the late 1940s. Following the first postwar exodus in 1946–1949, about 90,000 Jews remained in the country, many of them believing that they could rebuild their lives. However, when Jewish public life and political activity were eradicated in 1948–1950 as a rigidly Communist regime coalesced, it became clear that frameworks of independent Jewish life in Poland could hardly exist. This realization, coupled with the regime's constraints on occupational freedom and widespread nationalization of small private businesses, provoked an exodus that continued sporadically until shortly before the Six-Day War. Under the arrangements for Jewish migration from Poland in the late 1940s, those who wished to emigrate were allowed to obtain visas to Israel. From September 1949 until the end of June 1950, a total of 12,512 Jews left Poland on visas for Israel; by 20 October 1950,

---

[2] Meeting on Poland, 27–28 April 1966, Jerusalem Joint (JDC) Archives (henceforth AJJDC), box 76-A, p. 54 (henceforth: Meeting on Poland).

their numbers had climbed to 27,150.[3] Many of these emigrants were middle-class owners of private businesses and shops whose decision to leave was inspired by the regime's economic policies. The emigrants also represented the younger segment of the community—almost a quarter of those who left between September 1949 and June 1950, for example, were children under the age of 18.[4]

From late 1950 until 1956—the period known as the "Stalinist era" in Poland—Jewish emigration was not significant: 3,500 Jews, for example, left for Israel in 1951 and only 200–600 emigrated in each of the subsequent years.[5] Jewish emigration resumed, however, after Gomulka's return to power in October 1956. Nearly 50,000 Jews, or almost all of those who had hitherto remained in the country, departed by 1960 in this second large exodus.[6] This would have spelled the end of the community, had its ranks not been supplemented by approximately 20,000 Polish Jews who had spent the war years in areas annexed to the Soviet Union and who were repatriated to Poland in the years 1957–1959. Between 1960 and 1967, emigration again declined to an annual average of 400–900, according to data gathered by the Cultural-Social Association of the Jews in Poland (TSKZ, the community's official secular organization), and 1,500 annually, according to JDC estimates.[7]

Hence, by the early 1960s, Poland had a rump Jewish community that had lost almost all of its active social and Jewish elements to emigration. Many of the emigrants in the second half of the 1950s had held various positions in the previous Stalinist regime. The reform policies introduced by Gomulka after his return to power led, among other things, to the dismissal of an entire stratum of officials in the state system. Most of the Jews who were affected had held low- or middle-level positions in the public or Party apparatus. Some veteran Communist functionaries of Jewish origin, including those who had joined the Party in the 1920s and 1930s,

---

[3] Report on the state of emigration to Israel up to October 20, 1950, Archiwum Akt Nowych—Warsaw (henceforth AAN), KC PZPR 237/V-98; Sz. Zachariasz to Secretary of PZPR Central Committee Boleslaw Bierut, 2 March 1950, ibid.

[4] Report by E. Sluczanski, secretary of the PZPR Committee of Repatriates from the East, to Sz. Zachariasz, 16 May 1950, AAN, KC PZPR 237/V-98.

[5] M. Glanz, "Niektore problemy emigracji z Polski w ostetnim cwierwieczu," June 1971, AAN, KC PZPR 3048, 8 (henceforth Niektore problemy emigracji z Polski).

[6] Based on data gathered by the Polish Interior Ministry on emigration in the latter half of the 1950s: Centralne Archiwum Ministerstwo Spnaw Wewnetrznych (MSW), File 26/9, 49.

[7] Meeting on Poland, 55; Niektore problemy emigracji z Polski, 9.

preferred to stay in Poland after 1956 even after they were fired or pensioned off.[8] Quite a few repatriated Jews who had served in various capacities in the Soviet Union also stayed, believing that the new Polish regime would permit Jewish educational and cultural frameworks to flourish in the context of a "Polish path" to socialism. From the standpoint of most others, however, repatriation to Poland was a springboard for emigration to Israel.[9]

Figures vary with regard to the number of Jews remaining in Poland just prior to the crisis of 1967–1968. The JDC estimate put the number at 18,000–20,000 Jews, whereas the Israeli embassy in Warsaw reported a figure of some 23,000. All of these numbers are lower than those reported officially elsewhere in the West, where, in calculating the level of financial aid to be sent to Poland, an estimate of 25,000 Jews was used. For similar reasons, officials at the TSKZ placed the number of Polish Jews at 30,000.[10]

In explaining the circumstances of Polish Jewish emigration, Communist leaders pointed to conflicting trends. On the one hand, they construed the cessation of mass emigration in the early 1960s as a result of the continued Arab-Israeli conflict: the reality of relentless attacks, they claimed, deterred Jews who would otherwise have wished to emigrate to Israel. On the other hand, they also noted the change in public climate in Poland after 1956, which had a "crowding out" effect on the Jewish community. Here they were referring to the anti-Stalinist wave that had swept Poland, in which Jews were singled out for having been among the builders and designers of the previous regime.[11]

It is hard to accept the first part of this explanation, given that a new wave of Polish Jewish emigration to Israel began in October 1956, precisely at the time of the Sinai Campaign. The second explanation seems more plausible. Our own conjecture is that it was the prevailing anti-Jewish social climate in Poland in the second half of the 1950s, coupled with the relative ease of emigration to Israel from Poland, that led to the large outflow. It would appear, moreover, that the Jews of Poland—nearly all of whom were Holocaust survivors—retained some attachment to the Jewish

---

[8] Jaff Schatz, *The Generation, The Rise and Fall of the Jewish Communists of Poland* (Berkeley and Los Angeles: University of California Press, 1991), 272–73.
[9] Yisrael Gutman, *The Jews in Poland after World War II* (in Hebrew) (Jerusalem: Zalman Shazar Center, 1985), 111.
[10] Meeting on Poland, 4; A. Kohane to Boris Sapir, 10 May 1965, AJJDC, box 384.
[11] Niektore problemy emigracji z Polski, 9.

people, perhaps even to Zionism, even after a decade of Communism. Of the tens of thousands of Jews who left Poland between 1957 and 1965, only 2,300 emigrated to Australia, 1,600 to the United States, and a similar number to Canada, Brazil, and various European countries rather than to Israel.[12] One cannot disregard the fact that the Jews often had difficulty in obtaining visas to these other countries, but ideology and sentiment must have played some role in their clear preference for Israel.

A more accurate appraisal of the Jews who remained in Poland in the mid-1960s was provided by activists in the JDC. In their estimation, most of the remaining Jews belonged to the group that had been repatriated from the Soviet Union; having once been uprooted, they were loath to relocate yet again. A second group consisted of Polish Jews who had non-Jewish spouses. Many in this group were understandably reluctant to go to Israel, and they were also hesitant to emigrate to countries such as Australia and the United States—not only because of the uncertain prospects of obtaining a visa, but because they feared being told that they did not qualify for assistance from local Jewish organizations. A third group included Jews who continued to hold positions in the public or Party apparatus. Some of them refrained from applying for passports, fearing that their applications would be turned down and held against them in their places of employment.[13]

Polish Jewry in the Mid-1960s: Demography, Economy, Culture, and Education

The demographic data gathered by the JDC in mid-1967 projected a gloomy future for Polish Jewry. According to its estimates, only five percent of Polish Jews were children under the age of ten; twenty percent were aged 10–25; fifteen percent fell in the 26–50 year bracket and sixty percent were above the age of 50. In other words, approximately 10,000 Polish Jews were above the age of 50, as against only 1,200 children under the age of 10.[14] In Krakow, only three of the 1,400 members of the Jewish community were children under 10 years of age.[15]

---

[12] Meeting on Poland, 56.
[13] Ibid., 54–55.
[14] Ibid., 4a.
[15] A. Kohane to G. Osrin, South African Jewish Appeal, 19 May 1967, AJJDC, box 344-b.00–405.

Left out of these figures were Poles of Jewish origin (either of Jewish birth or born to parents who had originally been Jewish), whose numbers could not be estimated with any degree of certainty. This group was out of touch with the two official Jewish organizations in Poland, the TSKZ and the Union of Religious Communities. JDC activists who liaisoned with the TSKZ were utterly unable to estimate their number. The conjectures ranged from several thousand to 50,000. None of them were affiliated with any component of Jewish life; in fact, they spared no effort to blur their Jewish origin and concealed their Jewish past or kinship from their friends and even from their children.[16]

Leaders of the Cultural-Social Association (TSKZ)—veteran Communists though they were—invested great efforts in attempts to preserve some semblance of Jewish life in Poland. Men such as Lejb Domb-Trepper (a former Communist official in the Soviet Union), David Sfard, and Salo Fiszgrund (a Bund leader in postwar Poland) tried to develop Jewish educational and cultural frameworks for a younger generation whose ranks kept dwindling. At a meeting of the Cultural-Social Association in March 1963, for instance, Domb-Trepper reported that there were twenty-one Jewish clubs for children and teenagers in Poland, with a total membership of some 2,000.[17] By January 1965—according to JDC relief distribution reports—1,754 Jewish children and teenagers took part in club activities nationwide. Only four cities (Warsaw, Lignica, Lodz, and Wroclaw) reported club membership of more than one hundred. The total number of club members declined to 1,551 in December of that year, and had gone down to 1,250 by the end of 1966.[18]

The disintegration of the Jewish community was also economic. In 1967, the community had the world's highest proportion of members receiving JDC relief benefits. About 40 percent of Polish Jews, as against 10 percent on average in other countries where the JDC was active, needed this kind of assistance in order to fend off utter destitution. In fact, the provision of welfare of various kinds—allocation of ongoing benefits, funding and operation of old-age homes in Warsaw, and medical and long-term custodial care—accounted for most of the JDC's activity in Poland.[19]

---

[16] Meeting on Poland, 4, 7; Gutman, *Jews in Poland*, 102.

[17] Plenum fun hoyft-farvolting fun kultur-gezelshaftlekhn farband fun di yidn in poyln, referent fun khaver Lejb Domb, March 1963, Archiwum Zydowskiego Instytutu Historycznego, Warsaw (henceforth AZIH), Leopold Trepper, t.3.

[18] AJJDC, Financial Reports, file F-2.

[19] *1967—Guide to Overseas Operations of the American Joint Distribution Com-*

Economic problems were not confined to the elderly or disabled. Younger Jews suffered as well, both from structural problems of the Polish economy and from legislative measures that affected Jews more severely than any other group. In the early 1960s, the state began to allocate more resources to heavy industry, especially in certain regions and cities (Silesia, Gdansk) where such industry was concentrated. This move stimulated demand for skilled labor in the fields of engineering, electrical work, and metalworking, none of which had a strong Jewish presence. Many Jewish breadwinners, especially women, found it hard to make a living.[20] Even in traditional occupational fields—the civil service, municipal government, the Communist party, and the media—Jews faced a collective crisis. Here, in contrast to the industrial sector, there was clear discrimination, albeit not primarily anti-Semitic in nature, that often resulted in Jews' being expelled from work. Many Jews, as noted, had been aligned with the previous Stalinist regime and were now identified with foreign and obsolete ideological influences. The new regime promoted members of the younger generation of postwar Polish functionaries and activists (their highest-ranking representative was Edward Gierek, the Party's First Secretary in Silesia, who subsequently replaced Gomulka), who emphasized a more pragmatic and technocratic brand of socialism. Moreover, good jobs and places of residence were scarce. Banishing Jews from their places of employment had the effect of opening up the ranks for younger Polish Communists.[21]

The harsh economic reality was compounded by many Jews' disqualification from full pension rights. According to a regulation promulgated in August 1964, men at age 65 and women at age 60 became eligible for a full pension if they had worked up to a certain wage level for at least twenty-five years. The law took into account those citizens who had worked in Poland during the Nazi occupation or who had been active in the Polish underground during the war. But these provisions were of no benefit to most elderly Jews in Poland in the mid-1960s, many of whom had been repatriated from the Soviet Union after the war, and so had not

---

mittee (Geneva 1966), 6; report on JDC activity in Poland, 11 April 1967, AJJDC, box 384.

[20] A. Kohane to L. Questle, 19 October 1964, AJJDC, box 344-b.00-406.

[21] Paul Lendvai, *Anti-Semitism without Jews* (New York: Doubleday, 1971), 169–70; Anonymous, "USSR and the Politics of Polish Anti-semitism 1956–68," *Soviet Jewish Affairs* 1 (1971): 23; Zygmunt Bauman, "The End of Polish Jewry—A Sociological Review," *Bulletin on Soviet and East European Jewish Affairs* 3 (1969): 4.

managed to accumulate the required twenty-five years of employment by the time they reached retirement age.[22]

It is not surprising, then, that many Polish Jews sought to leave the country. Of the Jews who chose not to emigrate, a majority continued to identify with one or both of the two major Jewish organizations: the Cultural-Social Association and the Union of Religious Communities.[23] During the years under review, the number of elderly Jews who joined either or both organizations grew in accordance with the number of those receiving monthly JDC benefits—which tends to confirm the JDC's belief that the motivation for joining was to receive services and economic assistance.[24] The JDC budgeted $400,000 a year for its operations in Poland during this time. In 1966, for example, 11,500 Jews in Poland received regular assistance from the JDC. These included more than 6,000 elderly Jews who received a monthly pension of 250–300 zloty.[25] Another 1,010 received assistance for the purchase of food; 105 elderly Jews lived in an old-age home maintained by the JDC in Warsaw; 670 Jews were assisted in covering urgent medical needs; 1,560 received benefits for cultural and educational activities, and 170 Jewish students were given monthly stipends (this latter group had declined from 219 in the previous year).[26]

Apart from direct aid from the JDC, many Polish Jews benefited from membership in JDC-sponsored cooperatives. In 1957, the organization had been given permission to restart cooperative ventures, a previous and more large-scale program having been nationalized in 1949.[27] In 1965, cooperatives employed 2,119 individuals, of whom 1,700 were Jews, and as such were responsible for providing sustenance to approximately 25

---

[22] Meeting on Poland, 16.
[23] A Kohane to Charles H. Jordan, 22 March 1965, AJJDC, file P-201. The membership of the TSKZ was 7,000 in 1966, and that of the Union of Religious Communities, 7,500. Many held dual memberships, however, so that membership figures cannot be used to calculate population.
[24] Meeting on Poland, 7.
[25] This sum equivalent to $3.50–$4.00 per month. The Polish State Bank gave the JDC 72 zlotys per dollar spent on operations in Poland. Notably, Poland had multiple exchange rates. The low (official) rate was three to four zloty to the dollar, but the government set other rates in accordance with types of economic activity. The highest rate, on the black market, was approximately 100 zlotys to the dollar.
[26] Initial report on JDC activity in Poland in 1966, dated 11 April 1967, AJJDC, box 384; report on the number of Jewish student assistance recipients in Poland for 1965, AJJDC, file P-204.
[27] See Yehuda Bauer, *Out of the Ashes* (Oxford: Pergamon Press, 1989), 160–61.

percent of the Jewish families still in Poland. According to Kohane, the Jews could not have survived without the cooperatives.[28]

Indirectly, the cooperatives were also responsible for funding many of the cultural and educational programs within the Polish Jewish community. Under the arrangement agreed to by the Polish government, the JDC did not operate an independent office in Poland but rather directed its efforts via existing official Polish Jewish institutions, the largest of which was the TSKZ. Of the cooperatives' yearly profits, 20 percent was funneled to the TSKZ. Additional revenue came from an arrangement whereby the JDC was allowed to transfer dollars to Poland at a preferential rate of 72 zloty to the dollar. The Cultural-Social Association then used this money to purchase raw materials and equipment for the cooperatives at the official exchange rate of 3 zlotys to the dollar. The differential became a major source of funding for a variety of other activities.[29]

ORT was also allowed, in 1957, to resume its activities among Polish Jewry. By 1966, some 12,000 Polish Jews had participated in vocational training programs sponsored by ORT and current enrollment stood at 1,225, of whom 752 were women and 473 were teenage boys and men. The disproportionate number of women in the courses reflected their attempt to find a place in the Polish economy of the mid-1960s, where private businesses were all but non-existent.[30]

By 1966, JDC and ORT officials were asking themselves a disturbing question: just what was the purpose of continuing their efforts in Poland? Assuming that 5–7 percent of the Jewish population would be emigrating each year and that most of the emigrants would be comparatively young, it appeared that a majority of those participating in vocational training programs would be pursuing their careers outside of Poland. There was some internal discussion of this question, but in the end, the programs continued until they were disbanded by the Gomulka regime in 1968.[31]

The decline of Polish Jewry in the 1960s was also manifest in the fields of culture and, even more so, in education. On the one hand, the "Yiddish Buch" publishing firm continued to publish literary works; there were still Yiddish theater performances, and the Jewish Historical Institute carried on its research and writing.[32] Moreover, five Jewish schools were operating

---

[28] Meeting on Poland, 14, 49–50.
[29] Ibid., 51.
[30] Ibid., 59–60, 64.
[31] Ibid., 21, 65.
[32] Ibid., 33, 37, 40.

in 1966, in which six to seven weekly hours were devoted to subjects taught in Yiddish. Yet enrollment in these schools was distressingly low— only seven pupils in the first grade at the Jewish school in Lodz, compared to twenty-two in the highest grade—and these institutions had received a further blow the previous year when the Ministry of Education decided that Jewish history could be taught neither as a separate subject nor in Yiddish. The educational value of the schools had long since lapsed, and their continued existence was deemed necessary mainly in order to maintain the legitimacy of the Cultural-Social Association.[33]

Nonetheless, leaders of the Cultural-Social Association toiled relentlessly, stressing the magnitude of their educational efforts and the need to intensify Jewish education among the young. In 1965, Salo Fiszgrund reported that there were 3,000 children participating in Jewish summer camps. Sketching out the Association's further plans, he confidently predicted expansion of the summer and winter "colonies," the young people's clubs, and other cultural activities. Like other veteran Communists, he envisioned a renaissance among Polish Jewry that would follow in the wake of expanded Jewish education. Regarding emigration, Fiszgrund argued:

> It is true that many are emigrating to America, Australia, Belgium, France, Chile, and everywhere else. Those who aren't looking for a national solution are seeking their fortunes in the embrace of capitalism. History, especially the seventeen years of the existence of the Jewish state, confirms our old contention: that Israel cannot and will not solve the problem of the future of the Jewish people worldwide, and that the fate of the Jewish people wherever they dwell in the world, including Israel, is linked to the forces of progress, democracy, peace, and Socialism.[34]

Fiszgrund's remarks demonstrated the vast gap between the activists' frame of mind and the far grimmer reality. While Jewish community frameworks continued to exist, the unequivocal fact was that Polish Jewry in 1967 was on the verge of disintegration. Anti-Semitism and Polish "affirmative action" had little to do with it; the factors were basically demographic. The process, which had begun in the latter half of the 1940s, was now reaching its culmination.

---

[33] Data on TSKZ cultural and education activities in the early 1960s, based on a survey by David Sfard, are presented in Gutman, *Jews in Poland*, 112–13.

[34] AZIH, S. Fiszgrund, *TSKZ w Polsce*, t. 12.

The Gomulka Regime and Government Anti-Semitism prior to the Six-Day War

With this background in mind, we can now analyze the anti-Semitic campaign that began in the wake of the Six-Day War and became more pronounced in the year that followed. The basic issues to be considered are what specific role the war played in promoting government anti-Semitism (as opposed to other, preceding, factors); to what extent the Polish reaction to Israel's victory differed from those of other Communist-bloc countries; and finally, what were the effects of the anti-Semitic campaign on the Polish Jewish community?

The period preceding the Six-Day War was marked by increasing political instability in Communist Poland. From the time of his resumption of power in 1956, Gomulka had followed a policy of maintaining a balance between liberalism and authoritarianism. Having regained power in the period of the Hungarian tragedy, Gomulka was aware of the dangers inherent in Poland's becoming too liberal, on the one hand—thus risking a confrontation with the Soviet Union—or too repressive, on the other. His strategy was to engage in what amounted to an unwritten pact: the Communist party maintained full control of the apparatus of political power, but carefully refrained from attacking a set of socially sacrosanct values that were rooted in Polish history, Catholicism, and the more recent struggle against Nazism. Church activities were not disrupted, and scholarly research, literature, and other forms of artistic endeavor were pursued more freely than in other East European countries. Gomulka, however, reserved full check-and-balance powers over Poland's political, social, and economic agencies. It seemed at first as though the new regime was intent on shaking up the entrenched bureaucracy and bringing about a new and more liberal form of Communism; even the Polish intelligentsia believed that a unique Polish path to socialism could be found.[35] By the early 1960s, however, it was clear that Gomulka's main goal was the retention of party control, rather than the introduction of urgently needed reforms.

Hence the opposition to the government, which came from various circles—revisionist economists, liberal political groups, and the church—whose main criticism centered on what they perceived to be Poland's polit-

---

[35] "'In Every Situation I Look for a Way Out,' Janka Jankowska Interviews Jacek Kuron," in *From the Polish Underground, Selected from Krytyka 1978–1993* (henceforth, Kuron), eds. Michael Bernhard and Henryk Szlajfer (Philadelphia: University of Pennsylvania Press, 1995), 301.

ical and economic stagnation.[36] The dissidents took a moderate stance; even the more active among them did not advocate the regime's overthrow. Instead, individuals such as Michal Kalecki, Leszek Kolakowski, and Kazimierz Moczarski wrote articles that advocated greater economic and administrative openness. The need for reform was also widely discussed in forums such as the Znak debating club in Warsaw, whose membership of 300 included economists, sociologists, and academicians, some of them former members of the Polish underground (Armia Krajowa). Two young Marxist intellectuals, Jacek Kuron and Karol Modzelewski, joined the dissenters with an open letter to the government in 1965 in which they argued against the entrenched Party bureaucracy; Kuron later admitted that he and his colleague had erred in assuming that the Marxist system could allow for "social sovereignty" or pluralism.[37]

The internal pressures in Polish society peaked in the mid-1960s. The government's economic policies—particularly the Five-Year Plan of 1961–1965—which was meant to boost the gross national product by 20 percent—had failed. There was virtually no change in the average citizen's standard of living, and disillusionment was spreading not only in liberal circles but also among the middle and working classes.[38] Moreover, Gomulka was facing opposition even within his own party. A few years before, there had been a number of tumultuous demonstrations by workers in Poznan, Silesia, and elsewhere. Among those who now attacked Gomulka for poor leadership was Mieczyslaw Moczar, the minister of the interior.[39] Moczar and a group of supporters known as the "partisans" (many of them had belonged to the Armia Ludowa) espoused a model of socialism that was strongly influenced by traditional Polish nationalism—and to some extent, by anti-Semitism. In their view, Jews, especially those who were active in the Party, were a hostile element that should be ousted from all positions of influence.

Yet, an upturn in the strength of liberal circles, including those associated with the Church, seems to have been Gomulka's greatest fear. The

---

[36] Jack Belasiak, "Social Conformation to Contrived Crisis: March 1968 in Poland," *East European Quarterly* 22, no. 1 (1988): 84–86; Andrzej Friszke, *Opozycja polityczna w PRL 1945–1980* (London: Aneks, 1994), 133–221; Jerzy Eisler, *Marzec 1968* (Warsaw: Panstwowe Wydawnictwo Naukowe, 1991), 321–37.

[37] Kuron, 304.

[38] Josef Banas, *The Scapegoats, The Exodus of the Remnants of Polish Jewry* (London: Weidenfeld and Nicholson, 1979), 81.

[39] Bielasiak, "Social Conformation," 88.

anti-intelligentsia campaign began even before 1967. As far back as 1963, Gomulka came out against revisionist trends that, he said, had been permeating cultural activity in Poland. In June 1964, at the Fourth Congress of the PZPR, Gomulka's close assistant and principal spokesman in matters of ideology, Zenon Kliszko, inveighed against intelligentsia circles that, he said, had introduced anti-Polish and anti-Socialist cultural influences. His remarks underscored the aim that the regime had chosen to adopt: the fashioning of a Polish Socialism imbued with national motives and a pronouncedly patriotic posture. In the regime's struggle with the liberal opposition, the traditional slogans were replaced by slogans typical of the interwar Polish nationalists.[40]

When Adam Schaff (a Marxist theorist of Jewish origin) published a book in 1965 in which he claimed that Polish anti-Semitism had not been eliminated despite more than twenty years of Communist rule, officials vehemently denied the charge, arguing that anti-Semitism had become marginal in Polish society.[41] In fact, it is difficult to gauge with precision the extent of anti-Semitism in the first half of the 1960s, though it is important to make several distinctions—foremost that between official government policy and various strands within the Polish Communist Party. Officially, anti-Semitism was outlawed. Polish identity cards, unlike those in the Soviet Union, did not contain a category noting national origin, and there were no patently anti-Semitic regulations on the books (although, as previously noted, certain regulations—for example, those concerning pension benefits—effectively discriminated against Jews). Anti-Semitic propaganda and publications were banned, and Jews were ostensibly granted full civic equality.[42] Within the Party, the reality was more complex. After 1957, almost all the Jews who held key positions in the party or the civil service were ousted, and those that remained either held secondary positions or were not identifiably Jewish.

Thus, the anti-Jewish climate that spread through Poland in the mid-1960s was the result of a policy fashioned by political circles and did not necessarily reflect widespread grassroots trends of thought. Although it was rooted in an internal struggle that had erupted in the power centers of the Party, it was undoubtedly fueled by the conviction in these Party circles that Jews—especially persons of Jewish origin even if not identified as

---

[40] Friszke, *Opozycja polityczna*, 197; Banas, *Scapegoats*, 77–78.
[41] See discussion of the controversy surrounding Schaff's book in Gutman, *Jews in Poland*, 114–16.
[42] Meeting on Poland, 4a–5.

such—had a negative influence on the systems of government. Government policy vis-à-vis the Jews did not change radically until June 1967. In retrospect, though, this date marked the end of a process rather than the beginning. The instability of Gomulka's regime, which originated in internecine struggle in the ruling circles and in social ferment—especially among students and young intellectuals—had begun several years earlier. Thus, the 1967 war in the Middle East was merely a catalyst that powered the political and social crisis in Poland, the indications of which were previously evident.

The Anti-Semitic Campaign of 1968

Israel's victory in the Six-Day War represented a double blow for the Polish government. For one thing, it exposed the widening gap between public opinion and the Communist leadership. The regime deplored the war's outcome, whereas ordinary citizens regarded it favorably—even the Polish primate, Jozef Cardinal Wyszynski, attended public prayer services for Israel in the midst of the war. Even more alarming were the war's military consequences. Relying on Soviet strategy, weapons, and training, the Arabs had suffered a stinging defeat, and this reflected badly on the military capabilities of all the Soviet-bloc countries. Gomulka was well aware of the danger of undermined confidence in his regime; at a summit of East European heads of state in Moscow on 9 June, he already declared the need to counter "anti-Soviet trends" and manifestations of support for Zionism.[43] Three days later he spoke on the same topic with Polish Communist leaders, and the following week made his "fifth column" speech at the conference of Polish trade unions.[44]

As noted, Gomulka in this speech portrayed "Zionist aggression" against the Arab countries as a menace both to world peace generally and to Poland specifically. At first glance, his propaganda seemed to be similar to verbiage that was flowing from Moscow all the way to East Berlin. But Gomulka went further, drawing a connection between the menacing "Zionist aggression" and at least some of Poland's Jews—transforming them in one stroke into Poland's existential enemies.[45] Clearly, the factors

---

[43] Daniusz Stola, *Kampania antysyjonistyczna* (Warsaw: Instytut Studiow Politycznych, Polskiej Akadami Nauk, 2000), 30.
[44] Bielasiak, "Social Conformation," 91–93.
[45] Adam Ciolkosz, "Gomulka's Political Suicide," *Jewish Quarterly* 16, nos. 2–3 (1968): 17–18.

operating inside Poland for years are the key to understanding this response. The events of the Six-Day War, coupled with Alexander Dubcek's reforms in Czechoslovakia, transformed the potential for social protest into reality.

Immediately after fighting erupted in the Middle East, Poland not only severed diplomatic ties with Israel (in common with all Soviet-bloc countries apart from Romania) but also shut down the major Jewish cultural, educational, and relief organizations. On 10 August, the JDC office in Geneva received and official letter ordering their organization to terminate its operations by the end of the year. ORT was informed in a similar letter that it would be unable to open its schools for the upcoming academic year.[46]

Other concrete measures against the Jews, however, were not carried out until several months later, in response to student protests that were seemingly unrelated to Jewish matters. In January 1968, Adam Mickiewicz's play *Dziady* (Forefather's Eve) premiered in Warsaw.[47] The play, parts of which could be construed as critical of Russia, met with a tumultuous positive response and was then quickly banned by the censor. Students instigated a wave of protests, demanding an end to censorship, and a number of them—including Adam Michnik and Henryk Szlajfer—were suspended. On 8 March, students at the University of Warsaw rallied to seek their friend's reinstatement. After police intervened at this rally, demonstrations and clashes with the police broke out in Polish cities at other campuses. More than 2,000 students (only several dozens of whom were of Jewish origin) were arrested.

These events gave Moczar and his group a convenient pretext for moving against Gomulka for his alleged failure to deal with the "Zionists," "revisionists," and other hostile forces lined up against the state. Anti-Semitic and anti-Zionist slogans became the leading tools of manipulation in this political struggle. Moczar accused the Jews (in his words, the "Jewish Muscovites") of imposing a Stalinist system on Poland. In response, Gomulka—making extensive use of the Polish media—denounced his opponents as scheming to create a nationalist regime that would shatter the Polish-Soviet solidarity deemed so vital to the country's continued

---

[46] Summary of Meeting on Poland, JDC Geneva, 4–5 September 1967, AJJDC, file 396-A.

[47] Events surrounding the play and its impact on the wave of protests that erupted in Poland are discussed in Eisler, *Marzec 1968*, 146–63.

development and stability.[48] Beyond this, however, Gomulka also enlisted anti-Semitism and anti-Zionism to his cause.

A spate of anti-Semitic cartoons began to appear in the Polish press, in which Israeli soldiers and leaders were likened to Nazis.[49] Jews were also portrayed as the masterminds of an ostensible anti-Polish campaign in the West. They were accused, in traditional manner, of having seized the reins of the economy and of public opinion in the West, from which position they were directing the putative anti-Polish campaign. Much was also made of the fact that there were now Jews living in West Germany, the country so often cited in Polish propaganda as a hotbed of anti-Polish hostility, whose leaders were continuing the Nazi tradition of aggression. Finally, anti-Semitic propaganda stressed the nationalist theme of "Poland for the Poles," which amounted to a *j'accuse* against Poles of Jewish origin.

Traditional anti-Semitic equations were now replaced. The prewar era had had "Jews=Communism=Cosmopolitanism." This was succeeded, in anti-Communist circles of 1945–1947 with "Jews=Communism=Government." Following Gomulka's resumption of power in the "Polish October" of 1956, the equation became "Jews=Stalinism." Now there was a new slogan: "Jews=Zionism=Reactionism," which was used interchangeably with another slogan long popular in the Soviet Union: "Zionism= Nazism."[50]

The anti-Zionist campaign in 1968 evolved in the direction of creating a "Jewish image" of a political significance that fit well into the regime's incitement tactics. First, a venomous propaganda campaign was launched against Israel and its "crimes" in the 1967 war. Afterwards, the anti-Israel campaign developed into an anti-Zionist campaign, in which Zionism was depicted as the embodiment of reactionism and accused of having adopted Nazi values. The third phase in the incitement campaign of the Communist regime in Poland was the creation of a tautology between the terms "Zionist" and "Jew." Thus, this political propaganda campaign, which

---

[48] Bielasiak, "Social Conformation," 96–99.
[49] The extent and magnitude of anti-Semitic literature in Poland in the late 1960s and early 1970s is discussed in Alexander Klukman, "Polish Anti-Semitic Publications and Propaganda" (in Hebrew), *Yalkut Moreshet* 13 (1971): 147–63.
[50] See for example, Jan Kowalski, *Stosunki Polsko-Zydowskie wczoraj i dzis* (Warsaw: Polska Agencja Interpress, 1968), 9–28; Benjamin Pinkus, *Russian and Soviet Jews, Annals of a National Minority* (in Hebrew) (Beersheva: Ben-Gurion Research Center, Sde Boker Campus of Ben-Gurion University of the Negev, 1986), 399–400; Eisler, *Marzec 1968*, 8; Krystyna Kersten, *Polacy Zydzi Komunizm, Anatomia polprawd 1939–68* (Warsaw: Niezalezna Oficyna Wydawnicza, 1992), 166.

began with guidelines sent from Moscow after the Six-Day War and continued with a futile attempt to cope with Poland's internal political and social problems, metamorphosed into a pronouncedly anti-Semitic campaign against the Jews of Poland.[51]

Anti-Semitic propaganda was the norm at this time in much of Eastern Europe. What made the Polish anti-Jewish campaign unique was its severe and almost immediate consequences. The regime pressured Polish citizens to quarantine the few Jews still in their midst, thus creating the conditions by which Polish Jews were dismissed from their jobs, deprived of their pension rights, and placed in a situation that left them no choice but to take up their belongings and leave.[52] The campaign obviously had nothing to do with any "Jewish problem" that existed in Poland. Rather, it was the outcome of a crisis in internal Polish affairs that was sparked by the political and economic situation, Dubcek's "Prague spring," and the wave of student protests not only in Poland but throughout Western Europe. According the Jewish sociologist Zygmunt Bauman (who was expelled from the University of Warsaw in 1968), the regime's anti-Semitic propaganda was aimed chiefly at the Polish middle class, especially that echelon of young, white-collar workers in the public and academic sector. Anti-government ferment was rife in this sector, hence the government's attempt to use the Jews as scapegoats.[53] Ironically, most of the young Poles had been born either during or after the Second World War. By 1968, their overall knowledge of Jews was so minimal that anti-Semitism was essentially foreign to them.

REFUGEES AND IMMIGRANTS

The final large Polish Jewish emigration began in July 1967 and continued until the early 1970s. Most of the emigrants—some 12,000 people—left on Israeli visas between early 1968 and the end of 1969. With their departure, the major Jewish centers in Poland were liquidated. Some 4,000 Jews left from Warsaw; 3,000 from Wroclaw; 1,200 from Lodz; 1,000 from Katowice; 700 from Szczezyn, and 200 from Krakow. Polish citizens of Jewish origin also joined the outflow. Some of them had been expelled

---

[51] Stola, *Kampania antysyjonistyczna*, 40–46, 80, 145ff.
[52] Michael Checinski, *Poland. Communism-Nationalism-Anti-Semitism* (New York: Karz-Cohl, 1982), 217.
[53] Bauman, "End of Polish Jewry," 4.

from their jobs and been forced to leave; others had searched for long-forgotten Jewish roots *in order* to be able to leave.[54]

The emigrants' occupational structure underscores, at least in part (since some elderly Jews remained in Poland) the nature of Polish Jewry by 1969. Some 2,800 of the emigrants had finished some form of higher education, and another 1,000 were students in various stages of studies. About 50 emigrants were professors in the social sciences and the humanities. Sixty were lecturers in medical schools; another 40 lectured in polytechnic and technological institutes, and 520 were university lecturers and teaching assistants at various ranks. There were 40 physicists and nuclear researchers, and 370 physicians. About 200 of the emigrants had worked for the print media, including 15 newspaper and magazine editors, and 20 senior employees of publishing houses. Sixty-one emigrants had worked for Polish television and radio, and 90 were performing artists, including 23 actors at the National Yiddish Theater. Civil servants were also well-represented: 525 in all, including 90 department directors. Sixty had worked for the judicial system, and 60 had been army officers (principally in research positions). Another 1,000 were pensioners, mostly from the public services, and 70 had worked for various Jewish organizations.[55]

Most of these Jews had considered themselves inseparably associated with Communist Poland. They had opted to stay in Poland during the previous exoduses, had integrated into Polish life, had contributed significantly to Polish culture and scientific life, and had held positions in academia and research. Some of them were loyal members of the Polish Communist party. Yet the wave of purges did not spare them. By April 1969, the Party had expelled from its ranks approximately 8,300 members, nearly all of them Jews. The activist core of the surviving Jewish institutions in Poland—who for years, out of conviction, had pursued what had amounted to a dead-end path—now saw their institutions faced with threat of closure. They tried to conciliate the regime by means of anti-

---

[54] Niektore problemy emigracji z Polski, 10; A. Kohane to Louis D. Horwitz, 13 October 1969, AJJDC, Box 119-b (Poland: 1969).

[55] Niektore problemy emigracji z Polski, 10–13.

[56] Schatz, *The Generation*, 306. A tragic manifestation of the impotence of these Jewish cultural activists and intellectuals in 1968 may be seen in a report by the important Jewish historian Artur Eisenbach, director of the Jewish Historical Institute in Warsaw on 6 April 1968. In this report, Eisenbach lists the many publications of his institute on Jewish-Polish relations during the Nazi occupation, stressing those who attest to the extent of assistance and relief that Poles extended to the persecuted Jews. AAN, Sz. Zachariasz, 476/22.

Zionist statements and ostentatious gestures of loyalty—but failed: the Jewish cooperatives, the Yiddish-language schools, the young people's camps, and the publishers of Yiddish-language books and newspapers were all shut down, and most of the Jewish leaders were banned from the Party.[56]

Those who left Poland dispersed in various countries, among them the United States, Australia, France, Denmark, and Sweden. Israel was not the main destination for most of the 12,927 Jews who left Poland in 1968–1971. Although officially they left the country on the basis of emigration visas to Israel, in practice only 1,349 Jews from Poland reached Israel in 1968 and only 1,735 did so a year later. In all, only about 30 percent of Jews who left Poland in the 1968–1971 outflux came to Israel.[57] In 1971, the Polish Communist party secretariat estimated that approximately 2,000 Jews had resettled in Europe; they were now, it was claimed, disseminating anti-Polish propaganda in Western intellectual circles. Among those singled out for attack were the sociologist Zygmunt Bauman, Nina Karsow, Stanislaw Wydodski, and perhaps best known, the actress and director of the Jewish theater in Warsaw, Ida Kaminska.[58] According to data collected by the JDC, about 1,500 Jewish emigrants reached Copenhagen by the end of 1969 and 2,030 came to Sweden by March 1970.[59] There are no precise data on the majority of emigrants because most of them chose not to remain in contact with Jewish organizations in their new countries of residence. The JDC data, however, provide a partial picture of the emigrants that agrees with the description of a highly assimilated group of Jews.

All but 300 of the roughly 3,500 refugees who came to Sweden and Denmark were of Jewish origin—or else married to Jews. As a group, those who went to Sweden were younger and better-educated. Only five percent of those settling in Sweden were above the age of 60, as opposed to a significant percentage of those in Denmark. The marked difference in relative age is explained by the emigrants' perception of Sweden as a more industrialized country that was more likely to offer work. Relatively more former Party members also gravitated to Sweden. Akiva Kohane speculated that Sweden, which did not belong to NATO, was seen as the most

---

[57] Stola, *Kampania antysyjonistyczna*, 213–14.
[58] Niektore problemy emigracji z Polski, 13–14.
[59] *Polish Refugees in Copenhagen,* report by Akiva Kohane on his visit to Jewish refugees in Copenhagen on December 12, 1969, Geneva, 23 December 1969, AJJDC, 333c/334a, 1; *Polish Refugees in Sweden,* report by Kohane on a similar visit to Jewish refugees in Sweden, March 22–26, 1970, Geneva, 9 April 1970, AJJDC, 333c/334a, 1–2.

"socialist" country in Western Europe.[60] Kohane further noted that few members of the emigrant group had any Jewish identity, though a connection to Judaism was more pronounced among the elderly and, in general, among those who emigrated to Denmark.[61]

Following this last exodus, several thousand Jews remained in Poland, most of advanced age, some without families, and none with any prospects of starting over in a new country. They continued to live on their small pensions and attempted to the best of their ability to conceal their Jewishness. In the short term, the Polish regime managed to quell the eruption of pro-democracy forces. However, the events of 1968 triggered a process in Poland that came to fruition in the 1980s. The "Jewish issue" became increasingly important in Polish opposition circles precisely at a time when almost no Jews remained in the country, and after all Jewish schools and cultural agencies that had survived until the last exodus had vanished. Action to commemorate Polish Jewry, quests for and studies on Jewish roots in Polish culture, and probing of the Jewish influence in shaping the image of Poland—all these began in the wake of the events of 1967–1968. They became part of the activity of oppositionist groups in Poland.[62] Most Polish Jews left the country after Party officials instigated a wave of anti-Semitism in the hope to exploit the Jewish issue to attain political goals. Many of these Jews would surely have left Poland over the years even without the anti-Semitic tide.[63] Over the years, however, the Jewish issue experienced a renaissance and a renewal of preoccupation that had no parallel in post–World War II Poland—a Poland in which no Jewish life remained.

---

[60] *Polish Refugees in Sweden*, 3–4.
[61] *Polish Refugees in Copenhagen*, 7.
[62] Iwona Irwin-Zarecka, *Neutralizing Memory, The Jew in Contemporary Poland* (New Brunswick, N.J.: Transaction Publishers, 1990), 63–65.
[63] Bauman, "End of Polish Jewry," 7

THE SIX-DAY WAR AND COMMUNAL DYNAMICS IN THE DIASPORA:
AN ANNOTATED BIBLIOGRAPHY

Haim Avni and Jeffrey Mandl
The Hebrew University of Jerusalem

THIS ANNOTATED BIBLIOGRAPHY represents a selection of material examining the influence of the Six-Day War on Diaspora Jewry. An earlier edition was published to coincide with an international academic conference held in Jerusalem, 19–21 December 1994, under the auspices of the Avraham Harman Institute of Contemporary Jewry of the Hebrew University of Jerusalem and the Department of Organization and Community Relations of the World Zionist Organization.

The Six-Day War is a rare instance of a single event that impinged upon all parts of the Jewish world. Its effects on Diaspora Jewish life were numerous and diverse. The research for this bibliography has had (and in its latter stages will maintain) as its scope the entire geographical span of the Diaspora and the broad range of issues pertinent to a comprehensive consideration of the impact of the 1967 conflict on world Jewry. It includes materials published in the more than a quarter century since the war. While a substantial number of works treat the subject extensively, most devote only a part of their attention to it, and so an effort has been made to specify the section of the item in which the topic is addressed.

The present selection comprises books and articles published in English. The entries are ordered alphabetically by the name of the principal author, and, in cases where no author's name appears in the source, according to the title of the work. Due to the limited number of selections in this sample, they have not been divided by category. The annotations reflect the views of the author(s) of the work and not those of the annotator.

"A 'Writers for Israel' Symposium: How the Six-Day War Affected Jewish Identity." *Jewish Quarterly* 15, no. 4. (Winter 1967/8): 10–16.

> This group of Anglo-Jewish writers, formed in the month of the Six-Day War out of a shared concern for Israel's survival, held a symposium in early December 1967 which addressed the implications of the recent conflict. Included are reflections of participants Lionel Davidson, John Gross, and Wolf Mankowitz.

Alter, Robert. "Israel and the Intellectuals." *Commentary* 44, no. 4 (October 1967): 46–52.

> This essay critiques the responses of intellectuals to the new image of an independent, powerful Jewish people resulting from Israel's display of military prowess in the Six-Day War. Alter is particularly disparaging of the assimilated, progressive American Jewish intelligentsia. He claims that, disliking this new image, they distance themselves from it by adopting a hostile posture towards Israel.

Aron, Raymond. *De Gaulle, Israel and the Jews.* Trans. by John Sturrock. New York: Frederick A. Praeger, 1969. 160 pp. Originally published as *De Gaulle, Israël et les Juifs.*

> This distinguished French scholar considers the implications of the Six-Day War for French Jewry. He is troubled by Charles De Gaulle's policy of neutrality during the war and its injurious effect on Israel. Commenting that other French intellectuals had remained silent, he responds to the harsh criticism De Gaulle leveled against Israel and the subtle anti-Semitism implicit in the French president's statements at an historic news conference in November 1967.

Avruch, Kevin. *American Immigrants in Israel: Social Identities and Change.* Chicago: University of Chicago Press, 1981. 243 pp.

> This in-depth study is based on fieldwork conducted in Israel between 1975 and 1977 primarily among *olim* who had immigrated to Israel after the Six-Day War. It briefly addresses the effects of the 1967 conflict on patterns of American immigration to Israel. Of those Americans who had made aliyah between 1950 and 1975, as many as 80 percent came in the years following 1967. However, though the war played a significant role in the increased volume of immigration, it was not directly or singularly responsible for this phenomenon. The socially and politically volatile American environment in the middle sixties and early seventies also

affected how American Jewry framed its relationship to the United States and to Israel.

Beirman, David. "The Impact of Arab-Israeli Wars since 1967 on the Jewish Communities of Sydney, London and New York." *Menorah: Australian Journal of Jewish Studies* 4, nos. 1–2 (December 1990): 132–47.

In this comparative study, the researcher observes that the 1967 Arab-Israeli conflict had a markedly similar impact on the Jewish communities of Sydney, London, and New York. Contributing to this phenomenon were analogous trends in the three English-speaking host societies. Although their national governments maintained neutrality as the war in the Middle East approached, their media and public displayed strong sentiment in favor of Israel before and after the conflict. In these largely parallel contexts, these urban Jewish populations, and their communal leaderships, all manifested intense identification with Israel, with the period around the war marking a high point in their Jewish solidarity.

Borowitz, Eugene B. *The Mask Jews Wear: The Self-Deceptions of American Jewry*. New York: Simon and Schuster, 1973, 222 pp.

This Reform Jewish theologian maintains that the immediate American Jewish response to the Six-Day War had clear religious overtones. In the anxious period leading up to the war, many Jews wondered privately whether God would permit another Holocaust. When they witnessed Israel's victory, and the Jewish reconquest of Jerusalem with the Western Wall, they sensed the intervention of a transcendent, saving power and unmistakably felt God's presence. See especially Chapter 3, which also considers the political and sociological implications of the Six-Day War for American Jewry.

Breines, Paul. *Tough Jews: Political Fantasies and the Moral Dilemma of American Jewry*. New York: Basic Books, 1990. 277 pp.

The author argues that the impressive display of Israeli military strength in the Six-Day War led to a new self-image among American Jews that was tougher, more masculine. He examines forty novels published since the war that he claims portray this Jewish toughness.

Cesarani, David. *The* Jewish Chronicle *and Anglo-Jewry, 1841–1991.* 1994. 329 pp.

> After the Six-Day War, coverage of Israel dominated the *Jewish Chronicle*, overshadowing domestic news. This development "reflected changes in Anglo-Jewish society and identity." For Jews in Britain, "Israel and Zionism became a central element of their identity and they wanted the *Jewish Chronicle* to quench their thirst for news, information and opinion on the relevant subjects." As soon as the war ended, the paper closely reported the Israeli internal debate over the fate of the territories the state had conquered, bringing this complicated issue to the attention of British Jewry.

Cohen, Naomi W. *American Jews and the Zionist Idea.* New York: Ktav Publishing House, 1975. 172 pp.

> This book includes an incisive analysis of how U.S. government interests in the Middle East together with American domestic socio-political pressures influenced the American Jewish response to Israel's crisis in 1967. The case is made that favorable American governmental policy and general public opinion toward Israel during the episode was what enabled American Jews to support the Jewish state. Had the war continued or had Israel fared worse, American Jewish support for Israel would have been tested, as the community would have had to decide whether to challenge the American position against military intervention in the conflict.

Cohen, Naomi W., ed. *Essential Papers on Jewish-Christian Relations in the United States: Imagery and Reality.* New York: New York University Press, 1990. 377 pp.

> A few of the articles in this collection, especially that of Franklin Littell, deal with Christian reactions to the Six-Day War. Although it appeared that Israel was facing annihilation, most church leaders remained silent during the war. Afterwards, the fact that Jews had emerged as victors rather than losers conflicted with certain anti-Semitic theological strains. With Jews no longer the object of pity, the sympathy of some Christians turned to the Palestinians instead. In particular, the liberal Protestant establishment became hostile toward Israel, straining its long-standing alliance with Jewish groups. Ironically, conservative Protestant elements were to increase their support for the Jewish State.

Davis, Moshe, ed. *The Yom Kippur War: Israel and the Jewish People*. New York: Arno Press, 1974. 362 pp.

> Nearly all the articles in this volume, treating the Yom Kippur War and its effect on Diaspora Jewry, refer to the Six-Day War. For this reason, the book is useful in understanding how the 1967 war stands in relation to the 1973 conflict; in particular, whether the Diaspora Jewish response to the later conflagration represents a continuity or break with patterns of reaction that emerged from the Six-Day War.

Dawidowicz, Lucy S. "American Public Opinion." *American Jewish Year Book* 69 (1968): 198–229.

> This article is a comprehensive early account of reaction to the Six-Day War witnessed on the American scene. It reports public opinion as reflected in survey data, the treatment the war received in the press, and the actions of public officials regarding the Middle East conflict. In all these cases, generally favorable attitudes toward Israel were manifested. Jewish responses to the war are also surveyed in detail. Moreover, Christian reactions to Israel's conduct in the war, ranging mostly from neutral to negative in character, are examined — especially for their effect on Jewish-Christian relations. Lastly, the essay deals with ideological antagonism toward Israel that emerged from the American Left.

De Felice, Renzo. *Jews in an Arab Land: Libya, 1835–1970*. Trans. by Judith Roumani. Austin: University of Texas Press, 1985. 406 pp. Original title: Ebrei in un paese arabo: Gli ebrei nella Libia centemporanea tra colonialismo, nazionalismo arabo e sionismo (1835–1970).

> With the outbreak of the Arab-Israeli war on June 5th, 1967, rioting mobs in the streets of Tripoli attacked Jews and their property. The Jewish community informed the country's leadership that it would take a neutral position toward the war and remain loyal to the monarchy. However, with unrest linked to anti-government forces, the Libyan regime was unable to guarantee the safety of Jews, most of whom had no choice but to flee. A large exodus ensued, facilitated by the government, in which the majority of Jews went to Italy. Most never returned and were able to recover only a portion of the assets left behind. See Chapter 9.

Eckardt, A. Roy. *Your People, My People: The Meeting of Jews and Christians.* New York: Quadrangle, 1974. 272 pp.

This Protestant theologian, a leading American thinker in the field of Jewish-Christian relations, critiques Christian responses to the Six-Day War and their deleterious effect on dialogue between Jews and Christians in a chapter written with Alice L. Eckardt entitled, "Christian Silence and Christian 'Neutralism': A Predictable Response."

Elazar, Daniel. "The Rediscovered Polity: Selections from the Literature of Jewish Public Affairs, 1967–1968." *American Jewish Year Book* 70 (1969): 172–237.

This bibliographical essay devotes substantial attention to literature related to the Six-Day War and its impact on Jews in the United States and other countries. See also by the same author, "Confrontation and Reconstitution: Selections from the Literature of Jewish Public Affairs, 1969–1971," *American Jewish Year Book* 73 (1972): 301–83.

Fackenheim, Emil L. *The Jewish Return into History: Reflections in the Age of Auschwitz and a New Jerusalem.* New York: Shocken Books, 1978. 296 pp.

Emil Fackenheim, a prominent Jewish philosopher, was prompted in part by the Six-Day War to reconsider the meaning of the Holocaust for contemporary Jewish experience. Particularly relevant is the essay, "From Bergen-Belsen to Jerusalem: Contemporary Implications of the Holocaust," in which he maintains that the Six-Day War, by threatening a second genocidal episode, reawakened in North American Jews their long-repressed distress and guilt over the Holocaust. Doing so dramatically changed their way of thinking about the European Jewish catastrophe, transforming their consciousness as Jews. See next entry.

Fackenheim, Emil L. *Quest for Past and Future: Essays in Jewish Theology.* Boston: Beacon Press, 1970. 336 pp.

In his opening essay, "These Twenty Years: A Reappraisal," Fackenheim compares the Six-Day War with the Holocaust, pointing out that in both Jews were singled out for destruction. He argues that the fact of their unique and threatened position in the world means that Jews can no longer hold a wholly universalist vision. In the spring of 1967, Jews heard the "commanding voice of Auschwitz," which called on them to dedicate themselves to the distinct goal of their own group's survival. See previous entry.

"French Citizenship and Jewish Identity — A Discussion." *Midstream* 14, no. 7 (August/September 1968): 44–60.

This is an English translation of an article originally published in the French liberal-Catholic monthly *Esprit,* in which four prominent French-Jewish intellectuals discuss their reactions to the Six-Day War with editors of the periodical. The Jewish interlocutors are Richard Marienstras, Pierre Vidal-Naquet, Rabi (a pseudonym) and Alex Derczansky.

Furman, Andrew. *Israel through the Jewish-American Imagination: A Survey of Jewish-American Literature on Israel, 1928–1995.* Albany: State University of New York Press, 1997. 223 pp.

In a chapter dealing with "Saul Bellow's Middle East Problem," Furman explores Bellow's *Mr. Sammler's Planet* (1970), written in the wake of Israel's Six-Day War. Furman considers the implications of the main protagonist's visit to Israel during the war, which mirrors Bellow's own tour of the country at wartime, when he worked as a correspondent for *Newsday* magazine. He notes Bellow's ambivalence in the face of the moral question: "Can the Jewish soul survive the political and military exigencies that must be acted upon to ensure the Jews' physical survival in Israel?" He comments also on how the war figures in the fiction of Philip Roth, Anne Roiphe, and other American Jewish writers.

Glazer, Nathan. *American Judaism.* 2nd. ed. Chicago: University of Chicago Press, 1972. 210 pp.

In the book's epilogue, entitled "The Year 1967 and its Meaning, 1956–1972," Glazer posits three reasons for the enormous impact of the Six-Day War. First, as it threatened Jewish genocide, it had obvious, horrible parallels to the Holocaust, and powerfully stirred American Jewish memory. Second, young Jewish radicals became disillusioned when black militants and New Leftists, with whom they had been allied, denounced Israel's military effort as Zionist imperialist aggression. Third, and finally, harsh Soviet anti-Semitism in the wake of the war underscored the predicament of Russian Jews and the need for a vast campaign of American Jewish support for brethren behind the Iron Curtain. Glazer concludes that the amalgam of liberalism and ethnic loyalty defining American Judaism in the 1950s, if it was already disintegrating, was nonetheless shattered after 1967. The Six-Day War problematized American Jewish liberal commitments and dramatically brought Jews in the U.S. to embrace the ethnic component of their identity.

Goldberg, J. J. *Jewish Power: Inside the American Jewish Establishment.* Reading, Mass.: Addison-Wesley, 1996. 422 pp.

In a full chapter devoted to the ramifications of the 1967 war on American Jewry, Goldberg presents a provocative thesis. Although the Six-Day War actually demonstrated Israel's strength and security, American Jewish anxieties about Israel's survival in the weeks before the conflict left some in the community with a sense of vulnerability and isolation. A passionate Jewish minority advocating a defensive Jewish nationalism took the reigns of power in the polity. These "new particularists" as Goldberg labels them, consisted of three distinct elements: religious nationalists who saw the Jewish conquest of large territories in Eretz Yisrael as signaling redemption, neoconservative intellectuals, like Irving Kristol and Noman Podhoretz, who found confirmation for their anti-communism in Soviet anti-Semitism, and secular Zionists. Ultimately, these groups, none of which was dominant earlier, imposed on the majority a new set of values: "loyalty to the Jewish people, commitment to its survival, and hostility toward its enemies."

Goldscheider, Calvin. "American Aliyah: Sociological and Demographic Perspectives." In *The Jew in American Society,* ed. Marshall Sklare. New York: Behrman House, 1974: 335–84.

This analysis surveys the history of the immigration of American Jews to Israel and attempts to identify the social characteristics of the immigrants. The author concludes that the causes for the unprecedented increase in American *aliyah* after 1967 are rooted in pre-existing trends whose pace was accelerated by the war.

Gorny, Yosef. *The State of Israel in Jewish Public Thought: The Quest for Collective Identity.* Houndmills, U.K.: Macmillan Press, 1994. 279 pp.

This monograph offers a comprehensive account of the influence of the Six Day War on major trends in Diaspora Jewish thought, particularly in the United States. Taking 1967 as the starting point of the "return to Jewish normalization," Gorny discusses the impact of the Arab-Israeli war on the ideologies and politics of left-wing Jewish students, mainstream Jewish liberals, and Jewish neo-conservatives.

Halperin, Irving. "An American Jew's Diary of June 5, 1967." *Dispersion and Unity* 10 (Winter 1970): 136–54.

This personal, introspective account reviews the day on which the war broke out. The author, a Jewish professor of English literature in the United States, recounts how he and his wife, upon hearing news in the morning that the war had begun, decided to visit the offices of the Jewish Agency in their city hoping to be of some help. They were put to work interviewing the scores of people that arrived at the Agency to volunteer for civilian service in Israel.

Hartman, David. *Joy and Responsibility: Israel, Modernity and the Renewal of Judaism*. Ben-Zvi-Posner and the Shalom Hartman Institute, 1978. 286 pp.

David Hartman, a leading Jewish religious thinker, recounts how the Six-Day War convinced him of the religious significance of Jewish history as it is presently unfolding. Excited by the spiritual potential of the contemporary Jewish community, he immigrated to Israel to be part of the Jewish national center. However, his expectations of collective Jewish renewal and transformation were not realized in subsequent years. In retrospect, he believes that dramatic historical events like the Six-Day War are not the principal force in Jewish development. Instead, he advocates progress and change in Jewish life that are informed by history but grounded in *halakhic* tradition. Note especially the introductory chapter of this work. See also by the same author, *Conflicting Visions: Spiritual Possibilities of Modern Israel*. (New York: Schocken Books, 1990, 292 pp.)

Henkin, Louis, ed. *World Politics and the Jewish Condition*. New York: Quadrangle Books in collaboration with the Institute of Human Relations Press, 1972. 342 pp.

In this collection, Zachariah Shuster reports that in Western Europe the Six-Day War enhanced Jewish solidarity with Israel but posed problems for relations between Jews and non-Jews as the political environment turned hostile toward Israel. Elements on the extreme right, the New Left and Communists aligned with Moscow, not to mention Arab groups, all publicly condemned Israel. Of major political parties, only Social Democrats and centrists maintained a pro-Israel stance, but even their support for Israel weakened under the impact of the war. Haim Avni examines the case of Latin America, explaining that the Six-Day

War worsened relations between Latin American states and Israel. The war coincided with the growing influence of communism in the region, and by pitting Israel against the U.S.S.R., eroded support for the Jewish state. This development did not bode well for Latin American Jewry, a community closely linked with the State of Israel. Zvi Gitelman explores the worsened Jewish position in Eastern Europe after the war. Aside from Romania and Yugoslavia, Eastern European states followed the Soviet line, severing diplomatic and commercial relations with Israel. While in some countries, like the U.S.S.R., Poland and Czechoslovakia, negative policy toward Israel carried over into harsh treatment of local Jewish populations, in others, like Hungary and Bulgaria, it did not.

Herman, Simon. *American Students in Israel.* Ithaca: Cornell University Press, 1970. 236 pp.

While conducting research on American students participating in a study program in Israel in 1966–1967, the researcher was afforded the opportunity of observing the effects of the Six-Day War on the group. While the war clearly had an impact on Diaspora Jewry generally, its impact was even more pronounced on these youth who found themselves within the war zone itself. Though their parents urged them to return home, not a single student left. In the crucible of the experience, a deeper identification with Israelis and a greater readiness for *aliyah* was forged among the students. See Chapter 11.

Hertzberg, Arthur. "Israel and American Jewry." *Commentary* 44, no. 2 (August 1967): 69–73.

This frequently-cited essay represents one of the earliest published observations of the effects of the Six-Day War on American Jews. Surprised by the intensity and unanimity of American Jewish support for Israel during the 1967 crisis, Hertzberg analyzes what transpired among American Jewry and considers its implications for the future of the community.

Heschel, Abraham Joshua. *Israel: An Echo of Eternity.* New York: Farrar, Straus and Giroux, 1974. 233 pp.

This influential Jewish theologian probes the Jewish spiritual and emotional landscape in the anxious period leading up to the war and in its triumphant moments of victory. First written in 1969, the work has been interpreted as a polemic responding to Christian criticism of Israel in the wake of the war. Heschel justifies in religious terms Jewish claims to the land and, by extension, Israel's right to sovereignty over it.

Himmelfarb, Milton. "In the Light of Israel's Victory." *Commentary* 44, no. 4 (October, 1967): 53–61.

This essay contends that the Six-Day War, by displaying Israel's isolation in the world, reinforced among Jews a growing disillusionment with the modern, universalistic outlook they had once championed. Many rediscovered the depths of their particular Jewish commitments, both ethnic and religious, and turned to parochial Jewish concerns.

Katz, Zev. "After the Six-Day War." In *The Jews in Soviet Russia Since 1917,* 3rd ed., ed. Lionel Kochan. Oxford: Oxford University Press, 1978: 333–348.

This essay examines a number of the repercussions of the Middle East war in the Soviet Union and the Eastern Bloc. Despite aggressive anti-Semitic propaganda campaigns undertaken in the Soviet Union, Poland and Czechoslovakia in the years immediately following the war, the non-Jewish populations appear to have admired and sympathized with Israel, and held in far less esteem not only the losing Arab side but also Soviet diplomacy for its failure in the episode. Criticism of Soviet policy toward its Jewry and toward Israel emerged in quarters of the international communist movement. Though the position of Soviet Jewry worsened in the wake of the war, many Jews assumed a new assertiveness, resisting pressures to support policies opposed to Israel, and more courageously still, demanding the right to immigrate to Israel.

Kaufman, Edy, Yoram Shapiro, and Joel Barromi. *Israel-Latin American Relations.* New Brunswick, N.J.: Transaction Books, 1979. 256 pp.

This volume makes frequent reference to the effect of the Six-Day War on Latin American Jewry. During the conflict, Latin American governments were, on the whole, favorably disposed to Israel's position. Although Cuba did condemn Israel, it nonetheless did not sever diplomatic ties with the Jewish state as did nearly all other communist countries. However, support waned in the next few years as the Arab League made inroads in the region, enlisting allies in its struggle against Israel's continued occupation of the captured territories. While conservative elements like the Latin-American military elite considered Israel a valuable bulwark against communist territorial advances, radical groups such as left-wing student organizations tended to adopt a pro-Arab stance. At the time of the war, public opinion surveys in Buenos Aires indicated moderately pro-Israel sentiments. In Jewish communities of the region, greater solidarity with Israel was forged, but funds and membership in the Jewish communal establishments did not increase substantially.

Kaufman, Jonathan. *Broken Alliance: The Turbulent Times Between Blacks and Jews in America*. New York: Charles Scribner's Sons, 1988. 311 pp.

This book contains a discussion of the effect of the Six-Day War on the complex relationship between African Americans and Jews. In the wake of the war, outspoken black radicals criticized Israel as an imperialist aggressor, leading to ruptures in the already strained black-Jewish alliance of the civil rights movement.

Kaufman, Menahem. "From Philanthropy to Commitment: The Six-Day War and the United Jewish Appeal." *Journal of Israeli History*. 15, no. 2 (Summer 1994): 161–91.

This analysis places the remarkably successful fund-raising campaign of the United Jewish Appeal (UJA) during the Six-Day War into the historical context of the institutional ties between American Jewry and Israel. In the 1950s and 1960s, links between the Jewish populations of the United States and Israel were relatively weak. However, the 1967 crisis dramatically intensified the relationship. The UJA, which mobilized effectively then to raise massive sums in the American Jewish community for Israel's behalf, emerged as the main organ through which American Jews showed their support for Israel. The momentum carried over into the next years as American Jews, notably non-Zionists among them, became increasingly involved in Israel, especially its socio-economic sphere.

Laskier, Michael. *The Jews of Egypt, 1920–1970: In the Midst of Zionism, Anti-Semitism, and the Middle East Conflict*. New York: New York University Press, 1992. 326 pp.

This history contains a detailed account of the harsh fate suffered by the Egyptian Jewish community following the defeat of Egypt in 1967. Within three days after the outbreak of hostilities between Israel and Egypt, the police rounded up and imprisoned the majority of Jewish males. Under international pressure, Egypt gradually released the prisoners, but three years elapsed until the last of the men was freed. Nearly all the twenty-five hundred Jews in Egypt left within a year after the war, though doing so necessitated renouncing their citizenship and leaving their assets behind.

Letters to Israel. Summer 1967. Selected and ed. by Jeremy Robson. London: Vallentine, Mitchell, Ltd. for the Volunteers' Union, 1968.

The letters assembled in this volume are a representative selection of many thousands received by the Israel Embassy in London, both before and after the Six-Day War. Written by members of the British Public, both Jews and non-Jews, they are a spontaneous expression of sympathy for Israel's plight.

Liebman, Arthur. *Jews and the Left.* New York: John Wiley and Sons, 1979. 676 pp.

A trenchant analysis of the repercussions of the Six-Day War in New Left circles is provided in a chapter entitled "The New Left and the Jewish New Left in the 1960s and 1970s." Militant black radicals and Marxists had become the most influential voices in the New Left by 1967, and would shape the movement's response to the war. After the Middle East conflict, these black leftists, identifying with oppressed Third World peoples, and Marxist elements, championing the cause of masses in underdeveloped countries fighting for liberation from Western dominance, praised the struggle of the Arabs against Israel, which they denounced as an imperialist tool. Most Jews in the New Left were alienated by the anti-Zionist thrust of the movement, and were sensitive to the criticism leveled against it by Jewish leaders. However, they were also unable to find their niche in the Jewish community, which was becoming increasingly conservative in the period. Some eventually would evolve an alternative, a Jewish New Left, which blended Jewishness and Zionism with radicalism.

Medding, Peter Y., ed. *Jews in Australian Society.* Melbourne: Macmillan, 1973. 299 pp.

In this collection, see especially "The Impact of the Middle East Crisis of June 1967 on Jews in Melbourne," by Robert Taft. The article reports on a survey conducted within the two weeks following the conflict whose results point to the Melbourne Jewry's intense emotional involvement with Israel's fate during the episode. Taft, in another contribution to the volume, specifically analyzes the response of young Melbourne Jews to the war. In other pieces, Dennis Altman contrasts his own sense of detachment from Israel and the Australian Jewish community during the Six-Day War with his far deeper concern for the war in Vietnam, whereas Sue Hearst recounts her surprise at discovering in herself a profound attachment to Israel in the spring of 1967.

Neusner, Jacob. *Israel in America: A Too-Comfortable Exile?* Boston: Beacon Press, 1985. 203 pp.

The Six-Day War was a revelatory experience for American Jewry. It awakened in Jewish consciousness three core concerns: strong emotional attachments to Israel; the traumatic memory of the Holocaust; and a profound sense of ethnic identity — all of which had remained quiescent since the late 1940s. This new matrix of collective Jewish self-understanding transformed and imparted fresh meaning to the American Jewish experience. See Chapter 1.

Penkower, Monty Noam. "At the Crossroads: American Jewry and the State of Israel," in *The Holocaust and Israel Reborn: From Catastrophe to Sovereignty*. Urbana and Chicago: University of Chicago Press.

Pinkus, Benjamin. *The Jews of the Soviet Union: The History of a National Minority*. Cambridge: Cambridge University Press, 1988. 397 pp.

This history attempts to identify the effects of the Six-Day War on the situation of Soviet Jewry, tracing the changes in Soviet-Israel relations, the Soviet anti-Zionist campaign and the government policy toward Jewish emigration in the years after the war. It suggests that the Six-Day War acted as a catalyst that accelerated a process of Jewish national revival begun earlier. See the last of the four sections in the book.

Porter, J. N. and P. Dreir, eds. *The Roots of Jewish Radicalism*. 1971.

Rabinbach, Anson,. and Jack Zipes, eds. *Germans and Jews Since the Holocaust: The Changing Situation in West Germany*. New York: Holmes and Meier, 1986. 365 pp.

In this collection, Anson Rabinbach observes that the German New Left, which had seen Israel's existence as just and necessary after the Nazi horrors, lost sympathy for the Jewish state after what it considered its display of imperialistic aggression in the Six-Day War. In another article,

Jack Zipes explains that the majority of Germans respected and admired Israel for its military campaign in 1967, which some likened to the "Blitzkrieg" in the Second World War. However, whereas the political right applauded Israel, the German New Left now came to view it hostilely as an instrument of American hegemony. Jews in the New Left were placed in a difficult position. For their identification with Israel and Zionism they were shunned by others in the movement; for their criticism of Israel they were branded as traitors by leaders in the German Jewish community. In the essays of Yudit Yago-Jung, Detler Claussen and Dan Dinur, there are brief reflections on the impact of the Six-Day War, some of an autobiographical nature.

Raphael, Marc Lee. *A History of the United Jewish Appeal, 1939–1982.* Chico, California: Scholars Press, 1982. 164 pp.

A chapter entitled "The American Jewish Philanthropic Response to the Six-Day and Yom Kippur Wars," examines its theme through a case study of the Jewish community in Columbus, Ohio in May and June of 1967.

Ro'i, Yaacov, and Avi Beker, eds. *Jewish Culture and Identity in the Soviet Union.* New York: New York University Press, 1991. 482 pp.

In this collection of essays, Jonathan Frankel places in historical perspective the anti-Zionist policy of the Soviet regime after the Six-Day War. Zvi Gitelman explains that the bitter realization among Soviet Jews that their government had allied itself with opponents to Israel's existence helped spur the growth of the Zionist movement in the U.S.S.R. Yossi Goldstein cites a survey of Soviet Jewish activists taken in the early 1970s revealing that the Six-Day War led many to become active in the Jewish national movement. Stefani Hoffman details how the Six-Day War enlarged the readership of Jewish *samizdat* and focused the content of much of this underground literature on *aliyah*. Alexander Voronel contends that the effect of the Six-Day War on Soviet Jewry can only be understood when viewed alongside other forces impinging on Soviet Jewish life in the period.

Roth, Steven J. *The Impact of the Six-Day War: A Twenty Year Assessment.* Houndmills, U.K.: Macmillan Press in association with the Institute of Jewish Affairs, 1988, 316 pp.

This collection of essays treats a number of the important implications of the Six-Day War, including those for the Jewish Diaspora. Leonard Fine sketches the situation of American Jewry in the decades preceding and following the 1967 crisis, describing the context in which the war became a transforming event for the community and pointing to the legacy left by the war. Zvi Gitelman charts the influence of the Middle East conflict on Jews in Communist Russia, contending that the Jews of the Soviet Union were probably more dramatically and lastingly affected by the Six-Day War than any other Diaspora Jewry. Finally, Nathan Rotenstreich argues that an increased sense of solidarity linking Diaspora Jewry with Israel after the war was an inadequate substitute for a long overdue Zionist ideological formulation that could encompass the full scope of the contemporary Jewish world and undergird the ties between Jewry in and outside of Israel.

Rubenstein, Richard L. "Homeland and Holocaust: Issues in the Jewish Religious Situation." In *The Religious Situation: 1968–1969,* ed. Donald R. Cutler. Boston: Beacon Press, 1968–1969.

Rubenstein, writing shortly after the Six-Day War, laments that Jewish theology, so long grounded in the experience of Diaspora Jews as a weak minority, cannot comprehend the significance of the Israeli reality of Jewish power. The war prompted his reflections, as Rubenstein acknowledges. Milton Himmelfarb, Arthur Cohen, and Irving Greenberg all respond in the volume to Rubenstein's essay.

Rubinstein, W. D. *A History of the Jews in the English-speaking World: Great Britain.* 1996.

Sachar, Howard M. *Diaspora: An Inquiry into the Contemporary Jewish World.* New York: Harper and Row, 1985, 539 pp.

This work briefly covers the effects of the Six-Day War on Jewry in many of the different countries of the Diaspora.

Sacks, Jonathan. *Crisis and Covenant.* 1992.

Sarna, Jonathan D. *JPS: The Americanization of Jewish Culture, 1888–1988: A Centennial History of the Jewish Publication Society.* Philadelphia: Jewish Publication Society, 1989. 430 pp.

After the Six-Day War, books relating to Israel for the first time became the largest subject category for the Jewish Publication Society, outnumbering even works on the American Jewish experience. In the decade that followed, it published as many as twenty-eight books of this type. Included among them were works on Israel and Zionism and translations of Israeli literature.

Schiff, Alvin. "Israel in American Jewish Schools: A Study of Curriculum Realities." *Jewish Education* 38, no. 4 (October 1968): 6–24.

This article reports the findings of a study of several hundred Jewish schools. A central question of the research is whether the Six-Day War affected the treatment of the subject of Israel in Jewish education. The conclusion reached is that although the war influenced the attitudes of students and their parents and teachers toward Israel, it did not as yet engender a different approach to Israel in the curricula.

Schnapper, Dominique, *Jewish Identities in France: An Analysis of Contemporary French Jewry.* Chicago: University of Chicago Press, 1983. 181 pp. (Trans. from the French by Arthur Goldhammer. Original title: Juifs et israëlites).

This sociological study of the French Jewish community touches upon the Six-Day War and suggests that it caused many French Jews to reembrace their Jewish identity. Though large numbers had abandoned Jewish life after the Second World War, the crisis of 1967, by forcing Jews to re-confront a threat against the continued existence of their people, instilled in them a sense of the significance of their own Jewish destiny.

Shimoni, Gideon. *Jews and Zionism: The South African Experience (1910–1967).* Cape Town: Oxford University Press, 1980. 428 pp.

Though the South African government maintained a policy of neutrality toward the Middle East conflict, there was widespread public sympathy for Israel and positive treatment of Israel in the press, stemming, at least in part, from an identification with Israel's apparent isolation. The Jewish leadership, impressed with the reaction in the country, appealed to the government to allow sending monies to Israel in spite of the ban on such transfer of funds, and the Prime Minister agreed to the request. In fact, the government was convinced by the results of the war that Israel served as a useful buffer against the spread of Soviet influence on the African continent. This realization helped lead to a normalization of relations between South Africa and Israel, which in turn further secured the position of South African Jewry. See the epilogue.

Silberman, Charles E. *A Certain People: American Jews and their Lives Today.* New York: Summit Books, 1985. 458 pp.

The Six-Day War marked the beginning of a Jewish revival. The depth of American Jewry's emotional involvement in Israel's fate, intensified by fears the war would end in another Holocaust, awakened Jews to the importance of their Jewishness. Abandoning a dominantly universalistic outlook, many came to embrace and assert their religious and ethnic distinctiveness. Moreover, estranged from former allies among Christians and the Left, Jews developed independent political activism to further specifically Jewish interests. See especially Chapter 5.

Sklare, Marshall. "Lakeville and Israel: American Jewish Reactions to the Six-Day War — A Study." *Midstream* 14, no. 8 (October 1968): 3–21.

In an attempt to discern the impact of the Six-Day War on Jews, this sociologist in 1968 interviewed seventeen Jewish residents of a suburb in the midwest of the United States (the site of an earlier, more comprehensive study carried out by the same researcher). The conclusion of the study is that although the Six-Day War elicited an immediate dramatic response from these individuals, it had no apparent profound and lasting effect on them.

Stillman, Norman. *The Jews of Arab Lands in Modern Times.* Philadelphia: Jewish Publication Society, 1991, 604 pp.

The last chapter of this work details events in Tunisia, where anti-Jewish rioting broke out as a result of the war. Not only was there looting of Jewish property, but the Great Synagogue was burned. Despite the government's condemnation of these anti-Semitic eruptions and official promises to bring the perpetrators to justice, the majority of the Jewish community of twenty-three thousand fled the country, most to France. Persecutions which occurred in Morocco and Algeria in this period also caused waves of Jewish emigration from these countries. Included in the book are two documents related to the Six-Day War: an eyewitness account of the riots in Tunis on June 5th, 1967, and a report on Egyptian Jewry in the aftermath of the war.

Stock, Ernest. *Beyond Partnership: The Jewish Agency and the Diaspora, 1959–1971.* New York: Herzl Press in association with Hassifriya Haziyonit, 1992. 259 pp.

> Just prior to the war, the Jewish Agency was beset with difficulties, as diminishing sums were raised from Jewry abroad. Then, as the war loomed, the Agency assumed palpable importance as the primary channel through which Diaspora Jewry would provide its massive financial support for Israel. Louis Pincus, the chairman of the Jewish Agency Executive, led fund-raising campaigns in various Diaspora Jewish communities. Moreover, after the war, a number of economic conferences took place in Israel with the participation of Diaspora Jewish businessmen in order to stimulate Jewish investment in the country. Of further interest, the many Jewish volunteers who came to Israel because of the war represented a potential pool of *olim* and the Agency tried to encourage their *aliyah* and handle their absorption, but with mixed results. In the end, the war led to structural changes in the Zionist movement, a new relationship between the Israeli government and the Jewish Agency, and the reconstitution of the Jewish Agency.

Stock, Ernest. "How 'Durban' Reacted to Israel's Crises: A Study of an American Jewish Community." *Forum on the Jewish People, Zionism and Israel* 23 (Spring 1975): 38–60.

> This article provides an in-depth analysis of how the Jewish community of one American city reacted to the Six-Day War (and later to the Yom Kippur War). The pseudonymous city of 'Durban,' taken as the subject of the study, is in fact Boston. Stock focuses particularly on the Jewish communal apparatus.

"The Religious Meaning of the Six-Day War: A Symposium." *Tradition* 10, no. 1 (Summer 1968): 5–20, and "Tradition Symposium: Reflections on the Six-Day War After a Quarter Century." *Tradition* 26, no. 4 (Summer 1992): 6–25.

> In both symposia, several prominent Orthodox Jewish thinkers consider the theological significance of the Six-Day War.

Tivnan, Edward. *The Lobby: Jewish Political Power and American Foreign Policy.* New York: Simon and Schuster, 1987. 304 pp.

This analysis explores the political relationships among the United States government, American Jewry and Israel in the years between the 1967 and 1973 Middle East wars. The argument is made that in this interim period, Prime Minister Golda Meir cultivated American Jewry's emotional attachments to Israel and their generous financial support, but suppressed their ability to exercise political pressure on Israel. Doing so precluded their potential criticism of her insufficient efforts at reaching a negotiated peace. Compounding the problem was the fact that American Jews, enamored with the Israelis after their impressive military victory, were not prepared to criticize them. In the end, Meir did not adequately confront either the peace plan proposed by United States Secretary of State William Rogers or Egyptian President Anwar Sadat's peace initiative in 1971, and the lack of a vigorous debate over the possibilities for peace may be part of the explanation for this. See Chapters 2 and 3.

Urofsky, Melvin I. *We Are One: American Jewry and Israel.* Garden City, New York: Doubleday (Anchor Press), 1978. 536 pp.

Chapters 14, 15, and 16 in this work represent one of the most comprehensive accounts of the response of American Jewry to the Six-Day War. The notes to these chapters provide an extensive list of sources on the subject.

"Volunteers for Israel During the Six-Day War: Their Motives and Work Careers." *Dispersion and Unity* 13/14 (1971/72): 68–115.

An in-depth study of the volunteers who came to Israel in late 1967 is reported in this article.

Wasserstein, Bernard. *Vanishing Diaspora: The Jews of Europe since 1945.* Cambridge, Mass.: Harvard University Press, 1996. 332 pp.

Wasserstein observes that the 1967 war made a deeper impression on most West European Jews than earlier Israeli crises. It "was followed on television screens in most Jewish living-rooms in Europe," and led, for the first time since the foundation of the state of Israel, to significant levels of Jewish immigration from North and Western Europe. In the eastern half of Europe, Jews were placed in a difficult position, as the Soviet bloc backed Egypt and Syria and denounced the Jewish state.

Weinberg, Henry. *The Myth of the Jew in France, 1967–1982.* Oakville: Mosaic Press, 1987. 181 pp.

> Just prior to the Six-Day War, French President Charles De Gaulle imposed an embargo on arms shipments to the Middle East, denying Israel an important supply of weaponry. Then, at a press conference held on November 27th, 1967, De Gaulle castigated Israel for undue aggressiveness in its prosecution of the war. To the dismay of French Jewry, he blurred the distinction between the policy of the State of Israel and the behavior of Jews in his criticism, referring to actions of the "elite" and "domineering" Jewish people. Although the president later denied that his statements were anti-Semitic, French Jews feared they would spark a revival of anti-Jewish sentiments, which had remained subdued since World War II. Moreover, because of their solidarity with Israel, Jews were anxious they might be subject to the charge of dual loyalty. Indeed, when they tried to present Israel's case to the government, they were treated with hostility by public officials and the press. See the first chapter of this volume.

Weinfeld, M., W. Shaffir, and I. Cotler, eds. *The Canadian Jewish Mosaic.* Toronto: John Wiley and Sons, 1981. 511 pp.

> In this collection, Harold Waller relates that in the wake of the Six-Day War the importance of the Zionist Organization of Canada in the institutional relationship between Canadian Jewry and Israel waned, because the major organizations in the Canadian Jewish community also became significantly involved with Israel and the centralized local federations appropriated responsibility for fund-raising on Israel's behalf. Howard Stanislawski explains that the Six-Day War, by mobilizing collective Jewish concern for Israel, led in 1972 to the establishment of the Canada-Israel Committee, the first professional lobbying group organized to represent Jewish interests at the Canadian government. Arnold Ages writes of the tensions between the Canadian Jewish community and the editors of the United Church Observer, who vilified Israel for its part in the war with what oftentimes seemed anti-Semitic rhetoric.

Wertheimer, Jack. *A People Divided: Judaism in Contemporary America.* New York: Basic Books, 1993. 267 pp.

> The events surrounding the Six-Day War, which drew record numbers of American Jewry to Sabbath services during the period, produced a more decidedly pro-Israel orientation in American Judaism. Indeed,

even the anti-Zionist splinter group from Reform Judaism, the American Council for Judaism, was virtually disbanded. Moreover, a greater emphasis on Israel was injected into Jewish religious education, both in curricula and in extra-curricular programs like those sending Jewish youth to Israel for the summer. The religious movements within American Judaism participated in the new Jewish political activism that emerged in the wake of the war.

Wiesel, Elie, *One Generation After*. New York: Random House, 1970, 3rd ed., 198 pp. (Trans. from the French by Lily Edelman and the author).

In a chapter entitled, "Postwar: 1967," this important moral figure responds to Israel's detractors. He complains that the world could not fully cope with Israel's victory because it did not conform to the widely accepted traditional image of a victimized Jewish people. He argues that Israel fought for no other reason than to protect its very survival, and its prosecution of the war was just.

Woocher, Jonathan. *Sacred Survival: The Civil Religion of American Jews.* Bloomington: Indiana University Press, 1986. 244 pp.

The Six-Day War mobilized philanthropic and political American Jewish collective action. Thus, "civil Judaism" (the activity and ideology of the American Jewish secular, organizational world) for the first time assumed central significance in the community. Underscoring this development was the newfound prominence of the federations and the United Jewish Appeal, which had raised massive, unprecedented levels of funds for Israel in the period of the crisis and were now recognized as the preeminent leaders of American Jewish communal life. See Chapter 3.

INDEX

"19th of April" 172, 175, 178, 181
27th World Zionist Congress 153, 156–57, 187, 199
28th World Zionist Congress 159, 192

Abitbol, Eliahou 133, 136
Acotto, Andres Lopoz 181
Afghanistan 223
Ahad Ha'am 136
Ahdut Ha'avoda 144, 154
AIPAC 92
Alexandria 257
Algeria 142, 225, 234, 238–43
Alianza Monte Sinaí 194 (in Mexico)
Aliyah Committee 195 (in Mexico)
Aliyah Conclave 158
Aliyah Congress of 1971 191 (in Mexico)
Allon, Yigal 90
Alon, Moshe 148, 153
Alvarez, Luis Echeverría 198
American Jewish Committee 143
American Jewish Joint Distribution Committee (JDC) 292, 296, 298–99, 305
American Jewish Year Book 235–36
Andropov, Yuri 270
Anielevich, Mordejai 181, 186
Anti-Defamation League (ADL) 108
Anti-Semite and Jew 134
Anti-Semitism 108, 126, 138, 140, 142, 147, 156, 164, 170–71, 174, 206, 228, 251–52, 254, 259–60, 264, 278, 287, 297, 300–3, 305–7, 310
Arab boycott 91
Arab League 231, 244
'Aref, Abd al-Salem 221
Argentina 5–8, 18, 22, 24, 34, 137–186
Argentine Commission for the Defense of Embattled Israel 148
Argentine Jewish Youth Confederation 179
Armenia 270
Art Scroll Siddur 102
Asociación Mutual Israelita Argentina (AMIA) 143–44, 150, 153, 159–63, 169, 177, 185–86
Assimilation 40, 126, 136, 251–52
Atlas, Petr 283
Australia 22, 34, 55, 295, 309
Azbel, Mark 259–61

Baccouche, Hashmi 232
Bagu, Segio 181
Balfour Declaration 206
Baltic states 251, 255
Barromi, Joel 212
Bauman, Zygmunt 307, 309
Begin, Menachem 91–92, 215
Belgium 34, 53
Ben-Gurion, David 52, 214–15
Ben Youssef, Salah 231
Bernard Lazare Circle 182, 185
Betar 206

333

Bick, Myer 87
Birman, Aleksander 283
Bizerte 226–29, 232–33, 238
Black September (1970) 198
Blejer, José 170, 181
B'nai B'rith 84–85, 87 (of Canada); 143
Bnei Akiva 206
Borges, Jorge Luis 148
Bourguiba, Habib 224, 226–32, 235–38, 242
Brazil 34, 147, 159, 295
Brezhnev, Leonid 56, 263
Bronfman, Samuel 84
Browne, Gerald 216
Buber Jewish cultural club 181 (in Argentina)
Buenos Aires 24
Bund 143–44, 177 (in Argentina)
Burg, Yosef 90
Burshtein, Nuchem 171
Bustamente, Norberto Rodriguez 181
Butman, Hillel 258

Cairo 257, 269
Calleti, Oberdan 181
Cameron, Ralph 74
Cámpora, Hector J. 141
Canada 5–8, 22, 34, 81–98, 159, 295
Canada-Israel Committee (CIC) 85–97
Canadian Friends of Peace Now (CFPN) 93, 95–96
Canadian Jewish Congress 84–85, 88, 95–96
Canadian Zionist Federation (CZF) 85–90, 96
Capdevila, Arturo 148
Cape Town 211
Cape Town Hebrew Congregation 206
Casablanca 240–41
Castillo, Abelardo 181
Castro, Fidel 182–83
Catholicism 138–40, 142, 170, 301
Central Committee for Mexican Jewry 194, 200–1
Cercle Gaston Crémieux 129–133

Chaikov, Iosif 283
Chile 34, 141, 173, 182
China 277
Chuvakhin, Leonid 255
Claridad 171
Clark, Joe 94
Clinton, Bill 103
Colloquium for Peace in the Middle East 183 (in Argentina)
Committee for Peace in the Middle East 185–86 (in Argentina)
Communism 143, 167–69, 173, 179–80, 263, 270, 292, 294–95, 297, 300, 303–4
Communist-bloc 301
Communist party of Argentina (PC) 168–72, 174–77, 180, 183
Communist Youth Federation 168 (in Argentina)
Conference of Presidents of Major American Jewish Organizations 99
Conseil Représentatif des Institutions Juives de France 130
Coordinating Committee for Emergency Aid to Israel 83 (in Canada)
Cuba 182–83
Cultural-Social Association of Jews (TSKZ) 29–94, 296, 298–300 (in Poland)
Czechoslovakia 56, 175, 265–66, 305

Damascus 257, 269, 272
Dayan, Moshe 72, 78, 90, 262, 270–71
De Gaulle, Charles 19, 53
Delegación de Asociaciones Israelitas Argentinas (DAIA), 139, 143–45, 150, 164, 169, 179–80, 186
Denmark 5, 309–10
Department of Jewish Education and Culture 37, 48 (in Israel)
Department of Torah Education and Culture 35, 47 (in Israel)
Diederichs, Nico 216
Djerba (Tunisia) 229

Index

Dobkin, Eliahu 149, 245
Domb-Trepper, Lejb 296
Dovtian, Vaagan 270
Drechler, Nachman 177
Dreyfus, André 227–28
Dubcek, Alexander 266, 304, 307
Dubnow, Simon 129
Dulzin, Leon 153
Dymshitz, Mark 259

East Germany 232
Easterman, Alexander 231–32
Eastern Europe 25, 120, 129, 131, 168
Egypt (U.A.R.) 53, 74, 77, 142, 147, 221, 223, 230–31, 241, 248, 255–57, 269
Ehrenburg, Ilya 259
Eichmann, Adolf 24, 254
Elfen, Henri 234–35
El-Kuneitra (Golan Heights) 257
Elnecave, Nissim 157
Emergency Campaign Committee for Israel 171(in Argentina)
Emissaries (*shlichim*) 14, 35, 37, 144, 162, 178, 220
Energy crisis 57
Enlightenment 126, 132–33, 136
Escovich, Abraham 178
Etcheverry, Delia 181
Ethiopian Jewry 118
Evseev, Evgeny 263
Exodus (movie) 71, 73–74

Faier, Iurii 283
Fascism 264, 270
Federated Zionist Organization of Canada 84
Federation of Jewish Communities of Argentina 143
Federation of Jewish Cultural Organizations of Argentina 167
Fiedler, Leslie 78
Finkielkraut, Alain 131–32
Fiszgrund, Salo 296
Forum (newsletter) 200

Frai Isroel (newspaper) 176
Fraie Schtime (newspaper) 175, 177, 179–80, 185–86
France 5–6, 8, 18–19, 22, 34, 53, 125–36, 151, 219, 225–27, 229, 236, 240, 243–44, 309
Freiheit (newspaper) 176
French embargo (pre-1967 War) 53
Frondizi, Arturo 24
Fund-raising 37, 40, 42, 44, 47, 49, 83–85, 87, 89, 146, 150, 208, 211, 214–15

Gaza 257
Gdansk 297
Geneva 305
German reparations 63
Germany 5, 270
Ghioldi, Americo 147
Gierek, Edward 297
Glasnost 249
Golan Heights 257
Goldberg, Itche 177
Goldberg, José 174
Goldenberg, Isaac 139, 144
Gomulka, Wladyslaw 175, 266–67, 291, 293, 297, 299, 301–4, 306
Gorbachev, Mikhail 249
Goren, Shlomo 76–77, 211
Govrin, Joseph 255, 265
Granados, Jorge García 198
Gulf of Aqaba 256
Gulf War 30
Gurevich, Mikhail 283
Gutkin, Elimelech 144

Habonim Zionist Youth 206, 215
HaKoah (sports assn. in Argentina) 144
Harat al-Yahud 226 (in Tunis)
Harbutt, Charles 76
Harris, Milton 95
Hashomer Hatzair 180–81
Hassan II, King of Morocco, 242–43
Hatikwa (youth org. in Mexico) 193
Hebraica (sports assn. in Argentina) 144

Hebraica Society 150–51 (in Argentina)
Hebrew language 118, 130, 164–65, 208, 251, 255
Hebrew University 56
Hegel, Georg W. F. 134, 135
Helwan 257 (in Egypt)
Herzog, Chaim 214
Herzl, Theodore 118
Himmelfarb, Milton 78
Holocaust (Shoah) 3–4, 15, 83, 107, 120, 127, 146, 205, 207–8, 212, 214, 245, 250, 252, 254, 285, 288, 292, 294
Homs 257
Howe, Irving 120
Hungary 170, 301
Hussein, King of Jordan 230

Idisher Cultur Farband (ICUF) 167–69, 171–178, 180, 185–86
IFT, see Popular Jewish Theater
Independence Day 102, 210
Independence Loan, see Israel Bonds
Inflation 26, 57
Institute for Leadership Training 34, 48 (in Israel)
Institute of Mexican-Israeli Cultural Relations 201
Instituto Judeo-Argentino 143
Interim Committee for the Management of the Affairs of the Jewish Community 225 (in Tunisia)
Intermarriage 112
International Congress of Intellectuals 183
Intifada 30, 94, 96
Iran 120, 221, 243, 247
Iraq 221, 223, 231
Ireland 111
Irgun 206
Islam 119, 223, 230
Islamic Congress 245
Israel Bonds (Independence Loan), 57–60, 64
Israel United Appeal 208–10, 214 (in South Africa)
Italy 34, 240, 243, 244
Itzigsohn, José 177, 181, 184
Izvestiia (newspaper) 276, 278–79, 286

Jabotinsky, Ze'ev 206
Jarblum, Marc 225
Javits, Jacob 79
Jenin 257
Jerusalem 73–76, 91, 136, 142, 150–51, 154, 158, 163, 187, 201, 211
Jerusalem Fund 60, 64
"Jerusalem Program" of the WZO 157
Jewish Affairs (journal) 212
Jewish Agency 14, 34, 57, 60–61, 63, 105, 149, 153, 158, 209, 227, 245
Jewish Agency for Israel (JAFI) 40, 42, 47
Jewish Community Council 235 (in Tunisia)
Jewish Cultural Association of Cordoba 179
Jewish Historical Institute 299
Jewish Identities in France 127
Jewish Literary Center and Max Nordau Library 172 (in Argentina)
Jewish National Fund 60
Johannesburg 211
Joint Public Relations Committee 86 (in Canada)
Jordan 74, 77, 230, 257
Judeo-Arabic 130
Judeo-Argentine Cultural Association 176

Kalecki, Michal 302
Kamenszain, Tuvia 144, 153
Kaminska, Ida 309
Kanee, Sol 87
Karsow, Nina 309
Kasirskii, Iosif 283
Katowice (Poland) 307
Katz, Jacob 11
Kehila Nidje Israel 194
Kennedy, John F. 111

Index

Keren Hayesod 37, 145–46, 150–51, 163, 188
KGB 288
Khrushchev, Nikita 252–53
Kibbutz Artzi 169, 178
Kliszko, Zenon 303
Kohane, Akiva 292
Kolakowski, Leszek 302
Kordon, Bernardo 181
Kosygin, Alexei 262
Krakow 295, 307
Kuron, Jacek 302

Labour party 91, 96, 154
Ladino 118, 130
Landsfarein 168, 171, 177
Lanusse, Alejandro Agustin 141
Lazare, Bernard 182, 185
Lebanon 91, 142, 221, 247
Lebanon War of 1982 86, 93, 96
Lévinas, Emmanuel 132, 134
Levingston, Roberto M. 140, 179
Lévy, Benny 133
Lewinthal, Simon 171, 177
Liberman, Arnaldo 177
Libya 223, 229, 239–43
Lieberman, Joseph 112
Lignica (Poland) 296
Likud party 86, 91–92
Lipsky, Meir 177
Lithuania 132
Lochamei Herut 193
Lodz 296, 300, 307

Maccabi (sports assn. in Argentina) 144
Magen David Adom 60, 150, 210
Maghreb 224, 231, 239, 241, 244, 247
Maguen David 194 (in Mexico)
Mahal army volunteers 207
Maki party 172, 176–77
Mapai party 144, 154
Mapam party 169, 171–73, 178, 181–82, 186
Mapam-Hashomer Hatzair party 160–61, 171, 177

Marienstras, Richard 129–31, 136
Marrus, Michael 95
Masmoudi, Mohammed 225
Mauldin, Bill 75
Meir, Golda 180
Meknes (Morocco) 240–41
Mendelevitch, Yosef 254
Mendez, Nicanor Costa 141
Mexico 4, 8, 34, 159, 187–205
Mickiewicz, Adam 305
Mizrachi-Bnei Akiva 215
Moczar, Mieczyslaw 267, 302, 305
Moczarski, Kazimierz 302
Modzelewski, Karol 302
Montebello Affair 95
Morocco 4, 142, 161, 221, 239–41, 243, 248
Movement for a Progressive Israel and Peace in the Middle East 176, 178, 180–81 (in Argentina)
Movimiento Sefardi Sionista (MSS) 157–59, 161

Nasser, Gamal Abdul 69, 142, 148, 221, 230–32, 238, 256, 265
Nazism 82, 145, 263–64, 272, 276, 286, 297, 301, 306
Neher, André 219
Neo-Destour party 224–25, 234
Netherlands 34
New York 108
New Zealand 34
Nikitina, Galina 256
Non-Aligned Movement 198
Nordau Library 172, 175, 178 (in Argentina)
Northern Exposure (TV show) 112

Oceania 55
Odessa 259
Onganía, Juan C. 24, 139–40, 148, 169–70, 179
Operation Exodus 42
Ordaz, Gustavo Díaz 198
Organization of Latin American

Immigrants 152–53
ORT 299, 305
Oslo Accords 248
Out of the Garden: Women Writers on the Bible 121

Palace of Education 160 (in Buenos Aires)
Palestinian Liberation Organization (PLO) 93–94, 128, 248
Pearson, Lester 84
Peres, Shimon 90
Perestroika 249
Peretz Cultural Center 180 (in Argentina)
Perez, Leon S. 182, 184
Perón, Juan Domingo 24, 138, 141
Peronists 140, 147, 162, 168, 174
Pincus, Arie 153–58, 187, 189
Pinzon, Mimi 177
Poalei Zion (Labour Zionism) 144, 153, 215
Poch, Leon 150
Polak, Miguel 181
Polak, Moisés 177, 180–81
Poland 4–6, 8, 131, 168, 170, 175, 251, 266–67, 291–310
Popular Jewish Theater (IFT) 168–69, 171, 179 (in Argentina)
Porter, Maurice 213
Poznan 302
Prague Spring 307
Pratt, Simcha 209
Pravda (newspaper) 272, 278–81
Preminger, Otto 71
Primakov, Evgeny 257
Project Renewal 88
Pzredborsky, Lanwl 177

Rabat 241
Rabin, Yitzhak 72–73, 93, 257
Rafi party 154
Raices (newsletter) 158
Rakach party 172, 175
Rama, Carlos 182

Reading Ruth: Contemporary Women Reclaim a Sacred Story 121
Renewal Front 192 (in Mexico)
Reston, James 76
Rheingold Beer 111
Rojas, Isaac 147
Romania 251, 265, 270, 277, 305
Roosevelt, Theodore 111
Roshal, Grigirii 283
Rozen, Gil 177
Rozencoff, Mauricio 182
Rozenmacher, German 174
Rozitchner, Leon 184
Rusinek, Alla 254, 260

Sabry, Husein Zulfikar 142
Sadat, Anwar 255
Saidel, Miguel 182
Sapir, Pinchas 52
Sartre, Jean-Paul 134–35, 185
Schaff, Adam 303
Scheininger, Les 95
Schliapochnik, Aizik 177
School for Overseas Students 56
Schwartz, Arturo 183
Selim, Mongi 228, 231
Sephardic Zionist Movement 157
Sfard, David 296
Sha'arei Tefillah (prayerbook) 102
Shazar, Zalman 11
She'erit Hapletah 207 (in South Africa)
Shipman, Mel 95
shlichim, see emissaries
Shukeiri, Ahmed 180
Silberman, Charles 108
Silesia 297, 302
Simchat Torah 255
Sinai 74, 256–57
Sinai Campaign 42, 59, 61–62, 70–71, 231, 281, 294
Sinay, Ruben 172, 174, 179
Sión, Nueva 185
Smith, Terence 76
Smuts, Jan 207
Sneh, Moshe 177

Index

Sneh, Simha 158
Solotaroff, Ted 117, 120
South Africa 4, 6, 8, 18, 22, 34, 55, 149, 205–16
South African Jewish Board of Deputies 207, 210–11, 216
South African Zionist Federation (SAZF) 205, 208–11, 215–16
Soviet bloc 6, 305
Soviet Union (U.S.S.R.) 4–5, 8, 15–16, 18, 24–25, 42, 48–49, 53, 55–56, 58, 62, 118, 120, 131, 141–42, 146, 164, 170, 175, 179, 184, 242, 249–291, 293–95, 297, 301, 303
Soweto 24
SS Theodor Herzl 146
Stalin, Josef 252–53, 297, 305
Stalinist era 293
Straits of Magellan 141
Straits of Tiran 74, 141, 256
Study Circle on Diaspora Jewry 217, 219, 238, 241
Suez Canal 75, 257, 288
Suez crisis 133
Super, A. S. 211
Super-Jew 78
Superman 78, 80
Sweden 5, 309
Symbolic ethnicity 113
Syria 53, 73–74, 77, 120, 142–43, 147, 161, 221, 223, 255–57, 265, 269
Syrkin, Marie 79
Szczezyn (Poland) 307

Tacuara movement 24, 143, 147
Tel Aviv 269
Tergevozhdian, Aram 270
The Imaginary Jew 131
The Trials of Rosie O'Neal (TV show) 112
Thirty-Something? (TV show) 112
Tito, Josip 265
Tnuat Aliyah 154, 156–57
Tolchanov, Iosif 283

Toubi, Tewfik 172
Tourism 28, 30, 32, 48
Trainin, Natan 181
Tri-Continental Conference 182–83
Trigano, Shmuel 136
Tripoli 239, 243
Troper, Harold 95
Tunis 224, 226, 234–38
Tunisia 4, 218, 221, 224–33, 235–43, 248
Turkey 221, 223, 243, 247

Ukraine 271
Ultra-Orthodox 133, 136
Union of Religious Communities 296, 298 (in Poland)
Union Prayer Book 102
United Communal Fund 209 (in South Africa)
United Emergency Campaign 178
United Israel Appeal 40, 42
United Jewish Appeal (UJA) 14, 37, 40, 42, 47, 60, 64, 84, 100, 151, 163
United Kingdom (Great Britain) 18–19, 32, 34, 241
United Nations 141, 202, 209, 212, 216, 228, 231, 256, 262
United Nations Human Rights Commission 148
United States 5–8, 18–19, 22, 34, 37, 40, 47, 49, 52, 54, 56, 60, 65, 69, 73, 99–124, 149, 160, 220, 240–41, 248–49, 265, 267, 269, 295, 309
United Zionist Association 215 (in South Africa)
Uris, Leon 70, 72
Uruguay 34, 146, 182

Va'ad Hachinuch 169
Va'ad HaKehillot 143, 145, 161
Vasena, Adalberto Krieger 140
Vatican 142
Venezuela 34
Verbitzky, Bernardo 184

Vergelis, Aron 283
Viamonte, Carlos Sánchez 148
Vichy France 73
Videla, Jorge 170
Vietnam 70, 173, 181
Vietnam War 22, 183
Vil'fkovich, Semen 283
Vilner, Meir 172
Viñas, Ismael 183
Vorster, B. J. 216
Voz Libre 176, 185

Wailing/Western Wall 75–76, 211
Wall Street 112
War of Attrition 56
War of Independence 3, 207, 221, 244–45
Warsaw 294, 296, 298, 302, 307, 309
Warsaw Ghetto 130
Weizman Institute 181
West Germany 232, 270, 306
Western Europe 52, 55, 65, 118, 136
White, Theodore 76
World Jewish Congress 194, 227, 231, 241
World War I 57, 73
World War II 3, 53, 57, 64, 72–73, 82, 108, 127, 130, 134, 245, 269, 272, 279, 283, 292, 307, 310
World Zionist Organization (WZO) 14, 35, 48, 105, 151, 153–54, 156–59, 162–63, 187, 189, 191, 201

Writing Our Way Home 117, 120
Wroclaw (Poland) 296, 307
Wydodski, Stanislaw 309
Wyszynski, Jozef Cardinal 304

Yanover, Héctor 177
Yéchiva des Étudiants in Strasbourg 133, 136
Yemen 223, 232
Yiddish 118, 129, 131–33, 164, 168, 171, 176–77, 185, 251–52, 283–85, 299–300, 308
Yom Kippur War 19, 28, 32, 34, 42, 44, 51, 54, 57–59, 91, 118, 183, 193, 216, 266
Yugoslavia 265, 270

Zionist Federation 191–93, 195, 200–1 (in Mexico)
Zionist General Council 195, 199 (in Mexico)
Zionist Organization of Argentina (OSA) 143–46, 154, 15–58, 162–63
Zionist Revisionist Organization 215 (in South Africa)
Zionist Youth Council of Johannesburg 208

FINANCING RECURRENT EDUCATION

The Institute for Research on Educational Finance and Governance (IFG) was established with a five-year commitment from the National Institute of Education in 1979 and is administered through the School of Education at Stanford University. IFG is devoted to a program of policy-oriented research, dissemination and training on educational finance and economics, educational politics, educational organizations, and law and education.

Current research programs at IFG include the following:

- A Comparative Study of Private and Public Schooling Organizations
- Legalization, Regulation, and the New Federalism
- Cost and Cost Effectiveness of Educational Interventions
- Postsecondary Education and the Labor Market
- Planning Models for Local District Decision Making
- Intergovernmental Issues in Education

The Organization for Economic Cooperation and Development (OECD) was set up under a convention signed in Paris on December 14, 1960, that provides that the OECD shall promote policies designed

- to achieve the highest sustainable economic growth and employment and a rising standard of living in member countries, while maintaining financial stability, and thus to contribute to the development of the world economy;
- to contribute to sound economic expansion in member as well as nonmember countries in the process of economic development;
- to contribute to the expansion of world trade on a multilateral, nondiscriminatory basis in accordance with international obligations.

The members of OECD are Australia, Austria, Belgium, Canada, Denmark, Finland, France, the Federal Republic of Germany, Greece, Iceland, Ireland, Italy, Japan, Luxembourg, the Netherlands, New Zealand, Norway, Portugal, Spain, Sweden, Switzerland, Turkey, the United Kingdom, and the United States.

FINANCING RECURRENT EDUCATION

Strategies for Increasing Employment,
Job Opportunities, and Productivity

edited by
HENRY M. LEVIN
and
HANS G. SCHÜTZE

Published in cooperation with the Institute for Research on Educational Finance and Governance, Stanford University, and the Organization for Economic Cooperation and Development

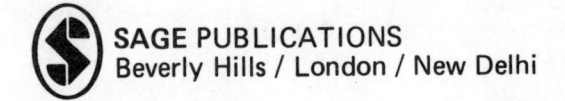

SAGE PUBLICATIONS
Beverly Hills / London / New Delhi

Portions of this book were previously published in *Education and Urban Society,* Volume 14, Number 3, May 1982.

Copyright © 1983 by Sage Publications, Inc.

All rights reserved. No part of this book may be reproduced or utilized in any form or by any means, electronic or mechanical, including photo-copying, recording, or by any information storage and retrieval system, without permission in writing from the publisher.

For information address:

        SAGE Publications, Inc.
        275 South Beverly Drive
        Beverly Hills, California 90212

SAGE Publications India Pvt. Ltd.   SAGE Publications Ltd
C-236 Defence Colony   28 Banner Street
New Delhi 110 024, India   London EC1Y 8QE, England

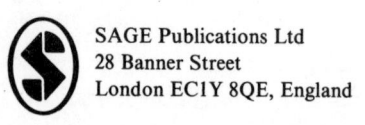

Printed in the United States of America

Library of Congress Cataloging in Publication Data

Main entry under title:

Financing recurrent education.

    Papers originally presented at conference sponsored by the Institute for Research on Educational Finance and Governance, and the Center for Educational Research and Innovation.
    Bibliography: p.
    1. Continuing education—United States—Finance—Congresses. 2. Occupational training—United States—Finance—Congresses. 3. Educational leave—Europe—Finance—Congresses. I. Levin, Henry M. II. Schütze, Hans Georg. III. Institute for Research on Educational Finance and Governance (U.S.) IV. Centre for Educational Research and Innovation.
LC5225.F56F56   379.1′215′0973   83-11214
ISBN 0-8039-2068-7

CONTENTS

Preface	7
Chapter 1: Economic and Political Dimensions of Recurrent Education *Henry M. Levin and Hans G. Schütze*	9

PART I: COMPREHENSIVE MODELS FOR FINANCING RECURRENT EDUCATION

Chapter 2: Individual Entitlements *Henry M. Levin*	39
Chapter 3: Individual Drawing Rights *Gösta Rehn*	67
Chapter 4: Intermediate ("Parafiscal") Financing Schemes *Werner Clement*	81
Chapter 5: Financing Mechanisms: Their Impact on Postcompulsory Education *Dieter Timmermann*	99

PART II: FINANCING RECURRENT EDUCATION IN THE UNITED STATES

Chapter 6: An Inventory of Programs and Sources of Support *Alan P. Wagner*	133
Chapter 7: Employer-Sponsored Programs *Gregory B. Smith*	159
Chapter 8: Unions and Postsecondary Education *Nevzer Stacey and Ivan Charner*	189
Chapter 9: Tax Limitation Measures: Their Impact in California *Harold E. Geiogue*	203

Chapter 10: An Opportunity Deferred: Lifelong Learning
ในthe United States
Pamela H. Christoffel 225

PART III: FINANCING PAID
EDUCATIONAL LEAVE

Chapter 11: The Swedish Model
Kjell Rubenson 237

Chapter 12: French Law on Continuing Vocational Training
Pierre Caspar 257

Chapter 13: The Federal Republic of Germany
Hans G. Schütze 273

Chapter 14: Paid Educational Leave: A Proposal Based
on the Dutch Case
Louis Emmerij 297

About the Authors 317

PREFACE

This volume had its origins in a conference on the costs and financing of recurrent education that was held at the Institute for Research on Educational Finance and Governance (IFG), Stanford University, in July 1980. That conference was cosponsored with the Center for Educational Research and Innovation (CERI) of the Organization for Economic Cooperation and Development (OECD) in Paris. Both the IFG and the OECD have devoted considerable resources to studying new approaches to financing postsecondary education generally, and recurrent education specifically. The outcome of the conference and a subsequent one in Bremen, West Germany, in October 1980 was *The Costs and Financing of Continuing Education and Training*—a volume on one of the most neglected aspects of recurrent education: its financing.

For reasons that are made explicit in the introductory chapter, we believe that recurrent education—a comprehensive strategy for distributing education and trainng over the life span of the individual in a recurrent manner with work and leisure—will become an important vehicle for addressing problems of employment, social mobility, and productivity. Yet, we are only in the early stages of discussing methods for financing recurrent education that are efficient, equitable, flexible, and comprehensive. The chapters in this volume draw upon a variety of ideas and experiences in the industrialized countries to provide alternatives for constructing such a framework. In this respect we are hopeful that the book makes an important contribution in advancing the necessary discourse.

We wish to thank both the OECD and the National Institute of Education for support of the intellectual activities and papers that led to this publication. We are also grateful to the German Marshall Fund of the United States for providing travel grants that enabled these scholars to attend the conferences at which their papers were first discussed. We are especially indebted to David Istance, Susan Peters, and Katherine Tobin for the many hours of capable devotion that they provided in helping to edit this volume. Of course, the views expressed in this book are those of the coeditors and authors, and not those of OECD, IFG, or any other institutions with which the authors are affiliated.

January 1983 Henry M. Levin
Hans G. Schütze

1

ECONOMIC AND POLITICAL DIMENSIONS OF RECURRENT EDUCATION

HENRY M. LEVIN
HANS G. SCHÜTZE

In the latter part of the twentieth century, the industrialized countries of the world will be facing a major educational and training challenge as labor force growth slows and technological change accelerates. There will be a rapid transformation of industries and occupations as economic shifts among nations and the introduction and application of new technologies create vast changes in the workplace. At the same time the growth of the labor force and particularly the entry of newly educated workers will fall to unprecedentedly low levels. Thus the newly trained labor market entrants can not be relied upon to sustain the changes that lie ahead. Without question the United States, Western Europe, and the other industrialized nations will have to pursue new educational and training strategies to prepare their existing labor forces for the new occupational demands. The purpose of this book is to address both methods and issues for financing a system of recurrent education that can accommodate the educational and training challenges that lie ahead.

In its broadest definition, recurrent education can be defined as follows: a comprehensive educational strategy for all post-compulsory or post-basic education, the essential characteristic of which is the distribution of education over the total life span of the individual in a recurring way, i.e., the alternation with other activities such as work, but also with leisure and retirement [OECD, 1973: 24].

This definition of recurrent education contains two essential elements: First, it offers an alternative educational strategy to the conventional concentration of all formal and full-time education in youth. It proposes to spread postcompulsory education over the full life span of the individual, and thus accepts the principle of lifelong learning.

Second, it proposes a framework within which lifelong learning will be organized, this being the alternation and effective interaction between education (as a structural learning situation) and other social activities during which learning occurs. This general definition of recurrent education contains two properties. It refers to educational offerings that are flexible in structure and content, and it refers to educational experiences that will be available over the life cycle of an individual.

Under present conventions, formal education and training for most individuals takes place prior to entering the labor force or in the first few years of work experience. During the remainder of the life cycle, further education and training constitute an exception for all but a few persons in relatively high-level occupations. For males the work career is often uninterrupted in the absence of unemployment or occupational change. For females, voluntary interruptions are more likely to address child rearing and family; there is surprisingly little pursuit of further education and training as a basis for labor market reentry. That is, present education and training practices tend to be relatively rigid, without accommodating the need to retrain for new careers or to adapt to technological change.

A system of recurrent education would alter this traditional pattern by providing opportunities for education and training throughout the life cycle. Typically, individuals would intersperse periods of work and education to meet both personal needs and those of employers. A system of alternative educational and training opportunities would be constructed that would incorporate existing offerings such as apprenticeships, extension courses, on-the-job training, college and university courses of study, correspondence courses, and technical schools, as well as new offerings and approaches that address previously unattended needs. Such educational and training experiences should be provided both inside and outside the workplace as well as through educational television and computer-assisted instruction. Availability of these offerings must be highly flexible, and opportunities must be provided on weekends and evenings as well as during regular work hours.

Many aspects of recurrent education already exist, but the present oportunities fall considerably short of an integrated system in two major ways. First, the present approach is highly fragmented: It is more a motley collection of confusing and uncoordinated educational possibilities than a systematic approach to recurrent education. Although a recurrent educational approach might surely incorporate all or more of the existing opportunities, they would become part of a more purposive and systematized approach to the overall educational and training strategies of societies. In this respect, availability, access, and comprehensiveness become of far greater concern than they presently are. Second, a system of recurrent education can provide a more systematic approach to the financing of recurrent educational opportunities and the provision of sufficient time away from the workplace to pursue them. Indeed, a major purpose of this volume is to consider alternative ways of providing a comprehensive system of financing recurrent education that will provide equity in access, flexibility and adaptability in responding to needs, and efficiency in the use of private and social resources.[1]

In summary, a recurrent educational approach would go beyond the existing offerings to provide a systematic approach regarding such matters as finance, information, coordination, educational leave for workers, and certification of training experiences. Heavy emphasis would be placed on a total system of opportunities for individuals, small groups, and employers in creating a menu of offerings suited to their needs and demands.

CONSTRUCTING A SYSTEM OF RECURRENT EDUCATION

Major components of recurrent education have been around for some time in the form of on-the-job training, adult education, correspondence courses, continuing education, extension courses, and the movement towards lifelong learning (Mushkin, 1974; Peterson, 1979). Certainly since the early seventies there has been a worldwide movement to improve the efficiency, equity, and flexibility of education through greater attention to lifelong learning (Faure, 1973; Emmerij, 1974). A crucial question that must surely be raised is why these movements have not been welded together into a system of recurrent education.

This question can best be answered by reference to the different concepts and notions of recurrent education. Although the terms "recurrent" and "lifelong" education have been used to refer to education and training over the life span, the generalization in terminology tends to gloss over the great diversity in underlying approaches as well as social and educational concerns. Table 1.1

TABLE 1.1 Different Versions of Recurrent Education

Motive	Rationale	Principal Clientele	Principal Forms
Increasing Productive Efficiency	Increase worker productivity and adaptation to technical change	Workers and persons reentering labor market	Job-oriented education and training
Reducing Unemployment	Use of recurrent education to share existing jobs	Labor Force	Educational leave and sabbaticals to rotate existing jobs
Reducing Overeducation and Underemployment	Providing educational opportunities throughout working life to reduce demand for tertiary education before entering workplace	Workers	Diversity of educational and training opportunities as needed over working life
Worker Participation	Improve conditions of work and worker participation	Workers	Training in skills and knowledge necessary for worker participation in decisions
Improving Quality of Leisure	Improve ability to use leisure hours productively	All adults	Emphasis on music, poetry, art and other forms of intellectual, cultural, and recreational development

Reducing Inequalities of Disadvantaged	Compensating for inequalities of worker social backgrounds and previous educational experiences to increase their mobility	Unemployed and unskilled workers	Basic academic skills and further job training
Improving Social Participation	Providing knowledge for greater social and political participation to improve their conditions	Nonprofessional and nonmanagerial workforce, housewives, and senior citizens	Political and family education as well as arts and human needs
Rescuing Educational Institution	New clientele and functions for postsecondary institutions faced with falling enrollments	Adults	Courses and degrees according to demand
Deschooling Society	Reducing coercion of mandatory schooling and bureaucracy of traditional educational institutions for greater individual freedom and choice by creating more flexible and responsive offerings	All persons beyond primary age	Whatever is demanded in the educational marketplace

provides a summary of nine relatively distinct motives that seem to be behind the arguments for recurrent education. Each of these tends to suggest a specific target clientele and set of offerings, and in many cases the overlap among clientele and offerings is minimal.

INCREASING PRODUCTIVE EFFICIENCY

The view that recurrent education can improve productive efficiency proceeds largely from the assumption that worker skills have a tendency to become obsolete under conditions of rapid technological change. As the nature of jobs evolves with new capital investment, workers will need to learn new skills or refresh old ones to adapt to new technologies. From this perspective, recurrent education provides the flexibility for retraining workers as skill rejuvenation is needed. Such an approach can improve worker productivity and earnings as well as increase the productivity of the firm and its profitability. Or, in time of rapid technical progress and change, recurrent education might be needed to maintain worker productivity which would otherwise decline. There is a particular incentive for employers to promote this approach, especially to the extent that recurrent education can reduce costs of training through economies of scale and can shift a portion of training costs from the private to the public sector.

The target clientele for this version of recurrent education is both the existing workforce and persons who are planning to reenter the workforce after periods of absence. (Housewives who have left employment to raise children are a good example of the latter.) Specifically vocational experiences would be offered to train persons for changing work roles and job requirements. The principal argument for public support of recurrent education that increases productive efficiency is that it would increase national productivity and economic growth while reducing inflation (through providing productivity gains commensurate with rising wages) and making products more competitive in world markets.

REDUCING EMPLOYMENT

A related motive for providing recurrent education is the role that it might play in reducing unemployment. However, what is referred to here is the use of recurrent education to rotate workers between periods of employment and periods of training, enabling a larger portion of the labor force to experience regular employment. By providing recurrent education for experienced workers at any point in time, job openings are provided for new members. Of course, to the degree that it improved the productivity of the labor force and made a country's goods more competitive in world markets, it might also contribute to job expansion.

The audience for such an approach is that of the labor force, but recurrent educational offerings can take several forms. Of most importance is the emphasis on recurrent education as an "active labor market policy" (Meidner and Anderson, 1973) as advocated in the chapters by Rehn and Emmerij in this volume. This approach must include provisions for inducing persons to leave the workforce to obtain further training or other types of education. One possible version is to create incentives for persons to take such leave when there is high unemployment in their industries or when retraining is needed in response to technical change. Other versions would make all workers eligible for such sabbaticals, with the expectation that they might be pursued most frequently when workers have incentives for retraining or switching careers to more prosperous sectors of the economy. While there is some overlap with the productive efficiency motive for recurrent education, the emphasis on the direct reduction of unemployment is grounds for viewing this approach as distinct.

REDUCING OVEREDUCATION AND UNDEREMPLOYMENT

In a very different sense, recurrent education may be used to reduce the number of overeducated members of the workforce —a considerable problem in many societies. Although there may be a growing shortage of certain skills in their economies as industrial reorganization and technical change accelerate, there is presently a surplus of persons with postsecondary education in virtually all of the Western industrialized countries. The phenomenon of overeducation or underutilization of educated labor is a waste of resources. Many people are trained who will not be able to obtain appropriate jobs in the careers for which they are trained (Freeman, 1976; Rumberger, 1981). At the same time it can represent a major source of social and political ferment as the job expectations of university and other postsecondary graduates are not fulfilled (Levin, 1976). The increasing costs of postsecondary education at a time of national fiscal crises in conjunction with an inability to employ graduates at appropriate job levels has stimulated a search for ways to reduce the demands by students and their families for traditional forms of higher education. However, given that education has been perceived as the main channel for upward mobility by the vast majority of the population, the demand for university participation will not be significantly reduced unless there are alternative channels of mobility.

In this respect, the provision of ample recurrent educational opportunities can be seen as a way of assuring secondary graduates that they need not undertake all of their educational experiences prior to entering the labor market. Presumably, under a system of recurrent education, employers would be expected to hire more secondary graduates and encourage them to seek out recurrent educational offerings that enable them to meet both their own needs and those of their employers. If such a shift from traditional timing and forms of postsecondary education to recurrent education were successful, it might reduce the perceived need for university training and thus reduce the number of overeducated persons. That is, recurrent education would be used to "cool off" the high demand for participation in traditional postsecondary education.

The main clientele would be secondary graduates who would enter the labor market at relatively lower levels and seek mobility through recurrent educational participation. The principal forms of recurrent education would be those that were highly related to job and career needs. The major obstacles to realizing this type of shift are that even fewer job opportunities are available for secondary graduates than for **university graduates, and employers tend to use credentials at the point** of labor market entry for assigning workers to occupational strata. Unless jobs become more plentiful at the secondary level and career mobility becomes closely linked with recurrent educational experiences rather than initial credentials, it is unlikely that there will be a profound shift in educational patterns.

WORKER PARTICIPATION

A rationale for recurrent education that is especially strong in Western Europe is its use in improving the quality of working life through worker participation. **An underlying assumption is that working life is oppressive because of the high degree of division of** labor and systems of managerial control that alienate workers from both the work process and their fellow workers. The response has been to develop a variety of ways in which workers can participate either directly or through representation in making decisions that affect the overall organization and functioning of the workplace as well as daily work operations.

Broadly speaking, this movement has come to be called "industrial democracy" or "workplace democracy." In part, employers have tried to increase the intrinsic attractiveness of the workplace through greater worker participation in order to reduce high levels of worker turnover and absenteeism and to raise productivity. In part, it has resulted from laws and collective bargaining agreements supported by labor that have mandated worker participation in the operations of the firm. For example, the codetermination laws of West Germany require that there be worker members on the boards of directors of large firms as well as worker councils for joint determination of employment and work operations (Furstenburg, 1977). Sweden has a national law requiring worker participation on all major decisions regarding employment and the nature and distribution of work (Ministry of Labor, Sweden, 1975). Other nations have also experienced increasing worker participation in their enterprises and government sponsorship of initiatives in this direction.

The need for recurrent education under such circumstances is to educate workers about their responsibilities and functions in a participative organization; to provide them with the knowledge that they will need to make good decisions; and to enable them to develop their other skills more fully for both occupational advancement and human development (Schuller, 1981; Turner and Count, 1981). Specific forms of recurrent education include the availability of educational and training sabbaticals, worker circles for discussion of all pertinent issues relative to the role of workers in such organization, and the availability of courses for workers on the basis of sufficient worker demand. Clearly the audience for this form of recurrent education is that of the present workforce.

IMPROVING QUALITY OF LEISURE

Advocates of recurrent education as a means of improving the quality of leisure often assume that a high standard of living in the industrialized countries requires a minute division of labor where most jobs have little skill content and are highly routinized. Therefore, they see little hope of transforming work into a more humane activity without a large sacrifice in living standards. But, they would argue that the redemption of this approach is that an "inhuman" technology has tended to shorten the work week and increase the amount of leisure that workers can enjoy.

Therefore, if the price of such affluence has been the destruction of the human spirit in the workplace—as Terkel (1974) has emphasized—the response must be to resurrect it outside of the workplace by bringing music, poetry, art, and other forms of cultural development into the lives of workers through recurrent or lifelong education. The clientele for recurrent education would include virtually all adults, and the opportunities would be scheduled during evenings, weekends, vacations, and other heavy concentrations of leisure hours. A major audience would be that of senior citizens who have retired from the workplace. Presumably, the alienation of the workplace or the home in the case of housewives would be compensated for in intellectual stimulation, spirituality, social interchange, knowledge, and human development provided by recurrent educational activities outside of work.

REDUCING INEQUALITIES OF THE DISADVANTAGED

Much discussion of recurrent education has viewed it as a way of redressing inequalities that emanate from the social origins of workers and their previous education (Levin, 1978). Because it has been evident that previous levels of educational attainment and their occupational rewards are heavily conditioned by the social origins of workers, recurrent education is seen as an opportunity for providing further educational opportunities for those workers who are least advantaged in labor markets. In particular, workers who are most susceptible to unemployment or underemployment by virtue of their previous educational experiences would represent the primary target for eligibility and financing of recurrent education. The expectation is that by using recurrent education to compensate this group for their labor market disadvantages, it will be possible to increase their occupational and earnings mobility. Indeed, this is largely the premise behind the various publicly supported training programs for the disadvantaged found in the United States (Mirengoff and Rindler, 1976) and Western Europe.

This approach to recurrent education focuses primarily on persons who are susceptible to unemployment and who are relatively unskilled. Recurrent education strategies include an attempt to provide basic academic skills where these were lacking as well as specific job training. A broader version of using recurrent education for reducing inequality would integrate a "prodisadvantaged" approach into a national system of recurrent education. The disadvantaged would be given greater financial assistance and a wider range of choices to meet their special needs. In this way, the concern for equalization could be integrated into comprehensive approaches to recurrent education for the entire population.

IMPROVING SOCIAL PARTICIPATION

A related perspective on recurrent education sees it as a means of increasing social participation in political, economic, and cultural life. In this framework, recurrent education is viewed as a way of increasing the democratization of political, economic, social, and cultural participation by providing educational experiences that enhance the ability of those who are least likely and least able to participate in these spheres of life. For example, persons from less advantaged educational and work backgrounds tend to participate less in the political process and tend to have greater difficulty in understanding complex political issues. Recurrent educational strategies could focus on increasing political participation by involving such persons in political discussions and enabling them to be more conversant with the important issues.

The attempt to increase social participation in all spheres of life by those who are most disenfranchised could extend to literacy, family planning, consumer knowledge, health and hygiene, and utilization of the political process to attain objectives. For example, senior citizens could be provided with instruction and other forms of experience that would increase their ability to organize collectively to meet their needs. Recurrent educational opportunities could also focus on greater involvement in the performing and fine arts and voluntary community services, as well as provide them with knowledge on nutrition and health care unique to their situations.

Clientele would be drawn largely from those groups who have the lowest levels of social participation and the fewest resources to improve their circumstances. These groups might include lower-level workers, housewives, the handicapped, senior citizens, and poverty populations. Essentially, recurrent education would be used as a way to provide the knowledge needed to increase participation and create social progress for those groups who are least able to provide such results on their own behalf. This approach to recurrent education is profoundly and overtly political, and it is inherently more controversial than the political motives of most other approaches.

RESCUING EDUCATIONAL INSTITUTIONS

At odds with the motive for using recurrent education to reduce overeducation is that of using it to rescue educational institutions that are losing enrollments because of reductions in the population of youth. Virtually all of the highly industrialized countries are experiencing historically low birthrates that have resulted in demographic shifts in the population (Acsadi and Johnson-Acsadi, 1980). As the population grows older, there are fewer persons in the age groups that in the past have pursued traditional forms of postsecondary education, so colleges and universities are facing declines in enrollments. Particularly affected are those institutions that proliferated and expanded to meet the demographic bulges of the "baby boom" period. A major strategy for maintaining enrollment levels has been for institutions to seek new clientele and educational directions.

Clearly, a major source of such clientele are those persons who are in the workplace or home and are beyond the normal age for postsecondary participation. By providing recurrent educational opportunities to these persons, it is hoped that empty classrooms and deficit budgets can be avoided. Indeed, the principal motive of many postsecondary institutions in promoting recurrent education is that of institutional survival. **Many strategies have developed to support this quest: Such institutions** have started satellite campuses in local communities and in corporate and government workplaces to attract students; have granted credits for "life" experiences to increase the attractiveness of further study towards a degree; have promoted more flexible degree requirements in terms of both scheduling and rigor with evening and weekend offerings and minimal library demands on students; and have expanded the range of offerings in both programs providing credit towards degrees and those that do not. Although many of these strategies have tended to compromise the quality of educational offerings, a deterioration of quality should not be considered intrinsic to the expansion of recurrent education.

"DESCHOOLING" THE POSTCOMPULSORY SYSTEM

A final motive for expanding recurrent education is to replace the highly institutionalized forms of traditional schooling. It is argued that mandatory schooling is coercive and that even traditional postsecondary education has become mandatory for those who seek to achieve placement in higher occupations. By making the routes for both training and occupational achievement more flexible and subject to individual demand and choice, much unnecessary schooling will be eliminated and coercion will be reduced. Since this view is often held by those who wish to see a "deschooling of society" (for example, Illich, 1971), it can be characterized under that rubric. The expectation is that such a system would be more flexible and efficient in the use of resources in addition to being more humane.

All persons beyond compulsory school age would constitute the clientele for such an approach, and the educational offerings would simply depend on what was demanded in the educational marketplace. Illich (1971) has suggested that every community could have documentation centers using the latest technology that would make information on any subject available through printed and electronic media. Individuals would learn how to use such centers to instruct themselves on topics that arose in their daily work lives, politics, or social relations, or on which they were curious. Issues of social priorities in what would be offered or who would be served would not be of importance under such an arrangement—it would be designed to minimize government regulations and other institutional encumbrances. However, it is conceivable that a regulated market approach might be developed with government-funded entitlements that could be used to pay for educational offerings that met certain stipulated criteria. Recurrent educational approaches responding to the deschooling motive could range from unregulated ones with little government support to highly regulated situations with continuing government funding and involvement.

POLITICAL AND ECONOMIC CHALLENGES

Thus far we have presented nine different motives for advocating the systematic expansion of recurrent education. For many observers at least some of them will represent persuasive arguments for recurrent education. Taken together, one might think that the political and economic support for recurrent education would be substantial. Yet, paradoxically, the very diversity of approaches may be the greatest political obstacle to adoption and implementation.

The political challenges can be seen most clearly if one looks at the different versions of recurrent education in terms of their rationales, clientele, and principal applications. Even a cursory comparison would suggest considerable differences among them that may inhibit the formation of political constituencies. Before reviewing these areas of potential discord, it is important to note that virtually all of the approaches can be viewed under three themes: those contributing to improvements in the functioning of labor markets and productivity; those contributing to improved social participation and equity; and those that are designed to achieve major institutional change.

> Labor Market and Productivity Strategies
> > Increasing Productive Efficiency
> > Reducing Unemployment
> > Reducing Overeducation and Underemployment
>
> Social Participation and Equity
> > Worker Participation
> > Improving Quality of Leisure
> > Reducing Inequalities of Disadvantaged
> > Improving Social Participation
>
> Institutional Change
> > Rescuing Educational Institutions
> > Deschooling of the Postcompulsory System

Even among these three major areas there are substantial differences in goals and constituencies. For example, the enhancement of social participation and equity may be important goals on their own merits, but they are not designed to contribute to institutional change or increase productivity. To some degree the various approaches are in conflict; at the very least, resources that are committed to one version may not be available for the pursuit of other approaches.

However, incompatability between the nine specific approaches (see Table 1.1) is even more acute. Even within major categories such as institutional change, the strategies differ immensely in objectives and clientele. For example, using recurrent education to broaden the mission of postsecondary educational institutions that are losing enrollments represents an attempt to strengthen existing institutional forms—a goal that is sharply in contrast with the motive of deschooling postcompulsory education. Using recurrent education to reduce overeducation or the underutilization of educated labor is also incompatible with using it to rescue traditional postsecondary educational institutions. As these conflicts are also evident in comparisons of many other categories, it is difficult to see how a single, comprehensive plan for recurrent education could encompass all of the various approaches.

Indeed, this situation has seemed to be a major political weakness of recurrent education in the past, especially in the United States. A single rubric has been used to refer to what are essentially a variety of competing and conflicting versions of lifelong education. By bringing them under a single descriptive term—recurrent education—it has been possible to get a large and diverse coalition to support the concept in the abstract. However, any implementation of recurrent education would obviously require that specific forms be adopted and financed that would either neglect or be incompatible with other forms. That is, once the broad notion of recurrent education is translated into particular strategies with particular goals, it becomes a narrower concept which may support the objectives of one constituency at the expense of another. In the United States there has been an indeterminacy in forging a politically acceptable strategy for implementation. This political challenge must be overcome in the future.

The economic obstacles are inherent in the present disincentives for individuals to undertake the recurrent education route in place of the traditional one. In order to make recurrent education vocationally relevant, a number of conditions must be met: (1) Employment opportunities must be readily available for persons who have completed high school and have not continued into postsecondary education; (2) career ladders and training options must be provided in conjunction with such jobs; and (3) later participation in and completion of educational programs on a recurrent basis must provide occupational advancement and income that are commensurate with the cost of those training programs and their value when they have been completed prior to entering the labor force.

The availability of employment is an obvious and important requirement for individuals seeking to take jobs prior to completing their formal education and training and then to pursue subsequent recurrent educational strategies. Presumably, individuals could begin their careers at entry levels and undertake additional education and training as needed. To do this, numerous work opportunities would have to be available for high school graduates. Unfortunately, unemployment rates for young high school graduates are substantial and considerably higher than for college graduates. For example, in March **1979 the U.S. unemployment rate for high school graduates 16-17 years** of age was about 24% and for 18-19 years olds was almost 12% although the overall unemployment rate for all groups was about 6% (U.S. Department of Labor, 1981: A-22). Thus, high school graduates who were under 20 years of age had unemployment rates that were two to four times the national average. Since that time unemployment rates have risen in all categories, and the relatively poor position of young high school graduates has deteriorated further. The data suggest that many individuals will have difficulty in finding the employment necessary to pursue a recurrent educational strategy, and the incentives may encourage improving employment possibilities through taking a college degree prior to entering the labor market in spite of the problems faced by those with college degrees (Freeman, 1976; Rumberger, 1981).

This disincentive is reinforced by the nature of entry-level positions. To a large degree these positions are not the first steps on a career ladder, but are "dead-end" positions that lead nowhere (Brown, 1982). Examples include one of the primary sectors for employment of untrained youth—fast-food restaurants. This industry is predicated upon operations that are largely determined by the machines and technology employed, and as a result the simple labor operations can be learned quickly and few skills are learned on the job. Further, there are few positions above this entry-level since relatively small numbers of supervisors can monitor very large numbers of workers in jobs that are so highly routinized. Although fast-food preparation in the past meant that individuals might develop skills as short-order cooks that could be transferred to more advanced kitchen and restaurant positions, this is not likely today.

Such jobs do not lend themselves to a demand for recurrent education and training for skill development because of the lack of career ladders in such employments. Rather, they reinforce the view that these are dead-end jobs, and the only way to improve one's employment is to get more advanced credentials that will provide employment opportunities in better occupations. Thus, both the relative dearth of jobs and the lack of career ladders for those jobs that are available tend to discourage individuals from considering recurrent educational strategies.

Beyond these disincentives to pursuing recurrent education in place of more traditional educational patterns, there is the related issue of the availability of training opportunities within firms. Unfortunately, many entry-level positions neither lead to career opportunities that require additional skills nor provide opportunities to learn new skills on the job. The most extensive training programs are generally provided for persons who have already acquired considerable formal education, generally at least at the level of a university degree. This also leads to incentives to complete postsecondary education prior to joining the labor force.

Finally, the issue arises as to whether individuals acquiring training and education in the recurrent fashion will do as well in the job market as persons who have acquired formal educational credentials prior to entering careers. For example, assume that a high school graduate decides to take a position as a clerical or assembly worker while pursuing a B.A. degree simultaneously on a part-time basis. The question is how that person will be viewed on the labor market when he or she completes the B.A. degree and applies for a management training position. One might think that a person with other work experience at lower levels would be even a more attractive candidate for a management trainee position than an inexperienced graduate with the same level of formal education.

However, it is not clear that firms behave in that way. An assembly worker or clerical worker with a new B.A. degree obtained on a part-time basis is more likely to be treated as an assembly worker or clerical worker who has overachieved, while the inexperienced worker with the newly acquired B.A. that was earned on a full-time basis is considered to be the more appropriate candidate for management training. In the United States one finds few recipients of law degrees or M.B.A. degrees who have studied on a part-time basis, being considered for the most prestigious positions that require these credentials. That is, firms do not seem to attach the same weight to part-time study as to equivalent full-time study in hiring and promotion decisions.

In summary, the logic of recurrent education for improving the efficiency and equity of utilization and training of human resources is not matched by appropriate incentives to individuals to forego traditional educational patterns for those of recurrent education. From all of the information available it seems reasonable to conclude that higher employment rates, better jobs and career mobility ladders, greater access to on-the-job training, and greater success in obtaining access to prestigious positions are available to those who enter the labor market with at the least the completion of a university degree. Finally, it is important to note that financial aid is rarely available for the part-time student, creating an additional disincentive to undertake a more flexible approach to post-secondary education and training. This situation does not serve to promote the more flexible work and study patterns associated with recurrent education. Yet, the near future appears to be a time when these challenges will be overcome and recurrent education will become more fully recognized as a force for improving training, employment, and productivity.

RECURRENT EDUCATION AS A RISING STAR

In the last two decades of the twentieth century, two phenomena will make recurrent education a vital strategy for promoting workplace productivity, employment, and occupational mobility. The first is the fact that enormous shifts in occupational skills will take place as old industries subside and new ones take their place. At the same time there will no longer be massive inflows of new workers with the latest training, so adaptation and retraining will necessarily need to focus largely on the existing workforce. Second, while relative expansion of high technology jobs will be substantial, such expansion will account for only a small proportion of new job positions. Since most of the expansion of employment will be in relatively low-skill areas that require modest initial educational qualifications, there will be a need for further education and training to create mobility and avoid a caste-like segmentation of large numbers of workers in low-skill jobs. Let us consider each of these in turn.

It is widely accepted that as the United States and Western Europe recover from the serious economic situation of the 1970s and early 1980s, the composition of industries and employment will change drastically. The production of steel, automobiles, and heavy machinery will have shifted substantially and will continue to shift to such Third World countries as Brazil, South Korea, and Taiwan—often under the aegis of multinational corporations that are headquartered in the industrial countries. At the same time, new industries will be rising and experiencing rapid growth in microelectronics, microcomputers, computer applications and software, robotics, and biotechnology. Beyond the rise and expansion of these industries themselves, their products will have profound effects on the nature of the work process and production in existing workplaces. The use of robotics and microprocessors to execute and control production will alter the characteristics of the workplace and the skills and training required of workers; biotechnology should have profound effects on the production of chemicals and pharmaceuticals.

Although the transformation of industry and the workplace has certainly been a constant feature of the nineteenth and twentieth centuries, the pace of change is accelerating because of rapid technological developments, information advances that permit extremely rapid diffusion of technology, and a desperate search for higher profits at a time of poor economic performance.

At the same time there will be a drastic decline in the inflow of newly trained workers: Falling birthrates in the industrialized countries have reduced the number and proportion of young persons. In the recent past, the need for workers with advanced skills was largely met through the introduction of newly educated workers into the labor force. This fact is reflected dramatically in estimates of the U.S. Department of Labor: While the labor force grew at an annual rate of about 2.2% between 1965-1975 and 2.7% in 1975-1979, the rate of increase will fall to 1.9% in 1979-1985, 1.3% in 1985-1990 and less than 1% in 1990-1995 (Fullerton, 1982: 49). Although there was a net addition of over 10 million workers to the labor force from 1975 to 1979, the net addition projected for the five-year period between 1990 and 1995 is less than 6 million (Fullerston, 1982: 51).

This means that to a sharply increased extent, the development of new skills to match the jobs generated by both industrial shifts and new technologies will have to be met through training and retraining of the existing labor force. It is difficult to see how this massive task can be accomplished efficiently without the initiation of a comprehensive system of recurrent education. Such a system must be organized to provide a level of comprehensiveness and adaptability that will accommodate the inevitable demands for workers that are qualified to meet the requirements of the new technologies and work tasks. If such a system is not forthcoming, it is conceivable that severe bottlenecks in production and costly inefficiencies in retraining will arise since the present approach to continuing education and employer training is probably not adequate to anticipate and accommodate the enormous changes that lie ahead. For this reason, concerns for future employment and productivity will be powerful stimuli for the development by both states and the national government of a systematic and responsive approach to the promotion and provision of recurrent education.

The second important reason that recurrent education is likely to become a more important factor on the political and educational agenda is the urgency of avoiding a permanent under-class of unskilled and low-paid workers. So-called high technology jobs will be expanding at a faster rate than many of the more traditional ones, but they will represent only a very small portion of the total number of new jobs that will be created in the next two decades. For example, although the number of positions for such jobs as computer operators is expected to double in the 1978-1990 period, this will amount to the net creation of only about 160,000 new jobs in that area (Carey, 1982: 42). However, during the same period, the number of new jobs for janitors and sextons is expected to approach almost 700,000; nurses' aides and orderlies—594,000; sales clerks—591,000; cashiers—546,000; waiters and waitresses—532,000; general office clerks—530,000; and food preparation and service workers in fast-food restaurants—492,000 (Carey, 1982: 40). In fact, among the 20 occupations that are expected to generate the most new jobs, there are no high-technology occupations represented, and no more than 4 seem to require any postsecondary education; professional nurses, elementary school teachers, accountants and auditors, and licensed practical nurses (if we assume that office skills can be acquired in secondary school). Even more important is the dearth of possibilities for career mobility, for in most of these cases there are no evident career ladders. That is, under normal circumstances, one does not move from the job of janitor to that of a skilled worker, and in many cases there are simply few higher-level positions of any sort in the firms that will hire this labor. Thus, we are facing an expansion of unskilled jobs that will typically lack opportunities for advancement in the absence of further training.

To a large degree, the sole hope for occupational mobility for vast segments of the labor force will lie in the establishment of a system of recurrent education that will prepare persons entering these jobs for the relatively smaller number of jobs in the economy that will require higher skills. That is, although large numbers of persons will enter jobs requiring little preparation and training, they will be able to advance to more demanding and remunerative work only if the opportunities to acquire appropriate training are available. By having such opportunities, incentives to take lower-level jobs and to perform well will be enhanced by the promise of more advanced training and opportunities. In this way, firms will be able to fill jobs at the lower levels, while workers who take those jobs can have access to the training required for upward mobility. At the present time, the very high turnover of workers in such positions is largely attributable to the routine nature and dead end careers associated with such jobs combined with a lack of access to further career training opportunities.

It may even be appropriate to tie eligibility for subsidized recurrent education opportunities to employment tenure so that individuals who spend a year or more in one of these ubiquitous low-skill areas will be rewarded with an expanded list of training options for higher-level employment. It is important to point out that much of such training must necessarily be made available outside of the place of employment, since many employers of low-skill workers will not have the resources or higher-skill positions to train workers for.

In summary, both the need to adapt an existing labor force to industrial shifts and changes in technology as well as the need to provide mobility routes for large numbers of workers who will be forced to accept employment in unskilled occupations that lack career ladders will necessitate consideration of a new system for the training and retraining of the work force. It is exactly these needs that are addressed most fully by a comprehensive system of recurrent education, and pressures from both directions will contribute to the formation of such a system.

FINANCING RECURRENT EDUCATION

As we stated at the outset, the goal of recurrent education is to create mechanisms that will promote alternative education and work patterns that can draw upon existing resources while providing incentives for new ones to emerge in a systematic way. Such a system would improve education, training, employment, and productivity by making access to a comprehensive system of recurrent education a universal option for individuals and firms, and would utilize educational resources more effectively than does the traditional pattern which places great urgency on completing one's formal education and training before seeking regular employment.

The focus of this volume is not to design a single approach to financing recurrent education as much as it is to set out alternatives for doing so. Depending on the goals of recurrent education and the existence of supportive resources, there are many different approaches that can be pursued. The following chapters provide a provocative discussion of these alternatives that enables one to evaluate them according to their strengths and weaknesses. This evaluation can be used as a basis for further discussion, planning, and action. The first part of the book addresses the complex issues surrounding overall models for financing recurrent education. The second part examines the financing of recurrent educational programs in the United States. Finally, the third part explores the financing of paid educational leave, using four case studies from Western Europe.

COMPREHENSIVE MODELS FOR FINANCING RECURRENT EDUCATION

The purpose of this section of the book is to set out several models for financing education that might be evaluated with regard to such criteria as equity, flexibility, comprehensiveness, efficiency, cost, and distribution of the cost burden. Three different financing approaches are presented, and they are assessed along with other financing possibilities in a common framework.

The chapter by Henry M. Levin on "Individual Entitlements" for recurrent education constructs the case for financing recurrent education through vouchers or entitlements that are issued to individuals when their compulsory education requirements are completed. The entitlements could be used for a wide variety of education and training opportunities including colleges and universities, employer- or union-sponsored training programs, correspondence courses, apprenticeships, and so on. Entitlements would be based upon both loans and grants, with the composition between the two dependent upon family resources. The ingredients of a system of finance, regulation, and information are discussed, and the GI Bill (by which educational entitlements were provided to military veterans) is used to evaluate the efficiency, equity, and responsiveness of the entitlement approach.

In contrast, Gösta Rehn proposes a different approach in the chapter entitled "Individual Drawing Rights." Each person would be able to use a portion of his social security account to take educational leave from work for retraining or preparing for other careers. The goal of this approach would be to maximize the ability of individuals to allocate their time among work, study, and leisure over the life span. These choices would be integrated into an active labor market policy that would create incentives for individuals to use their drawing rights for recurrent education when job prospects in their industries were declining and jobs were expanding in other industries. The plan might also augment drawing rights for the poor and handicapped in order to provide greater social equity. A major advantage is that existing social security accounts could be used as a basis for expanding individual choice and to support a diverse set of possibilities for participating in recurrent education.

A third approach is presented by Werner Clement in "Intermediate 'Parafiscal' Financing Schemes." In this approach, the focus for financing recurrent education would be on such intermediate entities as trade unions, employer associations, professional organizations, and other voluntary groups. The government would enable any such group to levy taxes on its members to support a program of recurrent education that would address its specific needs. Under such an arrangement, Clement suggests that people would be able to express their preferences for recurrent education through groups of a convenient size with common goals, and that costs would be reduced while participation would be encouraged.

In the final chapter in this section, Dieter Timmermann attempts to evaluate these three plans and others in "Financing Mechanisms: Their Impact on Postcompulsory Education." A number of criteria are established, and a self-financing or market model, a single-employer financing model, and a state financing model are assessed in addition to the use of entitlements, drawing rights, and intermediate institutions. Timmermann concludes that a mixed model incorporating aspects of each individual model might be most appropriate.

FINANCING RECURRENT EDUCATION IN THE UNITED STATES

Such traditional activities as adult education, university and college extension courses, on-the-job training, military training, other government training programs, and trade union educational and apprenticeship programs can all be incorporated into a comprehensive approach to recurrent education. But, since these educational and training programs are funded and sponsored by a wide range of state, local, and federal government agencies as well as private benefactors, it is difficult to know the extent of such programs, their sources of support, and the magnitude of participation and funding. This section of the volume represents a selective survey of recurrent education activities and their funding in the United States.

Alan P. Wagner attempts to piece together the myriad of existing programs in "An Inventory of Programs and Sources of Support." On the basis of his detective work, he concludes that in 1980 about 50 million individuals in the United States participated in at least one type of organized learning activity within the recurrent educational rubric, and the estimated costs were in the neighborhood of $55 billion. Wagner attempts to review the types and magnitudes of each type of program and the costs and sources of funding. Finally, he provides information on the characteristics of participants by sex, age, race, and employment status. Thus this chapter serves as a useful background for understanding the scope of present approaches to financing recurrent education in the United States.

Although employer-sponsored education is acknowledged widely as a substantial part of the existing system of recurrent education, surprisingly little systematic analysis of this mode has been carried out. This is the subject of Gregory B. Smith's chapter on "Employer-Sponsored Programs." Smith focuses on the purposes, forms, effects, and magnitude of training programs that are financed by employers. After this general survey, he addresses one of the most prevalent forms of employer-sponsored programs in recurrent education: tuition-assistance programs. Most of these programs suffer from low rates of employee participation, so Smith has chosen to review three relatively effective cases to ascertain what can be learned about making such programs more attractive and useful.

Clearly, unions also have an important stake in the recurrent education of their members. Only recently have there been concerted efforts to understand the extent of union involvement in recurrent education in general, and specifically the degree to which such provisions are financed by collective bargaining agreements. In "Unions and Postsecondary Education," Nevzer Stacey and Ivan Charner examine the role of unions. Specific types of programs and subsidies for recurrent educational activities are examined, and illustrative programs are indicated. The authors also reflect on emerging factors that may make such educational and training programs more important in the future, and they suggest that unions would be wise to consider these issues in their future policies.

Just as the recurrent education phenomenon began to become more fully articulated, a movement with important implications for public funding of programs gained momentum: the tax and expenditure limitation movement. In states such as California with Proposition 13 and Massachusetts with its Proposition 2½, state initiatives limited tax revenues from the property tax. Other states have passed expenditure limitation measures, and the substantial tax and expenditure cuts of the Reagan administration indicate that the thrust of federal policy is also in this direction.

In "Tax Limitation Measures: Their Impact in California," Harold E. Geiogue examines the impact of the $7 billion reduction in property taxes generated by the passage of California's Proposition 13 in 1978. Because of its weaker political constituency relative to that of the more entrenched forms of education, Geiogue found that recurrent educational offerings seem to have experienced greater funding reductions than did more traditional forms of postsecondary education. He concludes with an analysis and interpretation of this phenomenon—a view that is not optimistic with respect to the future of recurrent education under conditions of budgetary stress.

In the United States, much of the overall discussion of recurrent education has been situated at the federal level. In the autumn of 1980, the Education Amendments signed by President Carter provided an expansion of educational opportunity for adults and a commitment to recurrent education. In "An Opportunity Deferred: Lifelong Learning in the United States," Pamela H. Christoffel reviews the history of recurrent education at the federal level with major attention to the background and details of the 1980 amendments. Unfortunately, the exciting and productive changes that would have provided a federal stimulus to recurrent education did not receive funding appropriations at a time of severe budgetary distress. Nevertheless, they represent a background at the federal level for what might follow as the economy improves and job retraining becomes more pressing.

Overall, then, the rather rapid developments that took place in the United States in recurrent education have experienced setbacks in recent years, largely because of a poor economy and government fiscal stringencies. As we have argued above, we view this situation as a temporary one, for the realities of a slowdown in labor force growth and drastic changes in the structure of industries and occupations will create renewed pressures for more comprehensive ways of providing and funding recurrent education. An important aspect of that development might certainly be the provision of educational leave policies.

FINANCING PAID EDUCATIONAL LEAVE

Working individuals need more than just access to recurrent educational opportunities for pursuing further education and training over their working lives: They also need the time to dedicate themselves to further study. While in some cases this study can take place outside of working hours, for example during weekends and evenings, in other cases the intensity and depth of recurrent education and training will require a period of study that is unfettered by work obligations. In 1974, the International Labor Organization (ILO) Convention expressed a commitment to the granting of paid educational leave for training at any level. Many countries in Western Europe have moved in this direction by providing educational leave of absence provisions for workers. Since these may have profound consequences for future U.S. policies, this final section of the volume reviews four rather different approaches to financing educational leave.

It is generally recognized that Sweden has gone farther than virtually all of the Western European countries in providing training and educational opportunities for adults. In "The Swedish Model," Kjell Rubenson reviews the background and overall approach for financing recurrent educational opportunities in Sweden. Of particular importance is the integration of financial support for recurrent education that includes both the direct costs of the education and training as well as a stipend for covering the living costs of the participants. These programs are part of the overall labor market policies in Sweden, and they are designed to contribute to maintaining high levels of employment and productivity growth.

One of the earliest national laws regarding paid educational and training leave is the French Act of 1971. In 1979 almost 3 million French workers took part in training activities at a cost of almost $3 billion. In "French Law on Continuing Vocational Training," Pierre Caspar reviews the French experience as well as the patterns of financing and participation. Caspar suggests that there are a number of lessons to be learned from the French case, especially the need to avoid overregulation and the proliferation of detailed legal statutes on permissible program activities. He also suggests that many workers fear that if they take paid educational leave, their jobs may evaporate during their absence.

In contrast with France and its national laws, provisions for paid educational leave in West Germany are provided primarily at the state level. In his chapter on "The Federal Republic of Germany," Hans G. Schütze examines the provisions and experiences of the five states that have adopted extensive leave policies. Important comparisons are made of both the laws of the different states and their patterns of participation. Interestingly, although both the national setting and level of government sponsorship differ between the French and German cases, the Schütze chapter reports many parallels with respect to patterns of participation. The state-oriented nature of the Western German approach is likely to be of particular interest in the United States where much of the responsibility for education is concentrated at the state level.

The final chapter, "Paid Educational Leave: A Proposal Based on the Dutch Case" by Louis Emmerij, reviews the Dutch situation and makes a novel proposal: Emmerij suggests that the payments that are presently used for public assistance and unemployment compensation for unemployed workers be used to provide paid educational leave. Not only does he argue that such a policy would use more efficiently the funds that are already being spent on the unemployed by retraining them and increasing their marketable skills, he suggests also that systematic participation of employed workers in recurrent educational programs would open up considerable job opportunities for new workers. That is, the openings created by the constant movement of the experienced workforce into recurrent educational and training programs would serve to introduce new workers to those jobs and provide job mobility for workers at lower levels.

Thus, the variety of schemes for paid educational leave in Western Europe serves as a provocative set of experiences for U.S. consideration of such policies. The French and Swedish cases provide insights into national financing provisions and costs, and the West German case demonstrates how states might adopt and implement paid educational leave policies. As the Emmerij chapter suggests, such a policy can reduce unemployment and can be funded substantially from the various forms of public assistance and unemployment compensation that are presently used to support the unemployed. By implication, a U.S. policy might incorporate the participation of both states and the federal government, while integrating paid educational leave into overall policies for reducing unemployment and increasing productivity.

NOTE

1. For an earlier attempt at addressing these issues, see Benson and Hodgkinson (1974) and OECD (1975).

REFERENCES

ACSADI, G. T. and G. JOHNSON-ACSADI (1980) "Recent trends and determinants of fertility in developed countries," in A. A. Campbell (ed.) Social, Economic, and Health Aspects of Low Fertility. U.S. Department of Health, Education, and Welfare, Public Health Service, NIH Publication 80-100. Washington, DC: U.S. Government Printing Office.
BENSON, C. and H. L. HODGKINSON (1974) Implementing the Learning Society. San Francisco: Jossey-Bass.
BROWN, C. (1982) "Dead-end jobs and youth unemployment," in R. Freeman and D. Wise (eds.) Youth Unemployment. Chicago: Univ. of Chicago Press.
CAREY, M. L. (1982) "Occupational employment growth through 1990," pp. 34-47 in Economic Projections to 1990. U.S. Department of Labor, Bureau of Labor Statistics Bulletin 2121. Washington, DC: U.S. Government Printing Office.

EMMERIJ, L. (1974) Can the School Build a New Social Order? New York: Elsevier.
FAURE, E. et al. (1973) Learning to Be. Unesco, Paris. Toronto: Ontario Institute for Studies in Education.
FREEMAN, R. B. (1976) The Over-Educated American. New York: Academic Press.
FULLERTON, H. N., Jr. (1982) "The 1995 labor force: a first look," pp. 48-58 in Economic Projections to 1990. U.S. Department of Labor, Bureau of Statistics Bulletin 2121. Washington, DC: U.S. Government Printing Office.
FURSTENBERG, F. (1977) "West German experience with industrial democracy." Annals, 431 (May): 44-53.
ILLICH, I. (1971) Deschooling Society. New York: Harper & Row.
KUHLENKAMP, D. and H. G. SCHÜTZE [eds.] (1982) Kosten und finanzierung der beruflichen und nichtberuflichen Weiterbildung. Frankfurt am Main: Verlag Moritz Diesterweg GmbH & Co.
LEVIN, H. M. (1976) "Educational opportunity and social inequality in Western Europe." Social Problems 24 (December) 2: 148-172.
——— (1978) "Financing higher education and social equity: implications for lifelong learning." Social Rev. 86 (May) 3: 327-347.
MEIDNER, R. and R. ANDERSON (1973) "The overall impact of an active labor market policy in Sweden," in L. Ulman (ed.) Manpower Programs in the Policy Mix. Baltimore: Johns Hopkins Univ. Press.
Ministry of Labor, Sweden (1975) Proposals for an Industrial Democracy Act: A Summary of the Proposals of the Labour Legislation Committee. Vallingby, Sweden: Ministry of Labor.
MIRENGOFF, W. and L. RINDLER (1976) The Comprehensive Employment and Training Act: Impact on People, Places, Programs—An Interim Report. Washington, DC: National Academy of Sciences.
MUSHKIN, S. J. [ed.] (1974) Recurrent Education. U.S. Department of Health, Education, and Welfare, National Institute of Education. Washington, DC: U.S. Government Printing Office.
Organization for Economic Cooperation and Development [OECD] (1975) Recurrent Education: Trends and Issues. Paris: Author.
——— (1973) Recurrent Education: A Strategy for Lifelong Learning. Paris: Author.
PETERSON, R. E. et al. (1979) Lifelong Learning in America. San Francisco: Jossey-Bass.
RUMBERGER, R. W. (1981) Overeducation in the U.S. Labor Market. New York: Praeger.
SCHULLER, T. (1981) "Common discourse? the language of industrial democracy." Econ. and Industrial Democracy 3 (May) 2: 261-291.
TERKEL, S. (1974) Working. New York: Pantheon.
TURNER, R. and R. COUNT (1981) "Education for industrial democracy: an evaluation of the experimental trade union studies project." Econ. and Industrial Democracy 2 (August) 3: 371-394.
U.S. Department of Labor, Bureau of Labor Statistics (1981) Educational Attainment of Workers, March 1979. Special Labor Force Report 240. Washington, DC: U.S. Government Printing Office.

I

*COMPREHENSIVE MODELS
FOR FINANCING
RECURRENT EDUCATION*

2

INDIVIDUAL ENTITLEMENTS

HENRY M. LEVIN

Recurrent education is a theme that has come into widespread use throughout the Western industrialized countries. In general, this term refers to the broadening of both the scope and timing of educational and training activities in order to make such opportunities available over the entire lifespan and to encompass a spectrum of endeavors from traditional university instruction and apprenticeships to retraining programs and cultural enrichment (OECD, 1975, 1978; Stalford, 1978; Peterson, 1979). Under more conventional arrangements, education and training are typically limited to that period in one's life prior to entering the labor force and during the first few years of work. Under a program of recurrent education, the timing and nature of educational and training activities would reflect the specific needs of the individual to meet his or her occupational or nonoccupational goals as they arise over the lifecycle. While this definition represents only a general vision of the concept of recurrent education rather than a concrete description, its actual translation into specific forms is currently a subject for policy debate in the United States, Japan, Australia, and most of the countries of Western Europe.

The advantage of the recurrent education approach is its purported ability to meet specific individual needs for training and education as they arise as well as to incorporate a wider range of possible alternatives into the education and training system. Under the present educational and training approaches, the heavy emphasis on youth tends to neglect the periodic retraining, revitalization, and education necessary for the career mobility of adults. These needs are especially likely to be concentrated within the experienced workforce and among mothers who wish to enter or reenter the labor market after raising young children. The purpose of this chapter is to explore the use of a system of individual educational entitlements for financing recurrent education.

SOCIOECONOMIC CONTEXT OF EDUCATION AND TRAINING

Before describing a plan of individual entitlements for financing recurrent education, it is important to establish the terms of reference that will be assumed in the discussion. The most important of these refer to the socioeconomic context of education and training in the Western industrialized countries.

(1) With only a few exceptions, these countries are capitalist societies that are characterized by: (a) relatively few firms dominating most sectors of the economies; (b) distribution of income in which the top 5-10% of income recipients have a greater share of national income than do the poorest 40-50% of the population; (c) relatively low levels of economic growth for the foreseeable future; (d) relatively high levels of unemployment in comparison with the levels of 1945-1970; and (e) increasing pressures for expansion of social services to alleviate inequalities and hardships on the populations created by the "harsh edges" of monopoly capitalism.[1].

Taken together, these conditions suggest initial inequalities among individuals and families associated with the existing economic and social systems, increasing intervention by the states to cushion the inequalities and maintain the conditions of social reproduction, and a diminishing ability to provide the social resources to provide such services because of a falling rate of economic growth.

(2) These inequalities are reflected within the Western industrialized countries in the educational attainments of their populations (Levin, 1976, 1978a). The amount and quality of education received is largely a function of the social class origins, sex, and geographical location of the individual. Youngsters from families of modest income and occupational attainments, females, and persons from rural origins are likely to receive less schooling and schooling of a lower quality than males and persons from higher socioeconomic origins and from urban areas. Further, at the same level of educational attainment, persons from higher socioeconomic backgrounds have access to better jobs, occupational attainments, and incomes. In addition, there is considerable unemployment and underemployment at all educational levels, including that of university completion. The labor markets of these countries have shown an inability to absorb the large increases in recent years of university-educated young adults.

(3) During the compulsory period of schooling at the elementary and secondary levels, almost all schooling will take place in public institu-

tions. While inequalities by social class, sex, and geographic location still persist in these institutions, those inequalities have been diminishing over time. Moreover, there will continue to be substantial increases in the proportion of the young that complete secondary school, and especially those that obtain the qualifications for obtaining admissions to postsecondary educational institutions.

(4) The present system of providing postcompulsory education and training tends to provide the greatest public support for students from the most advantaged families, and the least public subsidies for persons from the least advantaged backgrounds (Levin, 1976, 1978b). This pattern is established by the fact that youngsters from lower-income families are least likely to complete secondary training, and therefore they are less likely to be eligible for postsecondary educational opportunities. Further, the most advantaged students will complete an academic course of study at the secondary level, so they will be eligible to attend the most highly subsidized part of the postsecondary educational system: the university. Students from lower socioeconomic backgrounds will be more likely to take postsecondary training—if they participate at all at that level—in community college, technical institutes, and short-course institutes. Programs associated with these alternatives tend to be of much shorter duration than university degree programs, and they also entail smaller resource requirements and public subsidies. Therefore, the present systems of postsecondary education and training tend to be inegalitarian with respect to their distributional implications.

(5) The present approaches to postsecondary education and training also introduce various distortions into both the educational choices of young people and the economic opportunities that will be afforded them later. First, public subsidies are not provided for all types of postsecondary educational and training experiences, but only certain types of orthodox educational alternatives such as the university and various other institutional training programs. While some countries provide training subsidies as part of their active labor market policies, even these are restricted to selected areas (see Lenhardt, 1978). The high level subsidization for some educational and training alternatives inevitably creates a bias in favor of choosing them in preference to those that are not subsidized.

Second, to the degree that the state assists the young in obtaining economic opportunities by providing such subsidies, it creates a bias towards overinvestment in "human capital" as opposed to physical capital. To a large degree these subsidies tend to stimulate the expansion of the supply of educated labor to corporate and government bureaucracies while reducing the training costs of these entities. Since most of the young who are fortunate enough to obtain postsecondary education and training do not have access to capital for creating self-employment, they must depend on the existing firms for jobs. These firms are able to take advantage of an expanding supply of trained labor with concomitant downward pressure on wages. Thus, indirectly the subsidies for postsecondary education and training represent a subsidy to existing owners of capital by reducing the wage costs of trained workers and by limiting the vast majority of the population to publicly subsidized investments in their training rather than providing assistance in obtaining ownership of capital.

IMPLICATIONS FOR FINANCING RECURRENT EDUCATION

What are some of the implications of this socioeconomic context for financing recurrent education? First, it would seem that *any system of financing recurrent education would necessarily have to be integrated with existing forms of postcompulsory education and training*. That is, it would seem that the design and finance of a system of postcompulsory education would include all education and training beyond the compulsory schooling period. This distinction between compulsory versus voluntary education and training represents the major distinction that characterizes adult recurrent education. That is, following the compulsory schooling period, one can choose the amount, type, and timing of further education and training. Thus, the existing set of postcompulsory opportunities must be integrated into the overall recurrent educational system, since all are voluntary options that are made *after* completion of compulsory schooling. Accordingly, a comprehensive approach to recurrent education must encompass all traditional forms of postsecondary education and training along with any new forms that may emerge.

A second implication is that no approach to recurrent education in and of itself will solve problems of inequalities that emanate from the nature of the economic and social systems of the Western industrialized countries (Levin, 1976, 1978a). The fact that the young will enter the postcompulsory period with different socioeconomic advantages and educational attainments is reason in itself to be wary of claims that adult recurrent education will resolve these inequalities that have not been resolved earlier. However, these inequalities should not be used as a basis for further unequal treatment in favor of advantaged populations. To the contrary, *the organization and financing of national systems of recurrent education ought to be distinctly equalizing in both intent and outcome.* As we will note below, this can be better achieved by providing entitlements with larger potential subsidies for further education and training to those populations that are the least advantaged.

A third implication is that *any system for financing recurrent education should be flexible enough to support a large number of nonorthodox educational and training alternatives as well as to provide a diversity of patterns of utilization.* That is, if only the traditional forms of postsecondary instruction are eligible for support, the ability to create diversity in types of educational training experiences as well as flexibility in their utilization will be seriously compromised. A system of recurrent education should be designed in such a way that various options that are presently unavailable or even beyond our existing imagination might emerge and be compatible with the overall system of finance.

A final implication is that even with future reductions in the number of youth who will be entering labor markets, problems of unemployment and underemployment are likely to continue into the future. *Accordingly, the organization and financing of recurrent education ought to promote increases in employment opportunities as well as the expansion of trained labor.* Vehicles for doing this will be discussed below.

THE NATURE OF INDIVIDUAL ENTITLEMENTS

Given this socioeconomic context and its implications, it is possible to present a plan for financing recurrent education through a plan of postcompulsory entitlements for individuals.[2] An entitlement approach refers to the provision of a guaranteed amount that would be provided by the government for each eligible person to obtain education and training in the postcompulsory education period. The entitlements could be used for a wide variety of educational and training experiences including universities, teacher-training colleges, short-cycle vocational programs, apprenticeships, on-the-job training, retraining programs, and both vocational and nonvocational adult education courses.

Essentially, the plan would work as follows. Each person would become eligible for an entitlement for further training and education at age 16 or the age at which the compulsory schooling period terminates. These entitlements could be used to obtain further education and training in any program that meets the requirements set out by the government for program eligibility. Such programs could be sponsored by governments, nonprofit agencies such as trade unions and religious institutions, or profitseeking institutions. They could include virtually all of the existing postsecondary institutions such as colleges, universities, and training programs, as well as apprenticeship and on-the-job training programs. The exact nature of eligibility would be determined by the goals of the recurrent education approach. Program eligibility to receive and redeem entitlements from students would be based on standards set out by the government such as financial accountability, educational and training content, procedures for handling complaints from participants, and the provision of sufficient and accurate information on programs.

Such entitlements could be composed of both loans and grants. The total amount and composition of the entitlement would depend upon the family resources and other background characteristics of the student. For example, one might expect that the lower the income of the student and his or her family, the larger the entitlement amount and specifically the grant portion would be. In addition, the entitlement might vary according to the student's choice of training or education, with more support being provided for study in those fields that are considered to have a high social priority and unusually high costs.

Perhaps the most important aspect of the entitlement approach is that individuals could use it for any combination of eligible training or education programs up to the maximum amount of the entitlement. Moreover, the entitlement could be drawn upon over a considerable period of time both prior to entering the workforce and during the working period. In fact, it might be reasonable to permit entitlement accounts to accumulate interest as an incentive for the participant to consider carefully the recurrent and continuing education and training possibilities that will exist over the life cycle. Programs would compete for students and their entitlements, and new offerings would arise in response to emerging training needs.

A public information system would be developed that would make entitlement recipients aware of particular education and training programs as well as the opportunities that are available in different occupational fields. This systematic provision of information would also keep potential providers of programs informed about which areas showed high student or trainee demand and which ones were less attractive. Government support of postcompulsory education and training would be vested predominantly in the form of entitlements to individuals rather than of grants to support institutions directly, and these entitlements would create financial support for institutions according to the choices of the student or trainee participants. Moreover, all of the existing sources of public funding would be coordinated into one overall system of financial support to replace the present confounding diversity of funding programs.

To summarize, a system of postcompulsory entitlements would have the following five general properties:

(1) Public support of postsecondary education and training would be channeled to the student in the form of a promissory note or entitlement.

(2) The entitlement would obligate the government to provide a specified amount of grants and loans that could be used for participating in education and training programs that had met eligibility requirements.

(3) The entitlement could be used over the lifetime of the student, and the unused portion would draw interest. The amount of the entitlement and its composition between grants and loans would be determined by the family resources of the student and other pertinent factors.

(4) Any education or training program approved as eligible by the government could accept students with entitlements and redeem these entitlements for cash from the government treasury. Such institutions would probably include most existing colleges, universities, training institutes and training programs of trade unions, government, and industry. New programs would also be eligible to participate by meeting the specified eligiblity requirements.

(5) Governments would sponsor an information and regulatory agency that would provide data for participants on training alternatives and their costs as well as program descriptions and job prospects among different occupations and training specializations. The agency would also set out the specific eligibility regulations to determine both the conditions of student and trainee participation on the one hand, and the requirements that must be satisfied for program eligibility on the other.

Within this framework there are a variety of plans that might be constructed, each responding to different objectives. It is not possible to analyze the consequences of a postcompulsory entitlement approach without discussing the main features that will determine its outcome.

The three major components of a postcompulsory entitlement plan are (1) the finance system, (2) the regulatory system, and (3) the information system.[3] The specific details of these three systems when taken together will determine the operation and outcome of the entitlement approach. The finance system refers to the determination of how much the entitlement will be and how it will vary according to the characteristics of the participants and the options that they choose. The finance component includes determination of how the entitlements will be composed—that is, the particular combination of loans and grants. The details of the loan and grant provisions, the method by which the government will obtain revenues for supporting the entitlement system, and the estimate of the total support requirements for the entitlement plan must also be determined through the finance system.

The regulatory system embraces the rules, regulations, and conditions under which the system will operate. These aspects include the definition of who is eligible to receive an entitlement, the amount of the entitlement as set out by the finance system and the conditions under which the entitlement could be used, the requirements of eligibility to redeem vouchers among providers of educational and training services, and the nature and responsibilities of the regulatory agency as it served to monitor the postcompulsory entitlement approach.

Since an entitlement approach places a heavy emphasis on alternatives and choice, an information system must be constructed to provide useful and accessible information on these choices for both the individual participants and for the institutions and enterprises that wish to offer education and training to entitlement recipients. Examples of information that might be needed by the individual participants include program descriptions, personnel qualifications, curriculum, costs, enrollments, facilities, placement services, experiences of graduates, and the proportions of students completing training. Information for potential providers of services might include the distributions and levels of enrollments by types of education and training, costs, geographical distribution, and changes in the patterns of these indicators from year to year that might reflect trends. Of course, data on occupational trends would be useful also. Finally, the regulatory agency would require data to evaluate the success of the existing provisions, and it would also need an efficient system for disseminating the information to the appropriate clientele.

Obviously the finance, regulatory, and information systems are not strictly independent of each other. For example, the definitions of eligibility for both individual participants and providers of training and educational services will have an important impact on the financial requirements of the entitlement plan. Likewise, the degree of equity that is desired will have implications for both the regulatory mechanism and the finance system in that requirements will be set out with respect to how the entitlement might vary with the financial resources of the family of the recipient. These regulations will affect the method by which entitlements are allotted as well as the distribution and level of financial support for postcompulsory education and training across the population. Thus, while each of the three component systems might be addressed separately for purposes of constructing a postcompulsory entitlement plan, their interdependence should also be recognized.

Before reviewing these three components more specifically with respect to their design and implementation, it is important to consider the potential of the individual entitlement approach for financing recurrent education and meeting the various criteria with respect to comprehensiveness, equity, flexibility, and the promotion of increases in employment that were set out in an earlier section.

COMPREHENSIVENESS

Individual entitlements enable a complete integration of existing forms of postcompulsory education and training as well as emerging ones, since the entitlement is neutral with respect to these alternatives. Under more conventional forms of financing postcompulsory education, educational and training institutions can only be established on the basis of a direct financing commitment from the government. This means that the provision of new opportunities must depend upon the acquisition of government support which creates cumbersome requirements for the initiation of new offerings as well as the loss of many potential training and educational programs that might be offered by private and nonprofit sponsors. In contrast, the entitlement approach enables adults to use their education and training subsidies directly, whether for traditional university education or any other eligible postcompulsory alternative. Indeed, the financing mechanism is neutral with respect to the type of education or training, so that new offerings can be considered on their own merits rather than on whether or not they fit a more traditional system of direct institutional subsidies. Individual entitlements enable a comprehensive approach to financing recurrent education that can not be found in the more "piece-meal" approaches that characterize the present system. And, they can easily encompass future alternatives that are not yet on the drawing board.

EQUITY

While no claim is made that the distribution of income or adult opportunities will become more equal under a plan of individual entitlements or any other system of financing recurrent education, there are strong reasons for believing that the distribution of educational and training opportunities can become more equal.[4] There are three bases for this: (1) By making each person aware of the existence of an entitlement for postcompulsory education and training, it is more likely that he or she will make use of it. Under the present approach, only those persons who are aware of available educational and training opportunities—generally the more advantaged members of society—will seek out those options.[5] (2) It is expected that under a system of postcompulsory entitlements, new education and training choices will arise that will be more accessible and attractive to the less advantaged members of society. That is, there will be an incentive by educational and training agencies to attract the "new clientele" who are not presently participating in postcompulsory education and training, but who will have the entitlements to do so under this new approach. (3) Under a system of postcompulsory entitlements, it is possible to tailor the size of the entitlement and the conditions of its use to favor persons from less advantaged backgrounds. In contrast, the present systems of financing postcompulsory education provide subsidies to institutions according to their educational and training costs rather than according to the socioeconomic backgrounds of their clientele. By providing larger entitlements to persons from lower-income families, such individuals will have a greater incentive to undertake postcompulsory education and training, and will have the ability to undertake a greater amount of such experience.

FLEXIBILITY

The individual entitlement approach maximizes the flexibility of the overall recurrent education approach, since the subsidy can be used for any combination of training and educational opportunities that are selected by the entitlement recipient. The entitlement can be partially utilized before entering the workforce and partially utilized during intermittent periods of training during the individual's career. Or, the individual can apply the entitlement to a university education immediately following his graduation from school. Alternatively, the use of the entitlement can be deferred for several years beyond the time of leaving school, until after the recipient establishes his career. All of these patterns can be accommodated without the need for special arrangements.

Further, the entitlement can be utilized for any combination of accredited educational or training activities. The government need only set out the various eligibility criteria with respect to the organizational requirements and types of education and training that will be eligible to be funded by entitlements. Both the state and private sector can offer education and training experiences, and there will be a strong incentive to meet the requirements and needs of students and trainees in order to attract adequate enrollments. Rather than the government facing the difficult challenge of setting out financing arrangements for large numbers of possible recurrent educational and training activities, the activities can be initiated with the knowledge that if they are attractive they will receive funding from the entitlements of their enrollees.

Finally, there is great flexibility in this funding mechanism, since particular policy goals with respect to equity or special educational needs can also be targeted in an effective manner. For example, larger entitlements can be given to persons from underdeveloped areas or persons who will study in fields of high national priority. As we stated previously, the entitlement can be "pro-poor" in providing more resources to those who have the least ability to finance preparation for their own careers and who lack other advantages that enhance adult opportunities.

INCREASING EMPLOYMENT

The mechanism of individual entitlements can also be used to increase employment for both individuals and groups of workers. The problem of both youth and adult unemployment is a very serious one, and the slow rates of expected economic growth as well as the rapid technological change (e.g., the revolution in minicomputers) may make the existing job situation even more dismal. Postcompulsory investments in education and training operate only on the supply of human skills and capabilities, not on the demand for them. Accordingly, policies for increasing jobs must accompany policies for expanding training and educational opportunities.

At the very least, active labor market policies must be pursued to provide appropriate employment for educated and trained labor, and these policies should be coordinated with any policy of recurrent education.[6] However, the individual entitlement approach has some attractive features for addressing both the retention of existing jobs and the creation of new ones. In at least three ways the entitlements can be used to create jobs for trained labor as an overall part of the recurrent education strategy.

First, many of the industrialized countries are experiencing plant closures by multinational corporations as these firms shift their activities to Third World countries that promise greater profitability because of low wages and state repression of trade unions. In many of these cases the activities that are being transferred are still economically viable, but not as profitable as in countries where the permissable degree of labor exploitation is considerably higher. In such cases, the closure of the firm creates unemployment and great public expense in the form of redundancy or unemployment payments and public assistance.

If the firm can be shown to be viable, the workers can be offered the use of their unemployment pay to purchase it with the assistance of government loans, and their remaining educational and training entitlements can be used to assist them in acquiring the training to undertake the management and operations of the plant. In this way, the state could assist the employees by training them at the employment site to operate their own firm as a producer cooperative or another form of self-managed enterprise. It would seem that entitlements might be part of an effective strategy to retain jobs under the aegis of worker-owned firms in such circumstances.

Second, the entitlements might also be used to create jobs through permitting groups of adults to combine their entitlements to prepare them for starting collective enterprises that might be owned and managed as cooperatives. For example, if a group of persons proposed the creation of a small enterprise to the government, the appropriate government agency might investigate the potential viability of such a firm. If the basic plan seemed sound, the government might lend the group the necessary capital while using the firm's assets as collateral for the loan.[7] But, one of the crucial determinants for successful operation would be the proficiencies of the labor force for operating the business in a viable manner. It is here that postcompulsory educational entitlements can be combined to cover a training program for the workforce. Such training might be provided by the government with funding from the entitlements, and the fact that it would be done collectively rather than individually would enable persons to be trained to work with a unique set of coworkers for the specific requirements of the firm that was being established.

A third area in which postcompulsory educational and training entitlements might be used for job creation would be to set out a policy in which a portion of the entitlement could be used to purchase tools and equipment that are required for self-employment. Many persons who receive training in particular careers lack the access to capital to be self-employed. Examples include the manual crafts such as carpentry, welding, painting, and so one as well as professional ones such as accounting, law, and architecture. Rather, persons with training in these areas must typically seek employment with existing firms.

An alternative arrangement would permit entitlement recipients to acquire education and training and to use the entitlements for those capital investments that are approved by the regulatory agency as being pursuant to their careers. In this way some persons could not only acquire relevant job skills, but they could create jobs for themselves by investing in the physical capital that is necessary for those careers.

The use of entitlements on both an individual and collective basis to provide training and the necessary physical capital could create additional jobs—especially in the service sector where large amounts of capital are not as necessary as they are in production. Such services include mechanics, carpenters, artists, bookkeepers and accountants, landscape architects, maintenance specialists, gardeners, and business consultants among others. While these uses of en entitlement approach would not address all of the employment problems of the industrialized countries, they could be part of a policy mix that combines education and training with a job creation and retention approach.

EVIDENCE ON THE POTENTIAL OF ENTITLEMENTS

Thus far we have asserted that individual entitlements represent a more comprehensive, equitable, and flexible approach to financing recurrent education, and we have suggested that they also have greater potential for combining education and training with job creation. Fortunately, there exists a substantial experience with individual entitlements in the United States, so it is possible to review the validity of some of these claims. Since 1944 the U.S. Government has provided educational benefits to military veterans under the GI Bill.[8] Eligible veterans are provided with monthly payments while they are enrolled in accredited education and training programs. In 1978, a single veteran who was studying on a full-time basis received $311 a month, and veterans with dependents received more. For example, a veteran with two dependents received $422 a month. Benefits could be used for up to 45 months of study. Thus, a single veteran was eligible for a total entitlement of about $14,000, and a married veteran with a child was eligible for an entitlement of about $19,000. An enormous variety of training and educational programs are accredited for GI Bill enrollees; an institution is required to meet educational, legal, financial, and reporting criteria for eligibility.[9]

Since 1944, more than 14 million veterans have received educational benefits under the three GI Bills that have been enacted during the last 35 years. In fiscal year 1976 about $6 billion was paid to veterans in educational benefits. This represented more than half of the expenditure on postsecondary education and training (O'Neill and Ross, 1976: 1). In sum, the GI Bill provides veterans with the equivalent of individual entitlements that can be used for a wide variety of educational and training options in both the public and private sectors. Further, it is a very substantial program with three decades of experience. Accordingly, it is interesting to observe the results of the GI Bill educational entitlements with respect to their comprehensiveness, equity, flexibility, and labor market effectiveness.

The comprehensiveness and flexibility aspects of the GI Bill can be reviewed together because of their obvious overlap. The comprehensiveness is evident in that the entitlements can be received for enrolling in a wide range of approved programs including most colleges and universities, training institutes, on-the-job training programs, correspondence schools, and so on. In the 1977 fiscal year, almost three-quarters of the GI Bill recipients chose to enroll in colleges and universities (Congressional Budget Office, 1978: 6). Of course, a substantial number of these were enrolled in the two-year community colleges in career training programs rather than in four-year academic courses of instruction. About one-tenth were studying in vocational and technical institutes, with almost an equal number engaged in on-the-job and farm training programs. The remainder were involved in correspondence schools, flight instruction, and high school completion. Among all veterans, almost 80% were in public institutions (Congressional Budget Office, 1978: 7).

Since the GI Bill permits veterans to utilize their educational benefits over the ten years following their military service, there is considerable time in which to choose and undertake educational experiences. Of course, even a decade is a limitation, so presumably participation would be higher over a longer permissable period. The use of the educational benefits can apply to part-time or full-time study, and they can also be used for correspondence school courses taken while one is fully employed. The benefits for anything less than full-time study are set at proportionately lower levels than for fulltime enrollees. The overall resut of this comprehensiveness and flexibility is a rather high rate of utilization of educational benefits, with the current estimate that significantly over three-fifths of recent veteran cohorts will use their educational benefits (O'Neill and Ross, 1976: 44). This proportion is considerably higher than the postsecondary participation of nonveterans, which is somewhere between 40-50%. Further, it has been concluded from statistical analysis of enrollments that about one-third of all veteran students would not have undertaken the education and training in the absence of the GI Bill benefits (Congressional Budget Office, 1978: 12-13).

Even more impressive are the equity implications of the enrollment patterns. Although in the general population the amount of postcompulsory enrollment of blacks is considerably lower than for whites, among veterans utilizing the educational benefits of the GI Bill the blacks showed slightly higher rates of participation (O'Neill and Ross, 1976: 53). After adjusting for test scores and prior educational attainments, the participation rate for blacks was found to be some nine percentage points higher than for equivalent whites (O'Neill and Ross, 1976: 58). Thus, the GI Bill entitlements seem to be considerably more effective in providing education and training to at least one major economically disadvantaged group than are the more traditional approaches.

But, of course, one question that might be raised is that of the quality of choices. That is, if the enrollees are simply using their entitlements in frivolous ways, the mere existence of a higher level and more equitable pattern of enrollments is not tantamount to a higher level of and more equitable educational benefits. Among a variety of sophisticated analyses comparing the earnings of veterans who had taken vocational training under the GI Bill and those who had not, it was found that earnings were about 10% higher per year among the GI Bill group.[10] This is about twice as great a gain as that associated with government-sponsored Manpower Development Training Act (MDTA) programs. For black veterans who used their GI Bill benefits, the gains were even greater—a differential of 15% higher earnings over comparable blacks with similar educational attainments and test scores but with no GI Bill training. Similar earnings gains were found for veterans who had used their entitlements for on-the-job training or college enrollments, although no racial comparisons were made.

In summary, extensive experience with the GI Bill has shown that a general system of individual entitlements can be more comprehensive, flexible, and equitable than the more conventional methods for financing postcompulsory education and training, and there is some evidence that it is more effective in imparting skills that are remunerated in labor markets. The fact that blacks participate more fully in postcompulsory education and training and receive relatively larger benefits than whites is also a rather remarkable finding. Indeed, the redistributive effect of the GI Bill entitlements is particularly surprising when one considers that no compensatory entitlements are provided on the basis of family background—blacks, whites, the rich, and the poor all receive the same entitlements. The experience of the GI Bill suggests that individual entitlements represent a forward-looking approach for constructing an overall method for financing recurrent education.

IMPLEMENTING A PLAN OF INDIVIDUAL ENTITLEMENTS

While the general description of a plausible entitlement plan can be described quite readily, the actual details require very careful formulation. At the end of the compulsory education period—for instance, at age 16—individuals would be registered with the national entitlement agency. Based upon the various criteria of eligibility, they would be informed of their "drawing rights" under the entitlement mechanism. Moreover, they would be assigned an identification number that would be used to keep records on their use of the entitlement so that one could ascertain quickly (through computerized access) the amount of entitlement that still remained and other pertinent information. In order to utilize the remaining value of the entitlement, the individual would apply to the entitlement agency to undertake additional study or training from an eligible provider. The agency would provide a draft or voucher that could be redeemed by the provider for cash by submitting it upon receipt to the government treasury.

All of the accounting and records would be maintained by the national entitlement agency, and an annual or periodic report would be issued to each registered individual regarding the drawing rights that where still credited to him. Possibly the unused balances would draw interest in order to compensate individuals who distribute their entitlement over longer periods. And, at retirement age it might be appropriate to refund to the individual any unexpended balance or it would be given to his estate in case of early death. In this way the entitlement recipients would not be pressed to utilize the entitlement in frivolous ways, and the returns to any use would be balanced against simply permitting the value to accumulate with interest until retirement. This would be an especially important provision for establishing equity for persons from less advantaged backgrounds, who historically have been less able and less likely to take advantage of postcompulsory schooling opportunities.[11]

FINANCE

A number of particular questions be resolved to construct the other financing details. These include (1) the source of revenues, (2) the size of entitlements, (3) the manner by which entitlements will vary according to the characteristics of the recipient and training choice, (4) composition of entitlements between grants and loans, and (5) total public support requirements. Each of these will be addressed briefly.

Source of Revenues

There is no single approach to the method of providing government revenues for postcompulsory entitlements. Different countries have different tax systems with respect to the degree that they rely upon value-added or turnover taxes, personal income taxes, excise taxes, and business taxes. But a strong case can be made for obtaining revenues from a broad-based tax rather than a payroll tax. That is, such a program should not be paid for by workers alone, but by all segments of the population.[12]

Unfortunately, much of the recent literature on the particular forms of recurrent education and training such as educational sabbaticals has focused on the use of a payroll tax that would provide a trust fund for such expenditures somewhat similar to the social security programs in the United States.[13] The principle underlying this view seems to be that educational leave and lifelong education are necessary ingredients for everyone—at least everyone in the labor force—and a provision should be made for this by imposing a mandatory tax on employers and employees that would be earmarked for such a function.

However, the use of a payroll tax for such purposes has a number of very serious deficiencies.[14] First, unlike the social insurance concept, the use of the entitlement is voluntary rather than based upon a certain event such as retirement or a contingency such as death or disability. Those persons who did not utilize their entitlements would nevertheless pay for them, and the historical record suggests that the least advantaged workers would be the least likely to utilize fully their entitlements (Rosenthal, 1976; Levin, 1976, 1978b; Cross, 1978; Harnqvist, 1978). Thus, a payroll tax on all workers would imply a subsidy of those who did use fully their entitlements by those that did not, a redistribution of wealth in favor of the more advantaged (unless unused entitlements were permitted to accumulate interest and revert to the worker at retirement or to his estate in case of premature death).

Moreover, payroll tax tends to be regressive. In fact, it has been found to be the most regressive major tax in the U.S. tax system (Pechman and Okner, 1974: 59). Since it is a tax on labor earnings rather than on sources of unearned income such as rents, dividends, profits, and interest), the very sources of income that characterize the rich are untouched while the working poor and middle classes are forced to support the entitlement system. That is, the one-third or so of national income that is derived from capital and that is concentrated among the wealthiest families in all societies would not contribute to the postcompulsory education and training system. If the tax is levied in a fashion similar to the present social security tax in the United States, it would apply as a constant tax rate up to a maximum level of earnings, and earnings beyond the maximum level would not be taxed. This too means that a higher proportion of a poor person's income will be taxed. Indeed, it was estimated for 1966 that the U.S.

payroll tax represented about twice as high a proportion of annual incomes for recipients under $15,000 as it did for those with incomes in the $30,000-50,000 range (Pechman and Okner, 1974: 59). Thus, the use of a payroll tax to support postcompulsory entitlements should be examined with great circumspection.

Size of Entitlements

The following factors would seem to be important in setting the size of the basic entitlements: the costs that the government presently incurs in subsidizing students in public institutions of higher education and public-supported training programs; the total direct cost of the various postcompulsory education and training programs; and the foregone earnings or the costs of maintenance for the normal living expenses of a student. The importance of the present government subsidy is that it gives a guideline for the level of support to postcompulsory education that the government has already shown a willingness to provide. The total cost of various types of training might be instructive for modifications of this amount. Finally, it is important to consider the other costs of obtaining postsecondary education and training that are reflected in the lost earnings of students or the costs of maintaining the student during his or her periods of study in order to ascertain whether these should be subsidized.

For example, the average subsidy per student in four-year public institutions in states such as California is about $2,500-3,000, suggesting that the state is willing to pay about $10,000-12,000 for the four-year course of studying leading to the B.A. degree. Of course, the state and federal governments provide other types of support for particularly needy or exceptional students as well as for those eligible to receive benefits under the programs for military veterans and social security. As a first approximation, it might be useful to think of this $10,000-12,000 as the basic entitlement that would be made available to all students, not just those who complete a four-year program at a public college or university.

But even this amount would not be adequate to cover the indirect costs of study reflected in foregone earnings and living expenses of students and trainees. Accordingly, it may be necessary to consider possible additions to the entitlements under some circumstances as well as the provision of loan programs for expenses beyond the entitlement. The composition of such loans and grants might vary according to the social-class background of the eligible individual and other factors.

Characteristics that Might Alter Basic Entitlements

While the setting of the basic entitlement is necessary for establishing a general baseline for the entitlement program, it is useful to consider the circumstances under which the entitlement might be varied because of the particular characteristics or educational choices of the recipient. For middle- and upper-income families an entitlement of $12,000 might be quite adequate for enabling their offspring to undertake postsecondary education and training. While $12,000 might not be enough to pay all of the direct costs and the living costs of the postcompulsory endeavor, such families have additional resources to provide such payments. Thus, a combination of family resources, students earnings from part-time summer employment, and loans could be used to supplement the entitlement.

But, persons from lower-income backgrounds are not in such an enviable position. Their families are less likely to provide either the additional direct costs of postsecondary education such as the balance of tuition or expenses for books and materials that might not be covered by entitlements. They are also less able to provide the living expenses and to forego the earnings that would be obtained from work. Finally, even their access to part-time work might be compromised relative to their more-advantaged counterparts because they lack the connections and information that often secure such jobs for middle and upper class youngsters.

Accordingly, it would seem that to obtain high levels of participation in postsecondary education and training among low-income populations it will be necessary to provide entitlements that would cover other educational expenses as well as the costs of maintaining the trainee or student. One important aspect of the finance system would be to design the entitlements to take account of differences in family backgrounds and resources.

A second situation in which entitlements might vary would be in the case of training programs that are of unusually long duration but have great social benefit. In those instances the amount of the entitlement might be increased to account for the relatively long training period and to encourage persons to enter those professions. Of course, this type of problem might also be solved by a liberal policy of loans that could be repaid from the future earnings of the recipients. Certainly, additional subsidies for the training of physicians will not in themselves expand the number of physicians who are trained, and such graduates can easily pay their loans out of the extraordinarily high incomes they receive during their professional lives (at least in countries like the United States and West Germany). Thus the adjustment of entitlements for long program duration and high program costs should be justified on the basis of associated social benefits; there should not simply be allocation of a larger entitlement for more expensive training.

Also, an entitlement might be increased in exceptionally meritorious cases in which it could be argued that the development of extremely scarce talent required the additional investment. For example, persons of exceedingly high scholarly, artistic, mechanical, or scientific merit might be chosen to receive highly specialized training beyond that which might be available for the average person. Again, the social benefits of developing such talent represent the basis for larger, special entitlements for talent that could be identified by some reasonable set of procedures. The social benefits of such a policy would be in the potential cultural, scientific, and technical discoveries, as well as in potential contributions to the artistic, cultural, and material well-being of the society.

Composition of Entitlements Between Loans and Grants

A very important issue that has arisen more generally in the debate over postcompulsory educational and training finance is the justification for providing loans rather than grants. According to some analysts the primary benefits from postsecondary investments are those received by the individual in the form of higher earnings. Accordingly, they recommend that assistance for such education and training take the form of income-contingent loans to be repaid out of the higher earnings received by those with the additional training.[15] An alternative argument is that the benefits of such educational and training endeavors are shared between society and the individual and some basis is supplied for providing a subsidy for postsecondary educational and training endeavors. These benefits include those of equalizing access to educational opportunities. Even in this case it is not argued that society should bear all of the costs of postcompulsory education, but only the portion that reflects the social benefits.

But, the territory between the social provision of complete grants for all postcompulsory training and education and that of just loans is vast, including all types of combinations of loan and grant plans. Thus, it is important to reflect on the composition of entitlements between loans and grants. We suggested at the outset of the entitlement design that one possibility would be to provide a $10,000-12,000 entitlement for everyone with some increase in entitlement for selected populations that are considered to be disadvantaged with respect to postsecondary education and training opportunities. We also suggested that a system of loans should be provided for persons who need more than the $10,000-12,000 or some other set amount.

But, there exist a number of other possibilities for combining grants and loans into "dual entitlements." For example, it may be more useful to think of every person as being eligible for a specified sum of grants and loans depending upon family background. In such an instance the person from a very wealthy background would only be eligible for a "loan" entitlement to be repaid out of his future income. The person from the most disadvantaged families would be eligible for a "grant" entitlement that would cover both the direct costs of education as well as living costs. Between these two extremes the plan would provide various combinations of loans and grants so that the person who came from the middle of the social-class distribution received the $10,000-12,000 grant entitlement and was also eligible for loans. An individual somewhat higher on the social-class scale would receive $8,000 in grants and loan eligibility.

Such an approach would have a number of advantages over the flat entitlement grant. First, individuals who came from families that had ample resources to pay for their postcompulsory training and educational experiences would not receive as large a subsidy as those from families who lacked such resources. Yet, even if the children in such families wished to establish independent status they would be eligible for loans so that they would not have to depend on their families' largesse. Since the loans would be repaid out of their future income and they would be likely to share in the financial resources of their families eventually, such an arrangement would provide flexibility, independence, and still a modicum of equity. Second, individuals from middle-income backgrounds would receive a dual entitlement of grants and loans that would provide an appropriate subsidy while accounting for their family resources. Again, a substantial amount of flexibility would be afforded the student and his family in choosing how much of the expense beyond the entitlement grant would be funded from savings and family contributions, part-time or full-time earnings during postcompulsory programs, and loans that would be repaid from future earnings.

Total Public Support Requirement

A final related issue on financing an entitlement plan is what it will cost government. The answer to this query depends on several factors: the size of entitlements and patterns of participation; the specific construction of the plan between loans and grants; and the degree to which public subsidies under existing grant programs to postcompulsory institutions, training programs, and individuals would be combined to underwrite an entitlement approach. The complicated nature of this problem is reflected by the fact that most direct support for postcompulsory education is provided to particular institutions with another portion going to students and trainees in the form of scholarships, fellowships, and maintenance grants or loans. These would have to be combined under an entitlement approach, and institutions would be required to obtain their support directly from student entitlements rather than from the government budgets.

Of course, it might be possible to provide direct support for institutions such as universities so that tenure obligations and budgetary planning could continue on the same basis as before while simply charging the student entitlement accounts for those persons attending the university. If student enrollments shrink below those that are adequate to provide entitlement support for university budgets, the government might require a long-run reduction of university resources for meeting student needs. However, this process would certainly cushion the short-run fluctuations that might disrupt the university planning processes if they were to depend for their income exclusively on the entitlements that they were able to obtain from one enrollment period to the next. Another alternative would be to require universities to obtain their support directly from the entitlements while permitting a substantial financial reserve to cushion short-run fluctuations from period to period.

For planning purposes it would be possible to estimate the approximate public expense for postcompulsory entitlements on the basis of a concrete determination of eligibility requirements for participants, size of entitlements, and fields in which entitlements could be used. This would be done by first ascertaining the number of eligible recipients and calculating the total amount of entitlements that they would receive in the forms of grants and loans. Next, we would need to assess the probable behavior of different subgroups with respect to the amount of their entitlement that they would utilize and the time pattern of utilization. This would yield an estimate of total annual entitlement costs for a particular cohort. For the United States, some data might be derived on these matters from the experience under the GI Bill.

REGULATION OF THE ENTITLEMENT SYSTEM

In addition to the financial arrangements for constructing a system of postcompulsory entitlements, it would be necessary to establish a regulatory system. In this section we review briefly the nature of this regulatory system and the types of decisions that must be made with respect to setting out regulations. A national entitlement agency would need to be established to administer the entitlements. This agency would have at least six major functions:

(1) The agency would process applications for entitlements, establishing the eligibility of the individual according to the law.

(2) The level and composition of each entitlement would have to be determined for each applicant on the basis of the appropriate criteria.

(3) Continuous and accurate records on the utilization of the entitlement and unexpended portions would be maintained for each individual.

(4) An information system would be designed and operated by the agency, and dissemination of accurate information to both individuals and institutions on educational and training alternatives would be provided.

(5) The regulatory agency would enforce eligibility standards for participating institutions and programs through initial screening of providers followed by periodic audits and reviews of complaints or violations.

(6) An adjudicatory mechanism would be maintained by the regulatory agency for settling disputes that might arise between program sponsors and enrollees.

In addition to establishing a regulatory agency to administer the entitlements for recurrent education, a number of laws and regulations would have to be created for the operation of the entitlement system. Among these are the following:

(1) Who is eligible to receive an entitlement?
(2) What are the characteristics that determine the size of the entitlement?
(3) What types of education and training experiences or other types of investments can the entitlement be used for?
(4) What are the eligibility requirements for accrediting educational and training institutions to receive entitlements?
(5) What kinds of information would the regulatory agency collect for purposes of dissemination on the characteristics and performance of the accredited educational and training institution?

The criteria for answering these questions and constructing an entitlement plan are reviewed at some length in a more extensive discussion on the subject (Levin, 1977b) so they will not be discussed in this chapter. However, the answers to these questions will depend clearly on national policy toward recurrent education as well as on other factors that are unique to each country.

SUMMARY

The whole notion of recurrent education is one that is characterized by diversity. Both the types of educational experiences and their timing over the lifespan would deviate from the predictable conventions of existing educational and training sytems. The very notion of recurrent education suggests that it cannot be codified easily according to existing educational and training institutions, experiences, or certificates. Rather, the offerings under such an approach are likely to evolve in directions that cannot be readily projected at the moment.

The individual entitlement approach represents a device for financing recurrent education that is perfectly compatible with both the diversity and uncertainty of future developments in this direction. Rather than proposing specific financing approaches for each type of recurrent education, individual entitlements enable a systematic solution to the financing issue. Further, we have asserted that the individual entitlement mechanism can provide a financing scheme that is more comprehensive, flexible, and equitable than present government educational and training programs. Finally, it offers greater possibilities for effectively integrating policies for job creation and retention with those for education and training.

One question that has not been addressed is the cost of individual entitlements in the aggregate. Obviously, it is impossible to provide any estimate of costs without a clear specification of a particular entitlement plan and the designation of a specific country. However, given some rudimentary notion of the particular arrangements for any society, it would be possible to provide an approximate picture of the costs. Of course, it should be borne in mind that not all of the costs associated with entitlements would be added ones. A very high proportion of them would be covered by funds that are already obligated for existing educational and training commitments since the proposed entitlements would largely replace the present system of postcompulsory education.

NOTES

1. Data on the income distributions are found in Jain, 1975. Economic growth prospects are summarized in the various issues of *Economic Outlook* issued regularly by OECD.

2. This presentation on individual entitlements builds on a number of previous papers written on the subject. See particularly Levin, 1977a and 1977b, and Kurland, 1977.

3. The detailed presentation and analysis of these three components are found in Levin, 1977b.

4. The distinction between the distribution of educational opportunites and outcomes, and adult opportunities and outcomes with respect to occupational attainments and income are addressed in Levin, 1978b.

5. In 1975 only about one-fifth of adult learners in the United States had not participated in education at the college level. That is, about four-fifths had undertaken at least some college training, and almost 60% had at least one college degree. See Cross, 1978: 9.

6. See the survey of these policies in Haveman and Christainsen, 1978, and Palmer, 1978. The origins of an active labor market policy are generally credited to G. Rehn. See Rehn and Lundberg, 1963, and Meidner and Anderson, 1973.

7. Government policies to promote employee ownership are discussed within a much wider framework in Meidner, 1978.

8. For recent evaluations and analyses of the GI Bill see Congressional Budget Office, 1978; O'Neill, 1977; and O'Neill and Ross, 1976.

9. These provisions are described in O'Neill and Ross, 1976: Appendix A.

10. All of the findings on earnings are in O'Neill and Ross, 1976: chap. 2.

11. See Harnqvist, 1978; Rosenthal, 1977; and Cross, 1978 for evidence on this contention, as well as Levin, 1976 and 1978b.

12. It may appear that because most payroll taxes require a mandatory contribution by the employer, that it is employers who are bearing at least that portion of the tax. However, it is generally agreed that in the long run such "employer" contributions are shifted to employees in the form of lower wages and salaries than would otherwise be received. See Brittain 1972: 60-81.

13. Suggestions in this direction are found in Kurland, 1974; Striner, 1972; U.S. Department of HEW, 1973: 126-134; and are reflected in actuality in the French Law of 1971 on educational leave for workers. See Levine, 1974.

14. See the useful discussion by Emmerij, 1979, especially with reference to the Dutch case regarding the use of social security funding.

15. A comprehensive treatment of student loan plans is Hartman, 1971.

REFERENCES

BRITTAIN, J. (1972) The Payroll Tax for Social Security. Washington, DC: Brookings Institution.

Congressional Budget Office (1978) Veterans' Educational Benefits: Issues Concerning the GI Bill. Washington, DC: U.S. Government Printing Office.

CROSS, K. P. (1978) "A critical review of state and national studies of the needs and interests of adult learners," pp. 7-19 in C. Stalford (ed.) Adult Learning Needs and the Demand for Lifelong Learning. Washington, DC: National Institute of Education.

EMMERIJ, L. (1979) "Paid educational leave with particular emphasis on its financial aspects." Prepared for the Project on Financing Recurrent Education, OECD, Paris.

HARNQVIST, K. (1978) Individual Demand for Education. Paris: OECD.

HARTMAN, R. W. (1971) Credit for College. New York: McGraw-Hill.

HAVEMAN, R. and G. CHRISTAINSEN (1978) "Public employment and wage subsidies in Western Europe and the U.S.: what we're doing and what we know." Discussion Paper 522-78, Institute for Research on Poverty, University of Wisconsin.

JAIN, S. (1975) Size Distribution of Income. Washington, DC: The World Bank.

KURLAND, N. [ed.] (1977) Entitlement Studies, NIE Papers in Education and Work 4. Washington, DC: National Institute of Education.

——— (1974) "Financing lifelong learning: proposal for an age-neutral educational entitlement program." New York State Educational Department, Albany. (mimeo)

LENHARDT, G. (1978) "Problems in reforming recurrent education for workers." Comparative Education Review 22 (October) 3: 452-463.

LEVIN, H. M. (1978a) "The dilemma of comprehensive secondary school reforms in Western Europe." Comparative Education Rev. 22 (October) 3: 434-451.

────── (1978b) "Financing higher education and social equity: implications for lifelong learning." School Rev. 86 (May) 3: 327-347.

────── (1977a) "Financing recurrent education with postcompulsory entitlements." Prepared for the meeting on Recurrent Education of the OECD, March 28-30. (To be published by OECD.)

────── (1977b) "Postsecondary entitlements: an exploration," chap. 1 in N. Kurland (ed.) Entitlement Studies, NIE Papers in Education and Work 4. Washington, DC: National Institute of Education.

────── (1976) "Educational opportunity and social inequality in Western Europe." Social Problems 24 (December) 2: 148-172.

LEVINE, H. A. (1974) "Strategies for the application of foreign legislation on paid educational leave to the United States." Prepared for the Career Education Program, National Institute of Education, NIE-C-74-0107.

MEIDNER, R. (1978) Employee Investment Funds. London: George Allen and Unwin.

────── and R. ANDERSON (1973) "The overall impact of an active labor market policy in Sweden," in L. Ulman (ed.) Manpower Programs in the Policy Mix. Baltimore: Johns Hopkins Univ. Press.

OECD, Centre for Educational Research and Innovation (1978) Alternation Between Work and Education. Paris: OECD.

────── (1975) Recurrent Education: Trends and Issues. Paris: OECD.

O'NEILL, D. M. (1977) "Voucher funding of training programs: evidence from the GI Bill." J. of Human Resources 12 (Fall) 4: 425-445.

────── and S. ROSS (1976) Voucher Funding of Training: A Study of the GI Bill, PRI 312-76. Arlington, VA: Public Research Institute.

PALMER, J. L. (1978) Creating Jobs. Washington, DC: Brookings Institution.

PECHMAN, J. A. and B. A. OKNER (1974) Who Bears the Tax Burden? Washington, DC: Brookings Institution.

PETERSON, R. E et al. (1979) Lifelong Learning in America. San Francisco, CA: Jossey-Bass.

REHN, G. and E. LUNDBERG (1963) "Employment and welfare: some Swedish issues." Industrial Relations 2 (February): 1-4.

ROSENTHAL, E. L. (1977) "Lifelong learning—for some of the people." Change (August): 44-45.

STALFORD, C. B. [ed.] (1978) Conference Report: Adult Learning Needs and the Demand for Lifelong Learning. Washington, DC: National Insititute of Education.

STRINER, H. E. (1972) Continuing Education as a National Capital Investment. Kalamazoo, MI: W.E. Upjohn Institute for Employment Research.

U.S. Department of Health, Education, and Welfare (1973) Work in America. Cambridge, MA: MIT Press.

U.S. Federal Trade Commission (1976) Proprietary Vocational and Home Study Schools. Bureau of Consumer Protection. Washington, DC: Government Printing Office.

3

INDIVIDUAL DRAWING RIGHTS
GÖSTA REHN

AIMING AT FREE CHOICE

This chapter is a plea for establishing a deliberate policy to promote diversification and flexibility in the regulation and allocation of time for work, study, and leisure (including retirement) allowing for the greatest possible freedom of individual choice (Rehn, 1974, 1977). While the arguments presented here range beyond recurrent education as such, an attempt is made to provide an important example of the application of such a system.

First, some of the general reasons why greater flexibility in working life is desirable in industrialized countries will be discussed. The basic starting point will be the value judgment that the desirability of individual freedom is indisputable in allocating one's time for different uses during a lifetime as well as during each year, week, or day. Second, the main features of a system of drawing rights will be presented—in essence, the right to utilize one's assets in a broadened social insurance system for income maintenance during nonwork periods with a greater degree of self-determination than traditionally is the case. A number of trends already observable in industrialized countries will be set forth that support the feasibility and desirability of such a scheme.

As a technical and administrative apparatus, the drawing rights model could be applied to achieve very different ends or meet a diverse set of priorities—for example, to influence the income distribution toward or away from equality. Because of the general nature of this system, its precise form and features must remain somewhat an open question, but in this chapter I express my personal inclinations towards specific goals and ensuing specifications.

In the last section of the chapter, more specific questions relating to recurrent education will be taken up and issues involved in furthering of adult studies by a drawing rights system will be discussed.

THE NEED FOR GREATER FLEXIBILITY

We have already stated the judgment that it is desirable for individuals to have greater flexibility throughout their lifetime as well as on an annual or weekly basis in allocating their working time. In reference to national or societal effects, we should also consider how a policy for influencing the allocation of time for work and nonwork could be integrated into labor market policies—policies for matching labor supply and demand, alleviating the unemployment-inflation dilemma, and promoting labor productivity. Freedom of choice in allocating periods of work, study, and leisure throughout the course of a lifetime presupposes the availability of a greater variety of work-time patterns and an apparatus for the transfer of liquidity (under risk-sharing insurance) between periods of directly productive work and other periods in each individual's life.

In an increasingly diversified and affluent society it is more effective to promote socially desirable behavior by economic incentives rather than by standardized rules. The question of economic incentives versus standardized rules straddles both individual and national perspectives. We will suggest a principle of individual self-determination combined with the offering of economic incentives designed to stimulate those who are willing and able to undertake adjustments in the labor market voluntarily (under partial utilization of their rights in the general insurance system) instead of making "social cases" of those who are most vulnerable to unemployment and least adaptable for new jobs by laying most of the burden of adjustment on the weaker groups.

A good deal of what we pay into the social insurance system is in reality a transfer of income between different parts of our own lives. These funds should therefore be regarded to a great extent as the individual's own property, the use of which could be substantially liberated from bureaucratic supervision. Instead, their use should be influenced by incentives that one may accept or reject according to one's own preferences. Furthermore, these funds can be used to rectify a number of inequities in some existing income transfer schemes for education and related purposes. The financing of university studies is a good example of such inequity: Everybody, including those in the lower-income brackets, has to pay taxes to provide advantages for the benefit of young people who can attend universities in order to enter the higher-income brackets. The suggested system of general income insurance and drawing rights would imply that those who were on the paying side in their young years would have at least some part of their payment as an account for use later in life for purposes of their own choice. Equity considerations can thus be included among the reasons for moving in the direction advocated here.

At the national level, there is a need for more rational policymaking that takes alternative allocations of working time into account. Decisions to reduce working time by lowering retirement age, prolonging vacations, lengthening young people's education, or shortening the work week have usually been evaluated separately; there has been little consideration of the extent to which the selection of one alternative inhibits the use of others, or of the actual preferences of particular groups or of the population as a whole. That is, there has been little explicit consideration of whether one sort of progress is preferred or quantifiably more valuable than the others.

Enhanced rationality would occur in two ways. First a new policy would streamline and coordinate what are, at present, quite separate funds and arrangements. Second, it should be possible to integrate its use into labor market policies. It ought to be possible to encourage workers' voluntary alternating between work and nonwork in such a way that the resulting changes in labor supply coincide with variations in the demand for labor. Periods of threatening unemployment could be changed into agreeable leisure or useful study. Clearly this has many implications for recurrent education and its economics. If abstention from directly productive work can ultimately improve one's future efficiency, the cost is obviously relatively low; if a period of destructive unemployment can be turned into one of agreeable or useful nonwork (leisure or training), the cost may even be converted into positive economic gain in addition to the social advantages involved.

The reforms envisaged here should also counteract the trend towards the limitation of individual freedom which is currently making itself felt in various ways in some countries (e.g., in the guise of guarantees of employment security and other incentives to work-force stabilization within the enterprise). As these protective rules reduce individual freedom by making a withdrawal from one's work place costly and risky (due to the ensuing loss of advantages built on length of service or enterprise-specific training), the need increases for counter-balancing arrangements that are designed to promote freedom without such loss. Inversely, the introduction of the latter types of security should reduce the need and demand for more rigid and counter-productive forms of protection that may function in some parts of the economy but not in all.

We should therefore promote this "security by wings" as opposed to "security under shells" to counteract the tendency towards a polarization of the labor force between those who can enjoy security and good incomes on condition that they stay where they once happened to settle, and those who are formally free from any ties but have to live in poverty and insecurity with only intermittent and marginal employment.

THE DRAWING RIGHTS SYSTEM: WHAT IT WOULD LOOK LIKE

What is therefore being recommended is a single comprehensive system for financing all periods of voluntary or age-determined nonwork that would replace the present systems for financing youth education, adult studies, vacations, old age retirement, and other leisure periods that need income maintenance (such as sabbaticals, long service leave and temporary retirement). Here every citizen would have his personal account (as already provided for in any retirement pension insurance system), registering year by year how much he or she is to be credited as contributions to the funds or streams of money going to those purposes. These contributions, however they may be gathered, would be counted as "points" with a constant value (i.e. indexed for inflation) which would represent the basis for the individual's right to receive benefits. The enjoyment of these benefits is now subject to strict rules such as age of retirement, level of pension, and number of vacation days to be taken every calendar year, with administratively determined conditions for receipt for subsistence money during studies. A certain part of the credits gathered under the consolidated system should be open to self-determination: a right to draw money on one's account at any time and for any purpose of one's own choosing. Obviously, this implies that money used for one purpose during one period will reduce the money that is available for another purpose or during another period.

The crediting of points may (as one possible alternative) function as do payroll taxes under present systems with due consideration of any change in the size of the benefits to be enjoyed. Self-employed persons would have to pay a similar proportion of their income according to their tax assessments.

It may be expected that the amount of normally enjoyed nonwork time will be further increased in the coming decades through laws or collective agreements regarding shorter working hours, prolonged vacations, increased access to education, lower age of retirement, and so on. It is mainly this increase in time for nonwork that could be presented as additionally accessible through income maintenance in the form of drawing rights for free use by the individual, but even part of current nonwork and income maintenance could be given this freer form.

The reduction of normal full-time work in a lifetime from the present average of about 80,000 hours to 70,000 hours in the space of one or two decades would imply a relative reduction of concomitant income. This would be counterbalanced by increased efficiency that could stem from reduced work fatigue and from improved skills conferred by more education, by the decline in unemployment that may be achieved through the reduction of working time if properly managed (see below), and by the increase in the activity rate induced by providing people who would otherwise be kept out of the labor market with greater access to part-time jobs and other flexible work opportunities. In any case, with the normal expected increases in incomes and salaries, we are actually considering a limited reduction in the rate of increase of income (in its distorted definition that fails to count voluntary leisure as part of the national or personal income).

The general and compulsory membership of all citizens in this financing system implies a guarantee that each individual will pay a certain amount to the general income insurance fund. This, in turn, makes one automatically credit worthy in relation to the system: He or she can be given the right to draw on his or her account even if in the beginning this implies an overdraft—something that is necessary in financing the studies of young people. The total amount of money to be made available to a person during a normal lifetime may be assumed to be equivalent to his or her contributions, with due actuarial allowance for risk-sharing and time-discounting. It would also be possible to use the system as an element of income redistribution. However, the drawing rights cannot be unlimited: The individual should not be able to empty his or her account to such an extent that nothing is left for old age pension, thus a considerable amount must be kept sacrosanct.

The introduction of such a general, integrated scheme would of course not mean that existing forms of insurance or income support would disappear. Disablement, sickness, and accident insurance would still function largely as at present. And individuals would always be free to keep to the ordinary unemployment insurance if they lost their job and did not wish to use up any part of their drawing rights in these circumstances.

Social and economic reasons have been emphasized for moving towards a general drawing rights sytem. It also needs to be noted that it would rationalize the jungle of existing forms of social insurance and reallocation of money between different parts of the individual's life. To keep track of one's rights to pensions, vacations, adult training, unemployment insurance benefits, redundancy payments, and so on is difficult, if not impossible, scattered as these are among the many different bookkeeping institutions. Therefore, while such rationalization would certainly assist one in using one's rights to study and leisure more freely and interchangeably, it would also be desirable in its own right.

The positive use of a flexible drawing rights system in labor market policies has been indicated in general already, but the possible uses of economic incentives to these ends still needs to be spelled out in a little more detail. Labor market authorities would be authorized to make an offer to workers in branches or areas with slackening demand for labor: Those in such branches who use their rights for recurrent education, their accumulated rights for intermittent long vacations, or for early, temporary, or partial retirement would not need to cover more than a part of their income maintenance during voluntary absence from work through drawing on their accounts because such voluntary absence would reduce the charge or the unemployment insurance system or other expenditure for helping the unemployed.

It must be expected that a number of workers in all categories would use these opportunities for leisure purposes, to study, or to train for jobs with a better future at less than normal cost. The system could be used equally to encourage temporary reductions of weekly working hours by providing income maintenance for the hours not worked and to stimulate use of those hours for vocational or theoretical studies through financial incentives. It could also be useful in situations of sectoral employment expansion by offering special stimuli to those who use their rights to train for occupations in growing demand to those on prolonged leave from one job who thus could be helped and encouraged to look for another job with better prospects in another geographical area. Determining the size of the financial incentives (i.e., the supplements to the drawing rights) needed to achieve the intended effects would have to be a matter for experimentation and experience.

FACTORS LEADING TO MORE FLEXIBILITY

In industrialized countries a number of trends can be noted that suggest that the demand for flexibility is growing and that the reduction of overall work time (which is assumed to be necessary in fully implementing these ideas) is already partially achieved.[1] While not all countries have shared equally in all trends and one can never be absolutely certain of the future, the trends lend support to the feasibility—apart from the desirability—of the arguments outlined above.

First, one can note certain trends in the duration of work time and out-of-work time. The progressive reduction of total hours worked in an average lifetime can be expected to continue along with an increase in the level of real income per hour. This will lead to greater variation and flexibility. Increases in the use of prolonged annual vacations lead one to question the principle that one's whole allotted vacation has to be used before a certain date (such as the end of the year). The reduction of weekly working hours increases the possibilities for deviations from "normal" patterns of work (such as flex-time and staggered schedules). As the age of retirement generally has been lowered and retirement pension provisions have been improved, arrangements around retirement age have become more flexible: There are now provisions for early or partial retirement, reduced work load through part-time work, and, conversely, the continuation of some form of work beyond the usual retirement age.

Two other factors can be mentioned in this context. One is the intergenerational inequality in educational experiences that resulted from the general postwar expansion of educational systems. This has been one of the principal factors behind the emerging demand for recurrent education. For this reason (and because there are those who may not wish to take up adult studies but who want some other form of advantage), the demand for greater interchangeability and flexibility will be all the more prominent. A second and different kind of factor is the increasing diversification of the economy and the increasing internationalization of production and trade. These changes frequently call for large-scale readjustments of the industrial structure and terms of the labor market which will be difficult to manage with just the traditional instruments of labor market policy.

FURTHER ASPECTS OF FINANCIAL EQUITY

In discussing any system of financing income maintenance, two aspects need to be distinguished. On the one hand, there is the question of how the money or revenue is to be raised in the form of social charges and other sorts of taxes. On the other hand, one must consider how the funds should be distributed to individuals and how these persons should be able to use their money for specific purposes (e.g., for recurrent education or for income maintenance in retirement).

With regard to the raising of revenues, in the field of recurrent education and training as well as other fields, there is a wide variety of schemes—both existing and suggested. They are intended to distribute the financial burden in precise ways between individuals and groups according to various notions of justice and equity. Moreover, these issues have been the source of considerable controversy in some countries. On closer examination, however, it becomes clear that there are only very limited possibilities to find out who *really* pays, no matter which system is in place.

An insurance fee or an indirect tax, formally paid by employers as a percentage of the wage bill or the sales volume, can be assumed to be borne largely by consumers through higher prices or by workers whose wages and salaries would be lower than what they otherwise would have been. Direct taxes that are levied progressively on income may have influenced these salaries upwards in a way that in turn affects the prices paid by consumers. Thus all tax systems that are based upon the registration of a money flow that is received by individuals from employers or other sources contain a large element of uncertainty and arbitrariness.

In order to keep the introductory presentation simple, the principle for raising revenues for the general income insurance and drawing rights system was assumed above to be a traditional payroll tax. We stress here, therefore, that it must be an open question what actually should be regarded and registered as the source of each individual's contributions—a part of income taxes, of payroll taxes, or a certain percentage of one's registered income, assumed to be paid via prices of consumer goods irrespective of the structure of the tax system. This structure should (under rational decision making) be formed in a way that promotes its equity and effectiveness regardless of what part of public revenues are formally earmarked as contributions by individuals to the general income insurance system.

When it then comes to the other side—the distribution of benefit rights to individuals—these rights may or may not be made equivalent to the (fictionally) calculated contributions. As in all social insurance systems, one can introduce modifications to that principle that can lead to greater or less equality or can stimulate desirable behavior by means of incentives. The main point is that everyone should constantly be able to see how he or she stands in relation to the system; that is, how great are the rights one has accumulated, what the consequences will be of using a certain amount immediately, and what temporary or permanent advantages society is offering in order to induce a desirable utilization of the drawing rights (e.g., extra advantages for sabbaticals during a slack period or for retraining towards jobs in growing demand).

One may perhaps ask why an individual should be compelled to pay taxes to a central fund and then give that person considerable freedom in its use? Why not let people save voluntarily for the various purposes of their choice? One reason is the general experience that adherence to private and voluntary insurance schemes is lowest and most difficult among those who need them the most for both themselves and their families. With compulsory membership and accounts supplemented by incentives, everyone can benefit roughly in proportion to what they are supposed to have contributed, with the additional possibility of modifications to favor the least privileged. It may also be true that having to abide by the same rules as everyone else can make the ensuring (relative) income reductions more acceptable and encourage a more careful use of these personal assets. However, at least as important is the fact that under this compulsory, general drawing rights system, the state can guarantee compensation for inflation better than smaller, private and segmented insurance institutions can, and that each individual is automatically credit worthy on reaching a certain age (the end of obligatory schooling being a possible starting point). This latter advantage of the system outlined here would mean that young people could finance part of their education out of their account in advance of actually accumulating their drawing rights through contributions. The availability of such drawing rights might well result in less advantaged young people increasing their participation in higher education.

A rather different advantage of the integrated system is that it is administratively cheap and simple. In this respect it can be contrasted with the current ideas and proposals in the debate on the "crisis of the welfare state" which suggest that more and more social needs should be covered by a highly segmented, differentiated insurance system, comprised of private agencies. This would, in fact, result in many additional costs, problems, and inequities. For example, each insurance company would have to engage in the expensive business of not only persuading people to take on that particular insurance in the first place but to do this with them rather than with a rival firm. It would also result in the mushrooming of contracts for old-age, sickness, and unemployment insurance between employers and trade unions, making for great complications for those who move between employers and insurance schemes. The experience of the United States in this respect is illuminating: It is a notorious feature of the American system that many people have great problems both in working out their rights and in ensuring that they receive what they are entitled to.

Indeed, it may be argued that an integrated system, despite the complications implied in the drawing rights, would cost less than the present maze of overlapping, inequitable, and often inadequate separate arrangements for income maintenance, which exist even in European countries despite their more centralized social insurance systems. Through a more integrated, general system, we could not only reduce the amount of involuntary unemployment and the amount of unpleasant and unproductive employment, we could also help the individual more efficiently and equitably to utilize the value of the productivity gains which accrue over his or her lifetime—namely, by facilitating the individual's adjustments to variations in economic structure.

THE USE OF DRAWING RIGHTS FOR RECURRENT EDUCATION

Recurrent education, as defined and discussed in various OECD publications and documents, is like the drawing rights model in that it is a general guiding concept which, if realized, would be shaped and molded by each country to its own traditions and institutions. And like the system of general drawing rights, it is envisaged that recurrent education would emerge through evolutionary reform rather than sudden, total change. Therefore, the question of how to apply drawing rights to recurrent education can only be treated in rather broad terms, short of developing very specific scenarios. It is assumed here, however, that the desirable development of recurrent education would mean that everyone would undertake some kind of postcompulsory study, and that menial jobs for which no particular qualifications are needed would be spread out more evenly and be regarded as a transition stage in the lives of most citizens.

One reasonable assumption is that it would not be economically possible to supply every citizen with drawing rights adequate to cover *all* education beyond compulsory schooling (i.e., equivalent to the customary two or three years of upper secondary school, four years of college or similar undergraduate studies, and additional years for postgraduate studies). In that case, much of the cost of postcompulsory education would still have to be paid with funds outside the drawing rights insurance system, including the traditional sources of student finance such as loans, stipends, parental or family support, and so on. Moreover, with all the different traditions for the financing of education in different countries, it would not be expected that a common or single pattern would apply universally to all the specific financing needed for recurrent education.

Nonetheless, whatever the tradition of educational finance in a given country, we suggest that the drawing rights system would make it possible for everyone to draw on their account to cover the cost of a certain amount of postcompulsory education. A feasible example would be that everyone would be offered three years of full-time postcompulsory study to be financed by drawing on their account. In theory, this would require roughly 10% of the average incomes of all taxpayers (three years being roughly 10% of the average number of working years per person). This would, however, not imply a concomitant increase in taxes as, at present, many people already receive income maintenance, tuition, or both through taxpayers' funds. The advantage of registering the equivalent amount of tax payments on each taxpayer's account is precisely the fact that the individual is thereby shown how much he or she is entitled to and can use this sum according to his or her own choice.

If the individual decides to use this opportunity for studies immediately after the completion of compulsory schooling, he or she would obviously have to go into overdraft. In this case, certain restrictions and controls would be necessary. For example, it might be stipulated that until age 30 using the drawing rights would only be possible for bona fide studies under similar regulations as those pertaining to traditional school and university stipends. It could also be stipulated that once the limit of the advance on the account was reached, a person would not be able to draw on the account for any further purpose until the overdraft had been compensated or paid back through one's automatic contributions. After age 30 the control would be relaxed and the individual could use his or her rights for education in the same way as for any other chosen purpose within the general regulations governing the drawing rights scheme. This is of course only one possible alternative.

Variations around the theme of developing recurrent education suggest a number of possibilities in these respects. Drawing rights for studies, for example, could be made available only at a later date than the completion of compulsory schooling, obliging the student who nonetheless wishes to continue his or her studies immediately to rely on the traditional sources of finance as at present. Or it would be possible to ensure that the number of points annually available for studies on each person's account would be relatively low during the first years after compulsory schooling, but would grow at more than the rate of interest up to a certain age (say, 30 years). This, too, would better meet the greater income requirements of adults compared with those of young people, most of whom have yet to acquire costly responsibilities. These different ways of discriminating in favor of older adults can be seen either as a way of discouraging the continuation of studies in the period immediately after compulsory schooling, or as a way of encouraging or compensating "second chance" entry into education.

It would, of course, be possible to modify the drawing rights system by introducing economic incentives that would make adult studies an attractive alternative. But if it is true that the marginal productivity of additionally expanding the education system or volume of studies is relatively limited, this too argues in favor of not restricting such incentives to education only.

A possible compromise between the interest of stimulating studies and the interest of economic equity among people with and without postcompulsory studies would be to provide all tuition free of charge (i.e., let taxpayers finance it irrespective of their own participation in such studies) but to let subsistence during studies be the individual's own responsibility. The need for liquidity would be met (beside by the traditional system of bursaries and easy loans) by access to drawing rights as described above.

CONCLUSION

A number of the possible ways in which a drawing rights system could be used for recurrent education have been discussed. It can be seen that the general features of the model, as outlined in the earlier parts of this chapter, would allow adults (and young people) to use their rights for educational purposes in a more flexible way than is possible in many countries at present. As envisaged here, the widespread use of economic incentives as a vehicle of labor market policy would to a great extent imply the promotion of education and training, thereby providing an important additional basis for the establishment of a more developed recurrent education system. On the whole, the drawing rights system would forcefully reduce the rigid compartmentalization of life in three distinct periods—study, work and retirement. Instead, it would promote freedom of choice, seen as both a social value and as a possibility for more rapid and humane forms of adjustment in the labor market—both of which are needed for full employment and improved rates of growth.

NOTE

1. In my earlier article (Rehn, 1972) and in later published versions the arguments for "flex-time" (free variations and timing of work *hours*) was an important element. As this can be implemented without income maintenance through drawing rights, this aspect is bypassed here.

REFERENCES

REHN, G. (1974) "Towards flexibility in working life," in S. Mushkin (ed.) Recurrent Education. Washington, DC: Institute of Education, Department of Health, Education, and Welfare.
―――― (1972) Prospective Views on Patterns for Working Time. Paris: OECD.
WIATR, J. and R. ROSE [eds.] (1977) Comparing Public Policies. Wroclaw.

4

INTERMEDIATE ("PARAFISCAL") FINANCING SCHEMES

WERNER CLEMENT

In the decades ahead, postsecondary education will very likely be one of the fastest growing areas of the educational system. Demographic factors, a probable increase in individual propensity for further learning, as well as other reasons of educational, social, and economic policy will all contribute to this growth. The existing plans of provision and those for the future make it likely that the organization of this educational area will differ significantly from the traditional models. Whereas in Europe, for example, formal education tends to be dominated by the state, alternative arrangements that comply with the manifold forms and expressions of recurrent education are needed and are being sought after.

Of course, reasons and rationales can always be found for any arrangement of provision and finance for recurrent education—whether it be a central-collectivist one, or an individualistic organization operating in a market. This depends largely on the ideology behind each proposal. Thus a tightly centralized, state-financed system may be discussed alongside one that operates as a market where individuals use vouchers for education. The major claim of this chapter is that a number of social factors and a range of theoretical considerations support a system which is neither purely public nor private—rather, an "intermediate" scheme for the provision and finance of recurrent education.

Further education within a recurrent framework is a sector in which there are high risks; there are those attached to government control on the one hand, and to market failures on the other. Therefore, if this area of education and training is not be "nationalized" or organized subject

---

AUTHOR'S NOTE: *I acknowledge gratefully comments made by C. Badelt, D. Istance, H. M. Levin, H. G. Schütze, D. M. Windham, and several participants of the Stanford Conference.*

to the criteria of private optimization, then a social and economic terrain—the contours of which have begun to be mapped only recently—must be entered. Provisionally, we can call it the "intermediary" sector.

While the analysis of this intermediary sector in economic theory awaits a much fuller treatment, there are nonetheless existing branches and strands of economics that are closely related to this idea which together can provide the basis of a more complete consideration. The economic theories of politics (theories of group behavior, clubs and collective action, and bargaining theory) and public choice theory (the nature of goods, externalities, and theories of intermediate "parafiscal" finance) together provide much of the conceptual apparatus required. Additional relevant branches include the new "third-sector economics," the economics of grants and of the institutional arrangements of quasi-public agencies. Pluralism, as political theory and constitutional reality, can also provide political and normative support to the theoretical development of this intermediary sector.

It would be a formidable task to exploit all these approaches with a view of building a "pure" theoretical model of the provision and finance of recurrent education. But by examining even briefly what already exists in countries, one finds an array of highly interesting institutional settings for further education which lie somewhere in the zone between state and that which is purely private. Examples are the Industrial Training Boards in the United Kingdom, the autonomous agreements ("conventions") and funds financed by special contributions in France, and arrangements under the Labor Promotion Act and paid educational leave regulations in the Federal Republic of Germany as well as many other similar devices in other European countries. More traditional settings, such as workers' education by trade unions or management courses given by employer federations, are equally relevant.

Yet, to conduct a simple stocktaking of these examples through national studies would not be sufficient to clarify the issues involved, nor could it provide a systematic analysis of these intermediate schemes and arrangements for the provision and finance of recurrent education. Such a systematic approach to the problems should make use of both theories and actual experiences drawn from case studies. For this reason the chapter is divided in two sections: the first discusses the theoretical considerations necessary to formulate the foundations of an intermediate scheme. This section, which can be skipped by a reader less interested in theoretical foundations, is followed by an attempt to conceptualize a realistic framework for such an intermediate scheme. The simple logic runs in the following way: Recurrent education may safely be considered a mixed good (using the language of economic theory) that has both public and private characteristics. For mixed goods, there is strong theoretical support that these goods should be provided by groups (as suggested by the analysis of the logic of collective action or theory of clubs.) For such provisions, an adequate scheme of finance has to be found.

Special funds or, more generally, financing schemes covered by the concept of parafiscality seem to provide the most suitable solutions. It is important then, first of all, that systematic guidelines for such intermediate financing schemes be elaborated that are general enough to fit the peculiarities of different countries. Although such an intermediate sector cannot totally replace state and private provision of further education and training, it can certainly be argued that it could well form a major part of total provision.

COLLECTIVE PROVISION OF RECURRENT EDUCATION AS THE RATIONALE FOR INTERMEDIATE (PARAFISCAL) SCHEMES

THE OPTIMAL PROVISION OF A MIXED GOOD

Education is usually viewed as a merit good or mixed good because it has both public and private chararacteristics. On the one hand, some education and training would be produced in the absence of public support because of the private demand created by individuals and their families. On the other hand, the production of education is believed to produce social benefits that are external to the individuals receiving the education: a more effectively functioning democracy and system of production, greater technological and cultural progress, and a "better" society (Bowen, 1977; Haveman and Weisbrod, 1977; and Weisbrod, 1964). Accordingly, education is viewed as having social merit and thus as deserving of both public and private support as a mixed good. Since it seems reasonable to view recurrent education in this light, we will assume that it is a mixed good also. It is therefore possible to apply the theoretical discussion on the provision of this category of goods to recurrent education. Beginning with the work of Tiebout (1956) and

Buchanan (1964), this area is usually considered under the heading of the "economic theory of clubs" (Sandler and Tschirhart, 1980).

A good starting point is the presence of a partial rivalry in consumption which is typical of mixed goods. Additional users joining the group of people who consume a mixed good collectively (i.e., the club) can create additional benefits for the original consumers, but only if every consumer takes part in financing the mixed good. Excluding it from certain people—"nonmembers"—prevents people from benefiting at others' expense (free-riding). However, once a certain level or number of club members is attained, rivalry occurs so that a further enlargement of the group may lead to higher marginal costs than marginal benefits to the existing members. This is usually labelled the "crowding" effect in the consumption of mixed goods.

Generally speaking, this problem can be formulated as a functional relationship between the average costs (which result from the provision of a mixed good) and the number of persons being engaged in its production and consumption. This was the original problem raised by Buchanan (1964) which was further developed by Oakland (1972) emphasizing that the crowding function is strongly determined by the frequency with which the club members make use of the mixed good.

One of the principal aims of the economic theory of clubs is to determine optimal club size given a certain amount of the mixed good. Optimal conditions can be formulated where both the amount of the good and the number of club members are variable. The optimal club size is attained when the net benefits from membership for an entrant equal the crowding costs resulting from that person's entire utilization of the mixed good. The optimal amount of provision is found when the marginal benefits from crowding reduction as a result of increased provision equal the marginal costs of provision (Sandler and Tschirhart, 1980).

These theoretical considerations give, albeit in extremely abstract form, some guide to the orientation of policy. Their application in reality would demand, however, a vast amount of concrete specification and empirical research. In particular, since the optimal club size in the case of recurrent education is determined by the benefits and costs of its provision, a functional specification of these two terms would be necessary. Independent variables that could be used for the specification of these relationships are, for example, the number of group members, the frequency with which clients use the educational facilities, and desired ratios between teachers and the consumers of recurrent education.

THE INSTITUTIONAL DECISION: INTERMEDIATE BODIES AS PROVIDERS OF RECURRENT EDUCATION

These optimum conditions do not a priori determine the institutional form that the club should take. Buchanan, for example, stressed that a club requires the organization of some sort of cooperative, sharing arrangement, that needs to be not only for nonprofit organizations (such as intermediate bodies) but may cover public arrangements and even profit-making firms (Buchanan, 1965).

It is argued here, however, that because of the "mixed good" nature of recurrent education, it can easily be demonstrated that institutional arrangements in the form of intermediate bodies have particular advantages over the others. First, it must be mentioned that the totally private provision of recurrent education is neither very likely to occur—due to the limited opportunities for profit in this field—nor would be desirable politically. That is, the high prices resulting from full-cost pricing would exclude the majority of potential consumers from access to education facilities and thus would not be acceptable. Second, one of the principal messages of economic theories of the voluntary sector is that state provision of public (or mixed) goods can present considerable disadvantages. As Olson (1965) has argued, the attributes of collective goods suggest only that they should be provided as a result of a collective decision-making process, because decisions at an individual level would fail. But collective need not necessarily refer to the state: Olson argues that it is necessary to analyze how smaller collectivities such as intermediate bodies would make these decisions (Badelt, 1981).

Apart from Olson's conclusions (which apply mainly to large groups), many educational institutions reflect already the basic idea that common valuations and preferences for continuing education may bring individuals together into groups engaged in the provision of education. There is, of course, a variety of motivations for participation: for example, social commitment (particularly expressed by churches and voluntary organizations); the desire for improving professional career prospects; a group feeling emanating from a common regional, social-class, or ethnic background; the desire to foster through education the ideologies and values of an organization;

and more immediate and personal needs such as those met by family or leisure activities. One can hardly deny that such attitudes and motivations have exercised a strong positive influence on developments of vocational and nonvocational adult education institutions.

While these are examples rather than an attempt to generalize, it should be stressed that by its very nature, the concept of recurrent education is flexible enough to include different institutional settings in its provision. What will be advocated here is that collective organizations (groups) are especially well adapted for such provision. A number of reasons, supported by theories of public choice and the emerging theory of the voluntary sector, may be forwarded in support of this view. The three arguments below underline that the state alone is unable to provide and cater for a sufficient supply of recurrent education (Weisbrod, 1978):

- governmental decisions are oriented towards short-term political criteria (for example, immediate popularity) that reflect neither "true" preferences nor politically desirable preferences (in the case of a merit good, such as education).

- governmental decisions have to be more or less centralized—a fact which has serious consequences in areas such as the dissemination of information.

- the ratio of costs to benefits is often much higher compared with alternative sources of provision.

The first of these three is elaborated by Weisbrod (Weisbrod, 1977; Weisbrod et al., 1978). He assumes that public policy, in pursuing maximization of votes, is oriented towards the demand of the median voter. This results in an undersupply of many collective goods and, in consequence, dissatisfaction among certain groups of consumers. One of the possible results is then "that a class of voluntary organizations will come into existence as extragovernmental providers of collective-consumption goods" (Weisbrod, 1977). The relatively low response of the eligible population to an extensive provision of recurrent education (as, for example, with the law of 1971 in France) may help explain why many governments were somewhat reluctant to make recurrent education a central political issue. On the other hand, such reluctance may leave many sections of the population without adequate opportunities. Again, therefore, the provision of education tailored to the needs of specific groups is one possible and feasible way out of that dilemma.

The second of the three arguments asserts that state provision of recurrent education has to be organized in a far more centralized way than is necessary with other forms of provision. However, centralization leads to limited and frequently biased information for decision makers (Downs, 1966; Orzechowski, 1977). This is particularly problematic for mixed goods which, as mentioned above, can be characterized by joint public and private consumption. It is certainly questionable to assume that any governmental institution could acquire the relevant information to cluster people who have more or less homogenous preferences. Yet this is the precondition to the realization of an efficient provision of recurrent education in the sense of a club.

In theory, there is only one way around this problem: This can be called "voting with the feet." This way of monitoring or showing preferences would suggest that governmental decisions should be decentralized until groups with relatively homogenous preferences emerge (Tiebout, 1956). This would require high mobility of consumers who would continue to move until they settled in a community where the provision of public goods largely corresponded to their preferences (Mueller, 1979). Although this theoretical alternative hardly could become directly applicable in practice—and certainly not in Europe—it has, nevertheless, the heuristic purpose of indicating that the problem of information can be relieved through decentralization in the public sector. One form of decentralization is precisely the provision and financing of recurrent education by parafiscal institutions.

The third problem, that of disadvantageous costs to benefits, is closely linked with the centralization issue. Drawing again on the economic theory of clubs, it suggests that the collectivity represented by the government would normally be considerably larger than the optimal club size. Hence, a reduction in the size of the club would save more in marginal costs than it would cost in marginal benefits, resulting in a net gain in benefits. One reason why larger units produce at relatively high costs is the existence of various forms of transaction costs such as those of information or of control. These aspects have been debated thoroughly and widely, often under the heading of "the costs of bureaucracy" (Tullock, 1965; Borcherding, 1977; Habermann and Loser, 1980).

To summarize: Neither the private profit-making nor the traditional public sector are capable of meeting the (potential) demand for recurrent education completely. Beyond these technical and theoretical arguments, a number of normative judgments related to recurrent education as a politically shaped concept can be used to underline the advantages of the provision of recurrent education by an intermediary sector. Such additional criteria, which carry implications for the specific institutional forms the provision of recurrent education should take, can be derived from the OECD model of recurrent education (OECD/CERI, 1977). For example, there are the objectives of providing a wide choice of learning opportunities, of allowing a significant degree of self-determination or self-management of the learning, and of allowing and encouraging innovation. The argument here is that an intermediary sector is particularly well suited to realizing these objectives.

THEORETICAL FINANCING SCHEMES FOR GROUP PROVISION

GENERAL ASPECTS

The economic theory of clubs also contains a nucleus of considerations concerning the financing of a mixed good. This is included in what is called the "toll condition" for the optimal supply of a mixed good. The toll condition basically requires financing of the provision at an equal rate or toll for all members. However, since utilization can vary between individuals, the total payment by each member need not be the same. Several authors have shown that the sum of ("efficient") tolls paid by all members suffices to finance marginal costs of provision.[1] Consequently, it fails to finance the mixed good completely whenever average costs exceed marginal costs (i.e., when increasing returns to scale are present). In this case, optimal financing of recurrent education—a mixed good—requires a two-part tariff: To avoid deficits, a fixed membership charge *and* a utilization fee are necessary. This is the basic message for optimal financing in the case of increasing returns to scale.

The applications of these theoretical stipulations to policymaking require consideration of some elementary rules for the financing of recurrent education. First, as discussed above, financing at full-cost pricing would exclude a considerable number of potential recurrent students and therefore, is not desirable. Second, the rules of "optimal" finance imply a basic standard contribution in order to balance out the potential deficit. In addition, there should be a fee payable on use, the size of which should be determined by the marginal costs of participation in recurrent education.

The question of what an adequate financing scheme for intermediate bodies would be has not been answered in a rigorous way. The economics of public finance tends to develop coherent frameworks for the finance of public or semipublic bodies either in a territorial or a functional perspective. This has meant that analytical public finance has been developed alongside the description of institutions and agencies.

Following this brief sketch of the analysis of finance, it is only fair to look also at the other strand of development in this area—the institutional findings. Here, a certain, if only partial, recognition of the role of intermediate bodies of finance can be found in Italian, German, and French economic thought—particularly in the concepts of organic finance and parafiscality.

THE MAIN CHARACTERISTICS OF PARAFISCALITY

Without attempting to give a comprehensive picture of fiscal institutions and mechanisms, some characteristic properties should be described (Smekal, 1969; Mäding, 1971; Tiepelmann, 1975). One can begin with their *objectives*. On the whole, parafiscal institutions are expected both to fulfill a public function and to be in accord with the needs of a population grouping. They are assumed to be able to do this more efficiently because of the possibilities of limiting membership or participation (the exclusion principle). They are also expected to realize the aims of decentralization and self-management through a far-reaching autonomy of decision making and action.

The above mentioned objectives cannot be attained without securing some minimum degree of *fiscal distinctiveness*. On the revenue side, traditionally it has been claimed often that one can only speak of a true "parafiscus" if the body in question has the right to levy taxes or contributions. However, strict adherence to this rule would eliminate an interesting range of fiscal institutions and narrow the subject down only to social security, unemployment insurance funds, and some professional corporations that have financial autonomy. Since the purpose here is to cover the areas of intermediate bodies more generally, our broader perspective will focus on intermediate bodies *that rely upon mixed revenues coming from different sources*. These may be state subsidies and transfers, contributions they levy themselves (e.g., through fundraising; Flanagan, 1977), and even revenues from economic activity (Weisbrod and Long, 1977) although the economic activity must not be profit-making. Even the earmarking of funds for specific purposes would not be a reason to exclude it, so long as a certain degree of financial autonomy were maintained (Kirchhoff, 1973).

The recognition of an intermediary sector between the state and private commercial activities and the establishment of criteria under which institutions would belong in this parafiscal area are loose indicators of the types of organizations that are meant to be included.

In order to provide greater specificity about true parafiscal *institutions,* the middle of the spectrum between state and private entities is the easiest to deal with. This covers institutions which are common features of the corporate state such as employers' federations, trade unions, chambers of commerce, and associations of the liberal professions— in short, interest groups and social partners. As one moves from the middle ground to the more governmental institutions, the social security system, public trust funds, and even "quangos" (quasi-autonomous nongovernmental organizations) might fall under the heading of parafisci. Whether or not a specific body should be included under this heading depends on the extent of its financial autonomy and self-ruling capacity.

Moving towards the private sector at the other end of the scale, syndicates, cooperatives, and companies acting for the public interest would not be considered parafisci because in these cases the criteria of raising and managing public finances and providing public goods certainly cannot be applied. The same may be true, if to a lesser extent, of voluntary associations.

Looking at the question of *financial planning,* parafiscal funds are earmarked for specific purposes. This is a major incentive for contributions from those who supply the finances, and it is also probable that the forces of group cohesion would soften if this principle did not hold. As to the relation between the contribution to and the benefits from a parafiscal institution, a certain difference from government taxation may also be discerned. Modern welfare-state budgets generally tax individuals according to their ability to pay and render services according to some principle of equity. While this idea also applies to parafisci, it does so to a lesser extent. One of the very reasons for their creation in the first place is that certain individuals are willing to pay more than the average on the understanding that they will receive an equal or comparable benefit from such a fund.

MAIN FEATURES OF AN INTERMEDIATE (PARAFISCAL) FINANCING SCHEME FOR RECURRENT EDUCATION

GENERAL ASPECTS

To make the principles of group provision and finance more operational, the theoretical rules and considerations need to be translated into criteria that specify how a functioning system actually would look. This cannot be done comprehensively or exhaustively here—the above discussion shows that intermediate schemes cover a widely ranging variety of activities and mechanisms. Not surprisingly, their aims, legal bases, activities, revenue structures, budgeting and bases of fiscal authority, and administrative and decision-making structures differ significantly. What is outlined here is only an overview of some of the more important issues raised under these headings.

THE REVENUE SIDE

Classifying the revenues of intermediate bodies is not difficult: Monies may come from individual contributions or fees, from the state through grants, subsidies, transfer payments, or loans, or from enterprises through voluntary contributions, compulsory levies, or loans. They may also come from the economic activities of the body in question and the management of portfolios. As stated before, the degree of financial autonomy is a central aspect of intermediary bodies of finance and provision. Within this general criterion, classification of revenues can reflect such features as the proportion of general or block grants as compared with earmarked funds, and can distinguish between the suppliers and the distributors of finance, between spending bodies, and between those who receive funds and those who use them (Peacock, 1967).

Taking *individual contributions* first, it is not difficult to see that basing them upon the expected benefits to the individuals of the education or training presents very difficult theoretical and practical problems (e.g., how to disentangle individual from social benefits, or general from vocational elements, or how to impute a precise figure to these benefits).

Moreover, as discussed above, individual contributions based on full-cost pricing would be a particular deterrent to those whose income is low, and any attempt to try to meet the costs fully through some formula for payments based on supposed subsequent pay-offs from the education (e.g., through loans or educational insurance funds) might be unduly discouraging to the would-be student. Therefore, participants' own contributions may only prove to be a marginal source for the necessary finance. Nonetheless, it is probably preferable that a certain portion be raised in this way—both as a reminder of the costliness of education and as a means of revealing actual preferences for education.

Turning to the *state,* it has already been emphasized that it cannot be the major source of the funds. A state contribution may nevertheless be required to ensure a "just representation" among the participants in the intermediate body. A possible upper limit to state grants could be set at the net costs—that is, the costs minus the direct benefits, which are open to approximate estimation.[2] Apart from these financing considerations, it may be stipulated that the state cover the capital expenditures in order to provide the initial capacities. This participation of the state might also be extended to include compensation for salaries foregone or incidental expenses of participation in recurrent education (as is done in Sweden).

Third, there are several reasons why *private firms* should share the financial burden of education and training that is organized and financed in this way. First, it can be assumed that they can afford it (especially if they can pass the costs on in prices) and that they will benefit in any case through productivity gains. But, they will tend to provide firm- or industry-specific skills that limit the value of training and its results to competitors. Insofar as this will lead to an under-supply and unjust distribution of educational provision, it argues for an industry-wide approach and the creation of a fund which is maintained through enterprise contributions to increase the supply of education and training and make the financial burden more equitable.

As to the basis of the levies or fees enterprises would pay, there are a number of possibilities; the choice between them is largely a technical one depending on circumstances. (The factors include the total number of employees or eligible employees, the value-added, the turnover, the profit, and the payroll.) The latter criterion—the payroll—does suffer from the problem of placing labor-intensive firms at a disadvantage (Hegelheimer, 1977). The net costs may prove a fairer basis if equalization of the burden is an aim of the fund enterprises contribute to. A case, then, can be made for the fund compensating firms for this difference, although in practice it may prove to be anything but simple to establish precisely what it should be. Therefore, different kinds of systems have been used such as that of the levy-grant, of the levy-grant-exemption, or the levy-premium systems used in the United Kingdom and France.

THE EXPENDITURE SIDE

The expenditure pattern is closely linked to the costs. These can be broken down as follows: capital-current costs, direct costs (for the participants, the firm, or the state), and indirect costs. The latter includes the foregone income of the participants, the loss of production (if any) due to staff reductions, and possible social costs that occur as negative spill-overs.

Among these, the most important items are the current costs of the teaching personnel and the compensation of trainees for loss of earnings. There is some debate about who should incur the payment of earnings foregone; in international comparisons, income foregone or the maintained payment of the salaries are rarely included at all. Significant differences are thus possible in the relative burdens for the spending bodies. In Britain, for example, it has been said that "at least two-thirds of post-initial vocational expenditures on adults is till financed ... by employers" (Drake, 1978). In France under the 1971 law, on the other hand, the state assumes two-thirds of the expenditures. Extreme caution, however, is required with this kind of comparison.

Another argument centers around the question of whether the financial resources should be allocated to people or to institutions. This may appear to be a misplaced question since it can be said that it is always people who ultimately receive the money. Yet in practice the difference may be of consequence. When the institution is the primary recipient of the subsidy, the advantage is that educational supply can be created and regulated in certain known ways. The risk, on the other hand, is that needs may be overlooked or provision may prove inadequate. Moreover, there may be risks of institutions behaving as bureaucracies and hence neglecting the consumers of education—the students. Advantages and disadvantages when finance is directed toward individuals are the converse of those just outlined.

DECISION MAKING AND POWER

The issue of the distribution of power is a central one, since parafiscal bodies can be distinguished not only by their relative degree of financial autonomy but also by their degree of self-government. When participation, fundraising, and determination of educational content all rest with the same interest group, there is little question about where the locus of power and control lies. Such a "closed-shop" situation may be justified on its own grounds, but not from a social perspective. Education is seen as a service for the members of the interest group, and sometimes may even be essential to ensure the stability of the group. This is reflected in the British case by the following:

> In the case of qualified manpower, valuable legal or conventional powers over training and access are vested in bodies like the Bar, the Law Society, the Royal Colleges of Medicine and in numerous chartered associations like the associations to which the 300,000 chartered and technical engineers belong [Drake, 1978].

Quite another type of situation arises when interest groups form a coalition and are induced by the state to establish educational provision. In this case, the power structure is usually tripartite and the stability of such a body is dependent upon the observance of the founding agreement (or law). Otherwise, there may be power shifts that would upset any initial balance. In fact, this is probably the most important and widely applied type of intermediate body as it conforms to certain principles of representative democracy. Examples are the Industrial Training Boards in Britain, the FAF (Training Insurance Funds) in France, and, to a certain extent, the *Bundesanstalt für Arbeit* in Germany.

In practice, the network of decision making and control is usually much more complex than is indicated by these general examples. First, there is considerable variety in the extent to which power is exercised over matters of finance alone or as it extends to education as well. Sometimes educational institutions are left relatively free and are financially supported on the basis of some index of man-hours of training delivered. More complicated criteria of support have also included stipulated educational standards (e.g., the system of *baremes* in France; see Glennerster, 1977; Blondel and Le Roux, 1975). An alternative arrangement is one in which control over finance and education is divided—for example, where educational institutions have to be recognized by the state or by some official body and funding is left to variegated schemes. A common arrangement is one in which intervention, information, and finance are examined and controlled through informal channels of different institutional structures. For higher education, a good example is the University Grants Committee in the United Kingdom, but other examples resembling this one also can be found in less mainstream educational settings.

CONCLUDING SUMMARY REMARKS

This chapter starts with the recognition of two very basic points. First, we can observe the fact that intermediate bodies (in education and training as well as in other fields and sectors) occupy a prominent position between purely private and public organizations. That is, they are an existing and very real fact of the world. Second, recurrent education has the properties of a mixed good, and therefore its provision and financing cannot be either exclusively private or public—further reason for seeing intermediate institutions as particularly suited to recurrent education. It can be added that the fact that recurrent education is a mixed good suggests that it is supplied best by groups.

Going beyond these two basic observations, we can observe that in pluralistic societies there are many movements or trends—such as the rise in participation in a variety of fields or the growth of voluntary organizations—that support the call for a truly intermediary sector. The fiscal form of this intermediary sector, organized around groups, would be institutions that are capable of raising funds under their own authority (at least to some degree) and can reflect the preferences of the individuals who comprise the group. The organizational forms this can take are funds, insurance, chartered associations, and voluntary groups. It is crucial to state that as soon as a group provision is recognized (according to educational standards) it may claim its right to be financed through this scheme.

One can foresee objections or potential problems with these proposals. For one thing, such intermediary organizations and financing may hardly provide an adequate basis for extensive recurrent opportunities. Nor, it might be added, do they provide reasonable assurance that various disadvantaged groups, who presently participate the least in adult education, would establish or join groups organizing education and training. Furthermore, except in the case of collective bargaining, national level coordination of group activities would seem unlikely without the assistance of some sort of state intervention.

The response to these potential criticisms reveals the flexibility inherent in such a system of intermediary provision and finance. It must be recognized that there is no one "best" solution to the development of such a sector for recurrent education. Hence an integrated system of education and finance must be sought, in line with the goals, institutions, and traditions of each country. Therefore, the state (for example) may take a role in ensuring that disadvantaged groups face adequate provision or in establishing a suitable mode of coordination without endangering the intermediary status of the bodies concerned. Added to this, it is likely that there may be much more rapid and flexible creation or adjustment of educational supply within such a sector than would otherwise be the case.

There are even grounds for believing that the overall level of provision of recurrent education would be increased if a more thoroughgoing intermediate sector were encouraged and developed. For this to be true, a number of holding conditions would probably have to be obtained. We might say that overall provision would increase if

- people would express and realize their preferences through groups of a convenient size;
- their willingness to do so thereby becomes greater than it is at present;
- sensible economies of scale would reduce the costs of the provision (e.g., through enhanced productivity);
- more people are thereby encouraged to join and participate with sufficient participatory power granted to participants in the management of the body, and in the management of funds in particular.

As with many questions concerning intermediary provision and finance, they have yet to be explored adequately and thoroughly. The fast growing body of literature that has been published since the presentation of a first version of this chapter is proof of the great interest in this area.

NOTES

1. For an overview see Sandler and Tschirhart (1980: 1496) and the literature mentioned there.
2. This is the approach of the German Edding Commission on Costs and Financing of Vocational Education and Training (see Kosten und Finanzierung der aussersculishen beruflichen Bildung, Bonn, 1974).

REFERENCES

BADELT, C. (1983) "Community action: success, failure, prospects," in M. Pfaff (ed.) Public Transfers and some Private Alternatives During the Recession. Berlin-München: Duncker and Humlot.

—— (1980) Soziookonomie der Selbstorganisation, Beispiele zur Burgerselbsthilfe und ihre wirtschaftliche Bedeutung. Frankfurt, New York: Campus. 120-124.

BENGTSSON, J. and H. G. SCHÜTZE (1979) "Developments in recurrent education and recent economic and social trends," pp. 11-41 in W. Clement and F. Edding (eds.) Recurrent Education and Berufliche Flexibilitätsforschung. Berlin: Duncker und Humblot.

BLONDEL, C. and C. LE ROUX (1975) Le financement de la Politique de Formation professionnelle et de Promotion en France. Paris: JJPE.

BOWEN, H. R. (1977) Investment in Learning: The Individual and Social Value of American Higher Education. San Francisco: Jossey-Bass.

BUCHANAN, J. M. (1965) "An economic theory of clubs," Economics 32: 1-14.

DOWNS, K. (1968) Inside Bureaucracy. Boston: Little, Brown.

DRAKE, K. (1978) "The financial, legislative and regulatory structure of vocational training in the United Kingdom." Prepared for the CEDEFOP, Berlin, April. (mimeo)

FLANAGAN, J. (1977) The Grassroots Fundraising Book. Chicago: Swallow Press.

GLENNERSTER, G. H. (1977) "The existing system of finance," in M. Keynes (ed.) The Finance of Education: Economics and Education Policy IV.

HABERMAN, G. and H. J. LÖSER (1980) Antiburokratie. Munchen: Moderne Verlagsgesellschaft.

HAVEMAN, R. H. and B. A. WEISBROD (1977) "Determining benefits of public programmes: some guidance for policy analysis," in R. H. Haveman and J. Margolis (eds.) Public Expenditure and Policy Analysis. Chicago: Markham.

HEGELHEIMER, A. (1977) Finanzierungsprobleme der Berufsausbildung. Stuttgart: Ernst Klett.

JANNE, H., P. DOMINICÉ, and W. JAMES (1980) Development of Adult Education. Strasbourg: Council of Europe.

KIRCHHOFF, G. (1973) Subventionen als Instrument der Lenkung und Koordinierung. Berlin.

MÄDING, H. (1971) Fondsfinanzierte Berufsausbildung, Gutachten und Studien der Bildungskommission 19. Suttgart.

MUELLER, D. (1979) Public Choice. Cambridge: Cambridge Univ. Press.

OAKLAND, W. H. (1972) "Congestion, public goods and welfare." J. of Public Economics (November): 339-357.

OECD/CERI (1977) "Conference on developments in recurrent education." Paris: Secretariat Synthesis.

—— (1975) Recurrent Education: Trends and Issues. Paris: Author.

—— (1973) Recurrent Education: A Strategy for Lifelong Learning. Paris: Author.

OLSON, M. (1965) The Logic of Collective Action: Public Goods and the Theory of Groups. Cambridge, MA: Harvard Univ. Press.

ORZECHOWSKI, W. (1977) "Economic models of bureaucracy, survey, extensions and evidence," pp. 229-259 in T. E. Borcherding (ed.) Budgets and Bureaucracy: The Sources of Government Growth. Durham: Duke Univ. Press.

PEACOCK, A. (1967) "A conceptual scheme for the analysis of data on educational finance," p. 285 in OECD (ed.) Methods and Statistical Needs for Education Planning. Paris: OECD.

SANDLER, T. and J. T. TSCHIRHART (1980) "The economic theory of clubs: an evaluative survey." J. of Econ. Literature 18 (December): 1481-1521.

SMEKAL, C. (1969) Die Finanzwirtschaft intermediarer Gruppen. Innsbruck: Universität Innsbruck.

TIEBOUT, C. M. (1956) "A pure theory of local expenditure." J. of Pol. Economy 64: 416-424.

TIEPELMANN, K. (1975) "Parafiski." WISU, Das Wirtschaftsstudium, 6: 295-300.

TULLOCK, G. (1965) The Politics of Bureaucracy. Washington: Public Affairs Press.

WEISBROD, B. A. (1978) "Some collective-good aspects of non-government activities: not-for-profit organizations," pp. 163-174 in H. C. Recktenwald (ed.) Secular Trends of the Public Sector, Proceedings of the 32nd Congress of the International Institute of Public Finance. Berkeley: Univ. of California Press.

—— [ed.] (1977) The Voluntary Nonprofit Sector, An Economic Analysis. Lexington: Lexington Books.

—— (1977) "Toward a theory of the voluntary nonprofit sector in a three sector economy," pp. 51-76 in B. A. Weisbrod (ed.) The Voluntary Nonprofit Sector. Lexington: Lexington Books.

—— (1964) External Benefits of Public Education. Princeton: Princeton University, Industrial Relations Section.

—— and S. H. LONG (1977) "The size of the voluntary nonprofit sector, concepts and measures," pp. 11-50 in B. A. Weisbrod (ed.) The Voluntary Nonprofit Sector. Lexington: Lexington Books.

WEISBROD, B. A., J. F. HANDLER, and N. K. KOMESAR [eds.] (1978) Public Interest Law, An Economic and Institutional Analysis. Berkeley: Univ. of California Press.

WEISSHUHN, G. (1980) Probleme ökonomischer und soziler Kosten—Ertragsrechnungen der Weiterbildung, Discussion Paper 54. Berlin: Technical University.

> # 5

FINANCING MECHANISMS
Their Impact on Postcompulsory Education

DIETER TIMMERMANN

This chapter will discuss the effects of various financing systems on recurrent postcompulsory education. First, a number of criteria will be introduced for assessing the probable impact of financing mechanisms on recurrent education. Second, several alternative financing models will be presented. Three models are presented in this volume (see Chapters 2, 3, and 4) so they will not be discussed in detail in this chapter. Other models which have not been proposed explicitly here will be discussed more fully. Third, an attempt will be made to evaluate each of the mechanisms in the light of the criteria—that is, to speculate on whether and to what extent the various systems of financing are likely to satisfy the objectives of recurrent education. One essential part of this discussion will be the identification of possible trade-offs between those objectives. The fourth step will be the attempt to find out which financing mechanism promises to fulfill the criteria most adequately. Such a "best" financing system very well may be a mixed one. Finally, the impact on macroeconomic activities of financing recurrent education as well as some caveats will be discussed.

CRITERIA FOR EVALUATING FINANCING MECHANISMS

In this section various criteria are set out for evaluating financing plans for recurrent education. Although much of the discussion of recurrent education has been limited to equality of educational opportunity and efficiency, several additional criteria will be introduced here.[1]

ENCOURAGING RECURRENCE

The first criterion is to encourage the replacement of traditional schooling patterns with a flexible and recurrent alternation of education, work, leisure, vacation, and retirement. This criterion is referred to as "encouraging recurrence," and advocates in particular part-time work as well as flexible work and vacation schedules. Also considered is the ability of alternative financing schemes to induce educational institutions to offer recurrent education.

INCREASING EFFICIENCY

The second criterion, "increasing efficiency," entails several different aspects of efficiency. The first is *internal efficiency,* which refers to optimizing the organization and mode of production within the educational industry by choosing cost-minimizing combinations of production factors, optimal firm sizes, time-minimizing decisions, and efficient management procedures. Internal efficiency also entails the matter of output quality—in other words, teaching contents. The second aspect is *external efficiency,* which is concerned with the efficient use of educational resources as it affects the functioning of the economic sector (i.e., of the labor market and its branches). While recurrent education is concerned with reducing unemployment, it also aims at preventing it by giving employed workers the opportunity to take part in recurrent education activities in order to alter their skills even before the threat of unemployment occurs. In this sense, external efficiency implies flexibility of the labor force (Clement and Edding, 1979).

As a result of recurrent education activities, productivity of the labor force is likely to increase in two ways: Recurrently educated workers and employees can be expected to be more productive than those who are not; and preventive recurrent education is likely to minimize the costs of structural and technological changes by ruling out or at least mitigating structural disequilibria in the labor market. Beyond this, external efficiency is also affected by the existence of external benefits and costs of education and the way they are taken into consideration by the financing schemes. Finally, achieving greater harmonization of labor markets through avoiding or mitigating cobweb cycles and over- or underinvestment in recurrent education will also enhance the external efficiency of postcompulsory education and training.

ENCOURAGING INNOVATIONS

The third criterion aims at increasing the innovative potential of the recurrent education system. The regulatory and financing mechanisms of the existing postcompulsory education systems are said to prevent drastic innovations in education. Thus scrutinizing the impact of alternative finance systems on educational innovations will be of interest. Some innovations can be easily sold in the educational market place and aim at increasing the market value of human capital (marketable innovations). Others may have a low value in the market place, but they have high social value.

ENCOURAGING MARKETABLE SKILLS

Fourth, a recurrent education system may be designed and financed such that primarily marketable skills and knowledge will be produced while nonmarketable abilities are suppressed, or vice versa. Hence, it is important to assess whether or not financing models for recurrent education foster a system that primarily produces marketable or nonmarketable skills or both in an appropriate mixture.

ENCOURAGING INTEGRATION

One salient feature of current activities in both continuing education and present postcompulsory education is the segregation of vocational training and general education as well as the lack of coordination among the diversity of other educational activities. Recurrent education stresses a systems approach to all recurrent offerings, so it is important to know if the various financing schemes foster the coordination of recurrent postcompulsory educational activities in a holistic and systematic way. It would be desirable to achieve an integration of the present subsystems and offerings of postcompulsory education and training into one general module system of recurrent postcompulsory education and training (Edding et al., 1974: 22). This integration should not be confined to the matter of organization and coordination; it should also refer to the integration of theoretical knowledge and practical know-how as well as of general education and vocational training. This criterion will be called "encouraging integration."

ENCOURAGING INDIVIDUAL CHOICE AND PERSONAL DEVELOPMENT

There is wide agreement among critics that in most countries present educational institutions and processes are marked by authoritarian hierarchical decision structures dominated by the state bureaucracy that do not give any significant decision-making power or influence to their clientele. Virtually all proponents of recurrent education project a system of postcompulsory education and training that will be tailored to the individual needs of learners, most of whom will be adults with some work experience and with specific perceived needs (Lowe, 1975).

For this reason, the criterion of increased individual choice and freedom for the learners is an important one for recurrent education. Hence, the sixth criterion for evaluating the alternative financing mechanisms will be the extent to which individual choice and freedom will be enforced. Such choice should foster personality enrichment and self-development, self-determination and self-responsibility, self-independence and self-control, democratization of educational decisions, and individual participation in shaping recurrent education activities. This criterion will be referred to as "encouraging individual choice and personal development." But note that this criterion (as well as others) very well may be in conflict with other criteria, as will be shown later.

EQUALITY OF EDUCATIONAL OPPORTUNITY

The seventh criterion is to promote equality of educational opportunity and encourage the demand for recurrent education. Here, the question will be whether and to what extent alternative financing modes are likely to encourage participation in recurrent education activities. Although precise information on the contribution of different factors to the demand for postcompulsory education and training does not exist, the available information on recurrent education suggests that several types of variables have an influence on the demand for it (O'Keefe, 1977).

First, there are ascriptive factors like sex, race, ethnic origin, and age. Second, career and promotion perspectives are said to be important determinators of recurrent education demand. This argument refers to the position of the potential learner in the job ladder and the labor market segment in which he or she is situated. In this context, some researchers have introduced the terms "recurrent education value" or "recurrent education closeness" of the respective jobs and work content. A related component is job security or the obligation to reemploy persons who have interrupted their work to undertake recurrent education activities.

A third set of variables likely to affect the demand for recurrent education is related to social background. The most common of these variables seem to be the education, social status, profession, income, and wealth of both the potential learner's parents and the learner as well as the number and kind of recurrent education activities he or she has already experienced.

Fourth, from a human capital theory perspective, the expected economic and noneconomic benefits—that is, the improvement of income or the expected rate of return from an investment in recurrent education—should exert a major influence on the demand for recurrent education. Fifth, the attitude of individuals towards mobility and change might be an important variable of demand. So might the sixth factor, the organization of work with respect to shift work, part-time work, and flexible work-time schedules.

Seventh, the recurrent education activities themselves (their regulatory as well as informational systems) are said to be important in motivating or discouraging demand for recurrent education. Important characteristics in this regard are as follows: the duration of recurrent education units, their contents and curricula, their module character, time schedule (during the day, evening, or weekends, and block or sequential), the regional distribution and the local distance of the recurrent education institutions, the variety of courses with respect to the clientele and their diverse interests, the mode of regulation of access, eligibility and admission rules, the degree of participation and learner influence on the activities, and the certification of performance and transferability of credits. The latter is likely to be of great importance as long as certificates are a prerequisite for entering career tracks and for promotion.

Finally, it is believed widely that the form and amount of financial contribution has a very strong impact on the willingness and ability of individuals to participate in recurrent education. The less the potential participants have to contribute out of their own pockets or through income foregone (at present in fees or in the future through loans) and the higher the subsidies, the more likely they are to demand postcompulsory education and training activities (Jackson and Weatherby, 1975). Encouraging additional demand for recurrent education is seen as an important criterion for assessing the impacts of diverse financing proposals. The view that it is desirable that the demand for recurrent education should behave in an anticyclical fashion reinforces this social perspective. The goal is that when demand for labor is low there will be more participation in recurrent education, and vice versa. Anticyclical behavior in the demand for recurrent education would not only relieve the labor market but also the public budget: It would reduce the need for unemployment compensation during recessions as well as avoid or mitigate "withdrawal effects" (losses of economic growth) in boom phases. Hence, it seems worthwhile to analyze the degree to which the financing schemes in question do initiate or enforce a specific demand behavior as to economic cycles.

Alternative financing mechanisms for recurrent education can affect the demand for recurrent education in two ways: first is the extent to which the potential participant has to pay for the education and has to forego income during the education period; second is variations in the types of recurrent education activities engendered that may result from different financing schemes. In comparison, social background and labor market as variables affecting the demand for recurrent education seem to be least alterable through different funding modes. The criteria of equality of educational opportunity and demand for recurrent education will be referred to as "encouraging demand for recurrent education" and "increasing equality of participation in postcompulsory education and training," respectively.

SOCIAL AND ECONOMIC EQUITY

The eighth criterion is that of "social and economic equity." It is comprised of a number of related aspects. The first one is equity among regions in the distribution of recurrent activities. The second facet has to do with equity of the financial burden between individuals, social classes, and generations, which brings up the "ability-to-pay" versus "pay-as-you-use" controversy. The third concern is directed towards equity of financial support for individuals, social classes, and generations, and the next means equity in the distribution of skills, education, and training between and within generations as well as equivalency of general education and vocational training. Finally, some researchers call for equity of financial and nonfinancial benefits of income, as well as of career outcomes and life chances between and within generations. All these different aspects of equity will be called "equalizing the distribution of recurrent education implications."

DEMOCRATIZATION OF EDUCATION AND WORK

The ninth criterion that is widely discussed in the literature and should be taken into consideration is "democratization" of education and work. However, as employment is beyond the reach of schemes for financing recurrent education, we aim at democratization of education alone, excluding the dominance of particular interests (Edding et al., 1974: 27). Furthermore, we should evaluate whether financing recurrent education models encourages activities and processes in postcompulsory education and training that are likely to endanger or enforce the social cohesion and integration of different social classes, races, or ethnic groups.

Some politicans and researchers are also concerned with the extent to which different financing schemes are likely to increase the total costs of education as well as specifically the burden upon the public budget. These concerns will be considered as the eleventh and twelfth criteria, respectively.

ALTERNATIVE MECHANISMS OF FINANCING POSTCOMPULSORY EDUCATION AND TRAINING

Six basic models for financing a recurrent system of postcompulsory education have been suggested in the past:

model 1: self-financing
model 2: drawing rights
model 3: entitlements (vouchers)
model 4: single-employer financing
model 5: parafiscal funds
model 6: state financing

Three of these models (the drawing rights model by Rehn, the entitlements model by Levin, and the parafiscal funds model by Clement) are presented in this volume. As the other three models (the self-financing model, the single-employer financing model, and the state financing model) have not yet been introduced and may be new to the reader, they will be described briefly before being evaluated.

The impacts of these financing models on recurrent education will be discussed with respect to the criteria introduced above. The discussion is followed by a matrix scheme that will show the impacts of the alternative financing mechanisms on the criteria. This scheme should also allow for a cautious comparison of the impacts of the various models that can then be used to draw some prudent conclusions as to what financing mechanism (a pure or a mixed one) seems to be most promising. These conclusions will clearly depend on value judgments with respect to the weight of the various criteria as well as to the assessment of the impacts; thus each weight-assessment system is likely to come to different conclusions. Hence, the choice or construction of a specific financing scheme for recurrent postcompulsory education and training is not possible without strongly involving personal and political preferences and judgments—in other words, without elements of arbitrariness.

THE SELF-FINANCING MODEL

A system of self-financing recurrent education requires individuals to pay for their own postcompulsory education and training out of their own resources. This can be achieved in a threefold manner: using up former savings, expending current income, or paying through loans which will be repaid out of future earnings. Individuals are assumed to consider themselves as consumers of and investors in recurrent education. In a free educational market, private producers would offer recurrent education services in order to make profits.

Yet it seems unlikely that this kind of free market provision for recurrent education would help meet the objectives that were implied by the preceding criteria. First, there is no reason why the recurrence of education and the alternation of work and education or training should be encouraged in a free market system of education to any considerable extent. Recurrent education is likely to increase the labor costs for employers; hence, they will prefer cheaper (i.e., traditional) forms of education and training, and so the demand for recurrent education by the mass of workers is not likely to emerge.

Second, pressure for internal efficiency can be expected to increase remarkably as consumers insist upon getting efficient services for their money and competition among producers forces them to look for cost-minimizing production. Thus, the production of recurrent education will tend to focus on the short run (and be more expensive for the demanders in the long run) and new production functions may reduce the production to only marketable outputs (i.e., to outputs that have a market value in the first place for the educational firm as well as for the demander). Those outputs that are not of value in the market but are of great value for society are more likely to be ignored.

Given a short-run orientation of a free-market system of recurrent education, overall external efficiency is not likely to improve very much either. First of all, as a response to structural or technological unemployment, recurrent education activities can be expected to be only reactions to unemployment—it is very likely that the motive of prevention will be absent. Second, the short-run market orientation of postcompulsory education will not help to increase flexibility in the labor force and the labor market; instead cobweb cycles of over- and underproduction of specific qualifications in various educational and labor markets are likely to prevail. Moreover, external effects of recurrent education will not be internalized at all, and in the long run private monopolies may emerge within the educational industries.

With respect to innovations, it can be expected that new educational technologies will be developed and used for recurrent education in a free-market system such that the internal efficiency of the education industry will increase as asserted above. Also, innovations in subjects, teaching contents, teaching methods, and so forth will emerge. However, these innovations are likely to be limited to marketable ones rather than be applied to those of high social import but little private demand.

As one consequence, the recurrent education system will focus on the improvement of marketable skills, whereas general education will be neglected widely. However, the integration of general education and vocational training as well as of the various activities of adult and further education in a recurrent education system will be encouraged, and the links between theoretical knowledge and practical know-how are likely to be strengthened (at least within postcompulsory vocational education).

There is no doubt that a free-market and self-financing system of recurrent education will strengthen and widen individual choice and freedom (Friedman, 1962; Coons and Sugarman, 1978; West, 1964) and consumer sovereignty. This will allow for a much broader variety of postcompulsory educational activities than is witnessed at present. It is likely that those broader activities will be shaped more to the specific needs of the buyers of recurrent education. But note that some inefficiencies can also result from individual choices based on individual purchasing power and preferences. First, there is the problem of imperfect information that may lead to "bad" or "wrong" decisions. Second, there is the problem of the short-run orientation in making choices: According to Bohm-Bawerk's law of time preference, the individuals' time preferences tend to overestimate present consumption with respect to a quick pay-off and to underestimate future benefits. This disposition implies a number of consequences which have already been mentioned above: short-run and quick pay-off demands for recurrent education, focus on marketable skills, cobweb cycles in the educational sector as well as in partial labor markets, and underinvestment in recurrent education.

Moreover, we would expect a self-financing system of recurrent education to have a detrimental effect on the demand for postcompulsory education relative to the effects of the subsidies offered by the present system. The increase in direct costs would discourage demand, particularly among disadvantaged and "education-distant" groups. We cannot foresee whether incentives created by increases in career and promotion possibilities, job security, and the "recurrent-education value" of work will occur and encourage demand for recurrent education.

Finally, demand for postcompulsory education and training seems very likely not to behave anticyclically with respect to the business cycle. Those laid off in phases of recession will lack the necessary resources to be able to bear the financial burden of paying for the direct cost of education. Many of those still employed who might be interested in pursuing recurrent education measures are likely to refrain because they may fear losing their jobs. Hence, most of the potential clientele for postcompulsory education and training can be expected to participate in recurrent education in periods of economic prosperity when the labor markets are tight and jobs rather secure. However, during such periods of full employment or even overemployment, withdrawal effects (output foregone) would be high, and wage as well as price pushes might occur in the wake of scarce labor. Generally, from an investment perspective, rational behavior would induce individuals not to postpone their education and training. Rather, to enjoy the maximum pay-off it would seem advisable to demand education in the early years as much as possible in order to get a high entry-level job and then receive on-the-job training afterwards (Stoikov, 1975).

Another important question is whether the self-financing (free-market) model of postcompulsory education and training would tend to reduce social and economic inequality. In this respect there is little reason to be optimistic. A free-market system would tend to enforce the disparities in the regional distribution of recurrent education activities such that the great bulk of offerings would be found in urban areas, where purchasing power and demand is concentrated, rather than in rural areas. Without subsidies,[2] the price of recurrent education, family income, and the expected return from the investment in recurrent education will be the main economic variables determining demand behavior.[3] *Ceteris paribus,* more recurrent education will be demanded by individuals of higher income. Individuals will demand postcompulsory education and training as long as they can pay for it. Therefore, the distribution of demand for recurrent education will probably mirror the present distribution of income rather than be more equal.

The drawing rights model as proposed by Rehn would use social security accounts to enable individuals to finance recurrent education as well as pensions and other periods out of the labor market. Inequal educational opportunities and life chances are very likely to continue from generation to generation. Also, equity of general education and vocational training will not be achieved.

Moreover, democratic participation in the decision and power structures of education as well as in the employment system will not be increased. The market mechanism is likely to reproduce these structures such that powerful interests in the economic sector will tend to dominate the choice of individuals. Self-financing and a market system in recurrent education also may lead to a higher degree of social stratification of the population and to social norms and values that might endanger social cohesion in the long run. While the total cost burden for education might decline substantially in such a financing system, the public sector would, of course, be relieved completely from the burden of financing postcompulsory education and training.

THE DRAWING RIGHTS MODEL

Before going into some detail on the drawing rights approach, two remarks seem necessary. First, the evaluation of the model depends to a great extent on the knowledge of the supply system of recurrent education. Rehn's model restricts itself to the demand side (the principles of raising, administrating, distributing, and using up the drawing rights from, among, and through potential demanders) but says nothing about the supply side of postcompulsory education and training. In particular he leaves open whether recurrent education activities should be offered in a free market by private firms, exclusively in a regulated market by state institutions, or in a partly regulated mixed market of private and public supplies (obviously, the latter currently prevails in most countries).

The structure and ruling principles of the supply system are of great importance for the way in which a recurrent education system functions, and hence for an assessment of it. Since Rehn stresses the freedom and responsibility of individuals for their own lives and the liberation of individuals from the bureaucratic state, it seems logical to assume that a free-market supply system fits best into his financing model. Hence, the completed model is basically a free-market system of postcompulsory education and training, differing from the self-financing model in one major way: Individuals are free to save for later consumption of or investment in recurrent education in the self-financing case, while in the drawing rights system individuals are forced to save a certain amount of their current income in order to acquire drawing rights which they then are free to use (for recurrent education or other activities). The basic contradiction in Rehn's model can be put as follows: Why should individuals gain more freedom for themselves by being forced to save? Why not allow them to decide whether to save or not and, if so, what amount to save?

Second, Rehn's model describes primarily a labor market strategy rather than an educational policy. However, the model can obviously be extended to serve as a strategy for financing recurrent education. The problem here is that Rehn tends to reduce the financing issue to solely a matter of bookkeeping. By doing so he overlooks the fact that shifting a financial amount from one account to another may induce substantial changes in the behavior of the respective account owners.

Generally, the drawing rights model is in many ways very similar to the self-financing model. That is why the following evaluation has been placed closed to the preceding one and, hence, can be shorter. Again, there is no reason to believe that a recurrent alternation of work, education, leisure, and training would emerge solely through the free-market forces. Within a free-market approach to recurrent education, alternation of work and education is more likely to be achieved through collective agreement or legislative actions rather than solely through the market forces which are independent of the way postcompulsory education is financed (i.e., whether through self-financing, drawing rights, or entitlements). As in the self-financing model, recurrent education programs will develop as a response to the respective demand. However, as drawing rights depend directly on earnings, the power for purchasing recurrent education will be distributed as unequally as earnings are. In addition to the remarks in the preceding evaluation, large quality differences within recurrent education are likely to occur in a free-market supply system.

Two other important issues are those of underinvestment in recurrent education and of equality of opportunity and life chances. First, it seems that underinvestment in recurrent education is very likely within the self-financing model. The drawing rights solution will also lead to that tendency because it does not restrict the use of the drawing rights to recurrent education but allows for leisure, early retirement, sabbaticals, vacation, and other activities too. We can expect that a great number of individuals will not use their drawing rights for education and training.

Second, the drawing rights model implies a strong relationship between earnings and the ability to pay for postcompulsory education and training. Earnings being distributed unequally, the opportunity to spend on recurrent education is also distributed unequally. Hence, those with high earnings accumulate more drawing rights than low-earners and are able to purchase more recurrent education. If education affects future earning power, those with high present earnings can increase their future earnings through recurrent education much more than those with low incomes. This mechanism will widen the inequality of educational opportunity as well as of the income distribution. Moreover, we can expect high-earners to be more likely to use their drawing rights for recurrent education than low-earners, who might use most of their drawing rights for leisure, vacation, and so on. Thus, inequality of education and of life chances would increase.

High earners who use most of their drawing rights for recurrent education while they are in their 20s and 30s will not only enjoy growing earnings but also a growing stock of drawing rights from these earnings. This will enable them to enjoy more leisure, sabbaticals, and other types of free time in their 40s and 50s. Moreover, the unemployed are not able to accumulate drawing rights during the unemployment period. This fact reduces their power to purchase recurrent education in the future. Finally, while the public budget will not be burdened in this model, it is impossible to estimate whether the total costs for education would increase or decrease. It is important to note that subsidies might be used to supplement drawing rights in meritorious cases such as those of the poor, as Rehn suggests.

THE ENTITLEMENT MODEL

The entitlement proposal has been introduced and discussed by Levin in this volume. Essentially, the government would guarantee a specified sum or entitlement for each citizen at the end of postcompulsory schooling that could be used for recurrent education. Like the two preceding models the entitlement scheme is a free-market model for the supply of postcompulsory education and training. The main difference lies again on the demand side. While demanders have to raise the budget for recurrent education totally out of their own resources (in the first case voluntarily, in the second case by requirement) in the preceding models, the entitlement solution requires the state to raise most of the financial resources. The state, then, has to transfer these resources to the individuals in the form of entitlements. These individuals are obliged to use them only for postcompulsory education and training but are free to choose among various suppliers.

The main characteristic of the model is the redistribution of income. This can occur through a system of finance that provides larger entitlements to the poor while requiring lower tax contributions from them. Again, as there are a number of similarities resulting from the free-market characteristics of both preceding models, the focus will be on the criteria in which substantial differences occur. Generally, as with the first model, efficiency gains will not be high except those resulting from competition and from a better-integrated approach to recurrent education.

The main effect of the entitlement solution may be the improvement of equality of educational opportunity and social equity. It should be clear that the strength of this effect depends on the size of the entitlement, its composition of grants and loans, and the incidence of the tax system. It seems safe to state that the higher the entitlement and the lower the loan component, the more demand there will be for recurrent education from disadvantaged groups and the less inequality there will be in educational opportunity. We can at least imagine an entitlement system in which educational opportunities and life chances are distributed rather equally. This would include the economic and noneconomic benefits of recurrent education as well as the distribution of skills, knowledge, education, and training within and between generations. However, that system is still likely to focus on vocational training, although this orientation may be weaker than in the two preceding models. The entitlement system is very likely to increase the total costs of education as well as the educational burden of the public budget.

THE SINGLE-EMPLOYER FINANCING MODEL

This model can be seen to be an extension of the on-the-job training system as well as of the apprenticeship system. Within this model, there are two investors: private or public employers who offer their own recurrent education activities to their employees (or apprentices) or pay for comparable activities offered by the (private or public) educational industry, and the employees who invest in their human capital through these activities. Both the employer and the employee enjoy a return on these investments in the resultant productivity growth: The employee experiences an increase of earnings, and the private employer experiences a higher profit. Also, the public employer is assumed to produce better (more productive) services (Becker, 1975: 15-80). Both parties are likely to pay for recurrent education in this system. The employer's expenses are for the direct educational costs and the subsistence of those employees engaged in full-time recurrent education; the employee foregoes income during the training periods and may be paid below his or her marginal productivity afterwards.

It is an open question whether this financing mechanism would encourage a recurrent alternation of work, education, and training. This would depend primarily on the needs of employers for such alternation and, beyond that, on collective agreement or legislative action. However, the educational activities in this system are very likely to be reduced to specific postcompulsory training (as expressed by Becker, 1975: 26) as employeers will aim at capturing the returns to postcompulsory training while trained employees could improve their earnings by changing employers (Mattern, 1979: 122). However, specific recurrent training seems very likely to restrict the mobility of employees: Such mobility might conflict with macroeconomic goals of encouraging shifts from declining industries to expanding ones. Hence, single-employer profitability calculations very well may conflict with labor market needs and reduce the external efficiency of the recurrent education system even though internal efficiency for a particular employer can be expected to be high (Sadowski, 1980: 5).

Employers will probably minimize the necessary time and cost needed for a certain amount of education and training. Moreover, it is likely that the single-employer financing mechanism will induce employers to seek a quick return by placing learners in productive work during their education and training period. Firms that are able to gain net returns from education and training through paying lower wages during the training period will be stimulated to train more individuals than they will be able to employ afterwards. This has been found to be true for most firms in the craft sector in West Germany (Mattern, 1979: 123; Sachverständigenkommission Kosten und Finanzierung, 1974: 93). Also, the large quality differences and the short-run orientation towards specific marketable outputs with respect to labor market changes indicate that a reactive (rather than preventive) policy of recurrent training prevails.

The single-employer financing systems can be seen to suffer from substantial external efficiency losses. Not only may individual profitability calculations conflict with labor market needs regarding the quality and quantity of recurrent training, employers who offer training will enjoy a significant competitive edge over those who do not (Sachverstandigenkommission Kosten und Finanzierung, 1973: 32).

A general tendency of underinvestment in recurrent education can be expected. Overinvestment in areas with positive (high) net benefits during the training periods will occur, while those areas with high net costs probably will be characterized by underinvestment in recurrent training. The inclination of these branches to invest in recurrent training will decline particularly in recession periods, while branches with net benefits will be induced to expand these investments by substituting cheap trainees for expensive workers. Moreover, those who are trained in net-benefit branches that do not find a job there probably will be able to find employment only in an unskilled or semiskilled position within another branch, thus their investment in recurrent training will not pay off. Inflexibility of the trained, cobweb cycles in the markets for trainees, overinvestment in one set of branches, underinvestment in others, a general tendency toward underinvestment, and competition biases will produce structural misallocations in the education and training market as well as in the labor market.

Another serious problem is that the unemployed would not be able to participate in recurrent education. Also, since innovations can be expected to respond to employer-specific marketable offerings, general, political, and cultural education will not be addressed by this financing system. Integration of general education and vocational training also will not be encouraged, while individual choice will be strengthened. There will be only a restricted range of educational offerings, mainly of specific training, and choices will be influenced substantially by employers.

It is hard to see how demand for postcompulsory education and training would be encouraged in this system, and particularly not that of disadvantaged groups. Career and promotion perspectives, job security, and recurrent-education value of work will not be affected to a substantial degree. Employers would restrict postcompulsory education activities to their economic needs. Restricted participation in recurrent education is not likely to reduce inequality in the distribution of skills and knowledge, of education and training between and within generations, of the distribution of career outcomes, or in the distribution of financial and nonfinancial benefits. The individual financial burden of trainees and individual financial support by employers may be subject to large variations. Sectoral, regional, and quality differences are likely to exist, and (an even more serious problem) the system is likely to imply a redistribution of burden and benefits in favor of those who can undertake the postcompulsory education and training activities. By means of a general wage reduction to below marginal productivity, by regressive tax-reduction incidence in the case of tax-deductible training costs for employers, as well as by the shift of training costs to the consumers, all workers and employees (as workers, consumers, and taxpayers) will pay for recurrent training but only a minority will profit. More concretely, those who remain unskilled or semiskilled workers or employees will help to finance the recurrent education of the skilled workers and of highly qualified workers. Hence, a redistribution from those with less recurrent education to those with more training is very likely to take place in the single-employer financing model. As in the first two models discussed, a polarization between qualified and unqualified manpower seems likely to develop. The dominance of particular employers' interests will prevail in the range of offerings. Total costs for education are not likely to increase, and the public budget will only be burdened in the case of tax reduction for training costs.

THE PARAFISCAL FUNDS MODEL

The finaincing mechanism of parafiscal funds has been analyzed in length by Clement in this volume. As should be clear from his analysis, in such a solution private and public employers are required to pay a levy on total wages (a payroll tax) or on value added into a funds system. The funds system can be organized into a central fund or a system of decentralized funds; the criterion of decentralization being alternatively professions, regions, or branches. (For discussion of the funds solution with respect to the German apprenticeship system and these alternatives see Hegelheimer, 1977; *Sachverständigenkommission Kosten und Finanzierung,* 1974: 245; Sadowski, 1980).

There are two possibilties of funding postcompulsory education and training within the model. One—which has not been discussed at all up to now—is an entitlement or voucher version. Under such a solution, the funds would transfer vouchers to employees at the beginning of their careers. Employees would be free to ask for recurrent education in those participating institutions and firms. Those institutions would be reimbursed for their training expenditures by redeeming the vouchers with the funds. The alternative possibility is direct institutional funding: The institutions and firms participating in the funds advance the expenditures themselves and are compensated directly from funding resources according to the regulations.

The parafiscal funds system has a number of favorable characteristics with respect to our criteria, although some serious problems remain. Generally, the funds system can be expected to encourage recurrent alternation of work, education, and training, and to initiate flexible work and nonwork schedules more than any of the models discussed before because a political will for establishing a recurrent education system within the funds is likely to develop. Comprehensive postcompulsory education and training programs may emerge. These programs would not only focus on specific short-run, marketable education and training, but would also stress general education, a long-run orientation toward training, and diversity. Hence, recurrent education could be freed from the cost-benefit calculations of single employers. Internal efficiency of recurrent education within training firms is likely to be high, although the funds may involve time-consuming and costly decision processes as well as high administrative costs, particularly for centralized funds.

As to external efficiency, ultimately postcompulsory education and training under parafiscal funds very likely will raise the flexibility of the labor force, and hence may contribute to the prevention of structural or technological unemployment. Structural disequilibria in the labor market are likely to be mitigated, and productivity gains can be expected.

However, there may be some aspects that would reduce efficiency. Different results may arise between labor-intensive and capital-intensive employers in favor of the latter, as well as between large and small firms in favor of the former. Differing abilities to shift the levy on to the consumers by raising prices will not only boost inflation but also will create new competition distortions. The expectation that the funds revenue will change in cadence with the business cycle (Hegelheimer, 1977: 102) seems attainable as the funds could accumulate a surplus in boom periods in order to support sufficient postcompulsory education and training in recession periods. This could contribute to steady development of recurrent education. But it is hard to foresee whether and (if so) why the funds system would be able to avoid cobweb cycles in recurrent education and the structural misallocations produced by them.

Innovations in postcompulsory education and training will be high within a funds system and will include nonmarketable innovations as the innovational risk will be shared by all institutions and firms. Moreover, by setting certain quality standards for the provision of general and specific education and training, not only marketable skills and knowledge will be improved significantly but also the general, political, cultural, and social qualifications that are desired by the members of the fund. The fund system may also encourage integration of general education and vocational training, theoretical knowledge and practical know-how, and various activities in adult and further education into the recurrent education system.

The major weakness of the parafiscal funds model is its inability to encourage demand for recurrent education and to diminish the inequality of participation in postcompulsory education and training, particularly with respect to disadvantaged groups, as long as job structures, job contents, and employment hierarchies remain unchanged. As long as job security does not exist and the recurrent-education value of work is not achieved for these groups (i.e., for the great majority of employees), the parafiscal funds system will suffer from the "law of participation" mentioned above. Another problem will be the fact that young people leaving the compulsory schooling sector and not finding an entry job, will be excluded from recurrent education.

With respect to the equity issue, the parafiscal funds model will not fare much better than the preceding models, with the exception of the entitlement solution. While the inequality of general education and vocational training might be lessened, and while the inequity in the regional distribution of recurrent education activities might be done away with completely through affirmative actions of the funds (Mattern, 1979: 128), the issue of inequality of educational opportunity and of life, income, and career chances is very likely to remain acute for the very same reasons presented in the context of the single-employers financing model. Through shifting the levy back on wages of all employees, forward on prices for all consumers, and, in the case of tax-reduction possibilities, forward to the tax payers, all employees and workers are condemned to bear the financial burden as wage-earners, consumers, and tax payers while probably only a minority will benefit (at least as long as the "participation with respect to demand law" is effective). Hence, there will be a redistribution over time of income from those who do not participate or who participate only a little in recurrent education to those who participate intensively. More concretely, the disadvantaged (the unskilled and semiskilled, the poor, women, blacks and ethnic minorities, and foreign workers) will pay for the postcompulsory education and training of skilled workers (white men) and particularly of highly qualified manpower. This redistribution effect could be overcome through self-financing contributions or income-contingent loans— funds that could make recurrent education available to those interested in taking part.

While the funds system would not necessarily increase individual choice for trainees, the funds system is likely to exclude the dominance of a particular employers' interest by establishing a kind of group democracy of trainees, employers, unions, parents, educators, and the state (Mattern, 1979: 129). However, this democratic participation in decision processes concerning recurrent education would be restricted to the administration of the funds and would not include the training activities themselves. On the other hand, a polarization between the trained and untrained parts of the labor force and between the disadvantaged and advantaged groups may emerge and grow within a funds system. While it seems difficult to see whether the total costs of education would increase in such a system, the public budget would be substantially relieved by shifting the largest part of the costs for postcompulsory education and training from the state budget to funds budget(s).

THE STATE FINANCING MODEL

The term "state financing model" may seem ambiguous in that the entitlement approach could also be understood to be a state financing mechanism because it is the state who issues the vouchers and redeems them (i.e., supplies the money). However, contrary to the entitlement approach, our state financing model assigns two functions to the state: first, that of financing postcompulsory education and training (as does the voucher approach); second, the function of producing and providing education and training through public institutions (which the entitlement approach does not do). This functional difference between the two models generates a number of differences in their impacts. Hence, our state financing model turns out to be a model for state finance and production of recurrent education. It extends the education monopoly of the state (which prevails in many countries in the schooling and higher education sector) to the whole postcompulsory education and training realm. Such a system could introduce a radically different system of education. The following is a description of one possible method.

(1) Compulsory schooling begins at the age of 6 for each individual and ends after having participated in a comprehensive school system at age 16 with the first high school diploma (high school diploma I). This would qualify a person for both work and for attendance in the second phase of high schools.

(2) The phase of postcompulsory education and training is organized according to the recurrent education concept. One becomes eligible attending the second phase of high school by earning the high school diploma I and accruing a minimum of four years of work experience. By way of exception, only extremely talented persons may be allowed to skip the work experience (in order to recruit scientists). The second high school phase ends after two or three years with the diploma II which again qualifies the individual for work and study. Admission to higher education is only possible for persons with diploma II or for those with diploma I and seven years of work experience. The attendance of high schools in the second phase and of institutions of higher education is possible on either a part time or full-time schedule.

(3) High schools and higher education institutions offer a highly stratified variety of education and training possibilities. These are developed in response to the various needs of individuals according to their work experience, their interests, and their educational prerequisites. Institutions of higher education carry out postgraduate studies in order to recruit young scientists.

(4) The state is the sole agent to offer all education and training activities during compulsory and postcompulsory education and training.

(5) The state bears all direct and indirect costs of education and training through the public budget.

(6) Each person with diploma I (i.e., who has completed compulsory education with success) gets a quota of "life education hours" or "points" in order to keep the demand for recurrent education within reasonable limits. These points can be used according to individual plans and preferences during the postcompulsory period. Only unemployed persons with specific characteristics (e.g., long unemployment) are restricted as to their freedom of choice: Unemployment compensation will be paid on the condition that one takes part in postcompulsory training activities.

(7) The state alone is responsible for the training and recruitment of teachers and trainers as well as for the size, structure and contents of education and training.

(8) Responsibility for the educational system forces the state to undertake research in qualification, technology, education, training, and the labor market in order to be able to carry through a plan of recurrent education. State planning of education is the dominant mechanism of allocation within the system of financing and producing recurrent education through the state.

Such a system could encourage the recurrent alternation of work, education, leisure, and training, and promote a general flexibility of work and nonwork time. Moreover, the integration of general education and vocational training and of theoretical knowledge and practical know-how would be likely to occur. Also, participation of the population in recurrent education can be comprehensive and equitable. Quality differences can be expected to be low, while the minimum standards of general education probably would be high. However, performance in vocational training might not satisfy employers. The regional distribution of activities would be equal, and social cohesion would generally be strengthened (Lowe, 1975: 44).

But note that a comprehensive high standard may imply uniformity instead of variety, and boredom rather than diversity. This characteristic may conflict with the postulate for more individual choice in education. Moreover, the federal structure of the state may be seen to endanger comprehensive solutions while it is feared that state responsibility for all kinds of education and training will reinforce the alienation between education and training on the one side and work on the other (Hegelheimer, 1978; Oberhauser, 1970: 27). We may also question the ability of this financing system to restrain the dominance of particular state interests in favor of the democratic participation of learners (Edding et al., 1974: 131).

The impact of the state financing solution on the efficiency of the recurrent education system is hard to estimate. Improvements of internal as well as innovational efficiency are unlikely to be substantial because of a lack of stimuli and of efficient possibilities of control, and also because of political and bureaucratic slowness in decision processes (Friedman, 1962; Levin, 1976; Weizsacker, 1975). External efficiency effects seem to be more complex: Efficiency may improve by internalizing external effects; these gains, however, may be lost through overinternalization—that is, encouraging overinvestment in recurrent education through a zero-price offer, creating a divergence between private and social rates of return (Friedman, 1962).

While we would expect the coordination between the education and employment systems to improve because of the productivity and flexibility of recurrently educated people and because of preventive training strategies, these efficiency gains may be compensated for (if not nullified entirely) by global and structural misallocations and misplanning by the state resulting from a lack of necessary information or political quarrels. Moreover, business cycles may destabilize recurrent education activities over time, and short-run interests of politicians are likely to cut resources for education in times of growing financial stress. Furthermore, recurrent education may become a victim of political conflicts and political cycles (Widmaier, 1976: 81; Downs, 1972).

The state financing model allows realization of social objectives in recurrent education (Edding et al., 1974: 127)—for example, equality of educational opportunity or similar equity principles—more than other models do. Through the progressivity of the tax system, the financial burden created by recurrent education can be redistributed to the benefit of those with low income. However, the basic question of whether the tax system actually can be constructed to work progressively is hard to answer. Apart from this problem, the lack of direct charges for recurrent education, new and flexible structures for work time, and attractive programs may suffice as incentives to attract those disadvantaged individuals and groups who are said to be education-distant today. Thus the possibility of enforcing equality of educational opportunity and of redistributing economic burdens and benefits in favor of the poor and disadvantaged supports the state financing model. In addition, the model could be extended by income-contingent loans or self-participation of those who are well-off in the case of a nonprogressive tax system. Finally, it seems very likely that such a model would increase the total costs as well as the state budget for education. This may again raise the question of an upper limit for the state budget.

CONCLUSIONS

The evaluation of the different financing mechanisms shows that none of the "pure" models can attain all of the goals. Each is characterized by deficiencies, although they are different for each model. This difference in deficiencies makes a comparison of the models very hazardous, particularly when this comparison is intended to identify the "preferable" financing mechanism. The assessment suggests a general trade-off between economic and noneconomic criteria (i.e., between efficiency and equality or social cohesion)—this trade-off becoming more significant to the degree that individuals are expected to finance recurrent education out of their own resources.

One way to determine the "best" financing system is to comprise a cost-utility analysis for each alternative model. First, this analysis would have to ask specifically which model is most able to meet each particular criterion. Each system would be evaluated on its ability to do the following: to maximize external and internal efficiency, minimize structural misallocations and efficiency losses, internalize external effects, maximize the quality of educational output and guarantee minimum quality standards, maximize innovation efficiency, minimize inequality of opportunity, maximize individual choice, prevent both underinvestment and overinvestment in recurrent education, minimize social and economic inequality, encourage demand for recurrent education, (particularly from disadvantaged groups and classes), maximize democratization and social cohesion, encourage integration, and so forth.

Second, in the course of such an analysis specific weights expressing the preferences of researchers, politicians, and others would have to be assigned to each criterion. This procedure would allow one to establish a definite order among the financing mechanisms and determine which is the "best" one. However, it is likely that there will be as many different orders and "best" financing modes as there are different preference structures.

My own evaluation of the impact of the various financing schemes suggests that a proper financing scheme for recurrent postcompulsory education should focus on entitlement, parafiscal funding, and state financing. These models seem to have a stronger impact on those criteria that should be met by a financing system of recurrent education than do the self-financing, the drawing rights, and the single-employer financing models. However, as the favorable models suffer from serious deficiencies as well, it seems obvious that we should attempt to construct a financing scheme that is composed mainly of various elements of the preferred models, but that capitalizes on their advantages while avoiding their deficiencies as much as possible.

A MIXED MODEL FOR FINANCING POSTCOMPULSORY EDUCATION AND TRAINING

The mixed model of financing recurrent education (model 7) should start with the assumption that the individual learner, the individual employer (public and private), and society in general will accrue monetary and nonmonetary economic as well as noneconomic benefits from postcompulsory education and training. Therefore, individuals, employers, and the state should pay for postcompulsory education and training. However, the extent to which each of these audiences should pay is open to discussions and political dispute since there is no knowledge of the distribution of these benefits among the individual learner, employers, and the society. In order to encourage demand for recurrent education, the contributions of individuals should strictly follow the "ability-to-pay" principle. The basic features proposed for this mixed model of financing recurrent education (model 7) are as follows:

(1) A parafiscal fund will be established, and all public and private employers will be required to contribute to this fund by a levy on their value-added. (A further question is whether a central fund or decentralized funds should be utilized. This question will not be discussed here.)

(2) The state pays a certain amount of tax money into the fund, for example as a fixed proportion of the state budget, with the proportion changing over time as needed. The fund will be administered by an agency, which is governed collectively by representatives of the state, employers' unions, and nonunionized laborers.
(3) Postcompulsory education and training is produced and offered by private as well as state institutions. Both have to meet high minimum standards of program quality and diversity in order to be accredited by the fund.
(4) The fund issues entitlements to every person who has completed compulsory schooling. Everyone is free to use the entitlements for any education or training activities in accredited institutions over their lifetime. The use is limited to recurrent education activities. Completion of compulsory schooling is the only prerequisite for admission.
(5) The entitlements consist of a basic grant for each eligible person and a dual component beyond the basic grant. The dual component generally consists of a grant and a loan element. The partition between the two elements depends on the ability of the eligible person to pay (i.e., based on income and wealth considering family responsibilities). This means that the grant (or loan) component decreases with increasing ability-to-pay (income and wealth), and vice versa, such that a disadvantaged low-income person may enjoy a full grant entitlement while an advantaged person who is more able to pay is likely to be supplemented in the form of a loan. Each person is free to pay out of present resources and refrain from using a loan.
(6) One becomes obligated to pay back a loan on reaching a specified income (for example, one that exceeds the income of a person without recurrent education).

This mixed financing system is likely to develop a comprehensive integrated system of recurrent education and recurrent alternation of education, work, leisure, and training as well as flexible work-time schedules. High minimum standards of output quality as well as a good diversity of programs that are tailored to the interests and needs of the learners seem very likely to emerge. Internal efficiency as well as efficiency in innovation are likely to increase, the latter with respect to nonmarketable as well as to marketable innovations The labor force will gain flexibility whereby labor market disequilibria very well may be prevented. An anticyclical investment strategy may prevail, and external effects will be internalized but not to the point of overinternalization. While the labor force will gain productivity, general over- or underinvestment may be avoided. General knowledge and specific mar-

TABLE 5.1 Impact of Financing Models on Recurrent Education

Criteria	Model 1 vl	l	p	nl	c	Model 2 vl	l	p	nl	c	Model 3 vl	l	p	nl	c	Model 4 vl	l	p	nl	c	Model 5 vl	l	p	nl	c	Model 6 vl	l	p	nl	c	Model 7 vl	l	p	nl	c
Encouraging recurrence				x			x					x						x			x							x							
Increasing efficiency internal	x		x				x					x					x					x		x			x					x	0		
external		0	0					x				0							0	0				x		0	0					x			
Encouraging innovation	x	0							0			x					x					x						x			x				
improving general knowledge				x					x				0				x		0				x	x			x		0				x		
improving marketable skills	x						x					x					x					x						x				x			
Encouraging integration									x					x			x		x			x						x				x			
Increasing individual choice	x			x			x					x						0	0													0	0		
Encouraging demand for RE and increasing equality of participation				x								x								x				x				x							
Decreasing social and economic inequality				x				x				0	0						x					x		0	0					0	0		
democratization				x				x					x						0	0				x			0	0					x		
Preservation and the enforcement of social cohesion				x					x						x			x					x				x							x	
Increasing total costs of education				x					0	0		x							0	0							x					x			
Increasing state budget burden for education				x	0				0	0		x							0	0				0	0			x						x	

1 = Self-financing model
2 = Drawing rights model
3 = Entitlement model
4 = Single-employer financing model
5 = Parafiscal funds model
6 = State financing model
7 = Mixed financing model

x = impact seems clear
0 = impact seems not very clear; either/or

vl = very likely
l = likely
p = possible
nl = not likely
c = contrary

ketable skills will improve within a system that is able to integrate general education, vocational training, theoretical knowledge, and practical know-how.

The entitlement component will enhance individual choice, and state and employers' participation in decision processes is likely to promote social cohesion. Demand for recurrent education will be stimulated, particularly among disadvantaged groups, because there will be no direct charge for recurrent education for those with less ability-to-pay, and also because we may expect strong efforts to change the job structure in order to increase the recurrent-education value of work.

The distribution of education and training as well as knowledge and skills will probably become more equal across regional and generational distinctions. Moreover, burdens and benefits will be distributed less unequally such that an overall drop in the extent of social and economic inequality would be likely. Furthermore, the dominance of particular interests will be broken and be replaced by democratic participation of all relevant social groups and institutions. While the total costs of education and training will increase, under such a system the state budget could be relieved. Generally, this financing model is likely to require the least trade-off between efficiency and equality. Apart from the problems of designing a financing method as well as the regulatory and information systems in detail, and leaving aside the problems of implementation, the mixed model (model 7) seems to be the most promising alternative. This can be seen in Table 5.1, which gives a summary of the model evaluations.

NOTES

1. All criteria are drawn from the literature on recurrent education. The sequence of introduction does not reflect priorities. Various references with respect to the objectives of recurrent education are to be found in Bengtsson and Schutze (1979); CERI (1973); Clement and Sauerschnig (1978: 12); Levin (1977, 1980) Mattern (1979: 9). More specific criteria have been proposed by Edding (1974), and Edding et al. (1974); and recently by CERI (1982), and Schutze (1982). The system of social indicators of performance of educational systems developed by the OECD (1973) is very detailed but has not been tailored to the needs of a recurrent education system. It has been constructed for the purpose of international comparisons in education rather than for comparing alternative financing models.

2. This is true only for public support. Private support (grants) by firms or other institutions might occur but is likely to remain an exception rather than the rule.

3. It does not seem very likely that loans will have a strong effect on demand (Mattern, 1979: 83).

REFERENCES

BECKER, G. (1975) Human Capital. Second edition. (New York and London: Columbia University Press).
BENGTSSON, J., and H. G. SCHÜTZE (1974) "Developments in recurrent education and recent economic and social trends," in W. Clement and F. Edding (eds.) Recurrent Education und Flexibilitätsforschung. Berlin.
BLAUG, M. (1970) An Introduction to the Economics of Education. London: Viking.
——— (1967) "Approaches to educational planning." Economic J. 57: 262-287.
CERI/OECD (1982) The Costs and Financing of Recurrent Education. Paris: Author.
——— (1979) Recurrent Education for the 1980s: Trends and Policies. CERI/CED (79) 12; ED (79) 16. Paris: Author.
——— (1973) Recurrent Education: A Strategy for Lifelong Learning. Paris: Author.
CLEMENT, W., and R. SAUERSCHNIG (1978) Empirische Grundlagen und Konzepte einer Bildungsfinanzierungspolitik in Österreich (Empirical Foundations and Concepts of a Policy for Financing Education in Austria). Vienna: Vertschafts verlag Dr. Anton Orac.
CLEMENT, W., and F. EDDING [eds.] (1979) Recurrent Education und Flexibilitatsforschung (Recurrent Education and Flexibility Research) Berlin: Dunker and Humblot.
COHN, E. (1975) The Economics of Education. Cambridge, MA: Ballinger.
COONS, J. E., and St. D. SUGARMAN (1978) Education by Choice: The Case for Family Control. Berkeley: Univ. of California Press.
DOWNS, A. (1972) "Up and down with ecology: The 'issue-attention-cycle'," The Public Interest 28 (Summer).
EDDING, F. (1976) "Ökonomische probleme des recurrent-education-konzepts," ("Economic Problems of the Concept of Recurrent Education") Jahrbuch für Wirtschafts— und Sozialwissenschaften, Heft 4: 287-301.
——— (1974) "Higher education in a future system of universal recurrent education," Paedagogica Europaea 9, 2.
——— (1974) "Educational Leave and Sources of Funding," in S. J. Mushkin (ed.) Recurrent Education. Washington, DC: NIE, U.S. Department of Health, Education, and Welfare.
EDDING, F., U. BOEHM, G. DYBOWSKY, and H. RUDOLPH (1974) Struktur und Finanzierung der Aus-und Weiterbildung (Organization and Finance of Continuing Education and Training). Gottingen: Verlag Otto Schwartz and Co.
FREEMAN, R. B. (1977) "The decline in the economic rewards to college education." Rev. of Economics and Statistics 59 (February) 1.
——— (1976) The Overeducated American. New York: Academic Press.
FRIEDMAN, M. (1962) Capitalism and Freedom. Chicago: Univ. of Chicago Press.
GLENNY, L. A. "Financing postsecondary education in the USA." Higher Education 5, 1: 103.
HANSEN, W. L., and B. A. WEISBROD (1969) Benefits, Costs and Finance of Public Higher Education. Chicago: Markham.
HEGELHEIMER, A. (1977) Finanzierungsprobleme derr Berufsausbildung (Problems of Financing Vocational Training). Stuttgart: Klett-Cotta Verlag.

JACKSON, G. A. and G. B. WEATHERSBY (1975) "Individual demand for higher education: a review and analysis of recent empirical studies." J. of Higher Education 46, 6: 623-652.

JENCKS, C. et al. (1972) Inequality: A Reassessment of the Effect of Family and Schooling in America. New York: Random House.

O'KEEFE, M. (1977) The Adult Education and Public Policy. Palo Alto, CA: Aspen Institute for Humanistic Studies..

KRELLE, W., M. FLECK, and H. QUINKE (1975) Gesamtwirtschaftliche Auswirkungen einer Ausweitung des Bildungssystems: Abschlussbericht (Macroeconomic Effects of an Expansion of the Educational System: Final Report). Tubingen: Verlag J.C.B. Mohr and Paul Siebeck.

——— (1974) Gesamtwirtschaftliche Auswirkungen von Änderungen der beruflichen Ausbildung und Weiterbildung (Macro-Economic Effects of Changes in the System of Initial and Continuing Training). Bielefeld: Bertelsman Verlag.

KUHLENKAMP, D., and H. G. SCHUTZE [eds.] (1982) Kosten und Finanzierung der beruflichen und nicht-beruflichen Weiterbildung (The Costs and Financing of Continuing Education and Training). Frankfurt Main: Verlag Moritz Diesterweg.

LEVIN, H. M. (1980) Individual Entitlements for Recurrent Education. Paris: OECD, CERI.

——— (1977) "Post-secondary entitlements: an exploration," p. 1 in N. D. Kurland (ed.) Entitlement Studies. NIE Papers in Education and Work 4. Washington, DC: U.S. Department of Health, Education, and Welfare.

——— (1977) "Financing recurrent education with post-compulsory entitlements." Stanford, CA: Stanford University, School of Education.

——— (1976) "Concepts of economic efficiency and educational production," in J. T. Froomkin et al. (eds.) Education as an Industry. Cambridge, MA: Ballinger.

——— (1975) "Educational vouchers and educational equality," in M. Carnoy (ed.) Schooling in a Corporate Society. New York: Longmans.

LOWE, J. (1975) The Education of Adults. Paris: Unesco Press.

MATTERN, C. (1979) Bildungsfinanzierung: Probleme unds neue Ansätze (Financing Education: Problems and New Approaches). Frankfurt-Berlin-München: Verlag Moritz Diesterweg.

MINCER, J. (1974) Schooling, Experience, and Earnings. (New York: Columbia Univ. Press.

MUSHKIN, S. J. [ed] (1974) Recurrent Education. Washington, DC: NIE, U.S. Department of Health, Education, and Welfare.

OBERHAUSER, A. (1970) Finanzierungsalternativen der beruflichen Ausund Weiterbildung (Alternative Financing Schemes for Initial and Continuing Training). Stuttgart: Klett Verlag.

OECD (1977) Learning Opportunities for Adults, Vol. I-IV. Paris: Author.

——— (1973) Indicators of Performance of Educational Systems. Paris: Author.

PECHMAN, J. A. and B. A. OKNER (1974) Who Bears the Tax Burden? Washington, DC: The Brookings Institution.

PFAFF, M., and G. FUCHS (1975) "Education inequality and life income: a report on the Federal Republic of Germany," p. 7 in OECD (ed.) Education Inequality and Life Chances, Vol. 2. Paris: OECD.

REHN, G. (1978) Towards a Society of Free Choice. Stockholm: Swedish Institute for Social Research.

——— (1974) "Towards flexibility in working life." University Q.: 276-286.

Sachverständigenkommission Kosten und Finanzierung der ausserschulischen beruflichen Bildung: Abschlussbericht (Expert Commission on Costs and Financing of Non-School-Based Vocational Training: Final Report) [1974]. Bonn.

Sachverständigenkommission Kosten und Finanzierung der beruflichen Bildung: Zwischenbericht der Kommission (Intermediate Expert Commission Report) [1973]. Bonn.

SADOWSKI, D. (1980) "Finance and governance of the German apprenticeship system: some considerations on market failure and its efficient corrections." Stanford, CA.

SCHÜTZE, H. G. (1982) "Das OECD-Konzept 'Recurrent Education' und Kriterien fur die Finanzierung lebenslangen Lernens" ("The OECD concept of recurrent education and criteria for financing lifelong learning") in D. Kuhlenkamp and H. G. Schütze (eds.) Kosten und Finanzierung der beruflichen und nicht-beruflichen Weiterbildung (The Costs and Financing of Continuing Education and Training). Frankfurt Main.

STOIKOV, V. (1973) "Recurrent education: some neglected economic issues," International Labour Rev. 109: 187-208.

THUROW, L. C. (1975) Generating Inequality: Mechanics of Distribution in the U.S. Economy. New York: Basic Books.

TIMMERMANN, D. (1982) "Das Staatsfinanzierungsmodell als Finanzierungsalternative fur Recurrent Education" ("The state financing model as an alternative to financing recurrent education") in D. Kuhlenkamp and H. G. Schütze (eds.) Kosten und Finanzierung der beruflichen und nicht-beruflichen Weiterbuldung (The Costs and Financing of Continuing Education and Training). Frankfurt Main.

―――― (1979) Bildungsmarkte oder Bildungsplannung: eine kritische Auseinanderstzung mit swei alternativen Stuerungssystemen und ihren Implikationen fur das Bildungssystem (Educational Markets or Educational Planning: A Critical Review of Two Alternative Regulatory Systems and Their Implications for the Educational System). Erweitertes Manuskript des Habilitationsvortrags vom 20.6. Bielefeld.

WEIZSACKER, C. C. v. (1975) "Hochschulstruktur und Marketsystem" ("The structure of higher education and the market system") in U. Lohmar and G. E. Ortner (eds) Die deutsche Hochschule Zwischen Numerus clausus und Akademikerarbeitslosigkeit. Der Doppelte Flaschenhals (The German University and the Double Bottleneck of Limited Access and Graduate Unemployment). Hanover-Dortmund-Darmstadt-Berlin: 306.

WEST, E. G. (1964) "Private versus public education: a classical economic dispute." J. of Pol. Economy 5 (October): 465-475.

WIDMAIER, H. P. (1976) Sozialpolitik im Wohlfarhtsstaat (Social Policies in the Welfare State). Reinbek: Rowohlt Tachenbuch Verlag GmbH.

WINDHAM, D. M. (1976) "Social benefits and the subsidization of higher education: a critique." Higher Education 5, 3: 237.

II

FINANCING RECURRENT EDUCATION IN THE UNITED STATES

6

AN INVENTORY OF PROGRAMS AND SOURCES OF SUPPORT

ALAN P. WAGNER

In 1980, 50 million individuals in the United States participated in at least 1 type of organized postsecondary learning activity, at a total cost of $55 billion. While the actual numbers are imprecise, the volume of and investment in learning beyond high school are impressive. The purposes of this chapter are to estimate the participation in different types of postcompulsory education and training programs in the United States, to compare the costs of and funding for these activities, and to consider differences in the attributes of participants among programs.

As sources of improvements in the productive capacities of workers, all postcompulsory education and training programs merit the attention of policy makers. The more detailed focus on the different types of education and training is important for several reasons. First, efforts to improve productivity through post-high school education and training may be less successful if public policies ignore sources of training outside of postsecondary educational institutions. Beyond identifying the available sources of training, the comparison may reveal which providers tend to be most efficient in producing trained manpower. Second, eligibility for public subsidies might be extended to nontraditional programs as a means of reaching those most in need

AUTHOR'S NOTE: *The author appreciates the helpful comments and suggestions of* R. Anderson, R. Boaz, W. Bruno, C. Byce, R. Calvert, T. Chase, B. Clayton, J. Green, A. Sinaiko, P. Smith, *and* F. Woods.

of training (such as the disadvantaged or the older worker with technically obsolete skills).

For the purposes of this article postcompulsory education and training programs are identified as those that include any formal, organized sessions of instruction. The definition excludes self-directed study, on-the-job training, and programs designed to transmit information only. Even with this restriction, the numbers must be regarded as "order of magnitude" estimates, principally because the data, culled from several published and unpublished sources, are inconsistent and, in some instances, quite dated.

I begin with a discussion of the enrollments in different types of postcompulsory education and training programs. Estimates of the costs of, and sources of funding for, these programs are considered in the next section, and a discussion of differences in the attributes of participants among the programs follows. The last section presents several implications for public policy.

VOLUME AND TYPES OF PROGRAMS

Estimates of the number of participants in postcompulsory education and training programs vary. The Carnegie Commission (1973) estimated that 74 million individuals participated in some organized learning activity in 1970 (projected to 108 million in 1980). This is reasonably close to the ETS estimate of 62 million learners for 1972 (Carp et al., 1974), but much higher than the 27 million reported in companion census surveys (NCES-sponsored Survey of Adult Education and the Census Bureau's own October school enrollment surveys). More recently, Peterson and others (1979) estimated the participation in organized post-high school education and training at 64 million. My own estimate, for 1980, is 75 million (see Table 6.1), although this figure (and the others) probably overstates the unduplicated count of participants by about 30%.

What types of education and training programs are chosen? During 1980, nearly 58% of the enrollees attended programs other than those offered at postsecondary education institutions. This finding is consistent with Peterson's estimate as well as figures cited by Smith (1973).

This and other interesting dimensions of current postcompulsory education and training programs emerge from the detailed distribution of participants by source of program in Table 6.1. As in other studies, the programs shown here are defined largely in terms of the *provider* (such as a four-year college or a tutor). Broschart (1977), among others, notes that this approach is but one of several ways of categorizing postcompulsory education and training.[1] The inventory of programs by provider, however, permits some comparisons with previous studies, reveals some differences in costs of and sources of funding for essentially identical training, and, in some cases, also distinguishes among types of education and training programs. To allow additional comparisons by type of program and funding, I have extended the general approach in two ways. First, estimates of participation by "type of program" (such as full-time, part-time, and noncredit study) are presented for some providers since differences in the type of course and the characteristics of participants are obvious. Second, some essentially similar programs offered within major employment sectors (private business or industry, armed forces, government) are considered separately, since these represent major providers of training.

Although good descriptions of the types of programs appear elsewhere (Fraser, 1980; Peterson et al., 1979; Calvert, 1977), several of the participant estimates merit emphasis. First, to better reflect the level of resources required to provide postcompulsory education and training, the participant data have been converted to equivalent class hours for each program. These estimates are shown in the last two columns of Table 6.1. Here, contrary to the distribution of participants, providers other than postsecondary educational institutions account for less than 30% of the total class hours devoted to postcompulsory education and training. Clearly, much of the training outside of postsecondary educational institutions is less extensive (fewer courses per participant) and relatively short term (fewer hours). As a result, those attending courses at postsecondary educational institutions spend over 200 hours in class, on average, while their counterparts receiving training from other providers average less than 100 hours in class.

Second, part-time (including correspondence) and noncredit enrollments represent about two-thirds of the 31 million enrolled in all postsecondary educational institutions. According to these figures, although full-time enrollment of 7.9 million students at a four-year institutions clearly dominates, part-time and noncredit enrollments represent a sizable proportion of this sector's clientele. These observations become all the more significant when viewed in light of recent enrollment trends: full-time enrollments rising at about 1% per year, part-time enrollments at about 6% per year, and noncredit enrollments (regis-

TABLE 6.1 Participation in Postcompulsory Education and Training Programs by Source, 1980

	Participants Number[a] (thousands)	Percentage	Participant Class Hours Number (millions)	Percentage
TOTAL	74,850	100.0	8,950	100.0
POSTSECONDARY EDUCATIONAL INSTITUTIONS	31,350	41.9	6,350	71.0
Four-Year Colleges and Universities				
Full-Time	7,900	10.6	2,600	29.0
Part-Time	3,500	4.7	525	5.9
Non-Credit	3,100	4.2	75	.8
Two-Year Colleges				
Full-Time	2,000	2.7	650	7.3
Part-Time	2,700	3.6	350	3.9
Non-Credit	3,450	4.6	100	1.1
Vocational				
Full-Time	600	.8	450	5.0
Part-Time	3,000	4.0	550	6.1
Proprietary				
Full-Time	600	.8	450	5.0
Part-Time	3,000	4.0	550	6.1
Correspondence (civilian)	1,500	2.0	50	.6
OTHER POSTCOMPULSORY EDUCATION AND TRAINING	43,500	58.1	2,600	29.0
Elementary and Secondary Schools	2,400	3.2	150	1.7
Business or Industry				
Apprenticeships	700	.9	100	1.1
Other organized instruction (off-the-job)	7,400	9.9	400	4.5
Professional Associations	5,500	7.3	125	1.4
Labor Unions	100	.1	25	.3
Armed Forces				
Initial training	1,050	1.4	500	5.6
Other organized instruction	750	1.0	150	1.7
Correspondence	1,000	1.3	50	.6
Prisons	75	.1	25	.3
Other Government Programs				
Manpower training	975	1.3	325	3.6
Cooperative extension	5,100	6.8	75	.8
Other organized instruction (off-the-job)	1,300	1.7	75	.8

(continued)

TABLE 6.1 Continued

	Participants		Participant Class Hours	
	Number[a] (thousands)	Percentage	Number (millions)	Percentage
Other Organized Programs (churches and synagogues, community organizations, libraries and museums, etc.)	16,000	21.4	575	6.4
Tutors	1,150	1.5	25	.2

SOURCES: Numbers represent best estimates, using published available data from census, private association, agency, and other surveys. Rounded to nearest 25 thousand of million. See text.

a. Overstates number of participants by about 30% due to multiple program enrollments.

trations) at about 7% per year over the 1976-1978 period (NCES, 1980; Dearman, 1980).

Third, nearly 15% of all participants in postcompulsory education and training receive off-the-job, classroom instruction provided by employers.[2] Although the estimates are "best guesses," these programs train 7.4 million persons in the private sector, plus 1.8 million in the armed services, plus 1.3 million in the public sector (federal, state, and local). According to Lusterman (1977) and the U.S. Office of Personnel Management (1980), this training takes place on or near the job site and tends to be job related.

Fourth, federal, state, and local governments *directly* provided postcompulsory education and training to over 25 million individuals in 1980. In addition to the armed forces and public employee training just discussed, the programs are quite diverse: adult and vocational education at elementary and secondary schools, CETA vocational training for the disadvantaged and unemployed or underemployed workers, a growing set of education programs in prisons (particularly at the postsecondary level), cooperative extension meetings, and programs of public community organizations, libraries, and museums. These programs are examined in more detail in other studies (see, for example, Congressional Budget Office, 1980b; Bell et al., 1979; U.S. Department of Agriculture, 1980; Kay, 1974; Peterson et al., 1979), but the nature and range of the learning activities should be obvious.

COSTS AND SOURCES OF FUNDING

In 1980, the instructional costs of postcompulsory education and training programs exceeded $55 billion (see Table 6.2). Although the figures are not strictly comparable, the Carnegie Commission (1973) estimated the 1970 costs at $28 billion. The 1980 figure excludes the indirect costs of the participants' time. If these are included, the total exceeds $100 billion in instruction and individual time resources devoted to post-high school education and training.

Selected measures of instructional costs by source of program are shown in Table 6.2. Particularly for programs provided outside educational institutions, the figures represent "best guesses." Again, however, some broad generalizations are possible.

First, the largest share of total cost, by far, appears in four-year colleges and universities ($24.5 billion, or 43.4% of the $56 billion expended). Perhaps the single most important reason for this result is the relatively high number of participant class hours at these institutions. In fact, over 70% of the dollars for postcompulsory education and training are spent by postsecondary educational institutions.

Second, employer-sponsored, off-the-job training programs account for over $11 billion in instructional costs, or about 20% of the total. In particular, private industry spent $7.2 billion for classroom instruction at the job site. The armed forces allocated over $2.8 billion for initial training and $8 billion for advanced instruction at military installations and schools. Instructional costs for government employee training came to an estimated $.6 billion in 1980.[3] One should recall that these cost figures *exclude* employee wages. From the employer's point of view, the wages of trainees represent a sizable part—perhaps as much as 50%—of the costs of their training programs.

Third, sizable differences emerge in direct costs per participant and per participant class hour. These figures control, to some extent, for the size of the programs offered by each provider, and hence give a better indication of differences in the cost of providing training. However, even these cost measures conceal important differences. For example, the high cost per class hour in postbaccalaureate study has been averaged with relatively low cost per class hour in noncredit courses. Further, flight programs in proprietary or vocational schools, or in the armed forces, tend to be considerably more expensive than other programs offered by these providers.[4]

Even with the "concealed" differences, the range of instructional costs per student is revealing: from $2675 for initial training in the armed forces to about $1700 in four-year college and university programs to less than $100 per participant for extension, tutored, and other organized community programs.[5] Differences remain even when costs are measured per participant class hour, although the ranking of providers is somewhat altered. University or four-year college programs run almost $8.00 per hour compared to $5.00-$5.50 in armed services training. Principally because few class hours are required, correspondence courses are estimated to cost over $18.00 per hour. This finding is also consistent with the Carnegie Commission's (1973) estimate for 1970.[6]

How are these costs of instruction met? Data on all sources of funding for all providers are quite sketchy, but enough information exists to suggest relative differences among programs in sources of funding. The amounts from each funding source used to meet the costs of instruction for each provider are shown in Table 6.3. Public funding consists of: (1) appropriations made to the provider from federal, state, or local governments; (2) grants and scholarships awarded through federal, state, or local government programs; and (3) tax expenditures for tuition aid, charitable contributions, and spending for training (private providers only). Private sources of support include: (1) employer tuition aid and expenditures on in-house training (net of tax expenditures); (2) other support derived from charitable giving (net of tax expenditures), or through nonprofit organizations; and (3) out-of-pocket spending by participants and their families (a residual). Many of the published figures on sources of support for individual programs were adjusted to include only the amounts used to defray instructional costs. Thus I have attempted to exclude, among others, the wage costs of participants (and the employers' support of these costs), and student aid used primarily to support living costs. Obviously, these adjustments required strong, somewhat arbitrary assumptions.[7] Given these cautions, several useful patterns in sources of funding emerge.

Taken together, public funding (including tax expenditures) provides $34.2 billion, or about 60% of the total cost of instruction of postcompulsory education and training programs in 1980.[8] Even though the larger amount of this public subsidy ($24.0 billion) is allocated to postsecondary educational institutions, the *share* of instructional costs met through public funding for nonpostsecondary school providers (61% of the $16.9 billion expended) is about the same as in the postsecondary education sector.

However, wide differences in the form of the public subsidy do appear. Postsecondary educational institutions receive $18 billion in institutional appropriations, compared to a little over $7 billion allocated to other providers. Even considering the larger costs of instruction in the postsecondary education sector, the difference is large: Institutional appropriations meet 49% of costs at the schools, while providing only 43% for other sponsors.[9] A similar difference in levels of support occurs in the distribution of student aid grants. Here, the $4.8 billion awarded to students meets 12% of instructional costs at postsecondary institutions. The $.05 billion in grants awarded to participants in nonschool programs represents less than a 1% share of costs.[10]

Third, the sectors also differ in the amount of support received from private sources. Here, almost 90% of the $5.4 billion provided by employers goes to support nonpostsecondary school programs of postcompulsory education. The $5.05 billion supporting these other providers of training meets 30% of the instructional costs in this sector. This also helps explain the $2.7 billion in tax expenditures ($2.5 billion for employer-provided in-house training alone), as private sector employers, treating training costs as a business expense, reduce their taxable income by the total cost of their programs.

Fourth, the share of all costs of instruction undertaken by employees primarily at their employers' expense exceeds $10 billion, or almost 20% of the total. Included here are all private sector employer spending ($5.4 billion), plus armed forces training (total: $4 billion), plus government employee in-house training (at $.6 billion).

Finally, some interesting differences emerge in sources of funding for different types of postsecondary education. University and four-year college programs meet about 40% of costs ($10.3 billion) through institutional appropriations, and perhaps 12% through public and private grants. At 2-year or vocational institutions, 70% to 80% of the funding ($3.9 billion and $3.4 billion, respectively) comes from institutional appropriations, with student aid grants and out-of-pocket family support accounting for another 15% each. This pattern is reversed for proprietary and correspondence school programs, where 80% to 85% of costs are met through the participants' own resources.[11]

CHARACTERISTICS OF PARTICIPANTS

Whether differences in public funding across providers serve to meet public policy goals depends, in part, on the extent to which particular types of individuals participate in the training. In Tables 6.4 through 6.8, participants are distributed by age, race, sex, employment status, income, and provider. These comparisons suggest which providers currently serve (or do not serve) potential target groups, and which programs are likely to grow or contract.

Differences in the distribution of participants by age suggest the providers that best meet the concept of recurrent education, and, importantly for policy purposes, which programs are likely to grow most rapidly through the 1980s. Table 6.4 presents the approximate age distribution of participants in each type of postcompulsory activity. From the estimates, those providers and programs serving the middle-aged group (age 35 to 54) include part-time postsecondary education (where 30% to 36% of the provider's participants come from this age group). Private employee in-house organized training, professional association training, and government employee in-house training draw even more heavily from the middle-aged group, accounting for 39% to 42% of the participants in these programs. As might be expected, younger learners represent the largest shares in full-time postsecondary education (ranging from 90% at four-year colleges and universities to 46% at proprietary schools), initial training in the armed forces (92%), and government manpower training (56%). Significantly, these programs serving younger age groups tend to utilize public funding, while the programs serving the middle-aged groups rely more heavily on private sources of funds.

Differences in the distribution of participants by race and ethnic group and by sex seem to indicate differences in the level of subsidy and in the type of training received by these groups. As shown in Table 6.5, although whites are heavily represented in postsecondary education, they also constitute a larger than proportional share in private employer in-house organized instruction (93%), professional association (94%), and public employee organized instruction (93%). On the other hand, blacks, accounting for 10% of the civilian adult population, tend to be more heavily represented in armed forces and government manpower training (at 16% and 34%, respectively). These training programs rely exclusively on public funding.

TABLE 6.2 Selected Measures of Instructional Costs of Postcompulsory Education and Training Programs by Source, 1980

	Total Cost[a] Dollars (millions)	Total Cost[a] Percentage	Per Program Participant[b] (in Dollars)	Per Participant Class Hour[c] (in Dollars)
TOTAL	56,475	100.0	750	6.25
POSTSECONDARY EDUCATIONAL INSTITUTIONS	39,600	70.1	1,275	6.25
Four-Year Colleges and Universities	24,525	43.4	1,700	7.75
Two-Year Colleges	5,675	10.0	700	5.25
Vocational Schools	4,300	7.6	1,200	4.25
Proprietary Schools	4,050	7.2	1,125	4.00
Correspondence Schools (civilian)	1,050	1.8	700	18.25
OTHER POSTCOMPULSORY EDUCATION AND TRAINING	16,875	29.9	400	6.50
Elementary and Secondary Schools	350	.6	150	2.75
Business or Industry Apprenticeships	350	.6	475	3.25
Other organized instruction (off-the-job)	7,200	12.7	975	18.00
Professional Associations	550	1.0	100	4.50
Labor Unions	25	*	225	7.25
Armed Forces Initial training	2,825	5.0	2,675	5.50
Other organized instruction	775	1.4	1,000	5.00
Correspondence	700	1.2	700	18.25
Prisons	100	.2	1,225	4.50
Other Government Programs Manpower training	1,475	2.6	1,500	4.75
Cooperative Extension	350	.6	75	5.75
Other organized instruction (off-the-job)	575	1.0	450	6.50
Other Organized Programs (churches and synagogues, community organizations, libraries and museums, etc.)	1,500	2.6	100	2.75
Tutors	100	.2	100	4.00

SOURCES: Numbers represent best estimates, using published available data from census, private association, agency, and other surveys. See text.
a. Rounded to nearest 25 million.
b. Rounded to nearest 25 dollars.
c. Rounded to nearest 25 cents.
*Less than .1%.

The differences in the distribution of participants by sex and provider (Table 6.6) suggest that women may be less likely to receive employment-related training than men. In particular, men make up the majority of participants in apprenticeship, professional association, and both private and public employee organized training. The latter programs are particularly important, since they may facilitate promotion in the company or agency. Elementary and secondary school, cooperative extension, and community-based programs—programs that are more likely to be avocational—enroll larger proportions of women.

Finally, participation in all programs tends to be linked to employment and income, as can be seen in Tables 6.7 and 6.8. However, those not working represent a majority of the participants in full-time study (50% to 70%) and in manpower training programs (96%). Similarly, over 90% of the trainees in government manpower training programs come from the lowest income quartile.

CONCLUDING REMARKS

The $55 billion spent in postcompulsory education and training programs in 1980 represents an important investment in probably the most important factor of production: human resources. Yet the data presented in this article suggest that sizable differences exist in the types of, costs of, and sources of funding for these programs. Three findings with broad implications emerge.

First, although over half of the participants enroll in programs offered outside of postsecondary educational institutions, the major portion of postcompulsory education and training costs are incurred in the postsecondary education sector. In part, this reflects the amount of participant time devoted to the learning activities. However, even though similar proportions of the instructional costs in both sectors appear to be met through public funding, this parity disappears when government-provided programs (armed forces, manpower training, public employee training) are separated out of the nonschool sector. This contrast suggests potential administrative and financial barriers to providing further education and training outside of schools. If these barriers were eased (through voucher or institutional funding), larger numbers of individuals might be able to participate in types of programs of particular importance to policymakers (such as job-related training provided by employers and professional associations).

TABLE 6.3 Costs and Sources of Funds for Postcompulsory Education and Training Programs, 1980

	Cost of Instruction (millions of dollars)	Public — Institutional Appropriation[a]	Public — Student Aid Grants[b]	Public — Tax Expenditure[c]	Employer[d]	Private Other[e]	Student and/or Family[f]
TOTAL	56,475	25,425	4,850	3,875	5,425	2,000	14,950
POSTSECONDARY EDUCATIONAL INSTITUTIONS	39,600	18,050	4,800	1,150	375	1,500	13,775
Four-Year Colleges and Universities	24,525	10,300	2,900	1,050	200	1,400	8,675
Two-Year Colleges	5,675	3,925	850	50	75	50	775
Vocational Schools	4,300	3,450	600	25	50	25	150
Proprietary Schools	4,050	275	400	25	50	25	3,725
Correspondence Schools (civilian)	1,050	100	50	—	—	—	—
OTHER POSTCOMPULSORY EDUCATION AND TRAINING	16,875	7,375	50	2,725	5,050	500	1,175
Elementary and Secondary	350	300	—	—	—	—	50
Business or Industry Apprenticeships	350	150	—	75	125	—	—
Other Organized Instruction (off-the-job)	7,200	—	—	2,525	4,675	—	—

Professional Associations	550	–	50	50	100	225
Labor Unions	25	–	–	–	25	–
Armed Forces						
Initial Training	2,852	2,825	–	–	–	–
Other Organized Instruction	775	775	–	–	–	–
Correspondence	700	700	–	–	–	–
Prisons	100	100	–	–	–	–
Other Government Programs						
Manpower Training	1,475	1,475	–	–	–	–
Cooperative Extension	350	350	–	–	–	–
Other Organized Instruction (off-the-job)	575	575	–	–	–	–
Other Organized Programs (churches and synagogues, community organizations, libraries and museums, etc.)	1,500	125	–	75	125	375	800
Tutors	100	–	–	–	–	100

SOURCES: Numbers represent best estimates, using published available data from census, private association, agency, and other surveys. Rounded to nearest 25 million; amounts less than 12.5 million are omitted. See text.

a. Includes institutional appropriations from federal, state, and local jurisdictions allocated to provider.

b. Includes public grants and scholarships awarded directly to students through basic grants, supplemental grants, state grants, and 25% of Veterans Administration benefits (an estimate of the proportion of VA benefits covering tuition and fees expenses). Tuition waivers are funded by institutional appropriations (and included there).

c. Tax expenditures consist of reduced tax liabilities resulting from private tuition-aid plans, corporate and individual support of educational and training programs, and the implicit tax subsidy for programs offered in private industry.

d. Includes support of tuition-aid, on-site training programs in the private sector, and programs offered by other providers, net of tax expenditures.

e. Includes corporate, nonprofit, and individual support of educational and training programs, either to institutions or to students (excluding tuition aid).

Second, with the aging of the U.S. population, participation in programs outside of postsecondary educational institutions will continue to increase at a faster rate than full-time postsecondary education enrollments. Here the growth of noncredit, community-based, and

TABLE 6.4 Participants in Postcompulsory Education and Training Programs by Age and Source, 1978 (in percentages)

	Total 17 Years and Over	17-24 Years	25-34 Years	35-54 Years	55-64 Years	65 Years and Over
TOTAL CIVILIAN ADULT POPULATION[b]	100	20	22	30	13	15
POSTSECONDARY EDUCATIONAL INSTITUTIONS						
Four-Year College or University						
Full-Time[a]	100	90	8	3	–	–
Part-Time[b,1]	100	17	47	30	5	1
Two-Year College and Vocational-Technical Institution						
Full-Time[a]	100	84	12	4	–	–
Part-Time[b,1]	100	26	36	30	6	2
Proprietary						
Full-Time[b,2]	100	46	33	18	2	1
Part-Time[b,1]	100	22	35	36	6	1
Correspondence[b,3]	100	19	39	33	7	3
OTHER POSTCOMPULSORY EDUCATION AND TRAINING						
Elementary and Secondary Schools (part-time)[b]	100	23	34	34	7	2
Business or Industry						
Apprenticeships	na	na	na	na	na	na
Other Organized Instruction (off-the-job)[b,4]	100	15	37	39	7	1
Professional Associations[b,5]	100	9	36	42	10	2
Labor Unions	na	na	na	na	na	na
Armed Forces						
Initial Training[c,6]	100	92	7	1	–	–
Other Organized Instruction	na	na	na	na	na	na
Correspondence	na	na	na	na	na	na
Prisons[d,7]	100	38	38	21	3	–
Other Government Programs						
Manpower Training[e]	100	56	27	10	3	–
Cooperative Extension[f]	100	13	25	29	16	10
Other Organized Instruction (off-the-job)[b,4]	100	15	37	39	7	1

(continued)

TABLE 6.4 Continued

	Total 17 Years and Over	17-24 Years	25-34 Years	35-54 Years	55-64 Years	65 Years and Over
Other Organized Programs[b,8] (churches and synagogues, community organizations, libraries and museums, free universities, etc.)	100	17	35	33	9	5
Tutors[b]	100	20	33	32	10	4

SOURCES:
   a. U.S. Bureau of the Census (1979c: Tables 6, 17, 19).
   b. Boaz (1980); based on those 17 years old and older.
   c. Defense Manpower Data Center (1980)
   d. Bell et al. (1979: 15-18); U.S. National Criminal Justice Information and Statistics Service (1979: Table 2; 1980: Tables 1, 2, 3, 6, 9).
   e. U.S. Department of Labor (1979: 20, Table 2); U.S. Department of Labor, Employment and Training Administration (1980a).
   f. U.S. Department of Agriculture (1980: Table 7); the Gallup Organization (1979).

1. Includes noncredit enrollments.
2. Based on respondents enrolled full time in an occupational program of more than 6 months.
3. Based on distribution of course registrations.
4. Based on "labor/professional organization" distribution.
5. Based on "labor/professional organization" distribution.
6. Based on distribution of accessions.
7. Based on distribution of prisoners.
8. Based on "private organization" and "other" distributions.

employer training programs might be expected. The role for public policy in this area is not clear. Public funding for these nontraditional programs might be channeled to sponsors or to students. A voucher scheme would put funds at the disposal of potential participants, removing at least part of the financing constraint. Further, educational institutions may be encouraged to continue to expand their offerings into these nonacademic program areas.

Finally, although the level of public funding is substantial, the distribution across programs and hence across subpopulations is far from even. Currently, the major proportion of public funding supports programs serving younger, minority, male, and employed participants. Opportunities for supporting other postcompulsory education and training activities clearly exist, and should be explored.

(notes begin on page 154)

TABLE 6.5 Participants in Postcompulsory Education and Training Programs by Race and Ethnic Origin and Source, 1978 (in percentages)

	Total	White	Black	Hispanic	Other
TOTAL CIVILIAN ADULT POPULATION[a]	100	83	10	5	2
POSTSECONDARY EDUCATIONAL INSTITUTIONS					
Four-Year Colleges and Universities					
Full-Time[b]	100	84	8	3	3
Part-Time[a,1]	100	91	5	2	2
Two-Year Colleges and Vocational-Technical Institution					
Full-Time[b]	100	76	13	6	5
Part-Time[a,1]	100	89	5	4	2
Proprietary					
Full-Time[a,2]	100	76	16	6	2
Part-Time[a,1]	100	90	5	4	1
Correspondence[a,3]	100	93	5	2	—
OTHER POSTCOMPULSORY EDUCATION AND TRAINING					
Elementary and Secondary Schools (part-time)[a]	100	82	7	8	3
Business or Industry					
Apprenticeships[c]	100	82	9	5	4
Other Organized Instruction (off-the-job)[a,4]	100	93	4	2	1
Professional Associations[a,5]	100	94	3	2	1
Labor Unions	na	na	na	na	na
Armed Forces					
Initial Training[d,6]	100	75	16	4	4
Other Organized Instruction	na	na	na	na	na
Correspondence	na	na	na	na	na
Prison[e,7]	100	51	37	10	2
Other Government Programs					
Manpower Training[f]	100	48	34	13	4
Cooperative Extension[g]	100	95	4	1	—
Other Organized Instruction (off-the-job)[h]	100	82	11	3	4

(continued)

TABLE 6.5 Continued

	Total	White	Black	Hispanic	Other
Other Organized Programs[a,8] (churches and synagogues, community organizations, libraries and museums, free universities, etc.)	100	93	3	2	2
Tutors[a]	100	95	1	2	1

SOURCES:
- a. Boaz (1980); based on those 17 years old and older.
- b. Dearman and Plisko (1980: Tables 3.5, 3.6).
- c. U.S. Department of Labor, Employment and Training Administration (1980b); data refer to registered apprenticeships (about 60% of the total).
- d. Defense Manpower Data Center (1980).
- e. Bell et al. (1979: 15-18); U.S. National Criminal Justice Information and Statistics Service (1979: Table 2; 1980: Tables 1, 2, 3, 6, 9).
- f. U.S. Department of Labor (1979: 20, Table 2); U.S. Department of Labor, Employment and Training Administration (1980a).
- g. U.S. Department of agriculture (1980: Table 7); the Gallup Organization (1979).
- h. U.S. Office of Personnel Management (1980: Charts 13, 15) and unpublished tabulations.

1. Includes noncredit enrollments.
2. Based on respondents enrolled full time in an occupational program of more than 6 months.
3. Based on distribution of course registrations.
4. Based on "business or industry" distribution.
5. Based on "labor/professional organization" distribution.
6. Based on distribution of accessions.
7. Based on distribution of prisoners.
8. Based on "private organization" and "other" distributions.

TABLE 6.6 Participants in Postcompulsory Education and Training Programs by Sex and Source, 1978 (in percentages)

	Total	Male	Female
TOTAL CIVILIAN ADULT POPULATION[a]	100	47	53
POSTSECONDARY EDUCATIONAL INSTITUTIONS			
Four-Year College or University			
Full-Time[b]	100	53	47
Part-Time[a,1]	100	45	55

(continued)

TABLE 6.6 Continued

	Total	Male	Female
Two Year College or Vocational-Technical Institution			
Full-Time[b]	100	50	50
Part-Time[a,1]	100	37	63
Proprietary			
Full-Time[a,2]	100	50	50
Part-Time[a,1]	100	46	54
Correspondence (civilian)[a,3]	100	68	32
OTHER POSTCOMPULSORY EDUCATION AND TRAINING			
Elementary and Secondary Schools (part-time)[a]	100	28	72
Business or Industry			
Apprenticeships[c]	100	97	3
Other Organized Instruction (off-the-job)[a,4]	100	62	38
Professional Associations[a,5]	100	56	44
Labor Unions	na	na	na
Armed Forces			
Initial Training[d,6]	100	87	13
Other Organized Instruction	na	na	na
Correspondence	na	na	na
Prisons[e,7]	100	96	4
Other Government Programs			
Manpower Training[f]	100	46	53
Cooperative Extension[g]	100	32	68
Other Organized Instruction (off-the-job)[h]	100	65	35
Other Organized Programs[a,8] (churches and synagogues, community organizations, libraries and museums, free universities, etc.)	100	35	65
Tutors[a]	100	27	72

SOURCES:
   a. Boaz (1980); based on those 17 years old and older.
   b. Dearman and Plisko (1980: Tables 3.5, 3.6).
   c. U.S. Department of Labor, Employment and Training Administration (1980b); data refer to registered apprenticeships (about 60% of the total).
   d. Defense Manpower Data Center (1980).
   e. Bell et al. (1979: 15-18); U.S. National Criminal Justice Information and Statistics Service (1979: Table 2; 1980: Tables 1, 2, 3, 6, 9).

TABLE 6.6 Notes Continued

  f. U.S. Department of Labor (1979: 20, Table 2); U.S. Department of Labor, Employment and Training Administration (1980a).
  g. U.S. Department of agriculture (1980: Table 7); the Gallup Organization (1979).
  h. U.S. Office of Personnel Management (1980: Charts 13, 15) and unpublished tabulations.

1. Includes noncredit enrollments.
2. Based on respondents enrolled full time in an occupational program of more than 6 months.
3. Based on distribution of course registrations.
4. Based on "business or industry" distribution.
5. Based on "labor/professional organization" distribution.
6. Based on distribution of accessions.
7. Based on distribution of prisoners.
8. Based on "private organization" and "other" distributions.

TABLE 6.7 Participants in Postcompulsory Education and Training Programs by Employment Status and Source, 1978 (in percentages)

	Total	Employed	Not Employed
TOTAL CIVILIAN ADULT POPULATION[a]	100	60	40
POSTSECONDARY EDUCATIONAL INSTITUTIONS			
Four-Year College or University			
Full-Time[b]	100	50	50
Part-Time[a,1]	100	87	13
Two-Year College and Vocational-Technical Institution			
Full-Time[b]	100	57	43
Part-Time[a,1]	100	77	21
Proprietary			
Full-Time[b]	100	42	58
Part-Time[a,1]	100	82	19
Correspondence (civilian)	na	na	na
OTHER POSTCOMPULSORY EDUCATION AND TRAINING			
Elementary and Secondary Schools (part-time)[a]	100	65	35

(continued)

TABLE 6.7 Continued

	Total	Employed	Not Employed
Business or Industry			
Apprenticeships[c]	100	100	–
Other Organized Instruction			
(off-the-job)[a,2]	100	91	9
Professional Associations[a,3]	100	94	6
Labor Unions[c]	100	100	–
Armed Forces			
Initial Training[c]	100	100	–
Other Organized Instruction[c]	100	100	–
Correspondence[c]	100	100	–
Prisons[d,4]	100	69	30
Other Government Programs			
Manpower Training[e]	100	4	96
Cooperative Extension[f]	100	30	70
Other Organized Instruction			
(off-the-job)[c]	100	100	–
Other Organized Programs[a,5] (churches and synagogues, community organizations, libraries and museums, free universities, etc.)	100	67	32
Tutors[a]	100	63	37

SOURCES:
- a. Boaz (1980); based on those 17 years old and older.
- b. Smith et al. (1980) and unpublished tabulations.
- c. Author's estimate.
- d. Bell et al. (1979: 15-18); U.S. National Criminal Justice Information and Statistics Service (1979: Table 2; 1980: Tables 1, 2, 3, 6, 9).
- e. U.S. Department of Labor (1979: 20, Table 2); U.S. Department of Labor, Employment and Training Administration (1980a).
- f. U.S. Department of Agriculture (1980: Table 7); the Gallup Organization (1979).

1. Includes noncredit enrollments.
2. Based on "business or industry" distribution.
3. Based on "labor/professional organization" distribution.
4. Based on distribution of prisoners prior to incarceration.
5. Based on "private organization" and "other" distributions.

TABLE 6.8 Participants in Postcompulsory Education and Training Programs by Family Income and Source, 1978 (in percentages)

	Total All Income Quartiles	Lowest	Lower Middle	Upper Middle	Highest
TOTAL CIVILIAN ADULT POPULATION[b]	100	23	28	28	20
POSTSECONDARY EDUCATIONAL INSTITUTIONS					
Four-Year College or University					
Full-Time[a]	100	17	21	26	35
Part-Time[b,1]	100	7	24	36	33
Two-Year College and Vocational-Technical Institution					
Full-Time[a]	100	26	26	25	22
Part-Time[b,1]					
Proprietary					
Full-Time[a]	100	36	28	20	15
Part-Time[b,1]	100	12	28	35	25
Correspondence (civilian)[a]	100	16	23	34	28
OTHER POSTCOMPULSORY EDUCATION AND TRAINING					
Elementary and Secondary Schools (part-time)[b]	100	14	27	32	27
Business or Industry					
Apprenticeships	na	na	na	na	na
Other Organized Instruction (off-the-job)[b,2]	100	6	23	37	34
Professional Associations[b,3]	100	5	18	34	33
Labor Unions	na	na	na	na	na
Armed Forces					
Initial Training[c,4]	100	91	8	1	–
Other Organized Instruction	na	na	na	na	na
Correspondence	na	na	na	na	na
Prison[d,5]	100	79	12	7	3
Other Government Programs					
Manpower Training[e]	100	91	9	–	–
Cooperative Extension[f]	100	18	25	30	27
Other Organized Instruction (off-the-job)[g]	100	12	27	41	20

(continued)

TABLE 6.8 Continued

Other Organized Programs[b,6] (churches and synagogues, community organizations, libraries and museums, free universities, etc.)	100	11	26	33	30
Tutors[b]	100	12	21	30	37

SOURCES:
a. U.S. Bureau of the Census (1979c: Tables 6, 17, 19).
b. Boaz (1980); based on those 17 years old and older.
c. Defense Manpower Data Center (1980).
d. Bell et al. (1979: 15-18); U.S. National Criminal Justice Information and Statistics Service (1979: Table 2; 1980: Tables 1, 2, 3, 6, 9).
e. U.S. Department of Labor (1979: 20, Table 2); U.S. Department of Labor, Employment and Training Administration (1980a).
f. U.S. Department of Agriculture (1980: Table 7); the Gallup Organization (1979).
g. U.S. Office of Personnel Management (1980: Charts 13, 15) and unpublished tabulations.

1. Includes noncredit enrollments.
2. Based on "business or industry" distribution.
3. Based on "labor/professional organization" distribution.
4. Based on distribution of accessions.
5. Based on distribution of prisoners prior to incarceration.
6. Based on "private organization" and "other" distributions.

NOTES

1. For example, one could distinguish between job-related and avocational training. Unfortunately, the available participant and cost data do not permit these comparisons. Whether the participant's "purpose" should influence public support for the activity is, of course, a policy decision. Current policies are somewhat contradictory, and indirectly applied. For example, college students enrolled less than half time are generally ineligible for federal financial aid (in part because they are presumably less serious about their schooling). On the other hand, local governments underwrite a substantial share of the costs for avocational programs sponsored by community organizations.

2. This estimate excludes employees attending college or university courses, professional association training, and labor union classes at the employer's expense (that is, "sponsored" by the employer). It includes courses taught by consultants or other instructors, as well as in-house training staff, provided that the course is conducted at or near the job site. Anderson et al. (forthcoming) caution that some employer-provided "courses" serve purposes other than training, including evaluation of personnel, dissemination of product information, and executive perquisites (particularly when the "training" occurs in exotic locales).

3. The figures here are imprecise, for two major reasons. First, many firms simply do not know how much they spend for training employees in-house. Second, the definitions of formal training differ: Some include on-the-job learning as well as off-the-job class-

room instruction. As part of a broader project on financing adult education, Anderson et al. (forthcoming) are attempting to measure costs of training programs in firms, unions, community organizations, and other sponsors. Their findings may help to gauge more accurately the level of investment in training outside of schools. See also Goldstein (1980) and Smith (1980).

4. Most postsecondary educational institutions also impose higher fees for flight programs. However, only a few colleges or universities now charge graduate students (or upper-division undergraduates) higher tuition than lower-division undergraduates. Anderson et al. (forthcoming) have found a wide variation in instructional costs per class hour among employee training programs.

5. The cost per student estimates given here differ from those reported elsewhere (Bowen, 1979; Hyde, 1976), since my enrollment figures include those attending degree or nondegree credit courses anytime during the calendar year (rather than only fall degree credit enrollments), and my instructional costs are limited to those allocated for instruction.

6. I also find that per hour instructional costs tend to be somewhat lower in proprietary school programs than for the roughly comparable offerings in vocational schools. See Wilms (1975) for a further discussion of this point.

7. An earlier version of this article included 50 appendices, which spelled out the assumptions made. The appendices are available, upon request, from the author. Several examples will illustrate key assumptions: (1) I allocated institutional appropriations to postsecondary institutions among the teaching, research, and service functions in proportion to their shares of expenditures. (2) Under student aid grants, I exclude all social security benefits, three-fourths of the Veterans Administration benefits paid to postsecondary training participants, and all proceeds from subsidized work or loan programs. As noted in the text, I am assuming that these funds go primarily to support living costs, rather than instructional costs. (3) In the area of private programs, I assume an average 35% corporate tax rate.

8. Across all programs, Christoffel (1978) has estimated that programs for which *adults* (age 25 and over) are eligible were budgeted at $14 billion in federal aid in 1977.

9. In part-time or continuing education programs, Anderson et al. (forthcoming) note large differences in the level of public institutional subsidies by type of course (for example, continuing education at medical schools versus part-time undergraduate study) and among states.

10. These grants would meet the costs of public sector employees participating in professional association training programs (teachers, government employees, and members of the armed forces).

11. These overall averages mask important differences in the receipt of student aid. As Wagner (1978), the Committee on the Financing of Higher Education for Adult Students (1974), and Van Dusen (1975) document, the part-time postsecondary student is less likely to receive aid.

REFERENCES

ANDERSON, R. E., E. S. KASL, J. R. APPEL, S. VARDEN, and L. WEINSTEIN (forthcoming) The Costs and Finance of Adult and Continuing Education in the United States. Lexington, MA: D. C. Heath.

BELL, R., E. CONRAD, T. LAFFEY, J. G. LUTZ, P. VAN REED MILLER, C. SIMON, A. E. STAKELON, and N. J. WILSON (1979) Correctional Education Programs for Inmates. Phase I Report. Washington, DC: Government Printing Office.

BROSCHART, J. R. (1977) Lifelong Learning in the Nation's Third Century. Washington, DC: Government Printing Office.

BOAZ, R. L. (1980) "Participation in adult education, 1978." National Center for Educational Statistics. (unpublished)

―――― (1978) Participation in Adult Education: Final Report 1975. Washington, DC: National Center for Educational Statistics.

CALVERT, R. , Jr. (1980) Noncredit Activities in Institutions of Higher Education for the Year Ending June 30, 1978. Washington, DC: National Center for Educational Statistics.

―――― (1977) "Participation in adult education: United States," in Learning Opportunities for Adults, Vol. IV. Paris: Organization for Economic Cooperation and Development.

Carnegie Commission on Higher Education (1973) Toward a Learning Society. New York: McGraw-Hill.

CARP, A., R. E. PETERSON, and P. J. ROELFS (1974) "Adult learning interests and experiences," in K. P. Cross et al. (eds.) Planning Non-Traditional Programs: An Analysis of the Issues for Postsecondary Education. San Francisco: Jossey-Bass.

CHRISTOFFEL, P. H. (1978) "Current federal programs for lifelong learning: a $14 billion effort." School Review 86 (May): 348-359.

College Board (1980) "Students may apply for more aid funds as a result of expanded eligibility guidelines." College Board News 8 (March): 6.

College Scholarship Service (1980) Student Expenses at Postsecondary Institutions, 1980-81. New York: College Board.

Committee on the Financing of Higher Education for Adult Students (1974) Financing Part-Time Students: A New Majority in Higher Education. Washington, DC: American Council on Education.

Congressional Budget Office (1980a) Tax Expenditures: Current Issues and Five-Year Budget Projections for Fiscal Years 1981-85. Washington, DC: Government Printing Office.

―――― (1980b) Youth Employment and Education: Possible Federal Approaches. Washington, DC: Government Printing Office.

CROSS, K. P. and A. ZUSMAN (1979) "The needs of nontraditional learners and the response of nontraditional programs," in C. B. Stalford (ed.) An Evaluative Look at Nontraditional Postsecondary Education. Washington, DC: Government Printing Office.

DEARMAN, N. B. nad V. W. PLISKO [eds.] (1980) The Condition of Education. Washington, DC: National Center for Educational Statistics.

Defense Manpower Data Center (1980) "FY79 officer and enlisted accessions." Unpublished tabulations. Defense Manpower Data Center, Alexandria, Virginia.

FRASER, B. S. (1980) The Structure of Adult Learning, Education, and Training Opportunity in the United States. Washington, DC: National Institute for Work and Learning.

FROOMKIN, J. and R. J. WOLFSON (1977) "Adult education 1972: reanalysis." Joseph Froomkin, Inc., Washington, D.C. (mimeo)

Gallup Organization (1979) The Gallup Study of Participation and Awareness of the Agricultural Extension Service. Detailed Tabular Analysis. Princeton, NJ: Author.

GOLDSTEIN, H. (1980) Training and Education by Industry. Washington, DC: National Institute for Work and Learning.

HALSTEAD, D. K. (1979) Higher Education and Price Indices. 1978 Supplement. Washington, DC: National Institute of Education.

HYDE, W. D., Jr. (1976) Metropolitan Vocational Proprietary Schools. Lexington, MA: D. C. Heath.

JOHNSON, S. E. (1979) "Education enrollment statistics," in Inmate Programs Reporting System Cumulative Activity Counts Report 72.90 (and earlier numbers). Federal Bureau of Prisons. (unpublished)

KAY, E. R. (1979) Enrollments and Programs in Noncollegiate Postsecondary Schools. Washington, DC: Government Printing Office.

——— (1974) Adult Education in Community Organizations 1972. Washington, DC: Government Printing Office.

LUSTERMAN, S. (1977) Education in Industry. New York: Conference Board.

National Center for Educational Statistics [NCES] (1980a) "Opening fall enrollment, 1979." (unpublished)

——— (1980b) "College and university financial growth outpaces inflation in fiscal year 1979," in Early Release, NCES 80-345. Washington, DC: Author.

——— (1979) Financial Statistics of Institutions of Higher Education, 1977. Washington, DC: Government Printing Office.

National Home Study Council (n.d.) "Nearly three and one-half million Americans study by correspondence." (mimeo)

——— (n.d.) A Report on Current Educational Practice in NHSC Member Institutions. Washington, DC: Author.

PETERSON, R. E., K. P. CROSS, T. W. HARTLE, J. B. HIRABAYASHI, M. A. KUTNER, S. A., POWELL, and J. R. VALLEY (1979) Lifelong Learning in America. San Francisco: Jossey-Bass.

PUMA, M. J., S. MILLER, W. DELLEFIELD, D. GOEKE, and T. MUSSO (1980) "Study of the impact of the Middle Income Student Assistance Act (MISAA)." Office of Evaluation and Dissemination, U.S. Office of Education. (mimeo)

SMITH, G. B. (1980) Employer-Sponsored Recurrent Education in the United States: A Report on Recent Inquiries into Its Structure. Stanford, CA: Institute for Research on Educational Finance and Governance, School of Education, Stanford University.

SMITH, P. A., P. R. KNEPPER, J. P. JACKLEY, and C. HENDERSON (1980) "Financing undergraduate education in 1978-79." Division of Policy Analysis and Research, American Council on Education. (mimeo)

SMITH, V. (1973) "Restructuring education and its timing," in S. J. Mushkin (ed.) Recurrent Education. Washington, DC: Government Printing Office.

U.S. Bureau of the Census (1979a) CPS Tables—October 1978. (unpublished)

——— (1979b) Current Population Reports. Series P-20, no. 333. Washington, DC: Government Printing Office.

——— (1979c) Current Population Reports. Series P-20, no. 346. Washington, DC: Government Printing Office.

U.S. Department of Agriculture, Science and Education Administration-Extension (1980) Evaluation of Economic and Social Consequences of Cooperative Extension Programs. Washington, DC: Government Printing Office.

U.S. Department of Defense (1980) Military Manpower Training Report for FY 1981. Washington, DC: Author.

U.S. Department of Labor (1979) WIN: 1968-1978: A Report at 10 Years. Washington, DC: Government Printing Office.
────── Employment and Training Administration (1980a) "Quarterly progress reports and summary reports." (unpublished)
────── (1980b) "More women are now apprentices, BAT reports." ETA Interchange 6 (March): 8.
U.S. Department of Health, Education and Welfare, Office of Evaluation and Dissemination (1980) Annual Evaluation Report on Programs Administered by the U.S. Office of Education, Fiscal Year 1979. Washington, DC: Government Printing Office.
U.S. National Criminal Justice Information and Statistics Service (1980) Prisoners in State and Federal Institutions on December 31, 1978. Washington, DC: Bureau of Justice Statistics, Department of Justice.
────── (1979) Profile of State Prison Inmates: Washington, DC: Government Printing Office.
U.S. Office of Personnel Management (1980) Employee Training in the Federal Service, Fiscal Year 1979. Washington, DC: Author.
VAN DUSEN, W. D. (1975) "Financial aid for part-time students: status and issues." College Entrance Examination Board, Washington, D.C. (mimeo)
Veterans Administration, Office of the Controller, Reports and Statistics Service (1980) "Veteran's benefits under current educational programs." Information Bulletin 04-80-2.
WAGNER, A. P. (1978) "Financing postsecondary learning opportunity through existing federal student aid programs." School Rev. 86 (May): 410-435.
WILMS, W. W. (1975) Public and Proprietary Vocational Training: A Study of Effectiveness. Lexington, MA: D. C. Heath.
YOUN, T.I.K. and R. THOMPSON (1974) "A summary and analysis of the national commission's survey of noncollegiate institutions," in G. B. Weathersby and D. Nash (eds.) A Context for Policy Research in Higher Education. Washington, DC: Government Printing Office.
YOUNG, A. M. (1977) "Going back to school at 35 and over." Monthly Labor Rev. 100 (July): 43-45.

7

EMPLOYER-SPONSORED PROGRAMS
GREGORY B. SMITH

The purposes, forms, effects, and magnitude of private sector spending for work force education and training have become in recent years, for many and varied reasons, subjects of intense interest and speculation. Demand for detailed and accurate information on these subjects has arisen within industry itself, government agencies, education and research institutions, and organized labor. Stimulating that demand are a diverse array of interests and concerns. Among them:

- continuing anxiety about a declining rate of of productivity growth, and its effects on inflation and our competitive position in the world economy, combined with an appreciation that past and future levels and kinds of investments in skill and knowledge formation might well be part of the cause and solution of present problems;
- concern about the ways and means by which equal employment opportunity gains for minorities, women, older workers, handicapped, and other groups can be advanced or, more probable, sustained in the years ahead;
- concern about whether our public education and training establishments and practices are up to the task of accommodating, quickly enough, the changing skill and knowledge formation needs of our economy, especially in the face of a rapidly altering demography in the work place;
- concern about whether the aspirations and expectations of the work force of the 1980s can be accommodated within traditional pyramidal occupational structures and attendant rewards, in the absence of other human-growth options; and
- an emerging appreciation that to achieve mastery over the demands of everyday life and to participate in an informed way in political affairs require of Americans an increased sophistication obtained only through continuing learning, and in many instances only through organized learning.

We know now that during the past 30 years a vast and diverse educational enterprise has emerged within private industry—particularly large firms. We suspect that how and how well it functions and what kinds of opportunities it entertains will importantly condition how these concerns and national challenges are met.

What are the origins of the present-day structure of employer-sponsored recurrent education, of what Lusterman (1977) has called the "shadow education system"? What functions is this structure intended to perform, and what is its rationale from the viewpoint of management and the stockholder? What methods and modes of education are employed? What kinds of workers are reached by the recurrent education opportunities now offered? Which are left out? Where is equity's place in this system? How substantial are the costs of the present structure? What do we know about the effects of the levels and kinds of expenditures currently being made? What are some salient implications of the shadow education system for public policy in this new decade?

This is an attempt to speak to these questions and, in a few instances, to answer them through two separate but related discussions: the first a brief examination of the whole of the structure of employer-sponsored recurrent education, and the second a closer look at a wing of that structure—tuition assistance programs.

A central question examined here is how large the employer-sponsored recurrent education enterprise is in numbers of participants and in dollars spent. This question has inspired much conjecture. For the whole of recurrent education (deliberate education and training), reasoned estimates range from 37,215,000 to a high of 73,253,000 participants (Fraser, 1980: 11). For industry-sponsored recurrent education the numbers range from 2,605,000 to 16,000,000 participants. We shall look closely at this. On the matter of expenditures, the same enthusiasm for diversity obtains. Estimates of annual employer expenditures range from $2 billion to $100 billion. We will ponder these great differences, as well.

DIMENSIONS OF EMPLOYER-SPONSORED RECURRENT EDUCATION

IN THE BEGINNING

Employer-sponsored recurrent education, in its contemporary configuration, has its recognizable beginnings in the awesome crucibles of the Great Depression and World War II. Despite a rich history in the United States of progressive enlargement of educational opportunity for adult workers,[1] it is true, as Stewart (1980: 9) has observed, that prior to the early 1930s "a policy of no policy describes public policy as to worklife education for adult workers, while little other than formalization of on-the-job training was apparent in private company practice—this despite the much admired rationalization of the American productive mechanism in the prosperity of the Twenties as the United States assumed economic leadership in the world."

The first of these systemic shocks, the Great Depression, displaced and dislocated millions of American workers from industrial jobs and from the soil. The prevailing processes and structures of industrial skill and knowledge formation—the special American blend of "comprehensive" public education, vocational training (formal, informal on-the-job, and apprenticeships), and work experience—were overtaken by events and rendered incapable of sustaining the needs of the economy as industrial production began to rise again in the late 1930s. One reason for the obsolescence of prior skill formation processes was, of course, the fact that human capital accumulation by adult workers became static or indeed declined during the period between 1930 and 1940. Apprenticeship stopped. Formal training in industry was abandoned. Skill acquisition through work experience declined, simply because 1929 levels of employment were not regained until 1940-1941 (Stewart, 1980: 10) As late as 1938, well after human resource development programs such as the CCC and WPA were in full swing, unemployment (and skill atrophy) remained high: 10.4 million workers, 19% of the total labor force, stood idle (Wool, 1947: 638; cited in Stewart, 1980: 10).

The first event conditioned importantly the peculiar ramifications for industry of the second event, World War II. Between 1940 and 1945, the standing military forces grew by about 12 million and civilian employment increased by 7 million. Civilian labor force growth was nearly treble the expected growth of 3 million workers. School- and college-age youth, women 25-54, and men and women over 55 accounted for the 8 million additional workers (Jaffe and Stewart, 1951: 176-182; cited in Stewart, 1980: 10). In the main, these persons had no occupational experience or training, and only irregular work experience or exposure to work discipline.

At every occupational skill level, and in an array of new occupations, demands for labor grew. Every possible training facility was brought into use. With the advent of the Vocational Education for National

Defense Act (VEND Program), $80 million were invested annually in established state vocational systems, with the result that over 7 million prospective war production workers received institutional training at a cost of about $400 million (Venn, 1970: 151; cited in Stewart, 1980: 11). Of greater significance by most estimates was the radical alteration of industrial skill training on the job.

> Jobs were broken down so that workers with a few weeks training could perform the simplified single skill tasks. Supervisory training was especially emphasized so that skilled workers might be more effectively used [U.S. Department of Labor, Bureau of Labor Statistics, 1945; Woytinsky et al., 1953; cited in Stewart, 1980: 12].

The public policy aftermath of these major events is well explored. The unemployment insurance and social security systems were Depression-born initiatives that have played and may yet again play important roles in connection with expanded work life or recurrent education opportunity in the United States. Out of the war experience and immediate postwar concerns emerged the Servicemen's Readjustment Act of 1944, a most important legacy of World War II. The GI Bill of Rights afforded 7.5 million adults new work life education opportunities at a cost of $13 billion in the period from 1944 to 1956. One-half of World War II veterans exercised the education and training option (Stewart, 1980: 12). Then, too, came the Employment Act of 1946, Congress's reaction to the perceived threat of a serious recession from expected reductions in military spending. This act, while in the main procedural and hortatory, established the dominance of macro (demand management) fiscal and monetary policies in postwar management of the economy.

The private policy response—though by no means as separate and insulated from the public policy response as we might think in our more laissez-faire moments—is a far less visible and well-examined matter. We do know that many of the employee education programs of the major U.S. companies, such as tuition assistance programs, began during and just after the war years (Bureau of National Affairs, 1978). We do know that in many high-technology areas developed or refined during the war, industry stepped in with its own technical/functional skills training programs, in part to protect industrial secrets from unscrupulous competitors, but also because the apparatus required for training were often unique and highly expensive.

FUNCTIONS AND NEEDS

Skill and knowledge formation occurs through three modes: (1) general education; (2) vocationally oriented education at all levels, including professional; and (3) learning opportunities provided by employers either on the job or in special programs. The individual, the occupation, the industry, and the social milieu dictate how these three modes are combined. Employer-sponsored education is the capstone of the other modes. In the United States, its main function remains to adapt previously acquired general knowledge and skills to the needs of the job. It also serves, with increasing frequency, the function of compensating for the deficiencies of both general and vocational education. In both cases, employer-sponsored education must often provide general knowledge.

The employer's needs are dominant in the American arrangement. Among the needs that recurrent education offerings are designed to meet are:

- supplementing and focusing the general skills of new workers to adapt to the way work is done in the enterprise;
- orienting new workers to the policies, rules, and organization of the enterprise;
- upgrading employee skills for promotion;
- retraining employees where new production methods and processes have been introduced;
- equipping managerial personnel to deal with new products or new factors affecting the business, such as government regulations in occupational health and safety, environmental governance, and affirmative action;
- compensating for serious deficiencies in the work skills of current employees, such as special training programs for DC-10 maintenance workers following the O'Hare Airport crash of 1979, and establishment of the Nuclear Operations Institute to train operating staff of nuclear electric generating plants following the Three Mile Island incident;
- assuring or achieving occupational vitality, particularly as it relates to managerial and professional employees;
- stabilizing employment, reducing turnover, and filling needs for shortage skills from within;
- enhancing the recruiting capacity of the firm (Goldstein, 1980: 7-14).

The occupation and industry of the worker importantly determine what recurrent education opportunities are available. There are significant differences in the education and training opportunities afforded managerial employees, sales employees, supervisory personnel, craft and operative workers, clerical workers, and professional and technical workers.

The structure and technology of industries similarly affects their needs and the modes of education available to them. In certain high-technology sectors, the telecommunications industry for example, employers can hire trained workers in only a few occupations. Career ladder structure is another decisive factor. Industries with well-articulated promotional sequences and ladders have few hiring points or entry portals except at the bottom rung. Workers advance to skilled production or maintenance jobs through recurrent education opportunities of varying kinds in such industries as steel, automobile, petroleum, and chemical. In the health care industry, a two-tier system obtains. Hospitals employ many occupations for which training is provided by schools. Little or no posthiring education is provided by the employer. The employer-provided education that does occur has the limited purpose of qualifying untrained workers (some 60%-70% of hospital personnel in large cities) for employment upgrading within job groupings where some promotional opportunities exist (Kimmerly, 1979; cited in Goldstein, 1980: 11).

METHODS AND FORMS

Employer-sponsored recurrent education takes many forms, employs an array of methods, and includes a wide range of content depending on the skills to be imparted and the purpose of the education. It ranges from the most informal training to highly formalized academic instruction.

The traditional and probably dominant form of skill acquisition is through informal, on-the-job training using the buddy system or supervisor-monitor trial and error method. More formal training, emphasizing the why as well as the how, may be employed for complex organizations and jobs. This may consist of individual or small-group instruction held in a classroom at the work place, offering programmed learning or audiovisual aids such as electronic blackboards. Or it may entail programs located away from the work site at a school or other community setting, possibly involving some form of tuition assistance or paid release time (Goldstein, 1980: 14-15).

Of the various types of on-the-job skill training processes, apprenticeship is among the most systematic and venerable. While only about 1.5% of new workers complete formal registered or unregistered apprenticeship programs, apprenticeship is the preferred choice in many industries, particularly the unionized sector. (Swerdloff, 1978; cited in Goldstein 1980: 15).

Each method, each form, has benefits and costs, assets and liabilities worked out according to the employer's preference, in most instances, although not necessarily on the basis of any refined tradeoff calculus. There is some evidence that the incidence of formal training programs has risen on the whole.

TELLING TREES FROM FORESTS

Agencies charged with the deep reading of present and future dispositions and capabilities of other countries, allies and adversaries alike, closely watch the processes and structures of skill and knowledge formation. Extensive records are kept concerning at least some aspects of two legs of the knowledge/skill formation triad in the United States—general education and vocational training. However, for the third leg, employer-sponsored education and training, the knowledge base is slim and fragmentary. This is a curious state of affairs in view of the millions of Americans involved in the recurrent education system, the estimated billions of dollars spent, and the consequences hoped for in terms of firm productivity, worker income, U.S. economic competitiveness in the global economy, and occupational and social mobility.

That our knowledge base is so limited is in large part a reflection of the historical separatism between the public and private sectors in the United States and the prevalent opinion shared by both sectors that education in industry is "a private affair." Both that understanding and historical separatism have undergone substantial modification in recent years, in part because of the growing areas of interface between public policy and private policy in the human resource development area. Equal employment opportunity is one major avenue of public policy intervention into that "private affair." Others include the significant evolution of public-private interaction in the employment and training arena since the Area Redevelopment Act of 1961, including the more significant Manpower Development and Training Act of 1962, and, more recently, the Private Sector Initiatives Program under the amended Comprehensive Employment and Training Act of 1973.

Our present knowledge base about the central questions—who is providing how much of what kinds of recurrent education to whom and with what effect—is constrained largely by four factors: (1) National surveys of education and training activity in the economy have been infrequent and irregular; (2) the mode of education that appears to be most prevalent, informal learning under the tutelage of a supervisor or worker, is not captured in surveys because records of such training are simply not kept—even more structured modes of training, such as systematic rotation of workers in skilled crafts areas, are not surveyed for the same reason; (3) few surveys contain a representative sample of companies—many of the studies that have been done involved respondent firms whose interest in training was such that it led them to join associations concerned with training; and (4) despite the fact that nonresponse in surveys usually indicates lack of interest in or lower incidence of the behavior or characteristic being measured, neither of the two most recent surveys of employer-sponsored education (Lusterman, 1977; U.S. Department of Labor, Bureau of Labor Statistics, 1977; cited in Goldstein, 1980) used information obtained from nonrespondents or adjusted reported findings to account for the nonresponse (Goldstein, 1980: 22-23).

THE SIZE OF IT ALL

The first general survey of employer-sponsored education was conducted by the U.S. Department of Labor in 1962. This establishment survey showed that only one enterprise in five sponsored any type of formal training. Only 7% of workers were enrolled in formal programs. Half of the enrollees were in safety training. Only 40% of the enrollees or 3% of all employed workers were receiving skill improvement education. Of these, 10% were taking administrative and advisory training, 7% sales training, and 6% training for the skilled trades. Importantly, this survey captured sharp differences in the incidence of training on the basis of establishment size (U.S. Department of Labor, 1965; cited in Goldstein, 1980: 26).

In a 1957 survey of the top 500 corporations listed by *Fortune* magazine, 85% of the responding companies reported some sort of sponsored education program. Of these, 67% conducted both internal and external programs; 28% conducted only internal programs. The most common type of education was supervisory skills training, offered by 92% of the firms. Education programs for professionals followed, offered by 71% of the respondent firms. Education programs for factory operatives were provided by 45% of respondents and programs for clerical workers (mainly female workers) by 31% of responding companies (Clark and Sloan, 1958: 13-24; cited in Goldstein, 1980: 27).

The most frequently cited study of employer-sponsored education is the Conference Board's survey of all firms with 500 or more employees for the period 1974-1975. The sample included firms together employing about 32 million persons, or about half the wage and salary workers in private nonfarm establishments at the time. The response rate was 22%.

Given the importance attached to the Conference Board survey by industry researchers and public policy analysts, I quote at length here from the analysis of this study's findings and flaws offered by Dr. Harold Goldstein (1980: 27-31):

> In this survey the formal training modes were structured as follows: (1) *Company courses,* whether conducted by company personnel or outside institutions and contractors, and whether they are held on or off the company's premises; . . . (2) *Tuition aid programs* selected and arranged for by employees, who are reimbursed fully or partly by the firm; . . . (3) *Other outside courses* offered by such organizations as the American Management Association, the Conference Board, professional societies, trade associations or corporate suppliers of training. They are open to employees of more than a single firm and are taken during working hours.
>
> Among the 22 percent of firms responding, the following percentages reported having various types of training programs (Lusterman, op. cit., Table 2.6):
>
> | | |
> |---|---|
> | Tuition aid (for after-hours courses) | 89% |
> | Other outside courses (during work hours) | 74% |
> | Company courses (during work hours) | 70% |
> | Company courses (after hours) | 39% |
>
> The largest firms had the highest incidence of each type of program. . .
>
> On the critical question of the number of employees receiving training, their occupations, and the kinds of training they got, the survey report is unclear. It is possible, however, to piece together a rough estimate of the total incidence of training. Employees who had participated in company courses in the previous year totaled 4.4 million, or 13 percent of all workers in firms employing 500 or more; 3.7 million (11 percent) had participated in programs during hours, and only 700,000 (2 percent) in after-hours programs (Lusterman, p. 11). In addition to those participating in company courses, there were 1.3 million participants annually in

tuition aid programs, or 4 percent of all workers, according to a rough estimate by the author of the study based on a 1970 Conference Board survey (Lusterman, p. 11). To this must be added the employees who participated in courses other than tuition-aid provided by non-company sources. The report gives no estimate of the number involved, but this form of training absorbed 9 percent of the training expenditures (Lusterman, Table 2.7). Making a rough estimate on the basis of the cost figures, this group of workers may have added about 10 percent to the numbers receiving training, or about 600,000. If we assume that none of these four groups of workers participated in more than one type of course, the total number of workers involved in formal training was about 6.3 million, or about *one out of five of the 32 million workers employed in firms with 500 or more employees.*

The percentage of employees participating in company courses (13 percent, overall) was fairly uniform in the larger size companies (14-16 percent), but in the smallest size firms it dropped to 10 percent (Lusterman, Table 2.2). By industry there was less uniformity; manufacturing firms had only 7 percent participation, finance and insurance as high as 20 percent, and in the other sectors, the range was 12 to 15 percent. Most of the participation was in courses during work hours (Lusterman, Table 2.7).

Another measure of the relative emphasis among programs is the distribution of expenditures (Lusterman, Table 2.5):

Company courses	80%
Outside courses	
Tuition aid	11%
Other	9%

Smaller firms depended more on outside courses for their training: in firms in the 500-999 and 1,000-2,499 size groups, between 50 and 60 percent of the expenditures were for outside courses, while in the largest size group, 87 percent was spent in-house (Lusterman, Table 2.5).

In terms of expenditures and employee involvement, therefore, the most prevalent mode of employer-provided training in firms employing 500 or more workers was through company courses during work hours. The kinds of training given in such programs are shown in [the table].

The functional-technical category included such areas as production, maintenance, marketing, sales, service, office administration, internal systems, finance and personnel—i.e., mostly managerial and white-collar skills. Comparing these figures with the occupational distribution of the work force in the reporting companies—11 percent managerial, 12 percent professional and technical, 10 percent sales and marketing, and 67 percent all other occupations (Lusterman, Table 2.11)—the conclusion is inescapable that training through company courses in working hours, the most prevalent mode, was disproportionately concentrated on providing managerial and other white-collar skills. This was less true in the largest companies (those with 10,000 or more employees) where 81 percent of the expenditures were on functional-technical training, while in companies with 500 to 4,999 employees about half the expenditures were in such courses (Lusterman, Table 6.6). In only 21 percent of the companies—and in only 36 percent of the largest size firms—did hourly-paid employees participate in functional-technical courses, however, and low-salaried employees participated in 22 percent of all firms and 43 percent of the largest ones (Lusterman, Table 6.7).

Tuition aid programs, although found in 89 percent of the companies reporting and therefore the most widespread mode of employer-provided training, involved only a small proportion of employees; all after-hours programs, of which tuition aid is one component, involved only 2 percent of the employees of reporting firms. . . . As noted above, tuition aid and other outside courses were favored by smaller firms, who did not have the "critical mass" to make it worthwhile to employ training staffs or to offer courses in occupations with few workers.

THE COST OF IT ALL

In the absence of any systematic record keeping within industry it is not surprising to find earnestly proffered estimates of annual costs ranging from $2 billion to $100 billion.

In an attempt to estimate the costs of education and training to business and industry, Tracey (1974) enumerated previous estimates, ranging from Machlup (1962), $3 billion for 1958; Decarlo and Robinson in a Chase Manhattan Bank report (1962), $17 billion; Boozer (1971), $20 billion; to Otto and Glaser (1970), $25 billion. Tracey went on to report that in 1972 Willard estimated total training costs of $700 annually per employee in large firms—$200 in direct training and $500 in indirect costs (including lost productivity). Using the 1971 annual average number of employees of private, nonfarm, nongovernment establishments (57,836,000), Tracey (1974: 11) assumed that if 2 out of 3 employees received some training at an average cost of $700, total industry expenditures would be about $27 billion; if 3 out of 5 received training, the cost would be approximately $24 billion. One estimate of total costs of employer-provided education and training in the United States (including government employees) runs as high as $100 billion during 1975 (Gilbert, 1976). This represents 12% of all wage and salary payments that year. (All of these estimates are presented in Fraser, 1980: 37-38.)

Lusterman (1977) estimates direct costs were about $2 billion ($1.6 billion for internal programs and $.4 billion for external offerings) for the large firms surveyed. Goldstein estimates an additional $1 billion in direct training costs for the rest of the private sector and adds about $2 billion in salary costs of trainees. After figuring in overhead costs and additional salary costs for managerial and professional workers who receive the bulk of training, Goldstein (1980: 35) estimates a total training expenditure of approximately $10 billion.

Per capita education spending varies significantly by size of firm and type of industry. The median (per capita) direct expense in the Conference Board survey was $16. The mean direct expense was $60 annually. A small number of companies with high expenditures were responsible for pulling up the mean. Transportation, communications, utilities, financial, and insurance companies spent more than the average, while wholesale and retail firms were well below the mean.

One employer, the Bell System, reports that it spends $1 billion per year on employee education, including the salaries of trainees. With nearly 1 million employees, its annual per capita expenditure is therefore $1000. This is estimated to be in the neighborhood of 5% of its total wage and salary bill. Such an apparently atypical company gives currency to an estimate such as that of Gilbert, that is, $100 billion total industry spending.

AND WHAT DOES IT DO?

Whichever estimate one accepts, the conclusion is unmistakable that employer-sponsored recurrent education is a massive enterprise that provides significant learning opportunities for many American workers. At the same time it is clear that opportunity is unevenly available, and that there is nothing approaching a consensus within industry that education for employees is in the employer's interest. Part of the reason for this latter condition most assuredly is the absence of any clear measure of the value or yield of education investments or, more precisely, the ratio of benefits to costs. The condition appears to remain as reported by Clark and Davis (1975: 186; cited in Goldstein, 1980: 50):

> Surprisingly little progress has been made toward developing techniques for comparing the benefits of training with its cost. While many studies

have shown the returns to investments in formal schooling, a survey of 100 large corporations by the authors turned up no instances (among the 50 replies received as this chapter is written) of business being able to gauge the returns to investments in training with the same financial analysis that it uses before deciding to build a new plant or when choosing between alternative pieces of equipment. While some companies may be conducting formal financial analysis of their training, our findings reveal that business, in general, lacks sophisticated guidance in cost-effectiveness analysis.

This assessment has been confirmed in numerous conversations with industry education and training officials over the past 24 months. It is worth noting that both the Bell System and IBM Corporation have significant research projects under way to measure performance changes (the critical variable for evaluation research).

IN SUM

From these diverse surveys this shadowy picture emerges: Formal education opportunities are provided by fewer than half of all firms, but by more than 4 out of 5 of the larger firms. Among these larger firms about 1 in 5 workers is involved in education during any given year, with a much smaller proportion for all industry. Most education opportunities are provided during working hours in company-sponsored courses. Education for skill and general knowledge development (as distinct from company or product orientation, safety, or the like) is only a modest part of the total. Many of the formal skill training and education opportunities are for management and other white-collar skill areas, particularly professional and technical. Manual workers receive a disproportionately small share of formal training. Educational expenditures were probably in the range of $10-$20 billion dollars in the mid-1970s. Because training is often constrained during downsurges in the economy, expenditures may be lower currently than they were during 1975-1976. The effects of these investments on individual or firm performance are not now measured. In the absence of such measures, one can anticipate that the ambivalence toward education and training observed in many conversations and in industry behavior today will continue.

This is a picture of the whole. What of that category of employer-sponsored recurrent education most prevalent in American firms today?

How significant is it? What are its implications for the financing of work life or recurrent education opportunity in the years ahead?

TUITION ASSISTANCE PROGRAMS: PROBLEMS AND PROSPECTS

From the public policy vantage, one of the more intriguing and enigmatic elements of employer-sponsored recurrent education is tuition assistance. As indicated above, it is the most widespread mode of employer-sponsored education. Tuition-assistance programs represent a private basis for financing those education experiences most in keeping with the image of recurrent education, that is, a curriculum inclusive of, if not principally concerned with, liberal learning and general knowledge areas, from Plato to polymers, Socrates to cybernetics.

Until recently, little attention had been given tuition assistance in the United States by either education policy circles, union officials, or the training and development community within industry. (Some elements of the latter appear to remain especially chary of tuition assistance.) Four years ago the National Institute of Education contracted with the National Institute for Work and Learning (formerly the National Manpower Institute) to examine the prevalence, content, and objectives of negotiated tuition assistance programs in the private sector and the obstacles to worker utilization of them. The overall study was subsequently broadened to include a series of case studies of successful (highly used) tuition-assistance plans, a series of model work place demonstration projects, a policy development initiative, and other activities in the general area of recurrent or work life education. Thus, tuition assistance is a dimension of employer-sponsored recurrent education about which our knowledge is a bit more complete.

The data presented below were gathered in 1976-1977 through mail surveys and direct interviews with 51 company and 52 union officials and 910 unionized workers, and analysis of 79 major contracts containing negotiated tuition assistance provisions.

DESCRIPTION

Tuition assistance is an educational finance mechanism, nothing more nor less. The operational definition for the National Manpower Institute's 1976-1977 study follows:

> A tuition assistance program is any formal program through which a company offers financial assistance to some or all of its employees to encourage them to complete courses of study either at outside educational institutions or through other educational vendors [LeBel, 1977: II-27].

Negotiated tuition assistance is an unusual subphylum. The operational definition of negotiated tuition aid (from the same study) follows:

> Any formal plan in which a company has agreed within terms of a company union contract, to pay all or part of the tuition and related financial expenses incurred by employees covered under the agreement, while pursuing courses of study offered on or off company or union premises [LeBel, 1977: II-26].

Four distinct types of negotiated tuition assistance plans were identified in this study of collective bargaining agreements covering 1000 or more workers. In rank order of incidence, and by definition, these four types are described below.

Tuition Reimbursement and Tuition Advancement Plans

Tuition reimbursement plans are by far the most common form of tuition assistance negotiated between companies and unions in the United States. Tuition reimbursement and advancement plans pay all or part of tuition and related costs for enrollment in education and training programs outside the company.

- Employees are usually reimbursed by the company after submitting evidence of satisfactory course completion and of tuition payment. "Satisfactory" usually means a passing grade, although in a significant number of plans a specific grade requirement is established.

- Plans usually cover all or part of registration fees, student activities fees, laboratory fees, and graduation expenses. Other costs sometimes covered are books, supplies, CLEP fees, transportation, and meals. The prevailing practice is to allow higher payments for diploma or degree courses and for job-related education.
- Common eligibility criteria are the worker's job classification, accrued seniority, and satisfactory course completion. Most are open to all active employees who are working at least half time and who have six months or more of service.
- The plans usually specify acceptable institutions and courses of study. Often these institutions include colleges and universities, community colleges, technical and vocational schools, high schools, professional societies, labor unions, trade associations, and correspondence schools. In a large number of plans, courses must be for credit and/or must be job-, career-, or degree-related. (Only 3.9% of the NMI sample provided coverage for other than job-, career-, or degree-related courses.)
- Time off for course attendance or study is not allowed in most plans. Course work is not supposed to affect job performance. In several plans, however, employees may trade shifts or adjust work schedules to accommodate courses.

The criteria for eligibility, institution, and course approval and the application procedures mentioned above obtain for the other three types of plans as well.

Educational leave is granted to a worker for educational purposes for a specified period during working hours; *educational leave of absence* is granted for a more extended period of time. Either may but does not necessarily involve full or partial tuition payment. Under the *educational leave of absence,* leave time is usually credited as continuous company service for pension rights, and many companies will reinstate the worker at the individual's previous job classification (7.8% of the NMI sample had educational leave provisions).

Under *training fund* plans, employers contribute fixed amounts of money per employee into a central fund to finance employee education and training. Usually training fund plans are administered by a board of trustees as part of an industrywide or areawide program. Often the fund is used to underwrite the operational and fixed costs of training institutes or schools. The objectives of training fund plans are to improve job performance, upgrade skills, retrain workers, and reduce workers' educational outlays.

Scholarship and educational loan plans are the least commonly encountered form of negotiated tuition aid (NTA). Under scholarship plans, eligible workers are given funds to cover educational costs. Loan plans provide loans that require repayment according to an agreed-upon schedule. (In the NMI sample 9.8% had scholarship provisions and 15.7% had loan provisions.)

PERCEPTIONS

Management and labor share positive attitudes as to perceived *objectives* and *impacts* of NTA use. Both management and labor overwhelmingly concur that updated knowledge and skills, improved worker performance, and personal development and growth are each important objectives. In addition, 92% of the company officials surveyed view preparation for future assignments to be an important objective. Over 65% of the union officials surveyed consider as other important objectives preparing union members for job mobility and responding to local membership concerns. In sum, both companies and unions with NTA plans view tuition aid as a means for improving the position of workers in terms of their skills, personal development, and future occupational assignments.

As to *impacts*, company and union officials share the view that the three major potential outcomes of NTA are greater worker effectiveness on the job, heightened career development and job mobility, and increased worker satisfaction.

The workers surveyed by NMI share the views of company and union officials regarding the objectives and impacts of NTA benefits mentioned above. Most workers of the 910 in the survey consider further education and training to be important for many diverse reasons, such as degree completion, improved basic skills, better job performance, preparation for another job, and so on.

The consensus among company and union officials and workers disintegrates over the question of what factors prevent fuller participation by workers in tuition-assisted education and training. Through its study, NIWL sought the views of these groups on the relative significance of 20 structural, social, and psychological conditions that previous studies indicated to be of possible importance.

Conditions posited included:

(1) The company does not give time off or adjust schedules to promote participation.

(2) Workers' interest in attending courses on their own time is low.
(3) Insufficient incentives are used to reward participants.
(4) Management does not encourage participation sufficiently.
(5) The range of courses offered by local educational institutions is too limited.
(6) Supervisors do not encourage workers or employees under them to participate.
(7) Counseling services in the company or union are not sufficient.
(8) Workers do not have enough information about the program.
(9) Course schedules offered by local educational institutions are not flexible enough.
(10) Shop stewards do not encourage workers under them to participate.
(11) Eligibility criteria in the plan are too restrictive.
(12) Support services, particularly child care, are inadequate to give workers enough free time to participate.
(13) Workers lack information about educational opportunities in the community.
(14) The locations of classes are not convenient for workers.
(15) Plan application and approval procedures are too complicated.
(16) Workers object to paying income tax on tuition-aid payments.
(17) Workers feel inadequate to understand or complete courses that are available.
(18) Workers are unwilling or unable to pay the costs of courses.
(19) Workers do not participate because of social pressure from other workers.
(20) Sex, age, ethnic, or racial discrimination restrict participation.

Company officials tend to discount the importance of all of these conditions except one: low worker interest in education. Union officials, on the other hand, cite workers' inability to take time off or make schedule adjustments, low worker interest in education, and insufficient encouragement by management as important obstacles to fuller participation. Workers cite lack of company encouragement, inadequate information about available courses, lack of adequate promotional or income incentives, inflexibility of work schedule, and restrictiveness of course eligibility criteria.

On the matter of information, about one-third of the workers surveyed did not know or were not sure about either their eligibility for the NTA program or the approval process. All were eligible. Workers themselves overwhelmingly reject the idea that low worker interest in education is a major barrier to education.

THE EXTENT OF TUITION ASSISTANCE

NIWL estimates that 1 in 10 major private sector collective bargaining agreements in 1977 contained tuition-assistance provisions. Expressed differently, we estimate that in 1977 there were approximately 200 NTA plans covering nearly 2 million workers. Found in all types of industries, the incidence of NTA plans approximates the distribution of unionized workers, with the largest proportion in manufacturing. There is limited evidence that the number of these NTA plans is growing.

Of the 79 plans closely studied, tuition reimbursement or advance provisions are present in 60 (75%) of the agreements. Of the 60, 54 offer tuition reimbursement exclusively. Only 6 of the 60 contain tuition advance provisions. Educational leave plans appear in 13 (16%) of the agreements. Training fund plans appear in 22 (27%) of the agreements, and scholarships and loans are provided for in only 6 (7%) of the agreements studied.

The Bureau of Labor Statistics estimate of a 4% participation rate in NTA plans nationally in the mid-1970s has been supported by a number of other proximate studies in the 1970s (O'Meara, 1970; Bureau of National Affairs, 1978). Applying this 4% use rate to the total population covered (2,000,000 workers), and assuming a per capita annual expenditure rate of $250, one can estimate *annual outlays* under NTA of about $20 million. *On-paper commitments* under NTA programs are quite probably in the range of 1 billion dollars (2,000,000 workers × $500 average maximum allowance).

What do we know about the reach and characteristics of tuition-assistance programs of the more common nonnegotiated variety? We know very little for certain. Available evidence suggests that they conform closely in basic features and nomenclature to what was described above in the NTA plans. Available evidence also indicates that the use rate is in the 4% range for these plans and that it is the younger, better educated, higher paid, typically white, male worker who takes greatest advantage of these plans (for a detailed discussion, see Charner, 1979, 1980).

Several recent surveys suggest significant growth in the number of tuition-assistance plans on the American scene during the past 15-20 years. If estimates such as those of O'Meara (1970) and Lusterman (1977) are correct, there has been an increase. If these estimates are correct, then we have a situation in which over 80% of all establishments with over 500 employees have tuition-aid plans.

Using data from Lusterman, I have made some rough "guestimates" on the dimensions of tuition-assistance plan prevalence in the United States and the implications for enrollments in adult education resulting from incremental increases in the average utilization rate for TA plans. These guestimates will gain moment in the context of the brief discussion of participation rates achieved in several U.S. companies' tuition-assistance plans; they appear in the Appendix, with necessary caveats. In brief, I estimate that in 1975 between 17 and 24 million U. S. workers in private establishments were eligible to participate in tuition-assistance plans and that approximately 818,000 did so. If participation rates were increased by 1%, nearly one-quarter million additional adults would be participating in recurrent education programs.

The average maximum coverable education expense under the 79 plans examined in the NIWL study was approximately $500. If we assume that all plans have an annual per capita ceiling of half that amount, and if we simply multiply that sum by the number of potentially eligible workers, the upper and lower limits of *paper commitments* for tuition assistance in the private sector were $6.1 and $4.2 billion in 1976 (see Appendix).

THREE PROGRAMS THAT WORK

The 4% participation rate is by no means constant across programs. In 1978-1979, NIWL examined three programs that boast relatively high rates of worker utilization. The purpose was to attempt to identify factors in the program structure and administration, in the work force, and in the contextual environment (industry, community, education infrastructure, and so on) that seem to account for above-average participation rates.

A synopsis of each of the 3 programs examined in these case studies follows. These synopses suggest that every large employer in the country has available the wherewithal, via direct policy action, to enhance employee participation in voluntary education and training programs by a factor of 5 to 10.

The Kimberly-Clark Corporation's Educational Opportunities Plan (EOP), which originated in 1974, is regarded as the leader in innovative company-sponsored tuition-assistance plans. The introduction of this progressive plan, which has a participation rate of over 35%, was a dramatic departure from the previously limited and restrictive tuition-aid program at Kimberly-Clark (K-C), which claimed a participation rate of only 1%.

Kimberly-Clark, headquartered in Neenah, Wisconsin, is a fast-growing, worldwide marketer of fiber-based personal care products.

The EOP, which provides benefits to workers *and* their families for courses that do not have to be job-related, is open to nearly half of the almost 16,000 U.S. employees. Many of the eligible employees are concentrated around Neenah, an area rich in educational institutions. The majority of eligible employees are white-collar workers. The participation rates of hourly workers under the plan are lower than the overall 30+ percentage rate. The EOP was introduced by the top corporate leadership as a way to recruit, develop, and maintain a highly qualified and satisfied work force and to evidence K-C's commitment and trust in its employees.

The EOP includes the following major components:

- *Kim Ed account*—a personal "bank account," determined by formula, allotted to each employee for his/her educational use. After submitting a "self-development plan," the employee may draw on this account throughout the year. (The typical Kim Ed allotment in 1978 was approximately $450.) Kim Ed includes a provision for up to ten days of educational leave per year.

- *Fam Ed account*—financial assistance provided to employees *and* their families, based on a formula allotment, for current or future educational expenses. The company makes annual deposits to the account, and there are financial incentives for employees to save for the future.

- *extended educational leave*—a limited number of paid leaves for up to one year. Reportedly, this component of the EOP is rarely utilized.

While notable for the care and detail with which it has been designed, the EOP is also unusually flexible, with deliberate attempts having been made to include structural features that would maximize employee use of the plan. The most striking among these include:

- *liberal eligibility*—unlike many plans, the EOP is not limited to professional or salaried employees. There is a six-month seniority requirement.

- *coverage of non-job-related and cultural activities*—again, a rarity. Courses and institutions must be approved.

- *advance payment*—for tuition and other educational expenses.

- *no grade requirement or proof of course completion.*

- *unit coordinators*—in addition to full-time, high-level administration, a network of local coordinators provides crucial support services, including information on the plan and local educational opportunities.
- *extensive plan promotion and publicity*—through employee orientation, special announcements, bulletins, supervisors, and word of mouth.

Plan officials view the high participation rate as the best measure of EOP success.

The Kimberly-Clark Educational Opportunities Plan is a carefully designed program offered to employees within a corporate context of strong support for self-development in an area rich in educational opportunities. Many of the plan's features directly reduce or eliminate the structural barriers that commonly inhibit workers from using educational assistance (Rosow, 1979).

District Council 37 of the American Federation of State County and Municipal Employees in New York City offers an unusual array of educational programs and services to a large and diverse group of municipal employees. DC 37's Education Fund (EF) stands out because it is overseen by a board of union members and operates out of the union's headquarters. Fund programs are not only highly subscribed (the overall participation rate is about 10%-12% and many programs have waiting lists); they have managed to attract most heavily those groups normally viewed as least likely to take advantage of educational opportunities—lower-skill and lower-paid employees.

With over 110,000 members, DC 37 is the largest council of AFSCME. Known as a progressive, service-oriented union, it offers a wide range of benefits for its members, including a health plan, legal services program, retirees' association, and political action program. Through an agreement negotiated in 1971, the City of New York provides $25 annually for each of over 76,000 eligible employees to be used to meet a general set of educational objectives. The total annual fund budget is nearly $2 million.

The Education Fund evolved out of the union leadership's attempts, in the 1960s, to meet the perceived needs of workers for education and training that would lead to job upgrading and promotional opportunities within the city's civil service system. Because of the enthusiastic response of the membership, the initial emphasis on career development has continued and is evident in the focus of Fund programs today. Whether by learning English, passing a civil service test, or obtaining a diploma or college degree, career advancement is the primary objective of most participants and in the selection of course offerings.

In an attempt to fulfill the learning needs of a very diverse population, the Fund has, over the years, developed a wide range of educational programs and offerings. Most of these offerings are in basic *skills development programs* (including, for example, high school equivalency, English as a second language, and reading improvement), *college degree programs* (DC 37 campuses of Hofstra University and the College of New Rochelle, labor/liberal arts for women, and the tuition refund program), and *career-related programs* (clerical skills, test-taking preparation, accounting, nursing, and so on).

Key provisions and features of Education Fund programs attempt to reduce barriers to participation in education faced by working adults who are returning to school after a long absence. These features and provisions include:

- *Flexible, simplified admissions procedures* with a minimum of the bureaucracy and red tape that students reported encountering at other schools.
- *Scheduling arrangements* enabling many students to attend classes on their way home from work. Most classes are held evenings or Saturdays at union headquarters, and alternative arrangements often exist to accommodate work shifts. Students gain support from attending classes with their coworkers in the union setting.
- *A diversified, nonrestrictive curriculum.* Programs are designed to meet a variety of learning needs and styles, and degree programs are not required to be job-related.
- *Little or no out-of-pocket expenses* for students, made possible through the existence of a fund that is to be spent *only* on education programs, unlike some arrangements in which education is seen as a cost item for the sponsoring organization.
- *An accessible network of support services,* including widely available group and individual educational counseling, a learning lab for tutoring and individual instruction in basic skills, a library, and a staff of faculty and administrators who reportedly often act as advisors to students.
- *Widespread publicity* of the Fund and its programs, through the highly popular union newspaper, word of mouth, referrals, notices, and so on. Especially because of the former, there is a high level of awareness of the existence of Fund programs.

Overall, the fund is seen by the union as successful because it meets its stated objectives and succeeds in attracting large numbers of students, most of whom have positive reactions to its programs. In addition to career development, other reported major outcomes of

Fund use are: improved job performance; increased self-esteem, interpersonal skills, and self-confidence; improved family relations; greater readiness to pursue further education (in the psychological sense or in terms of credentials or skills); and increased involvement in the union as a whole.

As with Kimberly-Clark, the success of the Ed Fund can be attributed to an interplay of environmental and programmatic factors. Many Fund-eligible workers have a strong, clear need for education in order to advance within the civil service system or even to maintain their jobs. Thus, when faced with a highly promoted education program tailored to their particular social/psychological and learning needs and offered within a union that strongly encourages them to "own" and use such programs, many DC 37 workers choose to return to the classroom (Shore, 1979).

The importance of leadership commitment and innovation emerges again in an account of the successful *Tuition Assistance Plan of Polaroid Corporation.* The creation of a learning environment was central to the vision of Dr. Edwin Land, the unique founder of this unusual and successful corporation, headquartered in Cambridge, Massachusetts, an area brimming with educational opportunities. Ever since Land's founding of Polaroid's education program in 1957, the company has placed high value on maintaining a cadre of highly trained and skilled employees who will advance in the Polaroid system.

As a result, the Polaroid education program today is noted not only for its liberal Tuition Assistance Plan (TAP), but for an extensive and highly utilized internal education and training system. The effect of all this, reports one employee, is that "education is just in the air at Polaroid." The numbers are a striking testament to this. Fully 50% of the corporation's approximately 12,000 domestic employees participated in 1 or more internal or external educational opportunities in 1977-1978. TAP was utilized by 10% of the eligible work force and, of these participants, *40%* were hourly employees. These figures stand out for two reasons, in addition to the unusually high 50% figure. First, as is the case of DC 37, TAP manages to attract significant proportions of users from the ranks of those considered least likely to utilize education and, second, TAP sustains a high level of participation despite the existence of a comprehensive internal education program.

Why does TAP do so well? Again, a look at the key features of the program reveals provisions that do much to overcome major barriers to participation. TAP is an integrated component of the overall employee development program, which includes skills training, management and organizational development, technology-based seminars, and career counseling. It exists to finance both independently undertaken external education programs and company-initiated programs that require use of outside educational institutions.

Of crucial importance is the fact that TAP *prepays 100%* of the costs of approved educational programs successfully completed by employees (the money must be refunded if the employee fails the course or does not complete it). The plan formerly paid only partial tuition costs. Through an "equity provision," hourly and salaried employees are entitled to the same tuition-assistance benefits. The plan, with an annual budget of approximately $450,000, is open to all half- and full-time employees on a prorated assistance basis. Acceptable courses and programs are those defined, *very* broadly, as job-related. In this case, the term encompasses not only those programs related to the employee's current or future job at Polaroid but also basic skills courses and several degree programs.

TAP is widely publicized in a variety of ways—brochures, handbooks, supervisors, word of mouth—and the application process is easy and convenient. Furthermore, not only is educational counseling made *available* to employees at their work site, but it is required before financial assistance is granted, so as to ensure that the best educational match is made between student and course to meet the objectives of both Polaroid and the employee.

Available anecdotal evidence suggests that the education program at Polaroid, and TAP within it, does in fact meet its fundamental objective of promoting advancement within the company.

One begins to sound repetitive when outlining TAP's other success factors. Again, what emerges is a combination of contextual and programmatic features. Counseling, publicity, full prepayment, and simplified and liberal requirements and procedures all tailor the plan to the needs of working adults. Furthermore, Polaroid's "corporate personality" has exhibited a clear and continuing commitment to the education and development of all its employees (Knox, 1979).

Taken together, the three programs described here point to a number of actions that, if adopted by other employers, would significantly enhance the attractiveness and utility of their tuition-assistance plans. These are: (1) advance funds, eliminating or reducing employee out-of pocket expenses; (2) broaden the eligible course criteria (in Kimberly-

Clark's open program, 90% of courses taken are job- or career-related); (3) simplify admissions and approval procedures; (4) provide such support services as career counseling, education advisement, and educational brokering; (5) keep constant the flow of information on the plan and on education and training options.

Wirtz (1979: 31) offers a fitting summary to this discussion of the tuition-aid element of employer-sponsored recurrent education:

> The real reason, though, for restrained reaction here is that these tuition aid and broader worker education developments, especially as they are reflected in cases such as these three, appear to offer such almost limitless prospects that the most serious danger may be in expecting too much from them too quickly. It is hard even to conceive of the changes that might come, in terms of everything from productivity per person hour to people's higher use of the human experience, from breaking out of the time-trap illusion that education is for youth and work for adults and never shall the two worlds overlap. It has been a mistake to assume that the "bridges between the two worlds of education and work" are properly built only from the school side of the gap. Worker education, including tuition-assistance as part of its curriculum, could be as important a development in the 1980's as the community colleges were in the 1960's— or even as the land grant colleges were a century ago.

APPENDIX
Tuition Assistance in the Private Sector: Estimates of Its Coverage and Potential Implications for Adult Education

Size of Establishment by Number of Employees	Number of Establishments[1]	Number of Employees[1]	Estimated Percentage of Establishments with Tuition Aid Plans[2] +	Estimated Percentage of Employees Eligible to Participate	Estimated Number of Eligible Employees	Estimated Number of Employees Participating at Average 4% Rate	Estimated Effects on Number of Employees Participating in Adult Education Resulting from a Participation Rate Increase of: 1%	2%	3%	5%	10%
1,000 and more	4,702	9,240,672	92 (90%–95%)+	70% (65%–75%)	(6,583,978) high 5,950,992 @ 70%	238,039	+ 59,509	+119,019	+178,529	+ 297,548	+ 595,097
500–999	7,298	5,053,493	82 (30%–85%)	70% (65%–75%)	(3,221,601) high 2,900,704 @ 70%	116,028	+ 29,007	+ 58,014	+ 87,021	+ 145,035	+ 290,070
100–499	71,898	14,429,095	60 (55%–65%)	65% (60%–70%)	(6,565,238) high 5,627,347 @ 65%	225,093	+ 56,273	+112,546	+168,819	+ 281,366	+ 562,732
1–99	4,059,541	33,955,586	32 (25%–40%)	55% (50%–60%)	(8,149,340) high 5,976,182 @ 55%	239,047	+ 59,761	+119,523	+179,285	+ 298,808	+ 597,617
TOTALS					(24,520,157) high 20,455,225 (17,039,658) low	808,207	+204,550	+409,202	+613,654	+1,022,757	+2,045,516

WARNING: The data in this table are no more than informed guesses about the reach of tuition-assistance programs in the private sector. Survey research on the subject of tuition assistance plan incidence in the private sector has been made up of infrequent and by and large limited surveys of the largest employer establishments. Thus, we have no empirical basis for the assumptions made regarding plan incidence or percentage of eligible employees for establishments under 500 employees, wherein the majority of the American work force is to be found. These "guestimates" are based on an "if this is so, then this is so" logic. They should be viewed and used accordingly.

1. Data are from U.S. Department of Commerce (1978: Table 1B). These data exclude government employees, self-employed persons, farm workers, domestic service workers, railroad employees, and merchant fleet and foreign-based workers.
2. Estimates are based on Lusterman (1977: Table 2.1). For the 500-999 group and the 1000+ group Lusterman's estimates are used. No serious survey data are available on tuition-aid incidence in establishments below 500. Estimates here assume, based on anecdotal evidence, a lower incidence the smaller the establishment size. We estimated a constant intergroup drop of 20% below the 500 employee size level.
3. Estimates are based on O'Meara (1970: Tables 8, 9). The first of these tables examines categories of employee eligible, and the latter examines length of service criteria. These are the key determinants of eligible populations. O'Meara estimates, based on his sample of 200 large companies, that 84% are open to all employees and that 65% have no service time stipulation. For the top 2 establishment size groupings we assume a 70% eligibility. We estimate progressively lower percentages of eligibility for the smaller employer groupings, assuming that because of higher turnover rates in smaller establishments fewer employees would meet service time requirements.

NOTES

This article leans so heavily on the fact gathering and analyses of Dr. Harold Goldstein, Dr. Charles Stewart, Ms. Bryna Shore Fraser, Ms. Jane Shore, Ms. Leslie Rosow, Messrs. Willard Wirtz, Paul Barton, and Ivan Charner, and Dr. Herbert Levine that any claim to authorship of more than a fraction of what appears here would constitute utter fraud. This article's existence is properly understood as a budgetary convenience, nothing more.

The works drawn upon are, in the main, policy research monographs commissioned by the Project on Worker Education and Training Policies, with which it was my good fortune to be associated from 1978 to 1980. This project is one of several current activities of the National Institute of Work and Learning; it was made possible through funding support from the National Institute of Education. Ms. Nevzer Stacey has served as the NIE project officer since 1976, and is, as much as anyone, responsible for its being.

1. To be reminded one needs to note only a few examples: the Carnegie and other public libraries, Samuel Gompers's work place-based training programs for cigar makers, correspondence and proprietary schools, county extension agents, the workers' education programs of unions and radical political groups, debating societies and the nineteenth-century Chatauquas, and literacy classes for immigrants.

REFERENCES

Bureau of National Affairs (1978) Training Programs and Tuition Aid Provisions. Personnel Policies Forum, Survey 123. Washington, DC: Author.
CHARNER, I. (1980) Patterns of Adult Participation in Learning Activities. Washington, DC: National Institute for Work and Learning.
────── (1979) "Workers' educational benefits: an exploration into the non-use of tuition aid programs." Worker Education and Training Policies Project, National Manpower Institute.
CLARK, H. F. and J. C. DAVIS (1975) "Training in business and industry," in M. E. Strong (ed.) Developing the Nation's Workforce. Yearbook 5. Washington, DC: American Vocational Association.
CLARK, H. F. and H. S. SLOAN (1958) Classrooms in the Factories: An Account of Educational Activities Conducted by American Industry. Rutherford, NJ: Fairleigh Dickinson University.
FRASER, B. S. (1980) The Structure of Adult Learning and Education and Training Opportunity in the United States. Washington, DC: National Institute for Work and Learning.
GOLDSTEIN, H. (1980) Training and Education by Industry. Washington, DC: National Institute for Work and Learning.
JAFFE, A. J. and C. D. STEWART (1951) Manpower Resources and Utilization.
KNOX, K. (1979) Polaroid Corporation's Tuition Assistance Plan: A Case Study. Washington, DC: National Manpower Institute.
LeBEL, A. A. (1977) Final Task A Report: A Description of Existing Negotiated Tuition Aid Plans. Washington, DC: National Manpower Institute.
LUSTERMAN, S. (1977) Educational in Industry. New York: Conference Board.

O'MEARA, J. R. (1970) Combatting Knowledge Obsolescence: II, Employee Tuition Aid Plans. New York: Conference Board.
ROSOW, L. A. (1979) Kimberly-Clark Corporation's Educational Opportunities Plan: A Case Study. Washington, DC: National Manpower Institute.
SHORE, J. (1979) The Education Fund of District Council 37: A Case Study. Washington, DC: National Manpower Institute.
STEWART, C. D. (1980) Worklife Education and Training and the Ordeal of Change. Washington, DC: National Institute for Work and Learning.
SWERDLOFF, S. (1978) Report on Project to Develop Data on Nonregistered Apprentices, by Occupation and Industry. Washington, DC: U.S. Department of Labor, Employment and Training Administration.
TRACEY, W. R. (1974) Managing Training and Development Systems. New York: American Management Association.
U.S. Department of Commerce (1978) County Business Patterns 1976. Washington, DC: Author.
U.S. Department of Labor, Bureau of Labor Statistics (1945) Improvement of Labor Utilization Procedures. Washington, DC: Author.
VENN, G. (1970) Man, Education and Manpower. Washington, DC: American Association of School Administrators.
WIRTZ, W. (1979) Tuition Aid Revisited. Washington, DC: National Institute for Work and Learning.
WOOL, H. (1947) "Recent trends in the labor force." Monthly Labor Rev. (December).
WOYTINSKY, W. S. et al. (1953) Employment and Wages in the United States.

8

UNIONS AND POSTSECONDARY EDUCATION

NEVZER STACEY
IVAN CHARNER

During the past two decades, the United States has witnessed a significant growth in the participation of adults in postsecondary education. Moreover, there has been a parallel growth in the awareness of the needs and desires of adults for education. As a result, new programs for adults are being developed at postsecondary educational institutions and through business, community-based organizations, and unions.[1]

Although the overall rate of adult participation in education increased from 7.6% in 1957 to 11.6% in 1978 (Momeni, 1980), significant variations exist among population groups. Generally, younger, white, well-educated, higher-income, higher occupational status adults have the higher rates of participation in education (Charner, 1980c). This variation has maintained and in many cases furthered the inequity between groups in the U.S. population.

Organized labor in the United States has a long history of support for equality of educational opportunity. While the early support focused on educational opportunities for school-aged children, since the early 1900s unions have been interested in education for their members. Organized labor's interest in education of unionized workers began with a concern for social change. It then turned to more utilitarian objectives that reflected the practical needs of the union movement. Finally, the worker education movement settled on the more general concern of providing higher education to union members.[2]

Unlike most Western European countries, the United States does not have any federal or state legislation regarding educational leaves or tuition assistance, nor is any legislation envisioned in the near future. In the United States, workers must rely on company-sponsored educational plans that are unilaterally offered or collectively bargained for. Organized labor, through its collective bargaining efforts and through its own financial support, has created a variety of mechanisms to allow members and their families to pursue education.

Our interest in this article is with union programs that provide educational opportunities to their members. While there are a large number of programs available to nonunion working adults, this article will focus only on union programs. We focus on union programs for two reasons. First, unions represent almost one-quarter of the paid work force and, second, unions play a strategic role in representing the long-range interests of their members, of which education is clearly one.

In 1977, labor unions represented 23.8% of the 81.3 million employed workers. Of these unionized workers 56% are blue-collar workers, 35% are white-collar; and 10% are service workers. Manufacturing and services industries account for 58% of the workers represented by labor unions (U.S. Department of Labor, Bureau of Labor Statistics, 1979).

As far as earnings are concerned, workers who are represented by labor unions earn more than those who are not; in 1977, on the weekly average, unionized workers earned $41 more, due primarily to higher earnings by blue-collar workers. The widest earnings margin between unionized and nonunionized workers is achieved by skilled workers in the building trades. For example, construction carpenters and craft workers in 1977 made on the average, $119 and $116 more per week than their nonunionized counterparts (U.S. Department of Labor, Bureau of Labor Statistics, 1979).

While unions have helped workers maintain and increase their salaries, they have also been concerned with skill upgrading and mobility potential of their members. As such, they have negotiated for and provided educational opportunities for their members. In this article we examine the history and present status of educational programs created by labor unions and collective bargaining agreements and explore the possibilities of developing further opportunities for union members to acquire postsecondary education. By "postsecondary" education we mean education that is beyond the age of compulsory schooling. We include any formal or organized activity undertaken with the intent of bringing about changes in information, knowledge, understanding, or skills. This definition includes courses offered by unions and employers as well as the more traditional education providers. For workers the pursuit of postsecondary education may be job-related, for career change, for personal development, or for social or political reasons.

THE ROLE OF UNIONS

As suggested earlier, labor unions have always supported education. Union involvement has taken several routes. As early as 1829, the New York Workingmen's Party urged the creation of a public school system in New York City open to all. In 1903, at the Twenty-Third Convention of the American Federation of Labor (AFL), the first permanent Committee on Education was established. The committee urged the introduction of textbooks that "will be more in accord with modern thought, social and political economy." It was during the early 1900s that educational departments were established in several unions, including the International Ladies Garment Workers' Education Department in 1917 and the Amalgamated Clothing Workers' Education Department in 1919. In the 1930s workers' education began to respond to the needs of immigrant workers, taking on an added role of providing education for union organizing and day-to-day union work.

Labor unions have played a major role in shaping federal educational legislation. The 1917 Vocational Education Act and the 1963 Amendments to the Vocational Education Act are among the benchmarks of union involvement in shaping educational policy in the United States. The 1917 Act gave the states federal funds to establish vocational education programs in industry, agriculture, and home economics for high school students, to train teachers, and to buy equipment. The amendments of 1963 extended vocational education to students in all vocational fields and gave the states and the federal government the responsibility to review vocational education programs periodically to determine whether programs matched projected manpower needs and job opportunities (United Auto Workers, 1974).

While a review of labor union history reveals that education has been and is a concern for the American labor movement, the emphasis of union education activities has changed in response to the changing needs of members. When unions experienced rapid expansion they focused their educational activities on teaching the fundamentals of trade union organizing and leadership. After the 1940s, when expansion slowed, the unions began to establish relationships with institutions of higher learning in pursuit of access to postsecondary education for their members. These relationships of unions with a variety of educational institutions have taken several forms.

UNION INVOLVEMENT IN POSTSECONDARY EDUCATION

Through funds provided in collective bargaining agreements and through their own financial support, unions have created a variety of mechanisms to allow members and their families to pursue additional education. There are two major approaches: direct subsidy and indirect subsidy. Direct subsidy is usually provided through funds allocated directly from the union's treasury to an individual or to an institution to support educational activities. Indirect subsidies involve employers or other sources of funding (Charner, 1980b).

DIRECT SUBSIDIES

Unions provide scholarships and loans so that members and their families may attend institutions of their choice. The United Auto Workers (UAW) alone spent $848,500 on scholarships in 1979. Some union scholarships pay for tuition only, while others pay a host of education-related expenses (books, stipends for living costs, and so on). Most union scholarships are awarded on the basis of economic need or on a first-come, first-served basis. In relation to total expenditures for postsecondary education, direct subsidy to individuals through scholarships constitutes the smallest single program, and most union scholarships are awarded to members' children, although some have gone to workers.

Another financing mechanism is direct union support of educational institutions where members attend prearranged programs. There are two types of arrangements under direct institutional support. In the first arrangement a specific union (or group of unions) makes educational programs available to its members through an agreement with a college, university, or other educational institution. There are several very successful programs of this kind in operation today. Programs that offer degrees in labor education are currently available in 47 institutions of higher learning. They have "open" admission policies and are strongly supported and advertised by the unions. Students are mostly adult union members. Programs include specific labor-related courses for workers and are run on both full-time or part-time bases. These programs provide bachelor's and some master's degrees to participants in union-related subjects. The Rutgers University Labor Education Center, the New York State School of Industrial and Labor Relations at Cornell (ILR), Empire State College, the College of New Rochelle's campus at the union headquarters of District Council 37 of the American Federation of State, County and Municipal Employees (AFSCME) in New York City, and Wayne State University's Weekend College are among the outstanding programs in this category.

A second type of direct institutional subsidy is the education center that is run as well as funded by a union. One outstanding example of this type of arrangement is the UAW's Family Education Center. The Walter and Mae Reuther Family Education Center, which is not affiliated with any formal higher education institution, spent $5,350,000 in providing education and training to members of the UAW in 1979. While the George Meany AFL-CIO Labor Studies Center and the Labor College in New York have affiliations with other institutions, the programs are designed exclusively for union members and are supported by the unions.

In the third kind of direct subsidy, members' dues support union education departments. The majority of courses offered by union education departments focus on teaching union skills ranging from collective bargaining to fiscal management. Although most of the union officials who take advantage of these courses do not receive credits for these courses, they are provided with opportunities to be better skilled and knowledgeable in understanding economic, social, and political issues.

In direct subsidy programs, the unions play an advocacy role and are closely involved in the management, administration, and curricular aspects of the programs. The participation of union members in these programs is high; in fact, most of them are oversubscribed.

INDIRECT SUBSIDIES

Unions and management establish collaborative relationships to provide education and training to their members through contract provisions that range from simple on-the-job training periods (for both entry-level jobs and promotions) to elaborate apprenticeship programs.

According to the most recent information available from the Bureau of Labor Statistics (BLS) of the United States Department of Labor, as of June 1980 there were 153 collective bargaining agreements covering 1000 or more workers that include in the contract a provision for *educational leaves of absence*, 788 contracts for *apprenticeship* programs, 705 contracts for *on-the-job training*, and 103 contracts providing *tuition aid*. These contracts cover over 7 million workers and represent over four-fifths of all the private sector contracts covering 1000 or more workers. The steelworkers, auto workers, and electrical workers, in particular, are parties to a significant number of contracts that include negotiated training and retraining provisions. Let us examine some examples of the arrangements through which unions provide postsecondary educational opportunities to their members through collaboration with management.

Educational Trust Funds

In this arrangement labor and management establish a trust fund into which employers pay a fixed sum of money on a specified basis. This payment varies based on cents/dollars per hour, or per worker, or may be a total lump sum for the length of the contract. The funds may be administered by the union alone, as in the case of District Council 37 of AFSCME in New York City, or by a board composed of management and union officials. In the case of District Council 37, the City of New York contributes $25 per employee per contract term. There are currently 76,000 covered employees in this contract, so fund contributions total almost $2 million per year. Courses offered under this arrangement range from college-level studies to vocational and career training. According to a survey conducted in 1973, 60% of the District Council participants had not previously gone to college and one-fifth had not finished high school; 60% of the workers earned less than $16,000 per year and 40% less than $12,000.

Recent interviews conducted under a study done by the National Institute for Work and Learning (NIWL)[3] with funding from the National Institute of Education (NIE) revealed that the majority of the participants in the District Council 37 program are females, clerical and hospital workers, who are in lower economic status positions. Attractions of this program are the location of the educational facilities at the union hall, the flexible scheduling arrangements, the close ties of the curriculum to state licensing requirements, and the perception it has instilled in participants that this is the workers' own program, designed and administered to meet their needs. The program also includes counseling to help workers overcome their fears about returning to school. With an estimated 10% participation rate among eligible workers, its developers consider the program highly successful (Shore, 1979).

A similar program is run by Local 3, International Brotherhood of Electrical Workers and New York Electrical Contractors. According to an agreement signed on 1 July 1964, between Local 3 and industry representatives, all employers remit to an educational and cultural trust fund an amount equal to 2% of their gross weekly production payroll. This fund supports a variety of activities, including a year-round residential education program at Bayberry Land, New York, and subsidizes the New York City Labor College associated with Empire State College.

Participants in education programs at Bayberry Land attend courses without loss of income for time away from work. The fund also provides scholarships to the children of members as well as opportunities for workers to take part in cultural activities in New York. In addition, for eligible employees and their spouses who meet certain criteria, the trust fund provides a college tuition reimbursement program. During fiscal year 1978-1979, the fund spent $408,160 on tuition reimbursement.

Tuition Aid

Originally conceived as an employee benefit provided unilaterally by the employer, tuition-aid programs are now also covered by many collective bargaining agreements. According to a recent study conducted by NIWL for NIE, there are approximately 198 plans in firms with 1000 or more employees, covering a total of about 1.6 million workers. Such plans vary with respect to the amount of reimbursement and types of courses, institutions, grade requirements, and eligibility requirements (Charner et al., 1978).

These plans are found in all types of industries: 54% of all plans are in manufacturing, 18% are in transportation and utilities, 19% are in service industries, and 9% are in construction. However, in all usage is low; only approximately 4%-5% of eligible workers and 2%-3% of hourly wage employees attend. Although the amounts negotiated for tuition vary from contract to contract, the General Motors and United

Auto Workers contract, for example, pays $900 per year per worker, whereas a contract between the State of Connecticut and the Connecticut Employees Union pays only $50 per course.

The barriers to participation in tuition-aid plans do not seem to be only financial. The NIWL study on "Work Life Education and Training Policies" (Charner, 1980a) identified perceived barriers to education as:

- inadequate employee information about tuition aid;
- inadequate counseling of employees;
- reimbursement rather than advance payment for courses;
- nonresponsiveness of postsecondary institutions to workers' needs; and
- difficulty in getting courses approved.

Apprenticeship

Another category of programs under direct subsidy to individuals is that of apprenticeship training arrangements. Apprenticeship programs provide credentials to individuals that entitle them to specific wage rates. Apprenticeship training is now available in the 415 recognized skilled occupations. Almost all large craft unions, including United Auto Workers (UAW), International Brotherhood of Electrical Workers (IBEW), International Union of Operating Engineers (IUOE), Sheet Metal Workers Union, and International Brotherhood of Painters and Allied Trades, have successful apprenticeship programs.

The financing schemes of trust funds for apprenticeship programs differ from union to union. An example of a joint labor-management program is the National Training Fund created by the Sheet Metal and Air Conditioning Industry and the Sheet Metal Workers Union. It was established in 1971 and is administered jointly by a committee of union and industry officials. The industry pays 4¢ an hour per employee. On the other hand, the National Joint Apprenticeship Training Committee for Operating Engineers receives no regular contributions. It is supported entirely from the sale of its training curriculum, workbooks, and materials. However, the local Joint Apprenticeship and Training Committees (JATCs) are financed by contributions negotiated under collective bargaining agreements whereby the employer contributes a set amount into the training trust fund for each hour worked by persons covered by such agreements. Such contributions range from 3¢ to 29¢ per hour worked and are considered to be tax exempt as educational institutions by the Internal Revenue Service.

There are currently 73 local apprenticeship programs administered by JATCs for Operating Engineers, representing over 336,000, or 81%, of the IUOE membership. It costs between $3,000 and $8,000 to train an apprentice over the designated period of his or her indenture (Israel, 1981).

An innovation in apprenticeship programs worth mentioning is the Operating Engineers' "Dual Enrollment Programs" sponsored by IUOE through its National Joint Apprenticeship Training Committee. This program combines apprenticeship with college study, thus enabling an individual to receive an associate degree at the end of his or her training. The operation of each local dual enrollment program is locally financed, and some even offer financial assistance to individuals, mostly in the form of a tuition reimbursement after successful completion of a course.

DEMOGRAPHIC CHANGES AND IMPLICATIONS FOR TRAINING AND EDUCATION

Having discussed briefly the existing programs in which unions play a significant role in providing postsecondary education to adults, we now turn to some of the possible advantages to union members if they participate in education and training programs. Although it is risky to rely too heavily on projections, we know that several demographic, technological, skill, and value changes will affect work places and organizations.

Over the last decade, large numbers of people joined the labor force for the first time, and an increasing proportion of these workers were women. In addition, the average age of the labor force is continuing to rise. The number of young people seeking jobs is likely to drop, especially after 1985. These developments point to the declining capacity of public and private pension and social security plans to support retirees. An aging work force also suggests a greater need for retraining. Coupled with these demographic changes, an increasing percentage of poorly skilled, non-English-speaking individuals will enter the labor force. As a result of these developments, the labor force will be highly heterogeneous and will contain an increasing number of workers with poor prospects for upward mobility. The demographics of the future suggest that mobility within internal labor markets will be limited and that education and training of the work force may be especially important for minorities, women, and older workers.

Another reason to suspect that worker training will be needed increasingly in the years ahead is the decline in the growth of American productivity. The causes and possible remedies of this slow but steady decline in the productivity growth rate are of the utmost importance to the economic well-being of the United States and its position in the world market. Although the effect of training on productivity has not been established empirically, there is evidence that productivity is related to rising educational levels (Goldstein, 1980). If general education contributes significantly to rising output per worker (Denison, 1976), then training that enhances work skills may also contribute. Large investments in research and development, more rapid application of new technology to industry, more rapid retraining of workers, and different styles of management to increase worker participation in decision making are also being investigated as possible remedies for declining productivity.

Two technological trends also suggest the increasing significance of employee training and education: technological changes in existing industries, and rapid technological innovations resulting in the creation of new industries. Technological changes generally require retraining of production workers, and most large high-technology companies are already spending large sums of money for this purpose.

The shift in the United States toward high-technology industries is requiring more skilled workers even at lower-level jobs. Some of the industries that reflect these changes are data and word processing, communications, pharmaceutical manufacturers, energy, transportation, heavy equipment manufacturers, and marketing. In the electronics field, the extensive use of micro chips will change the function of jobs by decreasing the need for workers at one level and increasing it at other levels. For office work, word processing machines and electronic filing systems are expected to cut the demand for secretaries and clerks. In the health sector, increasing labor costs will probably bring about the widespread use of electronic diagnostic machines operated by technicians rather than by physicians. These are some examples of innovations that will substantially change the nature of many jobs in the future, eliminating some repetitive, manual tasks and increasing the demand for workers with higher levels of technical knowledge. Such predicted changes in the nature of jobs will necessitate more training and education for workers in the future.

Both basic skill levels and work values have changed in the last decade. Although educational levels attained by individuals are higher then they have ever been, many employers are finding that new workers have inadequate reading, writing, and math skills. In addition, some new workers appear to have different expectations and motivations than their predecessors.

RECOMMENDATIONS

Since these changes will probably take place in the coming decade, it seems that workers who are members of unions must reexamine their education and training opportunities from a different perspective. Once the reasons to acquire further education and training become clear, alternative routes to provide mobility must be made available. What is vitally important to note is that not only should the programs be attractive to workers, but they must also be of high quality.

To be accessible, programs have to be offered at convenient times, based on the type of jobs the worker carries out. Second, education for workers should be at no cost to the workers, at least initially. Reimbursement at the completion of a course or partial payment prior to completion constitute barriers to participation. Third, support services for special groups are essential. For example, for single-parent families it is difficult enough to find child-care facilities during work hours, let alone to make arrangements for their children so that they can take courses after work. Fourth, workers have to feel secure in their learning environment. Adults who have been out of school for many years find it very difficult to compete with traditional students. It is important to conduct courses where workers feel comfortable, in their union halls or other places where the majority of the students are workers with similar problems or academic needs.

The programs that are made available to workers must have high academic standards. It would be a tremendous disservice to workers to raise their aspirations and help them overcome their fears of returning to school only to have them realize at the end of their course of study that their institution or course of study is viewed as less than desirable by others. With the mushrooming of educational providers, unions and workers are faced with myriad institutional options. Employers, too, are confronted with a variety of marketing approaches that make purchasing education not unlike purchasing cosmetics. Workers need counseling and advising services, not only in assessing their own career aspirations and past education and work experiences, but also the quality of courses they are about to take. Such counseling can only be done by individuals who know the work place and are not part of the educational "establishment." If union officials and managers were to provide assistance, the workers may have a real chance to pursue education and training worth their time and energy.

If workers state that their reason for pursuing education and training is to improve their career options, then they should be given training for occupations in which there are likely to be real job openings. Horizontal job mobility must be discussed with workers, and education and training to facilitate the "crossing" to a new occupation must be supported by unions. From the examination of recent data on tuition aid we know that use of educational entitlements dramatically increases in programs where tuition is allowed for courses that are not strictly job-related, but rather *career-related* (Rosow, 1979).

In recent years, organized labor has put a priority on increasing educational opportunities for workers. Through collective bargaining, cooperation with colleges and universities, and their own educational departments, unions have supported the higher education of workers through financial subsidies and program delivery. Union education programs for workers can affect the character of organized labor, the quality of the work force, and the higher education system. Their success is dependent on the ability of unions to cooperate with industry and education and to increase the participation of workers in these programs by overcoming the barriers faced by workers and responding to the diverse educational and training needs of workers.

If union leadership is able to do this, we would expect their ties to workers would be strengthened and their role in society would be enhanced. Involvement in the education of their 20 million members would revitalize their role in our changing society and regain for them the status they rightfully deserve.

NOTES

1. Charner (1980c) examines the possible reasons for this growth.
2. Dwyer (1977) provides a more complete historical delineation of union education.
3. The National Institute for Work and Learning was formerly the National Manpower Institute.

REFERENCES

BOAZ, R. (1978) Participation in Adult Education, Final Report, 1975. Washington, DC: Government Printing Office.

CHARNER, I. (1980a) "Investing in your employees' future." Training and Development J. (May): 100-104.

—— (1980b) "Union subsidies to workers for higher education," in H. Tuckman and E. Whalen (eds.) Subsidies to Higher Education: The Issues. New York: Praeger.

—— (1980c) Patterns of Adult Participation in Learning Activities. Washington, DC: National Institute for Work and Learning.

—— K. KNOX, A. LeBEL, H. LEVINE, and J. SHORE (1978) An Untapped Resource: Negotiated Tuition-Aid in the Private Sector. Washington, DC: National Manpower Institute.

DENISON, E. F. (1976) "Some factors affecting productivity growth," in The Future of Productivity. Washington, DC: National Center for Productivity and the Quality of Working Life.

DWYER, R. (1977) "Worker's education, labor education, labor studies: a historical delineation." Rev. of Educ. Research 47 (Winter): 179-207.

GOLDSTEIN, H. (1980) Training and Education by Industry. Washington, DC: National Institute for Work and Learning.

ISRAEL, P. H. (1981) "Education and training programs of the International Union of Operating Engineers," in P. Doeringer (ed.) Work Place Perspectives on Education and Training. Boston: Martinus Nijhoff.

LEVINE, H. and M. FRIED (1978) "Expanding options for worker education," in P. Barton (ed.) Implementing New Education-Work Policies. San Francisco: Jossey-Bass.

MOMENI, J. (1980) Adult Participation in Education: Past Trends and Some Projections for the 1980's. Washington, DC: National Institute for Work and Learning.

—— and I. CHARNER (1979) Tuition-Aid Plans for Workers: Characteristics, Operations and Consequences. Washington, DC: National Manpower Institute.

ROSOW, L. (1979) Kimberly-Clark Corporation's Educational Opportunities Plan: A Case Study. Washington, DC: National Manpower Institute.

SHORE, J. (1979) The Educational Fund of District Council 37: A Case Study. Washington, DC: National Manpower Institute.

United Auto Workers (1980) Annual Report. Detroit: Author.

—— (1974) Labor's Historic Support of Public Education: A Chronology. Detroit: Author.

U.S. Department of Education (1980) The Condition of Education. Washington, DC: Government Printing Office.

U.S. Department of Labor, Bureau of Labor Statistics (1979) Earnings and Other Characteristics of Organized Workers, 1977. Report 556. Washington, DC: Author.

9

TAX LIMITATION MEASURES
Their Impact in California

HAROLD E. GEIOGUE

This chapter will discuss the impact of voter tax limitation initiatives in California on public postsecondary recurrent education efforts. Proposition 13, Proposition 4, and the influence of Proposition 9 are forcing policymakers to order priorities for public expenditures both among and within program areas—where will recurrent education fall on the priority list?

This article will first present background on the structure and scope of California's public postsecondary education system, followed by:

- recurrent education within this system;
- a discussion of the recent "taxpayers revolt";
- the impact of Proposition 13 on recurrent education; and
- the difficult position occupied by education, particularly recurrent education, in the alignment of public expenditure priorities in the 1980s.

CALIFORNIA'S PUBLIC POSTSECONDARY EDUCATION SYSTEM

STRUCTURE

California's system of public postsecondary education is the largest in the nation. It currently consists of 135 campuses serving over 1.4 million students. This system is separated into three distinct public segments—the University of California, the California State University and Colleges, and the California Community Colleges. (In addition to the public system, there are approximately 300 independent colleges and universities serving 185,000 students.)

To provide guidelines for the orderly development of three public segments, the Master Plan for Higher Education in California was developed and its recommendations were largely incorporated into the Donahoe Higher Education Act of 1960. The purpose of the act was to define the function and responsibilities of each segment and to establish a systematic approach to the needs of higher education. A coordinating agency, the California Postsecondary Education Commission (CPEC) was established to assist in meeting the objectives of the act.

The University of California (UC). The UC system consists of 8 general campuses, 5 medical schools, and numerous special research facilities located throughout the state. To govern the University of California, the state constitution grants full power of organization and governance to a 26-member Board of Regents, the members of which serve 12-year terms. The regents have substantial freedom from legislative or executive control.

In addition to the function of instruction, which is basic to all three segments of public higher education, the University of California is designated as the primary state-supported agency for research. Instruction is provided to both undergraduate and graduate students in the liberal arts and sciences and in the professions, including teaching. The University has exclusive jurisdiction over graduate instruction in the professions of law, medicine, dentistry, and veterinary medicine. It has sole authority for awarding the doctorate degree, with the exception that in selected fields joint doctoral degrees may be awarded with the California State University and Colleges.

The UC regents have established their admission standards in conformity with guidelines in the original Master Plan that called on the University to limit admissions to the top one-eighth of California's high school graduates.

The California State University and Colleges (CSUC). This system comprises 19 campuses and is governed by a statutory 23-member Board of Trustees generally serving 8-year terms. Although the Board of Trustees does not have the constitutional autonomy of the UC regents, the Donahoe Act of 1960 did provide for centralization of policy and administrative functions that are carried out by the Chancellor's Office.

The primary function of CSUC is to provide instruction to both undergraduate and graduate students in the liberal arts and sciences, in applied fields, and in various professions, including teaching. The granting of bachelor's and master's degrees is authorized, but doctorate degrees may not be granted except under the joint doctoral program with UC. Faculty research is authorized only to the extent that it is consistent with the instruction function. Admissions are limited to the top one-third of California's high school graduates.

The California Community Colleges (CCC). A 15-member Board of Governors was created by statute in 1967 to provide direction to the 70 community college districts (with 106 campuses) that constitute the system. Unlike UC and CSUC, community colleges are administered by local boards and derive some funds from local property taxes.

Instruction in public community colleges is limited to lower-division levels (freshman and sophomore) of undergraduate study in the liberal arts and sciences and in occupational or technical subjects. The granting of the associate in arts or the associate in science degree is authorized.

Admission to the community colleges is open to any high school graduate or person over 18.

SCOPE

The statement that this is the largest public higher education system in the United States is supported by both enrollment and fiscal data. In the fall of 1978, UC enrolled 8% of the state total, CSUC enrolled 21%, and the CCC enrolled the remaining 71%. Part-time enrollees represented 73% of the CCC figures but only 7% of UC undergraduates (see Table 9.1).

A summary of estimated expenditures for 1979-1980 is shown in Table 9.2. total support for all higher education in 1979-1980 amounted to nearly $5.6 billion. Of the total support budget, the state general fund provided $2.8 billion, or 50%.

Considering there are a total of 135 institutions, 1.4 million students, and an annual state expenditure of $2.8 billion, there is indeed a large recurrent education movement.

RECURRENT EDUCATION IN CALIFORNIA

UNIVERSITY OF CALIFORNIA

Traditionally, off-campus instructional activities of the University of California have been associated with UC Extension and UC Agricultural

TABLE 9.1 California Public Postsecondary Education Enrollment (Headcount), Fall 1978

Segment	Full-time Number	Full-time Percentage	Part-time Number	Part-time Percentage	Total Number	Total Percentage
University of California						
Undergraduate	84,305	93	6,656	7	90,961	100
Graduate	35,067	95	1,853	5	36,920	100
					127,881 (8%)	
California State University						
Undergraduate	167,752	70	70,508	30	238,260	100
Graduate	15,065	22	52,850	78	67,915	100
					306,175 (21%)	
California Community Colleges	285,133	27	762,034	73	1,047,167 (71%)	100
Totals	587,322	40	893,901	60	1,481,223 (100%)	100

SOURCE: CPEC (1979).

Extension. In contrast to CSUC Extension activities, UC Extension operates relatively independently of UC on-campus programs. A very small proportion of UC faculty teach in its programs. The majority of instructors are either working professionals or are employed in one of the other educational segments. UC considers its extension program to be chiefly a noncredit program. Matriculated students constitute a minor role in UC Extension. UC Extension course credit may be applied to a degree program if the student makes special arrangements with his or her academic department, but such arrangements are relatively rare. UC Extension enrolled an estimated 375,000 people in 1979-1980.

UC enjoyed state general fund support for administrative and development costs for extension programs until 1968-1969, when state support was withdrawn. (At its apex the share of state support was approximately 16%.)

Unlike some public institutions that historically have served large numbers of matriculated part-time students and offered extensive pro-

TABLE 9.2 Summary of Estimated 1979-1980 Budget for
California Higher Education (in millions)

	State General Fund	Federal	Other	Total
University of California	$964.3	$1,151.5	$854.9	$2,970.5
California State University	821.5	53.2	292.7	1,167.4
Community Colleges	1,000.2	92.5	270.5	1,363.2
Miscellaneous	55.0	15.4	–	70.4
Totals	$2,841.0	$1,312.6	$1,417.9	$5,571.5

SOURCE: California State Department of Finance (1980-1981).

grams in the evening, the University of California over the years has focused primarily on full-time students and has made no scheduling or tuition arrangements designed expressly to serve part-time students. While the University has always had students who did not carry a full-time academic load, it had no programs for part-time students, as such.

One exception to this policy occurred in 1971 when the University developed plans for the UC Extended University (EU). Its first pilot programs were implemented in 1972. The Extended University was planned as a three-year pilot program designed to help the University learn how to serve a new group of qualified, part-time, older, working citizens by increasing opportunities for them to participate in UC degree programs—off campus as well as on campus. The Extended University was established as an entity separate from UC Extension and was placed under the administration of a university vice president headquartered at the systemwide administration building in Berkeley. Although extension personnel were involved on two of the campuses that participated in the EU program, the Extended University did not function as part of the self-supporting UC Extension program. During 1973-1974 the Extended University received $806,949 from the state general fund. In 1974-1975 the amount was increased to $1,312,434.

Students in Extended University pilot programs attended classes in the evening or on weekends. About half of the programs were offered off campus, emphasizing the point that some of the access barriers that had been lowered were not associated with geographic location. Because of the amount of funding granted the Extended University, it was in a position to make more extensive use of the media. Lecture demonstration courses were recorded on videotape for some programs; modules of instruction were on video cassettes in the nursing program; and microwave TV communication was utilized to beam courses to various cities.

In 1972-1973 the Extended University offered 7 graduate and undergraduate programs; 19 were offered in 1973-1974; 23 in 1974-1975. Over 1600 Extended University students were enrolled in the 23 degree programs offered that year by 7 of the UC campuses. More than half were enrolled at 33 off-campus locations.

All programs were regular University of California degree programs developed and offered by regular campus departments following regular academic procedures and regulations.

State funding of the Extended University was discontinued by the governor in 1975-1976 on the grounds that the University should maintain the program, beyond its initial phase, from the regular University budget. The regents' 1976-1977 budget included a request for $2.6 million for the Extended University as an augmentation (not within the regular budget) but the request was not included in the governor's budget. The state legislature passed a bill that appropriated $2.6 million, but the bill was vetoed by the governor. The Extended University is currently being phased out.

There is considerable evidence to support the view that the University's effort to extend its traditional approaches into nontraditional and off-campus areas was a partial response to criticism that the University was an "elitist" institution, unconcerned with new instructional techniques, with part-time study, and with older and underrepresented clientele. Another reason for the establishment of the Extended University undoubtedly was the genuine concern among many members of the University community that the criticism had some validity.

What also seems clear, however, is that the University's commitment to the concept of the Extended University was not strong. The fact that the decision was made to phase out the program once state funding was terminated, rather than attempt to continue it under an alternate funding arrangement, such as higher student fees or the use of internal University resources, indicates that the program occupied a relatively low priority within the University family. The fact that University Extension was so well established, and the fact that much of what the Extended University purported to do could also be done through Extension, probably contributed to the decision to abandon the program. At this time, there is little desire at the official levels of the University to continue formal degree programs beyond the confines of the traditional, campus-based setting dealing with top quality undergraduate and graduate students.

Despite this, California has developed a large recurrent education activity in its other two public segments—the CSUC and the CCC.

CALIFORNIA STATE UNIVERSITY AND COLLEGES

The California State University and Colleges offer four distinct approaches to off-campus and extended degree opportunities: (a) State University Extension; (b) miscellaneous courses provided at off-campus locations; (c) external degree programs; and (d) the Consortium of the CSUC. Administratively, extended degree programs and extension offerings are operated under the auspices of State University Extension, miscellaneous courses through the campuses, and the Consortium through its own administration in the systemwide Chancellor's Office.

State University Extension. Begun in 1932, this program is quite similar to most university extension operations. A variety of courses are offered featuring fee support, short duration, a focused audience, and little degree credit. As of 1978-1979, CSUC Extension enrolled 73,526 people, or the equivalent of 5,693 full-time students.

Miscellaneous courses. Conducted at off-campus locations, these courses, both degree-related and non-degree-related, are a rubric within which fall the thousands of efforts to reach adult learners who are isolated from a campus by either distance or time. These courses are classified separately because they are not related to a formal, organized, degree program. Unlike Extension, they do not require special fees. In 1979-1980 it is estimated that 4000 people will enroll almost equally in the degree- and non-degree-related miscellaneous courses.

External degrees. The CSUC system embarked on major efforts to establish formal degree programs for the on- and off-campus recurrent education student through external degree programs and the Consortium of the CSUC.

In 1971, the CSUC chancellor called for a major expansion of off-campus and extended educational opportunities. Noting the perceived "rigid system," which primarily served students in residence, he called for an alternative that included "television, correspondence courses, self-study combined with short-course on-campus programs, taped lectures with study guides to comprise programmed learning, as well as classroom instruction on or off campus," all to be on a self-supporting basis.

The proposed expansion in the nontraditional sector was endorsed by the Board of Trustees with the establishment of the Commission on External Degree Programs, which was charged with the establishment, on a pilot project basis, of policies and procedures for implementing off-campus degree programs. The activities of the commission resulted in the concept of the "1000-mile campus" and the CSUC system now has established policies that govern the development of external degrees.

At present, external degree programs are developed by the individual campuses and, after review by the Chancellor's Office, are forwarded to the commission for approval. These programs are fully self-supporting, although a small amount of funding is provided for fee waivers. By the fall of 1975, enrollment in these programs was 3733.

The Consortium of the California State University and Colleges was established in 1973 as the result of a recommendation by the Commission on External Degree Programs. Its purposes were to:

- serve the needs of highly mobile adult students who through circumstances are required to transfer from one college to another, thereby losing degree credit;
- develop statewide or regional external degree programs to serve sparsely populated geographical areas, or students with special interests who are dispersed over a wide area;
- conduct programs in geographic areas where the local CSUC campus is unable to meet the need with its own resources;
- encourage reciprocity of residence credit and core degree requirements between campuses and to begin building toward the development of a common "credit bank" or curricular records for students; and
- develop strategies for assessing the prior learning experiences of adult students, whose varied backgrounds of work and schooling make admissions decisions more complex.

TABLE 9.3 CSUC Recurrent Education Activity FTE, 1977-1978 to 1980-1981

	1977-1978	1978-1979	1979-1980	1980-1981
Extension	6,112	5,693	5,288	4,942
Miscellaneous Courses	1,002	819	816	816
External Degree	2,122	793	830	835
Consortium	423	318	225	375
Total	8,659	7,623	7,159	6,968

SOURCE: CSUC, Office of Institutional Research (personal communication).

As of 1977-1978, total FTE enrollment in the Consortium was approximately 500, a figure that was reduced to an estimated 300 for the 1979-1980 fiscal year. Although originally supported by the legislature ($46,252 in 1972-1973, with increasing amounts to $200,000 in 1976-1977), it is currently self-supporting. The Western Association of Schools and Colleges granted full regional accreditation to the Consortium in 1976.

A summary of full-time equivalent (FTE) enrollment in all four CSUC recurrent education activities is shown in Table 9.3.

CALIFORNIA COMMUNITY COLLEGES

Of all students enrolled in recurrent education in California's 3 public segments, the majority in the inventory of off-campus locations and programs in fall 1978 (62.4% of the off-campus locations and 81.3% of the course registrations) were in the CCCs. Although this is a decrease from 1976 figures of 67.7% and 84.8%, respectively, the community colleges are clearly the principal providers of recurrent education services.

The figures are also dramatically higher than the total reported in the fall of 1972. At that time, there were 1,363 off-campus locations with an enrollment of 190,000 students, over 98% of them part-time. By contrast (although they are not directly comparable), course registration four years later were 472,153, and six years later, 363,899. The 1,363 locations reported in 1972 had grown to 2,985 in 1976 and then dropped to 2,507 in 1978. Thus it is apparent that something caused a dramatic growth in enrollment between 1972 and 1976, and that something else caused a decline between 1976 and 1978. (This decline will be discussed further below.)

Recurrent education occurs primarily in the off-campus setting. In order to obtain information on off-campus programs offered by community colleges, CPEC sent a questionnaire to 20 colleges of varying size, geographic location, and commitment to off-campus operations. Of these, 14 responded.

Table 4 shows the number and types of courses, and types of faculty. The faculty are categorized as "full-time, on-load," "full-time, off-load," or "part-time." The first of these refers to regular, full-time faculty who are teaching an off-campus course as part of their normal assignment. "Full-time, off-load" refers to regular, full-time faculty who are teaching an off-campus course in addition to their normal assignments. "Part-time" refers to individuals who are not regular faculty members with full-time teaching contracts but are hired on a course-by-course basis.

As shown in Table 9.4, there is no consistency among the 14 colleges as to the distribution of credit and noncredit classes. College K offers all of its courses for credit, while 92% of College J's courses are in the noncredit category. Similarly, Colleges C and G have 75% and 85% of their courses in the noncredit area, respectively. Of the 14 colleges, 10 have a majority of credit offerings while 4 have most classes in the noncredit category. The fact that one of these institutions also maintain both the high school adult program and the regular community college program helps to explain the preponderance of noncredit offerings, but this is only a partial explanation.

Part-time faculty are currently teaching 84.4% of the off-campus courses in the 14 colleges, while the total number of part-time faculty is about two-thirds of all community college faculty on a headcount basis. Given the urgings of accrediting agencies for greater use of regular faculty in off-campus programming, the implications of such overwhelming reliance on part-time instructors are significant.

Table 9.5 shows course lengths and fee charges in the 3660 courses noted in Table 9.4. Community colleges use off-cammpus facilities to conduct classes very similar in format to those offered on campus, either during the day or in the evening. This format is the standard lecture/discussion system. The fact that 76.4% of all classes are quarter or semester length indicates the similarity with on-campus programming. The fact

TABLE 9.4 Courses and Types of Faculty Teaching at Selected Off-Campus Locations in the California Community Colleges, Fall 1979

College	Total	Courses Credit	Noncredit	On-Load	Faculty Off-Load	Part-time
A	254	228	228	71	11	172
B	110	110	71	6	11	93
C	767	194	573	149	10	608
D	231	210	21	71	5	155
E	119	100	19	15	2	102
F	453	277	176	9	5	439
G	226	33	193	26	11	189
H	72	34	38	1	2	69
I	445	435	10	96	9	340
J	480	39	441	22	9	449
K	226	226	0	39	8	179
L	113	109	4	0	2	111
M	56	34	22	1	4	51
N	108	100	8	13	0	95
Totals	3,660	2,090	1,570	519	89	3,052
Percentage	100	57.1	42.9	14.2	2.4	83.4

SOURCE: CPEC (1980).

that about 16% of the classes are not of a traditional length indicates flexibility in meeting special needs. Of the 583 courses reported to be under 10 weeks long, 312 of them are offered for credit and 271 are noncredit.

FISCAL PRIORITIES IN AN ERA OF RESOURCE RESTRAINT

With the foregoing discussion of California's postsecondary education structure in mind, I now address:

- the so-called California taxpayers' revolt;
- the impact of Proposition 13 of 1978 on recurrent education efforts in public institutions; and
- recurrent education's position in the political priority structure.

TABLE 9.5 Course Length and Fees Charged in Off-Campus Classes in 14 California Community Colleges, Fall 1979

	Number	Percentage
Course Length		
2 Weeks or Less	93	2.5
2-10 Weeks	490	13.4
Over 10 Weeks	2,795	76.4
Unknown	282	7.7
Totals	3,660	100.0
Course Type and Fee Status		
Credit		
Fee Charged	169	4.6
Fee Not Charged	1,850	50.6
Noncredit		
Fee Charged	311	8.5
Fee Not Charged	1,220	33.3
Unknown	110	3.0
Totals	3,660	100.0

THE TAXPAYERS' REVOLT

The decades of the 1960s and 1970s witnessed an extraordinary growth in the level and scope of government services. For example, during the past 10 years, the percentage increase in federal spending far outstripped the rate of inflation (170% versus 104%). The expansion was even more dramatic in California, where state spending increased nearly 2.5 times the percentage increase in prices.

The extraordinary growth did not just happen by accident. The citizens of California and the nation demanded that it happen. The rise of social consciousness in the late 1960s and early 1970s created public pressure for better schools, health care, air quality, and environment. Government action was viewed as the panacea for the creation of "the great society." Consequently, our elected representatives were just following orders.

It is important to understand the form that these demands took. The public did not demand that government grow and the private economy contract, nor did they demand that government take an increasingly large share of income. The public demands were focused on individual programs and services, rather than on the bottom line of total cost.

As we move into the 1980s, we are told that a taxpayers' revolt is in progress in California and perhaps nationally. There are many manifestations of this revolt, including:

- Propositions 9 and 13, as well as other measures aimed at reducing taxes;
- indexing of income tax and other measures aimed at reducing the growth in taxes;
- Proposition 4 and similar measures aimed at limiting the growth in spending; and
- efforts to balance the federal budget.

The concern, then, is not that elected representatives are failing to respond to the public's demands, but rather that they are doing too good a job of it, and the public does not like the fiscal consequences. While the public has become disenchanted with government spending in general, there is evidence that large segments of the public continue to believe that government can and should take on society's problems—the "there ought to be a law" attitude seems to be surviving despite the revolt. Evidence of this is widespread. In California, for instance:

- The number of bills introduced in the legislature last year was only slightly lower than the number introduced in the previous legislature.
- The testimony taken by legislative committees is indistinguishable from that taken prior to the enactment of recent initiatives—representatives of the public invariably plead for bigger budget appropriations and there has been no outpouring of public sentiment aimed at reducing individual items in the budget.
- The success of incumbents seeking reelection to the legislature has been very high. In November 1978—5 months after the voters expressed great dissatisfaction with government by approving Proposition 13—they reelected nearly 90% of those incumbents on the ballot.

What is new about the "taxpayers' revolt" is the feeling in many quarters that the public's appetite for government services is too healthy—that they demand more from government than they are willing to pay for. The expression "a million here, a million there, and pretty soon we are talking about real money" sums up the problem. Legislative bodies are caught up in the absurdity of trying to maintain spending for each of the individual items in the budget while concurrently being pressured to reduce the level of total spending.

It is this frustration—this recognition that representatives say "no" to individual progams—that has led many to advocate the kinds of broad limitations on government revenues and expenditures that are associated with the "taxpayers' revolt." The argument goes like this: If the amount of revenue that government receives, or the level of expenditures that it can make, is arbitrarily limited, willpower will of necessity be enhanced.

The point is simply this: It is not clear that the public has "sorted out" its priorities regarding government as yet, and until it does—until there is a balance between what is expected of government and what the public is prepared to spend on government—the public sector is going to be in a state of flux.

PROPOSITION 13's IMPACT ON RECURRENT EDUCATION

This brings us to the concern for recurrent education in the context of fiscal restraint. I am not referring to a moderate recession in financial support that all programs can survive with modest belt-tightening; I am talking about a time of deep academic recession caused by declining enrollments of up to 20% occurring in an era of limited resources. There will be the required analysis of the priorities of programs—some programs will expand, most will be fortunate to just retrench, while yet others will be reduced or eliminated. Based on my analysis of the impact of Proposition 13 of 1978, it is the last category into which recurrent education is likely to fall.

A brief orientation would be useful to those who are unfamiliar with the California voter initiative process. The California initiative process was established by special election on 10 October 1911. California became the tenth state in the nation to enact the initiative and referendum.

The initiative provides the people a mechanism to propose statutory revisions and constitutional amendments, and to adopt or reject those proposed by the legislature. The initiative allows the voters to bypass the legislature and have an issue of concern put directly on the ballot for voter approval or rejection.

In order to qualify a direct initiative for the ballot, a title and summary must be obtained from the attorney general, petitions circulated and signatures gathered, and the petitions must be filed with the county clerk of each county in which signatures were collected. Petitions supporting statute revisions must be signed by registered voters equal in number to 5% of the total number of votes cast for all candidates for governor in the last gubernatorial election; those for constitutional amendments require 8%.

An initiative that qualifies for the ballot goes before the voters at the next statewide election held at least 131 days after it qualifies. The governor may call a special statewide election for an initiative measure.

Any initiative measure approved by a majority of the votes cast at any election takes effect the day after the election unless the measure provides otherwise. An approved initiative is not subject to a governor's veto, nor may it be amended or repealed by the legislature without a vote of approval by the electors.

Proposition 13 on the 1978 June ballot was a constitutional revision initiative designed to limit the amount of revenue that could be derived from the taxation of property. The proceeds of such were used primarily to support local government and schools (including the community colleges).

Technically, Proposition 13 added Article XIIIA to the California Constitution, limiting property tax revenue to 1% of the market value of property plus an amount necessary to repay existing voter-approved debt. Article XIIIA also rolled back the assessed value of property to 1975 levels, limited increases in assessed values to 2% per year, and restricted the imposition of nonproperty taxes by state and local governments. The electorate approved the measure by a vote of 2 to 1.

Proposition 13 did not specify how the remaining property tax revenue would be distributed among taxing jurisdictions. Chapter 292 (SB 154) and Chapter 332 (SB 2212), Statutes of 1978, provided for this distribution of property tax revenue and provided $4.4 billion of state funds as fiscal relief to local governments in order to partially offset the loss in property tax revenue.

Proposition 13 reduced city, county, school district, and special district property tax revenue by about $6.9 billion, or about 55%, from the estimated property taxes that would have been levied in 1978-1979 if Proposition 13 had not been enacted. The property tax reduction was about $5.9 billion, or 51%, when compared to 1977-1978 collections.

TABLE 9.6 Comparison of the Property Tax Revenue Loss Resulting from Proposition 13 (in millions)

	1977-1978	1978-1979 Without Proposition 13	Actual
Property Tax Levies	$10,277	$11,258	$5,047
State Subvention for Homeowners' and Business Inventory Examptions	1,172	1,217	536
Total Property Tax Revenues	$11,449	$12,475	$5,583
Reduction from 1977-1978	–	n.a.	–$5,866
Reduction from 1978-1979 (Without Proposition 13)	n.a.	–	–$6,892

SOURCE: Office of Legislative Analyst (1980).

Table 9.6 provides information on property tax reveues in 1977-1978 and 1978-1979. The extent of the reduction in total revenue to each city, county, and special district varied according to: (a) the proportion of total revenue the city, county, or special district collected from property taxes; (b) the entity's legal authority to offset the property tax revenue losses with alternative revenue sources and the extent to which such authority was used, and (c) the amount of replacement revenue received from the state government.

Proposition 13, of course, is not an expenditure limitation, but merely a limitation on one source of revenue, the property tax. Proposition 13 does not say anything about whether total government expenditures can grow 20%, 30%, or 40%; it just says that you cannot fund government by more than "x" from the property tax. And because of this its primary impact in postsecondary education was on the community colleges. Prior to June 1978, community colleges in California were 60% to 70% funded from the local property tax, with the remainder from the state (20% to 30%) and federal (10%) governments. So it was clear that the community colleges had to adjust their planning to take account of fiscal constraints.

More interesting, however, is the fact that, as shown in Table 9.7, Proposition 13 has also had a direct impact on support for the University of California and the California State University and Colleges, which had no property tax support. In fact, the most bewildered people

TABLE 9.7 State General Fund Support to Postsecondary Education Pre- and Post-Proposition 13 (in million)

Segment	1977-1978	1978-1979 Pre-13 Estimated	1978-1979 Post-13 Actual
CCC[a]	$1,218	$1,303	$1,124
UC	737	819	767
CSU	666	734	683
Totals	$2,621	$2,856	$2,574
Reduction from 1977-1978	–	n.a.	–$47
Reduction from 1978-1979 (Without Proposition 13)	n.a.	–	–$282

SOURCE: Office of Legislative Analyst (internal office data).
a. State and local support.

in the capitol after the passage of Proposition 13 were from those segments of postsecondary education.

What developed, obviously, was a political environment involving the fiscal condition in general, and not just the property tax. The general climate of opinion was against government spending in all forms. Postsecondary education was not given any special high-priority protection (for reasons I will discuss), nor was recurrent education.

Details of Proposition 13's impact on recurrent education are sketchy, but some synthesis is possible. I will briefly discuss its impact on UC, CSUC, and CCC, recurrent education.

Of course there was no impact at the University of California, which had abandoned its External University program prior to 1978. In the CSUC system, as shown previously in Table 9.3. The development of recurrent education came to a halt. This is because the legislative fiscal committees began to question the very purpose of recurrent education activities. There was a general concern that much of the growth of recurrent education had occurred without adequate legislative involvement or oversight, especially with regard to enrollment levels, instructional quality, and equity of student charges. The postsecondary education commission was directed by the legislature to "define and study the various kinds of extended education. . . . Such study shall address questions of access, support, student needs, and quality." This study was conducted, however, as of this date, a final policy on the CSUC recurrent education activity remains unresolved by the legislature.

Community colleges reported that, within the operating budget, outlays for credit instruction were reported to be down by 1% while noncredit instructional expenditures were reduced by 27%.

Proposition 13 affected the colleges' ability to carry out the community college mission and functions. While few programs were cut, 6% of 60,000 courses and 13% of 125,000 course sections were eliminated statewide. The average size of remaining course sections increased by 4%, from 23 to 24 students. Courses qualifying for Vocational Education Act support (that is, with occupational objectives) were least affected. In fact, these courses increased slightly in number while all other courses were decreased in number by 16%. As shown in Table 9.8 noncredit courses were most affected. Of these courses, 20% were eliminated and another 10% were shifted to fee-supported community service status. Community service activities, in turn, were reduced overall by slightly more than one-third. All but four districts reduced overall by summer session offerings due to the uncertainty of funding and timing of Proposition 13-related decisions. Statewide, the number of summer courses declined by about 50%.

Community college staff were reduced by about 10,000 employees (14%) from 72,000 to 62,000 between spring 1978 and fall 1979. Of the 1,500 decline in full-time employees, two-thirds was attributed to normal attrition; but in most cases, the empty positions were not filled. Of the total decrease, most (7,000) took place among part-time faculty. In nearly all cases, part-time faculty were not rehired either due to classes that were not offered because of buget reductions or were offered then canceled due to inadequate enrollment. In many cases, noncredit classes experienced low enrollment due to the charging of fees. There was a 23% decrease in part-time staff, but just a 9% decrease in ADA. Consequently, many full-time staff took over part-time duties on an overload basis.

Prior to the passage of Proposition 13, the Department of Finance had projected increases of 3% in enrollment for community colleges during 1978-1979. The actual enrollment change between fall 1977 and fall 1978 was a decrease of 162,000 students, or 12.3%.

The fall 1978 enrollment loss was greater among part-time than among full-time students, greater among males than among females, greater among older than among younger students, and far greater among those enrolled only in noncredit courses. The enrollment of those taking only noncredit courses decreased by more than 50%, and the enrollment of full-time students attending only in the evening declined by one-fourth. There is little doubt that the bulk of the enrollment loss can be attributed to budget and programmatic cutbacks directly related to the significant reduction in fiscal resources caused by Proposition 13.

TABLE 9.8 Comparison of California Community College Enrollments for the Fall 1977 and Fall 1978 Terms, by Program of Studies[a]

	Total			Full-Time			Part-Time		
Category	Fall 1977	Fall 1978	Change	Fall 1977	Fall 1978	Change	Fall 1977	Fall 1978	Change
Head County Enrollment									
Credit Only	803,868	760,132	−5.4	233,362	206,918	−11.3	570,506	553,214	3.0
Credit and Noncredit	19,778	10,114	−48.7	7,481	4,309	−42.4	12,297	5,835	−52.5
Noncredit Only	45,227	19,668	−56.5	—	—	—	45,227	19,668	−56.5
Unknown	6,166	3,013	−51.1	306	43	−85.9	5,860	2,970	−49.3
Total	875,039	792,957	−9.3	241,149	211,270	−12.4	633,890	581,687	8.2
Percentage of Total									
Credit Only	91.9	95.9	4.0	96.8	98.0	1.2	90.0	95.1	5.1
Credit and Noncredit	2.2	1.2	−1.0	3.1	2.0	−1.1	2.0	1.0	−1.0
Noncredit Only	5.2	2.5	−2.7	—	—	—	7.1	3.4	3.7
Unknown	0.7	0.4	0.3	0.1	—	−0.1	0.9	0.5	−0.4
Total									

SOURCE: CPEC (1980).
a. Based on data from 81 of 106 colleges.

PRIORITIES

While it is difficult to make clear comparisons and conclusions, it appears that Proposition 13 had a major impact on postsecondary education in general and recurrent education in particular. There are a variety of reasons for the "softening" of the public priority for postsecondary education:

(1) The unprecedented increase in enrollment and expenditures for higher education. This not only makes it a highly visible segment of our public budget, but also causes a natural fiscal conflict between institutions of higher education seeking to maximize funding and elected officials seeking to minimize taxes.
(2) In addition, competition for money from new social programs, such as energy conservation and medical services, places pressure on decision makers to examine closely traditional programs and stress the reallocation of resources between and within agencies.
(3) The apparent vacuum of leadership in higher education. Right or wrong, academic leadership has the appearance of weakness. This vacuum is partially the result of the perception that leadership in higher education responds to internal special interest constituencies, particularly faculty, rather than to public needs. Also, the high turnover of academic leaders and their reluctance to be assertive contributes to this perception.
(4) The dissident students and faculty bringing higher education's dirty laundry to government's door.
(5) The push for access by women, ethnics, and disabled into the mainstream of society focuses attention on higher education as the gatekeeper.
(6) Reports of unemployment and underemployment of college graduates, particularly graduates of high-cost graduate programs, undermining some of the major rationales for support of higher education—economic development and social mobility.
(7) Finally, there is concern about competitive practices for student enrollments such as the lowering of entrance and retention standards and financial aid bidding. Elected officials see these actions as weakening the social fiber through lowering academic standards in order to assure institutional survival.

With these general concerns in mind, attention can be focused on recurrent education's position within the postsecondary education community. It is my thesis that, for a variety of reasons, recurrent education in California, and perhaps elsewhere, is in a politically vulnerable position given the politics within postsecondary education. While there are those like Daniel Perlman (1975), who see financial crisis as a stimulus for the expansion of recurrent education, I would argue that as it affects public institutions, just the opposite is true. The expansion in the 1970s was mostly due to the social pressure for increased access to higher education. Thus there was expansion in recurrent education despite leveling enrollments and financial difficulty—perhaps we can call this a state of "benign neglect." In a time of financial crisis, however, priority for recurrent education appears to be low due to a variety of factors, including:

- Its low visibility due to limited curriculum, limited staff, limited support services, and limited "alumni" hinders attempts to develop a broad-based constituency.
- Its organizational position, usually outside the academic institutional mainstream, exemplified by not being represented (a) in academic master plans, (b) in academic senates, or (c) in the line organization of the academic vice president's office, weakens its position in academic "in-fighting."
- Its heavy reliance on part-time or low-ranking regular faculty raises questions of quality.
- Its service to a clientele that is often employed, white, and middle-class encourages the budget agencies to promote a self-support financing plan for recurrent education.

CONCLUSION

These factors lead to the conclusion that, within academic institutions that have been in existence for decades and within the society they serve, recurrent education is still the new kid on the block. It is constantly under the burden of proof—and it is our job to establish such proof. Perhaps this can be accomplished through a stronger alliance with the forces of vocationalism in business, industry, and organized labor. Perhaps through an expansion of the type of student served—a "more broadly casted net" if you will. Perhaps the answer lies in a better system of governance.

A few words on governance. As I see it, we need a governance system

- that reduces uncertainty and confusion by being easily understood by all parties;
- that provides an effective accountability mechanism without reducing institutional autonomy;
- that places governors and legislative bodies in their proper role of oversight, not detailed intrusion into administrative matters; and, finally,

• that provides that the tough reallocation questions be addressed systematically across the whole of the higher education community.

If there are negative decisions to be made (closings of departments, layoffs, and so on), they must be determined rationally. Decisions should not be based on who has more muscle in the state house, but on who delivers necessary quality teaching, research, and public service in a reasonably cost-effective mode.

REFERENCES

California Postsecondary Education Commission [CPEC] (1980) Degrees of Diversity: Off-Campus Education in California. Sacramento: Author.
—— (1979) CPEC Information Digest, 1979. Sacramento: Author.
California State Department of Finance (1980-1981) The Governor's Budget. Sacramento: Author.
California State University and Colleges [CSUC] (1977-1978) Statistical Digest, Continuing Eduction, 1977-78. Long Beach: Author.
—— (1975-1976) Statistical Digest, Continuing Education, 1975-76. Long Beach: Author.
McCABE, G. (1979) Discussion Draft: Should the State of California Finance Off-Campus Instruction by the California State University and Colleges? A Study of the Issues. Long Beach: California State University and Colleges.
MAYHEW, L. B. (1976) "The closing door: national tragedy or a shift in social values?" Presented at the National Forum of the College Board, New York, October.
Office of Legislative Analyst (1979) An Analysis of the Effects of Proposition 13 on Local Governments. Sacramento: Author.
PERLMAN, D. H. (1975) "External degree programs: alternative delivery systems for higher education." Liberal Education (October).
RICHARDS, L. (1979) Results of Lifelong Learning Priority Issues Study. Los Angeles: University of Southern California and the Association of Independent California Colleges and Universities.
SALNER, M. B. (1976) Continuing Education in the California State University and Colleges. Long Beach: California State University and Colleges.
TEMPLIN, R. G., Jr. (1977) "Lifelong learning and the politics of education," in Politics of Higher Education and Public Policy. Washington, DC: American Council on Education.
University of California Systemwide Administration (1978) Report of the Systemwide Committee on University Extension. Berkeley: Author.
University of California Systemwide Study Committee on Extension (1978) University Extension at the University of California. Berkeley: Author.

10

AN OPPORTUNITY DEFERRED
Lifelong Learning in the United States

PAMELA H. CHRISTOFFEL

On 3 October 1980, President Carter signed into United States law the Education Amendments of 1980, Public Law 96-374. The legislation, which extended and revised federal postsecondary education programs through 1985, took significant new steps toward expansion of educational opportunity for adults. The result of a two-year legislative development process, the new law amended the Higher Education Act of 1965, which provides the basic statutory authority for a variety of federal student aid and postsecondary educational institution assistance programs. Much of the existing legislation was extended unchanged. Portions of the law dealing with recurrent education were subjected to extensive debate in the Congress over the two-year period and received considerable support in both the House of Representatives and the Senate at that time.

The new law focused only on postsecondary (postcompulsory) education programs, including those serving adults.[1] Overall, it included a wide variety of programs and opportunities for adult learners. It provided more equitable treatment of adult students in financial aid programs and limited expansion of some financial aid programs to less-than-half-time students, many of whom are adults. The law authorized a refocused program of state and federal recurrent education grants directed toward adults who have not participated in such programs previously. New emphasis was placed on recurrent education in statewide postsecondary education planning activities. Adult learning studies were to be carried out by the National Institute for Education. The existing Educational Opportunity Center program was modified to include a sharpened focus on serving adults through community-oriented programs. And finally, colleges and universities with schools of education were to receive support for the retraining of elementary and secondary teachers and postsecondary faculty.

However, in November 1980 Ronald Reagan was elected president and Republicans took over political control of the Senate from the Democrats, and with these changes came resolve on the part of government leaders to cut back federal spending for social programs. The spring and summer of 1981 saw the Congress, encouraged by the Reagan administration, undo much of what was accomplished in the Education Amendments of 1980. This article reviews the development of the original recurrent education legislation enacted last year and outlines how the new administration and the Congress have used a complex budgetary process to revise and rescind much of the new law even before the bulk of the changes it authorized were put into effect.

BACKGROUND

Development of the new recurrent education legislation grew out of some fairly clearly defined policy objectives. First, Congress at that time was determined to find ways to improve educational opportunities for adult learners, especially those adults who were not then participating in recurrent education activities. The encouragement of equal education opportunity had long been a cornerstone for traditional federal involvement in postsecondary education. The new law extended this commitment to those adults outside the mainstream of postsecondary education in the United States. Legislators agreed that the primary focus of the federal government in adult continuing education should be on promoting access, particularly for older persons, the less educated, minorities, low-income persons, and those living in central cities or rural areas.

The Congress was also anxious to achieve several more pragmatic policy objectives, including program consolidation and improvement of the federal-state partnership in support of postsecondary education. Both of these objectives were included as themes in the recurrent education portions of the new law.

Finally, the legislators were concerned about predictions of sharply declining enrollments of postsecondary students in the more traditional 18-to-22-year-old age group and sought to rechannel existing postsecondary education resources into this emerging sector of recurrent education, where unmet educational needs still existed.

These policy objectives, as stated by the U.S. Congress, grew out of considerable research and data collection carried out in the past few years. Work by Peterson et al. (1979), and more recently Wagner (1980), Smith (1980), and others, has documented the extent of recurrent education undertaken currently. As an area of endeavor, continuing education has undergone dramatic growth in this decade: More and more adults are participating in formal education, and more and more institutions—among them colleges and universities with an eye on the diminishing pool of traditional college-age students—are seeking to serve them. The extent of this growth is substantial.

However, while current adult participation in education spans a wide range of backgrounds, previous educational experiences, and incomes, it tends to be greatest among one broad group: Today's adult learners are disproportionately young, white, well educated, and earning salaries above the national median family income. For example:

- 15.8% of those between 17 and 34 years of age take advantage of adult educational opportunities (excluding those enrolled full time in high school or postsecondary institutions), whereas only 4.4% of those over the age of 54 participate.
- 12.5% of white adults participate in adult education, whereas only 6.5% of blacks participate.
- 26.8% of those with four years of college or more participate, while 11.2% of those with only four years of high school (and only 3.4% of those with less than high school diplomas) participate.
- 17.7% of those with annual family incomes of $25,000 or more participate, while only 8.4% of those whose income is between $5,000 and $10,000, and only 5.4% of those with incomes below $5,000, participate.

Equally important, recent research (Aslanian and Brickell, 1980) indicates that the majority of adults enrolled in education have returned to formal learning because of specific job- or career-related factors—to obtain or keep employment or to avoid job or skill obsolescence—or because of dislocations in their personal lives such as divorce or death of a spouse. Women are returning to the work place in unprecedented numbers and many seek education to refresh skills or learn new ones. Older adults seek education for second careers or to help them adjust to retirement.

Yet the disparities remain, so as Congress began developmental work on the Education Amendments of 1980, it was faced with very real and well-documented needs. And it appeared unlikely that major improvements would be accomplished without some federal intervention. The next problem was to examine and choose among alternative methods for federal financing of recurrent education programs designed to meet these needs. Again, much research has been carried out in this area, both in the United States and abroad, including that of Levin, Kurland, and others (Windham et al., 1978). Support for individuals in the form of entitlements, loans, grants, and other methods has been debated widely, as have models that would provide funds to educational providers—colleges, universities, unions, local community centers, radio and television, and other nontraditional institutions and organizations. After reviewing the research, the Congress decided to write new legislation that would utilize a variety of financing schemes, some in current practice and others as yet untried. Financial aid was provided to individual adult learners in various ways. Modest grants were to be made available, through the states, to a wide assortment of educational providers. And a limited amount of federal funds was designated for state government agencies responsible for planning educational activities within the states.[2] In fact, the new legislation was viewed as a sort of test of alternative methodologies. More intensive use of one or another models was discussed by the Congress and rejected for the time being. The legislators decided that the variety of financing schemes included in the new law ought to be utilized and examined over the next five years, at which point new decisions based on observed demand for and success of the alternative strategies would be made.

DEVELOPMENT OF THE LEGISLATION

Work on the development of this legislation began in 1978. Representatives from a wide variety of Washington-based educational associations and other interested organizations began a series of meetings to frame the new legislation and sharpen the federal role in support of recurrent education. Among the more than 50 members of this working coalition were the American Library Association, the Adult Education Association, the American Association of Community and Junior Colleges, the American Association of Retired Persons, the United Auto Workers, and the College Board. This coalition representing education, unions, senior citizens' and womens' groups, and minority interests was a unique phenomenon, reflecting the breadth of interest in recurrent education across the country. Using as background a study defining the future federal role in this area (Hoffman, 1980),[3] coalition members testified repeatedly on the need for recurrent education programs at congressional hearings. Congressman William Ratchford (Democrat from Connecticut), a member of the subcommittee and former commissioner of aging for the State of Connecticut, took the congressional lead and introduced the major section of recurrent education legislation. The subcommittee reacted favorably to these various efforts, and the Education Amendments of 1980, containing new adult provisions, passed the full House of Representatives in November 1979.

Meanwhile, the Senate was moving at a more deliberate pace. But, after considerable delay caused by controversy over other portions of the draft legislation, the measure was finally approved by both houses of Congress and signed into law by President Carter on 3 October 1980.

The following is an outline of the various recurrent education provisions of the amendments intended to benefit adults.

Programs	Relevant Provisions
Financial Aid to Individuals	
Pell Grants	Grants provided directly to students. New law eliminated number of years students are eligible for these grants, and provided more equitable treatment of financially independent students (many of whom are adults). Home equity was eliminated in calculation of assets in determination of financial aid.
Supplemental Educational Opportunity Grants (SEOG)	Grants to students through the postsecondary institutions they attend. New law eliminated number of years students are eligible for these grants, and permitted (not required) up to 10% of these federal funds to be used for students studying less than half time (some of whom would be adults).
College Work-Study (CWS)	Part-time jobs for students with 80% of wages paid by federal funds. New law

	permitted (not required) up to 10% of these funds to be used for students studying less than half time (some of whom would be adults).
State Student Incentive Grants (SSIG)	Federal funds go to states, which then make grants to students. New law permitted students studying less than half time (many of whom would be adults) to participate in this program if the individual states chose to include them.
Guaranteed Student Loans (GSL)	Loans for students made by private lenders and supported in part by federal funds. New law increased the amount that financially independent students (many of whom are adults) may borrow.

Grants to Educational Providers and States

Continuing Education Program and Planning	Grants to states, which then make grants to eligible organizations and institutions, with 10% of the funds reserved to the secretary of education for direct grants. New law focused grants on needs of disadvantaged adults, expanded eligible organizations to include unions, business and industry, local community centers, and others and required states to plan for recurrent education programs and provide educational information.

Grants for Other Recurrent Education Activities and Research

Educational Opportunity Centers	Centers that provide education information, counseling, and tutoring to students. New law focused the efforts of these centers on adult students.
Teacher Training	New law established grants to train postsecondary education faculty and set up a new fellowship program to retrain elementary and secondary teachers of the handicapped.

National Institute for Education	New law established an additional research priority to focus on older, part-time, and "nontraditional" students.

In summary, what the Congress sought to do was to

- recognize again the importance of learning throughout a lifetime;
- focus the federal role on promotion of equal educational opportunity;
- sharpen the federal focus on unserved and disadvantaged adults;
- ensure a diversity of innovative programs;
- provide *some* flexibility by giving individuals some freedom of choice (particularly through the Pell Grant program); and
- meet the requirements of relative efficiency and, certainly, feasibility at that time.[4]

A final note about context must be made here. These new federal recurrent education provisions, had they all been implemented immediately, would have encouraged only a small part of the overall level of U.S. adult learning activity. Second, any funds appropriated would have remained only a small portion of the total level of federal dollars going to more traditional postsecondary educational programs and students. In addition, only a *very* small portion of these federal funds can be used to support recurrent education activities outside of schools (see Wagner, 1980, for an inventory demonstrating the extent of such activities).

THE REAGAN REVERSAL

January 1981 saw the inauguration of Ronald Reagan as president and the beginnings of a new mood of fiscal conservatism across the country. Hardly had the new president taken office when he sent to Congress a sharply reduced budget request, with the proposed cuts falling most heavily on federally supported social programs (especially education).

Prior to this move, it was expected that implementation of the new Education Amendments of 1980 would take place over the next 2 years. Some sections of the law became effective immediately, such as the 10% possible set-aside of CWS and SEOG funds for less-than-half-time students. Other changes in the student aid programs that affected adults were to be implemented in 1982. Planning to begin operations under the new Title I started in the fall of 1980 and was expected to continue, with new grants starting in the fall of 1981.

However, the sharply reduced Reagan budget proposals put an end to hopes of immediate implementation of these new adult provisions. The overall problem with the new legislation was discovered even before the new president took office. It was one of runaway costs within the basic programs contained in the amendments.[5] Many hours of congressional debate on the legislation had centered not on the merits of the individual programs but on the overall cost of the programs to the federal treasury. The two federal student loan programs, National Direct Student Loans (NDSL) and GSL, were identified in particular. While some changes were made in the two programs (and those few relating to adults were noted earlier), the balance of the GSL program especially was retained intact in the new law. Thus no control was placed on the soaring costs of the GSL program (up from less than $500 million three years before to a projected $2 billion in 1981).[6] At the same time, increased demand and the effects of inflation put additional pressure on funding levels for the other programs contained in the law.

The new administration moved quickly to stem this tide of rising costs. By manipulating the complex congressional budgeting and appropriations processes, the president, with the aid of the Republican-controlled Senate, succeeded in legislating changes designed to cut the rising costs of the GSL program, substantially reduced the funding levels of other programs, and eliminated appropriations for others altogether. The effect on the new recurrent education provisions of the programs is devastating:

- Pell Grants—authorization funding levels have been reduced.
- SEOG—federal funds can still be used for less-than-half-time students, but overall dollars available are not sufficient to meet demand, so institutions have not put this new provision into practice.
- CWS—same as SEOG, above.
- SSIG—same as SEOG, above.
- GSL—the increased amounts that independent students could borrow under new law has now been reduced back to the old limits ($2,500 annually and $12,500 total). In addition, GSLs are now limited to those

with family incomes of $30,000 or less and to those above $30,000 based only on defined need. These and other changes seek to cap the rising costs in this program.

- Continuing Education (Title I)—appropriations for Fiscal Year 1981 were cut to $2.2 million (only enough to keep the administration of the program operating), down from $15 million the previous year. Fiscal year 1982 levels, not yet decided, cannot exceed $8.0 million and could well be zero.
- Educational Opportunity Centers—these have survived unscathed so far.
- Teacher Training—no funds will be available.
- National Institute of Education—overall funding for research was cut substantially and little money for new grants will be available.

While much of the legislation aiding adult learners remains in effect (GSL changes being an exception), the lack of significant appropriations for the programs has significantly delayed the implementation of these new adult provisions. Just when the prospects for new funding can be expected to improve is, at this point, very uncertain. The extent of the reversal has been unprecedented. While there remains substantial support for the policies and premises of recurrent education around the country today, there is much less agreement about what the federal role, supported by public tax dollars, should be in this area of adult continuing education.

Over the next several years, it is expected that the Reagan administration will continue to sort out its priorities for spending on federal programs. Until the American citizens have a chance to analyze the effects of these new conservative spending policies, little change can be expected. For the time being, the federal policy supporting recurrent education in this country, particularly that aimed at disadvantaged adults, is enacted in legislation but remains an opportunity deferred.

NOTES

1. A comment on terminology is also necessary at the outset. Earlier federal legislation, which remained unfunded, used the term "lifelong learning." Members of Congress objected to that term, citing its vagueness. Recurrent education is not a term used widely in the United States. Therefore, the new law uses the phrase "continuing education," intending, however, that all three terms are essentially the same. I use the phrase "recurrent

education," finding that the definition used in the 1973 OECD report (Recurrent Education; Paris OECD/CERI, 1973) is applicable to this discussion.

2. State governments themselves are sources of major funding support for public (and to some extent private) postsecondary educational institutions within their borders.

3. This work grew out of a three-year $1.6 million grant from the Exxon Education Foundation to the College Board to examine "Future Directions for a Learning Society." The project sponsored research, demonstrations of innovative recurrent education techniques, dissemination of information, and promotion of public policy.

4. This list is matched against a similar list of criteria for financing systems for recurrent education found in a report by the Centre for Educational Research and Innovation (1980: 10).

5. This section draws heavily upon the "Report from Washington" (College Board, 1980).

6. Appropriations for GSL are nondiscretionary, and the federal government is obligated to pay these costs.

REFERENCES

ASLANIAN, C. B. and H. M. BRICKELL (1980) Americans in Transition: Life Changes as Reasons for Adult Learning. New York: College Board.
Centre for Educational Research, OECD (1980) "The costs and financing of recurrent education." CERI, Paris. (mimeo)
College Board (1980a) Paying for Your Education: An Aid Guide for Adult Learners. New York: Author.
——— (1980b) "Report from Washington." College Board, Washington, D.C., Office. (mimeo)
GLADIEUX, L. E. (1980) "What has Congress wrought?" Change (October): 25-31.
HOFFMAN, E. (1980) The Federal Role in Lifelong Learning. New York: College Board.
National Center for Educational Statistics (1980) Participation in Adult Education, 1978. Washington, DC: Author.
PETERSON, R. E. and Associates (1979) Lifelong Learning in America. San Francisco: Jossey-Bass.
PURGA, R. (1978) "Financial aid and the adult learner: federal and New York State financial aid programs." Adult Learning Services Office, New York State Education Department. (mimeo)
SMITH, G. B. (1980) "Employer-sponsored recurrent education in the United States: a report on recent inquiries into its structure." National Institute for Work and Learning, Washington, D.C. (mimeo)
U.S. Congress (1980) Education Amendments of 1980. 96th Congress, Second Session. P.L. 96-374.
WAGNER, A. P. (1980) An Inventory of Post-Compulsory Education and Training Programs in the U.S. and Sources of Support. Stanford, CA: Institute for Research on Educational Finance and Governance, School of Education, Stanford University.
WINDHAM, D. M., N. D. KURLAND, and F. H. LEVINSON (1978) "Financing the learning society." School Rev. 86 (May).

III

FINANCING PAID EDUCATIONAL LEAVE

11

THE SWEDISH MODEL

KJELL RUBENSON

During the 1970s, the eduational rights of adults came to occupy the focal point of Swedish educational policy. Higher education was opened to mature students, and other resources for adult education became the cornerstone of these activities, and the 1975 Higher Education Act stated that all subsequent planning of the education system was to be based on recurrent education as a regular model for the individual person's educational planning (OECD, 1980).

The Swedish reforms naturally reflect the prevailing political, economic, and cultural conditions. Before going into further detail concerning the changes in question, this chapter shall describe briefly the two aspects of Swedish society that have done the most to influence the direction and development of policy concerning recurrent and adult education: the trade unions' intervention in educational policy, and the educational explosion.

There are many conditions that must be met in order for a thoroughgoing transformation to take place in the direction indicated by Swedish policy on recurrent education. This chapter will analyze two of them: educational leave and finance, with the main emphasis being on finance. Finally, some concluding remarks regarding the strengths and weaknesses of the system will be made and directions for change will be suggested.

THE INCREASING POWER RESOURCES OF THE TRADE UNIONS

By the mid-1960s it was clear that the course of social development that generally had been presumed to be condusive to greater equality was tending to perpetuate inequality instead. The Swedish Survey of Living Standards revealed that, despite steady economic growth, a vast difference still existed between socioeconomic groups (Johansson, 1970). This contributed to a radicalization of the trade unions.

In the early 1970s, at the insistence of the Swedish Confederation of Trade Unions (LO), the Social Democratic Government appointed a number of official commissions to draft legislation designed to increase worker influence in working life. At the same time Social Democratic policy was reorganized, a process in which LO came to play a leading part. In this way the union movement broke with the established practice whereby developments in the labor market were governed by agreements between employers' associations and workers' unions, with the state remaining neutral (Korpi, 1978: 356). This process culminated in 1976 in the passing of the Co-determination Act, which formally abolished the sole right of employers to direct and allocate work and to hire and dismiss employees. The Co-determination Act was an important step toward increasing the power resources of workers and their unions.

Korpi's analysis of the Swedish working class and welfare capitalism leads him to propound that workers' demands can be expected to grow with their power resources. There is little likelihood, therefore, of workers being induced by rising living standards to accept their subordinate position as wage labor (Korpi, 1978: 356). Korpi's interpretation is that the collective power resources and social awareness of the Swedish workers have developed to such a degree that they will no longer acquiesce in the hegemony of capital in economic life (Korpi, 1978: 364).

Korpi's analysis and discussion are concerned mainly with the relationship between political and economic democracy in view of the fact that, despite 40 years in power, the labor movement has failed to achieve one of the essential goals of socialism—namely, economic democracy. Thus the radicalization of the unions included reforms in adult education as well as in the labor market.

But there is another dimension of vital importance, that of cultural democracy. The interest taken by workers' associations in educational questions is connected partly with the growing educational requirements entailed by the realization of reforms in working life. However, the increased activity in educational affairs may imply that the growing collective resources of workers have led them to generate renewed demands for "cultural democracy."

The growing interest taken by the labor movement in educational questions during the 1970s is also to be viewed in the light of the thorough school reforms introduced under the Social Democrats. Party ideologists regarded education as one of the most important instruments for achieving a more egalitarian society; education was to be the spearhead into the future. However, by the late 1960s scepticism and disillusionment concerning the role of schooling as the great leveler of social inequalities had become widespread. The labor movement therefore demanded not only changes in the system of youth education but also improvements in educational opportunities for adults, so as to influence the educational choices of young persons (LOVUX III, 1974).

Exaggerating somewhat, one might say that the labor movement is doing nothing less than challenging the traditional view that social changes are achieved through the compensatory influence of the school system. Instead of primarily transforming the situation of children, attention is drawn to the conditions of adults in society.

THE POSTWAR EDUCATIONAL EXPANSION

For a long time schooling in Sweden was dominated by a highly selective and hierarchical system of parallel schools in which those who were well situated financially received a very different education from those who were less fortunate. At the end of World War II, the Social Democratic Government embarked on a thoroughgoing reform of the education system. This resulted in a uniform school system in which all pupils receive nine years' elementary schooling, after which the majority go on to upper secondary school, most of them following study routes that qualify them for university entrance. The reform of the school system and a rising demand for higher education transformed the university and produced an explosive increase in the student population (OECD, 1980). According to OECD data, Sweden had the highest average growth rate in higher educational enrollments among the OECD counties between 1950 and 1965 (Premfors and Ostergren, 1978: 9).

By the mid-1960s it was clear that the great transformation and expansion of the education system had presented educational planners with a number of acute problems such as rising costs, and so ongoing expansion of the education sector had to be restrained. Educational planning and labor market planning required closer integration. The substantial prolongation of youth education had caused wide gaps between the generations, and these gaps would make themselves felt for the rest of the century. It was in this environment that the idea of recurrent education emerged from the 1968 Education Commission (U 68).

The interest taken in recurrent education as a planning strategy probably was not due solely to the expectation that such a system would confer economic and educational benefits and lead to a more egalitarian recruitment. One of the primary reasons for this interest was probably the question of total enrollment restrictions in higher education (OECD 1977: 50).

Another important factor was the effort to achieve the closest possible adjustment between the needs of the labor market and the output of the educational system. At the time of the U 68 commission, there was a general awareness of the difficulties involved in assessing society's future need of qualified workers and in predicting student flows. In the final report of the U 68 commission (SOU 1973: 2, 584), recurrent education was referred to as a means of partially offsetting the unpredictability of the future labor market (Stahl, 1968: 115).

It is arguable that adult education and recurrent education have been governed by different concepts of equality. The general policy on recurrent education appears to be based on the establishment of equal opportunities, while adult education policy is aimed at equality of results. Adult education policy could be regarded as an effort to maintain a minimum "equality threshold" beneath which it would be unjust to exclude people.

SWEDISH EDUCATIONAL LEAVE

In 1970 the Swedish Employers' Confederation (SAF) asked the LO and the Salaried Workers' Confederation (TCO) to collaborate in an investigation by a joint group of experts of educational leave. These discussions, however, failed to produce a consensus of opinion. Instead, a considerable disagreement between the parties was revealed. LO and TCO broke off the negotiations and turned to the Ministry of Education to get the principle of entitlement to educational leave established by the Swedish Educational Leave Act (OECD, 1976).

This law, which came into effect on 1 January 1975, guarantees the right of all public and private employees to take leave for educational purposes during working hours. To qualify, an employee must have worked for his company for six months or at least twelve months during the past two years. This minimum employment qualification, however, does not apply to trade union training. The right to educational leave covers all types of education—general, vocational, and that which is provided by trade unions. The act does not stipulate a maximum or minimum duration of leave, nor does it say how many employees from a company may be absent at the same time. Responsibility for these arrangements lies with employer representatives and those of the employees, and these points must be settled by negotiation. The act entitles an employer to postpone leave in individual cases, but he is required to inform the trade union in advance whereupon the union is entitled to discuss the matter with him. If educational leave is postponed for more than six months, the employer must obtain permission from the local union organization. The six-month postponement period is reduced to two weeks when trade union training and leave of absence are of one working week or less.

The act also assures the employee of the right to return to his job after a period of educational leave and to resume the status and income he had before. This applies even if the employee does not complete the course of education for which leave was granted. The local trade union has the last word in the event of a dispute. If either party wishes, the matter can be dealt with at a higher level; in that case, the central employee organization has to agree to the desired postponement

Lack of statistics makes it very hard to gauge the utilization of the act. According to a rough estimate by the Employers' Confederation, the total volume of educational leave corresponds to one week off for 1-2% of all employees.

The Employers' Confederation has objected to the act, calling for restrictions on entitlement to educational leave and a review of the statutory rules. The main grounds for this criticism are that the existing rules impede the planning of production. The employers also allege that overall the various leave of absence reforms in recent years have inflicted serious injury on Swedish enterprise. The objections raised by employers to the Educational Leave Act are primarily to be seen as a manifestation of their displeasure with the general increase in opportunities for leave of absence, not with the value of selective educational leave. Increased absences created by the act have led the Minister of Labor to appoint a commission to review the total effects of the legislation on leave of absence. Thus it is possible that the existing Educational Leave Act will be revised on a more restrictive basis.

It is sometimes said that the fundamental weakness of Swedish recurrent education policy is its lack of a suitable finance policy to support entitlement to educational leave. One of the basic principles of the Swedish legislation is the free choice of studies. A free choice combined with paid educational leave would produce an immense educational explosion. This, however, is precluded by the limitations of resources. Instead Sweden has chosen to separate educational leave and finance. Thus the adult education assistance introduced at the same time as the Educational Leave Act enabled a limited number of persons from a specified target group to study during paid leaves of absence. In this way finance during educational leave ties in with the general aims of present educational policy in such a way that the system of subsidies for students acts as a general steering instrument of adult and recurrent education policy.

FINANCE

There are three distinct systems of subsidies for students that are relevant to recurrent education (see Table 11.1). *AMS Grants* pertain to labor market trainees. The *loan-grant assistance* scheme applies generally to postsecondary students and to adults (persons who are 20-years-old and over) receiving elementary and secondary education. Finally, the *adult study assistance* scheme is primarily designed for undereducated adults intending to study at the elementary or secondary level. Adult study assistance also includes a special grant to facilitate short-term studies sponsored by an adult education association.

As has already been made clear, the structure of financial support for students is highly incoherent. Although the various types of benefits are planned for students in a particular sector, it is not uncommon for all three types to occur in the same case (e.g., in municipal adult education). The size and consruction of assistance (see Table 11.1) may be said to reflect the responsibility assumed by society for various groups according to their economic and social conditions. Those who are out of jobs and pursuing labor market training are given the most generous terms, while those who are attending higher education are given the least advantageous conditions. All types of education covered by any of the three systems of financing are entirely free of charge, although in practice there may be some expenses for study materials.

AMS GRANTS

Active labor market policy was developed towards the end of the 1940s by the LO economists Gösta Rehn and Rudolf Meidner. This

TABLE 11.1 Different Forms of Financing Recurrent Education

	Folk High School, Elementary, and Secondary Schooling for Adults	Higher Education	Labor Market Training	Short-Term Folk High School Courses, and Adult Education Associations	Benefits as of 1 April 1980 Grant/Month (SKr.)	Benefits as of 1 April 1980 Loan/Month (SKr.)	Estimated State Expenditure 1981-1982 (Skr. millions)
AMS grants	x		x		3,410-4,620 (taxable)	—	1,875
Loan-grant assistance scheme	x	x			242	2,263	2,672
Adult study assistance[1]	x			x	2,216-3,003 (taxable)	800-1,000	544

NOTE: The Swedish kronor is valued at $4.1503 using market rate figures for the second quarter of 1980.
1. Adult study assistance is not given for higher education with the exception of 700 persons at postsecondary vocational education (YTH). The adult study assistance also include a special hourly and daily assistance for short courses.

model was characterized above all by its assertion that an active labor market policy is a principal factor of economic stability. Full employment was to be aimed at, but not by generating a high level of demand in the economy which would lead to inflation. Since labor demand at any given moment inevitably varies from one economic sector to another, it was more effective to try to maintain moderately high demand in the economy and combine this with selective measures aimed at influencing the employment situations in sectors that were threatened with unemployment. These specific measures were to include public employment projects (known as relief work projects), sheltered employment, support for firms in regions of high unemployment, and efforts to stimulate the mobility of workers between different localities, sectors, and occupations.

In this connection, labor market training has come to be an important component in achieving mobility. The labor market training system arose out of the need to act swiftly against imbalances in the labor market. First, the system helped underemployed and unemployed workers to improve their employability in occupations with better opportunities. Second, it increased the supply of skills in industries where a shortage of suitably trained personnel tends to exacerbate inflationary pressures. The labor market training system now has a running capacity of more than 1% of the total labor force. With courses lasting for an average of four to five months, more than 3% of the labor force can be reached in the space of one year.

The main provisions of the scheme are as follows. Persons can attend training courses arranged by the labor market authorities in collaboration with school authorities or with employers under the following conditions: (1) if they are unemployed or their employment conditions are precarious (in the sense that they are threatened with unemployment either because they work in declining sectors or because of personal difficulties); and (2) if they are willing to leave their jobs (or take educational leave) in order to train for shorthanded occupations. Courses are free of charge and trainees receive taxable AMS grants of SKr. 3,410-4,620 ($852-$1,155) per month. These grants exceed daily unemployment benefits and amount to some 80% of ordinary wages after taxes.

The courses vary in duration and level of qualification. Some are short introductory courses designed to acclimate participants to working situations outside their experience. Others are two-year courses for skilled workers and technicians, some of which are at postsecondary levels. One of the important functions of this scheme is to pave the way for women to enter the labor market. In recent years, half the participants have been women.

Most training takes place at permanent or temporary centers. The training is administered jointly by the Labor Market Boad and the National Board of Education. These boards delegate responsibility to their county subsidiaries or make arrangements with vocational schools, (which are now integrated with the system of upper secondary education). There were 78,000 participants in this kind of training in 1978-1979.

The primary objective of labor market training is to provide unemployed persons with steady jobs. Regular follow-up studies have shown that some 85% of persons who have taken vocational courses and then entered the labor market have obtained jobs within three months of completing their courses. Approximately 85% of these successful job applicants obtained work in the occupational sectors for which they trained.

The AMS grants are not geared to the education sector but are related directly to labor market policy. In a system of recurrent education, however, the present boundary between education and labor market training loses its raison d'être. This applies not least to the present-day discussion of persistent labor shortages and the role of recurrent education as a means of securing a more equitable distribution of work, education, and leisure between different age groups and social groups. However, until now there has not been any closer coordination of recurrent education policy and other social sectors (e.g., labor policy and social policy).

LOAN-GRANT ASSISTANCE

The present system of loan-grant assistance was introduced in 1965 with two objectives: first, the expansion of higher education recruitment by means of social benefits for students so as to eliminate social and geographical bias; and second, general improvements to the economic terms offered to those who are pursuing or have pursued higher studies (SOU 1963: 74, p. 32).

Loan-grant assistance consisting of (repayable) loans and (nonrepayable) grants can be awarded to upper secondary students of age 20 and to postsecondary students. The loan-grant assistance payable to a person studying full time for nine months during the academic year 1980-1981 was $5,636 or Skr. 22,546 (Skr. 2,500 per month). At present

90% of this amount is repayable. As a rough comparison, the average industrial worker gets about SKr. 3,500 ($875) after tax per month.

Repayable assistance does not carry interest in the normal way, but outstanding obligations are adjusted upward each year by means of an index. At present, debts on study assistance rise by 3.2% annually. The amortization period is usually over 20 years.

The main question or relevance for present purposes is whether the loan-grant system encourages or impedes recurrent education. As stated earlier, recurrent education was made part of the Higher Education Act. The primary aim was not to introduce recurrent education as a norm but to make it an equivalent educational alternative as far as possible (Govt. Bill Prop. 1976-1977: 59, p. 44). Turning to the system of finance, the goal as interpreted here implies that the system should be neutral with regard to the student's choice between the recurrent pattern and the traditional pattern of education. The neutrality of the system of finance should be viewed in relation to the transition in economic resources and material living standards of the student, both during and after studies.

The loan-grant system cannot be said to satisfy the requirement of neutrality by any stretch of the imagination. It creates special difficulties for those adults who have earned incomes because it does not cover even the loss of quite small earnings. Consequently, a person who wishes to study extensively and previously has been employed gainfully has to accept a reduced living standard. Calculations by the National Board of Statistics have indicated that a transition to full-time studies would result in a drastic increase in the number of households falling below the subsistence level (SCB, 1981).

Study assistance today consists mainly of benefits that are repayable after the completion of studies. The grant portion has remained almost stationary ever since the system was introduced in 1965. At that time the maximum grant payable was one-quarter of the total volume of loan-grant assistance, reducing the grant portion to 11%. Since the essential purpose of the student grant is to reduce the burden of indebtedness after the completion of studies, we may note that education policy has been developed in favor of recurrent education but the structure of study finance has tended to favor direct transitions.

Thus Blaug and Mace (1977) have argued that educational finance in Sweden is not supportive of a true effort to achieve a system of recurrent education. To be fair to the policymakers, the introduction of a separate financing system for adult education should be mentioned. However, this system was set up in order to help bridge the educational gap—not to favor recurrent education.

ADULT STUDY ASSISTANCE

The reform of adult education in the 1960s substantially augmented the opportunities for study and education open to adults. Municipal adult education was introduced in 1968 to give adults the chance to obtain formal education qualifications corresponding to those conferred by youth education. Improvements were made in the support given to independent and voluntary popular education, and radio and television were used more widely for educational purposes. One of the guidelines for the reform of adult education was that it should limit losses in production that result from removing workers from their enterprises during working hours. Accordingly, it was intended that studies be pursued in leisure hours and and combined with work in the home or outside it. The government, however, anticipated that full-time studies were destined to become increasingly important, and in 1968 a government commission on adult study assistance—the SVUX Committee—was appointed. This committee's proposals resulted in 1976 in the introduction of a separate system of study assistance for adults.

The overrriding goal of adult education is to bridge the gap between adults and youth. The question of resource requirements and priorities depends on the magnitude of the education gap in the Swedish society. Estimates of the gap and finance requirements are made in order to limit the effect of inadequate finances on enrollment. Total expenditures for meeting the calculated demand were estimated by the committee to be a resource increment of roughly SKr. 40-50 million ($10-12 million). It was recommended that plans be made to cater to the demand over a period of 20 years by means of gradual expansion. During this period, adult education would be given high priority in new education reforms. A phased expansion in itself would reduce the resource requirement to about SKr. 25 million ($6.25 million) due to the decline in educational predisposition with advancing age and the annual cohort's attainment of the age of 65. However, the committee did not believe that these were adequate to channel such heavy new resources into adult education, and a more modest and realistic build-up was suggested (SOU 1974: 62, 215).

The first five-year period was completed in 1980-1981, and it is possible to compare the actual allocation of resources with the proposed build-up. During the first two years there was a close correspondence between suggested and actual funding, but in the ensuing years a slowdown in economic growth and high levels of inflation contributed to a rising discrepancy which will probably continue to increase during the second five-year period. The discrepancy can also be expressed in number of grants. According to the committee's plan there should have been 50,000 one-year full-time grants in 1980-1981; instead there were only 15,800.

Adult study assistance is financed by means of a payroll tax surcharge equalling .25%. In 1980-1981 the revenues from this surcharge provided Skr. 588 million ($147 million) for purposes of adult study assistance. The following is a summary of the content and conditions of the various forms of adult study assistance.

Special adult study assistance

Special adult study assistance is available only for studies requiring prolonged and continuous periods of time. It is payable on either a full-time or part-time basis—that is, for a period of at least half a month's full-time studies (15 days) or for a full month's half-time studies (30 days). Special adult study assistance is awarded primarily for studies at the elementary and secondary school levels. At the postsecondary level it can only be awarded to students undergoing postsecondary vocational education (YTH).

The following factors have to be taken into consideration in the distribution of special adult study assistance:

- short-term previous education
- educational difficulties due to disability or for other reasons
- long-term vocational activity or its equivalent
- numerous dependents
- any previous receipt of special adult study assistance.

The assistance comprises a taxable grant and a tax-free loan and varies between Skr. 2,300 and Skr. 3,000 ($575 and $750) depending on income. The money allocated for the special adult study assistance 1981-1982 covers 15,500 grants of a nine-month duration.

Hourly study assistance

Hourly study assistance is payable to persons attending study circles and incurring losses of earnings as a result. Hourly study assistance in

1980-1981 stood at SKr. 33 ($8.25) per hour and was taxable. By way of comparison, the average hourly earnings of LO members on continuous triple-shift work in 1980 were SKr. 41.75 ($10.44). In the course of a fiscal year, assistance may be awarded for 70 hours. Hourly study assistance can be applied for by individual persons or collectively by a trade union organization. Most assistance awards are made in response to collective applications.

Hourly study assistance can only be awarded to a limited number of persons (25,000), and priority is given to those who have

- inconvenient working hours, especially as regards shift work;
- physically and mentally strenuous working conditions, whatever the arrangement concerning working hours;
- short-term previous education.

The resources available for hourly study assistance have not been fully utilized. The main reason for this is the problem of exercising entitlement to educational leave. Many people are unwilling to take time off out of loyalty towards their employers and fellow workers. The narrow range of subjects and the smaller amount of study assistance income in relation to average earnings have also had a negative effect (Stockfelt and Öberg, 1979; Naslund, 1980).

Daily study assistance

Daily study assistance can be regarded as a supplement to hourly study assistance. This type of assistance makes it possible for circle studies to be combined with short-term subject studies at folk high schools for additional depth. Daily study assistance in the course of a single fiscal year is subject to a maximum of 10 study days and 2 travel days per student. Daily study assistance can be applied for individually, or collectively by a trade union organization. There were 14,900 daily study assistanceships available in 1981-1982.

As the above description has shown, the reform of adult education financing (unlike the general study assistance) is geared to a particular clientele. The expansion of adult education in the 1960s and 1970s made policymakers aware that too much faith had been placed on the potential of a general augmentation of adult education resources. When one attempts to fulfill both allocation and the service-policy goals of individuals, the allocation effects turn out to be very limited and are accomplished at the price of great service-policy costs.

THE EFFECTS OF THE THREE SYSTEMS

Measuring the effects of changes in the field of adult education finance is highly complicated in terms of both the more theoretical considerations and empirical measurement. How can the effects of educational change be discerned in the complex process whereby present and future society is shaped in a permanent interaction of economic, political, and organizational forces at local, national, and international levels?

The reform of adult financing in Sweden has not been subjected yet to evaluation, so the only data available are annual study assistance statistics. By comparing these figures with the national educational statistics, which deal with adult education participation generally, one can, however, obtain some view of the recruitment effect of adult study assistance.

Available data indicate that the special adult study assistance has gone to the target group, at least insofar as that group is defined in terms of previous education (CSN, 1979; SCB, 1980: 5). The material does not say anything about how these individuals would have acted if no subsidy had been available. In other words, would these persons have participated in any case? However, there is research suggesting that a large proportion of the students would not have been able to participate without the special adult study assistance (see, e.g., Lövgren, 1978).

As an important part of the reform of adult education, outreach activities were given state grants and grouped together with adult study assistance. Grants towards outreach measures at work places are awarded in response to applications by trade unions. The passing of the Shop Stewards Act (1974) and the Educational Leave Act (1975) are important in this connection. The Shop Stewards Act entitles union representatives to engage in outreach activities at their own work places. The amount of time devoted to these activities has to be determined in consultation with employers.

The different reforms in Sweden have made it possible for outreach activities to be linked directly to the legislation concerning educational leave and study assistance in order to offer as favorable a study situation as possible. However, the existing statutory opportunities often are difficult to utilize. For example, in small work places workers have been reluctant to take leave because of the difficulties their absences create for their workmates (the Kronoberg Project, December 1977: 73).

The special adult study allowance in combination with eligibility for leave of absence has increased the proportion of daytime students. There are some indications that this might have led to a decline in dropout rates from the municipal adult schools. A 1973 study of evening courses showed that just over 30% of the participants completed the whole program (Borgström et al., 1979), and a follow-up study found that as many as 65% completed day courses (Rubenson, forthcoming). Thus with more people getting the chance to study full time, one might expect growing efficiency as reflected by a decreasing number of dropouts.

The existing evidence concerning hourly and daily study assistance does not testify to any substantial recruitment effect (CSN 1979; SCB, 1980: 5). However, hourly and daily study assistance benefits are not only aimed at recruiting the undereducated, they are also intended to facilitate educational activity on the part of workers with inconvenient work shifts or physically and mentally strenuous jobs. The available statistics tell us nothing about the effects achieved in these respects.

There has been criticism of the designation of hourly study assistance for participants in certain categories of study circles. When this special grant was introduced, its main purpose was to facilitate participation in study-circle activities aimed at eliminating the educational gaps. Surveys concerning the attitude of undereducated persons toward adult education have shown, however, that a freer choice of subjects geared to the working and everyday situation of the individual would be preferable to general education (Rubenson et al., 1977).

In order for allocation policy to be fulfilled, the following two conditions must be met. People with low resources (such as skills and income) have to be recruited, and by participating in this activity they should be able to obtain greater skills, income, and other resources. The crucial point with regard to a differentiated financing of adult education programs is which programs can be instrumental in redistributing resources. So far, owing to poor conceptualization, research in the field of adult education has little to offer regarding this question.

Parallel to the efforts made in recent years to reduce the social gaps in society, increasing attention has begun to be focused on the position of women and inequalities between the sexes. This has had repercussions on the structure of social benefits for students. When adult study assistance was introduced, it was resolved that no "needs test" would be imposed in relation to the spouse's income. As a result, homemakers are excessively compensated because they do not suffer any direct loss of income, so that the amount of assistance they receive exceeds any conceivable increase in expenditure entailed by a transition to education CSN, 1980a). There are two main reasons that this situation is harmful to the overall program: First, many applications are turned down because of the limited resources available; second, many gainfully employed persons are undercompensated because the maximum benefit rate does not cover their loss of earnings.

Where general study assistance is concerned, the rule before 1981 was that loan-grant entitlement was affected by the spouse's income—a rule that had been criticized ever since the introduction of the loan-grant system in 1965. The fundamental objection to a spouse's income being included in the assessment procedure was that in this way adults were not treated as independent individuals. Inclusion of the spouse's income has therefore been considered unacceptable for reasons of sexual equality. The problem with this approach is that it entails a conflict of goals between sexual equality and social equality. In considering social equality, the family's combined liberty of economic choice is most significant; in other words, how is the family's economic situation affected by choosing educational activities?

The elimination of spouse's income as a criterion for obtaining loan-grant assistance has tended to provide financial help for many women from advantaged backgrounds. The resources that are now going to these women could be used for specific measures designed to influence the educational interests of other hard-to-recruit groups. Exaggerating somewhat, one might say that social equality is being sacrificed on the altar of sexual equality.

CONCLUDING REMARKS

In the review of educational finance, it was pointed out that despite everything that has been done, the fundamental weakness of Swedish efforts to establish recurrent education was the lack of a scheme of student finance combined with entitlement to educational leave. The demands of the U 68 commission for special measures concerning social benefits for students have not been implemented. These measures were judged necessary if recurrent education was to become a realistic alternative to the traditional study route.

The critique should be analyzed with respect to the far reaching changes that were anticipated. When the idea of recurrent education was propounded in connection with the reform of higher education, the minister of education at that time stated the following:

> I anticipate that recurrent education—as a pattern for the utilization of the educational machinery—will gradually become a realistic alternative to the present order of things which is primarily based on continuous education during childhood and adolescence [Govt. Bill 1975: 9, 431].

Underlying the present debate is the conviction (evidently entertained by the planners) that recurrent education could evolve as a "harmonious model" without the need for a more distinct definition of priorities. Developments have shown that it was a mistake to suppose that in a situation characterized by limited resources, recurrent education could be developed without sacrificing harmony. New discord has come into being now that the issue at stake is not only the distribution of educational resources between different socioeconomic groups but also their distribution between young and mature students. This conflict is accentuated by the present economic crisis and approaching "hump" in the younger generation.

Another critical problem is the imbalance that has developed between the education sector and the labor market as a result of the economic crisis. One of the fundamental aims of Swedish economic policy today is to stimulate a structural transformation of enterprise and at the same time limit the growth of the public sector. This involves heavy pressure for a transformation of the education sector. The demand for the relatively cheap higher education designed for the public sector may conceivably diminish and be shifted to more expensive technical education, meaning that within a given financial constraint the number of places will be reduced.

We may note that the current situation has certain points in common with that which existed when the idea of recurrent education was first raised. Thus the demand for higher education among the younger generations is once more rising steeply and exceeding resources. The great difference today is that there is a powerful body of opinion against measures that would impair the ability of young persons to go straight on to higher education from upper secondary school. It is not surprising, therefore, that the Riksdag resolved to alter the rules of higher education entrance from 1981-1982. These alterations will tone down the importance of job experience and reinforce direct transitions. Thus in the present economic situation development of the more far-reaching approach to recurrent education whereby direct transitions are counteracted has come to a halt. Recurrent education in the form of in-service and further training, however, can be expected to gain strength in connection with the structural transformation of enterprise.

One possible alternative is to start charging fees for certain courses at universities and colleges. Enterprises and individual adults would then be able to purchase education. This policy would probably mean that Sweden would move in the direction of the French arrangement where paid leave of absence is closely bound up with a limited repertoire of mainly vocational courses.

Anything more radical that may happen in the area of financing is likely to be linked to developments in working life; for example, the trade unions might seek and get greater control of the education sector in enterprise. If this is the case, Sweden would be heading towards a situation in which the education provided by the community is geared more closely to employment. For example, collective agreements could be struck concerning entitlement to paid educational leave and a greater element of general education could be provided within the framework of in-service training.

REFERENCES

ARONOWTIZ, S. (1973). False Promises. New York: McGraw-Hill.
BLAUG, M. and J. MACE (1977) "Recurrent education—the New Jerusalem." Higher Education 6, 3: 277-300.
BORGSTRÖM, L. et al. (1979). Elementary School Studies for Adults. Summary report from the GRUV-project, 27. Stockholm: Pedagogiskt centrum, Stockholms skolförvaltning.
BROSTRÖM, A. and G. EKEROTH (1977). Vuxenutbildning och fördelningspolitik. Uppsala: Sociologiska institutionen, Uppsala universitet.
CERI (1973). Recurrent Education: A Strategy for Lifelong Learning. Paris: CERI/OECD.
CSN Studiestödsstatistik 1978-1979. Sundsvall: CSN June, 1979.
CSN October 29 (1980a) Det Särskilda vuxenstudiestödet—ATP villkoret och stödets storlek.
———August 27 (1980b) Anslagsframställning för budgetaret 1981-1982.

EKSTEDT, E. (1976). Utbildningsexpansion. En studie över den högre utbildningens expansion och ekonomins strukturella omvandling i Sverige under efterkrigstiden. Stockholm: Almqvist & Wiksell International, Uppsala studies in economic history 14.

Govt. Bill Proposition 1975: 9.

Govt. Bill Proposition 1976-1977: 59.

Govt. Bill Proposition 1980-1981: 20.

HOLMES, B. (1965). Problems in Education. A Comparative Approach. London: Routledge and Kegan Paul.

IPF, 1980: 4. Trender och prognoser, 1980.

JOHANSSON, S. (1970). Om levnadsnivåundersökningen. Utkast till kap. 1 och 2 i betänkande om svenska folkets levnadsförhallånden. Stockholm: Allmanna Förlaget.

KIM, L. (1979). Två års erfarenhet av de nya tillträdesreglerna till högskoleutbildning. Stockholm: UHÄ, 1979: 13.

KORPI, W. (1978). Arbetarklassen i välfärdskapitalismen. Stockholm: Prisma.

LOVUX I (1969). Fackföreningsrörelsen och vuxenutbildningen. Rapport från LO: s arbetsgrupp for vuxenutbildningsfrågor. Stockholm: Prisma.

LOVUX III (1974). Ny vuxenutbildning—ny skola. Stockholm: Prisma.

LÖVGREN, J. (1978). Yrkesteknisk högskoleutbildning 1975-1978. Erfarenheter från de två första försöksomgångarna. Stockholm: UHÄ 1978: 21.

NÄSLUND, N-E. (1980) LO och vuxenstudiestödet. Stockholm: LO.

OLOFSSON, L. E. (1980). Recruitment in the context of allocation policy," in R. Höghielm and K. Rubenson (eds.) Adult Education for Social Change. Lund: CWK Gleerup.

PREMFORS, R. and B. ÖSTERGREN (1978). Systems of Higher Education: Sweden. NY: International Council for Educational Development.

RUBENSON, K., (forthcoming). Till frågan om studieavbrott i vuxenutbildning. Stockholm Department of Educational Research, Stockholm Institute of Education.

—— U. BERGSTEN and B. BROMSJÖ (1977). Korttidsutbildades inställning till vuxenutbildning. Utbildningsforskning nr 26. Stockholm: Liber Läromedel/ Utbildningsförlaget.

SANDLER, R. (1937). Mångfald eller enfald. Stockholm: Tidens forlag.

SCB (National Central Bureau of Statistics) 1980: 5. Deltagare i allmänna studiecirklar läsåret 1976-1977.

SOU (Governmental Commission) 1977: 31. Studiestöd. Alternativa utvecklingslinjer.

—— 1974: 62. Studiestöd åt vuxna.

—— 1973: 2. Högskolan (1968 års utbildningsutredning).

—— 1971: 80. Vuxna-utbildning-studiefinansiering.

—— 1963: 74. Rätt till studiemedel.

STAHL, I. (1968). Utbildningsprogram och arbetsmarknadspolitik. Särtryck ur Tio Ekonomer om Arbetsmarknaden.

STOCKFELT, T. and S. ÖBERG (1979). Vem blev uppsökt och vad hande sedan? Sundsvall: CSN 5/1979.

TCO (1973). Vuxenutbildning, återkommande utbildning. Stockholm: Prisma.

12

FRENCH LAW ON CONTINUING VOCATIONAL TRAINING

PIERRE CASPAR

Over the past decade, there has been a great deal of international interest in the French system of continuing vocational training, particularly since the act of 16 July 1971 which called for the reorganization of vocational training under the more general heading of continuing education. Continuing vocational training in France has become both a right and a prominent aspect of economic and social life. In 1979, 2,900,000 members of the national labor force took part in training activities.[1] Total expenditures for these workers were some 15.8 billion francs (or $2.9 billion) of which 9.5 billion ($1.7 billion) were covered by firms and 6.3 billion ($1.15 billion) funded by various forms of state aid. (These figures do not include apprenticeships—that is, initial vocational training.)[2]

The 1971 act made it mandatory for firms employing more than 10 persons to devote at least 0.8% of their wage bill to educational spending. This was no more than a recognition by parliament of the prevailing practices of many enterprises; in fact, average expenditure by enterprises at the time amounted to about double the figure requested by law. The act encompassed and extended a number of arrangements made under a national interindustrial agreement signed a year earlier, on 9 July 1970, by most of the organizations representing labor and management. On the employer's side, these included the *Conseil National du Patronat Francais* (CNPF) and the *Federation des Petites et Moyennes Entreprises* (CGPME). For labor, the trade unions included the *Confederation Francaise Democratique du Travail* (CFDT), the *Confederation Generale du Travail* (CGT), the *Confederation Generale du Travail Force Ouvriere* (CGT-FO). Therefore, the 1971 act introduced a number of innovations into the French continuing training system based on a broad national consensus.

Continuing training in France, although slow to develop, has a long history. As long ago as the French Revolution, the creation of the *Conservatoire National des Arts et Metiers* (CNAM) in 1794 may be said to have marked the first stage of a national system for the training of adults—one that is open to all, multidisciplinary, and able to bridge the various sciences, crafts, and trades. Towards the end of the nineteenth and the beginning of the twentieth centuries came the creation of the *Universites Populaires* and the *Associations de Culture Populaire* and, alongside them, the vocational training courses given official status by the Astier Act (25 July 1919). Together they laid the foundation of the present-day state-provided, free, technical education, leading to the *Certificat d'Aptitude Professionnelle* (Certificate of Vocational Proficiency). In 1934, the first adult vocational training centers were established, which later culminated in the *Association pour la Formation Professionnelle des Adultes* (Association for Vocational Training for Adults; AFPA) which in 1979 was responsible for training more than 90,000 people.

Various other provisions and opportunities were developed during the twentieth century, but the system of vocational training was to take on a different and more coherent form after 1959 and even more so after 1968. It is this system which is described in the present Chapter, together with the rules and principles governing its financing and the special question of training leave.

THE LEGAL FRAMEWORK

The present statutory and regulatory framework took shape and became organized between 1968 and 1971. During this period, the government's approach was to get labor and management to study and integrate the main aspects of the organization and regulation of continuing vocational education in France before they coordinated and endorsed any resultant contractual system. Furthermore, the broad guidelines of current practice became clear during this time: compulsory contributions by employers to the financing of continuing training, wage-earners' entitlements to training leave, the remuneration of trainees, and the division of responsibilities between firms, unions, and government. The development of vocational training was explicitly linked to enterprise and national requirements for growth and technological progress, and to the need to improve employment throughout France.

Two milestones in continuing education resulted from this process. First is the national agreement already referred to between employers and unions of 9 July 1970. Among its agreements, two major rights of wage earners were defined as follows:

- the employees' right to absence from and continued remuneration during working hours to attend training courses of their own choice provided such training is approved by the employer/union commission of the appropriate industrial sector in which they work; and
- the employees' right to training paid for by the employer in the case of unemployment for economic reasons.

Second is the act of 16 July 1971, which was the response of the French government to this agreement. While most of the agreement was incorporated into the act, some new provisions were added, including the following four:

- All employees are entitled to training leave for training of their choice arising from their own initiative. Under the act, training proposed or offered by the firm as part of its own training program must therefore be distinguished from training personally requested by employees to further their knowledge in an area that interests them.
- All firms employing more than ten people are obligated to earmark 0.8% of the total wage bill for the vocational training of the staff. It was originally planned to raise this contribution gradually to 2%, and the current mandatory contribution is 1.1%. This sum must be used to pay for training activities inside or outside the firm or to purchase certain types of teaching equipment. Any money not so spent must be paid into the French Treasury (a stipulation that has frequently been erroneously described as a vocational training "tax").
- Employees, through their representatives on the works committee,[3] are able to have some say on matters of training since the firm must consult with the works committee on its annual training program. Failure to do so entails a fine (see Table 12.2).
- The state participates in remunerating trainees (see the following section for further details). Special provisions were also made for training of the self-employed.

Further measures were taken between 1974 and 1980 in order to improve the remuneration of trainees and the financing of training leave courses. These measures were also necessary in order to adapt the system to changing work and employment conditions—particularly for young people—following the economic downturn that began in 1974. Therefore, between 1971 and 1981 a considerable number of directives, additional clauses, counter-cyclical measures, and statutory acts have amended, clarified, and broadened the system outlined above. Among the most representative provisions are the following:

- *The Employment-Training Contract* (contrat emploiformation), introduced by decree (4 June 1975), is a work contract open to young people between the ages of 17 and 26[4] in which it is mandatory to include between 120 and 1,200 hours training. The employer receives a state subsidy for each eligible trainee taken on under this scheme.

- *The National Employment Agreements* (pactes nationaux pour l'emploi)[5] which are to help young people and people of certain other social categories seeking to enter or reenter working life. Supplementing the employment-training contracts mentioned above, the agreements aim at promoting apprenticeships by exempting them from social security charges. In addition, they provide opportunities for training periods that are paid for by the employer who is partially reimbursed by the state. These agreements offer practical guidance and a basic knowledge of the actual working conditions in an enterprise over a six-month period.

- *The Act of 17 July 1978,* which defined the scope of training leave in broader terms by explicitly including a cultural and social dimension. In the words of the act, "Training activities should enable a worker to change his job or occupation and to acquire a wider cultural and social outlook. Part or all of the training shall take place during working hours." The act also improved the provision of remuneration of workers on training leave. (Details of this will be spelled out below.) Finally, the act gives all employees an opportunity to take unremunerated "teaching leave" to engage in teaching activities for a maximum of one year. The teaching can be either full- or part-time in a public or private educational or training establishment or in a state-approved training course. Employees retain the same status as if they took training leave; that is, they remain members of their enterprises or establishments and are entitled to seniority privileges and paid annual leave.

THE FINANCE OF VOCATIONAL TRAINING

Adult training has become an important aspect of community life in France. Nearly 3 million people in 1979[6] (or one worker in seven) undertook training with a total of 350 million hours during the year and a budget of almost 16 billion francs ($2.9 billion). The total expenditures for 1972-1979 are set forth in Table 12.1. The contribution of firms accounts for over three-fifths of the total budget. It deserves, therefore, more detailed examination. The general data are given in Table 12.2.

TABLE 12.1 Training by Source of Funding: 1972-1979

	1972	1976	1977	1978	1979
Number of Workers in Training[1]					
State	958,000	805,000	894,000	993,000	1,041,000
Firms	1,049,000	1,814,000	1,856,000	1,831,000	1,686,000
Training Insurance Funds[3]	—	190,000	164,000	195,000	2,900,000
Jointly[2]	1,760,000	2,770,000	2,880,000	3,000,000	2,900,000
Trainee Hours					
State	182,000,000	189,000,000	206,000,000	250,000,000	242,000,000
Firms	78,000,000	107,000,000	107,000,000	104,000,000	92,000,000
Training Insurance Funds[3]	—	15,000,000	12,000,000	18,000,000	15,000,000
Jointly[2]	241,000,000	309,000,000	317,000,000	370,000,000	350,000,000
Budget (billion francs)					
State	1.7	3.1	5.1	6.8	6.3
Firms	2.8	6.5	8.0	8.7	9.5

NOTE: The figures given in this chapter do not include apprenticeships (i.e., initial training governed by an entirely different scheme and financed by a separate apprenticeship levy).
1. These are trainees enrolled in a course or part of a course during the calendar year.
2. Some sources are financed jointly by government and industry; this explains why the combined figures of rows 1 and 2 do not tally exactly with those of row 3.
3. Training insurance funds are handled by agencies empowered to collect finances and use them for training required by firms taking part in the scheme as well as by employees.

The figures in Table 12.2 reveal that while the rate of financial participation fixed by law is 1.1% of the wage bill, in fact the average amount spent in 1979 was significantly higher—1.8%. Participation in training varies considerably according to the level of qualification of the employee. Only 15% of trainees were unskilled workers, 47% were skilled workers, 23% were technical and supervisory personnel, and 15% were executive staff. Women accounted for no more than 25% of the trainees.

As Table 12.3 shows, the size of the firm also has a considerable influence on the scale of contribution. Whereas big enterprises with a staff of 2,000 or more spend on the average 2.88% of their wage bill on training, those on the 500 to 1,999 range spend 1.63%. The proportion then drops to 1.29% in the 50 to 499 range, and only 1.05% for firms with a staff of less than 50 people. It stands lower still at 0.94% for the very small firms that employ between 10 and 19 people.

In summary, we can look at the ways in which firms that are covered by this law meet their obligations under the 1971 act. Of the 1.1% they are obliged to spend on adult training, 0.2% is to be paid to the state to finance activities for young people and women seeking employment. Concerning the remaining 0.9%, there are several possibilities open to the employer:

(1) direct financing of vocational training schemes initiated by the firm itself, which may take several forms:
  - training programs, provided by the enterprise;
  - training by training associations (ASFOs)—that is, interenterprise sponsored;
  - training set up by a group of employers or an industrial sector;
  - training provided by training centers run either by the government (GRETA) or privately (chambers of commerce, private centers, etc.);[7]

(2) payments to a training insurance fund (FAF);

(3) payments to approved research institutes (up to 10% of the total amount required by law);

(4) payment to the French Treasury of any sums not spent in the above ways. In 1978, such repayments amounted to 221 million francs ($40 million).

The government may monitor the way these sums are used, but only by verifying whether or not statutory provisions and regulations are respected. The overall financial contribution of the state was 6.3 billion francs ($1.15 billion) in 1979. Of this sum, 2.8 billion were spent on trainee remuneration, 0.3 billion on equipping centers, and 3.2 billion on course operating costs.

TABLE 12.2 Finance and Participation in Training Financed by Firms: 1972-1979

	1972	1976	1977	1978	1979 Provisional
Total number of firms	113,000	124,000	127,000	126,000	126,000
Total wages paid (billion francs)	207	398	451	497	555
Minimum stipulated contribution (million francs)	1,700	3,908	4,513	5,465	6,090
Proportion of wage bill required as contributions (in percentages)	0.8	1.0	1.0	1.1	1.1
Actual outlay on training (million francs)	2,800	6,470	7,950[1]	9,070[1]	10,210[1]
Actual proportion of wage bill paid on training (in percentages)	1.35	1.62	1.76	1.82	1.84
Payments into French Treasury (million francs) for inadequate funding of training activities	170	250	209	232	225
fine for failure to consult works committee	7.5	12	10	10	11
Total number of employees	9,760,000	10,433,000	10,500,000	10,382,000	10,342,000
Number of trainees	1,050,000	1,814,000	1,856,000	1,831,000	1,862,000
Percentage of employees participating in a training course	10.7	17.3	17.7	17.6	18.0
Total number of training hours (millions)	77.6	106.8	106.7	103.7	101.8

1. Including financing of training activities for young job-seekers.

TABLE 12.3 Finance and Participation in Training by Size of Firm: 1979

	10-19 Employees	20-49 Employees	50-499 Employees	500-1,999 Employees	2,000 Employees or More	All Firms
Number of firms	47,000	49,000	23,000	2,000	400	121,500
Amount of wages paid (million francs)	32,600	74,300	154,700	92,200	169,800	523,600
Actual outlay for (million francs)	296	781	1,998	1,505	4,892	9,472
Proportion of wage bill paid on training (in percentages)	0.94	1.05	1.29	1.63	2.98	1.81
Payments into French Treasury (million francs)	74	92	39	3	—	208
Number of employees	669,000	1,536,000	3,135,000	1,704,000	2,769,000	9,813,000
Number of trainees	21,000	80,000	389,000	340,000	856,000	1,685,000
Percentage of employees participating in a training course	3.1	5.2	12.4	20.0	30.9	17.2

The average length of training varies considerably according to its nature. While reorientation and refresher courses for a given job last 140 hours on average, the average number of hours for qualifying or upgrading courses is 400 hours. For pretraining courses (the great majority of which are intended for young job-seekers and are financed entirely by the state) the average is 720 hours.

Of the employment-training contracts for young people mentioned earlier, 57,000 were signed in 1979, while another 30,000 signed in 1978 were still being completed. Of the trainees 57% were boys and 47% were girls.

Looking at the age of these trainees, 29% were under 18 years of age, 41% were between 19 and 21, and 30% between 22 and 26. At the end of courses 50% of the jobs were provided for relatively unskilled staff, as compared to 43% for skilled personnel and 5% for executive or technical staff.

Nearly 90,0000 people undertook an AFPA (Association for Vocational Training for Adults) training course in 1979.[8] All AFPA activities together total 53,830,000 trainee-hours and represent a budget of 1,271 million francs.

The preceding sections have thus outlined broadly how vocational training is financed in France and the way funds are used. Next, some of the technical and psychological difficulties that may arise and cause discrepancies between legal principles and actual practice will be examined with respect to the specific question of training leave. This is one of the most novel features of the French system.

TRAINING LEAVE: THEORY AND PRACTICE

RIGHTS AND REGULATIONS

Apart from the training leave provided for in the 1971 act and subsequent legislation, various provisions for leave for educational purposes are contained in a number of laws. These provisions enable beneficiaries to do the following:

- to work as teachers (teaching leave) as has been mentioned earlier;
- to prepare for certain examinations (examination leave);
- to request special training leave for young people;
- to enroll in trade union courses (workers' educational leave);
- to train for responsibilities in youth projects (leave for youth leaders and organizers).

On what condition is training leave available? To be eligible for training leave under the 1971 act, an employee must have worked in a given occupation for at least 24 months (not necessarily consecutively) with at least 6 of them at the firm concerned. Those who have changed their job because they were laid off for economic reasons do not have to meet this requirement as long as they have not taken any training course between terminating the old job and finding a new one.

It should be noted that a minimum interval has to be observed between one period of training leave and the next depending on the legnth of the previous course. For example, this interval[9] is set at six months when the previous training course was 80 hours or less in length, or one year if it was between 81 and 160 hours.

How long can training leave be? The duration of training leave may not exceed one year in the case of continuous full-time training, or 1,200 hours if it consists of periodic or part-time courses. Exceptions, however, can be made for certain state-approved courses.

What training may the wage-earner choose? The purpose of training leave is "to acquire a higher qualification, to change one's type of work or occupation and to acquire a wider cultural and social outlook." The wage earner has a free choice among specific training courses, although they must be directed towards the acquisition of theoretical or practical qualifications and must have a set curriculum. In no case may training leave be used for the organization of leisure pursuits or for relaxation.

Can an employer refuse a request for training leave? An employer cannot refuse a request for training leave, and may only defer it for one of two reasons. First, it can be deferred if he or she considers that the absence of the employee concerned will hamper the efficient running of the firm. In such a case, the request may be deferred for not more than one year, and then only after the works committee has been consulted. Second, it may be deferred if that would mean that more than 2% of the firm's personnel are on training leave, paid or unpaid, at the same time. For firms with fewer than 200 employees, the limit is fixed at the equivalent to 2% of the hours worked annually by the staff as a whole (including executive staff).

Under what circumstances is the worker entitled to remuneration while on leave? If the worker is to be paid during leave, the course selected must be either state-approved or recognized by the competent joint labor-management committee. In order to alleviate the financial burden on enterprises, the law fixes a ceiling on the number of workers who are entitled to be paid while on leave. Thus, paid training leave is granted to employees up to a limit of 0.5% (0.75% in the case of executive personnel) of the staff. For firms employing fewer than 200 people this figure is equivalent to 0.5% (0.75% in the case of executive personnel) of hours worked annually. If such a contingent of "working hour credits" is not used or not fully used, it can be accumulated over four years.

Regulations vary, however, according to whether the training course is state-approved, is recognized by a joint labor-management committee, or is not recognized by either. In the first case, the employee on training leave who attends a state-approved course is entitled to pay and continues to receive his previous wage. This is paid during the first part of the course by the employer and during the latter part by the state. Table 12.4 shows the conditions of remuneration.

When the training course attended by the employee is recognized only by the joint labor-management committee in his employment sector and not by the state, only the employer is required to maintain the worker's pay. The upper limit is either the first 160 hours or 4 weeks when the course is less than 500 hours, or the first 500 hours or 13 weeks when it is greater than 500 hours.

When the course attended by the employee is recognized neither by the state nor by the joint labor-management committee on employment for the sector concerned, the training leave is simply a leave of absence and neither the employer nor the state is obliged to pay the employee's wage. Employees may, however, request their employers to maintain their wages, since it is open to the employer to include the requests of individuals in the firm's own training program. If the firm subscribes to a training insurance fund, the fund may cover the employee's wage and training expenses either partially or in total.

Who pays the training costs? Training costs generally include registration fees, teaching materials, and in some cases the cost of travel and/or board. By law, employees on training leave are given preference in admission to state-aided courses which are usually free. Travel expenses are partly paid by the state if the worker is remunerated by the state. If the employee attends a course recognized by the appropriate joint labor-management committee, the employer is responsible for the training costs only if the course lasts more than 500 hours, in which case the firm reimburses actual costs up to a ceiling of 31.10 francs ($5.65) per hour. Above this ceiling, the employer pays an allowance equivalent to two-thirds of the training costs, but this allowance may not exceed 70.69 francs ($12.85) per hour. When the course attended by the employee is

TABLE 12.4 Conditions of Remuneration of Paid Training Leave for State-Approved Courses

Length of Course	Trainees' Occupational Category	Remuneration Paid by the Employer	Remuneration Paid by the State
Less than 14 weeks or 500 hours	All employees (executive and nonexecutive)	For the first 4 weeks or the first 160 hours: previous wage	With effect from the 5th week or 161st hour: previous wage up to a ceiling equivalent to three times the SMIC,[1] calculated on the basis of legally established weekly working hours
From 13 weeks or 500 hours minimum to one year or 1,200 hours maximum	Nonexecutive staff	Previous wage from the start of the course for 13 weeks or 500 hours	Previous wage up to a ceiling equivalent to three times the SMIC,[1] calculated on the basis of legally established weekly working hours with effect from the 14th week or the 501st hour
	Executive staff	Previous wage from the start of the course for 16 weeks or 600 hours	Previous wage up to a ceiling equivalent to three times the SMIC,[1] calculated on the basis of legally established weekly working hours with effect from the 17th week or the 601st hour
Over one year or over 1,200 hours	Nonexecutive staff	Previous wage from the start of the course for 13 weeks or 500 hours	120 percent of SMIC[1] with effect from the 14th week or the 501st hour
	Executive staff	Previous wage from the start of the course for 16 weeks or 600 hours	120 percent of SMIC[1] with effect from the 17th week or the 601st hour

NOTE: In 1980, the minimum wage was 13.66 F per hour ($2.48), which is 2,367 F per month ($430.50) based on a work week of 40 hours.
1. SMIC: The guaranteed minimum wage (Salaire minimum inter-professionel de croissance).

not a recognized one, the employer is not required to reimburse the training costs but may agree to do so in the same way as applied to the case of the employee's wage.

TRAINING LEAVE IN PRACTICE

From the rules and regulations, the right to training leave appears to offer workers comprehensive opportunity to meet their vocational training needs. In practice, however, the use of this right is not as simple as was intended originally. In spite of the legislation, it is still more difficult for the worker to exercise his right to training leave than for the employer to frame his own in-house training policy. In most cases, the employee has to choose between the training provided by the firm (which is organized during normal hours and therefore remunerated) and the training of his or her choice. For the latter, finance may not necessarily be secured because of the type of training sought (i.e., if it does not meet recognized criteria).

For reasons of clarity, it should be stressed that under the 1971 act there was no obligation on the part of the employer to remunerate an employee for training while on training leave. Such an obligation was only introduced by the act of 17 July 1978 which established a new system providing for combined remuneration by employer and state subject to the conditions discussed in this section. Firms that signed the July 1970 agreement as well as those that subscribe to a training insurance fund are obligated to maintain an employee's wage during training leave. However, an employee who has a choice between training available outside the firm and in-house training (which may enhance his or her image in the employer's eyes) will be tempted to choose the second alternative rather than run the risks of the first unless the outside training seems to be particularly advantageous. This is confirmed by a 1972 survey showing that 93% of hours spent on training were provided by the employer.

Another restrictive difficulty is that the law provides financial assistance only for previously approved training courses. This may, in some cases, limit access to cultural activities that have no direct vocational content and have no chance of obtaining official recognition. For instance, while a decree of 11 July 1972 expressly aimed to increase recognition of educational cultural activities, firms in fact have received only a few requests for training leave for such purposes—in most firms, only a handful each year. While the 1972 decree may be considered a sophisticated legal instrument that offers workers a wide variety of choice, the decree is difficult to use for both financial and psychological reasons. This explains the rather limited utilization of this provision.

POSSIBLE FUTURE DEVELOPMENTS

The right to training leave can be considered an innovation of great value, but it has suffered from the tendency in France to create endless legal texts in order to cover every conceivable situation. This has reduced much of its creative potential significantly. In 1974 it was calculated (light-heartedly) that more than 487 pages of official texts on the subject had appeared already and that in the whole of the country there were not more than three or four specialists capable of saying exactly what the position was when a particular question was raised. While this may be somewhat overstated, the picture is not that far removed from the actual situation.

It is also true that there is a contradiction between the definitions laid down and the opinions voiced since 1971 concerning continuing training and the system of values and down-to-earth realities of industrial life. This may indicate that some of those who are trying to promote a system of continuing education and training in France act as though it is possible to find technical solutions to political problems. There is a tendency to believe that decisions on economic and social questions can be taken regardless of the relationships between social forces—as if they concerned personal choice alone.

Many of the efforts made during the 1960s to promote training for the individual failed because they overestimated the value of knowledge in power relationships. Today this illusion has faded, but at the same time the tendency to confine training within purely technical bounds deprives the concept of training leave of its full meaning. It can be said safely that as long as the remuneration question has not been settled satisfactorily and while there is still wide-spread unemployment, very few people will be prepared to assert their right to training leave in view of the financial risk involved and the danger of later jeopardizing their employment. Although training leave is a right, it is understandable that many will think, "What will become of me if I leave my job for six months or a year to train in something that interests me personally, only to find that when I come back my employer has learned to do without me?"

The trade unions clearly have an important role to play by putting forward demands that are more precise, backed by better information, and based on a consensus of their membership. But it would appear that adult education and training must, for the time being, recognize the far-reaching implications of unemployment and the economic crisis.

Any debate on future developments of training leave therefore is bound to reflect the question of regulations and legislation less and concentrate more on the concept and status of training itself as perceived by both policymakers and workers. It must consider the very structure of employment in the world today. As part of this problem, one must consider the question of the mobility of workers which depends on a number of factors beside education. Further developments must consider the ability of workers to make plans for themselves, to conceive these plans realistically, and to realize them as a normal expression of individual choice that is still in keeping with the society around them. The individual's ability to act as a responsible partner in an industrial democracy in the midst of economic and political constraints is of paramount importance.

SUMMARY AND CONCLUSION

In summary, continuing vocational training is characterized by two central features. First, enterprises are obliged by law to provide their employees with the opportunity for continuing training and to devote 1.1% of their payroll to that end. Second, all employees have the right to leave for training purposes during normal working time.

Both features, although based on the same law of 1971, are not linked directly to each other; while the former provision has resulted in massive training efforts by the enterprises, only a relatively small (and declining) number of employees has made use of individual training leave. In 1978 more than 1.8 million workers participated in training provided by enterprises, but only 49,000 took leave for a training course outside the firm (as compared to 58,000 in 1976 and 68,000 in 1975).

There are three basic factors responsible for this poor result. First, more often than not the employee exercising his right and asking for training leave does not receive any remuneration while on leave; moreover, he or she is left with the instruction costs as well. Only where the state or the joint labor-management committee have accredited the training activity does the employer or state pay remuneration. Therefore the employee often cannot afford to take training leave.

Second, employees are only entitled to training leave, if the enterprise does not offer a similar course as part of its training program. Since enterprises, especially bigger ones, offer a variety of training activities under their 1.1% payroll obligation, the justification for the demand for a leave to participate in an outside training activity is often difficult to establish. Third, as is the case in other countries with educational leave provisions, there are particular problems concerning the exercise of the right to training leave in small and medium-size firms.

The 1978 law has clarified and ameliorated the problem of wage maintenance and extended the scope of eligible educational activities by including courses with social and cultural components rather than just the purely professional. However worthwhile the intentions of this law and the improvements it actually introduced, there remain considerable problems in the complete and effective utilization of the employee's right to training leave.

NOTES

1. Not including civil servants, who are not covered by the same scheme.
2. Calculated on a basis of $1 U.S. = 5.50 French francs.
3. According to the law, there must be a works committee (comite d'entreprise) where more than 50 people are employed.
4. In certain circumstances women of all ages who wish to resume gainful employment may also benefit under this contract.
5. These were first enacted on 5 July 1977 and have been renewed annually since then. To give some idea of the scope of these agreements, the third (dated 10 July 1979) provided opportunities for 280,000 young people.
6. The figures that follow are those currently available, namely the 1979 figures as given in the 1981 draft budget.
7. These are known as the groupement d'etablissements scolaires—that is, training provided by high schools or colleges, established to provide continuing training for the firms' staff.
8. AFPA offers 297 types of instruction in 32 subjects at 125 vocational training centers for adults. Skilled workers usually undergo six months of full-time training, and technicians are trained for nine to twelve months.
9. This is called a *"delai de franchise."*

REFERENCES

ADAMS, R. J., P. M. DRAPER, and C. DUCHAME (1979) Education and Working Canadians: Report of the Commission of Inquiry on Educational Leave and Productivity. Ottawa: Ministry of Supply and Services.
BESNARD, P. and B. LIETARD (1976) La Formation Continue (Continuing Training). Paris: Editions PUF Collection Que Sais-je, 1655.
DAVID, M. et al. (1976) L'Individuel et le Collectif dans la Formation des Travailleurs (The Individual and the Collectivity in the Training of Workers). Paris: Editions Economica.
DELORS, J. (1973) "French Policy on Continuing Education," in S. Mushkin (ed.) Recurrent Education. Washington, D.C.: U.S. Government Printing Office.
HERTZ-LEBRUN, C. (1979) La Formation Professionnelle Continue. Paris: Lamy.
SCHWARTZ, B. (1977) Une Autre Ecole (A Different School). Paris: Flammarion.
STRINER, H. E. (1972) Continuing Education as a National Investment. Washington, DC: W. E. Upjohn Institute for Employment Research.
VON MOLTKE, K. and N. SCHNEEVOIGT (1977) Educational Leaves for Employees-European Experience for American Consideration. San Francisco: Jossey-Bass.

13

THE FEDERAL REPUBLIC OF GERMANY

HANS G. SCHÜTZE

In 1976 the Federal Republic signed the resolutions of the 1974 ILO Convention Concerning Paid Educational Leave committed

> to formulate and apply a policy designed to promote, by methods appropriate to national conditions and practice and by stages as necessary, the granting of paid educational leave for the purpose of training at any level, general, social and civic education, [as well as] trade union education [art. 2].

Before adopting the convention, educational leave in certain forms had been an established practice in Germany. For example, over half of the West German youth undertake vocational training under the "dual system" in which apprentices spend part of the week in the firm and part of it in vocational school (College Entrance Examination Board, 1979). Employer-sponsored training programs are also provided for employees beyond the apprenticeship age through training programs on the employers' premises or through employers organizations such as the Chambers of Commerce. These are indeed the most important training programs in terms of enrollment and expenditures. The focus of this chapter, however, will be on a narrowed set of programs—those concerned with educational leave. Not all workers are entitled educational leave (*Bildungsurlaub*), yet all provisions conform to the basic characteristics of educational leave (i.e., the individual right to educational leave with the guaranteed right to return to the working place). Most of these provisions maintain the employee's full salaries or wages or a percentage of wages during the period of leave. however, what has emerged in recent years has gone far beyond these approaches by increasing the role of individual choice in electing to take educational leave.

THE SETTING

Western Germany is a federal republic consisting of 10 federal states (Länder) and West Berlin. The latter has most of the characteristics of a state but retains a unique status as a result of the division of that city and the German nation in the wake of World War II. As in the United States, the federal states have the power to regulate educational matters autonomously. In fact, this power is the only really important responsibility of the states—unlike the United States and Canada where the states (or provinces, respectively) have retained many other important powers which in Germany are the domain of the federal government. In order to maintain some degree of uniformity, there is a Standing Conference of the States' Ministers of Education which coordinates educational policies and ensures equivalence among the states of educational qualifications, diplomas, and so on. The federal government has limited jurisdiction in educational matters. It is responsible for establishing the general principles and the institutional framework of higher education, for the promotion of scientific research, student aid and, most importantly, for all non-school-based vocational training (College Entrance Examination Board, 1979).

Educational leave falls under the jurisdiction of the federal government because of a clause in the West German constitution that gives the federal government the power to legislate on economic and labor market matters. In the absence of such federal legislation, the states are free to regulate the provision of educational leave.

Although the federal government expressed its intention as early as 1969 to introduce a bill on paid educational leave, it has failed to do so due to resistance from employers who would have been obligated to bear most of the costs (Görs, 1978: 51; OECD/CERI, 1976: 157-158). However, laws on paid educational leave have been passed in five of the federal states, including Berlin. The other states have so far preferred not to pass similar laws, although some of them have paid-educational-leave bills under consideration.

Although there is no general federal law on paid educational leave, there are a number of provisions in federal laws that give certain groups the right to paid leave for specific educational purposes. For example, civil servants and judges are provided with recurrent opportunities for continuing education. More importantly, under the Enterprise Constitution Act *(Betriebsverfassungsgesetz),* members of enterprise councils *(Betriebsrat)* have the right to educational leave for courses that provide knowledge needed in exercising their functions as worker representatives. Earnings are continued during the period of leave as required by law.

Similar clauses exist for employee representatives in public administration, as well as salaried physicians and civil engineers charged with health and security matters within enterprises (von Moltke and Schneevoigt, 1977). Most important, however, both in terms of people affected and expenditures, is the Federal Labor Promotion Act of 1969 *(Arbeitsförderungsgesetz)* which provides educational costs and maintenance allowances for the unemployed and those threatened by unemployment who participate in continuing training or retraining programs.

In addition to the provisions contained in various Länder and federal laws, there are a number of collective agreements that provide for educational leave, both paid and unpaid. This chapter will limit itself to a description of the main features of some important leave schemes, and a discussion of participation, finance, and costs of recurrent education under these leave schemes.

LAWS FOR PAID EDUCATIONAL LEAVE IN THE FEDERAL STATES *(LÄNDER)*

The Berlin diet (the regional legislature) passed the first law pertaining to educational leave in 1970. This law granted 10 working days leave per year to workers, employees, and apprentices up to age 21. The law was amended in 1975 to include young people up to the age of 25. Its stated purpose was to enable young people to participate in educational activities, enhance participation in public life, and promote vocational education beyond the dual training system.

Laws for the four other Länder sponsoring educational leave were passed in 1974. Despite the seemingly concerted timing, these laws are not uniform but have diverging features concerning the eligibility of participants, the contents of accreditable courses and activities, and the procedure for accreditation. The only basic provision that is identical in all four laws is that they give the beneficiaries the right to leave for one working week per year or two working weeks for two consecutive years. The leave entitlement in Berlin amounts to two working weeks per year. During this leave, the salary or wage is maintained by the employer.

There are some restrictions to this leave entitlement, however. In the cases of Berlin, Bremen, Hamburg, and Hesse, the worker or employee must be employed for a minimum of six months before becoming eligible. This does not apply to Lower Saxony. However, in this state a ceiling has been fixed whereby the employer can refuse a request for leave if the total number of days during the course of one year is 2.5 times the number of eligible staff. This formula implies that no more than 25% of the staff is entitled to leave during the same year. Moreover, all of the state laws specify that a request for educational leave can be denied temporarily, if the functioning of the enterprise might be imperiled, or if there are requests for leave by other members of the staff with higher social priority.

As Table 13.1 shows, the Berlin and Hesse laws limit eligibility to apprentices and young workers up to age 25 while the other three state laws do not have an age ceiling. As in Berlin and Hamburg, the Hesse law is confined to courses of civic education or continuing vocational training; general education cannot be accredited. The Bremen and Lower Saxony laws, however, include continuing general education in the range of accreditable activities.

According to the ILO Convention on Paid Educational Leave, one of the objectives of such leave is to promote "the competent and active participation of workers and their representatives in the life of the undertaking and of the community" (art. 3,b). Although the wording of the definition of civic education in the German Länder Laws is slightly different, they essentially state the same objective—namely, to help workers understand their function, role, obligations, and rights, and to enable them to participate actively in social and public life, exercise their rights, and fulfill their functions. Under this definition, trade union education is part of—not separate from—civic education. In fact, about 50% of the courses and programs offered for this type of education are sponsored by the trade unions and those voluntary organizations that have strong links with the unions. The bulk of programs and courses of continuing education and training, however, are offered by the local popular academies *(Volkshochschulen)* sponsored by local government, while other voluntary organizations (like the churches) account for the remainder.

TABLE 13.1 State Laws on Paid Education Leave

	Berlin Law of 7/16/70 amended 12/17/76	Hamburg Law of 1/21/74	Bremen Law of 12/18/74	Lower Saxony Law of 6/5/74 amended 12/17/74	Hesse Law of 6/24/74
Eligibility	Wage and salary earners, apprentices; Age limit: under 26 years	Wage and salary earners, apprentices; No age limit	Wage and salary earners, apprentices, home workers and other dependent workers; No age limit	Wage and salary earners, apprentices, home workers and other dependent workers; No age limit	Wage and salary earners, apprentices; Age limit: under 26 years
Entitlement	10 working days per year; beyond this period there is a right to unpaid leave	10 (12) working days in two years	10 (12) working days in two years	10 (12) working days in two years	5 (6) working days per year
Contents of Courses	Civic education and continuing vocational training	Civic education and continuing vocational training	Civic education, continuing vocational training and general education	Civic education, continuing vocational training and general education	Civic education and continuing vocational training
Restrictions of Entitlement	after six months employment with the same firm; exercise of right can temporarily be denied by employer if and as long as there are compelling reasons regarding the functioning of the enterprise or if there are demands for leave of other salaried workers with higher social priority	after six months employment with the same firm; exercise of right can temporarily be denied by employer if and as long as there are compelling reasons regarding the functioning of the enterprise or if there are demands for leave of other salaried workers with higher social priority	after six months employment with the same firm; exercise of right can temporarily be denied by employer if and as long as there are compelling reasons regarding the functioning of the enterprise or if there are demands for leave of other salaried workers with higher social priority	employer can refuse, if a ceiling is reached. The annual ceiling is defined as a total of **days per firm equivalent 2.5 times the number of employees** exercise of right can temporarily be denied by employer if and as long as there are compelling reasons regarding the functioning of the enterprise or if there are **demands for leave of other salaried workers with higher social priority**	after six months employment with the same firm; exercise of right can temporarily be denied by employer if and as long as there are compelling reasons regarding the functioning of the enterprise or if there are demands for leave of other salaried workers with higher social priority

While the objective of continuing vocational training is to maintain, improve, or expand vocational qualifications and occupational flexibility (Hamburg law: sec. 1, par. 3), there is no comparable legal definition of general education in the two state laws that include general education in their range of accreditable activities. This leads occasionally to difficulties when employers refuse to grant educational leave to their employees for general education courses not related to job requirements (such as full-time language programs) or for courses such as sailing or yoga. Some of the workers have carried their cause to the labor courts which have, in the first instances, ruled that such courses are indeed covered by the term "general education." While results of these cases are at present pending before the Supreme Labor Court, there is growing resistance among employers against what are viewed as leisure-time activities. This resistance may eventually lead to a revision of the law on this point.

The Länder laws also differ considerably regarding the procedure for course accreditation. In Hamburg, the agency charged with implementation of the law is required to check every education or training course in terms of its compatibility with the law. In Hesse, it is confined to the accreditation of institutions and other providers of education and training. The courses offered by these accredited sponsors are then automatically recognized as eligible for paid leave. While Bremen and Berlin have similar provisions, Lower Saxony has adopted a blend of these two principles, allowing employees to seek recognition for courses provided by some nonaccredited institutions.

PARTICIPATION AND CHARACTERISTICS OF PARTICIPANTS

As can be seen from Table 13.2, participation in paid educational leave under the Länder laws is generally low. Although the participation rate is slowly increasing, it varies between less than 2% and 6%, and of a total of 3.75 million eligible employees only 87,000 exercised their right in 1980 (2.3%). Even taking into account the upward trend over the years, participation has neither lived up to the hopes and aspirations of the trade unions which were the driving force behind the Lander legislation, nor has it warranted the fears of employers who resisted it because of concern for the costs and the possible loss of productivity.

It is difficult to analyze the underlying reasons for this low participation or to assess the relative weight of the factors that contribute to it.

TABLE 13.2   Paid Educational Leave According to State Laws: Participation, 1975-1980

	Berlin	Hamburg	Bremen	Lower Saxony	Hesse
1975					
(a) eligible	105,300	614,926	330,000	2,011,595	403,692
(b) participants	4,277	3,000	3,190	8,985	6,407
(c) rate	4.0%	0.5%	0.9%	0.45%	1.6%
1976					
(a) eligible	93,400	702,771	322,000	2,011,595	412,900
(b) participants	4,946	3,550	6,785	20,168	8,322
(c) rate	5.3%	0.5%	2.5%	1.0%	2.0%
1977					
(a) eligible	94,700	697,792	323,000	2,061,968	433,500
(b) participants	4,563	6,000*	8,257	24,625	10,119
(c) rate	4.8%	0.9%*	2.8%	1.2%	2.3%
1978					
(a) eligible	109,741	700,000*	315,000	2,061,968	430,200
(b) participants	5,723	8,400*	9,893	29,523	11,242
(c) rate	5.2%	1.2%*	3.8%	1.43%	2.6%
1979					
(a) eligible	114,465	700,000*	315,000*	2,137,521	435,300
(b) participants	7,154	9,800*	13,187	33,897	12,927
(c) rate	6.2%	1.4%*	4.4%	1.59%	3.0%
1980					
(a) eligible	119,456	700,000*	315,000*	2,180,990	433,800
(b) participants	7,366	11,200*	12,380	40,930	13,570
(c) rate	6.2%	1.6%*	4.3%	1.88%	3.1%

SOURCES: Länder reports; Görs, 1982.
*Own estimate.

The trade unions see continuing resistance from employers and workers' fears of negative sanctions as the most important obstacles to higher levels of participation (Görs, 1978: 184-211; 1982). Employers, of course, deny that any such sanctions exist. This would violate the spirit and intent of the laws which generally forbid pressures or sanctions against workers who want to exercise their right to educational leave. According to employers, paid educational leave increases fixed labor costs and therefore has a direct impact on employment and competitiveness. They emphasize that accredited courses and programs often do not respond to the real demand which, according to them, is the upgrading of occupational skills and knowledge. In particular, employers have strong reservations against what they see as trade union education in the guise of civic education, and leisure activities in the guise of general education.

Apart from this conflict of views—which underlines the polarized and highly political nature of the debate about educational leave in Germany—there are a number of more objective factors that play an important role. First, there is a widespread lack of suitable courses (i.e., programs that are tailored to the needs of both workers and employers and are of the appropriate duration) as the majority of the Länder laws exclude courses shorter than three or, in some instances, five working days. Second, despite the provision for salary maintenance, the instruction and travel costs are not borne by the employer and so must be met by the participants themselves or some other sponsor. In addition, there is often a marked lack of information about available courses and the procedure for requesting educational leave. This is particularly true in small enterprises where union influence and worker representation is low or nonexistent.

One of the main problems concerning participation is the impact of previous education on the demand for recurrent education. It is, therefore, one of the acknowledged objectives of a recurrent education strategy to enhance participation in further learning among those with a low level of educational attainment. According to Table 13.3, employees possessing only a high school diploma are heavily underrepresented. In contrast, those with a technical school or upper secondary school diploma (which are prerequisite for access to higher education) are significantly overrepresented. The data regarding the occupational status of participants show fewer differences as the official German distinction between blue collar *(Arbeiter)* and white collar *(Angestellter)* is no longer an accurate distinction in a modern, technological economy. They nevertheless give an idea of orders of magnitude. Apart from Berlin and Hesse (where eligibility is limited by an age ceiling, and hence the majority of participants are apprentices) the figures for Lower Saxony, which is at present the biggest and most representative state with educational leave legislation, reveal that workers are slightly overrepresented. While this seems somewhat at odds with the general dependence of participation on educational attainment, it shows that targeted outreach programs, in particular by the unions and the enterprise councils, have been successful in overcoming this barrier.

TABLE 13.3 Paid Educational Leave According to Lander Law: Characteristics of Participants: 1977 (in percentages)

	Berlin	Hamburg	Bremen	Lower Saxony	Hesse	Educational Attainment and Occupational Status of Total German Working Population*
Educational Attainment						
Without diploma	n.a.	1.1	2.0	n.a.	n.a.	n.a.
With high school diploma	n.a.	35.2	33.3	n.a.	n.a.	72.4
With intermediate school diploma	n.a.	42.7	30.1	n.a.	n.a.	17.5
With technical school diploma	n.a.	6.0	22.6	n.a.	n.a.	n.a.
Abitur or equivalent	n.a.	13.1	5.0	n.a.	n.a.	9.3
Nonclassified	n.a.	1.9	6.9	n.a.	n.a.	n.a.
Occupational Status						
Blue-collar workers	n.a.	n.a.	36.0	52.9	10.8	43.0
Employees	42.3	n.a.	55.7	36.9	15.1	35.5**
Apprentices	57.0	n.a.	8.3	10.2	74.1	5.4**

SOURCES: Lander reports on paid educational leave, Hönigsberger.
*Federal Statistical Bureau (microcensus of April 1978).
**Own computations.

The composition of participants is also highly variable from year to year, as can be seen by comparing the 1977 figures in Table 13.3 with the 1980 figures for Lower Saxony of 44.3% workers, 46.5% employees, and 9.2% apprentices, as well as from course to course. A Lower Saxony study for the year 1977 showed that in courses offered by an educational institution sponsored by the trade unions, enrollments of workers amounted to 76% of participants as compared to 29% for courses offered by the local popular academies. Even this latter figure is significantly higher than worker participation in continuing education outside employers' premises, which is generally below 5%. It is thus evident that workers have indeed benefited from paid educational leave.

A third factor of significance regarding participation is the size of the firm. Large firms can cope more easily than smaller ones with the short-term absence of a small number of employees because they represent a low proportion of personnel and because the large firm has possibilities for internal substitution. In addition, those enterprises with strong worker representation and unionization tend to be far more active than others because they provide information and stimulate demand for eligible leave. Since these are characteristics of large and medium-size firms, the marked differences shown in Table 13.4 are not altogether surprising. This may be partly due to the fact that 40.3% of all Lower Saxony participants in 1978 were employed by Volkswagen (Görs, 1982)—an enterprise which is not heavily unionized, but one in which the president of the powerful metal workers union is a member of the Board of Directors.

In summary, the experience with paid educational leave laws suggests that a variety of factors are contributing to their underutilization. Although the trend is an upward one, participation in paid educational leave may not live up to the hopes of its protagonists (i.e., the trade unions and the Social Democrats), at least not in the immediate future. On the other hand, it must be acknowledged that, because of these laws, some 85,000 employees a year participate in some kind of further education. Most of them are ordinarily underrepresented in continuing education and probably would not have participated otherwise. In addition, plans are under way in Northrhine Westfalia (by far the most populous and industrialized of the federal states) to pass paid educational leave legislation. If these plans succeed, the number of employees eligible for paid educational leave under the Länder laws will more than double, bringing the total number of eligible persons to around 8 million (i.e., more than one-third of the entire work force in the Federal Republic). Such legislation would considerably enhance workers' opportuni-

TABLE 13.4 Participants in Paid Educational Leave in Lower Saxony According to Size of Firm (in percentages)

	\multicolumn{6}{c}{Number of Workers Employed}				
	1-9	10-49	50-199	200-299	1000 and More	Public Sector
1977	2.9	6.7	8.5	17.4	51.0	13.5
1978	2.7	3.3	8.8	14.1	56.0	13.1
1979	4.7	9.5	10.1	15.9	44.1	15.7
1980	3.8	6.0	8.3	14.3	53.9	13.8

SOURCE: Lower Saxony Report, 1981.

ties for continuing education and can be expected to make paid leave an important component of recurrent education in Germany.

THE ENTERPRISE CONSTITITUION ACT: PAID EDUCATIONAL LEAVE FOR WORKERS' REPRESENTATIVES

The federal Enterprise Constitution Act regulates worker participation in management decisions of the enterprise and the procedures to be followed, and accords special leave to members of the enterprise council. This leave is granted for participation in seminars and courses that provide the knowledge required to be a workers' representative. In principle, this right is not limited to a specific duration, and the enterprise council as a whole determines which of its members is to attend a specific course. The council also considers the timing of participation with respect to the proper functioning of the enterprise and its process of production. If there is a conflict between the council and the employer, a mediation board makes the final decision.

In addition to this collective right, the law provides an individual entitlement for each elected workers' representative to three weeks per elective term of three years, amounting to one week per year. Members of work councils who are fulfilling this function for the first time are granted an additional week. During these leave periods the salary is paid in full by the employer. This individual leave entitlement is in addition to any right to paid educational leave an employee might have under one of the state laws or under one of the collective bargaining agreements.

As might be expected, courses are mainly provided by the unions (84%), while employers and their associations and voluntary organizations such as chambers of labor or educational institutions sponsored by political parties and the confessions account for the rest—5.6% and 10.3%, respectively (Federal Ministry of Labor, figures from 1978).

Enterprise councils are not a branch of the union. Even if the majority of council members are union members, they have responsibilities only with respect to their own enterprise. These responsibilities are enumerated and defined in the Enterprise Constitution Act. Confidential information about the enterprise obtained by council members in the exercise of their function cannot be passed on to third parties, including the unions of which they may be members.

According to the law, enterprises between 5 and 20 salaried persons have the right to a single representative. Those of 21 salaried persons or more are guaranteed the right to a work council whose size is determined in proportions to the number of its personnel (e.g., three members for 21-50 salaried persons; 5 for firms of 51-150; 7 for firms of 151-300, and so forth). For the elective period 1975-1978, a total of 191,000 workers' representatives in the Federal Republic were eligible for special leave under the Enterprise Constitution Act (Federal Ministry of Labor).

A rough estimate of participation is derived from the fact that there were 9,592 courses during the 1975-1978 term which on average lasted one week and accommodated between 20 and 30 participants (Federal Ministry of Labor, 1979). This constitutes an approximate total of 239,000 participants during three years, or almost 80,000 per year. This suggests a participation rate of approximately 42% which is significant in comparison with the participation rate of educational leave generally.

The Enterprise Constitution Act extends the same right to leave for youth representatives—that is, the elected representatives of those under 19 years of age, most of whom are apprentices. Educational leave of a similar kind is also foreseen for the representatives of handicapped workers and employees who are responsible for the working conditions of handicapped personnel.

PAID TRAINING LEAVE UNDER THE LABOR PROMOTION ACT

While participation in educational activities under the Länder laws on paid educational leave is regulated largely by what is often called "social demand," the provision of training and retraining opportunities under the Federal Labor Promotion Act of 1969 is strictly based on a manpower requirement approach. The law is an instrument of what has come to be called an active labor market policy. It states as its purpose the achievement and maintenance of a high level of employment, the constant improvement of the employment structure and, thereby, the promotion of economic growth (for details regarding the law see Striner, 1972, and von Moltke and Schneevoigt, 1977). More particularly the measures under the law aim at the following:

- preventing the occurrence or continuance of unemployment or underemployent, on the one hand, and labor shortages, on the other;
- safeguarding and improving the occupational mobility of gainfully employed persons;
- preventing, offsetting, or eliminating the negative effects that technical developments or structural changes in the economy may have on gainfully employed persons;
- improving the employment structure in different geographical areas and economic sectors;
- and providing employment opportunities for the handicapped, women, the aging, and other hard to employ groups.

In addition to regulations concerning job counseling and placement, the act provides for the promotion of vocational training, continuing training and retraining through financial subsidies to individuals engaged in such training. With respect to continuing training, such subsidies are paid to participants who have completed an apprenticeship or possess appropriate work experience and wish to participate in programs designed to maintain or extend their professional skills and knowledge, adopt them to technical developments, or enhance promotion. Such subsidies are also available for the retraining of the unemployed or employees threatened by employment who "participate in programmes designed to enable them to transfer to some other form of suitable employment, with the particular objective of ensuring or improving their occupational mobility" (sec. 47). Such programs are no longer than two years when attended full-time, but part-time participation, including study by correspondence, is possible where part-time provision is available. Participants are paid a maintenance allowance calculated on the basis of the wage previously earned; until the end of 1981, this stood at 80 percent of the net wage or salary.

Under the impact of heavy resource restraints which required important budget cuts, the act was amended in 1981. This reduced the maintenance allowance to 68% of the previous net salary and narrowed certain of the eligibility criteria. Among these, the criterion of "threatened by redundancy," in particular, which previously had been interpreted very widely, was made more stringent by restricting it to salaried persons who had either received a notice of redundancy or whose enterprises had been declared bankrupt.

Eligibility for further training and retraining subsidies is dependent on membership of the compulsory unemployment insurance scheme, since it is from this fund that subsidies are paid and the scheme is administered. These measures are thus financed—as with unemployment benefits, vocational counseling, and placement services—by equal contributions of salaried workers and employees on the one hand, and employers on the other, with additional contributions from the federal government to meet the deficit in the budget of the scheme.

In 1980, 176,500 salaried persons received subsidies for continuing training courses, of which 65,300 (37%) were unemployed at the time they started the course, while the others were in gainful employment. An additional 38,000 persons were in retraining courses of which 60% were unemployed. The total of these two groups was 214,500 employees, or about 1% of the total workforce.

As can be seen from these statistics—in particular from the fact that some 50% of those in continuing training or retraining programs were unemployed—we are not dealing here with educational leave in the proper sense but with a labor market program designed to upgrade professional skills and thus to enhance employability and upward mobility. While this scheme resembles paid educational leave schemes in some of its features such as the maintenance of a proportion of the salary of an employee engaged mostly in training off the job, it lacks one important characteristic of educational leave—it fails to guarantee the right of return to one's job in the same enterprise upon completion of the training activity.

Nevertheless, this scheme has been included in this chapter for two reasons: First, because this kind of investment in human resources is of general interest when talking about lifelong learning in a recurrent pattern. It may also prove that such an investment is a sound one yielding concrete benefits that offset the costs incurred. Thus, according to a recent survey by the Federal Employment Institute, one in two participants in the retraining program had found employment within one month of completing retraining, and a total of 87% were in positions commensurate with their newly acquired qualifications within two years after completing their retraining (for a fuller discussion regarding costs and benefits, see Striner, 1972).

The second reason for mentioning the program in this chapter is its particular mode of financing. Whereas in the case of paid educational leave both under the Länder laws and the Enterprise Constitution Act the wages are maintained in full by the employer; in this case maintenance allowances are paid by a collective fund financed by equal shares from workers and employers. This emphasis on continuing training and retraining as an instrument of enhancing employability, and hence employment and its mode of financing, find their parallel in the French system of continuing training (see Chapter 12 in this volume) whose underlying concept of collective or parafiscal finance is also discussed elsewhere in this volume (see Chapter 4, and more concretely with respect to training, Chapter 14).

PROVISION IN OTHER LAWS

Besides the leave schemes discussed above, there are a number of other federal and state laws that accord a right to leave for educational purposes to particular groups. Some have already been mentioned in passing (e.g., the provisions for security engineers and employed physicians responsible for occupational health). Among these, the scheme of providing full-time continuing education and training for members of the armed forces serving beyond the compulsory conscription period is probably the most important in numerical terms (von Moltke and Schneevoigt, 1977: 106-107). However, these laws must be considered to be marginal in comparison with the ones described above.

PROVISION FOR EDUCATIONAL LEAVE IN COLLECTIVE BARGAINING AGREEMENTS

A sizeable number of collective bargaining agreements contain clauses providing for leave, both paid and unpaid, for various reasons. Based on a survey by the Federal Minister of Labor in 1967, it was found that only 57 out of 900 agreements included in the survey had clauses that entitled every worker to educational leave, while the majority of leave provisions in the agreements were limited to union members or workers' representatives. The agreements also differ considerably with respect to the duration of such leave, the contents of educational activities allowed under these clauses, and the maintenance of wages (which was covered in only a small number of cases—18 out of 900 agreements).

According to a survey sponsored by the unions in 1973, agreements with educational leave clauses affected 2.2 million salaried employees, representing some 10% of the workforce. A later survey counted a total of 204 agreements with such clauses affecting a total of 2.8 million workers (i.e., 14% of the workforce). Of these, only slightly more than one-third were entitled to full wage maintenance by the employer while on educational leave, and about one-half of those eligible did not receive any wage or allowance from their employer during such leave (for details, see Görs, 1982).

Although these figures seem important, the leave provisions in collective bargaining agreements probably have a marginal impact in comparison with the various legal entitlements to paid leave. This is due to several factors, not least of which is the bewildering variety in content of the leave clauses in the various contracts as well as a considerable overlap with similar legal entitlements. Thus, while workers' representatives might be entitled to leave for labor union education under the collective agreement for their sector of industry, they are also entitled to essentially the same right under the Enterprise Constitution Act. Although these entitlements do not necessarily preclude each other, it is obvious that in practice they are not accumulated, given the stipulation contained in both the law and most of the agreements that the exercise of this entitlement must not negatively affect the production of the enterprise.

Given this rather marginal nature of leave clauses in collective labor contracts, it is not astonishing that there are not even estimates available as to the extent that these contractual entitlements are being utilized. It can probably be safely assumed that current utilization is very low.

COSTS

We have already referred to the resistance on the part of the employers to the wide scale introduction of paid educational leave on the grounds that such entitlements would further increase labor costs and would therefore impair the economy as a whole in its competitiveness with other industrialized countries. Strangely enough, no concrete figures of any degree of accuracy were put forward in support of these arguments. Estimates given ranged from DM 600 million to 5 billions per year ($300 million to 2.5 billion), but these figures were rejected by the unions as unreliable and far too high (Görs, 1978: 196).

There are only scant data on the actual costs of existing leave schemes. Two of the states with paid educational leave laws have suggested concrete figures. Thus the authorities of Berlin have assessed the total annual burden for the employers at almost DM 3 million, including wages and contributions to the social security fund. Divided among the number of participants, this would amount to around DM 415 ($207) per participant (figures from 1979). The estimates given by the Hesse authorities are lower still—DM 3.9 millions for 13,570 participants (in 1980), thus around DM 290 ($145) per participant which is not more than 0.00048% of the total wage bill of that state.

However accurate these official estimates may be, they are not representative of the levels of outlays normally incurred. As has been pointed out, both Berlin and Hesse laws contain an age ceiling of 25 years which means that the majority of participants consist of apprentices and young workers whose allowances and salaries are considerably lower than that of the average employee. Based on an average salary, the figure for a one week entitlement per year (5 working days) would amount to approximately DM 1,000 ($500) per participant. Based on the 1980 participation rate and making allowance for less costly participation of apprentices, one can estimate the total cost at approximately DM 150 million ($75 million) which German employers had to bear for income maintenance of their employees while on paid educational leave—not counting empoloyers' contribution to paid training leave under the Labor Promotion Act. This figure does not take into account, however, instruction and indirect costs that must be borne either by the participants themselves, by the various sponsors of education and training courses, or by the states via subsidies to such sponsors. Because of the enormous variety of sponsors and programs and the lack of relevant data, not even a cautious estimate can be given regarding such costs.

This is not the case for the Continuing Training and Retraining Scheme under the Labor Promotion Act mentioned above. For the 214,500 participants (in 1980) in continuing and retraining courses, instruction cost, transportation, housing, and contributions to the social security fund amounted to DM 752 million. Together with almost DM 1.5 billion spent for maintenance payments, the Federal Employment Institute spent a total of DM 2.25 billion ($1.22 billion), thus around DM 10,500 ($5,250) per participant. In comparing these figures to the above estimates for paid educational leave schemes, account must be taken of the fact that the duration of more than 20% of these courses is between 18 months and 3 years, and that half of them last between 4 months and 1 year. Table 13.5 gives an idea of the total outlays for educational and training leave in the Federal Republic for the leave schemes mentioned above. It must be emphasized that this table is not only incomplete with respect to other costs besides maintenance, but is also based in part on estimates. It serves the purpose however of indicating the order of magnitudes involved.

MODES OF FINANCING

There are two principle modes of financing educational leave schemes. In one, the individual employer provides for the maintenance of wages and salaries. This is the case for the leave schemes provided in the Länder laws, the Enterprise Constitution Act, and those collective bargaining agreements that contain a paid leave provision. The second mode of financing is a collective approach: Outlays for continuing and retraining under the Labor Promotion Act come from the Unemployment Insurance Fund which is financed by compulsory contributions from both the employers and employees and is calculated as a percentage of the wage bill.

In addition to these two main sources of funding, paid educational leave schemes are publicly subsidized in several ways. First, as wage maintenance costs can be written off against profits for tax purposes, the state contributes in the form of tax revenues foregone. Second, in spite of the principle that the Unemployment Insurance Fund is collectively funded by contributions from employers and employees, the federal government has been obliged in recent years to provide massive subsidies in order to balance the deficit resulting from rising unemployment. Finally, instruction as well as indirect costs are being publicly subsidized in a variety of ways, mainly through grants to education and training institutions providing eligible courses or through payments to the sponsors of such courses (such as voluntary organizations, churches, and

TABLE 13.5 Educational Schemes and Leave for Continuing Training and Retraining: Participants and Costs, 1980

	Participants (in 1000s)*	Outlays for Income Maintenance (in Mio DM)	Outlays for Instruction and Direct Costs
Lander Laws for paid educational leave	87**	79**	n.a.
Federal Law concerning paid educational leave for worker representatives (Enterprise Constitution Act)	80**	72**	n.a.
Provisions for Paid Educational Leave in other Laws	n.a.	n.a.	n.a.
Paid Education Leave according to Collective Bargaining Agreements	n.a.	n.a.	n.a.
Paid Leave for Continuing and Retraining (Federal Labor Promotion Act)		1,498	752,000

SOURCES: Federal Employment Office, Promotion of Training, Participants Statistics (December 1981).
*Numbers have been rounded.
**Own estimates.

unions). It is extremely difficult to quantify the amount of public funds contributed in this way to the financing of education and training leave, especially since such funds come from federal, state, and local budgets rather than from a single source. However, it can be assumed that these public subsidies are substantial.

Problems in this area of financing arise at two levels. First, small firms often find it difficult to release a worker and then to face the problem of maintaining his wage during his absence while it is easier for large enterprises to cope with replacements and the financial burden. This problem is reflected in the participation data which show that workers from larger firms are overrepresented and those from small firms are underrepresented. In order to remedy the financial burden on the small firm, it had been suggested in the discussion and debate on legislation on paid educational leave in Bremen and in Hesse that a hardship fund that would reimburse about half of the expenditure incurred by small firms on wages during such leave should be created. This idea was not adopted, but it is clear that the present mode of financing places small firms—and hence workers from such firms—at a disadvantage.

The second problem concerns the participants to the extent that they are left with part of the cost for instruction and other course-related costs. Although courses are often fully subsidized from either public sources or from the sponsors (e.g., union funds) still some costs are incurred that are not met by these subsidies. While a minor financial contribution on the part of the participant may not be a problem for the average employee, it might constitute a real barrier to those who are financially less well-off (Kiausch and Schenk, 1978).

LABOR MARKET EFFECTS

From the discussion of costs and who has to shoulder them, we now turn to the question of whether or not present paid educational leave schemes have concrete labor market effects, and how these effects can be quantified. Ironically, the main points of this discussion were formulated at a time when labor supply was a problem and the opposition to leave laws on the part of employers was partly based on the argument that the implementation of leave laws would create considerable supply problems.

Over the last few years, in Germany as in the rest of the Western industrialized countries characterized by excessive labor supply, this question has been taken up by the unions and widely used in favor of paid educational leave. Various model calculations have been put forward that suggest that paid educational leave could in fact be used as a labor market instrument in that it would reduce actual labor supply. While most of these calculations concerning the quantitative effects of educational leave schemes tend to equalize the amount of hours lost and the additional demand, it is fair to assume that the net demand is considerably lower. It is natural that enterprises will tend to keep additional hiring (and hence costs) to a minimum and will thus try to compensate by means of temporary changes in work organization and the mobilization and better utilization of existing human resources.

Thus the Institute of Labor Market Research (which is attached to the Federal Employment Institute) has estimated that the potential net employment effect of leave schemes is less than half of the calculated increase in demand (Reyer et al., 1979).

However, these calculations remain largely theoretical as long as participation is as low as it is at present and the full potential of paid educational leave for relieving the pressures of labor supply is not really put to a test. Nevertheless, it can probably be assumed that the employment effect would remain relatively small, even if the participation rate were higher, as long as the size of the leave entitlement remains at the present level (i.e., one week per year). But even with this level of entitlement, the necessity for an employer to hire additional labor might be greater than at present if entitlements could be accumulated over a number of years thus enabling the employee to take more sizeable periods of leave. The maximum leave time is currently two years.

A final word must be said concerning the order of magnitude of educational leave entitlements. When considering their employment effects, their relative importance should be assessed against the background of other kinds of leave entitlements. These have steadily grown in Germany over the last few years, and the total average annual leave entitlement for salaried employees was almost six weeks (30 working days) in 1981. In addition, there are 12 official holidays per year, and several special leave entitlements for certain groups such as handicapped employees who are entitled by law to another six working days of annual leave. Effective yearly working time has thus been reduced to 211.4 working days in 1978, compared to 248.3 in 1960 (Reyer et al., 1979). It is in this context that paid educational leave at present levels can be said to have comparatively marginal effects on labor supply.

CONCLUDING REMARKS

It has been argued in some quarters that given the relatively generous annual leave entitlement in Germany compared, for example, with the United States, there is no real need for additional leave for educational purposes, and hence the low level of utilization. Educational leave, however, cannot be treated as a holiday, any more than, for instance, an apprenticeship or studies for a college degree could be. And it is obvious that skilled automobile workers, even with six weeks of annual leave, cannot normally be expected to use their leave to enroll in a short-term education or training course, even if such a course were available and accessible. But reasoning that treats educational leave the same as other sorts of leave illustrates the current lack of understanding and acceptance of the need for educational leave.

This may be one reason that paid educational leave has not lived up to its potential or to the hopes of its proponents, but it is not the only reason. The low degree of utilization is also influenced by the lack of educational and training offerings that are suited to the needs and expectations of adults, particularly adults with little or no more than compulsory schooling. The lack of individual motivation and self-confidence with respect to organized learning is probably more of a barrier to participation than pressure from employers, although the fear of negative sanctions in times of high unemployment must not be underestimated. In order to overcome this barrier, the federal government has therefore sponsored some extensive model programs in which the needs, interest, and motivation of special target groups (e.g. young people, migrant workers, women, the unskilled or semiskilled, industrial workers) have been studied and evaluated in order to assess which kinds of outreach, counseling, and course content can best reach these groups.

Paid educational leave in Germany is at a beginning. Except for the important continuing and retraining program under the Labor Promotion Act and the special leave for members of the enterprise councils, educational leave is still marginal in quantitative terms. However, the **level of participation, although still very low, has been steadily growing** since the right to educational leave was first introduced. It can probably be expected that the introduction of a general legal right to educational leave in the populous industrial State of Northrhine Westfalia will provide new momentum and lead to greater recognition of learning as a **lifelong process and of educational leave of absence as an important** instrument for the widespread implementation of this general principle.

REFERENCES

ADAMS, R. J., P. M. DRAPER, and C. DUCHAME (1979) Educationa and Working Canadians: Report of the Commission of Inquiry on Educational Leave and Productivity. Ottawa: Ministry of Supply and Services.

College Entrance Examination Board (1979) The Educational System in the Federal Republic of Germany. New York: Secretariat of the Standing Conference of Ministers of Education.

DEGEN, G. R. (1980) Bildungsurlaub (Educational Leave of Absence). Dusseldorf: Landesinstitut fur Curriculumentrwicklung, Lehrerfortbildung und Weiterbildung.

GÖRS, D. (1982) "Erfahrungen und sozio-okonomische Probleme der Bildungsurlaubsregelungen in der Bundesrepublic Deutschland" ("Experience with Educational Leave in the Federal Republic and Related Socio-Economic Problems"), in D. Kuhlenkamp and H. G. Schütze (eds.) Kosten und Finanzierung der beruflichen und nicht-beruflichen Weiterbildung (The Costs and Financing of Continuing Education and Training). Frankfurt Main: Diesterweg.

——— (1978) Zur politischen Kontroverse um den Bildungsurlaub (The Political Controversy about Educational Leave). Cologne.

HÖNIGSBERGER, H. (1977) Bildungsurlaub nach Gesetz (Legal Provision for Educational Leave). Heidelberg: Arbeitsgruppe fur empirische Bildungsforschung.

KIAUSCH, U. and P. SCHENK (1978) Bildungsurlaub nach Tarifvertragen (Provision for Educational Leave in Collective Agreements). Weinheim: Beltz.

KUHLENKAMP, D. and H. G. SCHÜTZE [eds.] (1982) Kosten und Finanzierung der beruflichen und nicht-beruflichen Weiterbildung (The Costs and Financing of Continuing Education and Training). Frankfurt Main: Diesterweg.

MUSHKIN, S. [ed.] (1973) Recurrent Education. Washington, DC: U.S. Government Printing Office.

OECD/CERI (1978) Alternation Between Work and Education: A Study of Educational Leave of Absence at Enterprise Level. Paris: Author.

OECD/CERI (1976) Developments in Educational Leave of Absence. Paris: Author.

REYER, L., H. U. BACH, H. KOHLER, and B. TERIET (1979) "Arbeitszeit und Arbeitsmarkt-Volumenrechnung, Auslastungsgrad und Entlastungswirkung" ("Working Time and the Labour Market-Volume Calculations, Degree of Utilization and Net Employment Effects"). Mitteilungen aus der Arbeits und Berufsforschung 3/1979: 381-400.

SCHÜTZE, H. G. (1982) "Das OECD-Konzept 'Recurrent Education' und Kriterien fur die Finanzierung lebenslangen Lernens" ("The OECD Concept of Recurrent Education and Criteria for Financing Lifelong Learning"), in D. Kuhlenkamp and H. G. Schütze (eds.) Kosten und Finanzierung der beruflichen und nicht-beruflichen Weiterbildung (The Costs and Financing of Continuing Education and Training). Frankfurt Main: Diesterweg.

STRINER, H. E. (1972) Continuing Education as a National Investment. Washington, DC: W.E. Upjohn Institute for Employment Research.

TIMMERMANN, D. (1982) "Das Staatsfinanzierungsmodell als Finanzierungsalternative fur Recurrent Education (The State Financing Model as an Alternative to Financing Recurrent Education"), in D. Kuhlenkamp and H. G. Schütze (eds.) Kosten und Finanzierung der beruflichen und nicht-beruflichen Weiterbildung (The Costs and Financing of Continuing Education and Training). Frankfurt Main: Diesterweg.

VON MOLTKE, K. and N. SCHNEEVOIGT (1977) Educational Leave for Employees: European Experience for American Consideration. San Francisco: Jossey-Bass.

14

PAID EDUCATIONAL LEAVE
A Proposal Based on the Dutch Case

LOUIS EMMERIJ

Paid educational leave has the advantage of meeting a variety of societal objectives. Depending on the economic and social situation, some of those objectives should be given greater stress than others. For this reason, paid educational leave will be explored for its implications in addressing unemployment. It is my contention that the industrialized countries will be quite unable during the 1980s to return to full employment as it is defined today. This has much to do with the slowdown in the rate of economic growth in the industrialized countries relative to the number of people who enter the labor market in search of employment in the majority of Western industrialized countries.

The rate of economic growth will not be such that full employment can be maintained given present technologies and in particular the forthcoming microelectronic and information revolution. If it is impossible to create enough jobs, something different must be done to reduce unemployment. Constructive interventions on the supply side of the labor market must be flexible however; if, during the 1980s for example, a different labor market situation emerges—given demographic tendencies—it must be possible to adjust policy measures on the supply side of the labor market accordingly. This is an important constraint on any search to identify such measures for reducing unemployment. The debate has only just started in the countries of the OECD, and although much has been heard about measures such as shortening the working week and early retirement, no clear line of action has yet emerged.

PROPOSAL FOR A FLEXIBLE MIX OF WORK, RECURRENT EDUCATION, AND LEISURE TIME.

A different and more comprehensive approach is required to reduce the amount of time that individuals spend in the labor market during their life spans. Such an approach would not be limited to relatively unimportant measures of labor market policy, but would consist of a more global package including educational policies, labor market policies, and social policies, combined with economic restructuring and development cooperation policies.[1]

Consequently, a social and cultural policy package must be proposed in addition to purely economic proposals. The foremost characteristic of the new package is that its progressive policy would maximize the opportunity for an individual to increase his or her control over shaping careers and life patterns relative to the present. Such a global approach must also be able to deal with the allocation of labor, but as a byproduct rather than as its major—or even sole—objective. Therefore one must ask what the countours would be of such a global approach to the unemployment problem in industrialized countries.

The life of an individual is divided into three parts, separated in most countries by impermeable partitions:

(1) the period spent at school and, for the more fortunate, at a university;
(2) active life, whether spent on the labor market or not and whether remunerated or not;
(3) the retirement period.

These periods follow one another sequentially. We go to school at an early age and remain there until age 16 or 18 (depending on the country) or, in the case of university students, very often to the age of 25 or even older. Then we enter the period of so-called active life until the age of 60 to 65 when we are kindly but firmly asked to take retirement. It is very difficult—particularly in most European countries—to reverse the sequence of these three events. It is the essence of a system of recurrent education to transform this rigid sequential system into a more flexible recurrent system in which it will be possible to combine or alternate periods of education, work, and retirement throughout one's adult life.

The idea of recurrent education that spans the first two periods of life mentioned above was launched some 10 years ago and has been discussed ever since. The complementary idea of retirement "a là carte" (freely selected by each individual) has been discussed less frequently, but it is the logical extension and the mirror image of recurrent education because it encompasses the second and third periods. Individuals could even be given the opportunity to combine all three periods by, for example, taking a period at age 30 of six months of anticipated retirement in order to continue or resume further education. Although this sounds extremely straightforward and simple, in reality it amounts to a social and cultural change of the first order.

The advantages of such an approach for the various partners, social and individual, in OECD countries is important to stress. In the first place, this much more flexible approach would enable an equally flexible labor market policy to be introduced that would have advantages both for employers and for workers. The employers would obtain a labor force that could be more easily and more quickly retrained in response to technological changes; the workers would have easier and more frequent chances to reorient themselves.

The educational system as it exists at present is extremely rigid and has long time lags between policy changes and outcomes. These were some of the reasons why in the 1950s and 1960s forecasts of occupational and educational structures of the labor force became fashionable. These long-term forecasts reflected the long gestation periods inherent in the educational production process. Indeed, it takes approximately six years to complete each of the main levels of the educational system. Hence, the school will react very slowly to changes in technology, and this in turn has implications for the required skill structure of the labor force.

Experience has shown that it is almost impossible to make more or less reliable long-term forecasts of the occupational and educational structures of the labor force. It is therefore much more realistic and desirable to shorten the gestation periods because by doing so, the educational system will become more adaptable. In other words, the relationship between school and work will become closer, more effective, and more beneficial to all parties.

In the second place, there is a specific advantage to the individual in terms of self-fulfillment and of being able to better realize his or her full potential. We know that motivation occurs at very different moments in a person's life and not necessarily at those points in time required by the sequential educational system. Educational opportunities and achievements will definitely be enhanced if individuals can go back to school when they are motivated to do so instead of being pushed by parents or by other persons in authority to remain in school. In the present setup it is difficult to return to school after having dropped out.

What is true for educational opportunities is equally true for occupational and income opportunities. In the global approach favored here, one has more than one occasion to orient (or reorient) oneself in the labor market. Furthermore, individuals can be offered a period of anticipatory retirement earlier in life during which they do not necessarily have to return to school but can do other things that they are strongly motivated to do at that particular time.

In the third place, its flexibility also makes the suggested approach an effective anticyclical weapon. At times when a particularly strong but temporary economic storm flails our countries, more people could be encouraged to withdraw for a while from the labor force in order to benefit from recurrent education or from a sabbatical period.

In the fourth place (and this is also an antistructural weapon) fewer people on average will be in the labor market at each point in time than is presently the case because people will, on the average, spend more of this time in the first and third blocks of their life rather than the second. In this way, the total labor supply will be reduced.

Thus the approach advocated here is on the one hand a generalization of traditional trade union demands for shorter working hours, more holidays, and earlier retirement and, on the other hand, supportive of the more recent proposals with respect to part-time work, the sharing of jobs, and rationing of the labor supply in general.

This global approach thus kills several birds with one stone: Economic structural limits for once will be consistent with the sociocultural objectives of the individual. Instead of a diminishing majority that works harder and harder and an increasing minority that is expelled shamefully from the labor market, it is proposed here that available work be rationed more intelligently and more comprehensively than it has been so far.

POLICY REQUIREMENTS

Next, let us look at the various changes that will be required if we are to move toward these new policies. First, it is necessary to introduce a system of recurrent education following the compulsory schooling period. There are however many definitions of recurrent education. For many it is a second chance that is parallel to the full-time formal educational system. This is definitely not the case. Recurrent education, as it has been conceptualized, is a comprehensive and flexible postcompulsory educational system that combines the present formal educational branches and various types of adult education. Recurrent education, therefore, does not necessarily imply the creation of additional types of education and training, but rather the integration of the existing types into one harmonious whole.

In order to speak about recurrent education, four conditions must be met:

- it must be able to receive people from all age groups beyond compulsory school age;
- it must be one integrated education and training system;
- it must offer "educational units" of variable and flexible duration that can be used as building blocks for and stepping stones toward a diploma or degree; and
- it must have exit possibilities at different levels, all of which are to be awarded with a diploma or degree.

With respect to the first point, it is to be expected that most youngsters who decide at the age of 17 or 18 to postpone the continuation of their studies for a while, will resume their schooling between age 20 and 30. This makes sense from an individual and therefore private rate-of-return point of view. It also makes sense from the macroeconomic and therefore social rate-of-return viewpoint. Were people to decide to start their university education at for example 55, they could not expect to receive important material returns in terms of income during the rest of their lifetime—and neither could society. It is to be expected that as people grow older, they will prefer to use stretches of anticipatory retirement in order to do things other than return to school.

The second point is important because in the approach suggested here, individuals must be able to travel along alternative educational paths and still achieve the same educational goal. People must have the opportunity to obtain the same "credits" by spending, for example, 52 long weekends at school as by attending full-time education during a period of three to four months. This flexibility must be built into the recurrent system or it will not be able to cope with the increased variety of students and circumstances.

This is much more easily said than done—hence the third point: the need for educational units that in relatively short time periods can provide a well-rounded part of a given educational career. The student or participant can thus build up credits in a flexible manner. Since they contribute to the total credits necessary to obtain a particular diploma or degree, they can not be viewed as isolated experiences. The fourth and last point refers to the necessity for recurrent education to have exit possibilities at different levels so that we do not fall into the "all-or-nothing" trap of current educational systems.

In summary, the educational characteristics of the recurrent education system suggested here are as follows:

- to hold as many options open for as long a period as possible;

- to transfer to a later age the emphasis on pursuing higher levels of education in order to interrupt the current tendency to spend more and more years of education in the existing sequential system even when there is no real desire to do so;

- to integrate formal and nonformal types of education.

The next component is the labor market policy. The proposals advocated here will have positive effects on the structural, cyclical, and individual levels of labor market policy. These have been mentioned above, so a brief reference will suffice here.

On the structural plane, recurrent education will be instrumental in creating a better linkage between the changing skills that are required and the educational and training supply delivered by this recurrent educational system. There is no doubt that one of the more important structural problems faced in industrialized countries—namely, the growing disparity between skills required and qualifications supplied—will be effectively countered by this system of recurrent education.

On the cyclical plane, the government can use appropriate incentives to stimulate more people to leave the labor force temporarily during an ebb tide in the economy. Even more precise targets can be attained. For instance, the government could well direct such measures to a specific sector of the economy or to specific groups of workers in the labor force. This could be done by giving higher financial rewards to people working in that sector or in that specific group—higher rewards for withdrawing for a given period of time into education or training. In other words, paid educational leave need not necessarily be the same from one group to another, from one sector to another, or from one period of time to another.

On the individual plane the advantages for individuals to reenter the labor market or to change within it are obvious and reflect those mentioned under the structural and cyclical components. There is, however, one additional point which needs to be emphasized: the possibility of obtaining an orientation period on the labor market between the termination of one's compulsory schooling and the start of recurrent education and training. During this period youngsters who have not yet firmly decided on their professional career would be able to explore various job opportunities. This would replace the training periods of today—training periods which are very often neither education, nor training, nor work, but rather are an unsatisfactory combination of all three.

A third dimension of this package concerns income distribution. What would the implications of the system of recurrent education and leave be for the income distribution of OECD countries? The "perverse" effects on tertiary income distribution of additional educational and other facilities have frequently been noted. Indeed, in most cases education is provided at low cost to the student through government subsidies that come from taxes paid by all. On the other hand, those who attend higher levels of education frequently come from the higher social classes. Such a situation is a clear example of how the poor subsidize the rich. This is one illustration of the perverse effects of providing not only education but also health and other facilities at subsidized prices. Care must therefore be taken that paid educational leave is granted as a matter of priority to those who have not been able to benefit optimally from educational facilities when young. In other words, a positive discrimination must be introduced in order to offset the perverse effects.

With respect to income distribution, Jan Tinbergen has drawn on time series from the Netherlands to show that education has expanded faster than warranted on purely economic and technological grounds. This apparent educational oversupply has resulted in a narrowing of income disparities between people with different levels of educational attainment (Tinbergen, 1975). If his conclusions are correct and can be generalized to situations in other countries, it would follow that recurrent education could have further positive implications for income distribution while at the same time it could maintain a somewhat better balance between the demand for skills and the supply of qualified workers.

A fourth dimension of the proposed plan for recurrent education would be to create a better work climate. The genuine opportunity to withdraw occasionally from the labor force is likely to diminish the number of those who declare themselves sick or otherwise unfit for work. Absenteeism due to sickness is a growing problem in most countries. Very often it is due to the fact that people work for too long a period under great stress. The safety valve provided by voluntary withdrawal could make a big difference.

Moreover, people who withdraw voluntarily from the labor force are in a very different psychological situation relative to those who are forcefully expelled. Pressure on health facilities can therefore be expected to diminish, implying a considerable saving of money in the health and welfare sectors—money that can contribute to financing the proposed recurrent education scheme. Finally, this policy package will almost necessarily imply the harmonization of the entire social security system. This also means that the great variety of pension schemes now in existence must be integrated in such a way that people are no longer confronted with bureaucratic problems concerning the right to retirement benefits when moving from one firm to another or from one job to another.

THE FINANCING OF PAID EDUCATIONAL LEAVE

Many may be inclined to think that the approach proposed in this chapter is a positive way by which to alleviate unemployment by redefining the concept of full employment. On the other hand, the costs involved might be such as to render its realization unlikely, particularly if large numbers of people were to be involved during the initial stages of introducing paid educational leave, as probably would be the case. Part of the solution would be to use the money now invested in social security schemes of all kinds to finance the proposed recurrent education and leave schemes.

Two groups will benefit from the approach advocated here: first, youth who proceed immediately to the new forms of recurrent education after completing compulsory education; and second, those who, after having worked for a certain period of time, withdraw voluntarily into a period of paid leave.

The financing of these groups will come from different sources. The cost of the first is now carried by the Dutch Ministry of Education's budget, combined with tax and other facilities granted to the parents involved. In the approach advocated here, the financial resources, insofar as they come from different budgets, will need to be centralized. In practice, this will amount to granting a student salary and to replacing present taxes and other provisions.

During periods of paid leave, the incomes of those in the second category must come from the amounts that are now paid through social security arrangements to people who are involuntarily expelled from the labor market. These people include not only the registered unemployed but also a portion of those who are declared unfit for work or on prolonged "sick leave."

Calculations have been made for the Netherlands regarding people who receive unemployment benefits, unfit-for-work benefits, and sickness insurance, but who should in reality be classified as "structurally unemployed." In other words, these groups consist of people who are either openly unemployed or are unemployed in a more or less disguised manner, and who find themselves in those categories because of the structural unemployment problem in the industrialized world. The essence of such calculations is to estimate the number of people that can withdraw voluntarily into paid educational leave at any point in time without additional costs being incurred by society, as compared to the present expenses involved in unemployment and social security schemes of all kinds to ensure the incomes of those who comprise the unemployed.

In estimating the potential size of the group that could take advantage of paid educational leave in the Netherlands, one must start by examining the number of young people of age 17 or over who are at present in the educational system. (In the Netherlands the number is approximately 350,000.) Next, the total amount of structurally unemployed people must be estimated, most of whom are hidden in a variety of social insurance schemes. The situation in the Netherlands is illustrated in Table 14.1, which includes a breakdown of the 377,000 people at present in a position of structural unemployment.

The social insurance categories according to which these people are paid are indicated by numbers I-IV because the exact names would have little meaning to foreign readers. Categories I and II represent those social security programs that accommodate people who are declared unfit for work. Category I was introduced fairly recently and it includes most cases in which people who had working accidents or otherwise are unable to continue working for some period of time. Category II includes those who are in reality quite fit for work, but are often put under this umbrella for humanitarian reasons. (Approximately 50% of those so classified are in this group.) For example, about half of the labor force in the age bracket 55-64 are found in this category. It is unlikely that all these people are disabled, and the only realistic explanation is that doctors tend more easily to certify people in that age

TABLE 14.1 Estimated Possible Withdrawals from the Labor Market Without Additional Cost (in 1000s): 1976

Social Insurance Group	Total Number	Number of Which Are Structurally Unemployed
I	93	20
II	380	190
III	244	112
IV	222	55
Total	939	377
Pupils and students of age 17 and over		350+
People who could potentially make use of paid educational leave		727

SOURCE: Emmerij and Clobus (1978).

group as "unfit for work" when they are in any case about to lose their jobs. Since it is extremely difficult for such people to find new employment and since the amount of income received under Category II is favorable as compared to unemployment benefits, it stands to reason that this category hides large numbers of people who otherwise would be openly unemployed.

Category III is that of the openly unemployed. It is estimated that half of the people to be found here are structurally unemployed, and the other half are cyclically unemployed. In other words, it is concluded that in a country such as the Netherlands there will always be about 100,000 persons who are *frictionally* unemployed.

Category IV represents those who are "absent through sickness for longer than three days." Actual absenteeism through sickness in the Netherlands is double the amount given in Table 14.1, but most people report back to work within one to three days. A conservative estimate is that approximately 25% of these people are on "avoidable" sickness leave and thus fall under the category of structurally unemployed.

This leads to the astonishing outcome that close to 1 million members of the Dutch labor force are absent from work at any point in time—about 20% of the total labor force. Out of this large number, about

377,000 are absent because of structural unemployment. If 350,000 pupils and students aged 17 and over are added, the potential size of the group that could make use of paid educational leave without additional costs being incurred by society is 727,000 people. In other words, close to 730,000 people in the Netherlands could make use of recurrent education through paid educational leave and receive between 75 and 85% of their most recent income, or a student salary. This would not represent a greater financial outlay than is now found in the budgets of the Ministry of Education and Sciences and of Social Affairs respectively.

Instead of spending the billions of guilders involved for *negative* reasons—expelling people from their working environment or forcing young people to remain at school while the majority would prefer to do something else before eventually returning to the educational system—the same amount of money could be used for *positive* reasons. This approach creates a new form of income maintenance for periods of inactivity. The difference is that involuntary inactivity for some (normally the weaker groups in society) is replaced by voluntary periods of nonwork for all.

The reasoning so far has focused on the financing of people's income during periods of voluntary withdrawal from the labor force. It has been stated that there are no *additional* costs involved as long as one substitutes a positive use of social security funds for the present negative use. This does not mean that no *other* costs are involved.

For example, it is likely that more educational facilities in terms of buildings and teachers will need to be provided. But here again, one must first look at the existing capacity. The Netherlands is experiencing demographic changes that will result in smaller numbers of youth. This, in turn, will have consequences for the employment of primary and secondary school teachers and for the utilization of school buildings. The education industry, like many other industrial branches, no longer functions at full capacity. Buildings remain empty and many school teachers are unemployed.

In such circumstances, it would again be comparatively inexpensive to make use of existing idle capacity to enable more people to return to school through paid educational leave. This example is given to indicate that additional costs caused by introducing a scheme like the one presented need not be as disastrously high as opponents might suggest.

Returning to the utilization of social security funds for the financing of educational leave, there are clearly a certain number of problems, but also possibilities. First, one might wonder whether it is realistic and indeed responsible to use funds that are typically used to remedy cyclical difficulties for the solution of structural problems. In other words, the argument is that such funds are meant to help people in periods of difficulty that are normally of limited duration—for example, sickness or working accidents that make people unfit for work for a few weeks or a few months at the most, or unemployment of the frictional type.

In the present proposal, these funds are largely set aside for educational leave that is meant to be with us forever albeit for rotating groups of people. This argument is valid as far as it goes. However, social security monies are used more often to alleviate or to hide structural unemployment problems; this assertion has been quantified in Table 14.1. The statement that these funds are used mainly for cyclical purposes thus already seems questionable. In actuality, social security funds are increasingly used to face up to a structural unemployment situation which, as explained earlier in this chapter, will surely last throughout the 1980s. This being so, it would be more honest to recognize this fact and to separate out those funds that are to be used for cyclical purposes as opposed to the rest, as has been done in Table 14.1.

Some people, while agreeing with the reasoning so far, will continue to argue in favor of using the structural portion of the funds for the creation of employment, particularly in the public sector, rather than "throwing it away in favor of educational leave." Of course, the creation of employment opportunities must remain a top priority. But what is to be done when maximal effort in that respect is not sufficient to supply all those who present themselves on the labor market with productive work? *Productive work* is indeed the key phrase. We would presumably not be interested in simply creating jobs at any price, if they are jobs of the most unproductive and unnecessary kind. It may be much better and also more productive to use the structural money not only to give people the opportunity to return to the educational system but also time to do other things (voluntary activities in the public sector, for example).

The educational part of creative leave would make people more productive, more flexible, and in general more inclined to follow and anticipate changes in their work environment. The noneducational part of creative leave would enable individuals to channel themselves into activities that they themselves consider to be useful. The chances are high that such activities will at the same time be more useful, and therefore more productive, for society at large than the creation of hosts of additional jobs in the public sector which would then become top-heavy as well as increasingly bureaucratized and tainted by interest groups and other lobbies. This debate between those who favor expansion of the public sector through means imposed by the government on the one hand, and those who want to give opportunities and insights to individuals on the other, will become one of the principle controversies of the 1980s, amongst all of the existing political parties.

Legal constraints are a second problem in proposing to use social security funds for more positive purposes such as educational or creative leave. In some countries, for example, if an unemployed person types a letter to a sick relative and an inspector happens to look through the window while he is doing so, that person risks losing his unemployment insurance because he will be accused of working. In the case of the Netherlands, where stringent regulations also hold, there is a clear tendency to take a more positive view towards the flexible use of social security funds, including their use for educational purposes.

A third problem (or possibility) concerns the introduction of incentives and disincentives to stimulate certain groups in society to take educational leave or discourage others. Policy measures on the supply side of the labor market must be sufficiently flexible and even reversible since it is possible that as early as the 1990s we may face a totally different situation on the labor market. In other words, the concern is with the general problem of how to ensure that the "right" number of people with the "right" composition withdraw voluntarily from the labor market at any point in time.

Overall, the total number of people involved might be influenced by changing the percentage of income to be paid: Instead of proposing the payment during the leave period of, for example, 80% of the latest income, this could be increased to 85% and in certain cases even to 90% in order to make it more attractive for more people to take the opportunity. The economic particulars could be differentiated—for example, by proposing a higher percentage for people who want to enroll in educational courses that are in high demand on the labor market than for those who want to go elsewhere. Along the same lines, people working in certain economic sectors could be stimulated more than those working in other branches of economic activity. These steering mechanisms, which any government has at its disposal, should be used to the fullest extent; in fact, the possibility of doing so is one of the original features of this proposal.

Finally, there is the problem of how to implement the whole scheme, assuming that all other obstacles have been cleared. If the proposal is to be of any real benefit to the employment problem, it is essential that people who are not in productive employment decide at the outset to take up educational leave. But that is not all. Not only must there be many initial recruits, but their working places must be taken up by people who are now unemployed. Only in this way can structural unemployment be replaced in due course by educational or creative leave. Otherwise, we shall be faced with an accumulation of structural unemployment *and* educational leave. The whole proposal would then break down.

Therefore, a matching problem presents itself: How can we make sure that those who withdraw voluntarily into educational leave have more or less the same qualifications as those who are at present unemployed? In this connection, it is clear that one must begin by convincing those workers with the lowest educational and training backgrounds to remove themselves from the labor market. This will serve two purposes: First, these are the people for whom educational leave is relatively the most useful; second, it is in this category that we find the bulk of the unemployed. In other words, the matching problem in this situaton would be much easier than in any other, and also more productive. The question of how the initial recruits and all those who take advantage of educational leave thereafter can ever be reinserted into the labor market is very easy to answer. Once the operation has started, a group of people will be away from the labor market at any point in time. This will be an ever-changing, rotating group; by the time the initial recruits return from their educational leave, another group will have just gone into voluntary retirement. Their places will therefore be vacated and will be refilled by the initial recruits, and so on.

THE DEBATE IN THE NETHERLANDS

The question of paid educational leave and its sources of finance has been presented from my perspective. The point at which official discussions in the Netherlands have arrived shall now be considered.

The Dutch government ratified the ILO Convention on Paid Educational Leave 140 on 14 September 1976. One year later, in September of 1977, at the request of the Minister of Social Affairs and of several of his colleagues, the Committee on Paid Educational Leave within the framework of the tripartite Social-Economic Council was installed. In October 1978, this committee presented to the government a unanimous first report in which it set out the general guidelines for the introduction of paid educational leave into Dutch society.

From the outset, the Committee on Paid Educational Leave has given a broader interpretation to its mandate than can be found in the ILO Convention 140. Paid educational leave in the ILO convention 140 refers only to leave granted to a worker for absence from the working place during a given period of time in order to benefit from schooling and/or training. The committee considered that since the convention had been accepted in Geneva in 1974 quite a few things had changed in Dutch society in particular and in the industrialized countries in general that made it necessary to look at the target population in a broader manner. The following are some of the considerations that guided the committee to this conclusion:

- the fact that the unemployment problem has become more serious since 1974;
- the low participation in the labor force of women in the Netherlands as compared to surrounding countries;
- an increased demand for adult education suggesting that many groups in the Dutch population who missed educational opportunities earlier in their lives now want another chance;
- the discovery that a significant percentage of the Dutch population can neither read nor write, in spite of compulsory education;
- the fact that during the last few years the Netherlands has been confronted increasingly with the problem of minority groups in the population, while the phenomenon of migrant workers seems to have become a permanent feature.

In summary, one is unavoidably led to the conclusion that it would not be justifiable to distinguish between the working population on the one hand, and the rest of Dutch society on the other.

Hence, the committee's declaration that paid educational leave must, as a matter of principle, benefit all groups of the population *and* cover all educational programs. Moreover, the committee has stated that this broad approach must be obvious from the start. In other words, in the initial phase of the introduction of paid educational leave, the target groups should include not only workers, but also other categories who will be given first priority to benefit from such leave. The committee has explicitly stated that *the entire Dutch population* must eventually be able to benefit. It is understandable that this ultimate goal cannot be reached overnight. Therefore, the committee has had to indicate its initial priorities. As has already been implied, paid educational leave in the Netherlands will begin by identifying target groups and providing them with a significant period of leave and a wide choice of educational programs. In other words, the committee wants to start with a few groups of the population, but wants to give these groups periods of paid educational leave of a meaningful duration which can be spent in schools of their own unrestricted choice.

The first and main criterion established by the committee for selecting these target groups is that the educational gap between population categories should not be increased. This implies that positive discrimination is necessary. If such precautions are not taken, a well-known phenomenon is bound to occur; namely, those who recognize the benefits of the additional opportunities and are ready to take advantage of them are as a rule those groups who already have better education and better incomes. These people have "learned to learn." This aspect makes education a self-cumulating and reinforcing process for groups with better educational backgrounds. People with little education are more likely to regard anything new with apprehension and even distrust—not because they are not interested, but usually because they do not immediately recognize what it holds for them. This gives the impression that they are less interested than those with a better education.

The fact that the committee decided to use the levels of education and income as its main criteria (people with low education and income levels will thus be the first to be presented with the possibilities of paid educational leave) means that a campaign must be started to inform and stimulate the target groups.

The next significant criterion that was used in selecting the target groups for the first phase of paid educational leave is the necessity to select a broad sample of population groups and not only workers. The more detailed results of this selection process and the five target groups that were ultimately chosen are shown in Table 14.2.

Turning now to financing aspects of paid educational leave, the committee reached the conclusion that the main source of finance had to be government funds because of the broad and representative selection of societal groups. If only workers had been selected, it would have been natural to discuss at length whether employers should pay or at least make a significant contribution. In the Netherlands, however, as Table 14.2 shows, there are significant target groups who are not in the labor force. The only way to make a start with educational leave and to ensure

TABLE 14.2 Target Groups for Initial Phase of Paid Educational Leave

Categories

Target Groups	Workers	Self-Employed	Social Security Beneficiaries	Other
I. Lowest education (secondary modern or lower technical school at most) including women	Lowest educated, including migrant workers and elderly workers in prepensioning-off phase	Lowest educated self-employed, people in agricultural, horticultural, and middle-income classes (mostly small shopkeepers and tradespeople)		Lowest educated without wage-losses and nonsocial-security beneficiaries
II. Long term unemployed and unfit for work (including women)		Social Security category I*	Social Security categories I, II, and III*	
III. Women			Social Security category III*	In households, or helping in their own (or husbands') shops
IV. Threatened by unemployment	In enterprises confronted by merger, rationalization, or closing down	In enterprises confronted by merger, rationalization, or closing down		
V. Other				

*See Table 14.1.

that this will be the beginning of a continuous and sustained movement is to make the financing independent of sources that cannot be counted on as always available at the required levels.

Starting from this general point, the committee declared itself to be in favor of using social security funds in order to facilitate procedures in times of great pressure on the public budget. It is true that the committee has done so prudently by emphasizing the fact that target group II (see Table 14.2) should be allowed to use its income out of social security funds to take up educational leave. In this respect, the committee's proposal is more modest than the one proposed in this chapter. However, it is interesting to note the reaction of the Dutch Social Security Council to questions put before it by the Committee on Paid Educational Leave. The main observations of the Social Security Council regarding the use that may be made of its funds for purposes of educational leave are the following:

(1) If participation in educational leave is consistent with the compulsion that the unemployed have to get back to work as soon as possible, it can be maintained that educational leave contributes to shortening the period of their dependency on unemployment insurance payments in the long run. In such circumstances, educational leave would therefore be fully consistent with the goals of the council's funds. In other words, if reinsertion into the labor market is the prime motive for educational leave, there is no problem whatsoever in using social security funds.

(2) In general, educational leave could be financed through social security funds by stating that persons are entitled to such an income during the period of their educational leave, and by requiring that the social security funds grant them a subsidy.

Concerning the first of these positions, it should be borne in mind that when we are faced with educational leave *during regular employment,* present legal constraints are such that social security funds are not automatically available. The Social Security Council however, has made a point of stating that possibilities *do* exist in principle, even within the present legal framework, but that a special case must be made for each individual. With respect to the second position, a new piece of legislation must be introduced for this to become a realistic proposition.

This initial reaction by the Social Security Council is important in that it is evidently willing to take considerable steps toward a system of financing recurrent education and is in fact already going somewhat further than the recommendation made by the Committee on Paid Educational Leave.

CONCLUDING REMARKS

What has been proposed in this chapter amounts to profound changes in the social and cultural domains of society with a view to achieving a better balance between remumerative work and other aspects of human life. If these changes can be brought about, the employment problem could also largely be solved.

In the face of lower rates of economic growth and continuing upward trends in technology and labor productivity, we must move from a defensive to a constructive attitude. The proposed policy package combines a progressive policy with restoration of maximum initiatives to the individual.

It has been shown that the proposed changes can be financed from existing public funds by changing their purpose and destination. Only few, if any, additional funds will be required. The proposed changes will be *equitable,* partly because of the built-in positive-discriminatory component. Equal educational opportunites for everyone will be advanced and income distribution will consequently become less skewed. Weaker groups in society, who are now becoming more and more vulnerable, will become stronger as they are given additional opportunities to return to education and other forms of self-development.

The proposed measure will also be *efficient* because it will boost labor productivty and improve the working climate. It will also increase the flexibility of the labor market and facilitate adjustments to technological changes.

NOTE

1. This proposal is duscussed in more detail in Emmerij and Clobus (1978). Later in this chapter I shall compare my personal opinions on the matter with the ideas of the tripartite Committee on Paid Educational Leave of which I am the chairman.

REFERENCES

EMMERIJ, L. J. and J.A.E. CLOBUS (1978) Volledige werkgelegenheid door creatief verolf—Naar een maatschappij van de vrije keuz (Full employment through creative leave—towards a society of free choice). Holland: Kluwer, Deventer.

TINBERGEN, J. (1975) Income Distribution: Analysis and Policies. Amsterdam: North—Holland Publishing Company.

ABOUT THE AUTHORS

PIERRE CASPAR is Professor for Adult Education at the Conservatoire National des Arts et Metiers in Paris, France. He holds a degree in civil engineering, a Ph.D. in Sociology, and a Master of Science which he received from the University of California. His academic activities prior to his present position included part-time lectureships at the Sorbonne University and the Ecole Nationale d'Administration while he was serving as Director of a counseling firm servicing enterprises with respect to personnel management and employee training. Dr. Caspar has published a number of books in these fields and has served as a consultant to OECD for a number of years concerning questions such as training, adult learning, educational leave, and industrial democracy.

IVAN CHARNER is Director of Research at the National Institute for Work and Learning in Washington, D.C. His research and professional interests include worker education and training, adult learning, and youth school-to-work transitions. Recent publications include "Another Piece of the Financial Aid Puzzle: Tuition Aid Offered by Companies and Unions," and "Documenting Youth Experiences: The Concept of a Career Passport."

PAMELA H. CHRISTOFFEL, Research and Development Associate in the Washington Office of the College Board, has written numerous articles in the area of public policy and adult learning. Her current work includes an examination of the use of new technologies to assist the education of adults and research on federal student aid programs.

WERNER CLEMENT is a Full Professor of Economics, Institute for Economic Theory and Economic Policy, University of Economics, Vienna, Austria. He has served on many advisory committees and as a consultant to the Federal Institute of Labor, Germany, as well as to the Council of Europe, UNESCO, and OECD. His published works include papers on labor market policy and educational finance in Austria as well as youth unemployment and employment policy in France. His specializations include labor economics, economics of education, comparative economic systems, and theory of economic policy.

LOUIS EMMERIJ is Director of the Institute of Social Studies in The Hague. Previously he served as Director of the Employment Planning and Promotion Department of the World Employment Program of the International Labor Organization, and he worked with the OECD Directorate for Scientific Affairs. He is the author of *Can the School Build a New Social Order?* and other publications. He has been especially concerned with issues of education and employment.

HAROLD E. GEIOGUE is the Principal Program Analyst for Education with the California Office of the Legislative Analyst. He has been involved in state-level education policy decisions since 1968. His recent activities include service as Vice Chairman of the California Student Financial Aid Policy Study Group and as a member of the advisory council of the Western Interstate Commission on Higher Education's Project on Expanding Regional Cooperation in Graduate and Professional Education. Recent publications include "Statewide Coordination in Higher Education."

HENRY M. LEVIN is a Professor of Education and Affiliated Professor in the Department of Economics at Stanford University. He is also Director of the Institute for Research on Educational Finance and Governance. His specializations include the economics of education and educational finance, economics of evaluation, and economics analysis of workplace democracy. Previously he was the president of the Evaluation Research Society.

GÖSTA REHN is Emeritus Professor and former Head of the Swedish Institute for Social Research at the Stockholm University. He was Director for Manpower and Social Affairs in the Organization for Economic Cooperation and Development from 1962-1974. Earlier he was Economist for the Swedish Trade Union Confederation and the Swedish Ministry of Finance. He is a specialist in labor market policy and as such has served as a consultant to various international organizations.

KJELL RUBENSON is a Professor in the Department of Administrative, Adult and Higher Education, University of British Columbia. His current work includes research on the Swedish system of higher education.

He has written numerous articles in the area of adult and recurrent education. Recent publications include *Adult Education for Social Change: Research on the Swedish Allocation Policy Lundl,* "Adult Education Research: In Quest of a Map of the Territory," and *The Adults—Dreams and Realities in the Swedish System of Higher Education.*

HANS G. SCHÜTZE holds an LL.M. from the University of California, Berkeley, and a Ph.D. from the University of Gottingen, Germany. He is a senior research fellow at the Paris-based Center for Educational Research and Innovation (CERI) of the Organization for Economic Cooperation and Development (OECD). In this function, he has been involved in work on recurrent education, higher education, schemes for educational leave of absence, education and training for health care personnel, as well as the evaluation of training and special programs for unemployed young people. Currently, he is directing an international study on the development and utilization of human resources in the context of structural and technological change.

GREGORY B. SMITH has served as Assistant Director of the Department of Justice Services of Multnomah County, Portland, Oregon. He was Senior Associate and Director of the Worklife Education Program of the National Institute for Work and Learning, Washington, D.C. He is a graduate of the Fletcher School of Law and Diplomacy. His research work has ranged across policy issues involving both domestic and international affairs.

NEVZER STACEY is a Senior Associate at the National Institute of Education. She has designed and managed research and policy studies that address various aspects of education and training in the workplace. Her publications and professional interests include research on corporate and union investment in human resource development. Under her direction the National Commission on Working Women was created, bringing together representatives from unions, business, and higher education to examine the problems faced by women in nonprofessional occupations.

DIETER TIMMERMANN is a Professor of the Economics of Education and Educational Planning at the Department of Education, University of Bielefeld, Germany. He has published diverse articles about finance and governance of education. He is concerned with the issues of efficiency in education, allocation of resources in education, and the cost and financing of education.

ALAN P. WAGNER, Research Associate, Center for Educational Research and Policy Studies, State University of New York at Albany, is an economist continuing an extensive research program on the economics of postsecondary education and training. His published work includes papers on the role of student financial aid in institutional and student decision making and differences in the returns to a college degree among different types of institutions and among fields of study.

AUG 0 5 1989